18951

Parliament, Parties,
and Society in France
1946-1958

Parliament, Parties, and Society in France 1946-1958

Duncan MacRae, Jr.
UNIVERSITY OF CHICAGO

ST. MARTIN'S PRESS · NEW YORK
MACMILLAN & CO. LTD · LONDON

ST. MARTIN'S PRESS, INC.
New York, New York
MACMILLAN AND COMPANY, LTD.
London
THE MACMILLAN COMPANY OF CANADA, LTD.
Toronto

MANUFACTURED IN THE UNITED STATES OF AMERICA
BY THE BOOK PRESS INCORPORATED, BRATTLEBORO, VERMONT

To the memory of

V. O. Key, Jr.
André Siegfried
Samuel A. Stouffer

Preface

THE FOURTH FRENCH REPUBLIC IS dead, but it is not yet long enough dead to fall into the historian's province. Autopsies have been numerous and brilliant. One more analysis, especially by someone who is at some distance from the events, requires some justification.

My aim is to show that we can better understand the problems of the Fourth Republic by a more precise and less speculative analysis. Those who know the period and what has been written about it will find much that is familiar in these pages. Yet some brilliant speculations are supported, others are made more precise, and some are questioned. By regarding the speculative interpretations of the period as hypotheses to be tested, and by seeking systematic ways to test them, we sharpen our knowledge. This sharpening means not merely accepting or rejecting formulations such as "individualism," or "social cleavage" but translating them into a form that can be compared with statistical data. Statistical tables provide more information than the words that describe them, and this additional information not only provides procedures for comparison with other countries, but also renders our knowledge of familiar things more precise.

Since the mere sharpening of well-known conjectures is not easily perceived by the nonstatistical observer, let us list some of the conjectures that the data lead us to question seriously:

1. Cabinets tended to be brought down by the operation of a parliamentary game in which prospective ministers were the center of opposition.
2. Divisions within the parties, like those between the parties, reflected basic cleavages in French society, and therefore accentuated cabinet instability.
3. France at that time was a "mass society" because of a lack of intermediate groups between the individual and the state; she suffered unstable government because of a large floating vote.
4. The Gaullist *Rassemblement du Peuple Français* (RPF) was a party of the "extreme right."

On the other hand, another well-known diagnosis of France will be supported by the data in this book. This pictures France as socially divided and individual Frenchmen as separated from one another, both in their local communities and to some extent in Parliament. Centralization, carrying local problems to the overburdened agenda of a central government, the failure to resolve problems at every level—all these factors were related to cabinet instability. Most analysts of French politics and society agree on this picture, at least in its broad outlines. Yet it is useful to specify ways of testing its truth, and the degree to which it is true, by means of statistical data. I have brought together a variety of data that bear on this problem, including analyses of surveys, voting statistics, and legislative votes. But despite their value they represent only a fraction of the information on problems of social division that further research could generate and utilize. Comparative studies of community power systems, elite mobility, and small-group processes would all be relevant; so too would a far more penetrating analysis of electoral statistics for smaller areas. Detailed studies relating social divisions to the changes that many consider to have taken place in France in recent decades, as well as comparative studies of other countries, would also be desirable, to specify the limits within which my interpretations hold.

By bringing statistical methods to bear on the problems of the Fourth Republic, I hope to contribute to the general methods of analysis used both by students of national politics and by political sociologists. These methods are, however, more appropriate for some problems than others. In particular, they seem more applicable to the gradual breakdown of a set of functioning institutions, evidenced through a series of repetitive events, than to the more nearly unique sequence of events that led to the threat of a military coup in May 1958. I shall concentrate attention on the sources of cabinet instability. Other contributing causes of the fall of the Fourth Republic have been traced elsewhere: the plots of Algiers, the disaffection of the army, and France's international situation all made important contributions. But this study and the methods of analysis it uses are concerned with the internal weaknesses, related to France's parliamentary government, that contributed to the Republic's fall.

This book is written not only for readers primarily interested in French politics, but also for readers who wish to compare political behavior in France and elsewhere. This latter group includes political scientists, sociologists, and others who are interested in the analysis of politics by "scientific" methods. Surveys, statistics, and techniques for the study of legislative votes have been applied extensively to American politics. Comparative studies using the survey method are becoming frequent. But for these approaches certain correctives seem desirable. Studies of American politics should be compared with studies of a system that failed, to separate this type of research from an optimistic, even apologetic, functional analysis. They should be contrasted with studies of a system operating under strikingly different formal institutions, involving persons whose national character is different from the American, to reveal further unspoken assumptions. They ought to be extended over longer periods of time, to transcend the mere cross-sectional association of social characteristics with the vote. Analyses of leaders and citizens should be connected, to show how much and under what conditions each group affects government action.

As a contributor to the growing number of comparative statistical studies of national politics, I wish to present a more detailed study of a single nation —comparing it, implicitly and explicitly, with our own. Concentration on one nation permits more detailed coverage of the system studied, in space, time, and other aspects, than is possible in a comparison of many nations.

It poses the problems of comparability in their most difficult form, dealing with formal institutions and leadership behavior over time more directly than the cross-sectional survey approach. In this way I hope to contribute to an eventual combination of these various approaches in a comparison of many nations which will nevertheless be detailed and objective.

Because I am writing for those who study politics statistically, I include much material that is not original. This material occupies approximately the first half of the book and precedes the central analysis, which begins with the study of cabinet instability. I presume the reader has only a superficial acquaintance with France at the start; those who have more background may skim the earlier chapters, using the table of contents as a guide. The points at which I present original contributions can easily be identified, however, by the frequency of tables in the text. This is not to say, of course, that the tables tell the whole story, even though they tell parts of it better than words. They constitute building blocks whose placement in the larger structure requires judgment more than strict deduction or statistical inference. They limit the class of possible general hypotheses that can be entertained; the intersection of this class with that defined by speculative hypotheses such as have appeared in the literature will come nearer the truth than either alone. And even if my own choice of interpretations should be in error, the statistical data are presented in such a way that they can be used in other interpretations.

My first intended audience consists of students of political behavior. The limited time available for training these students and researchers makes it difficult for them to acquire both the research techniques and the familiarity with a foreign language and culture that would make possible a technically advanced comparative politics. And since statistics and mathematics must be learned in formal courses, it seems easier to provide an introduction to France than an introduction to statistics in this volume.

A second audience, however, exists among students of French politics, who may learn something of statistical research methods, since they need not expend the effort needed to study a foreign society. The increasing interest in modern techniques in comparative political research may lead to a broadening of the range of methods used. And although these readers may not consider the statistical procedures I have used to be self-explanatory, they may still assess the value of the results.

The point of view from which I proceed is the comparative study of the internal politics of nations. France is the source of much interest to Anglo-Saxon observers, who have studied her presumed values and shortcomings for both personal life and national policy formation. But I wish to regard France as facing problems analogous to our own—perhaps teaching us, through her experiences, something of the difficulties of government in the modern world. At numerous points in this study, and especially at the end, I make recommendations for government reform in France. I make them in the hope that my goal for France is not altogether foreign to that of Frenchmen—a representative government responding to the needs of the citizenry, maintaining the latitude and support necessary to form and carry out coherent policies, while at the same time training leaders for the future.

The beginning of this research was aided by a Fulbright Research Scholarship in 1956–57; during this period I was aided by members of the Fulbright Commission in Paris as well as the staff of the Fondation Nationale des Sciences Politiques. Salary for a semi-sabbatical leave from the University of California also contributed to this part of the study. Later financial aid was given by the University of Chicago's Social Science Research Committee, the American Philosophical Society, the Social Science Research Council, and the National Science Foundation.

Useful data were provided to me by the Institut Français d'Opinion Publique, as well as by various French scholars and officials. A number of men who had been members of the National Assembly during the Fourth Republic gave useful information in interviews, especially during my visit to France in the spring of 1960. I am also indebted to the Institut d'Études Politiques at Bordeaux for its hospitality during that visit.

Where quotations in English are cited from French works, the translations are mine. Full references to works cited in footnotes are given in the Bibliography.

In data processing, I was aided by the staff of the Operations Analysis Laboratory of the University of Chicago, particularly Frank K. Bamberger and Natalie Beller. Later computer work was done at the Biological Sciences Computation Center and the National Opinion Research Center, using programs written by Mildred L. Wilkerson.

Many conscientious and capable research assistants aided in various phases of the study: Alan Altshuler, Jack Liebert, Roger Masters, Sarah S. Inger, Jack Dennis, Deane Raley, Donald von Eschen, David Johns, Inge Powell, Frederick Gleeson, Milton Kotler, Jacques Noël, Giuseppe Petrosini, Carol Heron, Farley Maxwell, Charles Ehrensperger, Elsa Stone, Michael Wolfson, Walter Nicgorski, Ernst Benjamin, Mark Kesselman, Charles Butterworth, Donald Niemi, David Nichols, Jean de Bay, Leonard Miller, Theodore Feely, Noreen Cornfield, William Richter, Paul Epstein, and Jeanne Hahn. Useful suggestions were made by Reginald Bartholomew, Philip Converse, Georges Dupeux, Nathan Leites, Remi Clignet, David Greenstone, Harvey Waterman, and Aaron Wildavsky—none of whom, however, is responsible for my errors. Sonya Illianova typed the manuscript with care. Ronald Inglehart kindly helped with reading the proofs, and Jean Poulard with the index. My wife, Edith K. MacRae, was a constant source of encouragement.

I am grateful to the *American Journal of Sociology* for permission to reprint and adapt in Chapter 8 material from "Religious and Socioeconomic Factors in the French Vote, 1946–1956" (November 1958).

Contents

Preface vii

1. The Failure of the Fourth Republic   1

Government Impotence 1
Immobilisme and the French Political System 4
Social Divisions 5
Sources of Cabinet Instability 6
Voting, Opinion, and Representation 9

2. France's Internal Divisions   15

Family and Community 17
Occupations 19
Nationwide Social Ties and Divisions 22
Overseas France 24
Organized Political Interests 26
Voluntary Groups: Was France a "Mass Society"? 28
Mobility and Social Change 32

3. Political Parties and the National Assembly   41

The Party System 42
The Structure of Political Parties 45
Structural Differences Among the Parties in the
    Fourth Republic 47
Cohesion and Discipline in the Parliamentary Groups 55
Parties and Majorities in the Assembly 57

4. Cabinets and Issues in the First Legislature   65

The Rise and Fall of a "Typical" Cabinet 67
The First Legislature: Chronology 70
Patterns of Cabinet Coalition 87
Types of Intraparty Division 89
Clusters of Roll Calls and Their Interpretation 91
The Right 95
The Radicals and UDSR 100
The Mouvement Républicain Populaire 102
The Socialist Party 105
Cabinets and Issues in Intraparty Division 106

xi

5. Cabinets and Issues in the Second Legislature   113

    The Second Legislature: Chronology 113
    Patterns of Cabinet Coalition 132
    The Right 134
    The Radicals and UDSR 143
    The MRP 148
    The Socialists 150
    Cabinets and Issues in Intraparty Division 151

6. Cabinets and Issues in the Third Legislature   157

    The Third Legislature: Chronology 157
    Patterns of Cabinet Coalition 165
    The Moderates 166
    The Radicals and UDSR 169
    The MRP 173
    The Socialists 174
    Cabinets and Issues in Intraparty Division 175

7. The Assembly and the Cabinet   181

    The Placement of Deputies on Scales 182
    Ministrables and Cabinets 185
    Factions and Leaders on the Right 188
    Factions and Leaders Among the Radicals 197
    Factions and Leaders in the MRP 204
    Factions and Leaders Among the Socialists 208
    The "System" and Cabinet Stability 211
    Conflicts of Ideology and of Interest 213
    Consensus and Cabinet Weakness 216
    The Legislative Parties and the Fate of Cabinets 221

8. The Electorate: Stability in the Vote   230

    Basic Attitudes Toward Voting 230
    Stability and Variation in the Vote 232
    Referenda and Stability of Party Division 243
    Social Correlates of the Vote: Regression at the
       National Level 244
    Regression Analysis Within Individual *Départements* 250
    Geographical Strongholds of the Stable Parties 253
    Occupational Division and the Small-Town Vote 256
    Stable Voting and Unstable Government 259

9. The Electorate: Variation in the Vote   268

    Gaullism and Poujadism 268
    The Mendesist Vote 273
    Social Bases of the Changing Vote 275

The "Bandwagon Effect" and the Parties of the Center 279
Conclusion 282

10.   Assembly Votes and the Constituencies   286

General and Specific Constituency Influences 286
The Socialists 290
The MRP in the Constituencies 293
The Radicals' Constituency Relations 294
The Moderates in the Constituencies 296
The RPF in the Constituencies 299
Militants, Ideology, and District Influence 299

11.   Organized Opinion and the Assembly   306

Types of Opinion and Types of Response 306
Popular Premiers and the Assembly 309
The System Defends Itself: The RPF 313
The System Defends Itself: Mendès-France 315

12.   Basic Problems of the Fourth Republic   322

The Rules Governing the Assembly 323
Centralization 325
The Party System 326
Ideology 328
National Character 330
Social Divisions and Political Activity 333

Appendix A. Roll Calls and Data Processing 339

Appendix B. Procedures for Cluster Analysis and
    Cumulative Scaling 348

Bibliography 354

Index 364

Parliament, Parties,
and Society in France
1946-1958

»1«

The Failure of the Fourth Republic

O N JUNE 1, 1958, THE French National Assembly approved Charles de Gaulle as Premier, and on the following day it voted him special powers. Thus closed a chapter in French history. The Fourth Republic, inaugurated in 1946, was to be replaced after twelve years by a new constitutional form—one which, though still a republic, placed far more power in the executive, far less in the legislature.

This transfer of power was a recognition of the failure of the Fourth Republic. In the Algerian crisis, the previous cabinet had been powerless to act. Divisions within the National Assembly and disaffection in the army had greatly reduced the government's authority. De Gaulle's investiture was a grudging concession by the Assembly to forestall a coup by the "men of Algiers."

But what had failed—the men, the institutions, or France? Could France have solved her major problems if she had taken any of the other paths open to her after World War II? These questions, intensely debated in France, are the subject of our analysis. They lead us to consider influences ranging from the political institutions and the Assembly to the social structure and temperament of the French people.

Government Impotence

The chief charge against the premiers and cabinets of the Fourth Republic, both at home and abroad, was their impotence. At the end this was symbolized by the ability of de Gaulle, as a private citizen, to give orders to the army when the government could not.[1] Earlier it was the initiative of commanders in Algeria to order the bombing of the Tunisian town Sakhiet Sidi Youssef and the capture of the Algerian rebel leaders in their airplane —decisions that had to be accepted by the cabinets of the time.[2]

The Fourth Republic had also failed to solve many problems other than Algeria. The tantalizing tug-of-war over the European Defense Community showed an incapacity to say yes or no collectively. The efforts to hold Indochina and Algeria, though constantly pursued by various cabinets, were long constrained to immobility rather than guided by positive choices. Reform of the electoral system, though often and widely advocated in the Assembly, could not command any majority except under the threat of the Gaullist *Rassemblement du Peuple Français* (RPF) in 1951. Efforts to collect direct taxes more efficiently met the determined resistance of the Poujadists.

Inflation, the high incidence of alcoholism, and agricultural overproduction were continual problems. And the isolation of the working class from the centers of government was never solved during the Fourth Republic.

No government, of course, solves all its problems immediately and to everyone's satisfaction. The United States has many problems similar to France's.[3] Minor problems may remain unsolved for a long time without impairing the effectiveness of a government. Nevertheless, measured against the requirements of its time, French government under the Fourth Republic was strikingly inadequate.

A major underlying problem of the Fourth Republic was the inability of her cabinets to govern effectively. The duration of cabinets was short; and premiers could often prolong them only by failing to govern, preserving their parliamentary support by inaction. Over the entire span of the Fourth Republic, this powerlessness of cabinets contributed to many of the other weaknesses of government. The very expectation that a given cabinet would not last long led to the consolidation of other sources of power—other possible coalitions among the deputies, the possession of particular ministries for periods longer than the life of a given cabinet, and administrative autonomy.[4] Incapacity to take action on certain matters led to increasing disillusionment on the part of those affected, for example, the military in Indochina, or France's allies on questions of European military organization. The one greatest strength of most cabinets lay in the protective reflex of "republican defense," but this reflex proved to be a weakness as well. The two major movements that might have given decisive government to the Fourth Republic—Gaullism and Mendesism—were stopped by concerted defensive action in 1947–52 and 1954–56.

This paralysis of decision was known as *immobilisme,* and the men and customs embodying it in the Assembly were known as "the system." Although these problems did not originate with the Fourth Republic, cabinet instability was less damaging in the Third. As Hoffmann writes, "In Robert de Jouvenel's days politics was the hobby of Frenchmen, but not the condition of their lives. Today, unfortunately, it has become the condition of their lives, but also the object of their dislike."[5]

We assume, therefore, that government impotence and cabinet instability were pervasive and characteristic problems of the Fourth Republic. Yet it is well to examine the successes and failures of the Fourth Republic more closely, because there were at times bold new policies—Mendès-France's liquidation of the Indochinese war, or Mollet's organization of the Suez invasion; and there were successes, as in the field of economic development, during that period. Moreover, some of the failures of the French Republic may not be chargeable to the peculiar features of its constitution and its leadership.

Immobilisme played an important part in the failures of the Fourth Republic. But France's problems were unusually difficult because to her international situation and the problems of decolonization were added the wounds of World War II and Vichy. The Algerian crisis of 1958, for example, would have been a difficult one for any French government to handle. De Gaulle, whose power and authority exceeded those of any leader of the Fourth Republic, later faced two more armed uprisings of the Algerian settlers, as well as the intransigence of the Muslims in negotiation. Even at the end, the Secret Army Organization nearly provoked the Muslims to violence. It may well be argued that the external problems that faced the Fourth Republic would have seriously threatened any government, in France or elsewhere.[6]

Had metropolitan France—the mainland and Corsica—been hermetically sealed from the outside world, including North Africa, the Fourth Republic might have existed much longer. So might the Third, had there been no Hitler. Siegfried contended that France, blind to external threats, had preserved only a precarious equilibrium by looking inward rather than outward.[7] But whatever her lack of preparedness for Hitler's invasion, her position adjacent to Germany left her more vulnerable than Britain or the United States.

The blow struck at French national pride by her defeat and acquiescence to the Germans had lasting consequences. It, and France's declining power in the postwar world, led some Frenchmen to resist all the more any further retreat in the later crisis of decolonization. An anxious national pride, which moved the metropolitan population somewhat, was heightened for the Algerian settlers by fear for life and livelihood, and for the professional military by defeat in Indochina and retreat in Egypt. De Gaulle derived much of his support from the fact that he symbolized the nation's honor; this symbolic position, though normally a source of strength to him in policy-making, sometimes led him to untenable choices.[8] By calling postwar France to a grandeur beyond her means, he created problems for her, and by a sort of ironic justice he was called back to power by the demands of those who insisted on national prestige and honor.[9]

Not merely the Algerian crisis of 1958, but other problems of the Fourth Republic as well may have been beyond the powers of any French government to solve. The alienation of the army dated not only from Indochina, Suez, and Algeria, but also from World War II.[10] A breakdown of legitimacy had been fostered by de Gaulle's own defiance of the "legitimate" Vichy government; later the Algerian rebels modeled the title of their own organization (*Gouvernement Provisoire de la République Algérienne*) on that of de Gaulle's Provisional Government.[11]

The strength and centralization of the administration, which often nullified government policy, dated from before the Revolution of 1789. The widespread negative attitude toward government (*incivisme*) existed long before 1946. Cabinet instability had been chronic throughout the Third Republic. In short, the Fourth Republic may be regarded in many respects as a twelve-year cross-section of a set of continuing problems in French politics. Not only the problems, but France's response to them, evoke echoes of other problems and responses dating back at least to 1789. The relation of groups to one another and to government, as it existed under the Fourth Republic, was in large part a legacy of the Third. To examine the extent of this continuity requires asking how far, and how rapidly, the institutions of the Fourth Republic and the social structures underlying them, might have been changed.

Not only were many of France's problems under the Fourth Republic of long standing; they also were sometimes accentuated by the actions of others.

Roosevelt's distrust had initially hindered de Gaulle, and British and American pressure contributed to the establishment of the strong competing groups that induced him to resign in 1946.[12] American pressure for German rearmament and European union also intensified political conflicts in France. Later, Dulles' actions on the Aswan Dam and the Suez Users' Committee frustrated Egypt and France in turn, needling them into conflict. The bitter nationalism and revolutionary outlook of the *Front de Libération Nationale* (FLN), which showed itself during the negotiations in 1961, was very difficult to reconcile with terms that would be accepted in the *métropole*. And throughout the entire Fourth Republic, the Communist party represented Soviet interests as well as the interests of its French clientele.

Some successes may in fact be claimed for the Fourth Republic. France's economic and demographic development from 1946 through 1958 compared favorably with the rest of Europe. To some extent, this development may be attributed to government action.[13] Moreover, the governments of the Fourth Republic arrived at agreements with other European countries on the coal and steel pool, on atomic energy, and on the common market. The generous *loi-cadre* for sub-Saharan Africa, as well as negotiated independence for Tunisia and Morocco, were also to the regime's credit. When these successes are set against the numerous failures of the system, they require explanation in terms of specific conditions for success and failure.

The successes of economic planning under the Fourth Republic were possible in part because they circumvented the political roadblocks that obstructed other decisions.[14] Many decisions were made in the Economic Council, a less politicized body than the National Assembly. Conformity with the plans was rewarded by subsidies, which did not constrain individuals completely in their action; a similar feature characterized the family allowances. The goals of economic and demographic growth, moreover, were not the property of any one restricted political group, but had broad support.

Granting independence to Morocco and Tunisia and loosening ties with sub-Saharan Africa were easier than solving the Algerian problem, because of the separate legal status of the former areas and the relative absence of permanent European settlers there. Nevertheless, there were strong and continuing objections to a "liberal" policy in the North African protectorates, and these objections affected the fate of cabinets. Generosity in these areas was also perhaps stimulated by a view of the consequences of an immobile posture in Algeria. Thus the successes of the Fourth Republic, although worthy of attention, should not obscure the central fact of *immobilisme*.

Immobilisme and the French Political System

Numerous explanations have been advanced for *immobilisme*. Among them have been irreconcilable ideologies, a deeply divided society, a highly centralized government, and excessive concern of the deputies with their private parliamentary "game" and their careers, without sufficient care about principles *or* policy.

We shall argue that the basic problem was the coexistence of two rather separate political subsystems, within which quite different views of politics prevailed. On the one hand there was the subsystem of the National Assembly and especially of the potential ministers (*ministrables*) who tended to support one another. On the other was the socially and politically divided subsystem of the voters and party activists (militants), dissatisfied at the compromises of the deputies, even when compromise was necessary. As one form of this dissatisfaction, party activists often initiated the pressures that reduced the cabinet's support and led it to resign. The consensual system of the Assembly, hedged in by the "unavailable" votes at both extremes, then typically put another similar cabinet in its place. Frustration from this process built up—together with substantive demands—until a "surge" movement rose to prominence, expressing voters' protest in another form. But the Assembly system then neutralized the surge, and the process continued.

We place the blame for the failure of the Fourth Republic on both these systems, or rather, on their coexistence. The *ministrables* of the "system" were unable to carry through—or to permit—bold new policies when needed, while the party supporters in the districts were intolerant of the necessary compromises of politics. Possibly if either view of government had prevailed more fully, government would have been more effective; but this disparity in views made it less effective than either alone.

The reasoning that leads us to this diagnosis is complex. We wish to show not only that these two different subsystems existed, but that they differed in their action from the political system of the United States. Moreover, the time dimension is crucial for contrasting the two subsystems, for the consensual one which dominated the Assembly acted slowly, while a characteristic feature of the subsystem outside the Assembly was the rapid surge and decline of political movements. Thus we must analyze a series of comparable sets of data over time.

To establish that this interpretation fits the facts better than others, we shall draw several contrasts. First, French political and social data will be contrasted with data for the United States to show that the explanatory factors adduced are not universal ones. Second, the extent of consensus among the parliamentary leaders will be shown as a contrast to the dissensus that existed among the voters. Third, the different responses of the voters, to stable and "surge" parties, will be distinguished to show the lack of representation of rapid changes of opinion in the power structure of the Assembly; this difference will also be traced in the Assembly's responses to the two types of parties. Finally, the penetration of constituency influences into the Assembly will be analyzed to show which members of the Assembly, and which parties, most fully represented each of the two subsystems.

Social Divisions

We first consider an aspect of France widely considered to underlie her politics but to be little subject to change: the diversity and depth of her social divisions. France has long been known as a land of controversy over the role of church schools, differences between the working class and the bourgeoisie, arguments between "static" and "dynamic" regions. These differences can be traced in individual life histories, the ways in which friends or strangers interact, and the kinds of social roles available to Frenchmen. In personal relations and social structure, France is more divided than the United States (and probably than other European nations). To describe these divisions at the start (Chapter 2) provides an introduction to politically salient aspects of France. At the same time we can make refinements in previous descriptions of French social structure.

French citizens, rather than being members of an unorganized "mass society," had nearly as many voluntary group memberships as Americans, but joined groups of a different sort. Voluntary groups in France did not cut across the major social divisions as much as in the United States. Political parties encouraged campaign activity that was confined more to working with one's fellow partisans than to persuading the unconvinced. This homogeneity of political associations and interactions combined with the relatively fewer consensual functions of local or regional government to push problems to Paris, politicize them, and complicate parliamentary life. One such complication was the simultaneous holding of local offices by deputies, which kept even major public figures from devoting enough time and attention to national problems.[15]

The social divisions of the country were reflected to a considerable extent in the political parties (Chapter 3), but the correspondence was by no means perfect. The principal stable parties—ranging from the Communists to the Moderates (Conservatives)—displayed a variation in structure that covered almost the entire range possible in modern democracies. In addition, the "surge" parties or movements—Gaullism, Mendesism, and Poujadism—cut across the divisions of the stable parties, and recruited socially more heterogeneous sources of support by means of a different political style. Because of these differences among the parties in structure, goals, and beliefs, we must consider each party individually in order to trace the sources of division in the National Assembly.

Sources of Cabinet Instability

While a survey of social structure and party differences provides a useful introduction to the problems of the Fourth Republic, a more systematic examination of the weaknesses of the Fourth Republic can best be organized around the working of the parliamentary system (Chapters 4–7). Cabinets were invested by a majority[16] of the National Assembly, and generally stayed in office as long as they felt they had a sufficient majority in the Assembly to continue passing important bills.[17] The majorities of investiture and support were drawn largely from parties that also participated in the cabinets, though sometimes support was given without participation. The parties sometimes fragmented, and the problem of gathering and preserving a majority became progressively more difficult as the mutual vetoes among the parliamentary groups and factions increased. The cabinet's margin of support was usually small, since at any time about one-third of the members of the Assembly belonged to parties (Communist, Gaullist, or Poujadist) that could not become part of any pro-cabinet majority. The obstructive power of particular parties in the majority was considerable, and the temptation to exercise it through defection was strong; but as we shall see it was restrained by consensus among the leaders.

There was thus often a rapid erosion of the cabinet's majority, followed by the premier's resignation when the margin became narrow. The only innovative decisions that could be taken without strong opposition in the Assembly were ones that could be carried out irrevocably at a single stroke (e.g., Mendès-France's liquidation of the Indochina war) or those few that did not divide the parties supporting the cabinet from one another (e.g., the Suez invasion). Cabinet crises did in fact supply an additional stimulus to solve problems; sometimes a sufficiently long crisis led to new possibilities that did not exist at its start.[18]

The fate of each cabinet that remained in office as long as several months seemed to depend on a characteristic configuration of parliamentary forces. A combination not merely of certain parties but of certain factions and individuals within them invested the premier and cabinet and was steadily eroded. Usually this combination corresponded to a central issue, such as economic policy, the European Defense Community (EDC), Indochina, or North Africa. The supporters of the cabinet wanted to keep it in office in order to act (or refrain from acting) on this question, while the opposition wished to bring it down for the opposite reason. This "central issue" so dominated the legislative process that many other issues, not obviously connected with it, elicited the same divisions within the Assembly.[19]

This interlinking of issues through the fate of the cabinet made it difficult to act on individual issues separately. Often the opposition introduced an issue known to divide the cabinet, in order to bring it down—the church-school issue, for example, dividing Socialists from the *Mouvement Républicain Populaire* (MRP). Conversely, the premier might try to prolong his cabinet's life by introducing issues intended to solidify his support.

The limited range of decision on the part of cabinets, leading to the choice between immobility and rapid overthrow, was a constant source of critical comment during the Fourth Republic. A major critique along these lines was expressed by Debré[20] and to some extent included in the changes made when the constitution of the Fifth Republic was written. This criticism bore on many aspects of the system. As it concerned altering the institutional arrangements of the Assembly, it traced the lack of government authority to the ease with which a cabinet could be voted down, the possibility for a potential minister to advance his personal career from the overthrow of the cabinet, the lack of personal responsibility by deputies for their votes,[21] and the control of the Assembly over its own dissolution. These and other related diagnoses of the ills of the Fourth Republic rest on a number of hypotheses which we shall endeavor to test.

Underlying some shortcomings of the institutions of the Fourth Republic were certain informal practices of the political world which have also received their share of blame. Among these were the customs of the Assembly ("rules of the game"), according to which careful contingent calculations of timing, gain, and loss were normally made;[22] the internal structure of the parties, both their divisions in Parliament and the conflicts between militants and leaders; the fact that cabinets represented loose, heterogeneous, and temporary coalitions, rather than agreements to govern;[23] the multiple ideological incompatibilities of parties and factions within them; and the conflicting personal ambitions of potential government leaders.

One clear divergence among diagnosticians in this group of hypotheses is between the claims that ideologies, on the one hand,[24] and personal ambitions, on the other, were responsible for the downfall of cabinets. Detailed analysis of roll-call votes will lead us to support the former explanation and question the latter.

By considering the chronology of the rise and fall of cabinets, we shall see that the parties that last went into opposition to a cabinet before it fell— and these are the ones whom Parisian political commentators considered "responsible"—tended to be ideological parties. In the First Legislature the Socialists performed this function most often; in the Second, it was characteristically the ex-Gaullists; while in the Third, it was the Moderates. In each case, matters of principle rather than the quest for posts in succeeding cabinets were the main source of disaffection.

At the same time, the different meanings of division in the different parties can be clarified. The Socialists and MRP, when they divided internally, tended to do so in relation to particular issues. The Moderates and Radicals each divided in ways that were common to a variety of issues. These general differences must be qualified, however, by consideration of the particular political situations in the three Legislatures.

The identification of the issues that divided each party also permits placing each deputy in relation to his party colleagues on these issues—e.g., for or against social legislation, European union, or the vigorous prosecution of the Algerian war. But the very identification of these issues is clearer in some cases than in others, because of the involvement of some issues with the cabinet's fate or with persistent conflicts between coalitions or intraparty factions. This involvement, as we have suggested, varied within a given party from one issue to another. Certain issues were substantive and persistent, while others were more closely tied to particular cabinets and the corresponding alignments of deputies were thus more temporary. (Chapter 10).

On the issues that we shall identify, the deputies who were potential ministers (*ministrables*) tended to support the cabinet. It has been widely contended that the ambitions of potential ministers led them to oppose the cabinets; but in their public positions they supported the cabinet more, not less, than did their party colleagues. The chief exceptions to this support occurred under the Mendès-France cabinet and the first cabinet of Edgar Faure.

The agreement among the *ministrables* was also expressed in their opposition to bold, innovative leaders. It has often been contended that the customs of the Assembly prevented such men from even being invested.[25] Mendès-France was a rare exception to this rule, owing his investiture to the Indochina crisis of 1954. The weakness of cabinets thus went hand in hand with their instability, the two phenomena combining to produce *immobilisme*. But while cabinet weakness was largely due to the selective influence of the Assembly's leaders, cabinet instability was more the fault of the rank and file.

The most manifest sources of cabinet instability appear to have been substantive issues or ideological differences. The parties that characteristically brought down the cabinet did so for substantive reasons more than for calculation of places in future cabinets, and suspicions that *ministrables* undermined the cabinets find little support in their votes. Our next task is therefore to trace these substantive policy differences from the National Assembly back to their sources in the constituencies and in the country generally. In the electorate we shall see that two patterns of voting existed side by side: the persistent, organized interrelations of the stable parties (including the Communists), and the periodic surge and decline of more radical, innovative movements. The separateness of these patterns of voting reflected a basic problem of the Fourth Republic.

Voting, Opinion, and Representation

Among the problems of the Fourth Republic, those centering in the Assembly, the Constitution, and the behavior of politicians have been nearest to the attention of French political commentators,[26] and perhaps most accessible to voluntary change. Fundamental to these problems, however, were certain conditions: the divisions among voters, party allegiance, avenues of political access for various groups, attitudes toward politics and authority. To probe more deeply into these conditions, we shall ask: How different could Parliament have been? Might there have been elected, under some possible circumstances, an Assembly that could form and sustain cohesive cabinets? What could such cabinets have done (Chapters 8–11)?

The timing of elections influences their responsiveness to waves of public opinion. The British Prime Minister, though he does not necessarily call for an election when opinion swings against him, does not confront the reluctance to dissolve Parliament that the French leaders displayed. The attempt of Marshal MacMahon to consolidate his power by dissolving Parliament in 1877 (the famous *seize mai*) enhanced the already considerable distrust of government authority that existed in France, and the memory of this event was so strong that dissolution was not again tried until December 1955. The reluctance to hold elections, even when the Assembly failed to reflect the public's views on current issues, explains some of the restriction on "possible Assemblies"; but more important was the political interest of the parties controlling the cabinets in the Fourth Republic. Unlike Marshal MacMahon, they normally felt they had much to lose by dissolution; and even had it been easy, they would have had little motive to use it. Moreover, as we shall see, there is some question whether elections held at other times would have solved the problems of government ineffectiveness unless other institutions had been changed as well.

Regardless of when the elections might have been held, one might still ask whether coherent majorities might have been created. Such majorities might have arisen either through changes in the public's party preferences or through alteration of the electoral system. During the Fourth Republic, only minor changes in the electoral system were politically possible; the one change made counteracted the Gaullist surge of 1951, leaving the Assembly as divided as before. And while surges of opinion in other countries often go to increase the representation of an established party, strengthening its trained leaders, surges in the Fourth Republic characteristically went to new parties, whose leaders were politically unskilled and opposed by the old.

We shall show, using voting statistics and survey data, that the public's political preferences rarely shifted so as to give a major increment of support to the established parties. The major shifts of votes were to and from new or "surge" parties. Only two movements—Gaullism and Mendesism—gave promise of providing possible constructive alternatives through parliament, and neither won anything approaching a secure majority in the Assembly. Moreover, each elicited such bitter opposition—de Gaulle being accused of proto-fascism and Mendès of treason—that a series of highly effective road-blocks were placed in its path to power. When de Gaulle finally gained power in 1958, it was as though a supercrisis, not merely an ordinary cabinet one, had been necessary for this grant of authority.

The study of voting also reveals the effects of the nation's social divisions. Regression analysis of the vote for the stable parties by areas (*départements*) suggests that there was a more uniform division of the country, along lines that were similar from one region to another, than exists in the United States. Religious practice, urbanization, and class differences were associated with the votes of the corresponding areas in a consistent way. Survey data also suggest that France's political divisions went deeper than those of the United States at the same period. Whereas the relation of social class to political preferences was attenuated in small American towns, it persisted with nearly the same strength in small French towns as in large cities. Differences of this kind in political compartmentalization, as well as differences in styles of political participation, suggest important and distinctive features of French politics.

Side by side with this stable and pervasive division were the periodic surges of support to new parties or movements. The fact that shifts in the vote went largely to new parties—or political movements—calls attention to the two competing views of political life that existed. Public frustrations with the state of things were channeled into new movements; these were resisted by the parliamentary leaders of the older, stabler parties of the cabinet coalitions; and this resistance in turn drove some of the impatient voters away from the cabinet parties.

The new political movements, though alike in their demands for fundamental change, were far from alike in their specific programs or their sources of support. Mendès-France, who worked through the established Radical party, succeeded in becoming premier but had a less distinct electoral base than de Gaulle or Poujade. Gaullism and Poujadism also drew their support from different sources, both socially and geographically.

After analyzing the behavior of the electorate generally, we must connect this behavior with divisions between and within the parties in the Assembly. We must ask whether internal party divisions in the Assembly reflected corresponding divisions in the electorate. This question can be studied by comparing the positions of deputies, within a given party, with aspects of the constituencies they represented.

Those issues most likely to reflect constituency influence can be identified in terms of their continuity in dividing the party in question over the three Legislatures. When deputies' positions on these issues are related to constituencies, the results are quite different for different parties. The less organized parties, especially the Moderates, seemed to respond most to opportunities to form coalitions in the constituencies by absorbing smaller groupings and altering their positions accordingly. The Socialists' internal divisions were not strongly associated with social and economic characteristics of their districts, but leftist Socialists tended somewhat to come from districts where the Communists were strong. This relation is the inverse of what the Moderates showed: the Socialists may have been influenced by a dominant working-class orientation of workers in certain areas, but were not altering their positions simply to gain electoral strength. The MRP was split along lines related to the political and social characteristics of the districts, and tended to form local alliances with like-minded lists of other parties. The Radicals, apparently responding to the MRP's position when both parties competed in a district, tended to form alliances with the Moderates when the MRP did not, and conversely; their positions on issues varied correspondingly, being most conservative when they were locally allied with the Moderates.

Because the general issues related to constituencies were not the same as those most closely related to the fate of cabinets, these intraparty divisions do not seem to have channeled local social divisions into the Assembly. Rather, the voter's party choice was the main connection between social divisions in the general public and the central governmental processes. The divisions within the parties, though they contributed to the problems of the Assembly, need to be considered in their own terms rather than simply as reflections of social divisions.

The differences in constituency relations among the parties suggest, in addition, that the more highly organized parties (Socialists, MRP) did not bargain for local alliances as much as the parties with fewer militants (Radicals, Moderates). This difference between the parties supports the hypothesis, developed below, that the party militants, especially in the more organized parties, were a basic source of the divisions between the parties that were manifested by the rank-and-file deputies in the Assembly.

In analyzing constituency relations we have selected the aspects of the legislator's position that were most consistent over time. But to study the rising and falling "surge" movements, one must examine the stages in the development of each, and the ways in which the Assembly's leaders contrived to lessen its influence. We select for particular attention Gaullism and Mendesism, for each might have provided alternative responsible sets of government policies. Both these movements were systematically opposed by some of the same key leaders in the Assembly. Intraparty maneuvering, the timing of elections, and the choice of issues on which to put the new movement at a disadvantage were tactics used against both. In the study of the resistance of the Assembly's leaders to these movements one can see most clearly the irreconcilability between the "system"—the leaders who held office repeatedly in various cabinets and the rules of parliamentary action they embodied—and the "surges."

The basic attitudes of the French toward life, human relations, and politics may also have played their part in making French politics of that period somewhat different from American. Contributing to the extremeness of certain movements of "defense" (particularly Poujadism) was the strength of attachment to *situations acquises.*[27] Even the neatly compartmentalized way in which Frenchmen characteristically perceive the world (and structure their social relationships), while it contributes to the clarity of Gallic logic and legal principles, hinders the sort of *ad hoc* compromise that would come more easily to an American. We shall show that these represent aspects of French politics that are perhaps less easily changed and that set limits to change in the shorter run.[28]

NOTES

1. One account of this is given in Arrighi, *La Corse, atout décisif,* p. 140. Full references to works cited in footnotes are given in the Bibliography.

2. The contrast with Truman's firing of MacArthur was made by Alfred Grosser in *Le Monde,* 5 March 1958. Here and elsewhere we use the term "cabinet" to translate *gouvernement,* especially in the plural, where it might be ambiguous for the American reader.

3. See Williams, "Political Compromise in France and America."

4. This expectation may have made possible a greater evasion of responsibility, as has been suggested by Leites in *On the Game of Politics.* The devolution of power from unstable cabinet to administration is noted in Fauvet, *La IV⁰ République,* p. 157.

5. Stanley Hoffmann, "Paradoxes of the French Political Community," in Hoffmann, *et al., In Search of France,* p. 60

6. See Aron, *France: Steadfast and Changing,* p. 27.

7. Siegfried, *De la IV⁰ à la V⁰ République,* pp. 165–166, 261. See also Jean-Baptiste Duroselle, "Changes in French Foreign Policy Since 1945," in Hoffmann, *et al., In Search of France.*

8. E.g., when he sent Admiral d'Argenlieu to Indo-China and when his advice maintained him there. See Fauvet, *La IV⁰ République,* p. 106.

9. This was pointed out by Hughes, "De Gaulle in Power," 188. On French national pride and motivations in the Suez affair see also Luethy and Rodnick, *French Motivations in the Suez Crisis.*

10. See Ambler, *The French Army in Politics.*

11. The tradition of provisional governments in France, however, was a long one.

12. See Churchill, *Triumph and Tragedy,* p. 247, and Murphy, *Diplomat Among Warriors,* p. 265.

13. For a critical evaluation of the sources of French economic growth, see Charles R. Kindelberger, "The Postwar Resurgence of the French Economy," in Hoffmann, *et al., In Search of France.* Among the means of government action were nationalization, subsidies for modernization, revision of the tax system with indirect taxes (the tax on added value, TVA), and family allowances. American economic aid also played a part.

14. As to how this came about, see Bauchet, *Economic Planning,* Part I, Ch. IV, and Crozier, "Pour une Analyse sociologique de la planification française."

15. Siegfried, *De la IVᵉ à la Vᵉ République,* p. 216. Two of the most famous *députés-maires* were Herriot of Lyon and Chaban-Delmas of Bordeaux.

16. The precise conditions for investiture were altered, both by custom and by constitutional change, during the Fourth Republic, but these alterations did not greatly affect the functioning of the system.

17. One exception was Pflimlin's resignation in June 1958, because of lack of support *outside* the Assembly rather than in it.

18. Williams, "Compromise and Crisis," and his *Crisis and Compromise,* Chap. 29.

19. This hypothesis has also been suggested by Aron in *France: Steadfast and Changing,* p. 12. We shall see that it held particularly for the Radicals and Moderates.

20. See for example Debré, *Ces Princes qui nous gouvernent,* pp. 174–175, and Buron, *Le plus beau des métiers,* Part II, Chap. II.

21. Siegfried, *De la IVᵉ à la Vᵉ République,* p. 215.

22. Leites, *On the Game of Politics.*

23. Siegfried, *De la IVᵉ à la Vᵉ République,* pp. 193, 196.

24. *Ibid.,* p. 230.

25. See Duverger, *Demain la République,* pp. 15–20. The quality of personnel was also criticized by Lavergne in "La chute de la IVᵉ République et la nouvelle Constitution;" but he attributed this deficiency in part to the dependence of deputies on party organizations—an argument that runs counter to others' diagnosis of party indiscipline as a serious fault.

26. For example, Duverger, *The French Political System,* pp. 138–140.

27. This was stressed by Luethy in *France Against Herself;* the contrast in styles of reaction is illustrated by comparison of the positions of the Poujadists with those of American groups described in Lane's *The Regulation of Businessmen.*

28. Duverger attributes the "individualism" of the French population to its largely peasant origin and the characteristics of peasant society, in *The French Political System,* p. 187.

»2«

France's Internal Divisions

AMONG THE EXPLANATIONS THAT HAVE been offered for the failure of the Fourth Republic, many involve the internal divisions of French society. They concern not so much the specific working of the parliament, nor the legal forms of election and representation, as the relations of French citizens to one another. They trace political problems to the deep divisions in the body politic, the relative absence of voluntary groups with overlapping membership, and the low degree of social and geographic mobility. These explanations concern metropolitan France primarily, but they may also be extended to the overseas parts of the French Union that were represented under the Fourth Republic. For the most part, these aspects of French society have changed slowly; they existed long before the Fourth Republic and are likely to outlast the Fifth.

These explanations center about the multiplicity and separateness of social and political groups. City dweller and peasant, priest and public-school teacher, employer and worker lived in different social worlds. In these and other aspects, the number of significant bases of social division seems to have been greater in France than in the United States. Where lines of division in the two countries corresponded, those in France usually went deeper. And while multiple social divisions have been viewed as a source of unity in the United States, they failed to subject the French citizen to conflicting obligations, and therefore simply divided the society into a greater diversity of subunits.[1]

We shall contend that these social divisions—particularly those in metropolitan France—constituted a permissive but not sufficient condition for political division. They were closely associated with differences among voters in party preference; and though this association was by no means complete, it exceeded similar associations in the national electorate of the United States. Moreover, specifically political groupings such as interest groups had a self-sustaining and self-protective character that gave them, and particularly their active members, an important role in maintaining political divisions.

Our argument will be that social divisions and separate communication groups were potential channels through which divisive political communications could flow. Whether such communications were sent depended on other factors—in particular, on the existence of sets of intermediate political leaders divided on national issues, talking of national problems in different terms from one another, and not interpenetrating with one another. This

15

stress on the leadership, rather than the public at large, as the more fundamental source of division derives from two sorts of evidence. First, the degree of political involvement and concern with issues on the part of the French public in general was lower, not higher, than that of Americans. Second, the divided public showed a remarkable acceptance of consensual communications when they were sent—in municipal rather than national politics.

France's internal divisions cannot obviously be attributed to size, population density, or economic development. During the Fourth Republic metropolitan France had one-fourth the population of the United States, but four times the average population density. The average election district for the National Assembly had about the same population as a U.S. congressional district, but was represented under proportional representation by about six deputies; the representation of individual districts ranged from two to eleven. With a smaller and denser population, France might even be expected to have shown greater internal consensus than the United States.

In general economic development, France stood fairly in the middle of the countries of Western Europe. During the Fourth Republic, her per capita income was about equal to that of Norway, Denmark, or the United Kingdom, above that of Italy, Ireland, or Portugal, below that of Sweden. In industrial production she ranked lower.[2] In both these respects, she was about 25 per cent below the United States. Politically, the most significant concomitant of this difference was the importance of agriculture. About a fourth of the French labor force was engaged in agriculture, as against less than 10 per cent in the United States. Partly because of the numerical importance of the agricultural interest, but even more because of a cultural separation of peasants from city dwellers,[3] urban and rural interests were sharply divided.

More important than gross economic or demographic variables are certain social conditions underlying political controversy. The possibility of mobilizing people on opposite sides of a political conflict depends not only on their having potentially conflicting attitudes and interests, but also on the relative absence of social ties connecting the two sides.[4] These "crosscutting" social ties were less prevalent in France than in the United States, and when they existed they seemed to mitigate conflict less.[5] Their relative ineffectiveness can be traced to three aspects of French society in which it differed from American: (1) occasions for contact between politically distinct groups were limited; (2) when contact did occur, the substance of communication was restricted; and (3) even when people of different political views did discuss politics, they influenced one another less in France.[6]

To illustrate these differences we shall describe the structure of French society, while pointing out the political importance of various groups within it. By "structure" we shall mean what groups of persons interact with one another about particular matters (e.g., families, communities, economic enterprises); and how they interact (e.g., the substance of the interaction, the relations of influence and authority). For each of these aspects of social structure we are concerned with the social norms regulating interaction. A social norm ordinarily involves not merely a uniformity of behavior, but also a moral feeling and expectation on the part of the participants that one should behave in a particular way in a given situation. A cluster of social norms that are associated with one another define a status (e.g., a kinship or occupational status, or membership in a particular group).[7]

We shall describe these aspects of the social structure of France by starting with the smallest units—those earliest in the individual's life history—and working outward. Thus we shall consider family and kinship, the community and its culture, occupation and work, and those structures of association that extended across regions and nation.

Family and Community

Foremost among the self-contained social units in France is the family. The foreigner who visits France for any prolonged period learns that business or professional affairs do not easily intrude into the family sphere. Frenchmen who visit the United States sometimes remark on the absence of walls around American homes, and are often surprised that Americans invite strangers into their homes so easily. Those who stay longer accept this custom only with reluctance. In France gatherings of family and kin are more frequent than in the United States, and to some extent take the place of association among neighbors or coworkers.[8]

Métraux and Mead have pointed out that the notion of the *foyer* is a central one in French society; family and hearth have deeper significance and clearer boundaries separating them from the outside.[9] The French child learns about the boundaries of the family early. Sitting in a baby stroller, he typically faces the mother rather than facing forward as is customary in the United States. On the beach, he is not expected to play with strange children; better to play alone than with strangers.

Drawing clear distinctions between the family and the outside is an instance of a more general tendency to draw precise social and conceptual boundaries. Lerner, reporting on his interviews with Frenchmen, noticed a barrier that could be crossed only if the rules were carefully observed, but which did not hinder a very free expression of ideas after it was crossed.[10] Similarly, a stranger is not easily invited into a French home; but once he has been invited, the standards of hospitality are very high.

When kinship ties extend beyond the community, they retain a force greater than is common in the United States, even in our South. For example, migration from farm to city has been considered to exert a considerable influence on the political and religious attitudes of the rural residents left behind.[11] City dwellers often return to the family home in the provinces for their summer vacations. Pitt-Rivers, writing of Magnac, a small town in southwest France, describes the interchange between the town and its emigrants:

> These emigrants do not willingly sever their connections with the village as a rule. In this, they are similar to their neighbors of the Auvergne and the newspaper *Auvergnat de Paris* covers the area of Magnac, giving a weekly account of every recent event of social importance, village by village, for the benefit of the metropolitan exiles. They frequently come to spend a summer vacation with relatives in the village and some maintain a house there for the

purpose, to which they will perhaps return when they receive their pension and retire.[12]

This enhanced influence of kinship implies that "family" is understood more inclusively in France than in the United States: closer ties remain between the emigrants and parents, siblings, aunts, uncles, or cousins in the provinces.

The importance of family ties appears in economic and occupational life as well; the likelihood that one will be working with relatives is considerable. Family farms and family shops are numerous because of the prevalence of small farms, commerce, and artisanal enterprise. Among the upper bourgeoisie, the ownership and management of family industrial enterprises are relatively inbred.[13] Thus family and occupation may reinforce one another as sources of social division. The family enterprise is presumably less frequent in the more industrialized, "dynamic" parts of France, but its decline is slow and it has strong powers of self-preservation.

The self-contained character of the family is a potential basis for political division. But family ties might also constitute a basis for cross-pressures if young people married outside their social and political circles. Available data on the extent of intermarriage among occupational groups, however, reveal no pronounced differences between France and the United States.[14] Insofar as political heterogeneity is introduced into family relations through marriage, its effects seem to be lessened by the fact that fewer attempts are made to persuade others to agree with one's own position. Even when family ties bring together relatives of different political persuasions, "political discussion is avoided in family gatherings." Moreover, the nature of discussion in general in France seems to be more an exposition of positions than an effort to arrive at consensus.[15]

Within the rural community, men of different families typically meet at the café rather than at home. Adults may be acquainted yet because of a personal feud (*brouille*) refrain from speaking to one another for months. Those who are *bien* (on good terms) with one another may be so for political and religious reasons, or for similarity of views on other subjects; those who are *brouillés* may be so partly for disagreements of the sort. Wylie writes of these relations in the village of Peyrane:

> It would be an exaggeration to say that all the people who are enemies for personal reasons are also political enemies, as it would be false to say that all people who vote for the same candidates get along well together. Raymond Laurens and Henri Jouve are close friends, although Laurens is a Communist and Jouve is a devout Catholic. Raoul Favre and Chanon are enemies even though both of them are Communists. These cases are exceptions, however. It is more usual for persons who dislike each other for personal reasons to disagree politically. Of course, if personal grievances are too intimate to mention in public, then political differences become particularly violent, for politics carries the whole burden of hostility.[16]

This internal opposition among residents of the same community provides a basis for self-definition in that everyone knows what he is for and against.

To know all one's neighbors, and place oneself in relation to them, is a type of self-definition of course more characteristic of the small town than of the city. But among some of the city dwellers it has its counterparts: not only the association among migrants from a given area, but also the proliferation of sports clubs and other voluntary organizations, associated with the Communist party, in working-class *quartiers*.

Within the community, persons may be defined not only in terms of their membership in distinct groups (families, churches, ethnic groups), but also in terms of social ranking. Rank or prestige in the village community may depend on personal qualities, statuses such as occupation, or membership in traditional estates (nobility and clergy). Varieties of social structure, even among rural areas, give political advantages to various types of local leaders, over and above their party affiliations. Aristocrats, businessmen, professionals may draw on aspects of their social prestige for political purposes.[17] In those parts of France where the nobility are still respected,[18] the local personage with greatest potential political influence may be the count (e.g., the Comte de Chambrun, who represented the Lozère as a member of a small left-wing group) or duke (the Duc de Montesquiou sat in the Fifth Republic for one of the districts in the Gers). In Normandy, a businessman such as Joseph Laniel might capitalize on his reputation and that of his family in campaigning for the Assembly; or in Corrèze, where the old Radical tradition was strong, the physician Henri Queuille, representing the influence of the Republic through the Ministry of Agriculture, might draw the rural vote.[19]

Occupations

For the great majority of Frenchmen whose experience takes them beyond family and traditional relationships, and particularly for residents of cities and towns, occupation counts most as a basis of social ranking, both within the community and outside it. Occupational divisions in France are comparable to those in the United States, except that they are deeper and more detailed. The urban working class is more isolated, socially and politically, from the middle classes; special occupational groups, such as civil servants and small shopkeepers, have characteristic political interests that make it impossible to group them simply as "middle class"; and the use of the plural ("middle classes") better suggests the complexity of their situation.[20] Interest groups representing various occupations and industries proliferate and fragment more than in the United States.

In mainland France, occupational groups may be classified in two ways: by their urban or rural character, and by their social rank. In the urban areas a hierarchy of occupations exists, from owners and managers of large enterprises to skilled and unskilled workers. In between are various middle-class groups, including professionals, public and private bureaucrats, and intellectuals. Small entrepreneurs and artisans exist not only in the large cities but also in the smaller towns. Thus the Poujadist movement, which appealed to these groups, found its highest concentration neither in the largest cities nor among the peasants but in between.[21]

In the most thoroughly rural areas the characteristic occupation is that of small farmer. These peasants (a term used more during the Fourth Republic than now) represented the social stratum farthest culturally and politically from Paris. While some peasants were close to the church and others suspicious of it, neither group was at ease with international cooperation or technological advance. The larger farms, with more area and personnel, were less completely rural. Additional leftist tendencies could be found among farm workers, both in the Paris basin and in the large vineyards of the South, where there were more workers per farm. And both strata in these areas—the large farm owners as well as the workers—were potential allies of the corresponding groups in the cities.

Thus political alliances and divisions between occupational groups could be formed on at least two bases: stratification (owners versus workers) and ruralism. Evidence for the latter were the peasants' parties and movements, as well as Poujadism, which were not simply alignments of haves against have-nots.

The internal differentiation within broad occupational categories is best illustrated in the middle classes. Distinct attitudes toward occupation and politics may be found in different occupational groups with comparable income and prestige. Shopkeepers, white-collar workers, civil servants, and intellectuals seem to differ from one another more than do their American counterparts.

Owning one's own shop—stationery, grocery, shoemaking, and the like—typifies a widespread ideal of having security, perhaps on a small scale, but having it entirely within one's control. The virtues of prudence, tenacity, and conservatism (in the sense of holding firm to what one personally has) were most highly developed among this group—similar, in many ways, to the attitudes of the small landholder.[22] And yet this group was one of the first to suffer from economic and technological change. With an end of inflation, rising competition from department stores and supermarkets, and a government effort at tax collection, the merchants and artisans were hard hit; they reacted more strongly and more directly than their counterparts in the United States.[23]

Other occupations of the "middle classes," though similar to the merchants and artisans in income and social prestige, had quite distinct political leanings. The white-collar groups, working in large urban commercial and industrial organizations, most closely resembled their American counterparts. Sales and clerical personnel at the lower levels, for example, might confront problems of status definition with respect to skilled workers of equal income. White-collar groups seem to have given strong support to the Gaullist and Mendesist movements. In the upper reaches of industry, the organization professionals and managers included a group who were among the strongest advocates of technical progress and modernization—breaking away from the conservative family-firm notion that had predominated under the Third Republic.[24]

Those who worked for the government, however, had different occupational perspectives. The security of a *fonctionnaire*'s position appealed to the same prudent conservatism as did the small proprietorship; a merchant might aspire for his son to enter the civil service. However much the public criticized their treatment by civil servants, they esteemed the prerogatives of the office.

Civil servants, and especially public-school teachers, were highly organized in trade unions and closely affiliated with the Socialist party (and to a lesser extent with the Radicals). The teaching profession was a stronghold of *laïcité* (the belief in public, nonreligious education) and its members defended this position. Teachers and other civil servants constituted an important source of skills for the parties of the left in the Assembly.

Higher civil servants (*hauts fonctionnaires*) constitute a still different special case. Their prewar generation, highly selected and trained at the *École Libre des Sciences Politiques* in Paris, was an elite group with a particular style, connecting many administrative and judicial agencies through personal ties. The *École Nationale d'Administration* (ENA), created after World War II to democratize recruitment and improve the quality of instruction, continued to draw its students largely from the upper middle class and from Paris; and while it has sent an extremely competent and self-possessed group of young men into the central administration, the prefectures, and the administrative tribunals, it has also maintained the quality of the upper administration as a thing apart.[25] In American terms, it is as though every government bureau in Washington were populated in its upper reaches by alumni of a special school for administrators—a combination of Princeton and West Point—and as though these bureaus had close connections with representatives of the same group in key positions in every state capital and large city.

The intellectuals represent another segment of the "middle classes" with distinct political leanings. By intellectuals we mean those who live by the creation of symbols—teachers,[26] journalists, writers, artists—who in France have for some time tended to the left politically. To be of the left means to be suspicious of power and authority, of economically vested interests, of possible violations of freedoms of expression. The United States was seen by the left as the ally of the French bourgeoisie (except for a short period after the Suez affair); this was sufficient to render it suspect. Violations of civil rights and liberties in the United States, real or imagined, often became *causes célèbres* among French intellectuals; the Rosenberg case, civil rights cases in the South, the Chessman case, all attracted great attention. The same groups that made much of these also called attention to the accusations against the army in Algeria of torturing Muslim prisoners. And in spite of a close affinity for Marxism, some of these groups strongly opposed the Soviet suppression of the Hungarian revolt—far more than the rank and file of the Communist party. French intellectuals—including some professors who held multiple jobs—wrote columns for newspapers and contributed to weekly and monthly journals that occupied a place intermediate between scholarship and political propaganda. They felt a duty to protest against the use of power, though without expecting to participate in it.[27] As a heroine of Simone de Beauvoir's put it, "All the American intellectuals plead impotence. . . . You won't have the right to complain the day the United States becomes completely fascistic, or the day it starts a war."[28]

Occupational groups other than the middle classes showed a similar

degree of fragmentation. Employers were divided on the question of technological change versus conservatism, as were the producers of various agricultural commodities. The labor unions were separated by both the church-
school question and the problem of communism. All these differences found
expression in the fragmentation of the corresponding political interest
groups.

Nationwide Social Ties and Divisions

Although family, community, and occupation normally unite persons
living close to one another, each may extend its ties farther. Migrants retain
connections with family and community; families of the nobility who can
maintain a residence in Paris as well as in the provinces enjoy higher prestige thereby. The occupational system, too, may be seen as a bridge between
community stratification and national stratification. A skill or a profession
may be practiced in various places, and can thus confer status (as well as a
livelihood) far from one's native commune. Thus, particularly for urban occupations, there is a tendency for those in the same occupation to have
similar political preferences. This similarity may also be reinforced by
organizational ties.

But there are other social bonds as well that define the individual's social
position in the national (urbanized) society and link him to others. One of
the most important of these politically is the set of ties deriving from attitudes toward religion. The vast majority of Frenchmen are Catholics, at
least nominally; Jews and Protestants, though they occupy some key positions, are negligible in the vote. But French Catholics have been bitterly
divided since 1789 on the relation between Church and state. The more
devout or "practicing" Catholics are more likely to send their children to
private church schools (*écoles libres*), often participate in the many Catholic
organizations for agriculture, youth, labor, etc., and tended during the
Fourth Republic to vote for conservative parties or the MRP. Those Catholics whose church membership was only nominal, together with a minority
of freethinkers, tended to support the Communists, Socialists, or Radicals,
and to favor public as against church schools. These political differences
divided individual communities, and were extended to the national level
by both the Church and an opposing set of anticlerical organizations. We
have already seen that this division was related to the position of the teaching profession.

Ethnic and regional relations provide national ties and divisions as well.
France, like the United States, prides herself on a capacity to absorb peoples
and cultures.[29] But counting her history in centuries rather than decades,
she absorbs them slowly. During the Fourth Republic, her chief "un-
absorbed" groups were the Algerian Muslims working in France, some
Italian immigrants in the South, and postwar refugees from Eastern Europe.[30]

Within France itself, the heterogeneity of the various regions and their
cultural independence has given a regionalism to politics and an "ethnic"
character to internal migration. Alsatian, Basque, Breton, and Provençal are
distinct regional languages; and though not all are spoken in political gath-

erings, local accents and *patois* may make local politics unintelligible to the Parisian.[31] The Corsicans, though living in metropolitan France, are distinct in name and (somewhat) in political leanings in Marseille. The Bretons who came to Paris to work tend to live in particular *quartiers*.[32] Protestants, though few in number, occupy distinctive places in the French culture and economy, and vote characteristically on the left.[33] A latent anti-Semitism, which flared up in the Dreyfus case, is said to have been a factor in the accusations of disloyalty directed at Mendès-France; yet Jews and Negroes reached higher posts in the government of the Fourth Republic than in the contemporary United States.

Ties of common experience in adult life also link groups across a nation. The educational process, for those who have gone as far as the university and especially for alumni of certain outstanding schools (the *grandes écoles*), gives rise to close friendship groups and to self-conscious elites. The independence as well as the competence of the administration is in this way strengthened. Military service, like the school system, unifies French culture and connects otherwise disparate social groups. Recruitment classes into the army, based on year of birth, constitute bases of mutual classification and sometimes of friendship. But these connections produce only a sense of nationhood, a willingness to *defend* France when she is threatened—not a consensus on gradual internal political change.[34]

The educational system can thus be seen to have various effects on the social ties. First, by its uniformity it contributes to the sense of membership in the nation. Second, at its higher levels, it selects elite groups. The differential recruitment of sons of the urban middle class into the administrative elite also separates this elite from the peasantry, and this cleavage perpetuates itself. Even in the provincial schools for agronomists, relatively few of the students admitted are children of peasants. Third, it creates the opportunity for formation of close friendships among young persons of the same age. Bourricaud points out the importance of the age-grouping: "Our friends we have known since the time that we were students in the same college."[35]

Peer groups are formed in the school, away from family ties; but like the family, they appear to be very stable and self-contained. Pitts considers informal voluntary organizations, related in structure to the peer group, stronger in France than in the United States. And they are stabler, in both structure and beliefs:

> The individual enters them with more difficulty and leaves them much more reluctantly than the American. On the other hand, the French peer groups will not support activities which might put into question the prevailing patterns of economics or political leadership, or require confidence in the benefits of long-term change. . . . No wonder political change in France appears as charismatic movements (the teacher seducing the students) sandwiched between long periods of well-tempered anarchy. The peer group must be bypassed rather than bargained with.[36]

This interpretation of peer groups is parallel to our interpretation of the political parties: that they are structurally stable elements, sustained by be-

liefs in the legitimacy of preserving their place in the existing order, and
that when change is attempted, they are bypassed.

Peer relations mean more to the student than relations with authority.
Friendship with someone of another generation, independent of kinship, is
a rare exception. Only in restricted circles such as an aristocracy, where both
generations are secure in their status, or in the relation of patron and protégé,
can this relation be a close one. In the age structure of the French population there is a great gap corresponding to the birth years 1914–18, as well as
to the losses of soldiers in those years; this gap was an additional barrier to
communication between the generations in France.[37]

The school system also reflects a characteristic of oral argument and discussion that appears in many aspects of French life, including parliamentary
debates. A highly prized skill is that of polished oral presentation of one's
argument in competition with others; oral presentations of this sort are used
in many competitive examinations. What is important is the stylized *expression* of one's position, but not necessarily either persuasion of the lis-
teners or the speaker's own openness to change. This general tendency appears in political argument at private gatherings; if politics is discussed, one
expresses one's position, perhaps even dramatically, but without really
expecting that the others will be convinced. As Bourricaud describes it:

> The English compromise is a voluntary operation, maturely delib-
> erated. . . . The French repudiate this method. They see in it only
> weakness. To discuss, for them, is to show that one is right, to im-
> pose one's point of view. However, as the compromise constitutes an
> indispensable procedure in all social life, the French have recourse
> to it as do others, but without saying so. It is not a question of re-
> flective discussion, between two individuals trying to understand
> one another. It is a question of a tacit accord, one might say shame-
> faced, that things will rest in a state that one will not speak of. Let
> sleeping dogs lie.[38]

Overseas France

During the Fourth Republic, Algeria, sub-Saharan ("black") Africa, and
other French possessions throughout the world were represented in the
National Assembly. Algeria and certain other areas were considered legally
as *départements* like those of metropolitan France, while most of the African
possessions were represented as "overseas territories."[39] In proportion to
their population, these areas were not heavily represented; but they were
important for the government of France because of the tactical positions
taken by the small groups of deputies, chiefly Africans, who represented
these areas. The actions of the representatives and the political leaders of
sub-Saharan Africa are also instructive; for under similar legal conditions
to those of metropolitan France, and often with greater social divisions in
their constituencies, they showed less inclination toward ideological division.

The social divisions that we have discussed for France were magnified
many times in sub-Saharan Africa and particularly in Algeria. The determination of the European settlers to stay in Algeria was buttressed by
the legal status of Algeria as part of France, as well as by three or more

generations' residence. The Muslims, on the other hand, represented an ethnically and religiously distinct group who could seek moral and material aid from the other Muslim nations of North Africa. Their break with France was hastened by France's failure to grant them the equality her laws promised. Cultural values, occupation, wealth, education, all were parts of a deep gulf between the average French settler and the average Muslim.

The social groupings in Algeria and the French Union, like those of mainland France, could be classified in two respects: according to social rank, as before, and according to degree of Europeanization. The latter aspect, distinguishing the colonists at one extreme from the non-Europeanized tribal population at the other, is analogous to the urban-rural distinction in mainland France. For the indigenous population far from the cities, family, community, and traditional culture meant more than occupation.[40] We may regard "indigenous population" and "colonists" as on a cultural continuum, with partly Europeanized groups occupying various intermediate positions. Europeanization was not, however, equivalent to a pro-French political position.

In Algeria the settler population (10 per cent of the whole) was larger and more deeply rooted than in sub-Saharan Africa. In the latter area the resident Europeans were relatively fewer, and more of them were civil servants who considered mainland France their home. But in Algeria there were two distinct stratification systems for Europeans and Moslems. The European[41] population consisted of a small but powerful upper stratum and a large middle-class population. Those Muslims who were Europeanized could move in three alternative directions: the largest number became unskilled workers; those who received more training might either be drawn into cooperation with the Europeans, or turn to the Algerian nationalist movement. At the founding of the Fourth Republic, Algerian political organizations of various views existed, but a steady polarization occurred, speeded by terrorism. Because there were two distinct ranking systems, any classification by social rank is very approximate; a Muslim political leader, for example, could be admired by his followers but scorned, hated, or feared by the settlers.

Our separation of metropolitan France and Algeria contains still further important simplifications. Parts of the population that we associate with each resided in the other area. The officers and men of the French army were in Algeria in large numbers from 1955 on and were a key both to the downfall of the Fourth Republic and to de Gaulle's chances for success. Conversely, the many Algerian Muslims who went to mainland France to work provided the nationalist movements with valuable sources of funds.

The social divisions overseas, though profound, were along quite different lines from those of metropolitan France. The efforts of the French government to apply similar laws to both populations, and the efforts of the political parties to organize support both at home and overseas, revealed to some extent which divisions were social and which political.

On the church-school question, the overseas members of the main political parties voted in ways that would have been quite anomalous for mainland deputies. The African political leaders who temporarily took the Communists as allies and as an organizational model, later broke these ties with none of the bitterness and recrimination that have characterized such breaks in Europe or America. Communist doctrine seemed to have been simply a temporary means to their ends—not a secular religion, nor a position fixed by irreconcilable antagonism to the metropolitan bourgeoisie. Even when the African leaders were planning the organization of the RDA into a mass party, one of them (d'Arboussier) made clear his disapproval of the French intellectual tendency to concentrate exclusively on protests against the use of power: "At no price must we let ourselves succumb to the delight (*volupté*) of being a small group who are right and know it."[42]

Organized Political Interests

Most of the separate social groups we have discussed found expression in political organizations. Family and age groups were not so organized; but occupation, community, local economic interest, and the two sides of the church-school question were. The potential political divisions in France arose not merely from conflicts of individual interest, but also from the forms in which these conflicts could be organized. Political interest groups acted primarily through Paris, rather than the local community; any given interest tended to be more splintered than its counterpart in the United States; and in their actions, French interest groups were even more defensive of the status quo and of their specific vested rights and privileges than were those in the United States.[43]

French interest groups aimed their influence largely at national rather than local government. Even local influence tended to work through local branches of the national administration more than through processes of community decision. The executive of a French *département* was not an elective officer like a state governor, but a prefect, a civil servant functioning under the Ministry of the Interior. He held the power of dissolution over intractable municipal governments. Although local groups could try to influence the prefect, they had little direct political influence on him at the *département* level; a deputy, however, could influence the political control of the administration in Paris and thus cause dusty files to be opened and considered.[44]

It is likely that because of the weakness of local centers of decision in France, more group influence was brought to bear on the central government than there is in the United States. Most pressure groups had their central offices in Paris, and local interest representatives often had to travel to and from the Paris ministries to settle affairs. Many local mayors functioned principally as lobbyists for their cities in Paris, residing in Paris and "infiltrating" the parliament, just as representatives of the home distillers or the veterans did. Both the frequent overlap of local and national offices (the *cumul*) and the continual absence of local mayors from their towns were strong evidence that Paris was a decision center for the municipal affairs of the provinces.[45]

The separation of the French working class from the centers of power in Paris was accentuated by the Communist party's hold on the workers. Their difficulty in winning reforms in economic well-being through political action merely increased their alienation from the other parties; and a slowly growing apathy to the capacity of the Communist Party to affect government did not bring them closer to the other parties.[46] The peasants, too, continued to feel a distrust of Parisian government and of the central administration in which they were under-represented. Some of the functions of economic development in Catholic rural areas were often actually carried out by Catholic organizations rather than the government.[47]

Even aside from the centering of power struggles in Paris, there was additional splintering among French interest groups. Added to the influence of centralization were the diversity of the economy, religious and ideological sources of division, and the "veto group" character of the interest groups themselves.

The well-known contrast between "static" and "dynamic" France found expression in the structure of numerous French interest groups. Organized business was divided by an increasing gap between the modern and unproductive sectors of the economy. The butter-margarine conflict in France was complicated by another fight between the interests of home-produced and creamery-produced butter. Alcohol production was correspondingly represented by the home distillers (*bouilleurs de cru*) and the relatively larger beet growers.[48] Each sector exerted its own appreciable influence, but one was linked to the mystique of the small and the distrust of Paris, the other to the quieter influence of major industry.

The legitimacy accorded to interest groups differed greatly between France and the United States. Employers' groups were more diffident and secretive in France, agricultural groups more anxious to conceal their identity behind a "front" of small peasants.[49] Thibaudet's maxim that a party cannot write "interests" on its banner was still valid, but the interests of small peasants or small enterprise were elevated to the level of ideological principle.

The division between proponents of economic change and defenders of group interests cut across the entire range of French political parties. To a very rough approximation, it would appear that the political extremes were opposed to economic modernization while the center favored it. The "cult of the small" was at the same time a protest against the central authority and a defense of economically backward enterprises. The privilege of the *bouilleurs de cru* to distill alcohol at home was justified, in these terms, as a right associated with the revolution of 1789. The same mentality that defended backward agriculture and backward industry, though supported by the left, denied the urban working classes short-run material benefits. The essence of the leftist position, as taken by the Communist party for example, lay not in immediate material gains for the workers, but in influencing the power structure through which any changes were to take place. If the power structure could not be influenced radically, they would still resist changes taking place through the action of the right.

To the economic and organizational sources of division among and within French interest groups may be added religious and ideological divisions. The church–school issue was fought on both sides by organized groups.[50] There were separate Catholic and socialist trade unions, while the Communists dominated the *Confédération Générale du Travail* (CGT).

There were several distinct Catholic employers' associations; and in labor-management relations, divisions in the plant paralleled those in the community.[51] The vertical gap between employer and worker has also been related to the compartmentalized and self-contained character of groups and the maintenance of social distance.[52]

This system of interest groups was far better adapted to seize or consolidate power for narrow group goals than to form broad national governing coalitions. Railway workers could place more members on pensions than were working,[53] but they were not necessarily concerned with modernizing the railroads. Apartment dwellers could retain rent controls, but this protective action did not contribute to new housing construction. A mixture of socialized and free sectors of the economy imposed unplanned controls—governmental control without planning, in response to pressure-group action—and thus failed to attain the full benefits of either capitalism or socialism.[54] The successes that French planning did achieve were accomplished in spite of the action of political interest groups.

Voluntary Groups: Was France a "Mass Society"?

Political interest groups constitute only one type among the variety of groups that an individual may voluntarily join. Sport clubs, fraternal associations, religious groups, and veterans' associations, for example, may constitute alternatives for spare-time activity, and participation in a political party may be for some a more direct channel to political influence than support of an interest group. The entire range of voluntary associations is viewed by some sociologists as an important foundation for a properly functioning democracy.

Kornhauser has contended that one characteristic feature of French society, underlying some of her political problems, was the dearth of relations intermediate between primary group and nation. He asserts that there were few voluntary associations mediating between the family and the state.[55] These groups have been seen as fulfilling multiple functions. Politically, they are considered to counterbalance the power of the national government and protect the individual against it, as well as to train citizens in political skills. Psychologically, they are considered to anchor the individual's judgment against irrational or extremist appeals, and to give him psychic security.[56] A society whose intermediate groups are weak, though voluntarily joined, is said to have the structure of a "mass" society. It is widely believed that this sort of organization was less prevalent in France than, say, in the United States. In French politics there has been a long-standing distrust of *corps intermédiaires;* early in this century there were legal restrictions on such organizations.[57] One might imagine that the proliferation of political interest groups, noted above, was counterbalanced by their smallness, or that other types of voluntary groups were less numerous in France. Nevertheless, it is desirable to examine the extent of membership in such organizations more closely.

Survey data on organizational membership suggest that a peculiar characteristic of France's group structure were the types of groups as much as the numbers of memberships. A French survey cited by Rose indicates that in 1951, 59 per cent of the French sample were not members of any such groups. More recently, Almond and Verba report nonmembership of only 43 per cent in the United States, with 53 and 56 per cent for Britain and Germany respectively. Other data also suggest that the proportion of non-membership in the United States was at least 47 per cent.[58] Thus while the United States did exceed these other countries in extent of group membership, France was not greatly different from Britain or Germany in this respect.

If we examine the types of associations in which membership was most common, however, we find substantial differences, not only between France and the United States but also between France and some of her European neighbors. This difference in kind is suggested by the specific types of organizations mentioned in the French and American samples. The middle and right-hand columns in Table 2.1 show distributions of types of association for the United States, which permit comparison with the types of French voluntary associations classified in the left-hand column.[59]

The types of groups prevalent in France tended to combine like-minded persons, rather than to promote communication across political divisions. One difference between the two samples is that the category "political parties" is replaced by "civic groups" in the United States; presumably the latter combine members of more diverse political views. Members of the *département* federations and local sections of French party organizations were considerably more active than their counterparts in the United States, even in the big-city machines. National party organizations in France meet frequently, contrasting markedly with party organizations at any level in the United States.[60]

On the other hand, civic associations, activities in local government, and heterogeneous organizations like parent-teachers' associations, were far more characteristic of the United States than of France.[61] This difference existed outside the political domain as well as in it. Table 2.1 shows the prevalence of fraternal and social associations in the United States; only 4 per cent of the French sample belonged to fraternal or social groups, compared to 11 per cent in a similar category in the United States. Almond and Verba give data on related categories of groups: the "fraternal" category, used only for the United States, included 14 per cent of the respondents; the "social" category included 13 for the USA, 14 for Britain, and 10 for Germany.[62] Thus France fell considerably short of these countries while the United States exceeded them in this sort of group membership. Similarly, veterans' groupings were cited by 5 to 7 per cent in the United States and only 3 per cent in France.[63]

In the French sample, 15 per cent do cite membership in athletic, recreational, and cultural associations—categories not given in the 1953 American study. Possibly these organizations grouped persons of different political views, though they were often also separated along political or religious lines. More important, their functions, more specific than those of fraternal or social groupings, may have restricted political discussion.

This contrast supports the notion that organizations that reinforced existing social divisions were more typical in France, while those that cut across other divisions and made decisions at the community level were more characteristic of the United States. Presumably French political interest groups, as a particular type of organization, differed in the same way from those of the United States: they divided local decision units rather than uniting them. It was not so much *corps intermédiaires* as intermediate decision points, such as local government or local collective bargaining, that were weak in France. In sociological terms, conflicts tended to occur at the most inclusive level and influentials in the local community were forced to be "cosmopolitans."[64]

Table 2.1 Membership in Voluntary Associations in
France and the United States

	France (1951)	U. S. A. (1955)		U. S. A. (1953, families)	
Nonmembers	59%	47% or more		47%	
Members of one or more groups	41			53	
	100%			100%	
Members of types of groups:					
Occupational	30%	Unions	14%	Unions	23%
		Occupat'l, Prof'l, Economic	3	Prof'l, Learned	2
Athletic, Recreational	9	Social, Recreational	6		
Cultural	6	Cultural, Educat'l, Alumni	1		
Political parties	5	Political and pressure	1		
		Civic, Service	14	Civic	5
Fraternal, social	4	Lodge, Fraternal	11	Fraternal, Secret	19
				Neighborhood, Ethnic, Special interest	8
Veterans	3	Veterans, Military, Patriotic	5	Veterans	7
Religious	2	Church, Religious	9	Church sponsored	3
				Youth	
Other	2			Other categories	17
Total including duplications	61%		64%		86%

Data for France from Rose, *Theory and Method in the Social Sciences*, pp. 84–85.
Data for U. S. A. 1955 from Hausknecht, *The Joiners*, p. 84.
Data for U. S. A. 1953 from Wright and Hyman, "Voluntary Association Memberships of American Adults," p. 287. The question was, "Does anyone in the family belong to any sort of club, lodge, fraternal order, or union with ten or more members in it?" The total of 86% includes some memberships not classified in the major categories given. No other category exceeded 2 per cent.

Tocqueville's observations of American democracy stressed not only voluntary associations, but also local government and the absence of centralized administration. Possibly the latter aspect of his argument is more relevant for distinguishing the Fourth Republic from contemporary America. Organizations were formed and joined in a different spirit in France and in the United States; rather than grouping a heterogeneous membership for collective action on community or national issues, they simply overlay and expressed preexisting social divisions. Examples would be the network of Catholic organizations in Brittany or Communist-linked organizations in the working-class areas of Paris. The Catholic organizations, however, could engage in local community action, since in the areas where they were strong there was little defensive opposition to them.

A number of measures of the extent of centralization of French society have been given by Gravier. Administrative personnel and expenditures are concentrated at the national level; railroads all radiate from Paris; the educational system has its centers of highest prestige in Paris; and streams of migration have been strongly directed toward Paris. In addition, he points out that outlying areas of France have lost population, while neighboring areas of Switzerland (presumably because of local autonomy) have gained.[65] Phenomena of this kind led Brindillac to ask: "Internal autonomy for Senegal, why not for Normandy?"[66] And while there have been efforts to mitigate this centralization,[67] it is still a problem.

The view of French voluntary associations as more vertical—channeled to Paris—and more divided at the local level, supports certain aspects, but not others, of the contention that France is a "mass society." The mass society, in Kornhauser's terms, combines accessibility of elites with availability of nonelites. Their direct access to one another obtains when intermediate groups are weak and noninclusive.[68]

Yet the very strength and isolation of the French family—and behind this, an institutionalized inaccessibility of the individual—protects both elites and nonelites from unwanted social pressure. It is at least partly for this reason that France has been a second home for so many political and artistic refugees: they have a legitimate claim to privacy. This additional fact is necessary to explain why France, even without procedures for community consensus, is a land of freedom; it suggests, incidentally, that the pluralist freedom which Kornhauser prizes and sees in the United States is only one kind of freedom.[69]

Other alleged features of mass society are its uniform and fluid standards.[70] Even though they may exist in French politics—and even there it is questionable—they certainly do not in either administration or culture. The unity of the elite corps of administrators, backed by the rigidity of the *petits fonctionnaires,* makes their standards anything but fluid. And the firm resistance of the Académie Française and the newspapers to foreign intrusions in the French tongue is one among many examples of the resistance of cultural standards to sudden change.

A still more questionable application of the mass society concept to France is that mass man is "self-estranged" because of his separation from major social processes.[71] On the contrary, the French peasant character is one of autonomy, by virtue of self-restriction to the immediate and secure and avoidance of "adventure."[72] He *is* self-oriented (capable of shaping his own destiny)[73] by virtue of restricting his goals. Thus intermediate groups are not the only condition for individualism; institutions beyond the immediate environment may also be irrelevant. This analysis holds mainly for the peasant and rural dweller, but the influence of their milieu is pervasive. The urban dweller, concerned more with world developments, may conform more to Kornhauser's model. But even in the farmers' barricades or in the street mobs of Algiers there was a strong element of immediate material interest.[74] Only later was a remote and symbolic element added—a call for the Estates General, or a Government of Public Safety.

In mass society, "populist democracy" combines weak rule of law with strong representative rule.[75] It is true that France has taken constitutions lightly and her peasants have avoided taxes, but we should distinguish between Parliament-made law and administrative law. The administration and its own law have been continually strong—in part because representative rule was so ineffective through temporary and heterogeneous coalitions.

Thus France was far from the "ideal type" of the mass society. Voluntary groups existed, but those that were politically important followed administrative and political lines and channeled members' demands to Paris. France's voluntary groups performed some, though not all, of the functions that concern theorists of mass society, and they were aided in some respects by the family, the administration, and cultural traditions. The individual's judgment was anchored—perhaps excessively at times—by the family and cultural traditions, as well as by membership in vertically structured groups.[76] He derived psychic security also from strong family ties, as well as from the prohibition on unrealistic aspirations. The power of the government was checked by strongly resistant veto groups. But the political training given to citizens was deficient: "One does not ask a mayor to know how to administer his commune, but to be clever in intervening with the more or less occult authorities who control subsidies and priorities, to lunch from time to time with a minister. . . ." And as for the party militant in the provinces: "[Centralization] deprives him of nearby objectives; it forbids him any partial experience of government; it places him in a sort of exile. The life of the militant is directed toward the center, whence come the news, passwords, lectures. . . ."[77] The weakness of the political system was that the safeguards against the arousal of citizens (other than in narrowly defensive action) were in a sense *too* effective. Thus when the nation needed to make collective decisions, they were long delayed, and a degree of frustration arose in some segments of the population that did lead to crises and to support for new political movements. But French social structure, rather than being that of a "mass" society, requires analysis in other terms.

Mobility and Social Change

The notion of social structure as we have considered it so far is largely static. But we must also ask how much movement of individuals among statuses took place, and how rapidly the system itself was changing. In a biological analogy, an organism has not only structure, but also metabolism and a life cycle.

The compartmentalization of French society might well be related to limited social mobility. The greater class conflict in Europe than in the United States has sometimes been attributed to a lack of opportunities for widespread upward social mobility in Europe. Yet the study of comparative social mobility in recent years has cast serious doubts on this hypothesis; rates of intergenerational occupational mobility in the general population have been shown to be very similar, among urban occupations, in many industrialized nations. Only mobility into certain elites is more restricted in Europe.[78]

Possibly, however, a greater proportion of the population is mobile in the United States because of its more rapid urbanization. Since 1900 the distribution of the labor force among various occupations has changed much more slowly in France than in the United States. The proportions of the labor force (*population active*) in primary occupations (agriculture, forestry, fishing, and hunting) in 1900 were very similar in France and the United States—44.9 and 42.6 per cent respectively. But by 1950 these proportions had dropped to 30.8 and 15.4 respectively. In this fifty-year period, the proportion of workers in primary occupations in the United States dropped to 36 per cent of its former value, while in France it dropped to only 69 per cent. These percentages represent extreme values, in that the percentages for most of the countries of Western Europe lie between them.[79]

Over and above the gross changes in France's occupational distribution, the occupational mobility of individuals *within* their careers may also differ in France and the United States. The monthly "rotation rates" in industrial employment in the 1950's were about 3.5 per cent in the United States and only 1.5 to 2.7 per cent in France.[80]

One might also imagine that the compartmentalization of French society was maintained by low rates of internal geographical migration.[81] Frenchmen, with their conservative peasant mentality, would not be expected to migrate easily. Attempts to persuade some of the miners of the Cevennes to move to more profitable areas when their mines were exhausted met the reply: "Who will move the graveyard?" Yet available statistics only partly support this hypothesis. Data on migration among geographical subunits show relatively minor differences between France and the United States. The per cent of persons moving among France's 90 *départements* in a year (2.7) was very similar to that moving between the 48 states of the United States (3.2 for 1947–57).[82]

Data on migration since birth (i.e., proportion of population born outside the subunit of current residence) have also been very similar for France and the United States in recent decades. A century ago, the migration rate for the United States calculated on this basis was twice France's, even when there were only thirty-three states. But the French migration rate rose steadily and even somewhat exceeded that of the United States by the 1920's, as Figure 2.1 shows.

The younger generation of French social scientists and politicians, as well as some foreign observers,[83] often see hope for France in its economic development and social change. In this view, increasing social mobility, together with urbanization and industrialization, is an aspect of France that permits alteration of the old political style based on *situations acquises.* But it is not easy to demonstrate that mobility increased during the Fourth Republic. The intergenerational occupational mobility of persons 40 to 60 years old was actually greater than that of persons aged 20 to 40.[84] Perhaps this fact can be attributed to mobility within careers, or to the dislocations of World War II; but it fails to support the contention of marked increases in mobility.

National surveys in France and the United States also permit a rough assessment of the extent of change in occupational mobility over the past two generations. Table 2.2 shows the proportions of male respondents whose

Figure 2.1 Migration from Place of Birth in France and the United States

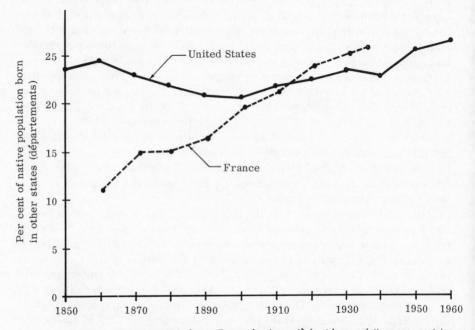

Sources: Goreux, "Les Migrations agricoles en France depuis un siècle et leurs relations avec certains facteurs économiques," *Études et Conjoncture*, p. 331n.; Beltramone, "Sur la Mesure des migrations intérieures au moyen des données fournies par les recensements," *Population*, 717; *Statistical Abstract of the United States*, 1956; United States Bureau of the Census, *Historical Statistics of the United States, Colonial Times to 1957: Continuation to 1962 and Revisions*, 1965.

fathers had been in the same occupation as themselves, and corresponding proportions for their grandfathers. For corresponding occupations, the proportional decline in occupational inheritance from fathers to grandfathers is not greatly different in the two countries.

Changes in the French economy have undoubtedly brought social changes, especially since 1952; the expansion of the tertiary sector of the economy, together with a rising material standard of living, have been cited as reasons for declining class consciousness. But this expansion has been far less rapid than in the United States.[85]

We must conclude that although social mobility is restricted in certain respects in French society, it is by no means generally lower than in the United States. Rather a detailed distinction is necessary between types of mobility that are restricted and those that are not. Concerning development

Table 2.2 *"Occupational Inheritance" from Fathers and Grandfathers in France and United States**

Occupation	France		Occupation	United States	
	Fathers	Grand-fathers		Fathers	Grand-fathers
Large proprietors, liberal professions	32%	16%	Professional	23%	15%
			Business	31	20
Higher civil servants, managers	17	10			
Lower civil servants, white-collar	31	11	White-collar	15	5
Merchants, artisans	54	36			
Farm owners	83	78	Farm	84	82
Farm workers	37	30			
Workers (nonfarm)	48	35	Skilled workers	30	18
			Semiskilled	19	8
			Unskilled	20	11
			Service	9	3

*Table entries are percentages in same occupation as respondents, among fathers and among grandfathers, based on the samples of those who gave occupations of fathers and grandfathers respectively.

Source: Bresard, "Mobilité sociale et dimension de la famille"; National Opinion Research Center (NORC), "Jobs and Occupations: A Popular Evaluation," in Bendix and Lipset, etd., *Class, Status, and Power*, pp. 424–425.

and renovation, the data lead one to look for long-run change, perhaps over another generation, rather than in a few years. In sum, the picture of a mobile society that is nevertheless compartmentalized supports the characterization of French society as one whose inner boundaries can be "crossed but not destroyed."[86]

NOTES

1. On the contrast between these two types of subgroup structure, see Coleman, *Community Conflict*, and Dahrendorf, *Class and Class Conflict*, pp. 215ff.

2. Chenery, "Patterns of Industrial Growth." French data are for 1952–54.

3. See Mendras, *Sociologie de la campagne française*, Chap. V.

4. See Lipset, Trow, and Coleman, *Union Democracy*, pp. 275–280, and Coleman, *Community Conflict*.

5. There remain, however, two major exceptions in the United States: the regional separation of the South and the social separation of the Negro.

6. A similar analysis of the social structure of India has been made by Morris-Jones in *The Government and Politics of India*, pp. 63–64.

7. This is a much simplified notion of social structure in comparison with detailed conceptualizations such as those in Parsons, *The Social System,* esp. pp. 51ff., or Merton, *Social Theory and Social Structure*, pp. 368–384. For systematic descriptions of French social structure see also John E. Sawyer, "Strains in the Social Structure of Modern France," in Earle, ed., *Modern France;* and Gurvitch, "Social Structure of Pre-War France."

8. In Paris, this is more true of the bourgeois and less true of working-class families, who visit more with their neighbors; see Chombart de Lauwe *et al., Paris et l'agglomération parisienne*, pp. 104–106. Among the upper class and nobility, family also counts for more.

9. Métraux and Mead, *Themes in French Culture,* and Martha Wolfenstein, "French Parents Take Their Children to the Park," in Mead and Wolfenstein, eds., *Childhood in Contemporary Cultures.*

10. Lerner, "Interviewing Frenchmen."

11. See de Vulpian, "Physionomie agraire et orientation politique dans le département des Côtes-du-Nord," 119ff., and Derruau-Boniol, "Le Départment de la Creuse," 54ff. Though the strength and distinctness of kinship ties protect the family against certain outside influences, the influence of emigrants through family ties may be an avenue of gradual change in rural France.

12. Pitt-Rivers, "Social Class in a French Village," 5.

13. See David S. Landes, "French Business and the Businessman: A Social and Cultural Analysis," in Earle, ed., *Modern France,* and Pitts, *The Bourgeois Family and French Economic Retardation*, Chaps. XIV–XVII.

14. See Bresard, "Mobilité sociale et dimension de la famille," 541; Institut National de la Statistique et des Études Économiques, "L'Enquête par sondage sur l'emploi de juin 1953," 40; Centers, "Marital Selection and Occupational Strata," 530–535. The general similarity between European and American rates of occupational intermarriage is also discussed in Lipset and Bendix, *Social Mobility in Industrial Society*, pp. 42ff.

15. See Wylie, *Village in the Vaucluse,* p. 211, and Crozier, "La France, terre de commandement."

16. Wylie, *Village in the Vaucluse,* p. 211. This aspect of personal relations is also described in Mendras, *Sociologie de la campagne française,* pp. 100ff.

17. Pitt-Rivers, "Social Class in a French Village," gives a similar example of a Socialist doctor campaigning on his personal prestige. He also points out that various criteria of social ranking may exist within a given community.

18. Chiefly Brittany; see Mendras' map in Fauvet and Mendras, eds., *Les Paysans et le politique,* p. 35.

19. He held this position several times during the Third Republic; see *ibid.,* pp. 262–263.

20. See Duverger, ed., *Partis politiques et classes sociales,* chapter by G. Lavau on middle classes.

21. This intermediate position of the artisans also appears in the community studied by Pitt-Rivers, "Social Class in a French Village."

22. See Landes, "Observations on France: Economy, Society, Polity."

23. A parallel between Poujadism and McCarthyism has been suggested by Lipset in *Political Man,* p. 170. But even though similar social groups were represented in the two movements, their expressions were quite different; direct protest against modernization and taxation has far less legitimacy in the United States.

24. See Ehrmann, *Organized Business in France.*

25. The social origins of the higher civil service are analyzed in Bottomore, "La mobilité sociale dans la haute administration française." Detailed statistics on the origins and later employment of ENA students are given in *Promotions.* Langrod describes the structure of French administration in *Some Current Problems of Administration in France Today.* An insightful account of the political views of this group is given by Brindillac in "Les hauts fonctionnaires;" he also observes that the ENA's recruitment did reduce the advantages of the *haute bourgeoisie* or "bourgeois dynasties."

26. Some intellectuals are also civil servants; but one may distinguish roughly between the teachers in *lycées* and below, who react more in terms of party and interest group, and the university teachers, who though civil servants tend to take more independent positions.

27. Among the French political leaders, however, were a number who had distinguished themselves in literature and were highly cultured.

28. de Beauvoir, *The Mandarins,* pp. 563–564. For further detail on the contrasting status and views of American and European intellectuals, see Lipset, *Political Man,* Chapter X, and Stanley Hoffmann, "Protest in Modern France," in Kaplan, ed., *The Revolution in World Politics.*

29. See Morazé, *The French and the Republic,* pp. 187–196.

30. See Girard and Stoetzel, eds., *Français et immigrés.*

31. See Pitt-Rivers, "Social Class in a French Village," and Williams, *Crisis,* p. 330 on General Koenig's linguistic shortcomings at Alsatian campaign meetings.

32. Chombart de Lauwe, *et al., Paris et l'agglomération parisienne,* p. 100. Though in America immigrants do likewise, internal migrants are less likely to do so.

33. Schram, *Protestantism and Politics in France.*

34. See Rémond, "Les Anciens Combattants et la politique." In the Gaullist politics of 1958, veterans of Indochina and of Algeria played a special part as activists.

35. François Bourricaud, "France," in Rose, ed., *The Institutions of Advanced Societies,* p. 511.

36. Jesse R. Pitts, "The Family and Peer Groups," in Bell and Vogel, eds., *A Modern Introduction to the Family,* pp. 266–286. That this state of affairs was changing has been suggested by Laurence Wylie in "Social Change at the Grass Roots," in Hoffmann, *et al., In Search of France.*

37. Morazé, *The French and the Republic,* p. 18, and Gurvitch, "Social Structure."

38. Bourricaud, "France," in Rose, ed., *The Institutions of Advanced Societies*, p. 520.

39. The overseas *départements* included French Guiana and the islands of Guadeloupe, Martinique, and Réunion. The overseas territories included Madagascar, St. Pierre and Miquelon, Oceania, New Caledonia, the Comores, and (for a period) the French possessions in India.

40. For a more detailed description of the social structure and customs of the various indigenous populations, see Bourdieu, *Sociologie de l'Algérie;* Little, "West African Urbanization as a Social Process;" Hodgkin and Schachter, "French-Speaking West Africa in Transition," 375–387. On the educated and politicized groups of sub-Saharan Africa, see Morgenthau, *Political Parties in French-Speaking West Africa*, Chap. 1.

41. Not necessarily French in national origin; Spanish and Italian names were frequent among the leaders of the settlers' political organizations.

42. Hamon, "Introduction à l'étude des partis politiques de l'Afrique française," 156.

43. See Brown, "Pressure Politics in France," 713.

44. See Chapman, *Introduction to French Local Government,* and Kesselman, *French Local Government.*

45. An analysis of a deputy's mail under the Fifth Republic suggests the administrative functions on which he was expected to do casework, that would not have concerned a congressman: e.g., individual housing problems, allocation of licenses for tobacco stores, work permits. See Lancelot, "Le courrier d'un parlementaire."

46. See Macridis, "The Immobility of the French Communist Party."

47. These organizations are described in Marcel Faure, "Action catholique en milieu rural," in Fauvet and Mendras, *Les Paysans et la politique,* pp. 345–360. See also Bosworth, *Catholicism and Crisis in Modern France,* Chap. 4.

48. See, respectively, Goguel, *France under the Fourth Republic,* pp. 154–155; Ehrmann, *Organized Business in France,* p. 321; Meynaud, *Les groupes de pression en France,* pp. 236–240; Brown, "Alcohol and Politics in France."

49. Georges-E. Lavau, "Political Pressures by Interest Groups in France," in Ehrmann, ed., *Interest Groups on Four Continents,* pp. 67, 77.

50. Brown, "Religious Schools and Politics in France."

51. Ehrmann, *Organized Business in France,* pp. 189ff., 335.

52. Crozier, *The Bureaucratic Phenomenon,* and Lavau, "La Réforme des institutions," 289.

53. According to Meynaud, in *Les groupes de presssion en France,* p. 262, the number of retired railway workers was 99 per cent as great as the working force in 1957, with an average retirement age of 57. Later the ratio passed 100 per cent.

54. See Baum, *The French Economy and the State.*

55. Kornhauser, *The Politics of Mass Society,* pp. 84ff.

56. See Lipset, Trow, and Coleman, *Union Democracy,* p. 80, for the political functions mentioned; the others are inferred from Kornhauser, *The Politics of Mass Society.*

57. See Arnold M. Rose, "Voluntary Associations in France," in his *Theory and Method in the Social Sciences.* That voluntary associations were fewer in France is also suggested by Gallagher, "Voluntary Associations in France;" but his only statistical data are on numbers of associations in two communities. He considers associations to be either linked to traditional social structures, such as nobility or community, or supplanted by them.

58. The French data are from a survey conducted by the Service de Sondages et Statistiques, reported in Rose, *Theory and Method in the Social Sciences*, pp. 84–85; the question was, "*Êtes-vous membre d'un groupement quelconque, tel que syndicat, club, parti politique, amicale, etc.?*" On Britain, Germany, and the United States see Almond and Verba, *The Civic Culture*, p. 302. Other United States data, from NORC surveys, are reported in Wright and Hyman, "Voluntary Association Memberships of American Adults: Evidence from National Sample Surveys." A 1955 study showed 64 per cent of a national sample as nonmembers, with union membership excluded. Since 17 per cent of adults were union members (see note *infra*), this suggests at least 47 per cent were nonmembers. The question used was, "Do you happen to belong to any groups or associations in the community here?" A 1953 NORC survey indicated 47 per cent of families as having no group member, again suggesting that at least this proportion of individuals were nonmembers. A similar figure was found in an AIPO survey in 1954 (45 per cent nonmembers), though not based on a probability sample; see Hausknecht, *The Joiners*, p. 23. A related comparison has also been made in Nordlinger, "Democratic Stability and Instability: The French Case."

59. The accuracy of certain figures here also receives support from other sources. A total party membership of 1.4 million, or 5 per cent of 29 million adults, is obtained by addition of figures from Williams, *Politics in Post-War France*, and Duverger, *Political Parties*. A study of the town of Auxerre showed 6 per cent of adults belonging to political parties, 43 per cent for occupational, 7 per cent for athletic-recreational, 10 per cent for cultural groups; see Bettelheim and Frère, *Une Ville française moyenne: Auxerre en 1950*. The U.S. union membership in 1955 was 17 million among 100 million adults, and Dupeux gives the same percentage for France in 1958; see "France," 44.

60. Only certain "amateur" movements within the American parties resemble the French in this respect; see Wilson, *The Amateur Democrat*.

61. Wylie writes of the youth club in Peyrane, a heterogeneous organization that failed: "Politics showed its head, and naturally that was the end of the club." *Village in the Vaucluse*, p. 211.

62. Almond and Verba, *The Civic Culture*, p. 302.

63. Almond and Verba, *ibid.*, give figures of 6, 5, and 1 per cent for the U.S.A. U.K., and Germany respectively. The lower figure for Germany may be attributable to her particular postwar experience.

64. See Coleman, *Community Conflict*, p. 23, and Merton, *Social Theory and Social Structure*, pp. 387–420. The mayor's role in influencing Paris is analyzed critically in Brindillac, "Décoloniser la France," 802. He was "cosmopolitan" in being concerned with Paris, even while aiming at action in the local community. See also Wylie, *Village in the Vaucluse*, Chap. 14.

65. Gravier, *Décentralisation et progrès technique*, pp. 37, 39ff., 49, 94–95. He also criticized French centralization in his earlier *Paris et le désert français*.

66. Brindillac, "Décoliniser la France," 799. For a more general treatment of these issues see Stanley Hoffmann, "The Areal Division of Powers in the Writings of French Political Thinkers," in Maass, ed., *Area and Power*.

67. E.g., in regional planning. See Bauchet, *Economic Planning*, Part I; Institut d'Études Politiques de l'Université de Grenoble, *Administration traditionelle et planification régionale*.

68. Kornhauser, *The Politics of Mass Society*, pp. 40, 84. "Noninclusive" means restricted to particular aspects of their members' lives.

69. The possible conflict between individual autonomy and the functioning of a complex society is pointed out in Winston White, *Beyond Conformity*. And Crozier points out that a tradition of individual resistance, rather than decentralized power, has compensated for French centralization; see "Le Citoyen," 205.

70. Kornhauser, *The Politics of Mass Society*, p. 103.

71. *Ibid.*, p. 108.

72. Lerner, "Interviewing Frenchmen," and his "The 'Hard-Headed' Frenchman."

73. Kornhauser, *The Politics of Mass Society*, p. 110.

74. See Gusfield, "Mass Society and Extremist Politics."

75. Kornhauser, *The Politics of Mass Society*, p. 131.

76. On stable social structure as a hindrance to mass movements in France, see Rémond, *The Right Wing in France*, pp. 293–294.

77. Brindillac, "Décoloniser la France," 802, 803.

78. This work is reviewed, and data are given, in Lipset and Bendix, *Social Mobility in Industrial Society*, Chap. II.

79. These values are calculated by interpolation from Fourastié, ed., *Migrations professionelles*, pp. 29–30.

80. Madinier, "La Mobilité du travail aux États-Unis et en France," 565, 572, gives figures for both countries and shows French rotation rates to have increased over time. But his method gives extremely low values of French rotation rates, seemingly not comparable with those of the United States. Thus the French figures we cite are based on studies of the textile industry in Organisation for Economic Co-Operation and Development, *Joint International Seminar on Geographical and Occupational Mobility of Manpower*, pp. 15, 26.

81. It is widely believed that the migration rate is considerably higher in the United States than in Europe; this supposition has served as basis for an interpretation of "other-directedness" in the United States. See Heberle, "A Note on Riesman's *The Lonely Crowd.*"

82. Sources: Institut National de la Statistique et des Études Économiques, "Les Migrations d'électeurs de 1949 à 1953," 6 (data are corrected by regression on net migration for entire population); *Statistical Abstract of the United States, 1952–1960.* More systematic examination of the effect of number of subdivisions on migration rates indicates that the French figure would have been about 2.3 per cent had there been only 48 subdivisions. This is based on an empirical approximation, tested for a number of countries, that the proportion migrating varies as the logarithm of the number of subdivisions.

83. Tannenbaum, *The New France*, and Wright, *Rural Revolution in France*, esp. Chap. 8; and several articles in *Daedalus*, 93 (Winter 1964).

84. Institut National de la Statistique et des Études Économiques, "L'Enquête par sondage sur l'emploi de juin 1953," 38.

85. See Aron, *France: Steadfast and Changing*, Chap. 3, and Fourastié, *Migrations professionelles*.

86. Stanley Hoffmann, "Paradoxes of the French Political Community," in Hoffmann et al., *In Search of France*, p. 4.

>> 3 <<

Political Parties
and the National Assembly

THE POLITICAL PARTIES OF THE Fourth Republic reflected many of France's internal divisions. The church-school question, the problem of state intervention in the economy, urban-rural conflicts, the distinction between "static" and "dynamic" France, the division of the working-class vote through the Communist party's obedience to Moscow—all contributed to the divisions between parties.

Yet not all political parties represent interests in the same way. They select among interests, stressing some at the expense of others. They organize interests and issues and even generate them from ideological principles. Like all organizations, they also develop interests of their own, centering about party survival, growth, or power. Thus some interests find representation through a single party, while others appeal to many parties or to none. Conversely, some parties are relatively inflexible in the interests they can represent, because of either doctrine or structure; others can alter their base of support over time, or gain support from diverse groups all at once. The parties of the Fourth Republic differed from one another in all these respects. To specify the elements of consensus and dissensus that they embodied, we must compare them with one another in structure and aims, both inside and outside the Assembly.[1]

The differences in structure among the major parties were reflected in the number and activities of their members and the social recruitment of their leaders, as well as in their formal organization and the conduct of party affairs. But the most important differences among the parties as they affected the decision power of the cabinets were those that made themselves felt in the Assembly. The parties differed greatly in their degree of discipline on votes, the Communists, Socialists, and MRP being generally most cohesive. This difference implied that a faction within one of the less cohesive parties in the cabinet's supporting coalition could challenge the cabinet openly in the Assembly, while a similar faction among the Socialists or MRP normally had to work through the party machinery to move the party as a whole into opposition.

Even more important than the structure of the parties in the Assembly was their numerical strength. The numbers of deputies belonging to parties that could support possible cabinets was sharply limited; for most of the

41

Fourth Republic, only about four hundred of the six hundred votes in the Assembly were conceivably available for support of some cabinet, and not all of these at the same time. Thus the differences in structure among the parties have to be considered in conjunction with the distribution of party strength in the Assembly, as we approach the critical question of cabinet instability.

The Party System

The major parties of the Fourth Republic in one sense existed in reciprocal opposition to one another. They would not have been what they were had it not been for the particular opposition they encountered. Thus MRP was forced to be a "clerical" party, partly because of the existence of the Radicals, and conversely; Gaullism existed in opposition to the immobility of the "system," and drew a strong defensive reaction from it; the Socialist party owed some of its lack of dynamism to its confrontation with the Communist party, while fears that the Socialists were inclining to the right contributed to Communist support.[2] The party system must therefore be explained before the parties.

In view of the social divisions we have considered and their historical roots, it is not surprising that France has had a multiparty system. Other explanations may be sought as well—in social relations and perceptual style or in the influence of the electoral system—but these may well reflect or express the same social divisions. Perhaps still another expression of the difficulty of achieving consensus is the fact that French political groupings seem unable to die gracefully. The United States normally has a two-party system; but if the Federalists, Whigs, Know-Nothings, Populists, Bull Moose Progressives, and Dixiecrats all still existed, we would have a very complex multiparty system.

Multipartyism in France has sometimes been attributed to her electoral systems.[3] Under the Fourth Republic, proportional representation was used in general legislative elections. With from two to eleven seats available in each district, more than this number of parties or factions normally aspired to election. The system of *apparentements* (electoral alliances) used in the 1951 and 1956 elections made it possible for even smaller parties to maintain candidacies without jeopardizing their larger allies' chances. The single-member run-off system (*scrutin d'arrondissement*), which existed during most of the Third Republic and is now used in the Fifth, tended to encourage fractionation on the first ballot followed by party alliances on the second. Only between 1871 and 1873 was there anything like the one-ballot plurality system of England and the United States.[4]

Since electoral systems that curtailed fractionation were so unpopular, we can infer that strong influences other than the electoral system favored party fractionation. But to admit that France's electoral systems have been partly a result of political divisions does not preclude their being a cause as well. Presumably these systems were chosen in order to preserve or enhance an existing fragmentation; and within the general family of fractionating electoral systems, one system may accomplish this end more fully than another.

The explanation most frequently given for French multipartyism traces it to a series of bitter internal controversies extending over a long period of her history. The revolutions of 1789, 1830, and 1848; the Commune of 1871; the struggles between the Republic and the Church at the turn of the century; the Popular Front, the pro-German collaborationists, and Vichy; the Algerian question, embedded in the larger context of France's place in the world—all have left their scars. In the United States the scars of the Civil War remain but Shays' Rebellion has disappeared, while disputes dating from 1789 leave traces in France;[5] the class consciousness of the IWW has subsided in the AFL-CIO, while French labor is still divided; the religious issue of 1960–61 affected a presidential election and Kennedy's legislative program but did not provoke the resignation of a cabinet member, as it did in the Debré cabinet.

The frequency and intensity of these controversies themselves require explanation. Some writers have attributed them to the fact that the overthrow of an absolute monarchy divided the country at the same period as religious questions and class conflicts, rather than at a different historical epoch.[6] Whatever their cause, they find expression in a divided social structure and pose chronic problems for the party system.

A cursory examination of the continuity and diversity of political tendencies in France from 1789 to the Fourth Republic shows not only the persistence of political groupings once they are formed, but also the continual addition of new ones. Monarchism had died out, and the MRP had emerged as a fullblown party; but in many respects the political tendencies of the Fourth Republic dated back to the Revolution and recognized their antecedents.[7]

The Jacobin tradition of 1789 in its extremism and subjugation of means to ends was still somewhat identified with the Communist party; during the Fourth Republic, history teachers in the *lycées* were suspected of Communist sympathies if they were too favorable to Robespierre. Public opinion data on preferences for historical personages showed clear party differences; voters of the left preferred Robespierre, of the right, Joan of Arc.[8] Left-wing Radicals formed a "Jacobin Club" in 1950 and later supported Mendès-France.[9] Socialists as well as Communists made the annual pilgrimage to the *Mur des Fédérés* where in 1871 the Communards were shot. And the official but seldom-used name of the Socialist party, *Section Française de l'Internationale Ouvrière* (SFIO), was itself an anachronism.

The somewhat less extreme Girondin tradition may have found its later expressions in the Radical party, and perhaps even in the present day SFIO, outflanked on the left by the Communists.[10] The bourgeoisie of the nineteenth century, and later the urban upper middle classes, supported Louis Philippe in 1830; the heirs of these groups later supported a series of conservative parties, up to the "Moderates" of the Fourth Republic. Plebiscitary support for a strong leader burst out periodically under the two Napoleons, and similar mass support developed later for Boulanger and de Gaulle. The legitimist tradition (support for the Bourbon dynasty) was strong until the 1870's, when the Count de Chambord threw away its chances by insisting on his white flag rather than the republican tricolor. With the *Ralliement* of the Church to the Republic in 1892, there arose a possibility for social Catholicism as well as conservative Catholicism; this movement became a major political party, the MRP, with the advent of the Fourth Republic.

Thus all the major political parties at the start of the Fourth Republic (except the MRP) had their roots a hundred or more years in the past. The divisions between them were reinforced not only by a series of political conflicts, but also by a remarkably persistent historical memory, refreshed by the continual acting out of old historical dramas in new circumstances. As Luethy writes, "Since 1789 events have been dated not by centuries, decades, or years, but by dates of the month."[11]

The MRP was the newest of the stable parties, and this fact was related to some of its peculiarities. It had a widely distributed electorate, especially at first, and was not deeply entrenched in local offices.[12] It thus favored proportional representation—the system under which it obtained more seats than even the Communists in 1946—against the greater localism of the alternative *scrutin d'arrondissement.*

The MRP also had a particular vocabulary and spirit and was less easily involved in local party alliances than some of the other stable parties—even while its deputies were more constantly involved in cabinet coalitions. But though the MRP was usually represented in the cabinet, its leaders, like those of the ex-Gaullists, were not those who conformed most to the informal rules of the Assembly's "game." Georges Bidault as Premier failed to resign easily as others did; and the MRP's share of cabinet posts was usually proportionally less than that of the other cabinet parties in relation to their supporting votes.

Although the major parties had deep historical roots, many minor ones, particularly the overseas parties, did not. In metropolitan France, some minor parties derived their existence specifically from Vichy and the Resistance: the Petainist UNIR and the UDSR are respective examples. Other small parties, such as the RGRIF, were mere heterogeneous alliances to meet requirements of the electoral laws. The principal parliamentary significance of minor parties resulted from the votes that some of them could supply to sustain a cabinet when needed. The UDSR benefited greatly from this fact, furnishing a disproportionate number of ministers. Some of the African parties also learned to derive material benefits from the system by using their votes judiciously.[13]

The leading politicians of sub-Saharan French Africa tended initially to affiliate in the Assembly with the metropolitan parties—Communists, Socialists, MRP, and later UDSR. But the major African party, the *Rassemblement Démocratique Africain* (RDA), was created in October 1946; in November 1948 an opposing party, the *Indépendants d'Outre-Mer* (IOM), was formed. The RDA first patterned its organization on the Communists and voted with them in the Assembly; but in 1950 they broke with the Communists and later entered several cabinets. As the African parties gained strength they came to have their own parliamentary groups rather than affiliating with the metropolitan parties. Earlier, however, they had profited from membership in multiple parties by concentrating their numbers in the committee on overseas affairs—a tactic commonly followed by nonideological interests such as agriculture. The African deputies elected in 1951 tended to be less militant, as they had benefited from government-rigged elections.[14]

In addition to the pro-cabinet overseas parties, more strongly nationalist parties were also represented in the Assembly. The group[15] *Triomphe des Libertés Démocratiques en Algérie,* represented by a few deputies in the

First Legislature, was the last parliamentary expression of the Algerian nationalist movement; several of its leaders later became officials of the National Liberation Front (FLN) and of the Algerian Provisional Government. The Madagascan nationalist movement was also represented in the First Legislature by three deputies, who later had to be recorded on roll calls as "unable to take part in the vote" as they were jailed after the 1947 revolt. They, too, were later represented in the government of the Malagasy Republic. But notwithstanding these open conflicts, the Fourth Republic succeeded in maintaining the sympathy of many of the leaders of sub-Saharan Africa for France even after independence.

The Structure of Political Parties

Political parties are organizations, but they should not be confused with bureaucracies. Their lower and middle levels may be actuated, far more than those of bureaucracies, by external sources of power. Subordinate employees in business or government administration do often depend on outside clienteles for their success; but they can rarely secede and take their clienteles with them, as some elective politicians can. Nor can they bargain so effectively within the organization by virtue of their outside influence. In a nation that practices representative government in decentralized units, the possibilities for independent influence through elective office are many.

A second difference between a political party and a Weberian bureaucracy[16] lies in the fact that some of its members do not have full-time, regularly remunerated careers in the organization. One of the advantages of the career politician over the part-time member lies in the personal resources he can devote to party affairs.[17]

The members (especially the more active "militants") nevertheless exert influence within the party; this upward influence and its legitimacy makes a party more like a voluntary association than a bureaucracy.[18] Still less involved than the members are those whose only relation with the party is their vote. Their allegiances and their political demands, which may be appealed to in campaigns, set limits on the policies of party activists, but scarcely ever determine the party's detailed strategy and tactics.

The structure of a typical party may be regarded as a pair of parallel hierarchies, geographically based, as in Table 3.1. At each level from the nation down, public officials are ordinarily chosen by popular suffrage,[19] and internal party officials are chosen by the party members but not by the electorate at large. The influence and membership of these two groups normally interpenetrates. Often an internal party organ will, by party statutes, include public officeholders. Conversely, the internally chosen officials of a party may have direct influence over the choices of its elected members. This could occur even in a relatively undisciplined party, as in the Radicals' Cadillac Committee, which determined whether a member of the party could enter the cabinet.[20]

The external part of a political party, based on holding public office, does not conform to the model of either a bureaucracy or a voluntary association. With the exception of the cabinet and the mayor, no elective element is directly chosen by the element below. Rather, the various levels are elected independently in constituencies of different size; their relations within the party depend on bargaining processes, in which the greater power normally goes with the larger constituency. But in France, as in the United States, municipal office in a large city may sometimes take precedence over

Table 3.1 Structure of a Typical French Party

Level	Public Office (External)	Party Membership (Internal)
Nation	Cabinet Deputies, Senators (organized in parliamentary groups)	Executive Committee (continuous) National Council (every few months) Party Congress (annual or less often)
Département (or parliamentary constituency)	*Département* Council (*Conseil Général*)	Federation
Commune (*canton*, urban *arrondissement*)	Mayor Municipal Council	Section (committee, cell)

a position in the national legislature, and other variations in personal power may cause departures from an ordering such as that of Table 3.1.

The parties of the Fourth Republic differed from one another in their various relations among these public and internal offices. In general, the public officers were more influential in parties of the right, and the internal organizations in parties of the left; the parties of the left tended to be more centralized. But a careful examination of party structure reveals exceptions to these generalizations, as well as differences in relations among party officials, members, and voters. These differences are important in the representation of district interests, accessibility to pressure, and possible cabinet coalitions.[21]

A major classification of French parties is of Duverger's, who distinguishes them primarily in terms of the organization of their smallest units.[22] Caucus, branch, and cell were typical basic units for parties ranging from right to left respectively; militia organization became relevant by 1958, when veterans of Indochina staffed some of the extreme nationalist parties. The parties of the right and right center were organized about restricted groups of well-known local personages (*notables*), the Socialist parties about branches for political education of the working class, and the Communist party about a tighter organization based largely on the workplace and adapted for secrecy.

In this classification Duverger considers the United States parties "archaic," denying that recruiting leaders among professional politicians makes a difference. Certainly the "courthouse gang" of the small county seat and the big-city organization are unconcerned with periodic meetings between elections for political education; but they differ from the traditional category of French *notables* in their capacity to become known through politics itself. Pure *notables* are recruited from strata with social prestige outside politics, and are thus likely to be conservative. Millionaires, generals, industrialists, journalists, and members of locally respected families have indeed capitalized on these statuses in American politics; but relatively more frequent is the politician who has acquired fame (or notoriety) through his own political activity.[23] The quest for votes does not force American party organizations to be conservative; rather it makes them temporary vehicles for many sorts of specific grievances. Whatever the shortcomings of localism or nonideological politics, the system permits political mobility.

In Duverger's classification, the internal structure of a party *is* the structure of the party.[24] This approach includes parties that do not possess public offices; but it may detract from the study of conservative parties or the American national parties, in which the actions of public officeholders predominate. In the present analysis, we are especially concerned with parties in the National Assembly; for this purpose it is preferable to consider a party as a dual organism, rather than restricting the term "party" to its internal part.

Structural Differences Among the Parties in the Fourth Republic

The parties of the Fourth Republic differed from one another both in their centralization (the influence of central versus local organs) and in the influence of their external and internal parts. Centralization is ordinarily associated with control by the internal part of the party, but not necessarily if the parliamentary group or an elected official exercises control. Decentralization may correspond to control over party decisions by local militants (as in the Socialist party), by local public officials, or by local influences outside the party framework.

Differences in centralization among the parties were reflected in their voters' acceptance of party decisions, as is shown by answers to two survey questions put to a sample of the public by the Institut Français d'Opinion Publique (IFOP) just before the October 1946 referendum (at which the Constitution of the Fourth Republic was adopted). The respondent was asked first how he would vote if his (national) party recommended that he vote *pour,* and then what his vote would be if his party recommended *contre.* The extent to which voters said their preferences would be altered by their party's recommendation reflects the party's influence over them, and inferentially, over the party's local officeholders (Table 3.2). This alteration may be measured by the difference in per cent *pour* (or *contre*) in relation to the party's stand. The decrease of central control from left to right is clear, if the MRP is placed to the left of the Radicals. We shall see that the MRP was more centralized and disciplined than the Radicals, but that in the church-school question and the competition for votes the Radicals were farther to the "left."

A related measure of voters' support for their national parties appeared in answers to a question asked in 1952 by IFOP: "Does the party you voted for have your entire confidence . . . ?" The rank order of parties was: Communists, 62 per cent "full confidence;" MRP, 51 per cent; Socialists, 48 per cent; RPF, 45 per cent; Radicals, 37 per cent; and Conservatives, 31 per cent.[25] The MRP, having lost most of its temporary Conservative supporters by 1952, enjoyed the fuller support of its remaining members. The RPF appears in an intermediate position, which reveals that its voters were not as unquestioningly loyal as General de Gaulle might have wished; this structural weakness foreshadowed the party's later difficulties in maintaining discipline in the Assembly.

Table 3.2 Influence of Parties on Voters at the October 1946 Referendum

		Communist PCF	Socialist SFIO	Chris- tian Dem. MRP	Radical RGR	Conserv- ative PRL	Entire Sample
Party recommen- dation	*Respon- dent's vote*						
Pour	Pour	85%	65%	42%	45%	35%	50%
Contre	Pour	18	26	20	25	21	20
	Difference	67	39	22	20	14	30
Contre	Contre	62	40	48	39	59	43
Pour	Contre	3	11	27	22	44	17
	Difference	59	29	21	17	15	26
	Average difference	63	34	22	18	14	28

Source: *Sondages*, October 16, 1946, No. 18, p. 239.

The degree of centralization of a party was also reflected in its national congresses. Congresses were held more often by parties of intermediate centralization, which required exchange of views between leaders and members, than by the extremes. The MRP held regular annual congresses, while Socialists and especially Radicals found it necessary to supplement them with extraordinary congresses. The RPF met almost annually through 1953, but its successor ex-Gaullist party, the URAS or RS, did not meet again till 1957. The Communists had only four congresses between 1946 and 1958, presumably on those occasions when an important policy was to be announced to the membership. The Conservatives met equally infrequently, their local units being so independent of one another that attempts at national consensus were unfruitful. When they met, it was often for *journées d'etudes*, which implied an exchange of views but not a collective decision.[26]

Not merely the frequency of national congresses but also the way they were conducted reflected a party's structure of influence. The leadership of the Communist party of course regulated the proceedings of its congresses closely. The RPF congresses showed great unanimity in their plenary sessions, but had active debate in committees dealing with special subjects, such as the church-school question. And even among the fragments of the

Figure 3.1 Membership Ratios for the Major Parties of the Fourth Republic

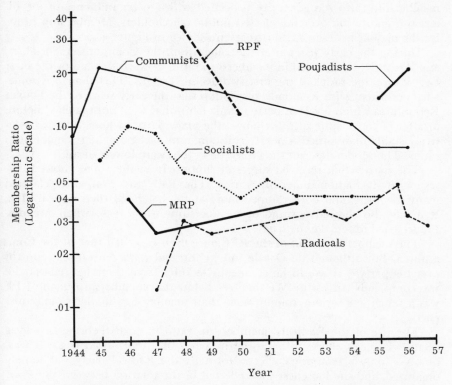

Source: The membership ratio is the ratio of members at the date specified to voters at the nearest preceding legislative election. When the party did not present candidates at a preceding election under the Fourth Republic, the following election is used. Total of voters, MRP, Radicals, RPF in Williams, *Crisis*, pp. 502, 108, 122, 139 respectively. PCF, Socialists, in Duverger, *Political Parties*, pp. 88, 82. MRP in Rémond, *Dépolitisation* Cahier, p. 89. Radicals in Bardonnet, *L'Évolution de la structure du parti radical*, p. 49ff. Poujadists, S. Hoffmann, *Le Mouvement Poujade*, p. 284. Data for specified months are plotted relative to July 1 of the year.

Radical party there were differences: after the split at the 1956 Lyon Congress, the dissident Morice faction conducted its later meetings with much less rank-and-file participation than existed in the major faction of the party.[27] The organization of the dissident Radicals, like that of the conservative parties, was decentralized, but public officeholders were dominant and the members as such (the internal part of the party) counted for relatively little.

The relative influence of the external and internal parts of a party may also be measured in various ways. These include (1) the ratio of members to voters, (2) the activities of the members, (3) the extent to which the deputies of a given party were recruited from occupations providing political skills, (4) the overlap between local offices and that of deputy.

Duverger has compared Socialist parties in terms of their "membership ratio"—the ratio of members to voters.[28] Although this ratio is sometimes difficult to measure accurately,[29] there were nevertheless substantial and consistent differences among the membership ratios of the parties. A higher membership ratio was generally associated with greater influence of the internal organization over the elected public officeholders. Membership ratios for the major parties in various years are shown in Figure 3.1.

During the early years after the Liberation, the Communists, Socialists, and Radicals all increased in membership ratio. Toward the end of the First Legislature, the ratios of the first two declined again. This change is somewhat consistent with Rémond's suggestion that the early years of the Fourth Republic saw high levels of party membership that were not matched before or after.[30] Yet in spite of this change, the main parties whose vote was relatively stable maintained a nearly constant rank order in their membership ratios. The Moderates, not shown in the graph, were lowest of all.[31]

The parties that received surges of support from the voters showed correspondingly high membership ratios. The RPF and Poujadists claimed many members, and both claimed more at the height of their appeal. The Radicals also showed a surge of membership in 1954–56, when Mendès-France tried to remake the party.

The membership ratio of the RPF once even exceeded that of the Communists. But although de Gaulle sought internal (and centralized) control over his party,[32] it would be erroneous to infer from these figures that he was completely successful. We shall see below that membership in the RPF was a much less serious commitment than membership in the Communist party.

The rise of the Radicals' membership ratio in 1956 (February) reflects Mendès-France's efforts to organize the party of a centralized basis; it was, however, only a temporary effect. Normally the Radical party was loosely organized, and the looseness was reflected in the relation between the Paris office and the local members. An accurate membership count was rarely available in Paris; local federations gained from this state of affairs by being able to buy up cards before congresses. When Mendès-France tried to enlist members directly through coupons on the party literature, the temporary afflux of membership was often reversed by the coolness of local committees to the newcomers.

A second indication of the extent of internal party control is the degree of activity of its supporters. Table 3.3 compares the parties with regard to the proportions of their voters who reported doing various kinds of political work for them.

The proportion of voters who attended meetings, gave money, or helped with publicity, like the ratio of members to voters, was high for the Communists and low for the Conservatives. In general the proportion of voters who engaged in these activities decreases from the more highly organized parties to the less. But the position of the RPF was anomalous: although it had the highest membership ratio of any party in 1948 its members reported (in 1952) a level of these kinds of activity slightly less than that of the Socialists. And unlike the MRP, the RPF did not gain much internal consensus as a result of its electoral losses between 1947 and 1952. Thus the membership claims of the RPF seem at best to have represented a different kind of membership from the other parties'. Membership involved allegiance to General de Gaulle, but not the voluntary devotion to a particular program and philosophy that characterized Communists, Socialists, or MRP.

Table 3.3 Respondents Reporting Various
Types of Political Activity

	France							USA		
	By reported 1951 vote								1952 vote (Pres.)	
	Entire sample	PCF	SFIO	MRP	RGR	Mod.	RPF	Entire sample	D	R
At last election, attended public meetings	30%	72%	44%	30%	38%	29%	35%	7%	9%	8%
In the past, gave money	20	62	35	22	21	9	34	4	6	4
sold newspapers, stuck posters	7	34	8	8	6	5	7	3	5	3
tried to convince others to support party	24	54	31	38	33	22	41	27	36	28
Number of cases	1412	142	159	122	87	87	150	1614	687	494

Source: Tabulations for France are based on IFOP survey No. 88 (February, 1952); data were supplied by the Survey Research Center, University of California, Berkeley. They agree approximately with those given in Williams, *Politics*, p. 453.
  U.S. data are from Campbell, Gurin, and Miller, *The Voter Decides*, p. 30. Question wording differed somewhat from the captions shown; see footnote 33.

The attempt to convince others to support one's party, however, was nearly as frequent among Gaullists as among Communists; Socialists, Radicals, and Conservatives proselytized less frequently. The meaning of this particular activity is more clearly seen if French participation is compared with data for the United States.[33] American voters were relatively lacking in the first three types of participation, but resembled the French voters in personal persuasion. These data suggest the relative importance of interpersonal persuasion in American politics. At the same time they suggest that the Gaullist "surge" appealed for votes in a way more nearly like that of an American party, as the RPF ranked higher in personal persuasion than in other activities.

A third indication of the influence exerted by the elective part of a party as against the internal (as well as of decentralization) was the extent to which its deputies had and exercised parliamentary skills. These skills can be inferred from the deputies' nonpolitical occupations. The large Communist parliamentary delegation, for example, did not need to include a high proportion of deputies with political power or competence in their own right; thus it included many working-class members and few professionals

Table 3.4 Occupational Composition of Parliamentary Groups vs. Party Candidate Lists, National Assembly, 1951*

Party	Industrial workers	White collar, artisans, merchants	Civil servants	Liberal professions	Business owners, managers, farm owners
Communists	+10%	0%	+ 5%	+ 3%	– 8%
Socialists	– 4	–14	+15	+16	– 8
MRP	+ 3	– 5	+13	+10	–14
Radicals	– 2	–12	+ 9	+19	– 7
Conservatives	– 2	–15	+ 3	+21	+ 4
Gaullists	– 4	–15	+10	+ 8	+ 5

*For each party, the percentage of candidates in a given occupation, successful or not, was subtracted from the corresponding percentage of deputies; the difference is the entry on the table. If the party had a larger proportion from a particular occupation among its deputies than its candidates, the difference is positive. Percentage differences do not add to zero because certain occupational categories, such as housewives, are omitted from the table.

Source: *Les Élections législatives du 17 juin 1951*, pp. 32f, 55f.

compared to other parliamentary groups. This disparity remains when the composition of the parliamentary group is expressed as a difference from the occupational distribution of its candidates, as in Table 3.4.

Normally the parties of the left draw their votes from lower occupational strata, those of the right from higher strata. To appeal to these votes and at the same time to reach out into other groups each party drew up its lists of candidates to form a judicious mixture. Such a list generally reflected the clientele sought by the party, biased toward people who had time to campaign and whose training allowed them to speak in public and perform other functions as legislators.

Each list included as many candidates as there were seats to be filled in the district. But only the top one or two persons on the list—in the order in which they were placed by the party—normally had any hope of election. The rest simply lent their prestige, or their symbolic and persuasive value, to the list. Thus the party, or the local committee that drew up the list, had two choices: whom to place on the list for campaign purposes, and whom to place at the top. If we contrast those placed on the lists by a given party with those who were actually elected, we may infer what characteristics the party valued in the Assembly, over and above what it presented to get votes.

To see how the figures in Table 3.4 were calculated, consider the first figure for the Communists. Of all the candidates on their lists in 1951, 30 per cent were industrial workers, but of the deputies elected, 40 per cent came from this group. The +10 per cent difference is unusual in two respects: it is highest in its row, indicating that the Communists favored workers differentially more than any other occupational group; and highest in its column, indicating that no other party did so to nearly so great an extent. The MRP, also associated with a large labor union (the CFTC), was the only other party to have an excess of workers among its deputies.

The Communists' stress on working-class deputies indicates that they valued class representation in the Assembly more than parliamentary skills. The party did not want deputies to become independent powers, and by 1951 did not expect its deputies to become ministers. If Table 3.4 had been extended to 1956, it would have shown a similar disregard for parliamentary skills on the part of the Poujadists, whose greatest excess was in the representation of merchants and artisans in the Assembly.[34] The MRP, on the other hand, had an excess of civil servants (+13) and of the liberal professions (e.g., lawyers) (+10) which was far greater than its excess of workers.

The Socialists and Gaullists actually put up higher proportions of working-class candidates than the MRP and elected fewer of them; the other parties put up fewer and elected none. The middle-class occupations other than civil servants (white-collar employees, merchants, and artisans), were underrepresented in 1951 among the deputies of all parties except the Communists. Civil servants were overrepresented in the parliamentary delegations of all parties, particularly among Socialists, MRP, and Gaullists. The Socialist party had an affinity for public-school teachers, and many civil servants were organized in its unions. The Gaullists, on the other hand, were closer to the higher civil servants and tended more to favor an impartial and skilled administration as an arm of a strong state.[35]

With the exception of the Gaullists, the parties reveal their leftist or rightist orientation by the relative values of the figures in the last three columns of the table. All parties had to recruit persons with political skills, but the leftist parties recruited more among civil servants, while the right recruited more from the liberal professions and from owners and managers. The MRP, in its lesser bias toward skilled occupations, seems to have been more internally controlled than the Radicals and perhaps more than the Socialists as well.

In summary, we see not only the unconcern of the Communists with extensive occupational skills in their parliamentary group, but also the different sources from which each of the other parties drew its necessary skills. The MRP's recruitment policies paralleled its doctrines of social reform; perhaps this consonance became possible after MRP had lost its conservative fair-weather friends to the RPF. The RPF, attempting to preserve internal and central control with a conservative clientele, seems to have been drawn toward candidates of the higher civil service (including some military officers) who would appeal to the voters yet be loyal to General de Gaulle.

A fourth indicator of the relative influence of elective officials in the different parties can be derived from the extent to which they possessed more than one elective office at a time. Deputies are permitted to hold local office at the same time; this practice is known as the *cumul,* and those who are

Table 3.5 Deputies Who Were Also Mayors

Elected	PCF	SFIO	MRP	Radi-cals	Peas-ants	PRL, Indep.	Gaullists		Poujadists
10 Nov. 1946	8%	19%	14%	34%	46%	17%			
							URAS	ARS	
1951	8	35	25	50	46	41	28	38	
							RS		
1956	9	38	31	43	31	45	50		2

Sources: *Annuaire de l'Assemblée Nationale, 10 novembre 1946; Annuaire de l'Assembleé Nationale, IIe Législature*, pp. 459ff.; *Les Élections législatives du 2 janvier 1956,* p. 65.

mayors are known by the title of *député-maire.* The proportions of deputies of the various parties who had this title are shown in Table 3.5.[36]

By 1951 half the deputies of the Radical party were also mayors, as were a similar proportion of the Independents and Peasants. The practice was somewhat less frequent among the Socialists and the MRP (from one-fourth to one-third), still less among the Communists (8 to 9 per cent), and least among the Poujadists, who had almost no mayors. Even in the First Legislature, the Radicals and Peasants led in the *cumul;* but its general incidence then was less, probably because the politicians emerging from the Resistance had not entrenched themselves locally. In the Second Legislature, the Radicals exceeded all other major parties in the *cumul,* reflecting a high degree of decentralization and external control. In the Third, Independents and Radicals again led; the Peasants, by then a small protest group, had fallen behind.

The rank order of the parties in placing independently powerful personnel in parliament was thus related to their placing skilled persons in parliament and to the extent of party influence over the voters. In this ranking the RPF stood in approximately the same position as MRP or SFIO; thus one would not expect the RPF as a whole to have been threatened by indiscipline of local officeholders. But one segment of it was more vulnerable. The ARS, which split off on the right wing of the RPF, contained a somewhat larger proportion of mayors than did the loyal URAS. The proportion of mayors among the Gaullists rose after the 1956 election because without General de Gaulle most Gaullists without local strength lost their seats; of the few that remained, half were mayors.

These statistics reveal a basic problem for a conservative party in maintaining discipline. Normally such a party puts up candidates with local prestige of their own. The loyal fraction of the RPF coped with this problem by selecting military officers, high civil servants, and other candidates of personal loyalty to de Gaulle. The Poujadists (who are difficult to classify on a right-left continuum) later sent to the Assembly a group of shopkeepers with no political skill or power; but even they were faced with the dual problem of desertion by deputies disloyal to Poujade, and the inability of the loyal deputies to induce their Assembly colleagues even to take them seriously.

The frequency of the *cumul* depends also on factors other than party organization. In small single-member districts (the *scrutin d'arrondissement*), the tie between the deputy and the locality is presumably close, and the overlap between parliamentary office and the offices of mayor or *département* councilor great.[37] Even under the Fifth Republic, with the great influx of "new men" in the Assembly, there have been many instances in which local officials—new only to national politics—succeeded the former deputies.[38]

Other formal conditions also influenced the extent of the *cumul*. In the early statutes of the Radical party, Radical municipal councilors were automatically members of the local committees. And the centralized French administrative system, which encouraged the overlap of municipal and national functions, made this manifestation of local power perhaps more evident in France than elsewhere.

Cohesion and Discipline in the Parliamentary Groups

Those parties with the greatest internal control and the greatest centralization were also the ones whose parliamentary groups in the National Assembly showed the greatest unanimity in their votes. The cohesion of these groups throughout the Fourth Republic is shown in Table 3.6. This table is based on analysis of a sample of 889 roll-call votes.[39] The votes studied may be classified according to the formal procedures under which they were conducted, the time and political situation at which they occurred, and the importance of the issue concerned.

During the Fourth Republic, the most frequent voting procedure permitted a deputy to vote by proxy. By giving his voting cards to another deputy, or to an official of his parliamentary group (the *boîtier*), he could vote *in absentia*. Because of the ease of this procedure 8550 roll-call votes were recorded during the Fourth Republic. Particularly on unimportant matters, many votes were cast along straight party lines in this way. A criticism of the Assembly's procedure under these rules was that deputies avoided personal responsibility for their votes through the proxy system.

On matters of importance, a personal vote (*scrutin public à la tribune*) could be called for.[40] As such a vote was initially used as a delaying tactic by the Communists, the conditions for holding it were at one time made more difficult. In 1955 a further procedural change was made so that all investiture and confidence votes were personal, and at the same time the majority required was changed to a plurality of those actually voting. The effect of this change was to increase considerably the number of personal votes after 1955, as well as to make their results less predictable.

In Table 3.6, the various types of votes are tabulated in separate columns. The left-hand columns refer to a sample of 739 roll calls considered sufficiently important by *L'Année Politique* (*AP*) for their numerical results to be cited in the text; the right-hand column refers to a random sample of

Table 3.6 Party Divisions in the Assembly*

	"Important" Roll Calls (Anneé Politique)				Random Sample of Remainder	Total
	Personal Vote	Proxy Vote			Proxy Vote	
		Investiture	Confidence	Other		
I Legislature						
(number of roll calls)	8	16	56	235	50	365
Communists	37%	-	-	-	-	
Socialists	87	-	1%	3%	-	
MRP	75	19%	16	10	8%	
Radicals	100	56	73	44	12	
Independents (RI)	100	87	89	48	18	
PRL	100	50	33	31	6	
II Legislature						
(number of roll calls)	10**	14	36	242	50	352
Communists	60%	-	-	-	-	
Socialists	70	-	11%	3%	-	
MRP	70	43%	42	21	4%	
Radicals	90	57	50	39	14	
Independents	90	36	55	28	2	
Gaullists (RPF)†	60	20	48	14	-	
URAS	100	89	87	36	8	
ARS	100	33	87	40	14	

III Legislature	Personal Vote				Proxy	Personal	
	Investiture	Confidence	Other				
(number of roll calls)	7	44	3	68	48	2	172
Communists	14%	61%		-	-		
Socialists	28	82		4%	2%		
MRP	43	70		9	4		
Radicals	71	100		57	21		
Independents	57	93		40	14		
Poujadists	14	45		12	10		

*Table entries represent proportions of roll calls on which the party in question had at least 10 per cent dissident members. Dissidence includes those who "did not take part in the vote," but not members of the cabinet. This classification is chosen for comparability with P. Campbell, "Discipline and Loyalty in the French Parliament During the Pinay Government."

**Includes five personal votes on questions of confidence, October–November 1955.

†The figures for the RPF and its successor fragments are based on smaller number of roll calls, since none of these groups existed for the entire Legislature.

150 roll-calls drawn from the large number not cited in *L'Année Politique*. All the votes of investiture and most of the official votes of confidence were included in the *Année Politique* sample. The personal votes that took place

were also heavily concentrated in this sample. The entries in each column are the proportions of votes in that category on which 10 per cent or more of the deputies in the party in question departed from their party's position (or did not take part in the vote).

Comparison of the right-hand column entry for any party, and for any of the three Legislatures, with the other columns shows that party cohesion was uniformly greater on the "unimportant" votes than on the "important" ones. This comparison is clearest when the two right-hand columns are compared, setting aside the influence of the personal vote or of the presence of a question of investiture or confidence.

On votes of investiture or confidence, even when the proxy vote was used, party division was generally still greater than on the other proxy votes in the *Année Politique* sample.[41] The relative division of the parties on investiture versus confidence votes, however, is not consistent, and few of the differences between the two types of votes are statistically significant in view of the small number of investiture votes. On personal votes, the degree of party division is still greater; but this is largely because we have counted absence as dissidence—a procedure justifiable for proxy votes, but less appropriate for personal votes and used here only for the sake of comparability.[42]

When the differences among the various types of votes are set aside a consistent picture of the relative degrees of party cohesion emerges. If we read down each column for each Legislature, the parties appear in approximate order from left to right, and from most cohesive to least. The ranking of parties thus obtained is largely independent of the type of votes used to assess cohesion: Communists and Socialists were most cohesive, MRP next, and Radicals, Independents, and Conservatives least. In the First Legislature, the PRL was somewhat more united than the Radicals. The MRP was generally less cohesive than the Socialist party, but much more so than the Radicals. The Gaullists (RPF) were highly cohesive from 1951 until the party split over Pinay investiture; after de Gaulle withdrew from politics in 1953, both of its remaining fragments (URAS and ARS) had much lower cohesion. In the Third Legislature the Poujadists were less cohesive than the MRP, indicating that Poujade as well as de Gaulle had problems in enforcing discipline; on votes of investiture and confidence, however, the Poujadists were highly disciplined, reflecting the importance of voting *"contre"* as against voting on mere issues. The ranking of the parties in terms of parliamentary group cohesion, therefore, was generally consistent with the other measures of centralization and internal control that we have considered. One exception is the Radicals, who were highest in division in the Assembly and at times in the *cumul*, but intermediate on other measures of internal control. The ranking of MRP and Socialists also varied from one type of vote to another. A final special case was the Gaullists, whose cohesion dropped sharply after de Gaulle's withdrawal.

Parties and Majorities in the Assembly

It was from among the parties' deputies that cabinets were normally formed, and from them that the cabinets drew their necessary support. We shall be concerned with the difficulties confronting cabinets—the disintegration of their supporting majorities, and the conditions under which these majorities could be held together. These difficulties showed themselves in different ways when they derived from the action of the more organized parties (SFIO and MRP) and the less organized (Radicals and Moderates). In the former case, the parties tended to divide less often on Assembly votes, and when they did divide, on more ideological grounds; in the latter, the divisions were not only more frequent but also more directly related to the fate of the cabinet.

To place the parties' action in perspective, we must outline the cabinet's situation in the Assembly, some of the customs of the Assembly, and the numerical distribution of party strength within which all cabinet and party action had to be calculated.

The investiture of cabinets and their maintenance in office were determined by the National Assembly, and were actually among the principal concerns of the Assembly.[43] The Council of the Republic was never really powerful during the Fourth Republic, though it did gain somewhat in power from 1946 to 1958.[44] The other assemblies created under the Fourth Republic—the Economic Council,[45] the Assembly of the French Union, and (for Algeria only) the Algerian Assembly, had even less power than the Council of the Republic. Studies of these chambers might reveal political divisions paralleling those of the Assembly; but because of their secondary roles they have received less attention.

Members of the National Assembly were jealous of their power, guarding it not only against the Executive but also against their own committees. Special powers, or the opportunity to promulgate decree-laws, were issued to cabinets only in emergencies; normally the fate of a cabinet and the daily agenda of the Assembly were under the continual control of the Assembly itself and could be altered by a simple majority vote.

A reform of the Assembly's internal regulations, delegating more work to committees, was proposed in 1952 but defeated by a large majority. The Assembly continually debated and voted on its own calendar, as well as on substantive legislation.[46] The agenda (*propositions de la conférence des présidents*) were often voted down, urgent priority was given to particular questions, and efforts to keep debate to a single subject were defeated— all through the deputies' urge for autonomy and independence from prior commitments. To this (as well as the proxy vote) we owe the extraordinary number of roll-call votes taken during the Fourth Republic. Siegfried summarized this characteristic attitude of the Assembly toward its cabinets: "This system, in which only the deputy counts, and the executive is his continually revocable delegate, . . . generates only anarchy."[47]

To be invested a cabinet required a majority of the Assembly, which amounted at first to over three hundred votes and later somewhat less. To stay in power the cabinet required at least a working majority sufficient to pass its program; various cabinets were overthrown either by failing a vote of confidence or by informal procedures leading to resignation when the government considered its majority too narrow.

Each of the three legislatures elected under the Fourth Republic contained a somewhat different configuration of forces in the Assembly and a correspondingly different set of alternative possible governing majorities.[48] Throughout almost the entire span of the Fourth Republic, as well as in the Fifth, cabinets depended on majorities of the center. They were generally opposed by the Communists at one extreme, and substantial fractions of the right at the other. Votes of investiture and confidence, as well as votes on substantive issues closely connected with the cabinet's fate, thus joined extreme left and right in opposition. From the Liberation to May 1947 the Cabinet's supporting majority was entirely on the left of the political continuum, since the Communists were in the cabinet. Majorities of the right, however, supported Pinay and Laniel during the Second Legislature and invested de Gaulle in June 1958.

After the departure of the Communists from the cabinet coalition in May 1947, the potential pro-cabinet vote remained about four hundred for the rest of the Fourth Republic. The one period that provided greater freedom of maneuver in forming cabinets was the latter part of the Second Legislature, when the ex-Gaullists had joined the other parties as potential government supporters; by the time Faure was invested in February 1955 nearly five hundred votes could be counted in potential support of one or another possible cabinet. Faure's investiture vote, not including the Socialists, was 369. These variations in the potential pro-cabinet vote are shown in Table 3.7.

Within the potentially pro-cabinet fraction of the Assembly, the conditions for attaining a majority included ideological and personal compatibility and party discipline as well as sheer numbers. The Socialists, who never broke party discipline on an investiture roll call until de Gaulle's investiture in June 1958, held special power by virtue of this fact. Of four hundred potential pro-cabinet votes, the Socialists' one hundred were essential to any stable majority except during the period March 1952–December 1955. Thus several cases of cabinet instability can be explained simply by a decision of the Socialist group.

The position of the cabinet was therefore continually precarious. A coalition of three or four major parties was normally essential to any cabinet; usually it was also necessary to cultivate the votes of minor parties or factions. The relative lack of maneuver created by a large "unavailable" vote was therefore a basic condition of the limited capacity of cabinets to govern. Wherever the specific responsibility for each particular cabinet's overthrow may have lain, the general composition of the Assembly made the formation of cabinets a continually difficult problem.[49]

It is extremely unlikely that this basic problem could have been remedied more than superficially by the Assembly's alteration of the electoral system. In the spring of 1951 and again in the latter part of 1955, long and tortuous debates on the electoral system took place. Dozens of electoral systems and amendments to them were rejected in succession by the Assembly. The only successful modification that occurred was the *apparentement* provision, largely a response to the threat of Gaullism. Not until de Gaulle came to power in 1958 was there an opportunity for a fundamental change; then France returned to the *scrutin d'arrondissement*.

One further possibility might have led to an Assembly of a different

Table 3.7 Pro-Cabinet and Opposition Vote During the Fourth Republic*

	Potential Pro-Cabinet Vote							Permanent Opposition Vote			
	PCF	SFIO	Rad.-UDSR	MRP	Cons.	ARS	URAS RS	PCF	RPF (Gaull.)	UFF	Approx. total
Dec. 1946–May 1947	182	102	69	166	74						0
May 1947–March 1949		102	69	166–154	74–79			181–3			182
March 1949–June 1951		99	59	154–144	62			182	24		206
July 1951–March 1952		107	91	86	96			101	115–121		220
March 1952–Jan. 1953		106	91	86	96	30		101	80–85		180
Jan. 1953–Dec. 1955		104	100	85	89–102	33	72	100			100
Jan. 1956–June 1958		96–100	93	74	95–108		22	150		52–30	200

*See also the tabulations of major Assembly votes in Williams, Crisis, pp. 498–501.

composition: dissolution and elections at a time when opinion had swung strongly in a new direction. But as we shall see, this solution was difficult because of the ways in which opinion fluctuated and because the decision processes that determined the date of new elections minimized the effects of swings and opinion rather than responding to them.

Because of these limitations, the formation and breakdown of cabinet coalitions in the Assembly is of central importance for an analysis of the functioning of the Fourth Republic. Barring an emergency of the sort that brought the Fifth Republic, the Assembly was doomed to form governing majorities with a restricted range of choice. Within this range, the diverse structures and aims of the parties and their factions determined the variability and decision capacity of the cabinets. In the chapters that follow, we shall trace the rise and fall of the cabinets that succeeded one another, and analyze the causes of their short duration and ineffectiveness.

NOTES

◆

1. We focus attention on the Assembly because it was the body to which cabinets were officially responsible. The second chamber (Council of the Republic) will be mentioned only in passing. The positions of parties and factions on issues will also be treated only incidentally in this chapter, but will be considered in Chapters 4–7.

2. See Macridis, "The Predicament of French Socialism."

3. See Duverger, *Political Parties*, pp. 206–255. This approach has been criticized, e.g., by Lavau in *Partis politiques et réalités sociales*.

4. See Peter Campbell, *French Electoral Systems and Elections*, p. 22, and Williams, *Crisis*, Chap. 22. *Scrutin d'arrondissement* differs from the Southern run-off primary in that it does not require a reduction of the field to two candidates on the second ballot. Key argued that the run-off permits multiple factions, in *Southern Politics*, pp. 416–423. French political scientists who argued along the lines of Duverger and Key were surprised by the results of the 1958 election, but attributed the sweeping UNR victory to the political crisis and de Gaulle's popularity; see Maurice Duverger, "Paradoxes d'une réforme électorale," in Association Française de Science Politique, *L'Établissement de la Cinquième République*, pp. 221–240.

5. This contrast is also used by Louis Hartz to support his contention that consensus has been greater in the United States than in Europe; see *The Liberal Tradition in America, passim*.

6. Middleton, *The French Political System*, p. 16, and Williams, *Crisis*, pp. 2–3.

7. See Rémond, *The Right Wing in France*, and Chevallier, *Histoire des institutions politiques de la France de 1789 à nos jours*.

8. *Sondages*, December 1949, No. 17, 178.

9. Bardonnet, *Évolution de la structure du parti radical*, p. 184.

10. It has been far less customary for parties of the left to trace their antecedents to the Girondins, and in fact Thibaudet traces provincial Radicalism to one aspect of Jacobinism in *Les Idées politiques de la France,* pp. 147ff. Nevertheless, the Girondin hostility to Paris (Chevallier, *Histoire des institutions politiques,* p. 78) was shared by many Fourth Republic Radicals. See also Stanley Hoffmann, "Paradoxes of the French Political Community," in Hoffmann, *et al., In Search of France,* p. 18.

11. Luethy, *France Against Herself,* p. 29.

12. That the internal part of the MRP antedated the elective is also noted by Capelle in *The MRP and French Foreign Policy,* p. 149.

13. Williams, *Crisis,* pp. 160, 174, 178–179, 181–182.

14. The history of the parties of French Africa is summarized in Thompson and Adloff, *French West Africa* and *French Equatorial Africa;* Morgenthau, *Political Parties in French-Speaking West Africa;* Hamon, "Introduction à l'étude des partis politiques de l'Afrique française"; and Blanchet, *L'Itinéraire des partis africains depuis Bamako.*

15. We use the term "parliamentary group" or simply "group" to designate the "legislative party." Parliamentary groups were organized at times, however, under different names from their members' election lists.

16. See Gerth and Mills, eds., *From Max Weber: Essays in Sociology,* Chap. VIII. For Weber's treatment of political parties see *The Theory of Social and Economic Organization,* pp. 407–412.

17. Michels, *Political Parties,* Chap. X.

18. See Etzioni, *A Comparative Analysis of Complex Organizations,* p. 24. But patronage, allocated like salaries, can produce a reverse effect.

19. Exceptions were the cells of the Communist party and the regional organizations of the Radicals, which had no elective counterpart. The President of the Republic, chosen by indirect representation, did not normally function as a party leader.

20. Bardonnet, *Évolution de la structure du parti radical,* pp. 125–129.

21. In this system of classification the parties of the United States are extremely decentralized and dominated by their elective officeholders. The French parties that they resemble most closely in structure are the Moderates and Radicals. American party congresses (conventions) at four-year intervals are extremely infrequent by French standards.

22. Duverger, *Political Parties,* Chap. I. His distinction between direct and indirect parties is of little consequence in France; only the Radicals had nonpersonal members. See Williams, *Crisis,* p. 119.

23. See Brindillac, "Décoloniser la France," 804, on the difficulty of doing this in France. But there were "achieved notables" in France as well; see Bartholomew, *The Politics of the Notable.*

24. E.g., Duverger, *Political Parties,* pp. 182ff., where he writes of relations between "the party" and "parliamentary representatives." An approach to parties as dual hierarchies, closer to the scheme used here, is presented in Leiserson, *Parties and Politics,* Chap. 5; the two hierarchies are there termed "electoral" and "governmental."

25. Williams, *Crisis,* p. 509.

26. *Ibid.,* Chs. 6–13, and *L'Année Politique,* various issues. In 1954 the Moderates changed to a congress; see Marcel Merle, "Les Modérés," in Duverger, ed., *Partis politiques et classes sociales,* p. 245. A detailed comparison of the parties is made in Peter Campbell, "French Party Congress."

27. Bardonnet, *Évolution de la structure du parti radical,* pp. 91–92.

28. Duverger, *Political Parties*, pp. 94ff. A similar index has been used to measure relative organization strength in American city politics; see Snowiss, *The Metropolitan Congressman*.

29. Parties inflate their claims of membership, and figures from different sources are inflated to different degrees. Use of the previous election as the denominator can also be misleading if a party's vote is changing rapidly.

30. See Vedel, ed., *La Dépolitisation: Mythe ou réalité?*, p. 90.

31. Even if subscriptions to the newspaper *France Indépendante* (about 20,000) were taken to indicate membership, the Moderates' membership ratio would have been less than .01. The ranking of the parties in ratios of members to voters is confirmed by 1958 survey data, kindly furnished by Philip Converse. If these data are corrected for under-reporting of the vote and for national turnout, the resulting membership ratios are: Communists, .15; Socialists, .04; MRP, .04; Radicals, .02; Independents, zero. The gradual approach of the MRP curve to that of the Socialists may reflect the greater homogeneity of their membership and electorate after 1951.

32. The national council of the RPF at first included no deputies; Williams, *Crisis*, p. 137.

33. Angus Campbell, Gurin, and Miller, *The Voter Decides*, p. 30. These questions concern only the 1952 campaign, while the French questions concern whether the voter had *ever* been active; Williams, *Politics*, p. 453. Thus only the relative frequencies of the various types of participation can be compared between countries. The same type of difference is also shown in more comparable surveys in France and the United States after the Fourth Republic; see Converse and Dupeux, "Politicization of the Electorate in France and the United States," 5.

34. Fifty-eight per cent of the Poujadist parliamentary group in 1956 were merchants or artisans, as against 43 per cent of the Poujadist candidates; *Les Elections législatives du 2 janvier 1956*, pp. 54f., 63f.

35. Though the RPF elected deputies from skilled occupations, we shall contend later that they lacked the skills of negotiation and compromise that characterized the senior leaders of the other "government" parties.

36. Many of these were mayors of very small towns; but even without distinguishing between towns of different size, the data show differences in party structure.

37. Williams, *Crisis*, p. 308.

38. The Assembly elected in 1958 had a higher proportion of overlap with local offices than did the Assemblies of the Fourth Republic: see Mattei Dogan, "Changement de régime et changement de personnel," in Association Française de Science Politique, *L'Établissement de la Cinquième République*, p. 259. Second-rank local politicians were advanced by the change in electoral systems; see Lesire-Ogrel, "Systèmes électoraux et vie politique," 3.

39. For the sampling procedure see Appendix A.

40. Lidderdale, *The Parliament of France*, pp. 143ff.

41. There were numerous "informal" votes of confidence as well, on which the premier staked the life of his cabinet without going through the official procedures. Many of these are included in the "other" important proxy votes.

42. The procedure used here follows that of Peter Campbell, "Discipline and Loyalty in the French Parliament During the Pinay Government."

43. See Chapters 4, 5, and 6 for evidence that the fate of the cabinet pervaded many votes that were not officially questions of confidence.

44. It gained over this period in its representation in the cabinet; see Williams, *Crisis,* pp. 287, 290.

45. See Lewis, "The Operation of the French Economic Council."

46. See Lidderdale, *The Parliament of France,* pp. 113–114. Also Williams, *Crisis,* p. 255: ". . . a determined cabinet could almost always persuade the house to disavow a recalcitrant committee. This did not justify the [committee] system."

47. Siegfried, *De la IVe à la Ve République,* p. 217.

48. In the preceding Constituent Assemblies, the three-party government of PCF, SFIO, and MRP arrived at most decisions outside the Assembly, and roll calls were of correspondingly less interest; see Williams, *Crisis,* pp. 386–387.

49. The details of internal division within the parliamentary parties and the allocation of responsibility for overthrow will be examined in the following four chapters.

»4«

Cabinets and Issues
in the First Legislature

WE RETURN NOW TO THE center of political decision—the National Assembly—and analyze the immediate causes of cabinet instability. We wish to show what factors impaired the capacity of cabinets to make decisions and carry them out. All cabinets of the Fourth Republic had short lifetimes; the longest, that of Guy Mollet, lasted less than sixteen months. This fact alone meant that an administrator, a pressure group, or a parliamentary faction opposed to the policies of a given cabinet could hope that it would not last long enough to put them into effect. The resources of time were on the side of those opposing innovative government action;[1] and organized interests that could influence a whole series of cabinets had particular advantages. The Algerian settlers, the beet growers, and the higher administration all profited from the brief lifetimes of cabinets.

Our first task is therefore to show what instigating factors were most important in bringing down cabinets in general. Was it the personal ambitions of *ministrables,* for example, or the incompatible ideologies of parliamentary groups forced to join in cabinets and their supporting majorities? In particular we want to relate the fall of cabinets, or constraints on their decisions, to some of the alternative causes cited by diagnosticians of the Fourth Republic: (*a*) the ideologies of deputies, factions, parties, and party militants;[2] (*b*) the interests embodied in pressure groups and constituencies; (*c*) personal ambitions, especially of would-be cabinet ministers;[3] and (*d*) personal antipathies and vetoes, as distinguished from ideological antagonisms.

To distinguish these various influences on the fate of cabinets—as they either hindered or aided the decision capacity of the cabinet—we must combine detailed analysis of the cabinet's life with a statistical study of the way individual roll calls exemplified more general bases for decisions for the deputies of each party. We shall first do this for one Legislature at a time, and then compare the alignments of each party across Legislatures.

For this statistical analysis, we first sort the various divisions of a party into clusters of similar roll calls, and then inspect the subject matter and political circumstances of the roll calls in each cluster. If the roll calls in one cluster dealt with a single issue, yet took place at different times under a variety of cabinets supported by different coalitions, we may infer that the issue in question was an important cause of that division. Such an issue may in turn be traced to ideological sources or to constituency interests, or both.

On the other hand, if a cluster of roll calls on different issues occurred under a single cabinet, we shall infer that the matter at stake was the support of a coalition specific to that cabinet. These two properties of clusters of roll calls will be called "issue-specificity" and "cabinet-specificity," respectively.

Those divisions in a given party that are issue-specific but not cabinet-specific can be sorted into questions of ideology and of interest by examining the types of arguments and groups that supported each side. The divisions that are cabinet-specific but not issue-specific can be analyzed to show the part played by personal ambition by relating votes to parliamentary careers. The existence of ministerial ambitions can be inferred, at least approximately, from a deputy's actually holding such posts, before or after the vote in question; and personal conflicts among leading deputies can also be used to explain mutual vetoes and factional antipathy, independent of the issues involved. The judgments that result are aided by statistical analysis but depend on nonstatistical inferences as well. We must decide when two roll calls involved the same or different issues; this distinction requires careful reading of the debates as well as knowledge of the nominal subjects of the votes.

We must also classify clusters of roll calls that have both issue and cabinet specificity. Certain clusters for the MRP and SFIO each dealt with a precise issue, but they were also concentrated in a particular cabinet's interval in office; we shall judge them to deal primarily with the issue rather than the cabinet. The Moderates in the First Legislature, on the other hand, were divided similarly throughout the entire Legislature on various issues in various cabinets; the underlying conflict was between Gaullism and the cabinet. The Radicals in the early part of the Second Legislature were divided similarly through several cabinets on a sequence of diverse issues that seemed to reflect an internal controversy between two wings of the party.

Another important intermediate case is the cabinet-specific grouping of roll calls in which one issue is dominant. Particular coalitions may support a particular cabinet not simply to combine votes but to pass or stop an important law or decision. Subsidiary matters will then be judged in terms of their effect on the cabinet's fate, and this in terms of the dominant issue. Such a dominant issue can be identified by its frequency and by the debates linking other issues to it.

After identifying these types of division in the parties we must relate them to the influences on a cabinet's longevity or downfall. This means not only judging whether the division of a given party helped or hindered the cabinet, but also judging whether the influence was direct—through the vote itself—or indirect—reflecting, for example, a corresponding division that would make itself felt within the party congresses on the question of support for the cabinet.

Our second major task is to show what factors in a cabinet's fall were related to the cabinet's (premier's) action. Was it true that decisive cabinets had shorter lives than *immobiliste* ones? What other factors influenced the duration of cabinets besides their choice of direction and type of action? Should Mollet, who undertook the Suez action, be considered *immobiliste*? Or should Pinay, who attained high popularity in the country by floating loans, restraining interest groups, and seeing prices stabilize?

Our third task is to trace these specific and instigating causes to the structure of the parties. It has been argued both that the parties of the Fourth Republic were too disciplined and that they were not disciplined enough.[4] We then ask what aspects of party structure influenced cabinet instability, given the general distribution of opinions represented in the Assembly. Whether this distribution itself could have been altered will be considered in later chapters.

From this analysis (in the next four chapters), we begin to develop the notion of two relatively independent political subsystems in the Fourth Republic. First we consider the immediate and precipitating causes of the fall of cabinets; we shall argue that they were more closely related to ideology than to personal ambitions. Then the major lines of division in the "government" parties will be identified. On the roll calls that define these divisions, we shall show that potential ministers tended to support the cabinet rather than to oppose it, and that the rank and file were more opposed. This finding points to a consensual system in the Assembly. But these conclusions will send us back to consideration of the voting behavior of the citizens, its relation to social structure, and the influence of party structure on it.

The Rise and Fall of a "Typical" Cabinet

To show the immediate and remote causes of the fall of cabinets, we shall examine the histories of the individual cabinets that were invested by the Assembly. In all, sixteen cabinets were invested and later overthrown.[5] Two others (Blum; Queuille 1951) resigned when the task for which they were called to office was completed; in 1958 Pflimlin resigned to make way for de Gaulle. And the de Gaulle cabinet of 1958, though invested under the procedures of the Fourth Republic, is not ordinarily considered as part of it.

The history of each cabinet includes comparable answers to a series of questions. Most important are: Who brought it down? What did it try to accomplish? What factors prolonged its life? What were the key roll calls by which its progress or regress could be measured? When was it generally believed in the Assembly that the cabinet was doomed?

The "typical" cabinet came into existence after a ministerial crisis—a period following the fall of one cabinet, in which various cabinets, premiers, and supporting majorities were considered more or less officially and more or less seriously. The longer this process continued and the more serious the problems awaiting attention, the graver the crisis was considered. After a series of these tries, which served to define the situation,[6] the premier actually invested was presented (*désigné*) to the Assembly by the President of the Republic and voted into office by a majority of the deputies. He then assembled his cabinet and again sought the Assembly's approval, usually by asking postponement of interpellations on the cabinet. This two-step approval by the Assembly was called the "double investiture."[7] When a new agreement had been reached on cabinet policy and Assembly support, the crisis was said to have been "resolved."

Before the vote of investiture, the premier-designate set forth his platform in his investiture speech. Like all political platforms, it usually contained intentional ambiguities; nevertheless it put forward the major positive policies he proposed. Questions that were avoided or glossed over were usually those that would divide the intended majority (e.g., EDC or the church-school question). The degree of specificity of the investiture declaration, and thus of the premier's "contract" with his majority, also varied with the urgency of the crisis preceding the investiture. When the Assembly felt a strong need to invest some cabinet, it might ask less explicit policy statements. Moreover, the degree of explicitness might depend on the receptivity of a key party to the premier-designate.[8]

After the cabinet was invested, it began a program of action. This could include action on Parliament (requesting legislation), action directly on the country (floating loans, persuading public opinion or pressure groups), or action on other countries (foreign negotiations or military action). The parliamentary schedule was influenced in both content and quantity by these choices. The cabinet, however, did not directly control the agenda of the Assembly. Particular bills had to be reported by the relevant committees, which sometimes disagreed with the cabinet; and the agenda were set weekly by an agenda committee,[9] functioning roughly like the Rules Committee of the U.S. House of Representatives but more often overruled. The Assembly as a whole could overrule either this committee or a specialized committee when it wished, but this fact did not necessarily aid the cabinet.

The development of the legislative program was also influenced by evidences of electoral swings. Cantonal,[10] municipal, or partial elections might give indications to the Assembly (or at least they were interpreted as such) of the changes that might occur at the next general election. A party that gained at such an election might increase its claims in the Assembly; one that lost might be treated less seriously by the others. The Assembly's schedule was also affected by the actions of private members and groups (e.g., the agricultural lobby, labor unions, or the church-school association). All these developments affected the sequence and timing of parliamentary activities.

On the parliamentary agenda, bills differed in their importance to the cabinet. Some originated with the cabinet and were part of its program. Others, originating outside the cabinet, received its support or opposition. Still others came to the floor without either an initiative or an official position by the cabinet.

Bills also differed from one another in the extent to which they involved the cabinet's fate. Were they, in the Assembly's terms, "political" or "technical"? Sometimes a cabinet that was kept in office for its action on one problem (e.g., Mollet on Algeria) could more easily take action on side issues (the Common Market) without endangering its existence. At other times, when the Assembly was ready to overthrow the cabinet, a peripheral or "technical" issue might be "politicized" and used as an excuse for bringing it down. Thus the transposition of an issue from political to technical or vice versa could influence the fate of both the issue and the cabinet.[11]

As issues succeeded one another in the Assembly, the cabinet's support normally began to dwindle. This process was neither uniform in speed nor irreversible; some premiers (e.g., Bidault) fought hard for their programs even when they had only a few votes to spare and remained in office for a considerable time thereafter. Others seeing their majorities decline seemed to lose the "will to live" and chose some convenient issue on which to bring the cabinet's fate sharply before the Assembly. The changing fates of cabinets were normally marked by a series of key roll-call votes, recognized by most political commentators.[12]

After a time rumors would begin to circulate in the corridors of the Palais-Bourbon that the cabinet's fall was imminent. Alternative majorities, premiers, and cabinets would be semi-openly discussed and their names reported in the press. The subsequent life of the cabinet would then be considered only a respite (*un sursis*). Eventually, the cabinet would fall and the responsibility for its overthrow would be attributed to some group, faction, or person.[13] The group thus held "responsible" would then normally be the first called on by the President of the Republic to resolve this crisis by trying to form a new government. The rare occasions when this nominee succeeded marked clear policy changes. Until the next premier was invested, the previous cabinet would remain in office in a "caretaker" capacity.

Responsibility for a cabinet's downfall was customarily attributed to the group, faction, or person who had last swung into opposition. Yet this formal rule was an oversimplification. A leading deputy who wanted to replace a sitting cabinet by another more favorable to his own ends could follow several alternative strategies leading to the downfall of cabinet without being held formally responsible. He might oppose the cabinet on earlier votes, bringing about a situation in which its fall was considered imminent; at this point he might either swing into support of the falling cabinet or absent himself on leave as the crucial vote approached. Alternatively, one group might try to induce the cabinet to follow a policy closer to its own, thereby giving an opposing group the choice between acquiescence and withdrawing its support from the cabinet. The formation of coalitions might also serve to conceal the hand of the initiator.

To identify the factors contributing to a cabinet's fall, we must therefore examine various sources of evidence. The customary attribution of responsibility must of course be considered. But in addition there are the commentaries of the press and of the deputies themselves. The customary interpretation of the order in which different groups went into opposition places undue stress on the last; perhaps the group moving into opposition just before the last contributed as much to the cabinet's fall. More generally, we shall examine the decisions made by groups that were part of the cabinet's supporting majority at its investiture and subsequently defected. By not including the "unavailable" votes of the Assembly (Communists, Gaullists until 1952, Poujadists) in this account, we simply attribute their part in producing cabinet instability to the voters rather than to their deputies.

One important hypothesis concerning the overthrow of cabinets is that the same groups of deputies were involved successively in the overthrow of several cabinets. As Robert Lecourt (MRP) expressed this, from the point of view of a party largely "faithful" to various cabinets: "The crises opened after a question of confidence are almost all due to [the] same nucleus of deputies passing from the majority [at] investiture to the opposition [on] the day the government is overthrown."[14]

A second hypothesis is that those deputies who brought cabinets down did so through ambition or the expectation of personal gain from changing cabinets. Were they themselves *ministrables?* Were they in the entourages of leaders who themselves took less clear positions?[15] Were their votes different on "political" and "technical" roll calls (i.e., in different clusters)? Were they or their "friends" disadvantaged by the choice of ministers in the sitting cabinet?

Thirdly, we must examine the part played by party decisions, as well as by the decisions of individual deputies, in bringing cabinets down. Particularly among the Socialists the pressure of the militants, expressed at party congresses, increased the party's opposition tendencies. Even those Socialist leaders who wished to participate in cabinets led by other parties (a position to which Mollet came by late 1950) could not make this decision on a purely individual basis. The official steps by which a party authorized its members' entry into cabinets are relevant, even for the divided parties.

The First Legislature: Chronology

The constitution of the Fourth Republic was approved by the French voters in a referendum in October 1946, and the first election of the National Assembly under it took place in November. For the previous two years, one Constituent Assembly and then a second had been drafting the constitution, an earlier version of which was rejected by the voters in May 1946. These same Constituent Assemblies—led first by General de Gaulle, and after his resignation in January 1946 by a three-party coalition—had been charged with governing France.

During these early years after the Liberation French political life was dominated by three highly organized political parties—the Communists, Socialists, and MRP. The parties of the right and center—Radicals and Moderates—had been discredited by association with the collaborationist Vichy government and seemed negligible in strength at the Liberation. A mood of reform dominated the country, and during 1944 and 1945 de Gaulle had already proceeded to nationalize some major industries. The Fourth Republic still bore with it at its inception the hopes for a brave new world that had grown as the Resistance envisioned a liberated France. In a few years these hopes were to give way to disillusionment.

The First Legislature (1946–1951) was dominated by the conflict between the coalition supporting most of the cabinets of that period and Gaullism. In the spring of 1947 General de Gaulle launched his attempt to regain power through the *Rassemblement du Peuple Français,* and a month later the Communists were forced out of the cabinet, never to return. The result was a precarious majority for the cabinet, a limited range of maneuver for its leaders, and a series of contests within the parties supporting the cabinet as to whether fractions of these parties should desert to Gaullism.

The Moderates, MRP, and Radicals were hardest hit. One of the Moderate groupings, the PRL, went over almost entirely to Gaullism and opposed the cabinets. The MRP, which had earlier claimed to be "the party of fidelity" to de Gaulle, lost a segment containing a number of important political leaders. The Radicals temporarily lost several of their leaders, but gradually regained them by 1951 as victory for the Gaullists began to appear less certain; only Jacques Chaban-Delmas among the better known Radicals succeeded in remaining Gaullist, taking the Gironde federation out of the party with him.

Among the remaining MRP deputies and the Socialists, the roll-call divisions related more to issues and principles than to cabinet coalitions, even though they were indirectly related to the conflict between Gaullism and the cabinet. The narrowing of the cabinet's potential base of support forced it to accept more votes from the right. The resulting conservative policies were of more concern to the working-class wing of the MRP, which had previously served in combination with only Socialists and Communists. Moreover, the center majority's delaying tactics against the RPF included postponement of the 1948 cantonal elections, and this tactic drew opposition from a segment of the remaining MRP deputies.

The Socialists, who did not divide on roll-call votes directly affecting the fate of the center cabinets of that period, nevertheless divided earlier on the proposed investiture of the Communist leader Thorez, and later on the electoral law of 1951, which disadvantaged both Communists and Gaullists. These divisions foreshadowed continuing dissent in the party in the Second and Third Legislatures and revealed internal controversies taking place even during the First. Though united in their votes on the cabinet, the Socialist deputies had to consider potential opposition at party congresses, which was reflected in certain Assembly roll-call votes on specific issues.

After the election of November 10, 1946, the Assembly was dominated by Communists, MRP, and Socialists, as the preceding Constituent Assemblies had been.[16] Unsuccessful attempts were made to invest Maurice Thorez (Communist) and Georges Bidault (MRP). Pending the election of the President of the Republic in January, Léon Blum then took office with a purely Socialist interim cabinet. In January the Socialist Vincent Auriol was elected President, and Blum accordingly resigned. He might have been re-invested, but a Communist veto was sufficient to discourage the attempt.[17]

Auriol then nominated the Socialist Paul Ramadier, who was invested by a vote of 549 to 0. Ramadier's cabinet extended from the Communists to the Moderates. Most of the policy problems confronting the cabinet had been intensified by the recent past: holding actions in the colonies, problems of budget and currency, labor-union demands. In early April 1947 General de Gaulle emerged from fifteen months' retirement and called for the formation of a broad political grouping, the *Rassemblement du Peuple Français*. Soon thereafter the Communists, even though represented in the cabinet, began taking anticolonial positions that contradicted the cabinet's policy. A series of strikes breaking out in May led the Communists into further disagreement with the cabinet; failing to resign, they were expelled by Ramadier for violation of cabinet solidarity in Assembly voting. For the rest of the First Legislature, there were only slightly over four hundred votes from which cabinet coalitions could be formed.

The departure of the Communists from the cabinet, which proved to be permanent, not only narrowed the range of parliamentary majorities but also provoked division among the Socialists. Governing with the Communists, they had been united; but as the left wing of the new majority, they were sharply divided in their congresses (though not on Assembly votes) as to whether to remain in office. The Ramadier faction narrowly prevailed against a group behind Guy Mollet, the recently elected secretary general of the party, and the Socialist ministers remained.[18]

The decline of Ramadier's majority is shown graphically in Figure 4.1. It shows the distribution of support and opposition among the Assembly

Figure 4.1 The Ramadier Cabinet and Its Support*

	Communists 182	Socialists 104	MRP 167	Rad. 43	26 UDSR	28 RI	35 PRL
1 Inv. Thorez** 4 Dec. 46							
2 Inv. Bidault** 5 Dec.							
4 Inv. Blum** 12 Dec.							
6 Blum cab. 17 Dec. 46							
20 Inv. Ramadier 21 Jan. 47							
22 Ramadier cab. 28 Jan.							
101 Communist mins. 4 May							
158 Q.c., ec. policy 4 July							
305 Algerian statute 27 Aug.							
316 Reorganized cab. 30 Oct. 47							

*The following conventions hold in this and similar succeeding figures:
The number of deputies indicated for each party (just below party name) is an average over all the roll calls shown.
Parties with fewer than 10 members are omitted.
—solid lines represent votes for premier or cabinet.
‒‒‒‒dotted lines represent abstention or nonvoting.
Blank space represents opposition.
On cabinet votes, shaded rectangles show by their width each party's vote for the cabinet, their height the ratio of ministers to supporting votes, and their area the total number of ministers. Junior cabinet members (secretaries and undersecretaries of state) are counted as one-half minister.
Dissidence of 5 or fewer members in a party is not shown.
**On nos. 1, 2, and 4, blank space represents any nonfavorable vote.

parties on selected major roll-call votes under his cabinet. At the top of the diagram are shown Thorez's support on his unsuccessful attempt at investiture (*scrutin* no. 1)[19] and Blum's massive support when he became the first premier. Between them was a vote on Bidault as premier, the only function of which was to show that the MRP could not form a cabinet.

Next is shown Ramadier's majority at investiture, and then the majority for his cabinet (no. 22). On the cabinet vote, each party in the majority is represented by a rectangle whose area is proportional to the number of its ministers, and whose width is proportional to the support it gave the cabinet. The height of the rectangle thus measures the ratio of cabinet posts to supporting votes. It can be seen that both Communists and MRP were relatively under-represented in Ramadier's cabinet.

Invested with the abstention (i.e., opposition) of only the PRL and half the RI, Ramadier saw first the Communists and fractions of the Moderates and Radicals move into opposition (nos. 101, 158).[20] Late in his ministry, when he succeeded in having a liberal Algerian statute passed,[21] he benefited from the Communists' abstention; even if they had opposed him, he would have lost only about ten votes from the previous roll call shown (nos. 158–305). As the autumn parliamentary vacation approached, his support in Socialist councils weakened and the fall of his cabinet was considered imminent, even after he had won a confidence vote on his economic policies by a margin of 49 votes. During the vacation, the RPF won a striking victory in the municipal elections, and attacks on the cabinet became more public. When Parliament reconvened, Ramadier reorganized his cabinet, but won "re-investiture" by a margin of only 20 votes (no. 316). His support had declined slightly among MRP, Radical, and UDSR deputies.

At this point the noncabinet Socialist leaders (Ramadier's own party colleagues) together with the MRP began negotiations toward forming a new, strong, united cabinet that would face up to the Gaullist threat. This movement was initiated by the MRP, but when Guy Mollet, the secretary-general of the Socialist party, announced at a press conference that Blum would be available for the premiership, Ramadier resigned.

The major problems of Ramadier's ministry had been the domestic economy (inflation and strikes) and the colonial situation. His government took the initiative on the Algerian statute; but on most other matters it was forced into action by events. Presiding over a large and heterogeneous cabinet, Ramadier had no clear "contract" at investiture and subsequently admitted having "neither a doctrine nor a policy." The major event for which his ministry is remembered is the departure of the Communist ministers and the move of their party into permanent opposition.

The customs that later came to define the "parliamentary game" were still being formed during Ramadier's ministry. It was he who, contrary to the spirit of the Constitution, revived the "double investiture." He instituted the "unofficial" question of confidence, by which the premier could threaten the cabinet's resignation if a vote were unfavorable without waiting a full day or requiring an absolute majority in opposition; it was first used for consideration of the Algerian statute.[22] He also initiated the custom of resigning in conditions other than the constitutional ones for overthrow of a cabinet—judging instead that he had insufficient authority to govern. Some other premiers were to hold fast in the face of attacks, even from within their own parties. But most were to resign before being overthrown by an absolute majority; this practice contributed to cabinet instability.

After Ramadier's resignation, Léon Blum stood for investiture on a "third force" program of firm opposition to both Communists and Gaullists.[23] But sympathy for Gaullism was considerable among the Moderates and Radicals, and Blum's firmness in that direction lost him essential votes. The next premier-designate would have to take a milder approach to gain

Figure 4.2 The Schuman Cabinet and Its Support

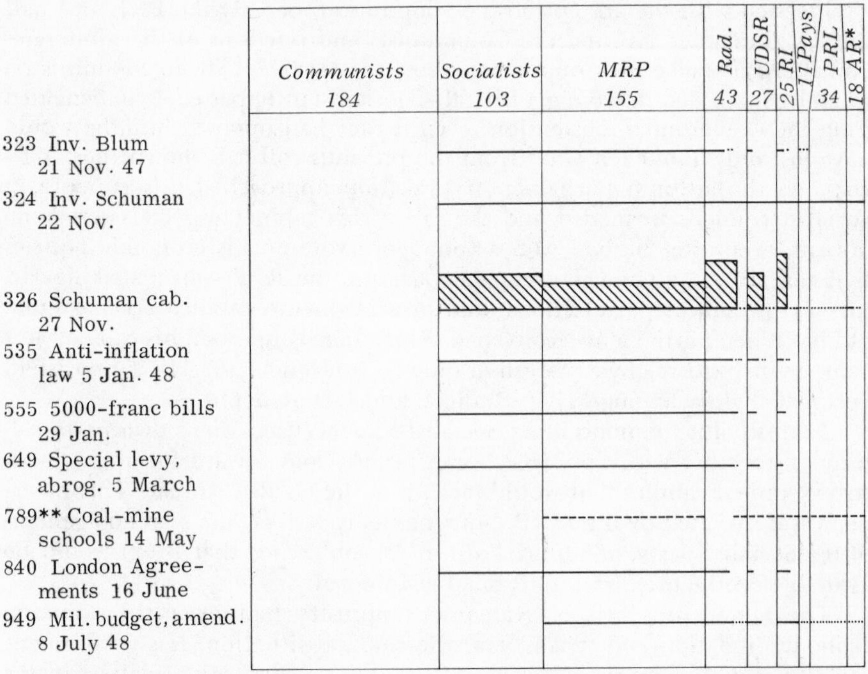

	Communists 184	Socialists 103	MRP 155	Rad. 43	UDSR 27	RI 25	Pays 11	PRL 34	AR* 18
323 Inv. Blum 21 Nov. 47									
324 Inv. Schuman 22 Nov.									
326 Schuman cab. 27 Nov.									
535 Anti-inflation law 5 Jan. 48									
555 5000-franc bills 29 Jan.									
649 Special levy, abrog. 5 March									
789** Coal-mine schools 14 May									
840 London Agreements 16 June									
949 Mil. budget, amend. 8 July 48									

Action Républicaine, a parliamentary group formed Dec. 29, 1947. Most of its members were ex-MRP deputies with Gaullist tendencies. On nos. 323-326 they were in two small groups.

**Dashed line on no. 789 represents "pro-clerical" votes on coal-mine schools question. Cabinet abstained; its members' votes are not shown.

the votes of Gaullist sympathizers; the center of gravity of the cabinet's support seemed to be moving toward the right.

At Ramadier's fall, several pro-Gaullist MRP deputies broke party discipline. They were expelled, some of their friends resigned in protest, and some UDSR deputies joined them. Thus the first "Gaullist" parliamentary group was formed, about eighteen in number.

The next premier, Robert Schuman (MRP), received personal investiture by a large majority (412–184, no. 324). But having appointed a cabinet containing only two Moderates (the Socialists vetoed a wider coalition that would have included the Moderate leader Paul Reynaud), he received a "cabinet majority" that was correspondingly narrower (Fig. 4.2). The ratios of cabinet posts to votes on the cabinet interpellations were approximately the same for all the parties represented.[24] The Gaullist group supported

Schuman's investiture, divided on his cabinet, and then largely opposed.

The Minister of Finance, René Mayer (Rad.), immediately began a series of measures to cope with inflation. First was a *prélèvement exceptionnel*, a new tax with the option of payment by subscription to a government loan. These forced savings were intended to remove money from circulation. The measure was passed in the Assembly by a margin of only 29 votes, and then defended successfully by narrow margins against a series of attempts to amend and abrogate it. Roll calls nos. 535 (one of a series of official questions of confidence) and 649 dealt with this measure. Mayer also took a second surprise step against inflation by removing all 5000-franc bills from circulation, allowing their holders to be reimbursed only gradually and after revealing their holdings (no. 555).

In the course of these votes Schuman made use of the "unofficial" question of confidence. Anxious for a favorable vote on no. 649, he circumvented the constitutional requirement for waiting a full day to put the official question of confidence. The deputies, about to go back to their districts for the weekend, might have wavered in their support for the cabinet's austerity measures.[25] Schuman received the support he needed, but he had given a further precedent to the custom that the cabinet resign when it could not pass new legislation. By the letter of the constitution, it had been conceivable for cabinets to remain in office until beaten by an absolute majority on a vote of confidence; it now became the practice to resign sooner. Schuman was the second premier to resign in the face of opposition less than the constitutional absolute majority; his resignation came after defeat on another unofficial question of confidence.

After Schuman's successful fight for his anti-inflation measures, his cabinet was weakened by the eruption of the church-school question. Some church schools in the northern mining areas nationalized in 1944 had been transferred to government control. Now the disposition of similar schools in southern mining areas had to be decided. Schuman proposed a compromise solution and persuaded his cabinet to vote for it. But in the face of a sharp attack from the Assembly's Education Committee and the brandishing of the issue of *laïcité* by the Socialist Maurice Deixonne, the cabinet lost the few votes it needed to keep control of the situation. Finally the committee's bill providing for complete nationalization prevailed (no. 789), while the cabinet abstained. This issue divided the cabinet, however, and hastened the subsequent departure of its Socialist members.

Negotiations were carried on at London for the creation of the West German Federal Republic, and the Assembly approved this action by voting a resolution[26] (no. 840). On this vote, also an unofficial question of confidence, Schuman retained his center majority by a narrow margin. The Marshall Plan was also adopted by a wide margin on July 7.

Schuman's break with the Socialists came in July 1948 over military appropriations. First he compromised with Radical and PRL deputies to persuade them to withdraw their amendments. But when he indicated that he would reject the Socialist amendment calling for a small cut in the military budget, the Socialists immediately left the cabinet's bench. Schuman waited for the unfavorable vote (no. 949) to resign.

Before a new cabinet could be invested, some agreement among the parties composing it on the wage-price problem seemed necessary.[27] Another important problem that would affect the outcome of the cabinet crisis concerned the cantonal elections scheduled for the autumn, in which further Gaullist victories were expected. Although the Socialists would have liked to hold the premiership again, the MRP deputies were bitter at them for their having overthrown Schuman. The conservative parties had also shown their power by giving or withholding support from Schuman, and would have to be given more attention in the future.

Figure 4.3 The Marie Cabinet and Its Support

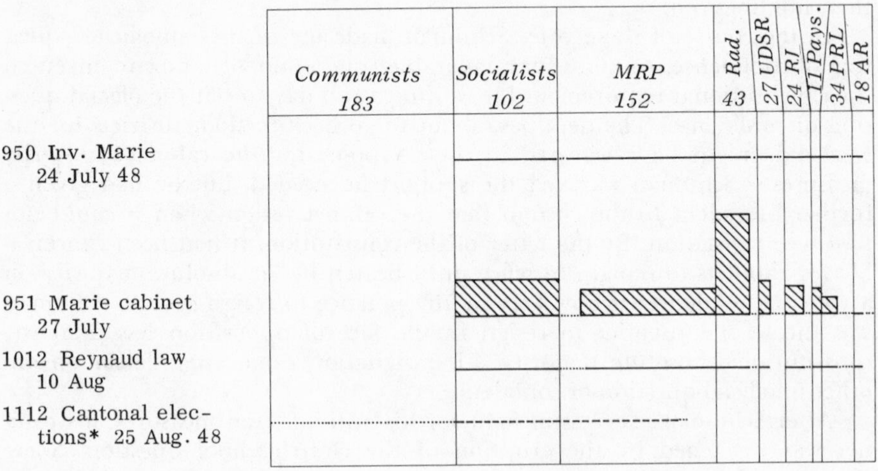

	Communists 183	Socialists 102	MRP 152	Rad. 43	27 UDSR	24 RI	11 Pays.	34 PRL	18 AR
950 Inv. Marie 24 July 48									
951 Marie cabinet 27 July									
1012 Reynaud law 10 Aug									
1112 Cantonal elections* 25 Aug. 48									

*Dashed line on no. 1112 represents votes in favor of postponing cantonal elections. Cabinet abstained; its members' votes are not shown.

The crisis was nevertheless resolved in only five days, after a series of interviews by President Auriol with party leaders.[28] With agreement in advance by both Léon Blum and Paul Reynaud to participate in a broadly based cabinet, the Radical André Marie was invested by 352 to 190 (no. 950). The Socialists, though willing to support such a cabinet, were quite reserved about the participation of PRL ministers, wishing to scrutinize the "republicanism" (i.e., non-Gaullism) of any ministers drawn from that party.[29]

Marie's investiture marked not only the broadening of the majority toward the right, but other political changes as well. The rise of a Radical to the premiership meant the return to power of the parties of the Third Republic, and was thus seen by some MRP deputies as a retrogression. The extension of cabinet and majority toward the right also reduced the importance of the UDSR's votes and deprived René Pleven, its president, of his veto power over cabinets.[30] Marie, as premier, increased the relative representation of the Radicals in the cabinet, while the MRP was again slightly under-represented (Fig. 4.3).

Two issues dominated the Marie ministry: the regulatory powers asked by Reynaud for organizing the economy, and the postponement of the cantonal elections for the *département* councils. On entering the cabinet Reynaud had asked passage of a bill permitting reorganization of the public services and nationalized industries. The bill also provided for measures to increase production, and for tax reform; a key vote on it was no. 1012. On this vote Marie's support was slightly less than on the composition of the cabinet. The opposition to this "Reynaud law" was based partly on Reynaud's position on the right (the left wing of the MRP abstained or opposed), partly on the delegation of legislative powers to the executive, and partly on the threat to various entrenched interests from Reynaud's proposed reorganizations. The passage of this bill was said to "end the crisis" by satisfying Reynaud's conditions for participation. But the later defection of the Socialists on the same issue led some observers to question whether there had been any real agreement on this issue at Marie's investiture.

Postponement of the cantonal elections was accomplished by the votes of the two major parties of the cabinet—Socialists and MRP—while the Communists did not vote (no. 1112). The Radicals and the parties of the right opposed, and the cabinet was neutral. The Fonlupt-Espéraber (MRP) bill was ostensibly a measure providing for the reorganization of the *département* councils, and the MRP denied official sponsorship of it. Yet its political motives were clearly recognized by the opposition and the press; it effectively permitted postponement of the elections to these councils, though without setting a definite alternative date for them.

Shortly thereafter, Reynaud began to translate his special regulatory powers into specific acts. They were to include a rise in the controlled prices of bread and milk, compensations for wage workers (such as an increase in family allowances) and budgetary economies.[31] But no sooner were they proposed than the Socialists made a counter demand for extensive wage increases, and Marie resigned. The timing of the crisis strongly suggested that Marie had never had genuine policy agreement from his supporting majority. The Socialist deputies, once the "mortgage" of the cantonal elections had been lifted,[32] moved away from government responsibility into sympathy with the wage demands of their worker clientele. Reynaud's conditions for entering the cabinet, when translated into concrete legislation, were precisely the conditions that the Socialists would not tolerate. Marie did not wait for an unfavorable vote to resign.[33] He chose not to try to reorganize his cabinet and stay in office; but both Ramadier's attempt to do so in October 1947 and subsequent experience showed that such reorganization was rarely successful.

To try to form the next cabinet, President Auriol first recalled Ramadier, who declined. He then recalled Schuman, who was invested by a smaller margin than any of his predecessors (Fig. 4.4, no. 1143).[34] The narrow investiture majority required the support of several minor parties: the five Independent Muslims, who could normally be counted on for support, joined three deputies from Upper Volta and four overseas *non inscrits* (deputies not in any parliamentary group) in support of Schuman. This vote foreshadowed many others in which the bargaining power of small parliamentary groups, including the nonideological overseas deputies, was augmented.

A week later, however, Schuman failed by six votes to gain the Assembly's approval for his cabinet. Failing on an official vote of confidence (no. 1144), though not by an absolute majority, the cabinet resigned. The custom of resigning after defeat by a mere plurality, which Schuman instituted in his first ministry and now confirmed, was no longer questioned. Even though supported by the Socialists, the Schuman cabinet was opposed by substantial factions among the Radicals, the UDSR, and the right. The defectors in-

Figure 4.4 The First Queuille Cabinet and Its Support

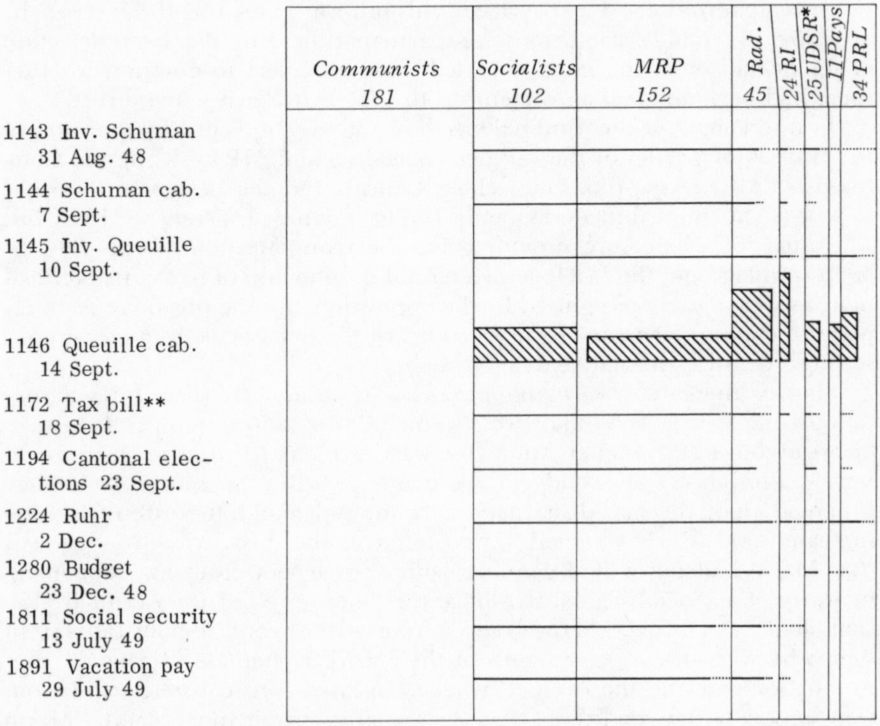

	Communists 181	Socialists 102	MRP 152	Rad. 45	24 RI	25 UDSR*	11 Pays	34 PRL
1143 Inv. Schuman 31 Aug. 48								
1144 Schuman cab. 7 Sept.								
1145 Inv. Queuille 10 Sept.								
1146 Queuille cab. 14 Sept.								
1172 Tax bill** 18 Sept.								
1194 Cantonal elections 23 Sept.								
1224 Ruhr 2 Dec.								
1280 Budget 23 Dec. 48								
1811 Social security 13 July 49								
1891 Vacation pay 29 July 49								

*By roll call no. 1891, 13 of the UDSR deputies had moved to a new Gaullist group.
**Placement of intraparty dissidence on "left" is only approximate, esecially for party divisions that do not appear in the scale clusters.

cluded a considerable number of Gaullists: a faction led by Giacobbi among the Radicals, almost the entire PRL, and the bulk of the UDSR deputies. Fauvet concluded from this vote that it was impossible to govern without either Communist or Gaullist support. The UDSR leader Pleven, he contended, had been "master of the game."[35] For although not officially a Gaullist, Pleven was for several years the advocate of a close alliance between the center parties and the Gaullist forces. The 22 UDSR votes that went into opposition did much to bring Schuman's cabinet down. This second Schuman cabinet, though short-lived, was the first to fall while the Socialists still supported it.

A cabinet was finally organized and approved under the leadership of Henri Queuille, a Radical of long ministerial experience in the Third Republic as well as the Fourth. He was supported at investiture by a majority similar to Marie's. Unlike Schuman, he lost only 11 favorable votes from the personal investiture to the vote on postponing the cabinet interpellations (nos. 1145–1146). His investiture only three days after Schuman's fall was partly due to the "government" parties' desire to avoid a power vacuum in the face of the Gaullist threat and pressing economic problems. Queuille's cabinet, like Marie's, included both Socialists and Moderates (Fig. 4.4).[36] Relative to its supporting majority, the cabinet had a high proportion of Radical and UDSR ministers and a low proportion from the MRP.

On the passage of a tax-increase bill (no. 1172), Queuille's support was reduced by 60 votes; but since some of the nonsupporters abstained, he still had the comfortable margin of 40 votes over the opposition. His losses of votes were primarily among the right, Radicals, and UDSR.

The timing of the cantonal elections then came to the fore again. The Fonlupt-Espéraber bill, passed under Marie, had permitted their postponement but had not specified when they were to be held. Queuille, skilled at postponing issues and avoiding conflicts, had taken no official stand on this issue at his investiture. Finally, however, he was forced to take a stand, and came out for postponing the elections till March 1949. In a series of close votes (for example, no. 1194), he won passage of this bill just before the summer parliamentary vacation. He then continued to face the wage–price problem, as well as a coal miners' strike in October.[37] In November the elections to the upper chamber (Council of the Republic) were held and marked another victory for Gaullism.

Shortly thereafter, the United States and Britain moved to associate the Ruhr with the new West German state. Several groups in the Assembly, having expected international rather than German control of the Ruhr, proposed resolutions criticizing the cabinet for allowing this association. Queuille succeeded in having a pro-cabinet resolution passed by a comfortable margin (no. 1224); but the 51 deputies who did not take part in the vote marked a Gaullist nucleus in the Assembly.[38]

On December 23 the Queuille cabinet brought its budget before the Assembly and passed it after a series of informal votes of confidence. One of these (no. 1280) is shown in Figure 4.4. A tax increase and a ceiling for civil expenditures (*loi des maxima*) were passed.

In February 1949 the Minister of Justice, André Marie, came under attack for alleged leniency in investigating a case of economic collaboration with the Nazis; he resigned on grounds of health. Although this reorganization did not threaten the cabinet, it altered the patterns of voting of the Radicals.

The cabinet was not seriously threatened again on an Assembly vote until July 1949. But this relative safety was gained partly because a 5 per cent loan floated by Minister of Finance Maurice Petsche required a corresponding parliamentary "truce." By May the possibility of the cabinet's fall was openly discussed and even some of its Moderate members were criticizing its policies. On roll call no. 1811, concluding a debate on the social security system, a pro-cabinet resolution passed by 293–264; the Independents, under Reynaud, moved into opposition.

On July 29 the cabinet came within three votes of defeat on a bill providing for vacation pay bonuses for employees in the social security administration (no. 1891). This victory depended on the votes of many small parties and fractions; two PRL ministers resigned from their party in order to vote for the cabinet.[39] Saved again by the summer vacation, the cabinet was generally expected to fall immediately thereafter. It actually fell near the end of the vacation when the Socialist Daniel Mayer resigned as Minister

Figure 4.5 The Bidault Cabinet and Its Support

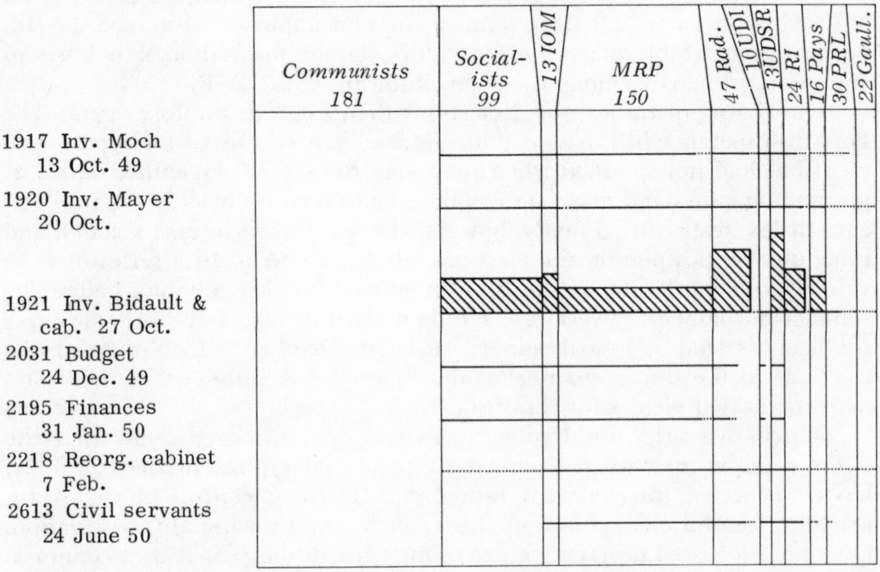

	Communists 181	Socialists 99	13 IOM	MRP 150	47 Rad.	10 UDI	13 UDSR	24 RI	16 Pays	30 PRL	22 Gaull.
1917 Inv. Moch 13 Oct. 49											
1920 Inv. Mayer 20 Oct.											
1921 Inv. Bidault & cab. 27 Oct.											
2031 Budget 24 Dec. 49											
2195 Finances 31 Jan. 50											
2218 Reorg. cabinet 7 Feb.											
2613 Civil servants 24 June 50											

of Labor. But although the Socialists were considered "responsible," the parties of the right and center, including such leaders as Pleven and Reynaud, had an important share in bringing the cabinet to the brink of defeat.

Daniel Mayer's resignation, approved after the fact by his party, led to the initial invitation to the Socialist Jules Moch to form another cabinet. Invested by only 311 votes, one more than the constitutional majority,[40] he was unable to form a cabinet for which he would get sufficient support. Though Moch had been more successful than Blum, it was clear that a cabinet led by a Socialist could not be invested; nor would there be another till 1956. The conflict between Socialist and Moderate principles told again in this case.[41]

President Auriol then renominated the Radical René Mayer, who was personally invested by a more substantial majority (341–183 on no. 1920). But he too was unable to resolve a controversy on cabinet places between the parties of his majority—Socialists and Radicals—and resigned. The conditions placed on René Mayer's cabinet by the Socialists were rumored to be a reprisal for his earlier hindrance of Moch.

Georges Bidault (MRP), benefiting from the length of the crisis, then succeeded in having himself and his cabinet invested in a single vote (no. 1921; Fig. 4.5). His wide margin at investiture quickly dwindled to a handful, however, as he put a series of questions of confidence on the budget (e.g., no. 2031). But instead of being overthrown, Bidault held firm; he stayed in office six months longer. His success seemed partly due to his own determination; for unlike some premiers faced with narrow majorities, he showed no signs of political "fatigue." Partly too it may be attributed to his facing difficult issues early in his ministry, when his credit with his supporters was high. His majority was in fact holding firm while the attacks on him were coming from deputies clearly outside the majority (Reynaud, Daladier).[42] The MRP was completely united in its votes for the cabinet, as it had not been under Queuille; and with Pleven in the cabinet the UDSR also gave nearly unanimous support. The Socialists could be counted on because at their party congress they had agreed as a test of the cabinet's policies to give it a respite at least until January.

After the close votes on the budget and taxes, a bill on collective bargaining was easily passed on January 4, 1950. The success of this bill was facilitated by Bidault's *not* having put the question of confidence.[43]

Another series of close votes on the budget took place on January 31. On one of several of questions of confidence put by Bidault (no. 2195), the vote was tied at 293–293, and an amendment favored by the government failed to pass. Bidault, however, considered this merely a "technical incident" rather than an occasion for resignation, and had it remedied in a subsequent vote. The failure of this amendment actually would have caused receipts to exceed expenses, and did not reflect a calculated effort to bring down the cabinet.

A few days later the Socialist ministers resigned from the cabinet; by supporting the cabinet without participating in it, they took an opportunity to solidify their position with their militants and voters. The cabinet was now under potential threats from both Socialists and Radicals, and in danger of losing support if it displeased either group.[44] Bidault then reorganized his cabinet, replacing most of the departing Socialists with members of the MRP: A confidence vote on the new cabinet (no. 2218) found the Socialists not voting. There was then discussion of the possibility of a cabinet crisis, but the Radicals knew the Socialists could not enter another cabinet before their national council meeting and refrained from pushing the attack. The cabinet was saved from falling also because the Moderates and Gaullists abstained rather than opposing on this vote.

The Socialists were further alienated from the cabinet by the revival of the "affair of the generals"—a dispute as to who had been to blame for attempts by two generals in 1949 to influence Parliament on policy in Indochina, as well as for the leakage of certain secret documents.[45] A committee of inquiry had been appointed by the Assembly in January and its report (under the chairmanship of the MRP deputy Delahoutre) was debated in early May. Parts of the report were considered by the Socialists unfavorable to Ramadier in his former capacity as Minister of Defense. A further source of contention between Socialists and MRP arose from the resurgence of the church-school question in Brittany.

The Socialists' gradual move into opposition was completed when they brought Bidault down in June (no. 2613). The distribution of favorable votes was nearly the same as on his "re-investiture" (no. 2218); but now most of the former abstainers, on left and right, were in opposition. Bidault, having been the most persistent of all premiers up to this time in the face of narrow majorities, was the first to be overthrown by the constitutional absolute majority.[46] The occasion of his fall was a vote on the reclassification of civil servants, which would affect their salaries; but the disagreements between Socialists and MRP were more general. That issue alone might conceivably have been compromised; but Bidault stood firm on it, knowing other pressure-group claims would immediately follow if he yielded. Moreover, he had seen from the tone of recent party congresses that there was a general and growing disaffection with the cabinet.[47]

The failure of the Bidault cabinet to obtain support on the right when the Socialists defected seemed to show again that the Socialists were essential for any supporting majority. But the antagonism between Socialists and Moderates was extending from domestic economic issues to include the issue of the European coal-steel pool (Schuman Plan) as well. The problem of electoral reform was also increasingly important. This issue had been in the background at Bidault's investiture and would come to complicate the fate of the Pleven and final Queuille cabinets.[48]

Bidault fell on the day the North Koreans invaded South Korea. The international implications of the invasion made it all the more urgent that France have something more than a caretaker cabinet. After several deputies had declined President Auriol's offer to form a new cabinet, Henri Queuille was recalled and invested (no. 2617: Fig. 4.6). But his apparently substantial support (363–208) was given only with reservations: the MRP revived the church-school question, and the Socialists, planning to support the cabinet without participation, gave the impression that their support would be on a day-to-day basis.[49]

Queuille formed a cabinet without Socialists but with more deputies from the center and right. Among the latter were Reynaud of the Independents and Giacobbi, recently returned to the Radical party after having been president of the Gaullist intergroup in the Assembly. But this move to the right was too much for the Socialists, who then brought down the cabinet when it was presented (no. 2618); they did so on the basis of its personnel alone, not waiting for its program. Paradoxically, it was the right wing of the Socialist group—those who would normally have been most favorable to Queuille—who were the strongest opponents of this cabinet; they needed to show that the cabinet was impossible without Socialist support in order to argue for Socialist participation in subsequent cabinets.[50]

The Socialists' defection on the cabinet vote left the MRP on the left flank of the majority. This position, which they were to occupy for the most of the Second Legislature, left them deeply divided, as their votes on no. 2618 show.

A *mission d'information* by Mollet then led to the designation of René Pleven (UDSR) as premier; he presented himself with a program drawn up by Mollet. On his personal investiture Pleven received ten more votes than had Queuille (no. 2619). Forming a cabinet including the Socialists,[51] he lost only about 40 votes as the cabinet interpellations were postponed. Invested in July, Pleven did not encounter serious opposition on any vote of importance in our sample until February 1951, when the electoral law came up. In the meantime, an incipient outbreak of the church-school controversy was suppressed, a pro-cabinet resolution on Indochina was passed, Naegelen was reappointed as governor-general of Algeria, the Pleven plan for a European army received a favorable vote,[52] and the Vichy amnesty bill

Figure 4.6 The Pleven Cabinet (First Legislature) and Its Support

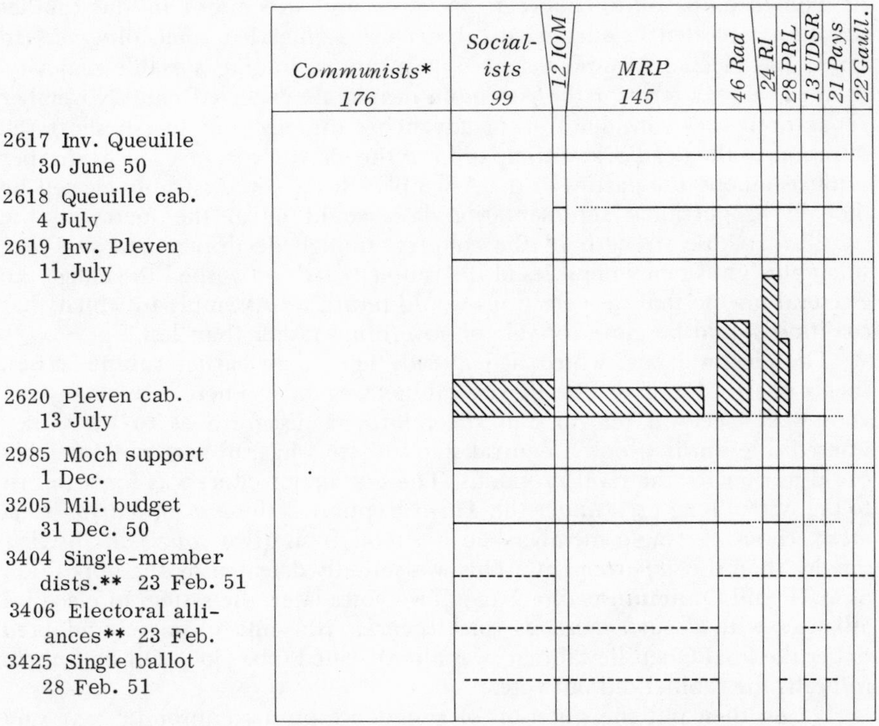

	Communists* 176	Social- ists 99	12 IOM	MRP 145	46 Rad	24 RI	28 PRL	13 UDSR	21 Pays	22 Gaull.
2617 Inv. Queuille 30 June 50										
2618 Queuille cab. 4 July										
2619 Inv. Pleven 11 July										
2620 Pleven cab. 13 July										
2985 Moch support 1 Dec.										
3205 Mil. budget 31 Dec. 50										
3404 Single-member dists.** 23 Feb. 51										
3406 Electoral alli- ances** 23 Feb.										
3425 Single ballot 28 Feb. 51										

*Not including the six RDA deputies, who split off on nos. 2985, 3205, 3404, 3425.
**Cabinet did not vote and members are omitted from diagram. Dashed lines represent the position closest to that of the cabinet coalition, when there is no official cabinet position.

was passed. In late October the cabinet was temporarily threatened by a disagreement between Socialists and MRP over the military draft bill; but this was settled and the bill passed by a substantial majority.

The greatest threat to the Pleven cabinet during this period occurred in a vote by secret ballot. Late in November the Communists revived the "affair of the generals," asking that Jules Moch (Minister of the Interior when the events occurred and now Minister of Defense) be impeached. On November 28 the Communist motion against Moch received 235 votes against 203; though failing of the necessary absolute majority, it was a serious defeat for the cabinet. Pleven offered his resignation to President Auriol, who refused it. He then put the question of confidence on support for Moch as well as the cabinet's general policy. On this vote (no. 2985) he was "reinvested" by a substantial margin. Most of the 70 deputies who abstained had some hesitations about the future general policies they were asked to endorse, but they did not wish to associate themselves with the Communists in opposition.[53]

In late December and early January a series of confidence votes occurred on the military budget, providing for France's rearmament. One of the closest of these was no. 3205. Pleven's supporting majority on this vote was nearly the same as on the initial approval of his cabinet (no. 2620).

The incompatibility between Socialists and Moderates in the cabinet coalition, revealed at successive cabinet crises, had led some observers to think that elections would be the only means of finding a viable majority. As the five-year term of the Assembly neared its expected end (November 1951), there was consideration of advancing the elections to cut short the duration of the deadlock; anticipation of the elections in fact led to sharper conflicts among the parties in the Assembly. But a new Assembly elected by the old proportional representation law would be at the mercy of the Gaullists, whose strength in the country, though declining, was still considerable. Thus many deputies of the cabinet coalition wished to change the electoral law, so that new elections would return an Assembly in which that coalition would be more capable of governing, rather than less.

The electoral law, which had already figured in earlier cabinet crises, then came to dominate the Pleven cabinet's agenda. There were many advocates of electoral reform, but the reformers disagreed as to what they wanted. Pleven first took a neutral stand to see what support the Assembly could muster for the rival proposals. The first major effort was for a return to the system long used under the Third Republic—the *scrutin d'arrondissement,* choosing single members on a runoff basis (two *tours*) in districts smaller than the *départements.* This was soundly defeated by the opposition of MRP and Communists (no. 3404). Two votes later, the system of electoral alliances with *départements* as constituencies (the one ultimately adopted under the final Queuille cabinet) was also defeated (no. 3406). On both these roll calls the cabinet did not vote.

Pleven then put the question of confidence on a compromise text supported by the cabinet and won by 243–216, the MRP abstaining. This bill was expected to be modified by amendment toward a one-ballot system rather than a runoff, and Pleven announced that he would accept this result if the Assembly voted it, even though the cabinet would remain neutral on it. But to the surprise of many, this delicate maneuver to advance electoral reform also failed (no. 3425). The cabinet was divided, six Socialists broke party discipline to oppose the bill, and it lost by sixteen votes. Pleven, finding there was no position he could take without losing either the Radicals or the MRP from his cabinet, resigned. Since it was difficult to assign responsibility for the cabinet's fall, President Auriol urged Pleven to remain in office, but he refused again, and a new ministerial crisis began.

This new crisis appeared difficult to resolve. The parties had just demonstrated that there was no electoral law on which they could agree. The single ballot at the departmental level seemed closest to succeeding, but the Radicals (among the pro-cabinet parties) had opposed it resolutely. In addition the Socialists and MRP now wanted to give priority to economic problems, while other parties were more concerned with constitutional reform or the electoral law.[54]

After unsuccessful explorations by several deputies, Guy Mollet was designated for an investiture vote. He obtained twenty-five votes fewer than Moch, the last Socialist to have sought the investiture. These losses were all from the parties of the center and right: MRP, Radicals, UDSR, Independents. The lesson of this vote was that no prospective premier could be invested as long as he antagonized important segments of the "usual" majority on the electoral-law issues.[55]

Henri Queuille then again accepted President Auriol's invitation to form a cabinet. He was to succeed where Pleven had failed. He had shown already that he was willing to work with different majorities at different times; his near fall on the vacation pay issue (no. 1891) found him supported by a leftist majority, while in his subsequent brief ministry he assembly a right-center cabinet without the Socialists. Now in the face of his own Radical party's initial opposition he succeeded in passing the only electoral law that the center majority would support. This was all the more impressive because the one point on which the usually divided Radicals had seemed to be united was their advocacy of the *scrutin d'arrondissement*.

In his investiture declaration Queuille was neutral on the electoral law, though favoring some reform embodying the majority principle. He declared himself to be "on leave" from the Radical party.[56] He proposed a limited program, including some anti-inflationary measures, minor constitutional revision, passage of the budget, and elections before the summer. The composition of his cabinet was to be almost the same as Pleven's. The Assembly, "weary" of the crisis, gave him solid support (no. 3428; Fig. 4.7).

Constituting his cabinet, Queuille promised to give priority on the Assembly's agenda to the electoral-law debate. On the cabinet roll call (no. 3429) he gained thirty votes at a stage where cabinets normally lost support. The general acknowledgment that there was to be no succeeding cabinet until after the elections may have aided him.

The break between Gaullists and the pro-cabinet majority now became sharper. The RPF forswore electoral alliances, and the Radicals opposed "bigamy" (joint membership in their own party and the RPF).

Initially, a single day was set for debate of the electoral law. The bill was successfully amended to provide for a single *tour* (rather than a runoff) and the majority principle (no. 3454). It was then modified, by a narrower margin, to provide for electoral alliances. The future electoral law began to take shape, but one day was insufficient for the details of drafting the bill to be completed. Four days later, however, after a long debate on electoral alliances, the Assembly reversed itself by rejecting the article of the bill providing for them (no. 3489). Two days after that, another all-night session (March 21) led to approval of the details of the bill again, and the entire bill was passed on a personal vote (no. 3618) on April 5. Some fifty deputies were absent from Paris and could not vote; the margin was only 263–251.

The Assembly's passage of an electoral-law bill represented a considerable advance over its previous confusion on the issue, but serious problems still lay ahead. The Council of the Republic, to which the bill would now go, was certain to substitute something nearer to the old *scrutin d'arrondisse-ment,* and might well do so by an absolute majority; then the Assembly to prevail would have to pass its own bill on second reading by an absolute majority (311) of its members.

There was still a possibility that Queuille would fall or resign; two of his ministers threatened to resign early in April. Queuille was considering

Figure 4.7 The Final Queuille Cabinet and Its Support

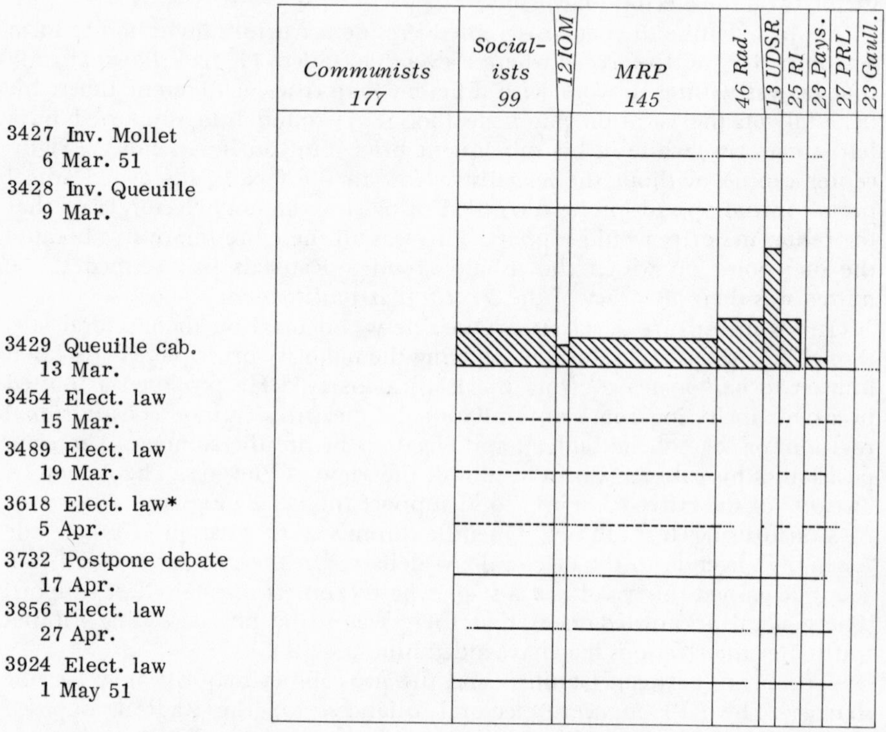

	Communists 177	Social- ists 99	12 IOM	MRP 145	46 Rad.	13 UDSR	25 RI	23 Pays.	27 PRL	23 Gaull.
3427 Inv. Mollet 6 Mar. 51										
3428 Inv. Queuille 9 Mar.										
3429 Queuille cab. 13 Mar.										
3454 Elect. law 15 Mar.										
3489 Elect. law 19 Mar.										
3618 Elect. law* 5 Apr.										
3732 Postpone debate 17 Apr.										
3856 Elect. law 27 Apr.										
3924 Elect. law 1 May 51										

*Personal vote; nonvoters allocated on graph in same proportions as voters, except for IOM, in which a majority failed to vote.

June 10 as a date for the elections, but if he fell the elections would have to be postponed. Some groups in the Assembly wanted to postpone the end of the Legislature in order to place the claims of various pressure groups on the agenda. On April 17 Queuille won the first of a series of confidence votes (no. 3732) supporting early elections and priority for the passage of the budget. Winning by 311 to 240, Queuille had lost about forty votes since his investiture.

On April 22 the Council of the Republic did in fact substitute the *scrutin d'arrondissement* by a large majority. It was not clear whether the Assembly would be able to override this vote, even on a compromise measure, nor was it likely that the Assembly would become converted to the Senators'[57] bill. Queuille, having maintained neutrality this far, now had to take a stand. The only position he could take that would keep his majority together was to favor the Assembly's former bill. The *scrutin d'arrondissement*, for example, would not only divide the majority but also require a long delay for redistricting. Queuille appealed for the re-passage of the law, though without putting the official question of confidence; on April 27 it missed receiving the absolute majority by three votes (308–270; no. 3856). As the cabinet members were preparing to walk out of the chamber, indicating their resignation, President Herriot of the Assembly saved the law by a parliamentary ruling, sending the bill back to committee. A rapid minor revision brought it back to the Assembly for a new "first reading." The parties became more unified—there had been Socialist and MRP dissidence —and the new bill was passed, this time on a question of confidence, by 339 to 251 (no. 3924).[58] This majority was increased six days later when the bill was finally passed again over the contrary vote of the Council of the Republic. The electoral campaign was on.

The elections were then set for June 17, the end of the Legislature fixed, and the budget voted. A final skirmish on tax exemptions for private schools did not prevent the Assembly from hastening to the end of its work.

Patterns of Cabinet Coalition

We may now summarize the factors bringing cabinets down in the First Legislature. We have considered seven cabinets that were invested and then actually or nearly overthrown by the Assembly.[59] In the fall of the first five, the Socialists played a major part and were considered "responsible." In Ramadier's fall it was Mollet, rather than the party as a whole, that gave the last push; but Schuman, Marie, Queuille (1949), and Bidault fell when the Socialist party as a whole went from support to opposition. Queuille's case was somewhat unusual in that Daniel Mayer resigned as Minister of Labor and only afterward received party support for doing so.

The last two ministries of the Legislature—those of Pleven and Queuille —ended under different circumstances. Pleven, trying to find a position on the electoral law that would retain his majority, lost unexpectedly when deserted by fragments of the rank and file, including some of the Socialists; but his failure on this vote was not charged to deliberate action by any party's official leadership. Queuille's last cabinet, which nearly failed on the electoral-law question, had the Socialists more firmly behind it.

Why did the Socialists play such a dominant role in the downfall of these cabinets? They were not essential to the cabinet's majority on a purely arithmetical basis, since together with the Communists they constituted an opposition of only 280 votes. Even after the Gaullist forces coalesced (in the ADS and RPI groups), the opposition numbered only a few votes over 300. Nevertheless, it was politically impossible to form a cabinet which the remaining parties supported unanimously. A few of the remaining deputies were ex-Communists or former leftist members of the MRP, while others were close to Gaullism without having formally left their own parties. For reasons such as these they could not all be marshaled behind a single candidate.[60] The difficulty of gaining support from a non-Socialist majority was shown by both Bidault's fall (no. 2613) and Queuille's unsuccessful second investiture (no. 2618): each failed by at least 100 votes.[61]

The Socialists were thus politically necessary, if not arithmetically so, to any cabinet's supporting majority in the First Legislature.[62] This means that when and if they decided to oppose the cabinet (after the Communists' departure), it would fall. But two important questions remain: could a cabinet have been brought down while the Socialists still supported it? And why did the Socialists not continue to support cabinets longer?

Only one attempt to form a majority *with* the Socialists failed: the abortive Schuman cabinet of September 1948 (no. 1144). This failure might be charged to Auriol's bringing Schuman back too soon after his previous fall. There were, however, several instances of cabinets that were very nearly overthrown while still supported by the Socialists. Ramadier was brought down to his twenty-vote margin by defections among the Radicals and Moderates before Mollet (and the MRP) finally undermined him. Schuman's first cabinet, Queuille's first, and Bidault's were all reduced to very narrow margins by the initial defection of these same parties. None was overthrown, and only in Queuille's case did this erosion of support lead to rumors of the cabinet's imminent fall. It is thus likely that at least some conditions permitted continued government by a majority including the Socialists, without many additional votes from the right.[63]

The stablest potential majority in the First Legislature after Ramadier was therefore one including the Socialists with a Radical or MRP premier.[64] Why, then, did this majority repeatedly distintegrate? The repeated moves of the Socialists into opposition seem to have been dictated by antagonisms that grew with time,[65] chiefly between the Socialist militants and the more conservative cabinet members, between whom the Socialist ministers were balanced in unstable equilibrium. Until Mollet's conversion to favoring cabinet participation under non-Socialist premiers, he drew his power within the party from successful advocacy of the militants' position. The affinity between Socialists and Communists was still recent enough that substantial segments of the party were uneasy about governing without the Communists. But when Mollet changed his mind and entered Pleven's cabinet on the program he himself had drawn up, the electoral-law issue was becoming dominant, and it was on this issue that the last two cabinets were threatened. If this analysis is correct, one might expect the early part of Pleven's ministry to have been the least *immobiliste* of all in the First Legislature, as the cabinet was most certain of Socialist backing; Pleven, however, had conciliatory tendencies. As the electoral-law controversy progressed, Mollet succeeded in enforcing party discipline and reducing dissidence so as to provide Queuille the few additional votes he needed in 1951.

It appears that the Socialist ministers made ambiguous agreements with their colleagues in these cabinets, and that the terms of these agreements were interpreted differently by the other parties, the Socialist ministers, and the Socialist rank and file. The break then occurred after a sufficient number of concrete instances had arisen to reveal this ambiguity. In the case of the "Reynaud law" under Marie, the break came as soon as specific decrees were issued; the parties of the right had not even had time to leave the majority.

Under Schuman, Queuille (1949), and Bidault, the issues chosen by the Socialists for the break were generally considered merely symptomatic of larger disagreements with the other parties of the majority.

Although the Socialists were most frequently charged with responsibility for cabinets' fall, they were not alone in seeking to overthrow them. Some Radicals and Moderates also made deliberate efforts in this direction—because an important weapon to influence cabinet policy was the threat of resignation or opposition. In this Reynaud resembled the Socialists. He opposed Queuille in 1949 and Bidault, though apparently for substantive reasons and not ambition for a cabinet position. Pleven and René Mayer also opposed Queuille in 1949, but their reasons seemed closer to personal ambition (or hostility); they entered the following (Bidault) cabinet. There were few Moderates in the cabinets of the First Legislature, and they were rarely mentioned as plotting new coalitions to place themselves in office.[66]

Types of Intraparty Division

Assessing final "responsibility" for a cabinet's downfall and identifying possible party combinations during a given Legislature tell only the broadest and most general conditions affecting the cabinet. Divisions within the parties are also of considerable importance; and when a party is divided on a vote that affects a cabinet's decision power, we wish to account for that division in terms of coalitions or issues.

Each roll-call vote could have two major consequences: action on the substantive matter at hand, and the continuation or downfall of the cabinet. Those votes that most clearly dealt with the cabinet's fate were on investitures, questions of confidence, and postponement of interpellations on the cabinet's policy or composition. But many other votes, apparently more concerned with substantive legislation, also affected the cabinet's fate. One of our central problems is to assess the extent to which these two considerations—substantive legislation and the fate of the cabinet—entered into any given vote and into votes in general.

The interrelation of issues through their involvement with a single cabinet was noted by Aron: "The very life of the government was in question at almost each moment, especially during the later years (but the phenomenon, to one degree or another had been present from the beginning of the Fourth Republic).[67] A similar relation between legislative voting and party control of the Executive has been observed in the United States;[68] it affects the President's legislative program, but not his tenure in office.

To distinguish clearly between issues and cabinets as factors in Assembly voting, however, we must be more precise. First, there is a question of degree. Within a given party, a basic orientation might persist throughout the entire Fourth Republic, but a few deputies might change their positions. Daladier, for example, shifted from extreme right to extreme left within the Radical party, but this shift alone is insufficient to show that divisions within the party altered fundamentally. A quantitative comparison is necessary.

A second problem concerns how closely cabinets were connected with particular issues. The issue of German rearmament under the Paris Agreements of 1954, for example, was specific to the Mendès-France cabinet, yet the votes on it did not merely reflect parliamentary maneuvering, nor were they closely related to other votes under Mendès. To some extent, the same problem arises for any cabinet: conservative economic policies, European union, "pacification" in Algeria, all were advocated by particular cabinets. We shall be most sure that a group of roll calls concerned coalitions more than issues, therefore, when a given voting configuration existed only under a particular cabinet, when it embraced a variety of substantive issues, and when each of these issues also elicited different configurations of voting under other cabinets. An issue that arose under only one cabinet renders the inference more difficult, in that it depends more on our classification of the subjects involved.[69]

A third problem in inferring cabinet as against issue specificity derives from the fact that two or more different cabinets may elicit the same coalitions, and for this reason similar voting divisions. If the same man was premier twice, or if two men from the same party formed cabinets of similar composition, the coalitions that supported them may have been similar. Thus it is not simply the specificity of a voting pattern to a single cabinet but its connection with a given coalition that matters.

Issue and cabinet considerations may be distinguished by analysis of the internal divisions of the parties in the Assembly. The relations *among* the parties do not provide full detail about the coalitions specific to each cabinet; the bulk of the Moderates, for example, may have opposed two different cabinets, but different groups of deputies may have constituted the opposition in the two cases. Only certain small parties near the center of the political spectrum (UDSR, Overseas Independents) revealed cabinet-specific coalitions by their positions *as parties*.

The distinction between issue-specificity and cabinet-specificity of votes is related to certain conflicting diagnoses of the weaknesses of the Fourth Republic. A central point of Leites' analysis is that tactical considerations of the parliamentary game weighed more heavily than the doctrines of parties, and that French political commentators exaggerated the ideological aspects of the parties.[70] Insofar as tactical considerations dominated, we should expect the configurations of votes to be relatively specific to particular cabinet coalitions and diverse in substance; if ideology dominated, these configurations would be expected to center about particular issues.

If we discover ideological or doctrinal positions through study of intra-party divisions, they will necessarily relate to the doctrines of factions rather than of entire parties. Multiple divisions existed within the parties as well as between them; deputies who voted on the left on one issue may or may not have been on the left on others, even within a single party. As long as a given issue (e.g., European union) continued to provoke the same divisions within a party, and these persisted independently of the cabinet coalition, these divisions are consistent with factional ideologies. A faction within a party could thus take a consistent set of positions on the major issues.

We shall judge these factional positions to have been more "ideological" than corresponding positions taken by United States legislators. Whether they meet the standard of the elaborate written works of ideological theoreticians is beside the point here. It may well be that some French commentators overestimated the ideological character of the Assembly; but our purpose is to compare French parliamentary processes with those of other countries in order to account for the peculiarities of French politics.

Our main reason for studying the internal divisions of the individual parties is that they yield a wealth of detail that might be concealed if we examined all the parties at once. When two or more parties are studied together, the clusters of similar roll calls that dominate the voting are those on which the parties tended to be united and in opposition to one another. As a result, the varieties of division within individual parties, which center more about particular issues, are harder to distinguish and more likely to combine in single clusters of roll calls.[71] Although some analysis of particular issues has succeeded in depicting the positions of a number of French parties at once,[72] we shall study single parties, or at most sets of closely related parties whose votes interpenetrated with one another.

Clusters of Roll Calls and Their Interpretation[73]

We wish to make inferences about general features of the divisions within each party—issues and factions. But these inferences have to be made from the votes of individual deputies on particular roll calls, recorded in the *Journal Officiel.* If we examine any particular roll call, such as the vote on the investiture of André Marie in 1948, we can imagine many reasons why deputies may have voted *pour* or *contre,* or abstained. The pages of debate and commentary devoted to any major vote in the Assembly often suggest dozens of factors that might have influenced the deputies' decisions. Some may be more prominent than others, but any or all might conceivably have played a part. In this perspective, each roll call is a unique event resisting our efforts at generalization.

But in spite of the apparent uniqueness of each roll call or each bill, there are elements in roll calls that lead a legislative body or a party to divide over and over again in similar ways. The same slogans and arguments and the same networks of factional relations come into play repeatedly—not only in the various stages of the fight for or against a particular bill, but also on different bills and on questions that to a casual observer might appear distinct. On these different occasions, even though there may seem to be different balances of force and different terrains of combat, closer observation will often reveal common elements. These common elements are the issues and factions whose existence and nature we wish to infer.

We must therefore examine the relations of votes on one roll call to those on others. By grouping together those roll calls on which a party was divided in similar ways, we can better judge whether a division was related to a substantive issue or a cabinet coalition. Then, instead of inferring the issues or factions involved in a single roll call, we can make inferences about the general issues or factional differences involved in a group or cluster of roll calls.

How shall we judge that the votes of a party are divided similarly on two roll calls? The simplest case occurs when their votes are divided identically on the two. If one-third of the party's deputies voted on the left and two-thirds on the right on one roll call, and the same one-third and two-thirds took opposite sides on a second roll call, we should call the divisions on the two roll calls not merely similar but identical. This is the most obvious type of similarity.

Another type of similarity is illustrated in Table 4.1, which shows the relation between the Moderates' votes on the investiture of Marie and on the budget under Queuille in 1948. We consider the 55 deputies who served only in the RI or PRL during the First Legislature. Thirteen of these were on leave or failed to cast meaningful votes on one or both roll calls; those in the Queuille cabinet were also among those excluded from the table. The remaining 42 are included. On each of these roll calls a *pour* vote was one favoring the cabinet and tended to be cast by deputies on the left wing of the Moderates, i.e., those toward the political center of the Assembly. On the Marie investiture, an abstention amounted to a polite form of opposi-

Table 4.1 *Relation Between Divisions on Two Roll Calls:*
Moderates (RI and PRL), First Legislature

Queuille budget (no. 1300)	Marie Investiture (no. 950)	
	-(*pour*)	+(*abst.*)
-(pour, abst.)	15	0
+(contre)	12	15

Source: Each roll call is identified by its official *scrutin* number, under which it is listed in the *Journal Officiel, Débats Parlementaires*.

tion, taken by the right wing of the Moderates; on Queuille's budget a *contre* vote was the rightist position.

We consider these two roll calls to be perfectly similar, not because they divided the Moderates identically, but because the divisions on both could have resulted from the Moderates' being arranged in a single rank order. Such a rank order—which might correspond to a single underlying issue or a single consistent factional grouping—can be seen if we study the table more closely.

Every Moderate deputy in the table who opposed Marie (right-hand column) also opposed Queuille's budget (bottom row). Conversely, every deputy in the table who supported Queuille's budget (top row) had also supported Marie earlier (left-hand column). The two roll calls divided the Moderates into three groups: a left wing (upper left cell) who supported both premiers, a right wing (lower right) who opposed both, and an intermediate group (lower left) who supported Marie but not Queuille. The three groups can be considered as left, right, and center in one common ordering. It is in this sense that we consider the two roll calls to be perfectly similar. This similarity results from the fact that there are no deputies in the upper right cell.

We shall measure "similarity" by an index that attains its maximum value, 1.0, for two perfectly similar roll calls, and has the value zero for two unrelated roll calls (a condition to be defined precisely below). The index we shall use will be based on the numbers in the four cells of the table relating the two roll calls. In Table 4.1, these numbers are 15, 0, 12, and 15; in general, reading the table like the page of a book, we designate them as *a*, *b*, *c*, and *d*. The index of similarity we shall use, Yule's Q-coefficient,[74] is defined by the formula

$$Q = \frac{ad - bc}{ad + bc}$$

For the numbers in Table 4.1, this becomes $(225 - 0)/(225 + 0) = +1.0$. More generally, whenever either *b* or *c* is zero, Q will be equal to ad/ad or 1.0. Thus not only in the case of two identical roll calls (for which b = c = 0), but also in the case exemplified by Table 4.1, Q will indicate perfect similarity between two roll calls by assuming the value 1.0.

This index has another property common to all indices of association for fourfold tables such as Table 4.1: when the dichotomies corresponding to the two roll calls have no association with one another (are independent of one another), it equals zero. This condition obtains when the ratios of the numbers in the two columns of the table are the same (a/c = b/d) or those in the two rows are the same (a/b = c/d). These conditions are in fact identical, and are equivalent to the equation ad − bc = 0. In order for the index to equal zero when ad − bc = 0, it has (ad–bc) as its numerator.

If, in Table 4.1, a few deputies had supported Queuille but not Marie, then the term *bc* in the expression for Q would not have been zero, and Q would have been less than unity. We shall tolerate some dissimilarity of this kind between a pair of roll calls and still accept the relation as "similar"; experience shows that it is reasonable to require a minimum value of Q = + 0.8, which will be our criterion.

A useful property of Q is that its value does not depend on the way the table is arranged. If the two roll calls are interchanged, Q does not change; and if the positive and negative categories of each are exchanged, Q is again unaltered. Only if the positive and negative categories are interchanged for one roll call, and not for the other, does Q change, and then only its sign changes.

We wish to infer what general types of divisions are exemplified by particular roll calls. To do this we compute all possible values of Q for pairs of roll calls in a given Legislature on which the party under study is divided.[75] For each major party or party grouping, in each of the three Legislatures of the Fourth Republic, such a "Q-Matrix" was computed. Our inferences about the bases of cabinet coalitions will be drawn from these matrices and from the clusters of roll calls found in them. The votes of the cabinet are omitted; they normally voted together, and we do not wish this custom to prejudice our results in favor of cabinet specificity of scales.

The discovery of clusters of roll calls that go together in this way gives useful information about the multiple lines of division in a legislative party. Issues that are sometimes thought to be similar may in fact divide a legislative body in distinct ways and may thus have to be distinguished more clearly. Conversely, issues that ordinarily seem distinct may turn out to divide the legislature in much the same way and can therefore be treated together. In this latter case, we need not conclude that the issues are substantively identical; it is the task of further analysis to distinguish issues from cabinets, for example, as bases for these clusters.

A portion of the Q-matrix for the Moderates in the First Legislature is shown in Table 4.2. This matrix shows the relations between all possible

Table 4.2 Q–Matrix (Selected Roll Calls) for Moderates in First Legislature (1946—51)*

Scrutin No. in Journal Officiel

	101	950	1080	1224	1300	1870	1942	2153	2617	2928	3202	3205	3406	3407	3425	3454	3455	3486	3847
101	2 x	8	9				9	8	8		10		8				8	8	9
950		1 x	9	9	10	8	8	9	9	10			10				8		
1080			2 x	8	8		9		8		8						8	9	8
1224				x	10	9		9	9	10	8	8	8	8	8		8		
1300					1 x	10	10	10	10	10	8		9				8		9
1870						x		8	10	10	8		9			8	9	9	9
1942							2 x				9		8				9		8
2153								x	9	10	9	8	10			8	8	8	
2617									1 x	10	9	8	8	8		8	8		9
2928										x	10	9	9			8	9		9
3202											3 x		10		10	10	10		
3205												2 x	8				8	8	9
3406													3 x		9	9			
3407														1 x			8	9	8
3425															x	9			
3454																3 x			
3455																	2 x	9	9
3486																		1 x	10
3847																			2 x

*Table entries are 10Q, unrounded, for instances in which Q is at least 0.8 in magnitude. These 19 roll calls were selected from the actual matrix of 77, to represent scale clusters 1, 2, and 3. The rectangular boxes indicate clusters of roll calls scalable at $Q_{min} = .8$. The number of the scale cluster is indicated to the left of the diagonal "x" corresponding to each roll call. Details about the roll calls in each cluster are given in Table 4.3.

pairs of nineteen selected roll calls.[76] For simplicity, only values of Q of at least 0.8 in magnitude are shown, and these are multiplied by 10 (un-rounded). For example, the association between roll calls 950 and 1300, based on the data shown in Table 4.1, appears in Table 4.2 as "10." The diagonal elements in the table, corresponding to each roll call's relation to itself, are indicated by the symbol "x".

Several characteristic features of Q-matrices may be seen in this example. One is that all the values of Q shown are positive. This means that the "positive" polarities on various roll calls may be chosen so that they fit to-gether in a largely consistent fashion.[77] We actually choose these polarities by examining the political circumstances of each roll call and the parties' positions on it. The votes on each roll call must be classified not as *pour* or *contre,* but as positive or negative in terms of the issue or basis of division involved. A *pour* vote on a crippling amendment or precondition usually places a legislator on the same side as a *contre* vote he might cast on passage of the bill. Thus we examine the substance and circumstances of the bill, motion, or amendment, and classify conservative votes as "+", leftist votes as "−". Errors of judgment in our classification of the sides on in-dividual roll calls may be rectified by inspecting the signs in the Q-matrix. As we shall see, some issues have no clear "left" or "right" positions; on such an issue, we need only choose the "+" polarity consistently over all the votes related to it, and then examine its relation to other issues by means of an index of association.

A second such feature is the distribution of values of Q. In the full matrix from which table 4.2 was selected, the relatively high proportion of Q's of at least .8 persists. In matrices for the more disciplined parties—MRP and SFIO—the proportion of high Q's is much lower.

For our purposes, the most important inference from a Q-matrix con-cerns the groupings of roll calls that are related to one another by high values of Q. To identify such groupings, we consider any value of Q of at least 0.8 to be "high." We look for the cluster containing the largest number of roll calls in the matrix, such that each roll call in the cluster has an as-sociation of at least .8 with each other. In Table 4.2 nine roll calls in cluster #1 may be identified by the number "1" to the left of the corresponding diagonal "x's". The roll calls in the first cluster are then eliminated from consideration, and the largest cluster among the remaining roll calls can be found. The result is an economical description of the various types of divi-sion within the party being studied. By placing deputies on the various issues, one can also obtain measures of the relations between them.[78] Since the procedures we shall use for this latter purpose are those of cumulative scaling, we shall refer to the groups of roll calls found as either clusters or scales.

The Right

We shall now apply this method to the delineation of the internal divi-sions in the major parties and groups of parties in the First Legislature. These groupings are the right, the Radicals and UDSR, the MRP, and the

Socialists. The Communists, essentially undivided on roll calls, will not be considered here; neither will small groups such as the Overseas Independents and the extreme left *Progressistes,* about whose internal divisions we cannot make reliable inferences.

We consider first that loose collection of parties, most thoroughly divided by roll-call votes, known as the "right." Included in this category are the Moderates, the Gaullists, and several small antiparliamentary groups which we shall not analyze. Probably the most familiar definition of the "right" has to do with class conflicts in domestic politics, the "right" being the expression of large business, its power, and its desire not to be constrained by government. But at least two social groups did not fit this definition perfectly: the nobility and the peasants. Though the deputies or parties that represented their views were considered "rightist," they did not always agree with big business on domestic policy.

It is also possible to define the "right" as being both anti-Communist and opposed to the parliamentary regime itself. In this respect the Gaullists were considered "rightist," and we shall classify them in this way as we consider the internal division of the parties in the Second Legislature. Yet on domestic issues the Gaullist deputies were by no means in full support of the positions of large business, and in foreign policy they sometimes found themselves allies of the Communists. Therefore we must simply point out that the category "right" is an approximation, and that the groups called "rightist" will be seen to differ from one another in their positions in the Assembly.

In the First Legislature, the principal groups in this category were the Moderate groups: the *Républicains Indépendants* (RI: 25–29 deputies) and the *Parti Républicain de la Liberté* (PRL; 27–38). We omit from analysis the Peasant party (7–23), except insofar as some of its members were also temporarily members of the other rightist groups considered.

During this period the RI and PRL could be scaled together easily. They were frequently divided on the same roll calls, and unlike the MRP or Radicals they never contained an extreme left wing that joined their right wing in opposing the government. Their members appeared to display an individualism that allowed the two parties to interpenetrate ideologically with relatively little evidence of party discipline.[79] Yet the scales that combine them also reveal general differences between the two parties in their positions on issues and their relation to the growth of the Gaullist movement.

From a Q-matrix containing seventy-seven roll calls, one dominant cluster of 33 items and three other clusters of 12, 5, and 4 items were found. The subjects of these votes and the premiers under whom they occurred are shown in Table 4.3. Scale I-1 (the cluster of 33 items) includes votes dealing with domestic, German, and colonial policy, as well as three investiture votes. In the designation "I-1," the Roman numeral indicates the Legislature, and the Arabic the order in which the cluster was found, from largest to smallest. The same numbering system is used for all parties.

We infer that Scale I-1 is a general left-right scale, not specialized to particular issues or premiers. One major political question underlying this scale is the choice between the cabinets of that time, and Gaullism; those who subsequently ran as Gaullists generally opposed the cabinet and appeared on the right in their scale positions.[80] The cabinets under which most of these roll calls occurred were headed by Radical or UDSR premiers; these were definitely left of the parties being scaled (RI and PRL) on domestic economic policies as well as the church-school question. Therefore the left wing of the RI or PRL was always the segment that gave most support to the cabinet. The right wing, on the other hand, not only opposed the cabinet, but also showed a greater sympathy for Gaullism. We shall see that this connection of votes under various premiers in a single scale was not so characteristic of the parties of the right in later Legislatures. Possibly this lack of cabinet specificity of scales in the First Legislature relates to the fact that there were relatively few rightist ministers in the cabinets of the period. Factions within the parties of the right may not have engaged so seriously in the contest for cabinet positions until later.

In the "polarity" columns of Table 4.3 we show the specific votes on each roll call classified as "positive" (rightist) and "negative" (leftist); the column "p_+" gives the proportion of these votes that were positive. These values give an approximate indication of the extent of the rightists' opposition to the cabinet on the roll call in question.

The rightists in the First Legislature were also divided by a second cluster of roll calls (Scale I-2); seven of the twelve roll calls in it dealt with the electoral law of 1951, which permitted electoral alliances (*apparentements*) between parties, benefiting coalitions of the center. The relation between Scales I-1 and I-2 may be shown by comparing the orderings of legislators that the two scales provide. To measure this relation we shall use the coefficient of association γ, proposed by Goodman and Kruskal.[81] This coefficient assumes its maximum value of $+1$ for two scale orderings that can be perfectly combined into a single ordering, and is equal to -1 for two scales that may be so joined after one is reversed. The coefficient Q for fourfold tables is a special case of γ. Values of γ are given in Table 4.3.

For Scales I-1 and I-2, the association between these orderings is $\gamma_{12} = +.67$; this is a fairly high association, and indicates that with some regularity the deputies farthest to the right on Scale I-1 tended also to be those who opposed the new electoral law. This association is consistent with the Gaullists' opposition to that law, which disadvantaged them.

Although Scales I-1 and I-2 ordered the deputies similarly, we can look for contrasts between the subject matter of the roll calls in them. Those roll calls in one scale whose associations with the other were lowest may be singled out for this purpose; in Scale I-2, these are nos. 101, 1942, and 3455. What distinguishes them from those in Scale I-1 is that they are somewhat more concerned with persistent issues and less with the particular problem of Gaullism. Roll call no. 101 took place barely after the founding of the RPF and dealt with the departure of the Communist ministers from Ramadier's cabinet; no. 1942 dealt with a substantive question (Germany) more than with the fate of the Bidault cabinet (in contrast to no. 2613, in Scale I-1); and no. 3455 was the first of a series of votes on the electoral law. This interpretation will be supported later by the fact that Scale I-2 showed greatest consistency with scales for the Moderates in the Second and Third Legislatures, in ordering the deputies.

Table 4.3 The Right (RI & PRL) in First Legislature:
Roll Calls in Scales

Roll Call	Premier	Polarity[1] +	−	p_+[2]	Subject	Association (γ) with Other Scales I-1	I-2	I-3	I-4
Scale I-1 (General Left-Right)							.67	.59	.87
950	Marie	a	p	35	Investiture				
951	Marie	an	p	37	Cabinet, postpone interpellation				
1012	Marie	a	p	39	Economic and financial recovery, entirety				
1039	Marie	an	p	40	Economic and financial recovery, entirety				
1145	Queuille₁	can	p	42	Investiture				
1172	Queuille₁	c	pan	54	Tax bill				
1199	Queuille₁	c	pa	60	Tax increase, after Council of Republic				
1210	Queuille₁	an	p	46	*Investigation of PCF and *Populaire*				
1222	Queuille₁	p	can	51	Ruhr, Capitant resolution				
1224	Queuille₁	n	p	36	Ruhr resolution, passage				
1251	Queuille₁	pn	c	44	Financial bill, budget procedure; RPF q. pr.				
1253	Queuille₁	c	pan	42	Financial bill, adoption				
1280	Queuille₁	c	pa	57	**Budget				
1282	Queuille₁	c	pan	60	**Budget				
1300	Queuille₁	c	pa	63	Budget, entirety				
1324	Queuille₁	c	pan	52	Budget after Council of Republic				
1371	Queuille₁	an	p	47	Delcos resolution for Marie				
1383	Queuille₁	pn	c	56	Legendre resolution against Marie				
1452	Queuille₁	p	cn	48	Terrenoire, prosecution of PCF				
1509	Queuille₁	pa	c	42	Censure, Capitant motion				
1654	Queuille₁	c	pan	40	Interpellation on RPF "plot," majority resolution				
		can	p	63					
1870	Queuille₁	p	cn	51	Atlantic Pact, Michelet amend.				
2153	Bidault	n	p	42	Mast-Revers affair, resolution				
2613	Bidault	c	pan	55	*Reclassification of civil servants (fall of cab.)				
2617	Queuille₂	can	p	34	Investiture				
2618	Queuille₂	ca	p	35	Cabinet interpellation (fall of cab.)				
2619	Pleven	an	p	36	Investiture				
2819	Pleven	p	can	56	Indochina, RPF-PRL resolution				
2822	Pleven	can	p	47	Indochina, majority resolution				
2928	Pleven	can	p	55	Indochina, majority resolution				
3407	Pleven	p	can	69	Electoral law: list, majority, alliance (André)				
3419	Pleven	can	p	53	*Electoral law, cabinet text				
3486	Queuille₃	c	pn	72	Electoral law, deptl. alliances (Bonnefous)				

Table 4.3 (continued)

Roll Call	Premier	Polarity +	-	p₊	Subject	I-1	I-2	I-3	I-4
						Association (γ) with Other Scales			

p_+ column label; Association (γ) with Other Scales spans I-1 I-2 I-3 I-4.

Roll Call	Premier	Polarity +	−	p_+	Subject	I-1	I-2	I-3	I-4
Scale I-2 (Electoral Law)						.67		.40	.78
101	Ramadier	an	p	69	*Communist ministers, resolution				
1080	Marie	an	p	53	Indochina, postpone interpellation				
1920	Mayer	a	p	64	Investiture				
1942	Bidault	c	pan	58	Germany, Scherer resolution				
3205	Pleven	c	pa	34	Military budget				
3455	Queuille₃	c	pan	63	Electoral law, alliances				
3481	Queuille₃	p	cn	65	Electoral law, national alliances (Barrachin)				
3847	Queuille₃	c	pn	51	Electoral law, initial text				
3856	Queuille₃	c	pn	55	Electoral law, entirety				
3883	Queuille₃	cn	p	39	Electoral law, elim. 5% reqt. for allied lists (Simonnet)				
3924	Queuille₃	c	pan	54	Electoral law, entirety				
4008	Queuille₃	c	pan	54	Electoral law				
Scale I-3 (Electoral Alliances)						.59	.40		.70
3202	Pleven	c	pa	23	*Military budget				
3254	Pleven	c	pa	30	Rearmament budget				
3406	Pleven	c	pn	69	Electoral law: list, alliance, single ballot (Delachenal)				
3425	Pleven	c	pn	60	Electoral law, single ballot (Delachenal)				
3454	Queuille₃	can	p	61	Electoral law, single ballot (Delachenal)				
Scale I-4 (Pleven)						.87	.78	.70	
2620	Pleven	ca	p	75	Cabinet interpellations				
2834	Pleven	c	pan	29	Pleven plan for EDC, cabinet resolution				
3255	Pleven	c	p	44	*Rearmament budget, art. 7				
3256	Pleven	a	p	76	*Rearmament budget, entirety				

*Question of confidence (as in similar tables hereafter).
**Unofficial question of confidence (as in similar tables hereafter).

[1]"Polarity" refers, in this and similar tables, to the division of possible politically meaningful votes in the Assembly into + (right) and − (left) categories. Votes are abbreviated in the following way:
p = "pour"
c = "contre"
a = "s'est abstenu volontairement" (abstention)
n = "n'a pas pris part au vote" (did not take part in the vote)
[2]The proportion of + votes on each roll call, for the party or parties studied, is designated as p₊, this information will be used later for the placement of deputies on scales.

Scale I-3 dealt with another aspect of the electoral law, while I-4, concentrated in the Pleven ministry, ranked the Moderates very similarly to I-1 and I-2.

The Radicals and UDSR

A second loosely organized set of parties, occupying positions ranging across the center of the political spectrum, are those we shall refer to as the "Radicals." Chief among these parties is the *Parti Républicain Radical et Radical-Socialiste,* the "official" Radical party, with headquarters on the Place

Table 4.4 Radicals and UDSR, First Legislature:
Roll Calls in Scales

Roll Call	Premier	Polarity +	Polarity −	p_+	Subject	Association (γ) with Other Scales I-1	I-2	I-3	I-4
Scale I-1 (Schuman–Bidault)							.79	.81	.41
458	Schuman₁	can	p	27	Anti-inflation law, entirety				
527	Schuman₁	can	p	32	*Anti-inflation law, amend.				
528	Schuman₁	ca	p	32	*Anti-inflation law, amend.				
529	Schuman₁	ca	p	32	*Anti-inflation law, amend.				
531	Schuman₁	can	p	32	*Anti-inflation law, amend.				
535	Schuman₁	ca	p	31	*Anti-inflation law, amend.				
537	Schuman₁	ca	p	30	*Anti-inflation law, passage				
555	Schuman₁	cn	p	29	5000-franc bills				
558	Schuman₁	cn	p	23	Regulation of exchange rates				
626	Schuman₁	c	pa	15	*5000-franc bills				
649	Schuman₁	pan	c	30	**Mayer levy, abrogate				
839	Schuman₁	c	pn	40	**London agreements (creation of West German state), Scherer et al. res., priority				
840	Schuman₁	c	pn	40	**London agreements, Scherer resoln., text				
2031	Bidault	can	p	53	*Budget, consideration				
2046	Bidault	cn	p	57	Civil and military credits				
2094	Bidault	ca	p	58	*Corporation tax				
2111	Bidault	c	pan	57	*Tax on road transport., Prigent amend.				
2113	Bidault	can	p	60	*Finances, entire bill				
2193	Bidault	c	pa	50	*Undistributed profits tax				
2195	Bidault	c	pa	47	*Finances, Simonnet amendment				
2197	Bidault	c	pn	54	Civil expenditures, Abelin amend.				
2856	Pleven	c	pan	23	Pétain release, reject Terrenoire motion				
3481	Queuille₃	pn	c	20	Electoral law, Barrachin amend.—natl. alliances				
3486	Queuille₃	cn	p	16	Electoral law, Bonnefous amend.—departmental alliances				

Table 4.4 (continued)

Roll Call	Premier	Polarity +	-	p_+	Subject	Association (γ) with Other Scales			
						I-1	I-2	I-3	I-4
Scale I-2 (Marie-Queuille)						.79		.69	−.05
326	Schuman$_1$	ca	p	17	*Composition of cabinet				
651	Schuman$_1$	pa	c	32	Mayer levy, Viollette amend.				
950	Marie	an	p	11	Investiture				
951	Marie	an	p	23	Cabinet interpellation, postpone				
986	Marie	pn	c	27	Economic and financial recovery, Triboulet amendment				
1012	Marie	can	p	17	Economic and financial recovery, entirety				
1039	Marie	ca	p	14	Economic and financial recovery, entirety				
1143	Schuman$_2$	an	p	36	Investiture				
1144	Schuman$_2$	c	pn	45	Composition of cabinet				
1145	Queuille$_1$	can	p	11	Investiture				
1199	Queuille$_1$	c	pan	38	Tax increase, after Council of Republic				
1222	Queuille$_1$	p	ca	11	Ruhr, Capitant resolution				
1300	Queuille$_1$	cn	p	20	Budget, entirety				
1308	Queuille$_1$	p	can	15	Budget, postpone application of tax reform				
1870	Queuille$_1$	pn	c	18	Atlantic Pact, Michelet amend.				
Scale I-3 (Bidault-Economic)						.81	.69		.36
1285	Queuille$_1$	pn	c	22	Budget, Crouzier amend., war damages				
1324	Queuille$_1$	can	p	20	Budget after Council of the Republic				
2093	Bidault	c	pan	41	*Production tax				
2112	Bidault	c	pa	47	*Finances, balance budget				
2192	Bidault	c	pa	50	*Production tax increase				
2194	Bidault	ca	p	65	*Tax on petroleum products				
2196	Bidault	cn	p	63	Civil expenditures, Abelin amendment, priority				
2198	Bidault	ca	p	63	*Budget, entirety				
Scale I-4 (Electoral Law)						.41	−.05	.36	
3847	Queuille$_3$	c	pan	65	Electoral law, initial text				
3856	Queuille$_3$	cn	p	51	**Electoral law, entirety, 2nd reading				
3873	Queuille$_3$	pn	c	55	Electoral law, Ginestet amendment, no alliances				
3874	Queuille$_3$	cn	p	57	Electoral law, majority vote, single ballot				
3924	Queuille$_3$	can	p	45	*Electoral law, entirety				
4008	Queuille$_3$	cn	p	43	Electoral law				

de Valois in Paris. Closely associated with it on many issues was the *Union Démocratique et Socialiste de la Résistance* (UDSR), a small group of political leaders originating in the resistance and preserving its identity separately. These two parties were joined in a loose electoral alliance known as the *Rassemblement des Gauches Républicaines* (RGR), which in 1955 became the vehicle for Edgar Faure after his expulsion from the Valois Radical party. The Radicals and UDSR were scaled together. The clusters of roll calls that emerged from analysis of the Q-matrix for the First Legislature are shown in Table 4.4. There is one dominant cluster of 24 items (Scale I-1) and the next largest cluster contains only 15. In comparison with the Moderates' scale structure, the first cluster is less dominant, and the electoral-law scale more independent of the others. Nevertheless, with the exception of the electoral-law scale (I-4), the other three scales order the Radicals and UDSR in much the same way; Scales I-1 and I-2 are very highly associated ($\gamma = .79$), and Scale I-3 is closely associated with both.

Titles are assigned to the scales in Table 4.4 on the basis of the cabinets and subject matter involved in the roll calls. It will be seen that Scales I-1 and I-2 include largely domestic issues, with the addition of a few related to Germany and the Atlantic Pact. Scale I-1, consisting largely of votes under MRP premiers, contains a considerable number of questions of confidence, while Scale I-2, with more votes under Radical premiers, contains four votes on investitures or on the cabinet. Scale I-3 resembles Scale I-1 more than I-2, in subject matter and MRP premiership as well as in its ranking of deputies. Scale I-4, on the electoral law, is the only one that is distinct in subject matter, as it is in its associations ($.41$, $-.05$, $.36$).

The relative independence of the Radicals' electoral-law scale, in comparison with that of the Moderates, may have been due to their different electoral situations. By 1951 the Radicals had recovered most of their straying Gaullists, and their electoral problems may have been more diverse and local rather than related to a contest with a single party throughout the country.

Compared with subsequent Legislatures, these divisions of the Radicals were relatively unitary and unrelated to particular cabinets. In comparison with the Moderates in the First Legislature, however, the Radicals and UDSR were divided in a somewhat more complex fashion, perhaps related to the Radicals' greater involvement in cabinet coalitions. Another possible source of this more complex division of the Radicals and UDSR was the presence among them of North African deputies, who voted differently from the rest, and the going and coming of certain deputies from Gaullism.[82]

The Mouvement Républicain Populaire

The Conservatives and Radicals contributed to the problems of cabinet formation through their fragmentation; individually outstanding deputies in these parties could enter or leave cabinet coalitions, taking parts of their parties with them. But in the more organized parties, individual deputies never enjoyed this tactical independence. The party organization controlled the entry of members into the cabinet; and when some entered against its wishes, as did three MRP deputies under Mendès-France, they were threatened with expulsion.[83]

Dissidence had some significance, nevertheless, in the MRP and the Socialist party, and perhaps even occasionally among the Communists. These cohesive parties may have contained more dissidence than their votes showed. Party congresses normally revealed more controversy than did the votes of parliamentary groups. But because the parliamentary position of a united party requires high cohesion for bargaining purposes, the party leadership sometimes adjusted its policies to reduce dissidence or to retain control.

At the same time, once a party policy was established, it was enforced by *discipline de vote*. Members were expelled from these parties, temporarily and sometimes permanently, for dissidence on key votes. Others resigned. Individual expulsion and resignation were less frequent on the right and among the Radicals; entire subgroups left these parties at times—the Peasants or the dissident Radicals—but party discipline was scarcely ever brought to bear on individual deputies. The loose structure of the parties of the right, and of the Radicals, permitted internal differences to develop to the point of group fission, while this point was never reached among MRP or Socialists.[84] Two small fissions did occur in the more disciplined parties over the Algerian crisis and Gaullism in 1958; Georges Bidault constituted his own splinter party from the MRP, and a minority of the Socialists formed the Autonomous Socialist Party (PSA; later PSU). But neither of these was a significant split *in parliament*. The ultimate sanction, actual or potential, of disciplined parties against parliamentary dissidence was denial of nomination.

The MRP parliamentary group at the start of the First Legislature was the largest non-Communist group in the Assembly during the Fourth Republic. Cohesion in the group was generally high.[85] Like several of the other parties, it lost members to the Gaullists during the First Legislature: three were expelled in November 1947 (Furaud, Michelet, and J.-P. Palewski), and several resigned (Lespès, Liquard, Livry-Level, and Terrenoire) after a split on a vote of October 30.[86] Others moved to the Overseas Independents, the Moderates, and the *non inscrits*. In our analysis we shall be chiefly concerned with those who remained in the MRP throughout the First Legislature.

Cluster analysis was particularly difficult for the MRP; for although the party was often divided, it was rarely deeply divided, and the same deputies did not usually join in the same combinations on successive roll calls. Inspection of their voting patterns suggests that control was brought to bear on dissidents after any deviation from the party's position, and that each dissident who wished to remain in the party may have had an approximate "quota" of deviant votes. This state of affairs was reflected in the Q-matrix by a scarcity of high Q's.[87] For this reason we shall analyze clusters of three roll calls for the MRP here, even though a minimum of four will be required elsewhere in our study.

Three distinct clusters of roll calls were found for the MRP deputies who remained in the party throughout the First Legislature. The roll calls entering into each cluster are listed in Table 4.5. The only divisions revealed by these votes were ones that split off small factions on the wings of the party—both left and right on Scale I-1, left on Cluster I-2, and right on Cluster I-3. Yet because of the size of the party, these small wings contain from twenty to forty deputies each, and reasonable inferences about the bases of their division can be made.

Table 4.5 MRP, First Legislature:
Roll Calls in Scales

Roll Call	Premier	Polarity +	Polarity −	p_+	Subject	Association (γ) with Other Scales I-1	I-2	I-3
Scale I-1 (Reynaud Law, Electoral Law)							.11	.16
986	Marie	c	pa	89	Reynaud law, Triboulet amendment			
1012	Marie	p	ca	85	Reynaud law, entirety			
1039	Marie	p	ca	90	Reynaud law, entirety			
3846	Queuille$_3$	p	c	10	Electoral law, amendment: single name, runoff			
Cluster I-2 (End of Session)						.11		.03
3837	Queuille$_3$	p	ca	77	*May 8 as national holiday, adjourn debate			
3839	Queuille$_3$	p	ca	83	*Salary zones, adjourn debate			
3840	Queuille$_3$	p	ca	88	*Eviction of tenants, adjourn debate			
Cluster I-3 (Cantonal Elections)						.16	.03	
1097	Marie	pan	c	24	Cantonal elections, Barrachin–Marin q. pr.			
1099	Marie	pan	c	21	Cantonal elections, Raulin bill			
1112	Marie	can	p	27	Cantonal elections, Fonlupt–Espéraber bill, entirety			

A certain specificity of the scales to particular periods of time can be seen. Scale I-1 was dominated by three roll calls on the "Reynaud law"; Paul Reynaud, Minister of Finance under Marie, asked special powers for government and economic reorganization. Those who opposed this bill were perhaps concerned more with the powers of the cabinet than with substantive interests.[88] Cluster I-2, which marked off another leftist segment of the party, centered about a series of motions to consider problems of substantive legislation, postponing the 1951 elections to do so. Those who opposed adjourning the debates on these problems were making common cause with the Communists to press the claims of deprived groups; the Queuille cabinet wished to set aside these claims and hold the 1951 elections on time.

On Cluster I-3, the right is marked off from the main body of the party by three votes on the 1948 cantonal elections. A bill sponsored by the MRP deputy Fonlupt-Espéraber was suspected by its opponents of aiming at postponing these elections for fear of RPF encroachments on the MRP vote.

We cannot, however, argue from this specificity of scales to cabinets that the MRP deputies were primarily concerned with the fate of cabinets. The membership of the right and left wings of the party, defined by these scales, showed considerable continuity across the three Legislatures. Moreover, the particular groups of roll calls that clustered in periods of time were concentrated on particular subjects far more than were those that we shall observe for other parties during particular cabinets.[89]

The Socialist Party

While more cohesive than the MRP, the Socialist party still contained consistent and significant internal divisions. Two issues in the First Legislature revealed certain of these divisions, and foreshadowed other divisions that were to occur in the Second and Third Legislatures. The first concerned the attempt of the Communist leader Maurice Thorez to be invested as Premier in December 1946. The Socialist leaders as well as the majority of the party supported Thorez; but twenty-five Socialist deputies nevertheless failed to vote for him. Nine of these men remained in the Third Legislature; and of them seven opposed de Gaulle's 1958 investiture while only two supported him.[90] The two types of opposition had a common feature— possibly the defense of the Republic—even though Thorez and de Gaulle would seem to have presented entirely different problems to the Socialists.

Table 4.6 Socialists, First Legislature:
Roll Calls in Scale

Roll Call	Premier	Polarity +	Polarity −	p_+	Subject
Scale I-1 (*Electoral Law*)					
3618	Queuille$_3$	p	can	81	Electoral law
3847	Queuille$_3$	p	can	88	Electoral law, initial text
3849	Queuille$_3$	p	ca	87	Electoral law, article 1
3856*	Queuille$_3$	pa	c	91	Electoral law, second reading

*The polarity and p_+ of this roll call diverge slightly from our general standards; it is included because of the scarcity of high values of Q.

The second major division of the Socialists in the First Legislature centered about the electoral law of 1951. A cluster of four roll calls on this issue was the only cluster satisfying our conditions; the Thorez vote, though important, was a relatively isolated instance of the type of cleavage it exemplified.[91] The four roll calls in the electoral-law cluster (Scale I-1) are shown in Table 4.6. Though they all occurred under the Queuille cabinet, they revolved about questions of principle, including the propriety of reducing the Communists' representation by means of the *apparentements*. The deputies who deviated from the party position on this issue were to be noted in later deviations from the party in 1958 and beyond.[92]

The mode of discipline in the Socialist party was similar to that in the MRP; dissidents were disciplined or expelled (e.g., Pouyet).[93] Some African representatives resigned from the group (Horma Ould Babana, Senghor), as did some metropolitan deputies as well (Rivet). Because of the discipline in the party, failure to "take part in the vote" was often considered a break with the party position and could not be viewed as politically insignificant, as it was for the Moderates.

A major issue among the Socialists during the First Legislature was whether the party should participate in cabinets or not. Guy Mollet first opposed participation, but later he favored it. After this change André Philip, Daniel Mayer, and Édouard Depreux became the leaders of the nonparticipation faction. Dissidence on this point was later stilled when the party went into opposition.[94] But although this issue was a significant one, it was manifested in party congresses rather than on roll calls in the Assembly. The fact that it did not divide the deputies is another bit of evidence that the divisions that did occur were concerned more with principle than with expediency or parliamentary tactics.

Cabinets and Issues in Intraparty Division

During the First Legislature none of the major parties showed internal divisions that were primarily related to the coalitions supporting and opposing particular cabinets. The parties whose scale clusters were most narrowly concentrated in particular ministries—the MRP and the Socialists—were actually the ones whose internal divisions were most principled; we infer this from the fact that the scale clusters were also narrowly concentrated on important issues that arose at particular times.

While the scale clusters of the right and the Radicals failed to show clear cabinet specificity, they were also less specific to particular issues than were those of the MRP and Socialists. The largest cluster for the right (Scale I-1 in Table 4.3) included votes on international, colonial, and domestic policies, and grouped cabinet votes together with votes on issues. Though it was certainly not specific to the coalitions around particular cabinets, it may well have related to a political situation—a set of opposing coalitions—that existed throughout the First Legislature. For this entire period, the Moderates were on the right of the cabinet coalition and had little chance for cabinet posts. And from 1947, they had the alternative of opposing the center coalition through support of the RPF. This alternative —slightly modified in the case of their electoral-law scale (I-2)—may have dominated the internal divisions of the right. Though not perhaps concerned with short-run tactics in cabinet support, varying from one cabinet to the next, it may still have concerned longer-term strategic positions toward alternative political coalitions, more than particular issues.

The Radicals' scale clusters shared this property with those of the right. Scales I-1, I-2, and I-3 (Table 4.4) were closely related to one another and nearly as heterogeneous in content as the main scale for the right. Domestic and international affairs, investitures and legislation, were joined in these scale clusters—a conjunction that did not occur for all parties or for other Legislatures. Consequently, it is not unreasonable to see the Radicals' major orientation during the First Legislature as also concerned with coalition strategy. Problems of coalition formation may have been relatively similar from cabinet to cabinet for the Radicals at that time. Not until the cabinet's supporting majorities moved to the center and right, during the Second and Third Legislatures, did cabinet specificity of scale clusters appear.

Two major political problems dominated the fate of the cabinets of the First Legislature. Within the cabinet coalitions, the conflicting positions of the Moderates and the Socialists prevented any cabinet from having a stable base of support. And on the right flank of the cabinets, the struggle between the cabinet coalition and Gaullism set another limit on what was possible. Defections of Gaullist deputies increased the number of "unavailable" votes and doomed the Third Force. The surge of Gaullist strength among the voters temporarily increased Gaullist support in the Assembly among Moderate and Radical deputies looking forward to the next election. But the delaying tactics of the leaders of the cabinet coalition permitted a decline in Gaullist strength among the voters, which was then reflected in the Assembly. This swing back to the center barely permitted Queuille to obtain passage of the new electoral law, which accentuated the Gaullists' disadvantage.

The skill that Queuille displayed against Gaullism, first in postponing the cantonal elections and later in revising the electoral law, was better suited to solving political problems than substantive ones. By delay, by conferences behind the scenes, and by compromise he succeeded in defending the governing coalition. But he did not propose clear-cut new policies at home or abroad, nor did he attempt to mobilize public opinion. His style of government—successful as it was in some respects—was what has come to be known as *immobilisme*. He and others like him were defending the Assembly against an outside mass movement. But he countered it by changing the laws rather than by challenging that movement to public debate, or by dramatic government action. Even a more activist premier, in his situation, might have been able to do little else, and might indeed have been less successful in doing what Queuille did. But the First Legislature already reveals the unfortunate conflict between advocates of drastic reform and altered substantive policies, outside the Assembly, and defensive, limited action by the governing coalition within it.

There is little evidence in the First Legislature for a parliamentary "game" embodied in shifting coalitions. The divisions within the Radical and Moderate groups were constant in comparison with what they were to become later. The immediate cause of the overthrow of cabinets was most frequently the action of the Socialist party; and although first Ramadier and then Mollet favored the party's participation in the cabinet, it was the party's militants rather than its *ministrables* who urged its withdrawal from office. As for the party fractions that went into opposition before the Socialists, we shall see later that it was also their rank-and-file deputies, rather than their prospective officeholders, who were most likely to vote against the cabinet.

NOTES

1. See Leites, *On the Game of Politics,* Chap. 4.

2. See Fauvet, *The Cockpit of France.*

3. This hypothesis was part of the Gaullist criticism of the Fourth Republic, and was embodied in the institution of *suppléants* in the Fifth.

4. Siegfried, in his summing-up of the Fourth Republic, implied that the disciplined parties precluded any representation of the public interest by individual deputies; see *De la IVᵉ à la Vᵉ République,* pp. 313–314. The notion that party fragmentation normally worked to the disadvantage of government majorities is suggested in Aron, *France: Steadfast and Changing,* pp. 19, 21. See also Siegfried, *De la IVᵉ à la Vᵉ République,* p. 196.

5. Only a minority were overthrown by the constitutionally required absolute majority of the Assembly; but we include in this category all cabinets that resigned when their majorities became so small that the premiers judged it impossible to govern.

6. They defined both the limits of possible majorities (Leites, *On the Game of Politics*) and the urgency with which compromise was required (Williams, *Crisis,* Chap. 29). On the types of trial candidacy see Williams, p. 415.

7. Starting after the fall of Mendès-France in 1955, only a single vote was required, on cabinet and premier together, and a plurality sufficed. From October 1955, this and all confidence votes were conducted by personal ballot; proxies were no longer permitted.

8. In June 1957 the Socialists asked detailed guarantees of Pflimlin, but immediately thereafter neglected to ask them of Bourgès-Maunoury.

9. The *Conférence des Présidents,* including leaders of parliamentary groups and committees and officers of the chamber.

10. These were to choose the members of the *département* councils—analogous to American state legislatures but far less influential. The electoral districts were *cantons.*

11. See Soulier, *L'Instabilité ministérielle sous la Troisième République,* p. 233, and Aron, *France: Steadfast and Changing,* p. 38.

12. See Appendix A on samples of "important" roll calls.

13. In political calculations of this sort the participants often have a higher confidence in their predictive ability than the facts justify. Fauvet's predictions of the sequence of designations in a crisis were usually accurate, but prediction of the outcome of key roll calls seems to have been subject to an error of about ten votes. Examples were the defeat of Pleven (1951), the investiture of Pinay (1952), and the defeat of Faure (1955) by an absolute majority on a personal vote.

14. *Journal Officiel, Débats Parlementaires,* 1955, 2951.

15. The entourages of parliamentary leaders may be identified in several ways: from commentaries on parliamentary life; from the political or electoral sponsorship of a junior deputy by a senior; and by their voting together in blocs, insofar as ideology can be left out of account.

16. The historical accounts that follow rely heavily on the daily *Le Monde* and the commentaries of its political columnists, especially Jacques Fauvet, René Puissesseau, and Raymond Barrillon. A summary of the events of the First Legislature appears in Taylor, *The Fourth Republic of France,* Part IV. A more recent account, drawing extensively on

interviews with leading deputies, is Elgey, *La République des illusions*. An account of all three Legislatures is given in Chapsal, *La Vie politique*, pp. 134–296.

17. *Le Monde*, 7 January 1947. On Blum's popularity see Gordon Wright, *The Reshaping of French Democracy*, p. 248.

18. This controversy is described in Elgey, *La République des illusions*, pp. 289, 291–292. The events leading to the Communists' expulsion are described in Fauvet, *Histoire du parti communiste français*, Vol. II, Part Four, Ch. 1.

19. Roll-call numbers cited in the text refer to the corresponding figures throughout Chapters 4–6. These are the official *scrutin* numbers from *Journal Officiel*. The arrangement of parties and factions in a single linear sequence in this and succeeding figures is less precise than our later arrangement of the members of individual parties separately.

20. The 68 abstentions at his investiture represented opposition, as a fixed majority was required. Prior to no. 158, Ramadier had seen his majority reduced to a margin of 59 votes on no. 142, a budget vote not included in the *L'Année Politique* (*AP*) sample. The Radicals' early opposition shows that at this time they were farther to the right than the MRP; they are so placed in the diagram. This placement was less clear, however, in the Second Legislature and in the voters' view.

21. Here and elsewhere "ministry" (for *ministère*) will be used to refer to the period during which a cabinet held office. The Algerian statute was never put into effect; see Williams, *Crisis*, pp. 349–350. Another Socialist, M.-E. Naegelen, was the Governor-General of Algeria who permitted its nullification. For its provisions, see Pickles, *Algeria and France*, pp. 28–29.

22. See Colliard, "La Pratique de la question de confiance sous la IV⁰ République," 226.

23. Fauvet, *Le Monde*, 23–24 November 1947. This cabinet crisis, and others during the First Legislature, were resolved rapidly because of the Gaullist threat.

24. In this calculation we count each junior cabinet position as equal to one-half a full ministry; a similar ratio was used in calculations by the parties themselves. We shall refer later to all cabinet members as "ministers," for simplicity.

25. Williams, *Politics*, p. 218, and *L'Année Politique*, 1948, p. 326.

26. The term *ordre du jour*, which we translate "resolution," refers to a policy declaration without specific legislative force, terminating a debate and returning the chamber to its agenda (*ordre du jour*). See Lidderdale, *The Parliament of France*, pp. 238–239.

27. Fauvet, *Le Monde*, 21 July 1948.

28. This initiative showed Auriol's view that he could take an active part in forming cabinets; see *Le Monde*, 10 December 1953.

29. Puissesseau, *Le Monde*, 23 July 1948. The persistent hostility of Socialists to Gaullism was to be an important restriction on cabinet coalitions in the Second Legislature.

30. Puissesseau, *Le Monde*, 17 August 1948.

31. *Le Monde*, 28 August 1948.

32. A "mortgage" (*hypothèque*) is a decision which, while unresolved, prevents action on another. On *la levée de l'hypothéque*, see Leites, *On the Game of Politics*, Chap. 3, and Melnik and Leites, *The House Without Windows*, p. 345.

33. See A. Chênebenoit, *Le Monde*, 29–30 August 1948.

34. Later experience was to show that the Assembly would never re-invest a former premier recalled when only a single ministry had intervened after his fall. Only Queuille, Pleven, and Faure were invested twice with cabinets; and in addition to a single ministry, either an election or one or more other ministries intervened.

35. *Le Monde,* 9 September 1948.

36. Fauvet wrote, *"Le ciment de cet assemblage c'est le refus d'un certain gaullisme."* *Le Monde,* 14 September 1948. Threats of opposition may be a general cause of cohesion in government coalitions; this hypothesis is suggested in La Palombara, "Political Party Systems and Crisis Government: French and Italian Contrasts," 133–134.

37. A dramatic account of the 1948 strikes, as well as those of 1947, is given by Matthews in *The Death of the Fourth Republic,* Chap. 12. The effect of these events on the cabinet's support, however, seemed slight.

38. The 182 "noes" came from the Communists and Progressives, while the Gaullists of various parties showed their disapproval by not voting; see Fig. 4.4.

39. Petsche had earlier resigned from the Peasant party in order to continue as Minister of Finance.

40. See Williams, *Crisis,* p. 214n., for the lengths to which the leaders had to go to assemble this majority.

41. Fauvet was already suggesting dissolution of the Assembly as a remedy for this conflict; *Le Monde,* 18 October 1949.

42. Fauvet, *Le Monde,* 25–27 December 1949.

43. Fauvet, *Le Monde,* 6 January 1950.

44. Fauvet, *Le Monde,* 5–6 February 1950.

45. See Werth, *France 1940–1955,* pp. 459ff.

46. Another such overthrow in eighteen months would permit dissolution of the Assembly; this may have made subsequent premiers more cautious.

47. Fauvet, *Le Monde,* 24 January 1950. Some Socialists were also personally hostile to Bidault.

48. Fauvet, *Le Monde,* 27 June 1950.

49. Fauvet, *Le Monde,* 2–3 July 1950.

50. Fauvet, *Le Monde,* 6 and 7 July, 1950. Moch, for example, was for participation, Mollet opposed. It was for this reason that Mollet rather than Moch was chosen to survey the possibilities for the next cabinet.

51. Mollet, who had brought about this combination, now took a place in the cabinet for the first time. He had obtained better terms for Socialist participation as a result of his *mission d'information.*

52. This plan, later known as the European Defense Community, encountered increasing difficulty in the Second Legislature.

53. On this vote the five deputies of the *Rassemblement Démocratique Africain* broke away from the Communists and supported the cabinet, showing a freedom from ideology that was rarely matched by ex-Communists of the *métropole.*

54. Fauvet, *Le Monde,* 2 March 1951.

55. Fauvet, *Le Monde,* 8 March 1951.

56. This was later reflected by cabinet divisions on a number of roll-call votes, indicating a greater neutrality than usual for the cabinet.

57. As the members of the Council of the Republic were called.

58. Neumann contends that Herriot's ruling was based on "highly questionable constitutional and parliamentary grounds"; see his "The Struggle for Electoral Reform in

France," 749. The question of confidence was put to avoid another personal vote, which would otherwise have been required; see Fauvet, *Le Monde*, 2 May 1951.

59. See also Macridis, "Cabinet Instability in the Fourth Republic (1946–1951)."

60. Aron, writing of the Third Legislature, asserts that a cabinet must count on 10 to 15 per cent dissidence in its supporting parties; *France: Steadfast and Changing*, p. 19. This may be a useful rule of thumb, but it seems more realistic to attribute dissidence to specific political factors rather than to a general characteristic of the parties.

61. In illustrating this point with specific examples, we follow the Assembly's custom of judging from a "parliamentary fact"; see Melnik and Leites, *The House Without Windows*, p. 345. The support for the various possible combinations would otherwise be difficult to predict.

62. We neglect the case of Socialist abstention, which always seemed temporary and was shortly followed by opposition.

63. Even at the end of the Legislature, Socialists, MRP, Radicals and UDSR together commanded nearly an absolute majority if they could have maintained their unity.

64. Socialist premiers after Ramadier could not be invested with their cabinets.

65. One model of coalition formation would lead one to expect a greater affinity between Socialists and their majority partners after some rightist elements had left; see MacRae, *Dimensions of Congressional Voting*, pp. 354–382. Thus the Socialists' departure seems due partly to increasing antagonisms with the center parties who remained.

66. Fauvet, *Le Monde, passim.* Closer analysis of the Moderates' votes will also show that their divisions were not highly specific to particular cabinets in the First Legislature.

67. Aron, *France: Steadfast and Changing*, p. 12.

68. Kesselman, "Presidential Leadership in Congress on Foreign Policy"; and his "Presidential Leadership in Congress on Foreign Policy: A Replication of a Hypothesis."

69. The introduction of·issues under particular cabinets for tactical reasons—e.g., the church-school issue under cabinets uniting SFIO and MRP—was also a complex combination of the short and the long term; it used a longer-term ideological division to further short-term goals.

70. Leites, *On the Game of Politics*, Chap. 1.

71. See MacRae, "A Method for Identifying Issues and Factions from Legislative Votes."

72. Wood, "Issue Dimensions in a Multi-Party System: The French National Assembly and European Integration."

73. An earlier version of this analysis was presented in MacRae, "Intraparty Divisions and Cabinet Coalitions in the Fourth French Republic." The corresponding material appears here in parts of Chaps. 4–7. Some of the explanatory text also parallels that in MacRae, *Dimensions of Congressional Voting*, p. 203.

74. See Yule, *Introduction to the Theory of Statistics*, p. 38.

75. Computer programs for producing this array of Q's were written first for the Univac I and later for the IBM 1401. A description of a simpler but closely related set of programs for analyzing United States legislative votes is given in MacRae, "IBM 1401 Q-Matrix and Editing Programs for Legislative Roll-Call Votes."

76. These were chosen from an actual matrix of 77 roll calls. For details of the procedure used in choosing roll calls, see Appendices A and B.

77. Often this corresponds to a general left-right division. In factor analysis it would correspond to a general factor.

78. Procedures for finding clusters and placing legislators are described in Appendix B; placement of legislators is also discussed in Chap. 7.

79. This was not true of the Peasant party in the First Legislature, in relation to RI and PRL; it is for this reason that the Peasants are not scaled for the First Legislature.

80. For an interpretation of this division see Marcel Merle, "Les Modérés," in Duverger, *Partis politiques et classes sociales,* p. 243. Positions of deputies are shown in Chap. 7.

81. Goodman and Kruskal, "Measures of Association for Cross Classifications," 749–751.

82. A separate analysis of Radicals without UDSR suggested that within the Queuille ministry (1948–49) a transition between scales occurred when André Marie left the cabinet after attacks on him as Minister of Justice.

83. Monteil was temporarily expelled; Buron remained in the party. *L'Année Politique* 1954, pp. 48, 70; 1955, p. 7.

84. The loss of a number of MRP deputies to the Gaullists during the First Legislature was not a fission in this sense, but a transfer to another political movement.

85. This cohesion was of an unusual type, however, as Peter Campbell shows in "Discipline and Loyalty in the French Parliament During the Pinay Government," p. 249. Of all the parties, the MRP had the lowest incidence of complete unanimity and the highest of divisions with a dissident fraction of less than five per cent.

86. *L'Année Politique,* 1947, pp. 215ff. The issue was support for a reorganized Ramadier cabinet, plagued by Gaullist and Communist threats to the public order.

87. Another peculiarity of the MRP was the inadequacy of the votes listed in *L'Année Politique (AP)* to give a clear picture of its internal divisions. A parallel analysis based on the *Journal Officiel* yielded a more detailed left-right scale, consisting largely of votes not in the *AP* sample.

88. Williams, *Crisis,* pp. 270–271. It is with this bill that roll calls nos. 986, 1012, and 1039 were concerned.

89. See, for example, the scales for the Moderates in the Second Legislature, as analyzed in Chap. 5.

90. André Philip, who had opposed Thorez, was also an active opponent of de Gaulle in 1958, though not in the Assembly then.

91. It was related to the divisions in Socialist party congresses in 1945–47; a scale based on these divisions was associated at $\gamma = .45$ with the Thorez vote. This supports the notion that the party was divided differently prior to Mollet's dominance of it; the electoral-law issue was one of the first of a set of divisions in which the left wing *opposed* Mollet. I am indebted to P. H. Auerbach for obtaining these data from SFIO headquarters.

92. See Chapters 8 and 10, sections on Socialists.

93. A number of Socialist militants were also expelled from the party over the laws opposing the Communist-inspired strikes in 1947; see Williams, *Crisis,* p. 171.

94. *Ibid.,* p. 90.

≫ 5 ≪

Cabinets and Issues
in the Second Legislature

THE ELECTION OF JULY 1951 produced a new configuration in the Assembly. The RPF emerged as a major group, and although its thrust was blunted by the new electoral law, it was strong enough to exercise a major influence on the cabinet coalitions and issues of the Second Legislature. By altering the electoral law the center parties had maintained their position but not enhanced the capacity of cabinets to govern.

The major developments of the Second Legislature centered about the disintegration of the RPF and the rise of European and colonial issues. While the breakup of the RPF made more votes available for possible cabinet coalitions from 1952 through 1955, it was accompanied by continued intransigent stands by the ex-RPF deputies on the new issues that arose. Consequently, except for the brief interlude of Mendès-France's ministry, the performance of the Second Legislature confirmed the immobility that had begun to set in during the latter part of the First.

Several of France's problems became more acute and moved into the parliamentary arena during the Second Legislature. The question of European union, which had begun with consideration of the European Coal and Steel Community, intensified when German rearmament was considered in the supranational framework of the proposed European Defense Community. Relations with Indochina provoked a sharp policy conflict that reached its height after the defeat at Dien Bien Phu. And the status of Algeria as an integral part of France came into the political arena with the outbreak of Muslim terrorism and the development of the National Liberation Front there. The economic problems that had divided cabinet majorities in the First Legislature receded into the background. A new conflict developed between the senior deputies who held most of the cabinet positions and another group who wished more radical changes in policy: the Mendès-France ministry was the latter group's one chance at power.

The Second Legislature: Chronology[1]

The revised electoral law permitted a prearranged coalition of parties in a district to take all that district's seats if it obtained a majority of the votes. The coalitions that were formed almost totally excluded the Gaullists and

Communists. Nevertheless, 119 Gaullists and 103 Communists were elected to the Assembly in June 1951.[2] The initial range of maneuver of the center parties was therefore narrower than it had been in the First Legislature. If the Socialists had joined the Communists and Gaullists in opposition (a total of 331 votes), no cabinet majority would have been even arithmetically

Figure 5.1 The Pleven Cabinet (Second Legislature) and Its Support*

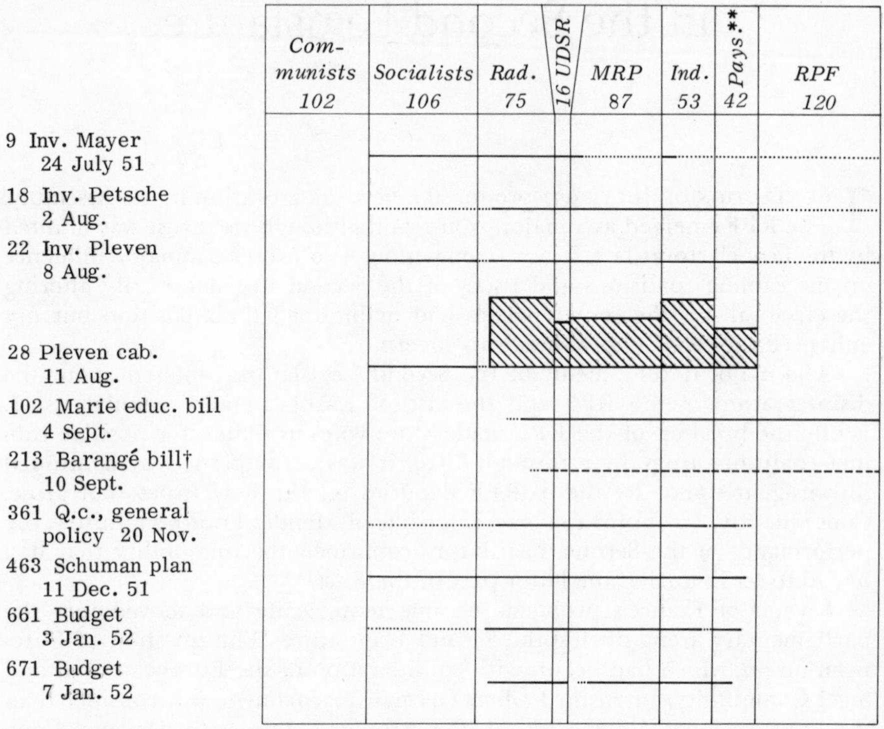

	Com- munists 102	Socialists 106	Rad. 75	16 UDSR	MRP 87	Ind. 53	Pays.** 42	RPF 120
9 Inv. Mayer 24 July 51								
18 Inv. Petsche 2 Aug.								
22 Inv. Pleven 8 Aug.								
28 Pleven cab. 11 Aug.								
102 Marie educ. bill 4 Sept.								
213 Barangé bill† 10 Sept.								
361 Q.c., general policy 20 Nov.								
463 Schuman plan 11 Dec. 51								
661 Budget 3 Jan. 52								
671 Budget 7 Jan. 52								

*Note that Radicals and UDSR are placed to the left of the MRP here, because of the dominance of the church-school question in this period.

**At no. 463 the Peasants split into two nearly equal groups. The Antier group supplied all the opposition on this and succeeding roll calls in the figure.

†Cabinet neutral, votes omitted.

possible. Moreover, the church-school question threatened to detach the Socialists from their cabinet partners. Yet the organizational fragility of the RPF proved to permit a greater diversity of cabinet combinations in the Second Legislature than in the First.

After some disputes on validating particular elections,[3] the Assembly settled down to the problem of choosing a premier. The first premier-designate to confront the Assembly was René Mayer. He received only 241 votes when most of the MRP and Moderate deputies abstained (no. 9: Fig. 5.1). Mayer had refused the MRP's request for cabinet neutrality on the church-school question. Possibly he was trying to regain the Socialist support he had lost two years previously when forming his short-lived cabinet; but his stand divided the MRP and forced it to abstain to maintain a degree of unanimity.[4]

Next to confront the Assembly was Petsche (Ind.). But again the school question came to dominate the investiture debate, and the Socialists abstained (no. 18). René Pleven, designated next, promised cabinet neutrality on the school question and further limited the possible bills on this problem to a range between those contemplated by Mayer and Petsche in their platforms. He was invested by a large margin, with Communists opposing and RPF abstaining (no. 22), and his cabinet was approved by nearly the same vote, with the RPF now opposing (no. 28).[5] The Socialists, though supporting the cabinet, did not enter it.

Bills on the school question quickly came to the fore, even though economic and international questions were also pressing. Both the RPF and the parliamentary association for the private schools favored this development; the former because they wished to encourage a split of the cabinet coalition,[6] and the latter because there was a clear "pro-clerical" majority in the new Legislature. André Marie, the Minister of Education, proposed a bill providing for scholarships and building funds, some of which would go to private schools. In September this bill was passed by a large majority (no. 102). Opposing were Communists, Socialists, and half the Radicals.

Immediately afterward on the agenda came a stronger bill for school aid, the Barangé bill, proposing aid to parents of children in primary schools, public and private. After numerous counter motions and votes on the articles, this too passed (no. 213) but by a smaller margin than the Marie bill; the cabinet now abstained. The important political result of this series of arguments over the school question was further to separate the MRP and Socialists from one another. This issue was to contribute to the MRP's voting more frequently to the "right" of the Radicals in the Second Legislature.

The cabinet also had to remain neutral on the salary scale bill (late September), which provided for an increase in the minimum wage in relation to a price index. Although Pleven opposed the bill, he could not make his opposition a question of confidence without splitting the cabinet.[7]

After the parliamentary vacation, which extended from late September to early November and included the cantonal elections, questions of foreign policy came to the fore in the Assembly. The economics of rearmament would require tax increases, and the problem of German rearmament under the "Pleven Plan" for a European army also began to divide the parties internally. Having avoided issues before, Pleven now had to put the question of confidence on his general policies to be able to carry on foreign negotiations. He did so on November 20, and won by 246–228 with the Socialists abstaining (no. 361).

The closeness of this vote reflected the majority's internal conflicts, which had been growing since the parliamentary vacation. At their Lyon congress, the Radicals had already acted as if they were ready to choose Pleven's successor. The Independents and Peasants were also uneasy about the austerity measures proposed by René Mayer, the Minister of Finance; before taking responsibility for such measures, some of them wanted to offer the RPF a chance to govern. On the vote of confidence, the Peasants had been divided, and Antier (Pays.) was dismissed from the cabinet for opposing its policies. Shortly thereafter, the Peasant Party split in two over the consequences of this incident.

On December 11 the Schuman Plan for a European Coal and Steel Community received strong support on a key vote. Pleven put the question of confidence against a motion to send the bill back to committee, and won by 376 to 240 (no. 463), making it certain that the Assembly would ultimately approve the Schuman Plan.

By 1952 the cabinet encountered increasing difficulty on the vote of the budget. The Finance Committee of the Assembly had already rejected it— the rejection in itself was not fatal. On January 3 Pleven won a vote of confidence for the consideration of the cabinet's budget bill rather than the committee's, but his margin was only seven votes (no. 661). The Socialists abstained; the Communists and Gaullists were joined in opposition by a Radical faction under Daladier as well as by the Antier Peasants. A chief point of contention was the proposal for *lois-cadres*[8] by which the cabinet might act to reform the nationalized railways and the social security administration and reduce their expense.

Four days later the Socialists brought down the cabinet. Mollet, now favoring abstention rather than opposition, had to give in to preserve his party's unity. Pleven fell by an absolute majority[9] on a question of confidence relating to the *loi-cadre* on railway and transportation reform (no. 671).

The question still remained whether the RPF could or would become part of a cabinet coalition. After Pleven's fall, President Auriol called first Christian Pineau (Socialist) and then Jacques Soustelle, president of the RPF group in the Assembly. But Soustelle declined, wishing first to see the non-RPF majority fail again and thus increase the RPF's bargaining power. After several other unsuccessful invitations, Edgar Faure (Rad.) was designated by Auriol. At the same time, Tunisia brought to the U.N. Security Council a complaint that France had not fulfilled her obligation to grant "internal autonomy" to her protectorate.[10] Although the effect of external events on the development of cabinet crises was often slight, the Tunisian affair seems to have aided Faure.

The large majority by which Faure was personally invested (401–101; no. 672, Fig. 5.2)[11] owed much to his skill in answering questions from the floor after his investiture speech. He had taken positions on taxes and for the salary scale, and proposed that the cabinet's accomplishments be reviewed only after three months. (It was actually to last only six weeks.) On the day Faure was invested the French arrested Habib Bourguiba in Tunisia as he was about to preside over a meeting of his party, the Neo-Destour; this action was taken by the Pleven cabinet, still in office. Faure, constituting his cabinet, faced a vote on Tunisian policy in place of the usual "cabinet investiture"; on this vote (no. 673) he retained his initial support, with only the RPF moving from abstention to opposition. Faure's cabinet, like Pleven's, was supported by the Socialists without their participation.

Faure, invested after a promise to engage in long-run planning, was confronted with two immediate problems: the balance of payments and the salary scale bill. He advocated the salary scale as part of a larger economic program and put the question of confidence on urgent priority for it (no. 696). On this he won by only seventeen votes, having lost the support of a considerable fraction of the Moderates as well as part of his own Radical party.

Figure 5.2 The First Faure Cabinet and Its Support*

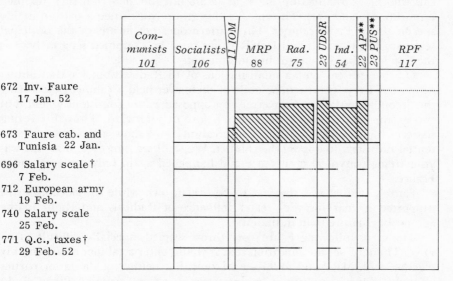

	Com- munists 101	Socialists 106	11 IOM	MRP 88	Rad. 75	23 UDSR	Ind. 54	22 AP**	23 PUS**	RPF 117
672 Inv. Faure 17 Jan. 52										
673 Faure cab. and Tunisia 22 Jan.										
696 Salary scale† 7 Feb.										
712 European army 19 Feb.										
740 Salary scale 25 Feb.										
771 Q.c., taxes† 29 Feb. 52										

*The MRP are again placed to the left of the Radicals because of the dominance of the issue of social legislation.

***Paysans d'Union Sociale* (PUS) are the Antier faction, more pro-Gaullist than Camille Laurens' *Action Paysanne* (AP).

†On nos. 696 and 771 it is extremely difficult to place the Radicals' dissident faction on the "left" or right."

A major debate on the European Army then took place. Faure put the question of confidence on a general resolution by Guérin de Beaumont and others favoring the European army under certain conditions. It was carried by 327 to 287 (no. 712). Most of the majority parties were divided, but none deeply, and the only group joining the Communists and Gaullists in opposition were the Antier Peasants. The Gaullists' opposition reflected not their anti-cabinet position, but their nationalism; later in the Second Legislature, when the Gaullist deputies were free to join cabinet coalitions, this nationalist opposition to the European army was still a source of important disagreements within these coalitions.

The salary scale bill then returned to the agenda; and after the defeat of a number of amendments, it was passed with Communist support (no. 740). The vote, although reflecting one of the rare instances of a "popular front" majority other than the school question,[12] produced an incomplete bill: no provision was made for the case in which salaries rose between 5 and 10 per cent.

The cabinet's budgetary proposals then came up, and Faure fell on the second of a series of questions of confidence (no. 771)—a proposal to increase

taxes by 15 per cent. Faure's failure was due partly to the Assembly's unwillingness to pay for its own military policy, partly to the ideological incompatibility of the parties of the center majority, and partly to personal
feelings among some deputies that Faure was a young upstart who should
not be permitted too great a success.[13]

An important contribution to Faure's fall was made by a group of Radicals who first abstained on the salary scale bill (no. 696) and then opposed
him (nos. 740 and 771). The votes of this group constituted a pattern highly
specific to the Faure cabinet. This pattern does not fit any of the principal
scales for the Radicals and UDSR,[14] but must be examined separately as is
the case for other important but unique votes.

On these three votes, a small nucleus of 16 Radicals outside the cabinet
supported Faure consistently; none of these ever held a cabinet post during
the Second Legislature. Conversely, 23 opposed Faure consistently, and 6 of
this group held cabinet posts either before or afterward. Thus this voting
pattern, highly specific to the Faure cabinet, did show a tendency for potential ministers to oppose the cabinet. We shall see, however, that this was
an extremely atypical occurrence and happened again only under Mendès-
France.

Faure's cabinet was the first to be overthrown while the Socialists still
supported it, marking the greater influence of Radicals and Right in the
Second Legislature than in the First.[15]

The crisis following Faure's overthrow seemed especially difficult to resolve. The RPF set the condition that it would enter a cabinet coalition only
together with MRP and SFIO—a relation that neither of the latter parties
wanted.[16] After some initial explorations by others. Antoine Pinay (Ind.)
was invited to form a cabinet. This attempt was generally regarded as simply
a matter of "lifting the mortgage on the right," i.e., showing that a rightist
majority was impossible, in order to clarify the later combinations. But on
this investiture the RPF divided; and a dissident group of twenty-seven RPF
deputies, together with the near totality of the MRP, Radicals, and Moderates, gave Pinay 324 votes. (The latter parties were unanimous because they
expected Pinay to fail.) The dissident RPF deputies were on the (socioeconomic) right wing of the party. We shall therefore now represent the
major faction of the RPF as on the "right center" of the political spectrum
(Fig. 5.3); we are thus arranging the parties more nearly in terms of their
positions on domestic social and economic legislation, rather than simply
their support or opposition to the cabinet.

Pinay's cabinet was approved by a somewhat smaller vote, RPF and
Socialists abstaining. The MRP apparently had to be given a larger number
of cabinet posts than usual to insure its support. Usually underrepresented,
it had a higher "cabinet ratio" under Pinay than did the premier's own
party (Fig. 5.3). On this vote (no. 776) the RPF regained its unity by abstaining, though it was sharply divided in its internal deliberations.

The new premier then undertook to restore public confidence, stabilize
prices, and balance the budget without increasing taxes. He floated a substantial loan and (with some help from the international economic situation) saw prices stop rising. Meeting with businessmen and pressure groups,
he used persuasion to get further price reductions. Early in April he brought

his budget bill to the Assembly, putting several informal questions of confidence on it. He won these by comfortable margins; on no. 838, for example, dealing with nonmilitary economies, he received the support of nearly two-thirds of the RPF group.

A key point in Pinay's program was an amnesty for previous tax evasion, designed to increase investment from hitherto hidden private funds. On

Figure 5.3 The Pinay Cabinet and Its Support

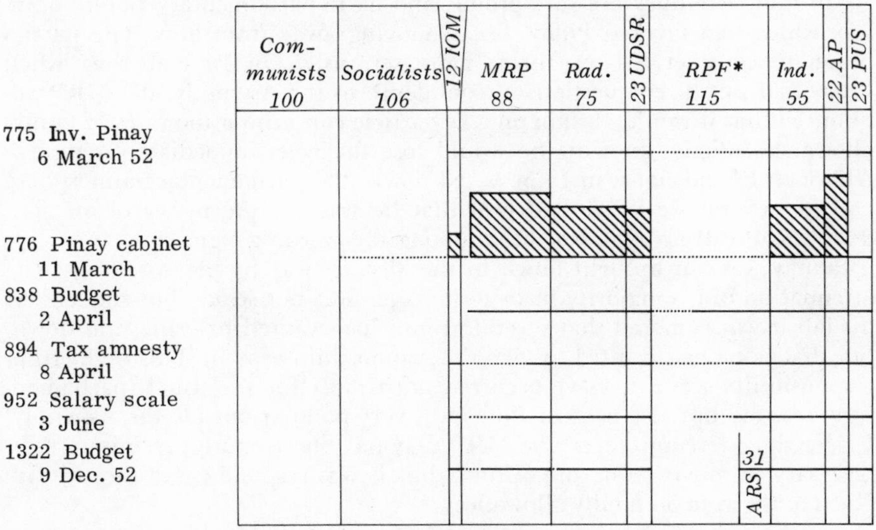

	Communists 100	Socialists 106	IOM 12	MRP 88	Rad. 75	UDSR 23	RPF* 115	Ind. 55	AP 22	PUS 23
775 Inv. Pinay 6 March 52										
776 Pinay cabinet 11 March										
838 Budget 2 April										
894 Tax amnesty 8 April										
952 Salary scale 3 June										
1322 Budget 9 Dec. 52							ARS 31			

*The RPF, which now divides on roll calls, is placed on the right center rather than the extreme right; it is the right wing of the RPF that supports Pinay (Ind.).

this vote (no. 894), most of the MRP and RPF deputies abstained, sympathetic with the Resistance rather than with Vichy profits; in this respect both groups were nearer to the Communist-Socialist opposition than were the Radicals. The division of the MRP on this bill reflected that party's difficulties now that it found itself on the "left wing" of the majority, with the Socialists in opposition.

The premier then argued that consideration of the salary scale bill should be postponed, and he won MRP support because of the incompleteness of the bill passed previously. On June 3 he put the question of confidence on his own version of the bill (no. 952), which was passed by a rightist majority. Again the RPF was deeply divided—into three nearly equal parts. Since a segment of the RPF had moved into opposition, the cabinet's margin of support was reduced to 42 votes.

A debate on Tunisia followed in June. On June 20 eleven resolutions on Tunisia were successively presented and all defeated. The proposed plans for reform in Tunisia were rejected by both the right (as too generous) and the left (as insufficient).[17]

In the fall the Vichy amnesty bill was considered, and a skirmish took place on the budget for overseas territories. In late November, however, the cabinet's difficulties began. Pinay, wishing to give priority to discussion of the budget, had to put several unofficial questions of confidence in order to prevail over the Assembly's wish to consider family allowances and old-age assistance. In December he twice put the official question of confidence in order to maintain priority for the budget. The closest of these was no. 1322, opposing a Communist motion. He won by a margin of nine votes; the largest segment of the RPF (loyal to de Gaulle) was now in opposition, while the new ex-Gaullist ARS group supported him.

In mid-December pressure groups and extra-parliamentary public opinion, which had favored Pinay, began moving away from him. The parties began to consider his overthrow more seriously. On December 22 when Pinay had put three questions of confidence to the Assembly, the MRP announced that it would abstain on a key article concerning the rates of family allowances. Pinay, knowing he would lose the vote, immediately resigned. Although he did not wait to be voted down, the parliamentary atmosphere had for several weeks warned him that he was "at the mercy of an accident." Roll call no 1322 had been among the warning signs.[18]

Pinay was not brought down in the "usual" way by the Assembly. The attenuation of his majority prior to no. 1322 was not steady but sudden. At his fall it was rumored that several groups had wanted to bring him down, but that none had wanted to take the responsibility for it. This flight from responsibility seems to have occurred not simply for the usual (parliamentary) reasons, but also because Pinay was very popular outside the Assembly. Under these circumstances, the MRP may have been more precipitate than necessary in moving into opposition; but it was responding to the priority given to the vote on family allowances.[19]

In the cabinet crisis that followed Pinay's fall, the key question was whether the "loyal" Gaullists would enter the governing majority. Among the unsuccessful candidates called by the President of the Republic, the most important in this respect was Jacques Soustelle. The parties deliberated his candidacy, but aside from his own RPF only the MRP encouraged him. Socialists and Radicals opposed him and the Independents were cool.

The premier under whom the loyal Gaullists entered the supporting majority was the Radical René Mayer, an international businessman. Although a deputy from Constantine (Algeria), Mayer was born in Paris and had run unsuccessfully in the Charente in 1945. With 81 RPF votes, he was invested by the comfortable margin of 389–205 (no. 1453: Fig. 5.4). Sixteen days later (January 22), his cabinet was approved by almost the same margin. The RPF, though supporting Mayer, did not enter the cabinet, thus offering the same conditional support that the Socialists had given to the preceding cabinets.

The entry of the RPF into possible supporting majorities appeared at first to enlarge the range of parliamentary maneuver considerably. All parties but the Communists could now enter into at least *some* cabinet coalitions. But the peculiar ideological configuration of the RPF imposed stringent conditions on its possible coalitions. On domestic social questions it tried to keep to the left; before supporting Mayer its leaders had set the condition of sharing power with the Socialists.[20] And among the parties of the Mayer majority, the RPF differed from most in its sharp opposition to European union, especially to the European army. Thus Mayer, a "European" himself, became the first of a series of premiers who had to walk a tightrope on the issue in order to keep the Gaullists' support without losing that of other parties. It was even said that the moment the RPF entered the majority the European Defense Community was dead.[21] A sign of this development was Mayer's replacement of the ardently pro-European Robert Schuman by his MRP colleague Georges Bidault as Foreign Minister.

Figure 5.4 The Mayer Cabinet and Its Support*

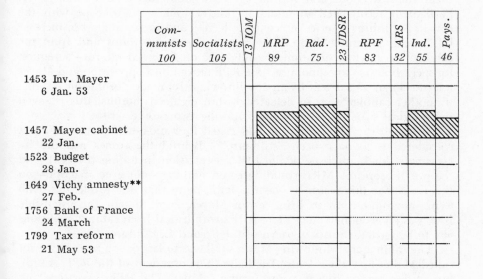

	Com- munists 100	Socialists 105	13 IOM	MRP 89	Rad. 75	23 UDSR	RPF 83	ARS 32	Ind. 55	Pays. 46
1453 Inv. Mayer 6 Jan. 53										
1457 Mayer cabinet 22 Jan.										
1523 Budget 28 Jan.										
1649 Vichy amnesty** 27 Feb.										
1756 Bank of France 24 March										
1799 Tax reform 21 May 53										

*Polarities of factions are difficult to assign for the right. The convention adopted here is that the opposition comes from the left in the RPF and ARS, but the right among the Independents and Peasants.
**No. 1649 concerns an amendment, thus the pro-cabinet vote is *contre*.

The decision of the RPF deputies to support Mayer was a close one, however. Some of the more "loyal" Gaullists such as Barrès and Gaston Palewski were opposed, while ex-Radicals such as Chaban-Delmas and Ulver favored supporting him.

Early in February André Boutemy, a Senator associated with powerful conservative lobbies, resigned from the cabinet under attack. On February 3 the Assembly refused to postpone an interpellation directed at him; before the date scheduled for the debate, he resigned.

During the early days of the Mayer ministry, the trial for the Oradour-sur-Glane massacre was being held at Bordeaux. In 1944 the Germans had massacred the population of this small village in the Charente; among the German troops were some Alsatian conscripts. Now, while the Southwest favored punishment, Alsace insisted on clemency. The cabinet supported a bill for amnesty of "Frenchmen forcibly incorporated in the enemy forces," and after being convicted, the Alsatians were freed. Although this issue did

not threaten the cabinet, it divided the MRP and to some extent the Socialists.

In March the Vichy amnesty bill was passed, after considerable debate
and some close votes. But it was not until March 24 that the cabinet's
margin of support was substantially reduced on an important vote: Mayer's
proposed convention with the Bank of France was then passed by only 257–
221, with RPF abstaining (no. 1756: an informal question of confidence).

A parliamentary "truce" reigned during the spring as Mayer visited the
United States. The municipal elections showed a turn to the left. General
de Gaulle, judging the RPF deputies lost to the parliamentary game, gave
them their freedom and retired again to Colombey-les-Deux-Églises. As
Parliament reconvened in mid-May, Mayer took steps to cope with the
deficit, publishing a series of economy decrees and presenting a tax increase
bill to the Assembly. Protests arose from pressure groups and from the
cabinet. On his first question of confidence on financial reform—a request
for special powers to economize—the RPF moved into opposition and Mayer
fell (no. 1799). His defeat by an absolute majority made dissolution possible
if another cabinet were so defeated within eighteen months; this changed
the political situation during the following two cabinet crises.

Although the Mayer cabinet had lasted four-and-a-half months, Fauvet
considered it to have been "stillborn."[22] Behind the scenes was the increasingly dominant issue of the EDC; a coalition including the RPF and
the pro-"European" MRP could agree on nothing—not even inaction—on
this issue. For this reason it was the RPF, more than the Moderates, who
went into opposition to bring down Mayer, even though the ostensible
issue was an economic one.[23] The RPF's withdrawal from cabinet coalitions
was to be a characteristic pattern of the Second Legislature.

The cabinet crisis following Mayer's fall was to last over a month. Auriol
called Mollet first, then André Diethelm (now president of the RPF group),
but neither was willing to try to form a cabinet. The RPF was stll asking
for a coalition with the Socialists, an impossible condition. First to be
officially presented were Paul Reynaud (Ind.) and Pierre Mendès-France
(Rad.), both of whom asked for stringent reforms and were defeated (nos.
1800, 1801; Figure 5.5). The division of the RPF on the Reynaud investiture
showed again that its position on many issues was "right center." Proposing
to fill his cabinet positions by negotiating with individual deputies rather
than party chiefs, Mendès split several of the parties.

Next Bidault asked for extensive economic and financial powers and
missed investiture by only a single vote (no. 1802). The Radicals were held
responsible for his failure; only 27 of them supported him, including 10
former ministers (under Mayer) who did so as a courtesy.[24] Next presented
was a Radical, André Marie, who put forward a conciliatory program but
also failed (no. 1804). His investiture was prevented by the abstention of
most of the MRP deputies and half of the RPF (now URAS).

Pinay having surveyed the situation and declined, the choice then fell
on Joseph Laniel, a lesser-known leader among the Independents. In his
investiture declaration he sidestepped the European issue, favoring the
"continuity" of French foreign policy; he also asked for increased taxes on
alcohol and gasoline, and special powers for economizing (but not for tax

reform). He was invested by a substantial majority, with essentially only the Communists and Socialists opposing (no. 1807); fifteen deputies on the left wing of the URAS abstained. His cabinet was also approved by a large margin (no. 1812), but two days later he adjusted the allocation of cabinet

*Figure 5.5 The Laniel Cabinet and Its Support**

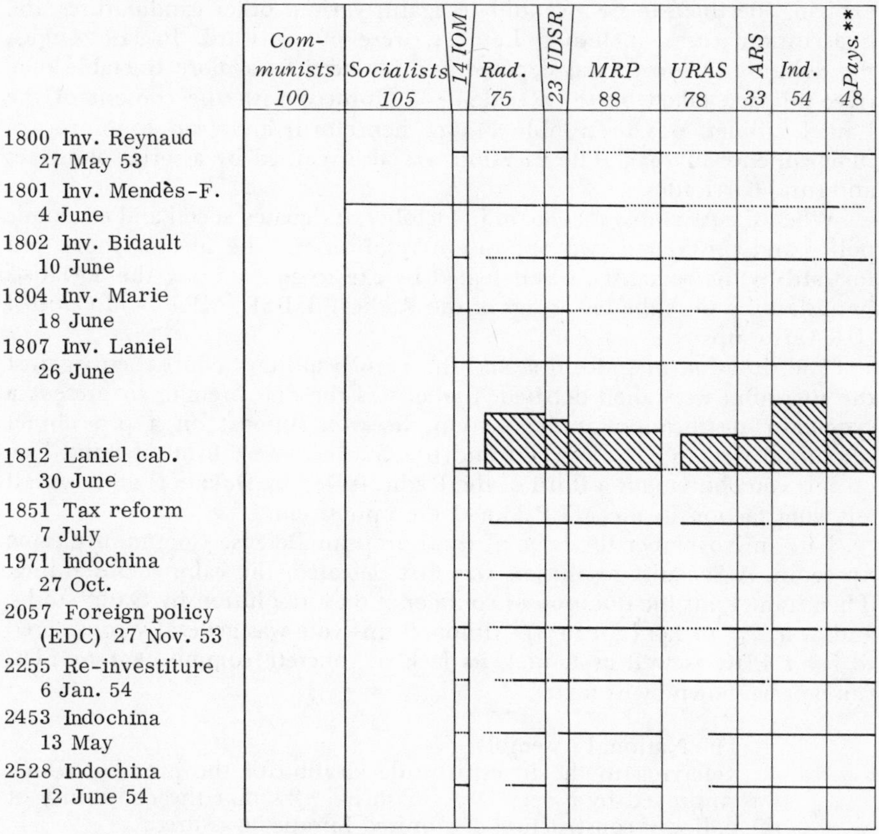

*The Radicals and UDSR are again placed to the left of the MRP, because on the colonial questions that arose under Laniel the Radicals were more likely to be in opposition. The small ARS opposition is now considered to be on the right wing of that party.

**From no. 2255, the Peasants were again divided into two groups.

posts by appointing sixteen Secretaries of State to serve under various ministers.[25]

A week after the approval of the cabinet, Laniel's financial bill was passed (no. 1851). On this issue, the first major substantive question considered in his ministry, his majority declined to 314–267—still a margin of 47 votes, but one that saw substantial fractions of MRP and URAS joining the Communists and Socialists in opposition. Pinay and eight of his "friends" also abstained on this vote, reflecting the factional divisions among the Moderates: their faction had failed to receive cabinet posts from Laniel.

Before the summer vacation, the Assembly passed a bill for revision of
the constitution, dealing with investitures and other parliamentary matters;
the reform finally went into effect in early 1955. The Vichy amnesty bill was
also passed in its second (final) reading. Both were passed by large margins
and neither involved the cabinet's fate. During the summer and autumn,
there was increasing discussion of the election of the President of the Republic, scheduled for December. President Auriol, whose seven-year term was
expiring, declined to be a candidate again; various other candidatures and
quasi-candidatures, including Laniel's, were put forward. In late August
the Sultan of Morocco was deposed and replaced by a more tractable relative; this act, taken by the Resident of Morocco with the consent of the
Laniel cabinet, was to trouble France henceforth and lead to Moroccan
independence in 1955. The vacation was also marked by a series of strikes
and rural barricades.

When the Assembly met again in October, it debated social and economic
policy and considered two opposition resolutions. The first of these, put
forward by the Socialists, was defeated by 242 to 299; joining the Socialists
or abstaining were the left wings of the Radical, UDSR, MRP, and Gaullist
(URAS) groups.

The situation in Indochina and the French military effort there against
the Vietminh were then debated. Laniel was the first premier to present a
systematic justification of that action; he won support on a pro-cabinet
resolution (no. 1971). The right and the Gaullists were firmly behind him
on this vote, but about a third of the Radicals (led by Daladier) and a small
left-wing faction in the MRP joined the opposition.[26]

Late in November the issue of the European Defense Community came
up again. A Socialist resolution was first defeated, the cabinet abstaining.
Then Laniel put the question of confidence on a resolution by Garet (Ind.),
and won, 275 to 244 (no. 2057). Although this vote was generally considered
to favor EDC as well as Laniel, its lack of concrete commitment to EDC
can best be shown by its text:

> The National Assembly,
> Referring to the investiture declaration of the premier, which
> was approved by a very large majority, asks that the continuity of
> the policy of construction of a united Europe be assured,
> Approves the declarations of the government,
> And, rejecting any addition,
> Passes to the order of the day.[27]

This motion, however, was enough to cause 60 URAS deputies to abstain,
and to reduce Laniel's margin to 31 votes.

Although the Assembly met in December, no important business was
transacted; the election of the President of the Republic occupied the center
of the political stage. The election was conducted at Versailles, by the Assembly and the Council of the Republic meeting jointly, under rules resembling
those of a U.S. presidential nominating convention. Only on the thirteenth
ballot was Coty, a dark horse, elected; meanwhile Laniel had been successfully stopped by the maneuvers of Senator Duchet (allied with Pinay). All
of those mentioned were Independents.[28]

Since new enmities had been created by the presidential election, and since in any event the President of the Republic has the right to designate the premier, Laniel submitted his resignation to Coty, as Blum had given his to Auriol in 1947. Coty declined it, and Laniel then presented himself to the Assembly for "re-investiture" (no. 2255). He won by a vote similar to that on his financial bill (no. 1851); on the re-investiture he had somewhat less support from the Radicals and more from the URAS.

On March 9 the cabinet again successfully defended its Indochina policy, winning by 333 to 271 on a supporting resolution. Among the Radicals Mendès-France and Mitterrand (resigned from the cabinet) had joined Daladier in opposition. But a week later Dien Bien Phu was surrounded, and the deterioration of the military situation began to impress both the public and Parliament. The Socialists voted against the military budget for the first time in the Fourth Republic (March 19). Dien Bien Phu fell on May 7, and on May 13 Laniel won support for his Indochina policy by a margin of only two votes (no. 2453). Since the earlier vote on Indochina (no. 1971), he had lost somewhat over forty URAS votes; in partial compensation, the MRP now backed him unanimously.

The defection of the URAS was not due entirely to the Indochinese situation, however. During the Easter vacation (April–May 1954) a date had been set for the debate on EDC. Merely to do this was for Laniel to lean too far toward the "European" side of his majority for the Gaullists' comfort.[29]

In June Laniel was soundly defeated on another resolution on Indochina. Putting the question of confidence on the resolution, he gained votes but still lost by thirteen (no. 2528) and resigned. Almost the entire difference between this roll call and no. 2453 was from the shift of sixteen more Radicals into opposition; together with the URAS, they had brought Laniel down.

Mendès-France, having attacked the Laniel cabinet forcefully and delivered the *coup de grâce,* was called next to form a cabinet. He promised to go to the Geneva conference and either make peace in Indochina within a month or resign, and he said he would take office only if he attained an absolute majority without the aid of Communist votes. His majority (no. 2529; Fig. 5.6) of 419 to 47 included 320 non-Communist votes—more than an absolute majority. He was solidly supported by the "anticlerical" parties of the Assembly, and received four-fifths of the ex-Gaullist vote as well.[30] Although invested by a narrow margin (some observers had predicted that he might fail of investiture again), he was to govern for some time with substantial majorities.

In forming his cabinet, Mendès again negotiated with individuals rather than parliamentary groups. The Socialists supported the cabinet but were unwilling to participate; Mendès' European and economic policies did not fit their views. The MRP opposed, largely from loyalty to Bidault, whose actions in the preceding cabinet had borne the brunt of Mendès' attacks. Mendès chose two MRP deputies as ministers, and their party promptly relegated them to a party limbo.[31] Mendès' cabinet was not neatly tailored to his supporting majority, but was rather to the right of it; and the normal balancing (*dosage*) of cabinet posts among the parties was not respected (Fig. 5.6). The cabinet consisted largely of new men drawn from the rank and file, in contrast to the "old team" who had taken turns at filling the posts in the previous cabinets. Among the Radicals the only holdovers were Edgar Faure, who continued as Minister of Finance, and Émile Hugues.

Mendès took up the Geneva negotiations, initiated a series of weekly radio addresses,[32] met with Paul-Henri Spaak, and postponed negotiations

Figure 5.6 The Mendès-France Cabinet and Its Support

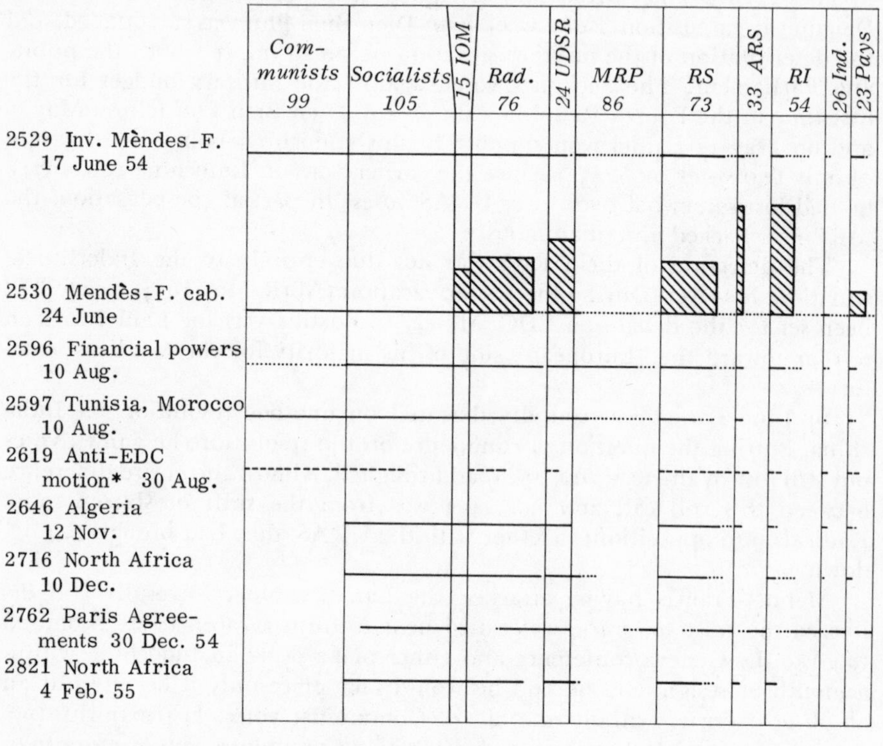

	Communists 99	Socialists 105	15 IOM	Rad. 76	24 UDSR	MRP 86	RS 73	33 ARS	RI 54	26 Ind.	23 Pays
2529 Inv. Mèndes-F. 17 June 54											
2530 Mendès-F. cab. 24 June											
2596 Financial powers 10 Aug.											
2597 Tunisia, Morocco 10 Aug.											
2619 Anti-EDC motion* 30 Aug.											
2646 Algeria 12 Nov.											
2716 North Africa 10 Dec.											
2762 Paris Agreements 30 Dec. 54											
2821 North Africa 4 Feb. 55											

*Cabinet nonvoting; these votes omitted. The wings classified as "left" among the ARS, RI, and Peasants are anti-EDC and pro-Mendès.

on the European Defense Community. Those who favored EDC, especially the MRP, were fearful that Mendès would kill it, as he had never taken strong stands in its favor; in his investiture declaration he had promised only to resolve the question. Talks within the cabinet on EDC were begun by General Koenig (ex-Gaullist) and Bourgès-Maunoury (Rad.); they got nowhere.

In July Mendès signed the treaty at Geneva partitioning Indochina; on his return he was given an overwhelming endorsement by the Assembly. In August he asked for special financial powers, and even with the Communists abstaining he won by 361 to 90 (no. 2596). On this vote he had a more clearly left-center majority than at his investiture, being supported by MRP as well as Socialists and Radicals.

On July 31 Mendès flew to Tunis and began negotiations toward Tunisia's "internal sovereignty." On the vote immediately following (no. 2597), an implicit question of confidence on Tunisia and Morocco, he gained a larger but differently composed majority. This "colonial" question recreated Mendès' investiture majority, Communists supporting him and MRP deputies largely abstaining.

Next on Mendès' crowded agenda was the European Defense Community. His efforts at compromise within his cabinet led first to the resignation of three of his six Gaullist ministers. Taking his compromise plan (which was too supranational for the Gaullists) to Brussels for negotiations of the six "European" powers, he was rebuffed: the representatives of the other nations thought his changes in the treaty too radical, and they were encouraged to oppose him by articles in the French press written by prominent "pro-European" deputies as well as direct personal communications on their part.

After the breakdown of the Brussels conference, Mendès flew to England and talked with Churchill. He then returned to France and brought the original EDC treaty (the one on which France's allies had insisted) before the Assembly, the cabinet now taking a neutral position. Some of the pro-EDC deputies now wanted the debate delayed, foreseeing a defeat. But Mendès kept his investiture promise; and the pro-EDC forces, by a parliamentary blunder, allowed a *question préalable*[33] sponsored by Aumeran (an extreme nationalist) and Herriot to come to the floor. This motion would remove EDC from the agenda. It carried, 319–264 (no. 2619), and EDC was dead.

Many of Mendès' critics never forgave him for allowing EDC to be killed in this way, contending that he could have passed it by backing it strongly. This argument neglects the fact that Mendès could not have gained the premiership or held it without Gaullist support. He could hardly have been himself had he relied on the MRP rather than the Gaullists for support; even at his unsuccessful investiture in June 1953 (no. 1801) the MRP had been only lukewarm to him, and MRP defections might have been considered responsible for his defeat. Moreover, the vote on which EDC was defeated may have found *more* deputies supporting EDC (opposing the *question préalable*) than would have backed the bill itself.[34]

The parties had long been deeply split on the EDC issue, and the Aumeran-Herriot motion revealed it. In Figure 5.6 the majority opposing EDC (dashed lines) resembled Mendès' investiture majority more than did the pro-EDC minority. The Socialist group was split nearly in half. The leaders of the anti-EDC faction (Mayer, Moch, Lejeune) were excluded from the party, but later allowed to return. The Radicals, too, were evenly divided, with the normally pro-Mendès segment opposing EDC. After the defeat of EDC, two Radicals and a UDSR member of the cabinet resigned. And although the MRP deputies voted with near unanimity, two deputies and a Senator were excluded from the MRP for dissidence on the issue.

Parliament then adjourned and Mendès went about the difficult task of replacing EDC. The two preconditions that Herriot had placed before EDC were settlement of the status of the Saar and British participation in the European defense organization. Mendès now proceeded to negotiate with

Britain, receiving considerable cooperation from Eden.[35] In early October the London Agreements for German rearmament were concluded; the Assembly approved them conditionally by a resolution passed on October 12. On this vote the Communists were in opposition, the MRP abstaining, and the Moderates divided; Socialist support carried the vote.

At this time, Mendès' support among Gaullists and Radicals was high. On October 13 he met with General de Gaulle. The following week he was received with great enthusiasm at the Radicals' Marseille Congress but made no effort to intervene in intraparty politics.

At the end of October, after negotiating with Adenauer over the Saar question, Mendès completed the Paris Agreements on German rearmament that were to be sent to the Assembly.

On November 1 Muslim terrorism broke out in Algeria. These incidents, plus the "leaks" of national defense secrets that had been publicized in October, gave an opening to Mendès' latent opposition. He was accused of disloyalty, softness, "abandonment" of the colonies and Algeria. On November 12, seeking postponement of interpellations on Algeria, Mendès saw his margin of support decline to forty votes (no. 2646).[36] Following this vote, Mendès left on a good-will trip to the United States.

By early November the Independents and MRP were already considering who should be Mendès' successor. Mendès tried to realign his cabinet by inviting six Socialists to join. The Socialist executive committee referred the question to a special party congress, which finally decided (after Mendès' departure on this trip) to impose doctrinal conditions that they knew he would refuse. One of Mollet's problems at this stage was to maintain his party's unity and his control over it; by maneuvering against participation he furthered these ends. His party nevertheless continued to support Mendès, and attained the degree of discipline Mendès needed on the final votes approving German rearmament under the Paris Agreements.

Criticism of Mendès mounted during his absence. Just before his return, his cabinet published a series of anti-alcoholism decrees. On December 10 another resolution supporting the cabinet on North Africa was passed but with a margin of only 29 votes (no. 2716). The MRP was said to have tried to bring him down on this vote.[37] His majority was similar to that on no. 2646, with the losses distributed mainly among the ex-Gaullists and Peasants. This roll call was later to be chosen by *L'Express* as one of the "test" votes by which Radical deputies' loyalty to Mendès was established for the 1956 elections.[38] In spite of the reduction of Mendès' margin in the Assembly, it was generally expected that none of the parties on which he relied would try to bring him down until after the passage of the Paris Agreements. The cabinet was firmly supported by the Socialists, ex-Gaullists, Radicals, and UDSR, as well as a scattering of votes from segments of other parties.[39]

The week beginning December 21 brought the Paris Agreements before the Assembly; all the votes on them were close. Losing by 21 votes on one of the early roll calls, Mendès had to put several questions of confidence. But on December 30 the entire bill was passed, 287 to 260 (no. 2762). The Socialists, largely supporting Mendès, held their dissent to 18 votes; the

MRP, largely opposing him, nevertheless gave him 16.[40] The Radicals were deeply split, and the 27 of his own party who opposed Mendès now included many of the left wing, his normal allies; Herriot was still against German rearmament. Mendès' success in getting the Paris Agreements ratified was an individual tour de force. Very few deputies supported him in the debates and some deserted him. Though there was no organized effort to overthrow the cabinet on this issue, the deputies were simply reluctant to vote for German rearmament.[41]

Undaunted by the deteriorating parliamentary situation, Mendès came out with a host of new proposals. First he proposed, and the cabinet supported, the reform of the electoral system and return to *scrutin d'arrondissement*. Next François Mitterrand (UDSR), his Minister of the Interior, announced a plan for reforms in Algeria.[42] Then Mendès reorganized the cabinet, appointed the Gaullist Jacques Soustelle (then considered "liberal") as Governor General of Algeria, and accepted a debate on North African policy for early February.

Late in January, however, there were signs of dissidence in Mendès' own party. A meeting of the Radical executive committee on January 26 was dominated by a debate between Mendès and René Mayer. Mayer accused Mendès of playing politics in the Soustelle appointment—a type of action that Mendès had condemned in others. If he was trying to consolidate a new and stabler majority, this was a maneuver in which no other premier had succeeded. Some of his opponents began to say that the time was "now or never" for his overthrow.

The *coup de grâce*[43] was given by Mayer himself on a resolution on North Africa on February 2 (no. 2821). Speaking for the Algerian Radicals, Mayer accused Mendès of setting no limits to France's concessions. The opposition converted the issue from a specific one on North Africa to a general one; the MRP, and other EDC supporters, felt more justified in opposing Mendès on his general policies than on the narrower issue of North African policy. In comparison with no. 2716, sixteen Radicals and ten ex-Gaullists swung into opposition, contributing the largest new blocs of hostile votes. Mendès was brought down by an absolute majority on a vote of confidence (permitting Faure to dissolve the Assembly in December). After the vote, rather than walking out with the cabinet, he went to the rostrum to deliver a summing-up speech—but was shouted down.[44]

A series of potential premiers were then called by Coty to survey the situation: Pinay (RI), Pflimlin (MRP), Pineau (SFIO, who failed of investiture on no. 2822; see Fig. 5.7), and then Mendès' Radical colleague and Minister of Finance Edgar Faure. Fauvet wrote: "One is more aware that [Mendès'] fall was knowingly provoked because five ministerial combinations had been in preparation for several weeks in the corridors."[45]

Late in Mendès' ministry, the constitutional revision bill had been enacted.[46] One provision went into effect with the Pineau investiture vote: premier and cabinet now stood for investiture only once, together. The "double investiture" was eliminated.

Pineau, opposed by the Communists, Moderates, and Gaullists, received only 268 votes (no. 2822). The Assembly, "tired" of the crisis, then invested Faure by a large majority (no. 2823), only the Communists and Socialists opposing. Faure had shown remarkable powers of survival: from the Laniel cabinet, through Mendès', now to form his own—this in spite of the great antagonisms between Mendès and the "old team" of *ministrables,* some of whom Faure brought back. There was speculation that President Coty had planned the evolution of the post-Mendès crisis in this way, so as to blunt Mendès' propaganda thrusts as he prepared for the next election.[47]

Among Faure's first major actions were the completion of two of Mendès'

Figure 5.7 The Second Faure Cabinet and Its Support*

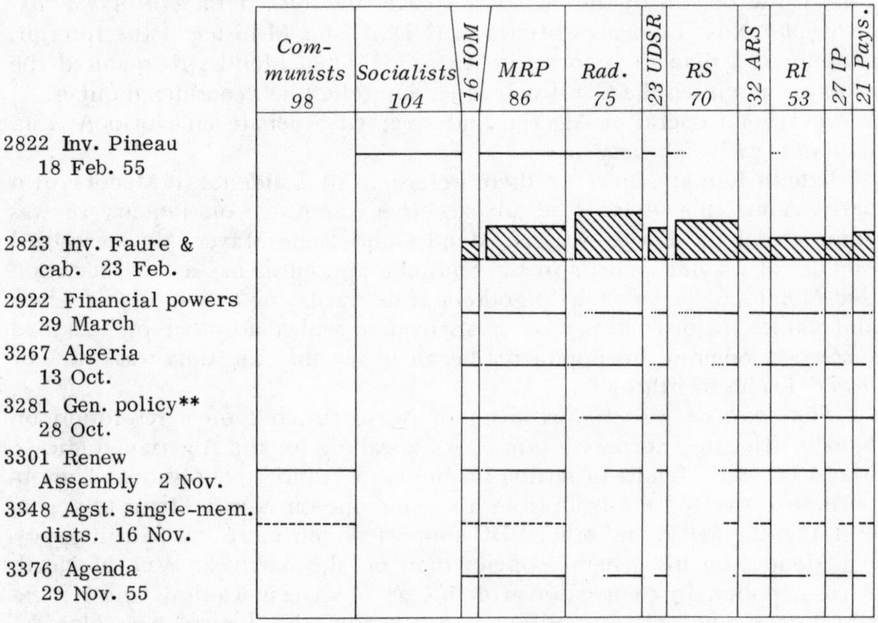

	Communists 98	Socialists 104	16 IOM	MRP 86	Rad. 75	23 UDSR	RS 70	32 ARS	RI 53	27 IP	21 Pays.
2822 Inv. Pineau 18 Feb. 55											
2823 Inv. Faure & cab. 23 Feb.											
2922 Financial powers 29 March											
3267 Algeria 13 Oct.											
3281 Gen. policy** 28 Oct.											
3301 Renew Assembly 2 Nov.											
3348 Agst. single-mem. dists. 16 Nov.											
3376 Agenda 29 Nov. 55											

*Identification of dissident wings as "left" or "right" is unusually difficult because of the multiple issues involved (domestic, colonial, electoral law), and the peculiarities of Gaullist ideology. Opposition wings of RS and ARS are classified as "left," but their basis of opposition was advocacy of firmness in North Africa.

**From this point on, all confidence votes are personal. In the graphs we shall allocate nonvoters in each party in the same proportions as those who voted. In the rare case when the majority of the group does not vote, this will be treated as abstention by the nonvoters.

programs: ratification in late March of the Paris Agreements by the Council of the Republic and conclusion of the Tunisian agreements. Though continuing some of Mendès' policies, Faure preferred a subtle and conciliatory approach. Also late in March, Faure asked for special financial powers. Among them were powers to check on tax payments, to which the Poujadists in the Assembly's galleries objected vociferously. On these special powers, the Radicals split (no. 2922); the dissidents appeared to intend continuing opposition to Faure. An emergency law for Algeria was passed. Soustelle, continuing as Governor General under Faure, was committed to the "integration" policy, intended to give Muslims more rights while insuring that

Algeria would remain French; at the same time he was coming to oppose the FLN more strongly.

The cantonal elections in April showed a swing to the left and large losses for the ex-Gaullists. Mendès meanwhile was gaining support from the "new left" and planning the reorganization of the Radical party. The Radical congress in May abolished the office held by Léon Martinaud-Déplat, administrative secretary of the party and an opponent of Mendès, and created a new administrative structure. Mendès became first vice-president, second only to Herriot and effectively head of the party.

In June Faure took steps toward a more liberal policy in Morocco. He first nominated as Resident the Gaullist Gilbert Grandval, who met strong opposition from the French in Morocco. Then in a series of conferences he arranged for the creation of a "Throne Council" that would permit the removal of Moulay ben Arafa, the puppet Sultan installed under Laniel.

On August 21 a series of massacres occurred in Algeria and Morocco. Both the settlers and the nationalist segments of the Assembly began to accuse Faure of weakness. Faure supported Soustelle in Algeria and derived support from his firmness there; but his continued negotiations over Morocco earned him distrust among ex-Gaullists and Moderates. Early in October three of his Gaullist ministers resigned because of their party's increasing opposition to the cabinet.

On October 13 Faure lost a vote on a resolution dealing with Algeria (no. 3267): most of the ex-Gaullists joined the Communists and Socialists in opposition. But by putting the question of confidence, Faure was able to reverse this result. Later in October he was again forced to put the question of confidence on a resolution on his general policy (no. 3281), in order to reverse an unfavorable vote.[48] By this time, the cabinet's policy included not only North African policies, but also a proposal to hold general elections in December 1955. By taking this position, Faure prolonged his ministry, as some deputies were afraid to vote against an early election. This latter proposal was attacked by Mendès in *L'Express:* he wanted both a return to the *scrutin d'arrondissement* and time to organize his electoral campaign.

On October 31 Faure put the question of confidence on holding elections for the new National Assembly without any change in the electoral law (no. 3301). He won handily (with Communist support), but the Mendesist opposition now claimed half the Radical party, as Faure had spurned their cherished *scrutin d'arrondissement.*[49] Faure's transfer of emphasis from North African policy to domestic political problems was made on the ostensible grounds that a new Assembly voting on issues such as those of North Africa would permit their clearer resolution; this hope was to prove as ill-founded as similar hopes had been in 1951. But the change of issues also helped Faure to forestall Mendès' campaign, as well as to stay in office a little longer.[50]

On November 14 the Assembly voted to consider the *scrutin d'arrondissement,* with Gaullist support (no. 3348). The cabinet was divided and took no official stand. But although Mendès' supporters might have been encouraged by the result, the Gaullists wanted only to embarrass Faure, whose

Moroccan policy they disapproved, and as a new party were not genuine adherents of the single-member district.

Faure pushed ahead with his proposals for early elections under a slightly modified electoral law. But the Assembly's agenda committee had set an agenda giving priority to interpellations on general policy. Faure then put the question of confidence on giving priority to his own agenda, and was defeated by 218 to 318, an absolute majority, on no. 3376. Only the Moderates, the MRP, and half the Radicals supported him at his fall. Coming within ten months after Mendès' fall, this vote allowed the premier to dissolve the Assembly. It was a surprise to the Assembly, both because the absolute majority was difficult to obtain on a personal vote, and because the personal vote had made the usual advance calculations and proxy manipulations more difficult. Faure decided on dissolution, and the electoral campaign was on.

Mendès immediately moved to exclude Faure from the Radical party. Faure and a group around him took refuge in the RGR, a loose federation of small parties with the Radicals, in which his friends happened to control a majority of the Radical party's delegates, Under Mendès, the party claimed the right to replace them by new delegates; Faure's group refusing, the Radicals excluded them all.[51]

Patterns of Cabinet Coalition

The Second Legislature, whose party composition initially seemed to allow less room for parliamentary maneuver than the First, was transformed by the Pinay investiture. The two preceding cabinets, Pleven's and Faure's, had marshaled and lost supporting majorities on issues continued from the First Legislature: domestic social and economic questions, on which Socialists and Moderates inevitably parted. Even at this stage, there were new elements in the game: some of the Radicals took a more active part in Faure's overthrow, and his cabinet could clearly be brought down while the Socialists still supported it. For in the Second Legislature the Socialists, MRP, and RGR together had almost twenty votes fewer than in the First— enough to make the difference between Bidault's early successes against attacks from the Right and Faure's failure in 1952.

An additional feature that distinguished the Pleven and Faure cabinets of 1951–52 from their predecessors in the First Legislature was the vigor with which the church-school issue was pressed. Previously it had been pushed by doctrinaire Socialists; now the RPF, backing the association of deputies who favored the church-schools, consciously strove to separate Socialists from MRP.

But the Pinay investiture, dependent as it was on miscalculation, changed the picture completely. The very availability of 27 RPF votes for his investiture enlarged the range of combinations; and the succeeding splits in the RPF went still further, both involving their factions more in cabinet coalitions and weakening de Gaulle's hold on them.

The "typical" coalition of the latter part of the Second Legislature was represented by the cabinets of Mayer, Laniel, and Faure (1955). All their cabinets were opposed by the Socialists while supported initially by the Gaullists. In the overthrow of these generally rightist coalitions, segments of the Gaullists always played an important part. The parties or factions actually charged with the cabinets' fall were not always the same, but Gaullism, later allied in the opposition with Mendesism, was a key element in the defection.

The most "atypical" coalition was of course that supporting Mendès.[52] His combination of Socialists, Radicals, and Gaullists depended on temporary and personal factors; and it was the only cabinet coalition of the first two Legislatures that did not include the MRP. Some have attributed its disintegration to Mendès' activism; but another view is that Mendès was invested to liquidate the Indochinese and German problems, and that he would not have been invested at all except for these emergencies.

In spite of the similarity among various coalitions in the Second Legislature, there was considerable diversity in the parties or factions bringing the cabinets down. Pleven and Faure (1952), fighting the parliamentary battle along the lines of the First Legislature, were felled by left and right respectively; in Faure's fall, his Radical colleagues also played a part. Pinay, moving the pendulum considerably to the right, was ostensibly brought down by the MRP, now on the left wing of his coalition. In the downfall of Mayer, Laniel, and Faure (1955), the Gaullists were important; but the Mendesist opposition led in Laniel's overthrow as well as in Faure's. The leader in Mendès' downfall was his party colleague René Mayer; thus the Radicals, though not known as a party of extremes, had generated internal hostilities and vetoes that added to the previous ideological incompatibilities in cabinet coalitions.

The Socialists were never ministers in the Second Legislature; but when they supported cabinets (Pleven, Faure in 1952, and Mendès), they did so without defecting. Perhaps their period in opposition from 1952 to 1954 made this position stabler under Mendès-France.

After the Pinay investiture, it was no longer necessary for Socialists and Moderates both to join in the majority supporting the cabinet; the Socialists were in opposition except for Mendès' ministry, and then a majority of the Moderates were normally in opposition. Thus although the short life of the Pleven and Faure cabinets can be explained in terms we have used for the First Legislature, the succeeding five cabinets cannot. Why, then, were their lives equally short?

The major factor in cabinet instability in the latter part of the Second Legislature was the behavior of the Gaullists. They were intensely concerned, as was de Gaulle, with France's position in the world, and with retaining the means to assert this position. Thus their nationalism on the issue of "Europe" and the EDC—diametrically opposed to the MRP's position—created an internal contradiction in the Mayer and Laniel cabinets at least as great as that between Socialists and Moderates on domestic issues. Moreover, the Gaullists were insistent on a firm and clear position in Morocco, and defected from Faure on this issue in 1955. Paradoxically, the Gaullists entered the parliamentary game at a time when the newly dominant issues set them apart from their majority allies.[53] Perhaps if they had entered sooner they would have compromised more easily on domestic issues; but on international issues they left the cabinets as fragile as before.[54]

The overthrow of Mendès remains to be explained, as it was due neither to domestic left-right controversies nor to Gaullist defection. Certainly he had made enemies—from the "Europeans" to the home distillers to the advocates of proportional representation to the Algerian settlers. The increasing opposition to him had not been a partisan matter; he divided all the parties except the Communists and (in their votes) the Socialists. The outstanding feature of this opposition seems to have been personal antagonism and distrust: a dislike for his style, a feeling of distance from him and his friends on the part of many party leaders and *ministrables,* and thus an uncertainty about his future actions.[55] This combination of attitudes resulted both from his disregard for the established channels and customs of the Assembly, and from his conception of a premiership less dependent on the continual supervision of the Assembly and the parties. These attitudes were to contribute greatly to his later failures as well.

The Right

The rightist parties in the Second Legislature were as follows: *Indépendants* (53–55 deputies); *Paysans* (two groups, 43–50); *Rassemblement du Peuple Français* (RPF: 121), and its subsequent fractions, *Union des Républicains d'Action Sociale* (URAS: 79) and *Action Républicaine et Sociale* (ARS: 34). Because of the difficulty of scaling all these groups together, we shall first exclude the Gaullists and examine the remaining deputies, and then return to consider the Gaullists.

The non-RPF rightist deputies, whom we shall refer to as "Moderates" to distinguish them from the more inclusive category of the "right," were divided in a more complex fashion than in the First. A swing to the right in public sentiment had augmented the number of rightist deputies in the Assembly, partly at the expense of the MRP. The Moderates had fought the election in an alliance of "Independents, Peasants, and National Republicans," which foretold a slightly greater cohesion of their deputies' votes. They later divided into an Independent group and two Peasant groups, but like the RI and PRL they can be scaled together. Seven clusters of roll calls were found in the Q-matrix, as shown in Table 5.1.

The scale structure of the Moderates in the Second Legislature is strikingly different from that in the First. Instead of one dominant thirty-three-item scale cluster, none of the clusters found contains more than eight roll calls. Moreover, the clusters are relatively specific to particular cabinets; Scales II-1, II-3, and II-5 to that of Mendès-France, Scale II-2 to the pre-Mendès period (especially Pleven), Scales II-6 and II-7 to Faure's 1955 cabinet.

These scales divided the Moderates in several distinct ways, as closer inspection of their associations (γ) reveals. In the first place, three of the scales including roll calls under Mendès-France are closely associated with one another: Scales II-1, II-4, and II-5. Scale II-4 consists mainly of roll calls under Faure, but apparently the colonial issue carried over from Mendès' ministry, and the same Moderates who distrusted Mendès' economic policies tended also to oppose Faure's Moroccan policy. Secondly, the two scales dealing with the electoral law, II-6 and II-7, are closely associated and quite distinct from all others. Free from their electoral struggle with the Gaullists, the Moderates apparently now divided on this issue in a way related to specific constituency problems. Thirdly, the division of these parties on German rearmament, Scale II-3, is relatively independent of the other scales and even of the others under Mendès-France. This issue is distinct from others for all the parties studied.

Finally, Scale II-2 ("Europe") is also relatively distinct from the others. Five of the eight roll calls in this scale deal with European union, but the other three concern domestic and North African policy. These roll calls split off a segment ranging from 25 to 40 per cent of the Moderates, who opposed the first three cabinets of the Legislature. This opposition seems to have been centered on European union, but to have been generalized to other issues through the fate of the cabinets.[56] The opposing group tended largely to come from the Peasant parties. Interestingly, the highest association of Scale II-2 is with Scale II-4, when the second Faure cabinet had restored the old coalition.

The notions of "left" and "right" begin to break down on the EDC issue. Among the conservatives, it was generally the left wing—those nearer the center of the Assembly on domestic issues—who were more favorable toward European union. The extreme right was both more nationalistic and, in its peasant base, more distrustful of the international urban culture that Paris represented.[57] The "extreme right" (actually a mixture of traditional conservatives, nationalists, and peasants alienated from Paris) opposed European union and the position of big business on ideological grounds (including nationalism) as well as in the defense of particular agricultural interests.

The ambiguity of the notion of "extreme right" is suggested by the relative positions of the Antier and Laurens factions of the Peasant group. The Antier faction, having separated from the other group on the occasion of Antier's pro-Gaullism while a member of the Pleven cabinet in 1951, actually represented a distinct social base. On EDC it was more nationalist, especially on the crucial Aumeran-Herriot motion that killed EDC. Later Antier joined forces with Poujade (1957). These positions are symptomatic of the affinity between the Antier group and the most rural peasants—those who most thoroughly distrusted Paris, large industry, and internationalism.[58] In contrast, the Camille Laurens faction of the Peasants divided in almost the same proportions as the Independents on the Aumeran-Herriot motion.

Though we have argued that specificity of scales to cabinets is often evidence that the party in question was playing a "parliamentary game" in making alliances with the cabinet, this notion does not apply exactly to the Mendès-France cabinet. It was not Mendès' coalition who played this game, but those who opposed him. The specificity of the scales thus seems to result from a combination of the issues posed by Mendès and the antagonism generated toward him on the part of the previously leading "players," because he tried to change the rules.

The "Mendès-colonial" scale for the Moderates is not restricted to

Table 5.1 Moderates, Second Legislature:
Roll Calls in Scales

Roll Call	Premier	Polarity +	−	p+	Subject	II-1	II-2	II-3	II-4	II-5	II-6	II-7
Scale II-1 (Mendès-Colonial)							.30	.68	.66	.62	.05	.02
2597	Mendès-F.	c	pan	69	**Tunisia and Morocco, postpone interpellations							
2617	Mendès-F.	c	pan	70	Tunisia and Morocco, Aubry et al. resolution							
2618	Mendès-F.	c	pan	78	French interests in India, Aubry resolution							
2634	Mendès-F.	can	p	74	*Budget, postal and telegraph							
2646	Mendès-F.	c	pan	73	Algeria, postpone interpellations							
2697	Mendès-F.	c	pan	74	Leaks, interpellations, Loustaunau-L. resolution							
2716	Mendès-F.	c	pan	66	North Africa, Mailhe resolution							
2743	Mendès-F.	c	pan	43	*Associated states, budget							
Scale II-2 (Europe)						.30		.37	.55	−.02	.39	−.06
463	Pleven	ca	p	26	*Schuman plan, André et al. motion, recommit							
473	Pleven	can	p	25	*Schuman plan, art. 1							
474	Pleven	ca	p	22	*Schuman plan, entirety							
661	Pleven	can	p	36	*Budget, 1952, balance: cabinet bill							
671	Pleven	ca	p	30	*Budget, 1952 balance, amends. (fall of Pleven)							
709	Faure$_1$	can	p	40	European Army, Beaumont et al. resolution, priority							
712	Faure$_1$	can	p	35	*European Army, Beaumont et al. resolution							
989	Pinay	p	cn	38	Tunisia, RPF resolution							
Scale II-3 (Mendès-Germany)						.68	.37		.29	.22	.13	.23
2622	Mendès-F.	can	p	47	*Foreign policy and London agreements, Aubry resolution							
2745	Mendès-F.	c	pan	25	Paris Agreements, art. 1 of first bill (Germany and Italy in Brussels Pact)							
2750	Mendès-F.	c	pa	19	*Paris Agreements, arts. 2 and 3 of first bill (Germany in NATO)							
2752	Mendès-F.	c	pa	19	*(Same as 2750)							
2762	Mendès-F.	c	pa	18	*Paris Agreements, entirety							
2821	Mendès-F.	c	pan	81	North Africa, Mailhe resolution (fall of Mendès)							
Scale II-4 (Mendès-Faure)						.66	.55	.29		.47	.17	−.12
2611	Mendès-F.	c	pn	60	Special financial powers, second reading							
3262	Faure$_2$	ca	p	45	Morocco, Depreux resolution (Aix-les-Bains agreements)							
3263	Faure$_2$	c	pa	48	Morocco, Depreux resolution (no additions)							
3264	Faure$_2$	c	pa	43	Morocco, Depreux resolution, entirety							

Table 5.1 (continued)

Roll Call	Premier	Polarity +	Polarity −	p_+	Subject	Association (γ) with Other Scales II-1	II-2	II-3	II-4	II-5	II-6	II-7
Scale II-5 (Early Mendès)						.62	−.02	.22	.47		.22	.24
2529	Mendès-F.	c	pan	28	Investiture							
2530	Mendès-F.	can	p	64	Cabinet interpellations, postpone							
2570	Mendès-F.	can	p	42	Indochina, Geneva agreements, Delbos resolution							
2571	Mendès-F.	can	p	44	Indochina, Delbos-Valabrègue resolution							
Scale II-6 (Single-Member Districts)						.05	.39	.13	.17	.22		.67
3292	Faure₂	c	pan	56	Single-member districts, Caillavet							
3325	Faure₂	can	p	53	Single-member districts, Naegelen							
3348	Faure₂	c	pan	55	Single-member districts, Devinat and Bénard							
3355	Faure₂	p	c	51	Electoral law, suspend debate until redistricting							
Scale II-7 (Electoral Law)						.02	−.06	.23	−.12	.24	.67	
3326	Faure₂	p	c	74	Electoral law, departmental ballot (Barrachin)							
3327	Faure₂	p	can	78	Electoral law, second Hugues bill							
3328	Faure₂	p	can	82	Electoral law, Bergasse bill							
3330	Faure₂	pan	c	58	*Electoral law, against all counter-bills							

colonial issues; it contains also a vote on the postal and telegraph budget and one on the defense information "leaks." These relations suggest that the colonial issue loomed large in the Moderate deputies' views of his cabinet, and that the suspicions which some on the right entertained of Mendès ("abandon," "playing the game of the Communists") did much to assimilate other domestic left-right issues to the colonial issues, as well as to undermine Mendès' position.

We may see the degree of specificity of the Moderates' scales to particular cabinets, and their independence of the issues involved, by tabulating the roll calls in them by cabinet and subject. For subject classification we shall use six major categories:

1. *Cabinet* votes. These are votes dealing directly with the fate of the cabinet as such, and not with any single substantive issue. They include investitures, votes on interpellations on cabinet composition, censure motions, and resolutions dealing with the cabinet's general policies.

2. *Domestic left-right* issues. These include taxation, currency, and budgetary measures, social services and welfare-state questions, civil liberties, the issue of government corruption, and proposals for special government powers for domestic reasons.

3. *Electoral laws.* Though domestic in application, the controversies of 1951 and 1955 about electoral-law revision produced quite distinct scales in several of the parties.

4. *European union.* This category includes proposals such as the Schuman Plan, EDC, Euratom, and the Common Market.

5. *Foreign affairs* (other). Most of the bills in this category concerned Germany (the Ruhr, the Saar, the Bonn republic, German rearmament), the Marshall Plan, NATO, or Suez.

6. *Colonial and Algeria.* These include measures dealing with Indochina, Morocco, Tunisia, and Algeria.

The distribution of the roll calls in the scale clusters among these categories is shown in Table 5.2. Each entry gives the scale cluster number, followed by the roll-call number. The chronological sequence is from top to bottom of the table, and the corresponding ministries are indicated in the left-hand column. The concentration of scales in particular ministries can again be seen, but now one scale can be compared with another more easily. Thus it can be seen that Scale II-2 is concentrated in the period from Pleven to Pinay, but no other scale contains roll calls in that period. Scale 2 combined domestic and "European" issues, with the domestic left wing also favoring European union. Also included was a single roll call on Tunisia under Pinay; this is noteworthy both for its inclusion in the same scale, and for the fact that subsequent votes on North Africa fell in different scales, restricted to the Mendès-France and Faure cabinets. There is reason to believe that the Moderates' votes on this roll call, ostensibly on Tunisia, were actually dominated by considerations of the more general foreign policies of Robert Schuman, the Foreign Minister.[59]

The remaining scales were concentrated in either the Mendès-France or the Faure (1955) ministry, with the exception of Scale II-4. Three of these dealt with specific subjects: Scale II-3 with German rearmament, and Scales II-6 and II-7 with the electoral law. Scales II-1 and II-5 were concentrated in two distinct periods of the Mendès-France ministry. Each combined roll calls on colonial and domestic affairs: Scale II-5 included Indochina and the installation of the cabinet, while Scale II-1 included votes on North Africa and on domestic affairs. The vote on which Mendès fell (no. 2821) was placed in Scale II-3, though it nearly entered Scale II-1. We infer that colonial affairs largely dominated the Moderates' votes under Mendès, and that other matters (including his investiture) were dominated by these questions in the eyes of the right.[60]

Scale II-4 included three items dealing with Faure's Moroccan policy. It aligned the Moderates in a way somewhat similar to the "Mendès-colonial" scale, but not identical with it ($\gamma = .66$). Thus two successive cabinets had similar salient issues and similar positions on them, yet drew support from somewhat different quarters among the Moderates. This sort of specificity of scales to cabinets, which is not obviously attributable to alteration of the substance of the issue, may well relate to the "game of politics," to coalitions, or to the connection between coalitions of support and cabinet portfolios. Between Mendès and Faure there was a sharp personal antagonism,

Table 5.2 Moderates, Second Legislature:
Scales by Subject Matter

Premier	Cabinet	Domestic Left-Right	Electoral laws	European union	Foreign (other)	Colonial, Algeria
Pleven				2-463*		
				2-473*		
				2-474*		
		2-661*				
		2-671* (fall)				
Faure₁				2-709		
				2-712*		
Pinay						2-989
Mendès-France	5-2529					5-2570
	5-2530					5-2571
						1-2597**
		4-2611				1-2617
						1-2618
					3-2622	
		1-2634*				1-2646
		1-2697				1-2716
						1-2743*
					3-2745	
					3-2750*	
					3-2752*	
					3-2762*	3-2821* (fall)
Faure₂						4-3262
						4-3263
						4-3264
			6-3292			
			6-3325			
			7-3326			
			7-3327			
			7-3328			
			7-3330			
			6-3348			
			6-3355			

*Question of confidence.
**Unofficial question of confidence.

Table 5.3 URAS, Second Legislature:
Roll Calls in Scales

Roll Call	Premier	Polarity +	Polarity -	p_+	Subject	Association (γ) with Other Scales					
						II-1	II-2	II-3	II-4	II-5	II-6
Scale II-1 (Economic)							−.03	.33	.89	.52	.08
886	Pinay	p	an	25	*Budget, art. 45 (tax frauds)						
887	Pinay	p	an	27	*Budget, art. 46 (sales without invoices)						
888	Pinay	p	an	21	*Budget, art. 47 (no state orders for condemned persons)						
889	Pinay	p	can	18	*Budget, art. 48 (filling out invoices)						
894	Pinay	p	can	10	*Budget, Denais-Paquet amendment (tax amnesty)						
895	Pinay	p	ca	18	*Budget, entirety						
922	Pinay	p	ca	18	*Budget, entirety (second reading)						
927	Pinay	c	a	14	**Loan bill, Finance Committee report						
931	Pinay	p	a	14	**Pinay loan bill						
1807	Laniel	p	ca	80	Investiture						
1844	Laniel	p	ca	65	Financial reform, special powers						
1851	Laniel	p	cn	60	Financial reform, entirety						
1867	Laniel	p	ca	58	Financial reform, second reading						
1943	Laniel	ca	p	89	Socialist resolution, social situation						
1962	Laniel	p	ca	84	Interpellations on agric. policy, resolution						
Scale II-2 (Mendès-Colonial)						−.03		.37	−.01	−.31	.44
2570	Mendès-F.	p	can	82	Indochina (Geneva agreements), Delbos resolution						
2571	Mendès-F.	p	can	83	Indochina, Delbos-Valabrègue resolution						
2596	Mendès-F.	p	can	73	*Special financial powers						
2597	Mendès-F.	p	can	59	**Tunisia and Morocco, postpone interpellations						
2611	Mendès-F.	p	can	68	Special financial powers (second reading)						
2617	Mendès-F.	p	can	65	Aubry et al. resolution, Tunisia and Morocco						
2743	Mendès-F.	p	can	79	*Associated states, budget						
3262	Faure₂	pn	c	14	Morocco, Depreux resolution (Aix-les-Bains agreements)						
Scale II-3 (Germany)						.33	.37		.26	.34	.66
2057	Laniel	pan	c	90	*Garet resolution, foreign policy						
2744	Mendès-F.	c	pan	57	Paris Agreements, Badie m. pr. (Saar)						
2745	Mendès-F.	p	can	44	Paris Agreements, art. 1 of first bill (Germany and Italy in Brussels pact)						
2748	Mendès-F.	p	can	44	Paris Agreements, second bill (rights of German Federal Republic)						
2752	Mendès-F.	p	can	50	*Paris Agreements, arts. 2 and 3 of first bill (German entry into NATO)						
2762	Mendès-F.	p	can	49	*Paris Agreements, entirety						
3264	Faure₂	pan	c	19	Morocco, Depreux resolution, entirety						

Table 5.3 (continued)

Roll Call	Premier	Polarity + −	p_+	Subject	Association (γ) with Other Scales II−1	II−2	II−3	II−4	II−5	II−6
Scale II−4 (Economic)					.89	−.01	.26		.64	−.24
838	Pinay	p can	56	** Budget, art. 6 (economies)						
841	Pinay	c pan	60	** Budget, Triboulet amend. (cut aid for merchant marine)						
843	Pinay	c an	59	** Budget, art. 6, Goudoux amendment						
852	Pinay	p an	55	Budget, art. 6 (economies)						
1812	Laniel	p can	75	Postpone cabinet interpellations						
2263	Laniel	c pan	83	Salary scale, Socialist resolution, priority						
Scale II−5 (Disaffection from Laniel)					.52	−.31	.34	.64		.16
2255	Laniel	p ca	71	Postpone interpellations ("re-investiture")						
2414	Laniel	p can	46	* Indochina, postpone interpellations						
2453	Laniel	pa c	37	* Indochina, postpone interpellations						
2521	Laniel	pan c	19	Indochina, Raingeard resolution, priority						
2528	Laniel	pan c	32	* Indochina resolution (fall of Laniel)						
Scale II−6 (Faure-Colonial)					.08	.44	.66	−.24	.16	
3162	Faure$_2$	p ca	75	French-Tunisian agreements						
3263	Faure$_2$	pan c	13	Morocco, Depreux resolution (no additions)						
3267	Faure$_2$	pan c	23	Algeria, Gaborit resolution						
3270	Faure$_2$	pn c	18	Algeria, Chevallier resolution						

a contrast in political styles, and a battle between "ins" and "outs." These additional considerations produced new cleavages and realignments in several parties during 1955.

The Gaullist deputies, placed on the extreme right of the Assembly's semicircle after the 1951 elections, first voted with high cohesion against all cabinets. But after the defection of the ARS and the withdrawal of de Gaulle from politics, the ex-Gaullists regained some freedom in their votes —enough to reveal more clearly their relative· positions on issues. These positions were by no means completely "rightist." The URAS supported the "leftist" Mendès-France while the ARS and other rightist parties opposed him; and its deputies also opposed the cabinets of Laniel and of Faure in 1955, while the traditional rightist parties supported them. The particular ideological position of the ex-Gaullists will emerge more clearly from a study of their votes.

The deputies of the URAS came to it largely from political obscurity, and returned to this obscurity at the 1956 election.[61] A few of them, however, had come from parties other than those of the right (Radicals, MRP, UDSR); and these ex-Gaullists, like their freshmen colleagues in the URAS, voted considerably more to the "left" than did the deputies of the other rightist parties. The ARS, on the other hand, contained a high proportion

of ex-conservatives who had been in the rightist parties of the First Legislature, voted on the right wing of these parties, and moved temporarily into
the RPF. These conservative deputies had longer careers before the Second
Legislature, and survived in greater proportions into the Third.

The terms "left" and "right" are at best an approximation to complex
organizations of positions on political issues; and for the Gaullists this approximation is less adequate than for the other parties. In order to examine
the Gaullists' positions on issues, we shall therefore consider a set of scales
constructed for the URAS alone. These scales have the value of extending
back to the Pinay ministry, in which period the ARS could not be scaled,
as they were still undivided in their votes. By considering the URAS alone,
we shall be able to compare the structure of these Gaullists' votes with that
of the conservatives on the earlier issues of the Second Legislature.

Six scales were found for the URAS; the roll calls comprising them are
shown in Table 5.3. Scales II-1 and II-4, both dealing with economic issues,
were closely associated ($\gamma = .89$). These scales defined the major domestic
division of the URAS, centering about support or opposition to the Pinay
and Laniel cabinets. The more loyal Gaullists and the leadership opposed
these cabinets and voted on the left,[62] while another wing of the party, more
sympathetic with the Moderates and the ARS, supported these cabinets.
Associated with these two scales, but somewhat less closely, was Scale II-5,
dealing with the Indochina issue under Laniel; while this scale still dealt
with support for a Moderate premier, the issue was colonial rather than
domestic.

Associated with all three of the scales mentioned (II-1, 4, 5) at a lower
level ($\gamma = .33, .26, .34$) was Scale II-3, dealing mainly with the Paris Agreements for German rearmament. On this scale the domestic conservatives
favored German rearmament, while the domestic left opposed. This polarity
is the *opposite* of that for the Moderates, whose right wing opposed German
rearmament. This difference between the Gaullists and the Moderates
reveals the particular Gaullist ideology which made it impossible to place
Gaullism on any single "left-right" continuum.

In its opposition to the regime, the Gaullist movement was classified
as on the right. Its opposition to rightist premiers, however, would seem
to have placed it somewhere in the center of the political spectrum on
domestic issues. In foreign and colonial policy, the Gaullists (like their
leader) were nearly impossible to place in simple left-right terms. They had
opposed the supranational EDC, some using arguments that came close
to the Communists'.[63] The same general alignment persisted in the URAS
leaders' opposition to the Paris Agreements. They took a principled position
on this issue, turning against Mendès-France whom they had supported previously.

Scales II-3 and II-6 also form a loose cluster ($\gamma = .66$) that is relatively
independent of the first three. Those URAS deputies who opposed German
rearmament also tended to oppose Faure's colonial policies. This combination of positions was shared only by the leftist parties in the Assembly.

The divisions in the URAS thus seem to have been largely ideological.
It is true that their attitudes toward the Pinay and Laniel cabinets showed
divisions that did not appear later; but even under Laniel, domestic and

colonial issues fell into different scales. The German issue, too, combined roll calls under Laniel and Mendès-France. But most important was the peculiar combination of nationalism and leftism which characterized the leadership faction of the URAS and set them apart from other groupings on the "right."

If the URAS did show divisions that were specific to a particular cabinet, they occurred in the early part of the Mendès-France ministry. The "Mendès-Colonial" scale (II-2) actually included two roll calls on domestic financial powers. It also had relatively low association with other scales. Those Gaullists who supported Mendès at this time backed his policies both at home and abroad, perhaps because of his activism and decisiveness, akin to de Gaulle's own desire to break with the habits of the "system."

The Radicals and UDSR

Seven scale clusters were found for the Radicals and UDSR[64] in the Second Legislature; the roll calls in them are shown in Table 5.4. Two of the scales each dealt clearly with a single issue: Scale II-1 with the school question, and II-3 with the Paris Agreements. At the other extreme, Scale II-7 included four roll calls each reflecting the bitter antagonism between the factions supporting Mendès-France and Faure in the party: Mendès' fall, Faure's 1955 investiture, and two votes affecting the next electoral campaign as the Second Legislature neared its unexpected end.

Scales II-2, 4, 5, and 6, which were fairly closely associated, reflected a general left-right division within the party. On Scale II-5 this was restricted to domestic economic matters, but Scales II-2 and II-4 showed that European and colonial issues were also related to them in the Radicals' divisions. The right wing, which supported the cabinets other than Mendès-France's, supported the European Army and the colonial holding action under Laniel, as well as conservative domestic policies. But primarily, these scales seemed to reflect the support given by a segment among the Radicals to the typical cabinet coalitions of the Second Legislature. Just as the Moderates in the First Legislature had to choose between the "system" and Gaullism, the Radicals in the Second chose between the typical cabinet coalition and protests against it.

But the protests in the Second Legislature came from within the Radical party itself, and split it deeply. They took somewhat different forms at different times. Protests against EDC by the left wing of the party found their place in Scale II-2. Perhaps the earliest vote reflecting this type of protest was Mendès-France's unsuccessful investiture in 1953, which appears in Scale II-6. His opposition to Laniel on Indochina is reflected in the Radicals' divisions in Scale II-4; and the final, most bitter antagonism between the groups around Mendès and Faure is expressed in Scale II-7. All four of these scales show moderate associations with one another.

On the question of EDC, it was the left wing of the Radicals who opposed German rearmament, and the right who favored it. Though Mendès-France was officially neutral, the crucial vote saw Mendès' normal supporters voting in opposition to EDC. This alignment on German rearmament was more like that within the Socialist party, or in the URAS, than like that in

Table 5.4 Radicals and UDSR, Second Legislature:
Roll Calls in Scales

Roll Call	Premier	Polarity +	Polarity -	p_+	Subject	II-1	II-2	II-3	II-4	II-5	II-6	II-7
						Association (γ) with Other Scales						

Scale II-1 (School Aid) — .14 .34 .52 .30 .42 .30

183	Pleven	pn	c	33	School aid: Barangé bill, art. 1, entirety
198	Pleven	pa	c	22	School aid: Barangé bill, art. 2, entirety
213	Pleven	pn	c	36	School aid: Barangé bill, entirety
259	Pleven	pa	c	37	School aid: Barangé bill, entirety (second reading)
1174	Pinay	p	cn	40	Scholarships for private high schools
1379	Pinay	cn	p	33	School aid increase, art. 32, separate consideration
1401	Pinay	p	can	25	School aid, new art. 72
2785	Mendès-F.	can	p	37	School aid, extend Barangé law; Lempereur q. pr.
2992	Faure₂	pn	c	25	Agricultural education, priority on agenda
3115	Faure₂	pan	c	20	Agricultural education, Laurens amendment
3151	Faure₂	pan	c	21	Agricultural education, entirety

Scale II-2 (European Defense Community) — .14   .46 .68 .69 .65 .56

709	Faure₁	p	cn	90	European army, Beaumont et al. resolution, priority
712	Faure₁	p	can	83	*European army, Beaumont resolution
1756	Mayer	p	an	81	**Convention with Bank of France
2044	Laniel	pan	c	56	EDC, Socialist resolution
2057	Laniel	p	can	53	*Foreign policy (EDC), Garet resolution
2305	Laniel	p	cn	63	Indochina, Sesmaisons resolution
2598	Mendès-F.	c	pan	69	Const'l revision, Badie m. pr. (EDC)
2619	Mendès-F.	can	p	56	EDC, Aumeran-Herriot q. pr.
2620	Mendès-F.	ca	p	39	Foreign policy, postpone interpellations
2843	Faure₂	c	pan	65	**Civil servants' pay; *charges communes,* separate consideration (Lamps)

Scale II-3 (Paris Agreements) — .34 .46   .43 .54 .36 .18

2744	Mendès-F.	c	pa	76	Paris Agreements, Badie m. pr. (Saar)
2745	Mendès-F.	p	can	59	Paris Agreements, art. 1 of first bill (Germany and Italy in Brussels Pact)
2748	Mendès-F.	p	can	66	Paris Agreements, second bill (rights of German Federal Republic)
2749	Mendès-F.	p	can	74	Saar agreements
2750	Mendès-F.	p	ca	58	*Paris Agreements, arts. 2 and 3 of first bill (Germany in NATO)
2752	Mendès-F.	p	can	56	*Paris Agreements (same as 2750)
2762	Mendès-F.	p	ca	58	*Paris Agreements, entirety

Table 5.4 (continued)

Roll Call	Premier	Polarity +	−	p_+	Subject	II-1	II-2	II-3	II-4	II-5	II-6	II-7
					Association (γ) with Other Scales							
Scale II-4 (Laniel-Indochina)						.52	.68	.43		.46	.54	36
210	Pleven	can	p	15	School aid: Barangé bill, separation of art. 4							
1971	Laniel	pan	c	61	Indochina, Kuehn resolution							
2414	Laniel	p	can	67	*Indochina, postpone interpellations							
2453	Laniel	pan	c	73	*Indochina, postpone interpellations							
2521	Laniel	pan	c	53	Indochina, Raingeard resolution							
2528	Laniel	p	can	44	*Indochina resolution (fall of Laniel)							
Scale II-5 (Economic)						.30	.69	.54	.46		.51	.42
1844	Laniel	p	ca	76	Financial reform, special economic powers							
1851	Laniel	p	ca	68	Financial reform, entirety							
1867	Laniel	p	can	68	Financial reform, second reading							
2882	Faure₂	c	pan	65	**Budget, Caillet m. pr.							
2922	Faure₂	p	cn	60	Special financial powers							
Scale II-6 (Investitures and Education)						.42	.65	.36	.54	.51		.58
1801	Mendès-F.	an	p	13	Investiture (failed)							
1804	Marie	p	an	87	Investiture (failed)							
2382	Laniel	c	pa	64	National education budget, Lempereur amendment							
2384	Laniel	p	ca	64	National education budget, entirety							
Scale II-7 (Mendès-Faure)						.30	.56	.18	.36	.42	.58	
2821	Mendès-F.	ca	p	34	*Mailhe resolution, N. Africa (fall of Mendès)							
2823	Faure₂	p	can	86	Investiture							
3301	Faure₂	pan	c	51	*Renew National Assembly without change							
3376	Faure₂	pan	c	50	*Against agenda (fall of Faure)							

the conservative parties. The alliance thus united the nationalist wing of the rightists and the left wing of the Radicals against EDC. The connection between the right and the "pro-Europe" position within the Radical party may have been related to the opposition between Mendès and the previous rightist cabinets of the Second Legislature; but it may also relate to the specific significance of "right center" in the French political spectrum. The "right center" represented large industrial and commercial organizations— some of them the *féodalités* against which old-time Radicals were continually on guard. This aspect of traditional Radicalism set it apart from the views of the "neo-Radicals," who were more ready to support large business.[65]

While underlying issues and factional contests can be seen in the Radicals' scales, the patterns into which these scales are organized are less clear

Table 5.5 *MRP, Second Legislature:*
Roll Calls in Scales

Roll Call	Premier	Polarity +	Polarity -	p_+	Subject	II-1	II-2	II-3	II-4	II-5	II-6
Scale II-1 (General: Leftist Bloc)							.46	.88	.65	−.10	.75
776	Pinay	p	a	88	**Cabinet interpellations, postpone						
838	Pinay	p	ca	87	**Budget, article 6						
922	Pinay	p	an	78	Budget, entirety (second reading)						
1322	Pinay	p	an	79	**Budget, against Midol m. pr.						
1693	Mayer	c	p	14	French in enemy forces, amnesty: Lipkowski amendment						
1844	Laniel	p	ca	88	Financial reform, special powers						
2305	Laniel	p	ca	85	Indochina, Sesmaisons priority o. j.						
2748	Mendès-F.	p	ca	81	Paris Agreements, rights of Bonn Rep.						
2977	Faure$_2$	p	cn	89	Algeria, emergency law						
Scale II-2 (Mendès-Colonial)						.46		.03	.42	.59	.53
1801	Mendès-F.	can	p	39	Investiture (failed)						
1971	Laniel	p	ca	84	Indochina, Kuehn o. j.						
2529	Mendès-F.	can	p	88	Investiture						
2570	Mendès-F.	c	pan	66	Indochina, Delbos o. j. (Geneva agreement)						
2571	Mendès-F.	ca	p	83	Indochina, Delbos-Valabrègue o. j.						
2597	Mendès-F.	can	p	79	**Tunisia and Morocco, postpone interpellations						
2618	Mendès-F.	ca	p	90	French interests in India, Aubry o. j.						
Scale II-3 (Germany)						.88	.03		.52	−.47	.50
1597	Mayer	p	can	89	French in enemy forces, amnesty: entirety						
1967	Laniel	c	pa	84	Indochina, SFIO o. j.						
2745	Mendès-F.	pan	c	26	Paris Agreements, Germany and Italy in Brussels pact						
2750	Mendès-F.	p	ca	18	*Paris Agreements, Germany in NATO						
2762	Mendès-F.	p	ca	16	*Paris Agreements, entirety						
Scale II-4 (Pinay)						.65	.42	.52		.16	.59
671	Pleven	p	ca	83	*Budget, amendments to balance (fall of cabinet)						
893	Pinay	p	a	16	*Budget, art. 6						
947	Pinay	pa	c	14	Salary scale, cabinet text						
1053	Pinay	p	can	52	*Salary scale, passage						
1225	Pinay	ca	p	87	Family allowances, postpone debate						

Table 5.5 (continued)

Roll Call	Premier	Polarity +	-	p_+	Subject	Association (γ) with Other Scales					
						II-1	II-2	II-3	II-4	II-5	II-6
Scale II-5 (Colonial)						−.10	.59	−.47	.16		.08
832	Pinay	p	cn	87	Tunisia interpellations, date						
2634	Mendès-F.	c	pan	83	*Budget, postal and telegraph						
2697	Mendès-F.	c	pan	43	*Affair of "leaks," interpellations, Loustaunau-Lacau						
2716	Mendès-F.	c	pan	74	North Africa, Mailhe o. j.						
2738	Mendès-F.	p	can	88	Associated States, budget, reject						
Scale II-6 (Cabinets)						.75	.53	.50	.59	.08	
895	Pinay	p	an	78	*Budget, entirety						
899	Pinay	p	an	79	**Salary scale bill, postpone						
1457	Mayer	p	ca	88	Postpone cabinet interpellations						
1800	Reynaud	p	can	43	Investiture (failed)						

These scales should not be interpreted as clearly distinct unless gamma is low; allocation of items depended on close decisions.

than for other parties. In part this complexity is due (as in the First Legislature) to the heterogeneity of the set of deputies under study, including UDSR and overseas deputies as well as traditional mainland Radicals. Thus Scale II-1 largely separates the UDSR and overseas deputies from the rest on the school issue.

We have noted above that another type of antagonism between the senior deputies of the party and the younger generation was reflected in the Radicals' votes under Faure's 1952 cabinet. The roll calls reflecting this split were few in number; the split was most clearly revealed if the UDSR were left out of account; and the division at that time was along different lines from the later ones centering about Mendès-France. But at that time, as well as later under Mendès, the major *ministrables* tended to oppose the "new men." Faure, however, learned his lesson and joined them later.

Between the First and Second Legislatures, the Radicals' alignment changed considerably; but this reorientation from one Legislature to the next can be explained in terms of the overall party configuration. While the Moderates remained to the right of the pro-cabinet majorities in both Legislatures, the Radicals found themselves on the other side of the majority in the Second. In the First Legislature, Socialists and MRP had regularly been in the cabinet; only on the church-school question did some of the Radicals outflank the cabinet on the left. In the Second Legislature, however, the Radicals were often to the left of the cabinet's majority. The Socialists were no longer participating, and a right-center coalition including the Moderates was more nearly the rule. Thus a consistent "opposition" position, or a consistent support of cabinets in general, would have led to a more complete shift by a Radical deputy relative in his party colleagues than by a Moderate.

The outstanding feature of the Radicals' divisions in the Second Legislature is that they did not realign internally on issues that realigned the other parties (EDC), but that they did show distinct internal divisions on issues that were not always distinct for the other parties (the school question, the Faure cabinet of 1955). The reason for this is that the Radicals were continually fighting their own internal battles, and assimilating the new issues of the Assembly to their own internal issues.[66]

The MRP

In the Second Legislature, the MRP was divided more deeply than in the First. By the election of June 1951, many of the conservative and Gaullist supporters of the MRP had left it, as had some of the deputies nearest to them. Yet during the Second Legislature the party's relation to right-center cabinets and to Mendès-France, as well as the problem of German rearmament, generated new divisions that were reflected in increased dissidence on roll calls. The scale clusters for the MRP in the Second Legislature are shown in Table 5.5.

While six scale clusters were found, their associations show that they fell into two fairly distinct groups. Those centering on roll calls under Mendès-France and on colonial issues (Scales II-2 and II-5) were associated fairl closely with one another ($\gamma = .59$). Their associations with the others were lower. The remaining scales (II-1, 3, 4, 6) involved roll calls from the cabinets preceding Mendès', several on German rearmament under Mendès, and one under the subsequent Faure cabinet. All of this group had associations of at least .50 with one another, while only one of the eight associations between this group and the two "Mendesist" scales exceeded .50.

The scale best reflecting the lasting divisions in the party was Scale II-4, whose roll calls were concentrated largely under the Pinay cabinet.[67]

Table 5.6 shows the relations between the MRP's scale items and the corresponding cabinets and subjects. Scales II-2 and II-5 are clearly identifiable as dealing with colonial issues. Scale II-2 includes only five votes on colonial affairs (one under Laniel) and two on Mendès' two investiture attempts. This suggests that the colonial question dominated the MRP deputies' attitudes toward Mendès-France. Even at his first investiture attempt, some MRP deputies were concerned about his position on Indochina;[68] and though he took no active part in the opposition to Laniel on Indochina on no. 1971, the division of the MRP was similar. Scale II-5 also deals primarily with colonial questions, including one such vote under Pinay and two under Mendès-France. But its items were concentrated in the latter part of the Mendès-France ministry, after the defeat of EDC, and differed from the earlier configuration in that a group of Alsatian deputies including Pflimlin had swung into support of the cabinet.

Scale II-3 dealt largely with Germany; this issue was evidently a distinct one for the MRP, since it fell into a different cluster from the other issues under Mendès, and the cluster also included a roll call under Mayer, on amnesty for Frenchmen in the German army.

Scales II-1, 4, and 6 were concentrated on domestic questions under Pinay and Mayer, with the addition of a vote under Faure's second cabinet

Table 5.6 MRP, Second Legislature:
Scales by Subject Matter

Premier	Cabinet	Domestic left–right	European union	Foreign (other)	Colonial, Algeria
Pleven		4–671* (fall)			
Pinay	1–776				5–832
		1–838**			
		4–893*			
		6–895*			
		6–899**			
		1–922			
		4–947			
		4–1053*			
		4–1225			
		1–1322**			
Mayer	6–1457			3–1597	
				1–1693	
Reynaud	6–1800				
Mendès-F.₁	2–1801				
Laniel		1–1844			3–1967
					2–1971
					1–2305
Mendès-F.₂	2–2529				
					2–2570
					2–2571
					2–2597**
					2–2618
		5–2634*			
		5–2697*			
					5–2716
					5–2738
				3–2745	
				1–2748	
				3–2750*	
				3–2762*	
Faure₂					1–2977

on the emergency law for Algeria. The unsuccessful investiture of Paul Reynaud was also included in this group. No easy distinction can be drawn among these three, except that Scale II-6 was most closely related to the fate of cabinets, consisting of two investitures and two confidence votes.

Even though the scales relating to Mendès-France and to the other cabinets were distinct, a clear inverse relation existed between the wings of the MRP that supported the cabinet in the two cases. The "polarity" column of Table 5.5 shows that positive or rightist votes were opposed to Mendès but favorable to the other cabinets. Scale II-2, measuring the MRP's alignment toward Mendès during the early part of his ministry, had associations of +.42 or higher with Scales II-1, 4, and 6.

The MRP's internal divisions involved a mixture of specific issues independent of the cabinet in office and dominant issues affecting the fate of particular cabinets and permeating other votes under those cabinets. The most specific issue for the MRP in this sense was that of Germany (Scale II-3). The dominant issues were the domestic left-right question, under Pinay and Laniel, and the colonial question under Mendès-France (beginning as a specific issue under Laniel).

In responding to these dominant issues, the MRP resembled the Moderates, whose votes in the Second Legislature had been specific to particular periods of time and the corresponding cabinets. The Radicals, on the other hand, had divided in ways dominated by intraparty antagonism rather than major parliamentary issues. But this similarity between MRP and Moderates is only partial, for the Moderates' scales were much more independent of one another than were the MRP's. Between the pre-Mendès period and Mendès' ministry, their scales were only weakly associated ($\gamma_{12} = +.30$), while the corresponding association for the MRP was higher ($\gamma_{12} = +.46$). Thus the MRP maintained a more consistent basis of internal division throughout the Second Legislature than did the Moderates.

The Socialists

In the Second Legislature, the question of German rearmament split the Socialist party deeply. The single six-item scale centering about this issue is shown in Table 5.7. This set of roll calls split off a "left" faction of the party, who opposed German rearmament; but no. 2619, the Aumeran-Herriot motion on which EDC was killed, split the party in half. This series of divisions had a major effect on the party's unity and Mollet's ability to keep control. His increasing intraparty problems may have given him another reason for not wishing the party to enter the Mendès-France cabinet.

This scale is clearly specific to a given issue, even though all the roll calls in it took place under Mendès-France. In the Second Legislature as in the First the Socialists were divided on a series of votes, all in fairly close succession, dealing with a single issue. In each case the issue provoked intraparty debate and conflict—far more in the case of German rearmament —because the party's policies were expected to be settled in internal discussions rather than by discordant actions of party factions in the Assembly. The Socialist dissidents on EDC and Germany were not seeking to join another cabinet coalition, but were expressing positions of principle on which they could not be constrained by party decisions.

The Socialists' division in the Second Legislature was not closely related to their division in the First; cross-tabulations of deputies' positions on the two would suggest that they were independent of one another. We shall see that this was because two distinct groups in the party joined in opposition to EDC.

Table 5.7 Socialists, Second Legislature:
Roll Calls in Scale

Roll Call	Premier	Polarity +	Polarity -	p_+	Subject
Scale II-1 (German Rearmament)					
2619	Mendès-F.	ca	p	50	EDC, Aumeran-Herriot q. pr.
2744	Mendès-F.	c	p	86	Paris Agreements, Badie m. pr. (Saar)
2745	Mendès-F.	p	cn	79	Paris Agreements, art. 1 of first bill (Germany and Italy in Brussels Pact)
2750	Mendès-F.	p	cn	82	*Paris Agreements, arts. 2 and 3 of first bill (Germany in NATO)
2752	Mendès-F.	p	c	83	*Paris Agreements (same as 2750)
2762	Mendès-F.	p	cn	81	*Paris Agreements, entirety

Cabinets and Issues in Intraparty Division

By the time of the Pinay investiture in 1952, the external Gaullist threat to the "system" was rapidly receding. When Mendès-France stood for the premiership in 1953, another rallying point for protest appeared. With some help from the Gaullists, Mendès-France attained the premiership in 1954 and posed a series of issues that tested all the parties in his majority. All the parties we have considered were realigned during this period. The MRP's realignment started first, with the opposition of a small group to Laniel's colonial policies. The Moderates realigned at Mendès' investiture, and maintained this pattern of division throughout his ministry. The Socialists were realigned on the German issue during Mendès' ministry, but this division had in fact been foreshadowed by a vote on the European army under Faure in 1952 (no. 709). The URAS changed its factional configuration after Mendès-France proposed the Paris Agreements, and continued its new alignment under Faure. Finally, the Radicals realigned at Mendès' fall. For the most part, the organized and ideological parties (Socialists and MRP) reflected the new issues earliest in their votes.

The Socialists' divisions on roll calls in the Second Legislature were centered about issues, as was true for both Socialists and MRP in the First Legislature. The divisions of the other parties, however, require closer analysis before their bases can be discerned.

The Moderates showed the clearest degree of specificity of scales to cabinets. While they voted on Germany and the electoral law as distinct questions, their other scales were largely cabinet-specific but general in issue content.[69] Their alignment prior to Mendès-France (Scale II-2) was clearly distinct from their alignments under him (Scales II-1, 5), in which colonial issues dominated. Only in a scale under Faure (Scale II-4, still involving colonial issues) was there some return to the pre-Mendès alignment.

The MRP also showed a certain specificity of scales to cabinets, but comparison with the Moderates suggests that the underlying considerations were related more to principles than to coalitions. For the MRP, as for the Moderates, a scale largely specific to the pre-Mendès period (II-1) and one largely specific to Mendès' ministry (II-2) can be found. As for the Moderates, these scales seem to reflect dominant issues, since their patterns of intraparty division extend to votes on other issues and on the fate of the cabinet. But there are differences: the MRP's "cabinet-specific" scales are more closely associated between the Mendès-France ministry and others, and they do not fit so neatly into exclusive sets of cabinets.

Even though the MRP's divisions in the Second Legislature were clearly more concerned with the fate of cabinets than those in the First, an emphasis on principle still distinguished the MRP from the Moderates.[70]

We have also argued that the relative independence of the Moderates' scales from one another is further evidence that the scales reflect coalitions (as against principles) more than in the case of the MRP. We make this argument only for scales representing "dominant issues" connected with the fate of cabinets. That is, a party that divides repeatedly in the same way on a series of votes on different subjects under a given cabinet may do so because of the problem of supporting a coalition or because of a vital concern with a major issue on which that cabinet must act. But if the party repeats this pattern of voting with an entirely different alignment of its deputies under the next cabinet, we must suspect it of being more concerned with coalitions than with issues. By contrast, a party such as the Socialists, which divided in quite disparate ways but with close relation to a particular issue each time, reveals a multiple ideological cleavage more than concern with the place of its factions in successive cabinet coalitions.

The scales for the URAS reveal a specificity to intervals of time, but they do not coincide with particular cabinets. The initial divisions of the URAS (on Scales II-1 and II-4) were largely restricted to domestic issues and extended through the Pinay ministry and part of Laniel's. But Scale II-5, beginning on the Laniel "re-investiture" vote, reveals an intraparty division related more to preferences for a particular cabinet at a particular period, especially in connection with its colonial policy. The URAS deputies were concerned with the cabinet's policies but also with its composition. Their scales distinguished Laniel's colonial policy from his other policies, but also from the colonial policies of Mendès and Faure.

The URAS' scales, like the major scales of the MRP, were fairly highly associated with one another. Thus we have reason to believe that the URAS, like the MRP, had consistent principles underlying its factions' support or opposition to various cabinets. As we have seen, the issue on which the Gaullists brought down several cabinets—that of "Europe"—was a highly ideological one on which the URAS was relatively united. We infer that the URAS was divided on matters of principle, even though its factions were also concerned with the fate of cabinets, and their actions strongly affected the cabinets' fate.

The Radicals and UDSR were repeatedly divided on one persistent issue—the church-school question—but in addition showed considerable consistency of division on different issues. The linking of many issues, before and during the Mendès-France ministry, in the closely associated Scales II-2 and II-5, might have been consistent with an ideological division within the party. But the party's division under Faure (Scale II-7) was also related to these and reflected hostility between two blocs in the party. Analysis of the scale clusters is thus consistent with the other evidence we have of personal antagonisms within the party as a major factor in the Radicals' divisions.

The "typical" cabinet of the Second Legislature was brought down by Gaullist defection. This defection was ideological in origin; but rather than deriving from lasting divisions in the constituencies (as Socialist defection might), it reflected the residue in the Assembly of a wave of protest, which represented less and less in the country as the Second Legislature wore on. The RPF came to the polls too late (in 1951) to win the conclusive victory its leader had wished; and its deputies then remained on the parliamentary scene too long to allow the other parties a chance to govern. They did aid Mendès-France somewhat; but Mendès' decisive style did not keep him in office long enough to begin his domestic economic reforms. For reasons of person or principle he antagonized segments of all the parties that might support him; and for their diverse reasons, these segments contributed to his overthrow. Faure, his successor, then restored the "system" to power.

NOTES

1. A useful source for Assembly lore during the Second and Third Legislatures is Faucher, *L'Agonie d'un régime*. Additional details on the Mendès-France ministry are given in Rouanet, *Mendès France au pouvoir*.

2. Had the old electoral law remained in effect for metropolitan France, these figures would have been 145 Gaullists and 174 Communists; Williams, *Crisis*, p. 314. Together these parties would have constituted an absolute majority.

3. Isorni (Pétainist), Thorez (Communist), Koenig (Gaullist).

4. Jacques Fauvet, *Le Monde*, 26 July 1951. In Fig. 5.1 we reverse the previous positions of Radicals and MRP; partly because of the dominance of the school question, the MRP came to ally itself more with the parties to its right, and the Radicals were closer to the Socialists on a number of major votes.

5. In both cases the RPF was effectively in opposition, since investiture required an absolute majority rather than a plurality.

6. It was difficult for the cabinet to abstain, since the parties in it had fought elections on the issue.

7. Fauvet, *Le Monde*, 22 September 1951.

8. "Framework-laws," the details of which the cabinet would then be empowered to specify by decrees.

9. By Article 51 of the Constitution, this absolute majority did not permit dissolution if another similar overthrow occurred within eighteen months; such a possibility arose only when eighteen months of the Legislature had elapsed before the first overthrow.

10. Matthews, (*The Death of the Fourth Republic*, p. 285) claims that this complaint had been provoked by a memorandum which the Pleven cabinet had sent to Tunisia, and that this memorandum had been strongly worded because Pleven needed the support of the colonists' lobby in his close budget votes.

11. In Fig. 5.2 the MRP is again placed to the left of the Radicals; its deputies' votes on the salary scale under Faure emphasize their leftist position on social legislation.

12. The other politically significant instance after 1947 was Mollet's program of social legislation in the Third Legislature.

13. Fauvet, *Le Monde*, 1 March 1952; Faure was referred to as one *"qui n'a pas été longtemps nourri dans le sérail."* This same attitude had also been held previously toward René Mayer. Fauvet later indicated that he considered the Moderates to have been responsible for Faure's overthrow; *Le Monde*, 23 May 1953.

14. It does not fit them because of (a) the specificity of the voting pattern to the brief Faure ministry; (b) the different voting patterns of Radicals and UDSR. This question seemed to concern the Radicals primarily, and the cluster of votes emerged more clearly in analysis of the Radical deputies alone.

15. Chapsal considers this vote to mark the end of the "Third Force," the Socialist-MRP-Radical coalition against Communists and RPF; *La Vie politique*, p. 190.

16. *Le Monde*, 2–3 March 1952.

17. Fauvet, *Le Monde*, 22–23 June 1952.

18. Fauvet, *Le Monde*, 24 December 1952. Chapsal notes that Pinay's cabinet was the last to be overthrown on a purely economic issue; *La Vie politique*, pp. 205–206.

19. Fauvet, *Le Monde*, 24 December 1952.

20. The *Rassemblement* did not wish to govern in a purely rightist coalition; *Le Monde*, 26–30 December 1952.

21. For the effects of RPF support on cabinets' positions toward EDC, see Fauvet, *La IVᵉ République*, pp. 226–227.

22. *Le Monde*, 23 May 1953.

23. Fauvet, *La IVᵉ République*, p. 228.

24. Fauvet, *Le Monde*, 12 June 1953.

25. The ARS had complained of its share, using the formula that counted one of these posts as half a regular cabinet post (*Le Monde*, 1 July 1953). On other occasions these junior posts were referred to as *"strapontins"* (temporary folding seats in the aisles of theaters).

26. Mendès-France was "on leave" on this vote; he had criticized the Indochinese war on the ground that France needed to choose clearly among uses of her limited resources, but did not vote in opposition till later.

27. *L'Année Politique*, 1953, p. 435. The ambiguity of this resolution is noted in Leites, *On the Game of Politics*, pp. 129–130.

28. A detailed account of the presidential election is given in Melnik and Leites, *The House Without Windows*. For Duchet's role see Fauvet, *La IVᵉ République*, p. 243.

29. Fauvet, *Le Monde*, 11 June 1954.

30. Former URAS, now known as *Républicains Sociaux*.

31. *"Hors du groupe parlementaire."* But Buron and Monteil eventually returned to the MRP group.

32. Published as Mendès-France, *Dire la vérité: Causeries du samedi, juin 1954—février 1955.*

33. Equivalent to a motion that the issue should not be brought up; Lidderdale, *The Parliament of France,* pp. 134–135.

34. *Le Monde,* 2 September 1954, p. 6. See also Grosser, *La IVᵉ République et sa politique extérieure,* p. 319.

35. *Ibid.,* p. 321.

36. Alexander Werth calls this "the first big attack" on Mendès-France: *Lost Statesman,* p. 147. But it was not carried through, for Mendès could have dissolved the Assembly if overthrown by an absolute majority before November 21—eighteen months after Mayer's fall. See Williams, *Crisis,* p. 238.

37. G. Mamy, *Le Monde,* 12–13 December 1954.

38. For the so-called Phrygian bonnets awarded by this newspaper to presumed loyal Mendesists, see Duverger, Goguel, and Touchard, eds., *Les Élections du 2 janvier 1956,* p. 128.

39. Fauvet, *Le Monde,* 14–15 November 1954.

40. Several, including Pflimlin, were Alsatians.

41. Fauvet, *Le Monde,* 7 and 8 January 1955.

42. Both Mendès-France and Mitterrand, however, favored forceful action against the Algerian "rebellion," a fact that was often forgotten by the partisans of "French Algeria."

43. Or in Mendès' own terms, *"le coup de pied de l'âne"*—the donkey's kick to the dying lion.

44. Mendès, like Pinay, refused to resign in the usual way. Both were suspected by the deputies of playing public opinion against the Assembly. But whereas Pinay resigned "too soon," Mendès did not leave the chamber soon enough.

45. *Le Monde,* 15 February 1955.

46. See Duverger, *The French Political System,* pp. 43–44, and Macridis, "A Note on the Revision of the Constitution of the Fourth Republic," 1015–1016.

47. Werth, *Lost Statesman,* p. 179.

48. By this time another procedural reform had gone into effect: personal votes would be required henceforth on all investitures and confidence votes.

49. This vote was also among those chosen by *L'Express* for the Phrygian bonnets, as an indicator of loyalty to Mendès.

50. *Le Monde,* 3 November 1955.

51. Among them was René Mayer, who had returned from his post on the European Coal and Steel Community to battle Mendès again. But as a deputy from Algeria, he had no seat in the Third Legislature.

52. Interestingly, the two supporting coalitions that were not "typical" were those of Mendès and Pinay, both of whom relied heavily on public opinion rather than the Assembly.

53. Chapsal (*La Vie politique,* p. 202) points out that the EDC issue allowed the RPF to regain its unity. But the fleeting unity that it attained at the start of the Mayer ministry

seems not the reason for its entry, but rather a stage in its disintegration. Thus it was more nearly coincidence that the RPF, like the SFIO in 1950, entered a cabinet just as the dominant issues changed.

54. Malterre and Benoist, *Les Partis politiques français*, p. 139: The ex-RPF *"a gardé de son chef les attitudes brusquées et les démissions subites, qui montrent que ses membres ne sont pas pleinement habitués au régime et à ses adresses."*

55. Hence the *procès d'intention* to which he was continually subjected, and René Mayer's remark, *"Je ne sais pas où vous allez."*

56. The fate of various cabinets prior to Mendès-France was closely linked to EDC; see Lerner and Aron, eds., *France Defeats EDC*, and Fauvet, *La IV⁰ République*, pp. 230ff.

57. But we shall see that among the Radicals the right wing was more favorable to EDC, while the left opposed it.

58. See Fauvet and Mendras, eds., *Les Paysans et la politique*, p. 137. The distinction between the two Peasant factions is also made by Merle in Duverger, ed., *Partis politiques et classes sociales*, p. 247. The "anti-European" position of the Antier group will also be shown in Chap. 7. Our analysis implies that Antier's support for the RPF was not based on similarity of constituencies.

59. *Le Monde*, 2 October 1952.

60. These interpretations assume the Moderates' votes on a given cabinet were centered about a *dominant issue*—in their eyes the most important matter that cabinet dealt with. This is not to say that the coalitions were concerned purely with cabinet posts and the internal politics of the Assembly.

61. A number re-emerged in 1958 and thereafter, however, as important figures in the Gaullist UNR.

62. Deputies' positions will be shown in Chap. 7. Note also a comment of Aron's, cited by Fauvet, *Le Monde*, 23 June 1950: "[Le RPF] *recueille incontestablement, en majorité, des voix de droite mais . . . son état-major, issu de la Résistance, vient en partie de la gauche."*

63. The Gaullists Vallon and Capitant had come close to the Communists over EDC; see Malterre and Benoist, *Les Partis politiques français*, p. 33, and Lerner and Aron, *France Defeats EDC*, pp. 40–41.

64. Though these two parties are scaled together, as before, we shall refer to them for convenience as the "Radicals."

65. See de Tarr, *The French Radical Party*, Chap. 5. In this respect the leftist traditional Radicals were akin to the "extreme right" among the Peasants.

66. Fauvet writes that the Radicals decide on *"considérations de personne et de politique intérieure"; Le Monde*, 12 October 1954.

67. See Chap. 10 for a discussion of cross-Legislature continuity of scales. The problems that the Pinay investiture created within the MRP are indicated by Raymond Barrillon, *Le Monde*, 9–10 March 1952, p. 2.

68. *Le Monde*, 4 June 1953.

69. The high degree of cabinet specificity would be reduced somewhat by choice of other party groups for scaling—e.g., the RI alone, or Moderates and ARS. Nevertheless, this quality still distinguishes the Moderates from the other parties.

70. MRP's scales were also less related to *ministrable* status (Chap. 7) and more to constituency interests (Chap. 10). See also Yates, "Power, Principle, and the Doctrine of the *Mouvement Républicain Populaire*."

>> 6 <<

Cabinets and Issues
in the Third Legislature

THE THIRD LEGISLATURE ENDED, HALFWAY through its expected span, with de Gaulle's accession to power. The election that began it had inspired hopes of a new "mandate," but these hopes were disappointed even more than in 1951. The majority that Guy Mollet mustered for his relatively long-lived cabinet was known to be the only stable one possible. The Algerian issue came to dominate the Assembly's deliberations and the fate of the cabinet. Other issues, such as European union, faded into relative insignificance. The parties splintered further and imposed more and more contradictory conditions on one another. Yet not till near the end of the Third Legislature did politicians in Paris think seriously of the possibility that the regime itself might be replaced.

The notions of "left" and "right," as used to characterize the alignment of the Assembly, were peculiarly inadequate in the Third Legislature. With the decimation of the ex-Gaullists in the 1956 election, and the relegation of the Poujadists to a noisy opposition, one might have expected the stable parties to align themselves in a familiar pattern. But the intensification of France's dilemma in Algeria brought about a situation where a Socialist premier, and two cabinets backed strongly by the Socialists, carried out a military holding operation there. This policy had many overtones of the political right, and if carried out by a rightist coalition it would have immediately elicited leftist opposition. But because of the initial direction of the policy by the Socialist leaders and their involvement in it afterward, Socialist opposition was muffled. The Socialists continued to favor social legislation, and thus encountered increasing opposition from the right; but at the same time the Socialist leadership could not prevent the development of leftist dissidence in their own party. The dissidents were joined by the Mendesist fraction of the Radicals, who outflanked the Socialist leadership on the left in their opposition to Mollet's Algerian policy. This ideological shift was compounded by the fact that Mollet's earliest and most loyal supporters among the Radicals tended to be on the "anticlerical *left*" wing of that party.

The Third Legislature: Chronology

The election of January 1956 again failed to yield an Assembly with coherent majorities. The strength of the Gaullist Social Republicans fell from 80 to 20 seats. The Poujadist vote, much larger than expected, caused the majority provision of the electoral law to work in only 11 districts; for the most part, proportional representation operated. The Communists' strength in the Assembly thus rose from 100 to 150 seats, even though their fraction of the popular vote remained much the same as in 1951. The 52 Poujadists in the new Assembly[1] brought the total of "unavailable" votes to about 200; and unlike the Gaullist deputies of 1952–55, these deputies showed little prospect of supporting cabinets later. But more serious were the increasing hostilities and mutual vetoes within and between the "majority" parties. In spite of a surge in its urban vote, the Radical party returned only about fifteen deputies who were to prove thorough Mendesists; the party was to fragment further. All the majority parties began to be split more and more on Algerian policy: leftist dissidence grew in the Socialist party, while "French Algeria" factions developed among the Radicals, Gaullists, and Moderates, and (to a small extent, with Bidault) in the MRP.[2]

In spite of this increasing division, the first cabinet of the Third Legislature, under Guy Mollet, was to be the longest-lived of the Fourth Republic. As the Assembly convened, the apparent victors of the election were the Socialists and Mendesists, hastily allied for the election in the "Republican Front." Mollet, leader of the strongest party in this alliance, was called first by Coty as premier, and invested by a large majority (no. 6; Fig. 6.1). Mendès, his ally, had been assured a major cabinet position; but he did not wish the ministry of either Finance or Algeria, and the MRP vetoed him for Foreign Affairs.[3] He thus became a Minister of State, without portfolio.

Mollet's investiture speech promised social legislation and a liberal policy in Algeria; the large investiture majority was expected to increase his authority. But when he went to Algiers to announce his policy (February 6) he was pelted by a mob, and he yielded to this show of violence, feeling that not only the wealthy settlers but even the European working class in Algeria opposed his policies. He had disregarded Mendès' advice to move quickly, and the nationalist agitators (including Poujadists) had had time to prepare demonstrations against him. Perhaps a more serious obstacle to his proposed policy was the fact that now communication with the Muslims was practically cut off. They were no longer represented, even nominally, in the Assembly, and Mollet talked only with Europeans while on his trip. He jettisoned the liberal General Catroux as Resident General (without consulting his cabinet) and put the Socialist Robert Lacoste in his place.

After Mollet's return to Paris, the Assembly considered domestic matters such as the church-school question (refusing by narrow margins to give it priority), and social legislation. Mollet encountered his first opposition on an amendment to his paid-vacation bill (no. 37).

At the same time, important decisions on Algeria were being made. At Lacoste's recommendation, the cabinet decided on a vigorous military effort in Algeria; Mendès joined in favoring large reinforcements in Algeria while offering negotiation. Mollet planned to ask the Assembly for special powers in Algeria; these provided for economic and social reform as well as for the renewal of police powers that the Faure cabinet had exercised. But the cabinet's action tended to be largely military, and nothing specific was said about negotiating with the rebel chiefs.[4] This parallel to Indochina worried both Mendès and Gaston Defferre, then a Socialist colleague in the cabinet.

At about the same time General André Zeller resigned as Chief of Staff, declaring that he considered that "the fluctuations of the military policy of successive cabinets did not permit him to fulfill his functions effectively."[5] He was succeeded by General Paul Ely.

Figure 6.1 The Mollet Cabinet and Its Support

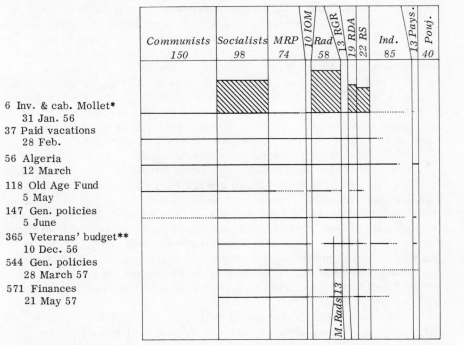

	Communists 150	Socialists 98	MRP 74	10 IOM	Rad 58	13 RGR	19 RDA	22 RS	Ind. 85	13 Pays.	Pouj. 40
6 Inv. & cab. Mollet* 31 Jan. 56											
37 Paid vacations 28 Feb.											
56 Algeria 12 March											
118 Old Age Fund 5 May											
147 Gen. policies 5 June											
365 Veterans' budget** 10 Dec. 56											
544 Gen. policies 28 March 57											
571 Finances 21 May 57											

*On this and other investiture votes of the Third Legislature, only a plurality was required. One consequence was that abstention and nonvoting were no longer equivalent to opposition.

**Morice Radicals were a separate party on this and succeeding votes. They are shown to the right of the Valois Radicals.

In early March the debates began on Mollet's proposals for Algeria. At the same time new terrorist outbreaks occurred. The bill for special powers was passed by a large majority; the Communists supported it and only some two dozen Moderates joined the Poujadists in opposition (no. 56). Through March and April it became more and more evident that no easy solution was possible in Algeria. The drafting of thirty thousand conscripts for Algeria was discussed; Lacoste decided that no overall negotiation with the "rebels" was possible because of their insistence on the recognition of an Algerian national state. Mendès made little headway in the cabinet in combating Lacoste's postion, only some of the dissident Socialists supported him.[6] The anti-Mendès faction of the Radicals published a manifesto insisting on firmness in Algeria and implicitly criticizing Mendès. Meanwhile Mollet brought his bill for a National Old Age Fund to the Assembly. Most provisions of the bill passed easily, with Communist support; but a less popular section, providing for tax increases, received a majority of only 260–138 (no. 118).

Communist votes were essential for the cabinet's victory on this roll call; the MRP abstained and many Moderates and Radicals opposed.

Late in May Mendès resigned from the cabinet. He remained head of the Radical party and continued his efforts to reorganize it. But in October at the Lyon congress a group under André Morice seceded, opposing his control. Mendès' basic problem during this period was that a large consensus had developed in favor of the prosecution of the Algerian war. On this issue, as on others before, he was concerned that France choose policies proportioned to her means, and make the necessary sacrifices to carry them out. On Algerian policy, while approving acts of firmness and force, he wished also to assure the Muslim population of just political treatment as well as economic aid from the French government. It was because he saw the Mollet cabinet failing to carry on these latter policies that he resigned.[7]

Early in June Mollet put the question of confidence on his general policies, with special reference to North Africa (no. 147). This vote combined what might have been different majorities on Algeria and the protectorates of Tunisia and Morocco; it was carried by only 271 to 59, with the Communists abstaining. In July Mollet won a series of votes on Euratom, an issue which momentarily took precedence over Algeria.[8]

Later in July the United States and Great Britain withdrew their offer to Nasser to build the Aswan Dam; a week later he nationalized the Suez Canal. Shortly thereafter, France and Britain began preparing for the Suez invasion, which was to take place at the end of October.[9] The unsuccessful invasion actually solidified Mollet's position as premier; even without Communist support, he was not seriously threatened until December, when he almost fell "accidentally" on the veterans' budget (no. 365). But after the budget votes he received a solid vote of confidence on his foreign policies. Meanwhile Lacoste was claiming that "pacification" in Algeria was going well and would soon succeed.

In December Mollet, confronted with criticism in his own party, reformed the municipal administrations of Algeria and replaced them with temporary ones. This act led some of the settlers to distrust Lacoste and to seek security in alliances with politicized elements in the army.[10] But in antagonizing the Europeans, Mollet gained nothing in his relation with the Muslims. His position on Algeria, expressed in Washington in late February, was that it was up to the "rebels" to make the next move. Meanwhile in January he had won two roll calls on the Common Market by comfortable margins.

In March 1957 the Moderates began to think of overthrowing the cabinet; they hoped another cabinet might slow inflation by reducing domestic expenditures.[11] Lacoste again claimed that great progress in "pacification" would be made in the following three months. On March 28 Mollet won another confidence vote on his general policies (no. 544) by 221 to 188. Substantial defection had occurred among the Radicals and RGR, and the Moderates now abstained. In May Mollet finally proposed to raise taxes to pay for the Algerian war. Putting the question of confidence on this issue, he was confronted with an ultimatum from the Moderates: no more alternating majorities using the Communists for social legislation and the Moderates for Algeria. Thus Mollet fell on no. 571, as a substantial bloc of Moderates swung into opposition.[12] The Radicals also voted to abstain (except for Radical ministers, who could support the cabinet) to preserve their internal unity.

The most important long-run cause of Mollet's fall was the FLN's refusal to negotiate on his terms: cease-fire, then elections. Even though the cabinet had obtained a respite from the UN, it had no way out of the Algerian impasse—especially no easy solution to present to the Assembly and the interested groups represented in it.[13]

The immediate cause of Mollet's fall—and one that would be crucial throughout the rest of the Legislature—was the defection of about forty Moderates who had previously supported Mollet or abstained.[14] As his fall neared, Mollet stressed his leftist policies; by doing so he may have consolidated support in his own party but made it easier for the Moderates to oppose him. But a more fundamental reason for the Moderates' defection was their feeling of growing strength in the country. They had gained in a series of by-elections since January 1956. Moreover, organized sentiment for maintaining a "French Algeria" was growing, and was particularly strong on the right. This position was held not merely by Moderate deputies, but also on their right flank by Poujadists and other splinter nationalist groups who thus exerted pressure on the Moderates.[15]

At Mollet's fall Mendès also lost control of the Radical party. In March he had negotiated new disciplinary rules for the Radical parliamentary group, in return for concessions on Algerian policy, at a party conference at Chartres. After debate and compromise, the group had voted that only the cabinet members would be allowed to support Mollet on the forthcoming confidence vote. But four others supported him as well, and two of the four neglected to appear at the disciplinary hearing. Unable to carry a vote in favor of their exclusion, Mendès resigned his leadership of the party.[16]

Pflimlin tried next to form a cabinet but was prevented by the Socialists' unwillingness to participate. Mollet then influenced President Coty toward the nomination of Maurice Bourgès-Maunoury, a younger Radical who had been Mollet's Minister of Defense, and persuaded the Socialists to enter the cabinet.[17] Bourgès-Maunoury was invested by the rather unimpressive vote of 240 to 194, with the MRP and some Moderates abstaining. He was to receive thirteen more supporting votes at his fall (see Figure 6.2).

Bourgès-Maunoury found it difficult to complete his cabinet; he was hindered by both policy disagreements and the vetoes of various party groups against potential ministers. Mollet, as a patron of Bourgès-Maunoury, wished his own tax program reintroduced by the new cabinet. Twelve days after the investiture a compromise tax bill was passed, providing for some increases; but the Assembly approved it only to avoid reopening the crisis.[18] The Socialists, still participating in the cabinet, were further divided by this position.

In July bills providing for Euratom and the Common Market were passed (no. 623).

Bourgès-Maunoury then proposed a bill providing for special police powers in Algeria with extension to mainland France. Aimed at possible Muslim terrorism, it provided increased powers of search, detention, and arrest. Though supported by the Moderates, it provoked dissent among both

MRP and Socialists; they were by no means sure against whom the powers were to be used, and some even feared that the press might be threatened.[19] Twenty-six Socialists failed to take part in this vote (no. 655), and most made a political issue of it.

Over the summer vacation, Bourgès-Maunoury drafted a *loi-cadre* for government reform in Algeria; but the Moderates' support was hard to

Figure 6.2 The Bourgès-Maunoury Cabinet and Its Support

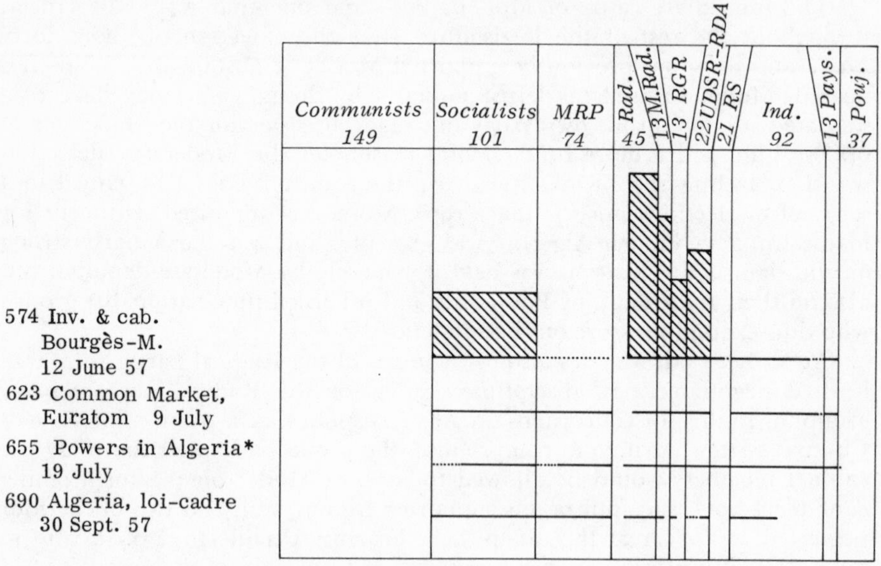

	Communists 149	Socialists 101	MRP 74	Rad. 45	13 M.Rad.	13 RGR	22 UDSR–RDA	21 RS	Ind. 92	13 Pays.	Pouj. 37
574 Inv. & cab. Bourgès-M. 12 June 57											
623 Common Market, Euratom 9 July											
655 Powers in Algeria* 19 July											
690 Algeria, loi-cadre 30 Sept. 57											

*Socialist nonvoting expressed left-wing dissidence.

retain on either the establishment of a decentralized executive in Algeria or the combination of Muslims and Europeans in a single electorate. Like Mollet's Algerian policy, it mainly represented an effort of the mainland French to agree among themselves.[20]

Calling a special session of parliament in September to deal with agricultural discontent, Bourgès-Maunoury brought the Algerian *loi-cadre* before the Assembly. But the cabinet itself could not agree on the text; André Morice, representing the "French Algeria" position, was continually opposed to his Socialist colleagues in the cabinet. Mollet and Roger Duchet, leader of the Independents, debated the problem at a "round table" instituted by the premier to try to resolve the disagreement.[21] But finally on September 30 Soustelle led the Gaullists and about forty Independents into opposition and brought the cabinet down (no. 690).

The cabinet crisis led first to a foredoomed effort at investiture by Pinay (no. 692; Figure 6.3). Then Mollet tried again, and many expected him to succeed; but the Moderates opposed him nearly unanimously and he lost by 63 votes (no. 693). He antagonized them unnecessarily in his investiture speech by mentioning labor–management co-determination in industrial relations. It is possible that he learned at the last minute that Socialist dissidence was so great that he might not be able to control his party if he became premier. An alternative interpretation is that the right abandoned Mollet once it thought Algeria "pacified."[22]

The premier finally invested was Félix Gaillard, a still younger Radical with relatively few enemies (no. 694). The crisis had lasted thirty-six days; this very fact exacerbated the Franco-Tunisian conflict, which was first to sustain Gaillard and then to become his undoing.

Figure 6.3 The Gaillard Cabinet and Its Support*

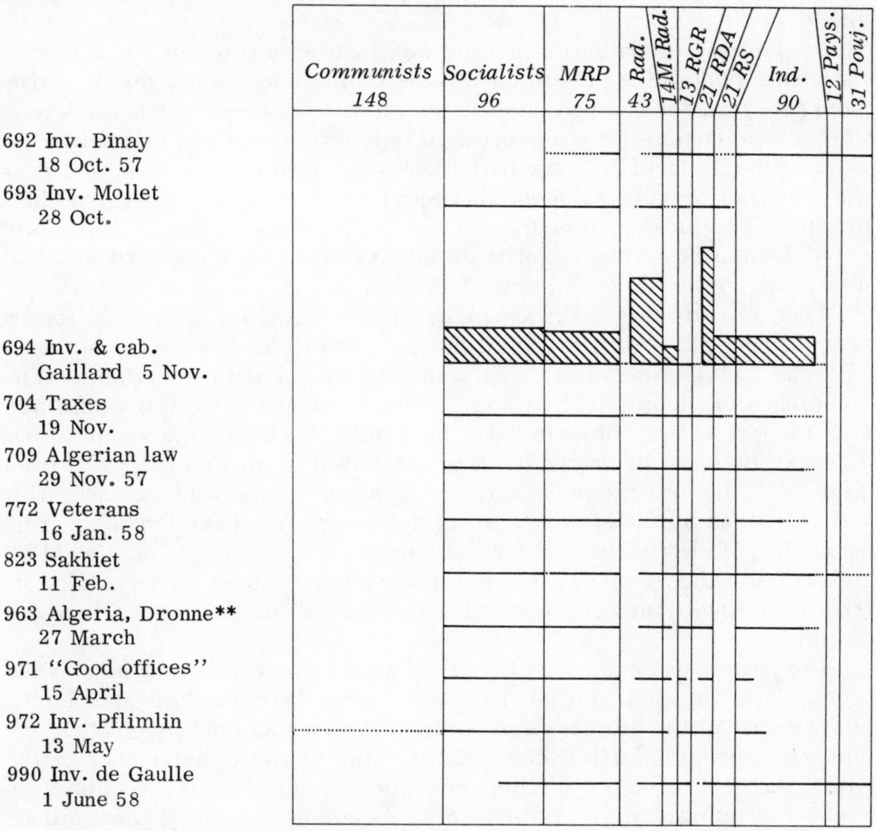

*Nonvoters are omitted from the diagram; disaffection expressed by nonvoting is not represented.
**"Contre" is pro-cabinet on no. 963.

Bourguiba, now President of Tunisia, was annoyed by France's assertion of her right to pursue FLN troops across the border into Tunisia, and sought arms to protect Tunisia's sovereignty. France, under the Bourgès-Maunoury cabinet, was reluctant to supply them. After waiting through the cabinet crisis, the United States and Britain offered to deliver the arms. Upon assuming office Gaillard insisted that no country other than France should supply arms. But he was unable to deliver them because of rightist opposition, and the Anglo-American deliveries were made.

Gaillard's effort to present himself as the defender of France against her enemies (and allies) overseas was of only limited value in retaining the Assembly's support. Proposing a tax increase two weeks after his investiture (no. 704), he saw his support reduced by 81 votes, half the Moderates abstaining. But the bill was nevertheless passed, and Gaillard's firm stand on the supply of arms to Tunisia may have prevented the result from being worse. Ten days later, Gaillard succeeded in having a *loi-cadre* for Algeria passed (no. 709)—a compromise less liberal than the bill on which Bourgès-Maunoury had fallen. An explicit electoral law added to this version of the bill assuaged some of the fears of the previous rightist opponents of the bill.[23]

On January 16 Gaillard's margin sank to twenty votes on a question of confidence opposing a motion on prisoners' allowances and veterans' retirement (no. 772). Succeeding threats to the cabinet promised to be more severe, since several factions were supporting it only provisionally at this point.

On January 11 FLN troops had attacked across the Algerian border near the Tunisian town of Sakhiet-Sidi-Youssef and taken four French soldiers prisoner. The incident was debated in the Assembly and the cabinet protested. Gaillard's narrow majority on no. 772 might have been still less had it not been for his firm stand toward Tunisia.

Then on February 8 French planes bombed Sakhiet in reprisal for repeated firing on French planes from the town. The bombardment, on a Saturday, found crowds in the marketplace and claimed many victims. The bombing, though initiated by local military commanders, was authorized after the fact by the cabinet in Paris. Bourguiba was highly indignant, as was Tunisian opinion; he demanded the withdrawal of all French troops from Tunisia. When an interpellation was proposed on the cabinet's action, it was postponed by the large margin of 335 to 179 (no. 823). On this "firm" action the Moderates backed Gaillard nearly unanimously; but the MRP and Socialists did so only with serious reservations. A week later Gaillard accepted an Anglo-American offer of "good offices" in the Franco-Tunisian dispute.[24]

The parties of the majority continued to support Gaillard as long as the "good offices" mission continued its negotiations between Paris and Tunis; but evidence of the cabinet's decreasing authority mounted. A police strike took place in mid-March.[25] General Ely, chief of the General Staff of the Army, was said to be considering resignation because of the Assembly's reduction of military appropriations. Still, as late as March 27, the Gaillard cabinet won by a large majority on an informal question of confidence (no. 963). Formally the vote was on the decrees applying the *loi-cadre* in Algeria; but actually the Gaullist Raymond Dronne, introducing a *motion préjudicielle*,[26] was attacking Gaillard for leaving so much authority to the "good offices" mission on North Africa.

By mid-April it became clear that Gaillard had failed to obtain from the "good offices" mission the minimum he had promised the Assembly. No control could be guaranteed over the airfields in Tunisia, or over the Algerian-Tunisian frontier. He may have promised too much.[27] The Moderates swung into opposition, and Gaillard fell (no. 971). The fall was harder because before the vote Gaillard had warned the assembly: "I hope no one will have the cowardice to abstain."[28]

The rest of the story of the last days of the Fourth Republic is not of primary concern to us here; its locus moves from Paris to Algiers, and from the National Assembly to de Gaulle's headquarters. No further cabinets were brought down by the slow attrition of their majorities. The crisis following Gaillard's fall lasted almost a month, and was resolved only on May 13, the day of the military takeover in Algiers. Bidault, who might have stood as a "French Algeria" candidate for the premiership, was precluded from doing so by a vote of his MRP colleagues. After long negotiations and trials by various *ministrables,* Pflimlin was finally called to form a cabinet. But his nomination was a danger sign to the Algerian activists; since he had opposed Bidault earlier, he was suspected of being too "liberal." He was invested by only 274 to 139, with the Communists abstaining—a majority not likely to enhance his authority.

Pflimlin's cabinet did little more than to transfer power to de Gaulle, and it resigned when Coty was ready to nominate the General. Finally the Socialists came around to partial support of de Gaulle, under Mollet's influence. The support of half the party—granted on a vote without party discipline[29]—was essential to de Gaulle, and at the same time revealed cleavages in the party that went back to the First Legislature. De Gaulle's investiture also owed a great deal to last-minute support from the Algerian settlers and army. One of the many events of this turbulent period that affected the Assembly was the Algerian group's seizure of the island of Corsica. This coup, joined by the Gaullist deputy Pascal Arrighi, led to the suspension of the latter's parliamentary immunity. But the conspiratorial history of these events has been told elsewhere;[30] we are concerned here only with the contribution that cabinet instability made to it.

De Gaulle's investiture itself served as a sort of litmus paper revealing some of the most deeply established customs of the Assembly. He had always favored a strong executive and criticized the subservience of the executive to the Assembly. When it came time for him to present himself for investiture —still under the rules of the Fourth Republic—there was serious doubt till the last moment whether he would deign to speak before the Assembly and solicit its votes. He finally made the speech but walked out immediately afterward rather than stay as an ordinary premier-designate would have done. Later, when asking for special powers, he stayed for the debate.[31] But his concession to the system was only temporary.

Patterns of Cabinet Coalition

All three of the cabinets of the Third Legislature were brought down by the Right; a group of some forty Moderate deputies supported them at their investiture (or abstained, in Mollet's case), and then moved into opposition. The Socialists were essential for any cabinet coalition and played a dominant part in all three cabinets. Thus in a sense the Third Legislature represented the converse of the First, in which the Socialists had normally gone into oposition over disagreement with the Moderates. The small band of Gaullists could no longer bring down cabinets alone, nor was their ideology of vital importance, even though they joined in bringing down Bourgès-Maunoury and Gaillard.

Changes had taken place within both the Socialist and Moderate parties, but they were changes of degree only. Mollet had become an advocate of participation in the cabinet, especially when he was premier. He continued to exercise his influence through the party's participation, even after his own ministry. But the forces favoring doctrinal purity in opposition remained, and he had to take account of them. At both the fall of his cabinet in May 1957 and his unsuccessful investiture in October, he took care to "fall to the left," i.e., to stress points of Socialist doctrine in his final speeches.[32]

On the other hand, the Moderates were more numerous, more accustomed to cabinet positions, and more strongly concerned with the dominant issue (Algeria) by the latter part of the Third Legislature than in the First. They had fallen away from the cabinet's supporting majorities in the First Legislature as well, but then they could not normally bring the cabinet down. In the Third Legislature, however, if they had all joined the Communists and Poujadists in opposition, the total opposition vote would have been about three hundred, enough for them to exercise a veto as effective as the Socialists'.

But although the main sources of defection from cabinet coalitions were similar in the First and Third Legislatures, the configuration of the center parties was not. The MRP, though normally supporting the Mollet and Bourgès-Maunoury cabinets, was somewhat divided and did not enter them; only under Gaillard did it participate. By October 1956 the Radicals were divided into three factions; and instead of playing their former role as a party of compromise and a possible source of premiers, they introduced new sources of division. After Mendès went into opposition, his followers simply added their votes to those of the Communists and Poujadists in determining the fate of cabinets. Thus there was opposition to the cabinet coalitions, not merely from the Communists and Poujadists, but also from factions of the "center" parties.

The Moderates

In the Third Legislature, six scale clusters were found for the Moderates;[33] the roll calls included in them are shown in Table 6.1. These clusters tended largely to be concentrated within particular ministries and particular intervals of time. Scale III-1 consisted largely of roll calls under Gaillard, Scale III-4 under Pflimlin, and the rest under Mollet. In subject matter, Scales III-1, 2, and 4 dealt largely with aspects of the Algerian problem; the others concerned domestic social-welfare legislation, together with votes on sub-Saharan Africa, the Common Market, and constitutional reform.

The associations between the scales, as shown in Table 6.1, do not fall into a neat pattern of clusters. Rather, those scales that contain roll calls near one another in chronological sequence tend to have high associations. Thus Scales III-6 and III-2, containing the earliest roll calls under Mollet, have an association of .66. This is true even though the former deals with domestic issues and the latter almost exclusively with Algeria. But apparently the Moderates' alignment on Mollet's Algerian policy between March and June 1956 was conditioned by their attitude toward him as a Socialist,

Table 6.1 *Moderates* (IPAS), *Third Legislature*:
Roll Calls in Scales

Roll Call	Premier	Polarity +	Polarity −	p_+	Subject	III-1	III-2	III-3	III-4	III-5	III-6
Scale III-1 (Algeria)							.50	.41	.54	.15	.34
171	Mollet	can	p	87	*Civil budget, art. 2 and entirety						
239	Mollet	c	pan	87	Civil budget, 1956 (sixth reading)						
690	Bourgès-M.	ca	p	46	*Algeria, *loi-cadre* (fall of Bourgès-M.)						
706	Gaillard	p	can	12	Algeria, Tixier-V. motion						
709	Gaillard	can	p	33	*Algeria, institutions						
710	Gaillard	can	p	34	*Algeria, election law						
777	Gaillard	can	p	13	Foreign policy (Tunisia), Rolland resolution, priority						
793	Gaillard	can	p	30	Algeria, *loi-cadre*						
807	Gaillard	can	p	29	Algeria, institutions, entirety						
Scale III-2 (Mollet-Algeria)						.50		.47	.51	.38	.66
53	Mollet	can	p	24	*Algeria, special powers, art. 1						
54	Mollet	can	p	33	*Algeria, special powers, arts. 3—4						
56	Mollet	can	p	32	*Algeria, special powers, entirety						
103	Mollet	c	pan	73	*Natl. Old Age Fund, agst. Jean-Moreau m. pr.						
147	Mollet	can	p	63	*General policies (Algeria, Tunisia, Morocco)						
Scale III-3 (Mollet—Domestic and Europe)						.41	.47		.27	.64	.48
164	Mollet	c	pan	38	*Old Age Fund, third reading, entirety						
187	Mollet	c	pan	22	*Old Age Fund, fourth reading, entirety						
363	Mollet	can	p	84	*Budget, 1957, price rebates on agricultural equipment						
419	Mollet	c	p	16	Common Market, interpellations						
420	Mollet	a	p	13	Common Market, Verdier et al. resolution						
Scale III-4 (Pflimlin)						.54	.51	.27		.34	.13
971	Gaillard	c	pn	71	**"Good offices" mission, postpone interpellations (fall of Gaillard)						
972	Pflimlin	c	pn	70	Investiture						
974	Pflimlin	c	p	58	State of emergency in mainland France						
977	Pflimlin	can	p	49	Special powers in Algeria						
983	Pflimlin	p	can	83	Arrighi; Vayron motion						
Scale III-5 (Mollet)						.15	.38	.64	.34		.35
25	Mollet	p	cn	13	French Equatorial Africa, date on interpellation						
118	Mollet	c	pan	83	*Old Age Fund, cabinet amendments						
119	Mollet	c	pan	83	*Old Age Fund, cabinet amendments						
120	Mollet	c	pan	63	*Old Age Fund, entirety						
Scale III-6 (Domestic)						.34	.66	.48	.13	.35	
35	Mollet	an	p	21	*Paid vacations, art. 1						
36	Mollet	can	p	22	*Paid vacations, art. 4						
38	Mollet	can	p	48	*Paid vacations, entirety						
884	Gaillard	can	p	12	*Constitutional revision						

and thus differed from their later alignments (also on Algeria) on Scales III-1 and III-4.[34]

Scales III-1 and III-4, last in the temporal sequence, deal with later stages of the controversy about Algeria. Scale III-1, the earlier of the two in time, is the more closely associated with the next earlier Scale III-3 ($\gamma = .41$). But the association between III-1 and III-4 is higher (.54) as they are not only in sequence but both deal with Algeria. We thus interpret these scales by a combination of temporal sequence and subject matter.

Table 6.2 Moderates (IPAS), Third Legislature:
Scales by Subject Matter

Premier	Cabinet	Domestic (nonbudgetary)	Budget	European union	Colonial, Algeria
Mollet		6–35*			5–25
		6–36*			
		6–38*			
					2–53*
					2–54*
					2–56*
			2–103*		
		5–118*			
		5–119*			
		5–120*			
					2–147*
		3–164*			
			1–171*		
		3–187*			
			1–239		
		3–363*			
				3–419	
				3–420	
Bourgès-M.					1–690* (fall)
Gaillard					1–706
					1–709*
					1–710*
					1–777
					1–793
		6–884*			1–807
					4–971** (fall)
Pflimlin	4–972				
					4–974
					4–977
					4–983

*Question of confidence
**Unofficial question of confidence

If there is one scale that is most closely related to the fate of cabinets, it is Scale III-1. Not only does it contain the vote on which Bourgès-Maunoury fell (no. 690); it is also more closely associated with that on Mollet's fall (no. 571) than any other scale, and it shows the highest association between *ministrable* status and support of the cabinet.[35]

The relation between temporal sequence and subject matter in these scales can be shown more clearly by tabulation of scales in subject categories chronologically, as in Table 6.2. Scale III-6 is concentrated at the start, except for roll call no. 884, which dealt with the problems of constitutional revision. Next comes scale III-2, which seems to be distinct in subject matter and overlaps Scale III-5 somewhat in sequence. The only apparent exception to its concentration on Algeria is roll call no. 103, which dealt with a *motion préjudicielle* raised against the Old Age Fund on the ground that the entire budget should be considered first. But here and elsewhere, the state of the budget depended largely on the Algerian war; it was this issue, therefore, that elicited the particular division on no. 103.[36] Table 6.2 is arranged, moreover, to show that other budget votes were also closely connected with the Algerian issue. Roll calls nos. 171 and 239, occurring under Mollet and alternating with votes in other scales, both dealt with the budget and both entered Scale III-1 ("Algeria"); the opposition among the Moderates to Mollet's budget thus resembled most closely their later opposition to Bourgès-Maunoury and Gaillard on explicitly Algerian issues.

Scale III-5, which dealt mostly with the Old Age Fund, also included a vote on French Equatorial Africa. The latter, then, was more nearly a simple left-right issue of the domestic type than it was related to Algeria.

Near the end of Gaillard's ministry, a vote on constitutional reform took place. This issue was evidently so devoid of Algerian overtones that it fell into Scale III-6, along with three votes on social legislation early in Mollet's ministry. But Gaillard's fall (no. 971) marked a new division of the Moderates, which was to continue under Pflimlin.[37] The issue on which Gaillard fell was his apparent weakness in asserting France's prerogatives in Tunisia, as against the recommendations of the "good offices" mission. Pflimlin, too, was viewed by the right as suspect for lack of firmness. Perhaps the change in scale divisions of the Moderates from Mollet to Pflimlin involved a change in complaints from excessive spending for social legislation to simple fears of weakness and "abandon."

The Radicals and UDSR

The election of 1956 at first appeared to be a victory for both Radicalism and Mendès-France; the Radical vote increased and the party's Assembly group included a half-dozen new deputies elected expressly on the Republican Front's platform.

This success was short-lived. Mendès, first a Minister of State in Mollet's cabinet, resigned over Algerian policy and found himself losing support among the previously loyal southwestern wing of the party. After the fission of the party at Lyon (October 1956), he took his followers (or was drawn by them) into a position that was often to the left of the Socialists'. This iso-

Table 6.3 *Radicals and UDSR, Third Legislature*:
Roll Calls in Scales

Roll Call	Premier	Polarity +	Polarity –	p_+	Subject	III-1	III-2	III-3	III-4
Scale III-1 (Mendesism)							.56	.19	.94
265	Mollet₁	p	an	66	Suez interpellation, resolution				
582	Bourgès-M.	p	can	50	*Financial bills, amendments and entirety				
646	Bourgès-M.	c	pn	36	Algeria, special powers, Dumas amendment				
655	Bourgès-M.	p	can	47	*Algeria, special powers				
693	Mollet₂	p	can	63	Investiture				
709	Gaillard	pan	c	69	Algeria, institutions				
		p	can	39					
710	Gaillard	pan	c	69	Algeria, electoral law				
		p	can	39					
714	Gaillard	p	can	40	*Restoration of economy				
745	Gaillard	p	n	63	Retrospective budget, 1957				
762	Gaillard	p	cn	52	Budget, 1958 (second reading)				
772	Gaillard	p	cn	46	*Motion opposing agenda (veterans)				
777	Gaillard	p	cn	52	Foreign policy (Tunisia), Rolland res., pri.				
778	Gaillard	p	cn	49	Foreign policy (Tunisia), Rolland res., pri.				
793	Gaillard	pn	c	59	Algeria, *loi-cadre*				
823	Gaillard	p	can	48	Sakhiet interpellation, Brocas resolution				
846	Gaillard	pan	c	73	*Military budget				
963	Gaillard	c	pn	56	**Algeria, application of *loi-cadre*, Dronne m. pr.				
971	Gaillard	p	c	66	**"Good offices" mission, postpone interpellation (fall of Gaillard)				
993	de Gaulle	p	can	71	Algeria, renew special powers				
Scale III-2 (Europe)						.56		−.05	.44
210	Mollet₁	p	cn	45	Euratom interpellation, Depreux resolution, priority				
211	Mollet₁	p	can	40	Euratom interpellation, Depreux resolution, amend.				
420	Mollet₁	p	can	58	Common Market, Verdier et al. resolution				
571	Mollet₁	p	can	21	*New financial arrangements (fall of Mollet)				
613	Bourgès-M.	c	pn	52	Euratom and Common Market, reject (Rieu)				
623	Bourgès-M.	p	ca	53	Euratom and Common Market, entirety				
807	Gaillard	pn	c	60	Institutions in Algeria, entirety (second reading)				

Association (γ) with Other Scales: III-1, III-2, III-3, III-4

Table 6.3 (continued)

Roll Call	Premier	Polarity +	Polarity −	p_+	Subject	Association (γ) with Other Scales III–1	III–2	III–3	III–4
Scale III–3 (Early Mollet)						.19	−.05		.64
103	Mollet₁	p	can	82	*Natl. Old Age Fund: agst. Jean-Moreau m. pr.				
254	Mollet₁	p	an	70	*Genl. policies (Algeria), interpellation, priority resolution				
362	Mollet₁	p	can	38	*Budget, 1957, aid to farmers' families				
363	Mollet₁	p	can	35	*Budget, 1957, rebates on agricultural equipment				
367	Mollet₁	p	can	52	*Budget, 1957, entirety				
Scale III–4 (Mendesism)						.94	.44	.64	
690	Bourgès-M.	p	can	48	*Institutions in Algeria (fall of Bourgès-M.)				
701	Gaillard	p	cn	56	Algeria, special powers				
748	Gaillard	p	cn	50	*Budget, 1958, entirety and amendments				
884	Gaillard	p	can	49	*Constitutional revision, arts. 3−6 and entirety (second reading)				

lated Mendès from the southwestern Radicals, who now tended to support their own *ministrables* Bourgès-Maunoury and Gaillard. At the same time some of the previous right wing of the party (e.g., André Morice) went still farther to the right in the "French Algeria" movement.

The Faure faction, excluded at the start of the Third Legislature, and the Morice group, who broke off at Lyon, could not be analyzed together with the orthodox Radicals. The scales obtained for the orthodox (Valois) Radicals and UDSR are shown in Table 6.3.[38] Four scales were found; they showed a fundamental division between the periods before and after Mendès-France's loss of control of the party (III-3 vs. III-1 and III-4), and a distinct scale dealing with the issue of European union (III-2). We shall treat Scales III-1 and III-4 as identical in content, as they are very closely associated ($\gamma = .94$).

The relation between chronology and issues is shown more clearly in Table 6.4, which relates the scale items to subject-matter categories. The one scale most nearly specific to a particular issue is Scale III-2 (Europe), which includes five roll calls under two premiers on European unification. The Radicals' division on this issue remained constant even while divisions on other issues were changing. One exception to this clear issue specificity is the inclusion of no. 571, the vote on which Mollet fell. This vote was not primarily concerned with Europe; but the small group of Radicals who broke party discipline to support Mollet also happened to be in favor of European integration. A second exception is no. 807, which dealt with Algeria and might nearly have been placed in Scale III-1 rather than III-2.

Table 6.4 *Radicals and UDSR, Third Legislature*:
Scales by Subject Matter

Premier	Cabinet	Domestic left-right	European union	Foreign (other)	Colonial, Algeria
Mollet$_1$		3-103*	2-210		
			2-211		3-254*
				1-265 (Suez)	
		3-362*			
		3-363*			
		3-367*			
			2-420		
		2-571* (fall)			
Bourgès-M.		1-582			
			2-613		
			2-623		
					1-646
					1-655*
					4-690* (fall)
Mollet$_2$	1-693				
Gaillard					4-701
					1-709
					1-710
		1-714*			
		1-745			
		4-748*			
		1-762			
		1-772*			
					1-777
					1-778
					1-793
					2-807
		1-846*			1-823
		4-884			
					1-963**
					1-971** (fall)
de Gaulle					1-993

Roll call no. 571 marks Mendès' loss of control of the party, and it also separates Scale 3 chronologically from Scales III-1 and III-4. Scale III-3 dealt with domestic and Algerian questions under Mollet. But rather than saying that there was a dominant issue during his ministry, we emphasize that this was the period in which Radicals' positions with respect to Mollet's policy coincided with positions on Mendesism; Mendès was the legitimate leader of the party. Throughout all the subsequent ministries, a single alignment dominated the party and was expressed by Scales III-1 and III-4. The only roll call in this later period, other than those on Europe, which failed to enter one of these scales, was no. 807, which just barely failed to do so. And to indicate that factionalism meant even more among the Radicals than among the Moderates, the vote on revision of the constitution (no. 884) also entered Scale III-4.

The Suez interpellation vote (no. 265) foreshadowed this reorientation. Conducted under the Mollet cabinet, it fell into the later scale cluster, Scale III-1 rather than III-3. But in other votes between October 1956 and Mollet's fall in May 1957, Mendès continued to support the cabinet. It was only after his loss of control of the party that he and his most loyal followers went into consistent opposition.

The Radical party in the Fourth Republic was rarely divided by two or more completely distinct cleavages at the same time. Its major controversies seem to have taken place between a persisting set of factions, which were aligned in much the same way on all the important issues under any given cabinet. In the First Legislature, support and opposition to Schuman, Marie, Queuille, and Bidault divided the party in much the same way; a dominant "left-center" bloc included Mendès together with many of his later enemies as well as a number of the southwestern group. In the Second Legislature, this bloc was sharply divided between Mendesists (together with the south-west group) and the "government" Radicals.[39] Finally, in the Third Legis-lature, Mendès lost all but a handful of new deputies; the southwestern group, under Gaillard, regained control of the party; and the "French Algeria" faction moved into rightist opposition.

In what ways did the structure of the Radical party contribute to cabinet instability and incapacity to govern? If it exacerbated the problems of the Fourth Republic, it was not through multiple cleavages but rather through the personal nature of its internal antagonisms. Central to these personal antagonisms was the dramatic and tragic figure of Mendès-France—a man who commanded admiration because of his will to govern and to choose but who left behind him deeper wounds than this policy alone might have entailed.

The MRP

For the MRP in the Third Legislature we find only one politically mean-ingful scale cluster,[40] whose roll calls are listed in Table 6.5. Five of its six roll calls dealt with Mollet's old-age-fund bill, and the sixth with the *loi-cadre* for France's overseas territories. Roll call no. 103, which reflected the Algerian question for the Moderates, evidently did not do so for the MRP.

Since only one scale appeared, it is difficult to infer whether the cabinet or the issue involved was more important. Study of the Q-matrix suggests, however, that the significant feature of this scale is the absence of the

Table 6.5 MRP, Third Legislature:
Roll Calls in Scale

Roll Call	Premier	Polarity +	−	p_+	Subject
Scale III-1 (Mollet, Social Legislation)					
82	Mollet	a	p	10	Overseas territories, entirety
103	Mollet	can	p	20	*Old Age Fund: against Jean-Moreau m. pr.
118	Mollet	can	p	85	*Old Age Fund, government suppl. amends. (taxes)
151	Mollet	can	p	80	*Old Age Fund, art. 1
162	Mollet	an	p	82	*Old Age Fund, art. 1 (taxes)
184	Mollet	can	p	82	*Old Age Fund, art. 1 (taxes)

Algerian question. At a lower threshold value of Q, other roll calls before and after those shown formed a cluster that seemed more closely related to Algeria. This indicates that the divisions were based on issues and again supports the notion that the MRP was a party concerned with principles.

The MRP, though increasingly divided, especially during the Second Legislature, does not seem to have experienced the deep internal wounds that the Radicals had at that time. Returning to greater unanimity in the Third Legislature, it remained able to tolerate a certain level of internal dissent without fission. Even the dissidence of Bidault (a founder of the party) on Algeria obtained relatively little support within the party. The MRP's vote structure thus reveals internal ties—of principle or morality—which may have restrained members from public disagreement on principle. Disagreements within the MRP gave the impression more of a party united in its basic philosophy, differing on matters of detail, and not carrying its internal quarrels to a larger public audience. Rarely did the fate of specific cabinets seem to determine the vote structure of the MRP; in this respect dissent in the party remained relatively individual and principled, rather than factional and tactical.

The Socialists

For the SFIO, as for the MRP, only one politically significant cluster of roll calls was found in the Third Legislature, as shown in Table 6.6.[41] This single scale was related to the investiture and powers of de Gaulle, and had a clear-cut relation to previous divisions in the party. Those who had previously opposed German rearmament tended largely also to oppose de Gaulle's investiture and powers. Those who failed to support Bourgès-Maunoury's request for special powers in Algeria were also largely found within this group.[42] The common characteristic of this set of votes would appear to be distrust of strong government power, especially when it is exercised by the center or right.

Table 6.6 Socialists, Third Legislature:
Roll Calls in Scale

Roll Call	Premier	Polarity +	Polarity −	p_+	Subject
Scale III–1 (de Gaulle)					
990	de Gaulle	pn	c	.47	Investiture
993	de Gaulle	pa	c	.57	Renewal of special powers for Algeria
996	de Gaulle	pn	c	.47	Full powers (special article)
1000	de Gaulle	p	cn	.47	Constitutional revision (article 90)

Cabinets and Issues in Intraparty Division

The "parliamentary game" was not observable in its pure form in the Third Legislature because of the dominance of the Algerian issue. During the long Mollet ministry, both Radicals and Moderates displayed separate patterns of voting on separate issues. But under Bourgès-Maunoury and Gaillard, most roll calls in scale patterns explicitly involved Algeria; this issue dominated others in its frequency, even if its characteristic divisions did not extend to all domestic votes. The Algerian question dominated the Moderates' divisions in 1957 and 1958 as completely as the Gaullist threat had done in the First Legislature; but the former was an explicit issue of legislative policy, while the question of countering the RPF had not been so openly involved in the substance of legislation.

The Radicals' divisions in the Third Legislature, though coinciding with the intervals of ministries, were actually due more to the power struggle within the party itself. In this respect the Radicals' realignment in the Third Legislature resembled that in the Second.

Socialist dissidence represented in part an opposition to Mollet's entry into the parliamentary game. Mollet was deeply involved in the process of forming cabinets, and his control over the Socialist party organization made the resulting combinations more stable.[43] Mollet, too, was the key person to be converted to support of de Gaulle and subsequently entered de Gaulle's cabinet. In this sense at least one faction among the Socialists was somewhat more involved in the "game" in the Third Legislature than before.

The distribution of party strength in the Third Legislature gave less room for parliamentary maneuver than in the First or Second. The short life of the Third Legislature and the increasing importance of the Algerian issue also provided less opportunity for shifting coalitions to reveal themselves. The Assembly was also more deeply divided in the latter part of the Third Legislature than it had been before. For most of the parties, the scales that most resembled their previous divisions were based on domestic issues under Mollet, before the Algerian issue became dominant. The party considered most "responsible" for the downfall of cabinets in the Third Legislature—the Moderates—showed less tendency for its *ministrables* to support the cabinet at the end of the Legislature than had generally been the case before.[44] And the leaders of the different parties came to disagree with one another more and more on Algerian policy, as the various "round table" conferences revealed. These developments suggest that the consensus among the leading deputies—those of the "system" as well as the Mendesists—was breaking down during the Third Legislature. Thus although cabinet paralysis had been a source of government weakness throughout the Fourth Republic, it was magnified in the Third Legislature through increasing disagreement among the leaders.

To summarize our findings on issues and cabinets in all three Legislatures, the main difference we have found is among the parties. The internal divisions of the MRP and the Socialists tended to center more about particular issues than did the divisions of the Radicals or the Moderates. Even the Gaullists in the Second Legislature seemed to divide on more ideological grounds than Radicals or Moderates. The Radicals tended to divide over questions of personality and faction, largely centered within their own party. The Moderates divided in similar ways on a variety of issues—over a long series of cabinets in the First Legislature and over shorter intervals in the Second.

The relations between issue and cabinet specificity in the parties can best be shown with the aid of a diagram. We may obtain an index of cabinet specificity for each party in each Legislature by counting the maximum number of roll calls in each scale that took place under any one premier, then adding these numbers for all scales and expressing the total as a proportion of all roll calls in all the scales. A similar index of issue specificity can be constructed by counting the roll calls in the modal issue-category. Figure 6.4 locates each party studied, in each Legislature, as a point whose horizontal coordinate is its cabinet specificity, and whose vertical is its issue specificity.

The most interesting feature of this diagram is that cabinet and issue specificity are not simply alternatives; rather, there is a slight positive association between the two. Moreover, we have observed that the most ideological parties—MRP and Socialists—had high specificity in both senses; the diagram now suggests that these two aspects tend to go together for other parties as well. For example, the opposite pole is represented by the Moderates in the First Legislature, whose leading general scale showed low specificity in both senses. And the Radicals in all three Legislatures, while varying in their relative degrees of cabinet and issue specificity, showed a low and relatively constant sum of the two. This suggests that the continuum from less to more ideological parties arrays them from lower left to upper right in the diagram—according to their *combined* cabinet and issue specificity, rather than according to any differential between them.

This interpretation sustains and generalizes the observations we have made about the relative lack of evidence for a parliamentary "game" in individual Legislatures. The alternative to "ideological" politics thus appears to be not the shifting and specific coalitions that might have supported various cabinets, but *general* coalition patterns that embraced a variety of both issues and cabinets. These coalitions, whether they dealt with the external threat of Gaullism or the internal feuds of the Radical party, were what distinguished the divisions of the Moderates and Radicals from those of the MRP and SFIO.

We thus reiterate, but in a more precise sense, that the question whether

Figure 6.4 Cabinet and Issue Specificity in All Three Legislatures

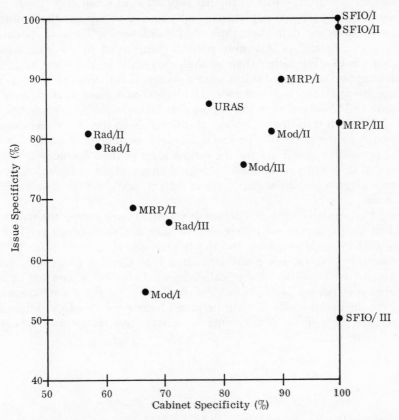

*The following procedures were used to measure cabinet specificity for a given party and Legislature. For each scale, the premier under whom the greatest number of roll calls were conducted, was identified. Then the number of roll calls under this premier was counted, and these counts were summed over all scales. This sum was expressed as a proportion of the total number of roll calls in all the scales.

For issue specificity, the same procedure was followed with the substitution of "issue" for "premier." The issue categories used were (1) domestic, (2) electoral law, (3) Europe and Germany, (4) colonial and Algeria.

issues or coalitions were more important has to be answered differently for different parties. But if we combine this finding with our knowledge as to which parties were most instrumental in bringing the cabinet down, we shall find that it stresses ideology as a cause of cabinet instability. For in the First Legislature it was the Socialists most often who dealt the final blow to the cabinet, and in the Second, the Gaullists. Both were parties whose internal divisions were primarily ideological.[45] In the Third Legislature it was the

Moderates who brought down all three cabinets, and in this Legislature the Moderates' votes were more closely related to particular issues than in the First. The particular scale for the Moderates that involved the cabinets' fall (III-1) did in fact reflect the dominant issue of North Africa, but the question involved seemed more a bitter policy disagreement than a mere "game" for cabinet positions.

This interpretation—that issues, or ideology, predominated in causing cabinet instability—will be further supported in Chapter 7. There we shall see that the potential ministers actually tended to support the cabinet more rather than less than their rank-and-file colleagues. To some extent, therefore, the "game" of Assembly politics contributed to the continuation of cabinets in office rather than to their downfall. In this view, the relations among parliamentary leaders were a source of consensus in the system, and the essential dissensus was more ideological and more characteristic of the rank-and-file deputies in the parties that brought the cabinets down.

We shall trace these ideological differences to the active members of the parties in the districts. The social divisions we described earlier are viewed as permissive conditions for the propagation of these ideological differences —that is, as distinct channels through which divisive communications could pass, given a particular party system with its activists and their positions on issues.

This explanation holds primarily for differences *among* the parties, more than for the intraparty differences we have analyzed, which are less clearly related to social structure. Intraparty divisions reflect coalitions within the Assembly that are not easily translated into election campaigns, and they usually reflect subtler ideological divisions than those separating the parties from one another. Nevertheless, the conflicts within the parties are related in some degree to ideology, both because of the pressure of the militants and because the policies of a cabinet are always one reason for supporting or opposing it.

NOTES

1. Soon reduced to 42 by invalidation of elections.

2. These factions developed without any direct representation of the settlers, since no 1956 Assembly elections were held in Algeria.

3. For the effect of this veto see Werth, *Lost Statesman*, p. 285, and Fauvet, *La IVᵉ République*, pp. 308–309.

4. Mollet later pursued fruitless secret negotiations with them through Socialist party officials; see Tournoux, *Carnets secrets de la politique*, pp. 119–120.

5. *Le Monde*, 1 March 1956, p. 2.

6. See Werth, *Lost Statesman,* p. 312.

7. For the program that he urged on the cabinet before resignation see Werth, *Lost Statesman,* pp. 306–307.

8. *L'Année Politique,* 1956, p. 70. See also Scheinman, *Atomic Energy Policy in France under the Fourth Republic,* pp. 157–165.

9. See Finer, *Dulles Over Suez.* Soviet troops entered Hungary only a few days before Israel invaded Egypt.

10. E. Mannoni, *Le Monde,* 12 January 1957.

11. They were also concerned about Socialist "colonization" in the bureaucracy, and about impending legislation on the schools; see Chapsal, *La Vie politique,* p. 255.

12. Jacques Fauvet, *Le Monde,* 8 March 1957.

13. Fauvet, *Le Monde,* 23 May 1957.

14. Their importance was pointed out by Maurice Duverger in an article, "Les Quarante," *Le Monde,* 22 November 1957, cited in Chapsal, *La Vie politique,* p. 257.

15. The Moderates' position is analyzed in Chapsal, *La Vie politique,* pp. 256, 259, 245.

16. See de Tarr, *The French Radical Party,* p. 231.

17. This sequence showed his tactical skill, which Fauvet suggests was not matched by a sense of larger political issues; see *Le Monde,* 9–10 June 1957, and *La IVᵉ République,* p. 331.

18. Fauvet, *Le Monde,* 26 June 1957.

19. *Journal Officiel,* 1957, 3775.

20. A. Chênebenoit, *Le Monde,* 6 September 1957.

21. On the failure of this and later "round tables," see Andrews, "Swan Song of the Fourth Republic."

22. See G. Mamy and Fauvet, *Le Monde,* 30 October 1957; see also Duverger, *Le Monde,* 22 November 1957.

23. Fauvet, *Le Monde,* 1–2 December 1957.

24. For a participant's account of the mission see Murphy, *Diplomat Among Warriors,* pp. 439–441.

25. This strike, at the Palais-Bourbon, revealed the incapacity of the government to assure the deputies access to their own chamber. See Arrighi, *La Corse, atout décisif,* pp. 3–7.

26. A preliminary motion which must be decided before the main one; see Lidderdale, *The Parliament of France,* p. 134.

27. Fauvet, *Le Monde,* 16 April 1958.

28. Fauvet, *La IVᵉ République,* p. 342.

29. See Hurtig, "La S.F.I.O. face à la Vᵉ République: majorité et minorité," 532.

30. See Arrighi, *La Corse, atout décisif;* Bromberger, *Les 13 Complots du 13 mai;* Tournoux, *Secrets d'état;* Meisel, *The Fall of the Republic.*

31. See *New York Times,* June 2, 3, 1958.

32. See Leites, *On the Game of Politics,* pp. 8, 119.

33. Including the *Indépendants et Paysans d'Action Sociale* (IPAS: 83–89 members), but not the *Groupe Paysan* (GP: 11–18) or the Gaullist *Républicains Sociaux*. Inclusion of this latter group would have sharply restricted the possible scales; their higher discipline, especially later in the Legislature, would have eliminated many roll calls from consideration.

34. This interpretation differs somewhat from that in Smith, "Algeria and the French *Modérés*: The Politics of Immoderation?"

35. See Chapter 7; also Smith, *ibid.*

36. Closer inspection of this last vote reveals that the Moderates' attention was drawn to Algeria during the debate. Laniel had spoken about Algeria, even though the speakers of the left had been more concerned with domestic issues (*L'Année Politique*, 1956, p. 50). Thus we can regard no. 103 as concerned with Algeria.

37. Roll call no. 971 was actually a transitional one, as closer inspection of the Q-matrix reveals; it could almost have been placed in Scale 1 as well as Scale 4.

38. These scales are based only on the votes of those deputies who remained in the Radical or UDSR group throughout the Third Legislature. An additional cluster for Radicals alone will be discussed in Chapter 7; see Table 7.9.

39. The latter, who supported the cabinets of the "system," were referred to by de Tarr, in *The French Radical Party*, as *radicaux de gestion*.

40. A second cluster found will not be interpreted, as it simply groups a series of personal votes held in succession, on all of which nearly the same deputies were absent.

41. Two other scales were found that simply marked off sets of deputies absent at particular periods and may be neglected as having no political significance.

42. The roll call involving his request (no. 655) would have been included in Scale 1 if the minimum value of Q had been lowered to .6. This roll call is the only one studied on which absence on a personal vote was politically significant by itself.

43. See Siegfried, *De la IVᵉ à la Vᵉ République*, pp. 120–121.

44. The relations between scales across Legislatures will be considered in Chapter 10, and the relation of scale position to *ministrable* status in Chapter 7.

45. A major exception was René Mayer's action in precipitating Mendès-France's downfall. This was a tactical decision rather than one resulting from a new issue.

»7«

The Assembly and the Cabinet

W E HAVE NOW EXAMINED THE gross attributions of responsibility for cabinets' fall during the three Legislatures, and the dimensions of cleavage within the major parties. We have seen that certain parties were charged with a great share of responsibility for the fall of cabinets: the Socialists in 1946–51, the Gaullists in 1953–55, and the Moderates in 1956–58. The final blow to the cabinet was not always reflected by a roll call included in our scales, however, for the party going into opposition was often unanimous in doing so.

Aside from the final votes on which cabinets were "killed" there were many other votes on which the fate of cabinets was involved that did appear in the scales—in certain scales more than others. On a scale including a high proportion of cabinet-related roll calls, the divisions of a party indicate the deputies' positions in relation to the fate of the cabinet. These positions may be distinguished from the same deputies' positions on scales that were less closely related to the cabinet. (We shall identify other scales, related to the constituencies, in Chapter 10.) In this chapter, the positions of deputies in each party during each Legislature will be contrasted where possible on scales of the two types.

We shall show that *ministrables* generally voted more favorably toward the cabinet than did the rank-and-file members of their parties—contrary to the widespread view that they were to blame for cabinet instability.

In inferring the meaning of a scale based on legislative votes, we use information about the legislature as well as the substance of the votes. This permits inferences about scale issues from the positions taken by particular deputies, as well as the examination of group influences on the votes—either coalitions in the Assembly, or alliances and pressures relating the legislator to his constituencies. We shall therefore present tables of deputies' names, showing how the members of each party were placed on representative scales. These tables show how the deputies' positions varied from one scale to another or from one Legislature to another. The names of well-known deputies, placed on the scales, immediately give further information about the meaning of the scales. Even for the less conspicuous members, careful study of their constituencies, their biographies, and their arguments in debate can be informative. The votes of *ministrables* can also help us to examine the behavior of the group of leaders who largely dominated the Assembly.

The Placement of Deputies on Scales

In Chapters 4–6 we identified, for each party, clusters of roll calls which divided that party similarly. Each cluster was identified from the corresponding Q-matrix, in which the similarity of each possible pair of roll calls was measured by the coefficient Q (see Chapter 4).

These clusters of similar roll calls can be used not only to identify the sources of division within each party but also to place deputies in relation to these divisions. If an issue is involved, the deputies are ordered according to their positions on it; if a cabinet is affected, they are placed by their degree of support or opposition. Our cluster analysis has been designed to permit this.[1]

Figure 7.1 Location of Legislators and Cutting Points Along a Scale

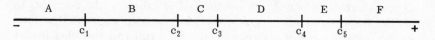

We must now show that each cluster of roll calls we have found can also be used to place deputies in a corresponding rank ordering, or scale. For this purpose we consider how we would identify a group of roll calls that ranked legislators along a single continuum. We shall see that the clusters identified from the Q-matrix also serve, to a good approximation, as bases of ranking.

Let us first imagine that such a continuum, or basis of ranking, exists. Examples might be the left-right division on social legislation, attitudes toward European union, the church-school question, attitudes toward the colonies, positions with regard to a cabinet, or intraparty factional divisions —bases of division that we have already discovered in the clusters identified in Chapters 4–6.

In order to see whether actual roll calls fit such a ranking, we must classify the votes on each roll call not as *pour* or *contre*, but as positive or negative in terms of the issue or basis of division involved. This polarity classification was made at the stage of computing and analyzing the Q-matrix.

When an ordering of this sort is found and a set of roll calls and legislators fit it perfectly, it can be represented by a diagram such as Figure 7.1. The legislators may be considered as arrayed along a continuum from "−" (e.g., a leftist position) to "+" (a rightist position). In the diagram, we assume there are five roll calls, each corresponding to a cutting point on the continuum: c_1, c_2, c_3, c_4, c_5. These cutting points divide the line into six segments, A, B, C, D, E, and F, each of which corresponds to a set of legislators. If we had analyzed six parties, each voting as a bloc, these segments might have corresponded to a sequence of parties shown in one of the figures of Chapters 4–6; A might have been the Communists, B the Socialists, and so on. But we are principally concerned with divisions *within* a given party (or a closely related pair of parties) and the segments therefore correspond more nearly to the party's left wing, its left center, and so on, to its right wing. Normally we shall not attach much importance to the particular points of division between these segments, simply observing that they occur where the roll calls happen to divide the party. In some cases, however, they identify the boundaries of recognizable blocs.[2]

Each cutting point then divides the legislators into two groups; for example, on the roll call corresponding to c_2, the legislators in segments A and B vote "−" (e.g., leftist) while those in C, D, E, and F vote "+". Since each cutting point forms two different groups in this way, the five cutting points allow us to rank the six segments of legislators relative to one another. We cannot, however, rank legislators within each segment; thus it is more correct to say that we assume a set of ordered or ranked categories than that we assume a complete ranking of all legislators relative to one another on a continuum.

Table 7.1 Response Patterns Corresponding to a Scale

Segment in which legislator is located	Number of positive responses	Votes on measure whose cutting point is				
		c_1	c_2	c_3	c_4	c_5
A	0	−	−	−	−	−
B	1	+	−	−	−	−
C	2	+	+	−	−	−
D	3	+	+	+	−	−
E	4	+	+	+	+	−
F	5	+	+	+	+	+

Once a legislator is classed in a definite segment or category, we know how he voted on every roll call corresponding to one of the cutting points. If he is in segment A, on the extreme left, we know he voted "−" on all five. If he is in B, he must have voted "+" on c_1, but "−" on the remaining four. A complete list of the voting patterns for legislators in each of these six segments is given in Table 7.1. If a set of roll calls fit these patterns, then deputies may be located in segments by their individual patterns of votes on these roll calls. The segments may be identified not only by letters, but also by the number of positive responses, as shown in Table 7.1. The number of positive responses will be used in our later treatment of scale segments, and will be known as the legislator's "scale score."

Although we shall find (and have already shown) clusters of roll calls that fit this ranking relationship quite well, such a fit would not occur easily by mere chance. In the case of five roll calls, the six voting patterns or "perfect scale types" that fit the ranking model perfectly are only a small fraction of the patterns that could conceivably occur. For with five roll calls, each of which permitted a "+" or "−" vote, a legislator could conceivably vote in $2 \times 2 \times 2 \times 2 \times 2$ or 32 different patterns of +'s and −'s. If the investigator can discover groups or clusters of roll calls that fit together to conform to a single ranking, he has reason to believe that some influence other than random voting is producing this simplicity. He normally infers that each cluster of roll calls that fit together in this way embodies some general basis of division, whether an issue or an opposition between coalitions.

The procedure we have chosen to identify clusters—analysis of the Q-matrix—is also a test of the conformity of groups of roll calls to the ranking model. We chose to use the coefficient Q because it attains the value of 1.0 whenever two roll calls have a perfect ordering, or scale, relation to one another. This can be shown by reference to Table 7.1. Consider first the relation between roll calls c_2 and c_4. The legislators in segments E and F voted "+" on both these roll calls; those in A and B voted "−" on both; those in C and D voted "+" on c_2 and "−" on c_4. No one voted "−" on c_2 and "+" on c_4. In other words, if we expressed the relation between the votes on c_2 and c_4 in a fourfold table the −,+ cell would be empty.

This relation holds for *any* two roll calls in Table 7.1, or in a perfect scale of this kind. For if the relation between any two of the roll calls in Figure 7.1 is expressed in a fourfold table such as Table 4.1, either the +,− cell (the upper right cell, designated as *b*) or the −,+ cell (lower left or *c*) will be empty. This means that the product *bc* will be zero in the expression for $Q = (ad - bc)/(ad + bc)$. As a result, Q will be equal to ad/ad, or + 1.0. The perfect relation between the Moderates' votes on the Marie investiture and the Queuille budget, in Table 4.1, is another example of this same type of relation. One could arrange from left to right the three groups of deputies distinguished in that table: those who supported both premiers, those who supported Marie but not Queuille, and those who opposed both. In order for the left end of such an array to correspond to the political "left," we consider a conservative or rightist vote to be "positive" in those cases where such a vote can be identified.

Our earlier decision to include in clusters groups of roll calls with Q's of .8 or more allows some departure from the scale model. The degree of departure allowed is measured by the product *bc*, in relation to *ad*.

We then use the scale model to assign scores to the deputies, equal to the numbers of positive votes in the corresponding perfect scale patterns. Each such score corresponds to one segment or category in an array such as that of Figure 7.1. For each roll call in a cluster, we know its proportion of positive votes (p_+). In a perfect scale, the value of p_+ for each roll call —that is, each cutting point as in Figure 7.1—measures the proportion of deputies who are to the right (positive) side of that cutting point. If we wish to work back from actual roll calls to the corresponding scale positions, we make use of the observed values of p_+. We arrange these values in order, and select individual roll calls, or groups of roll calls with values of p_+ that are close together, to define cutting points on the scale. When a group of roll calls is thus combined into a single hypothetical roll call, this defines a cutting point; each deputy's preponderant vote on these roll calls is converted to a single vote on that hypothetical roll call. This procedure has the advantages of averaging out some of the "errors" or departures from the perfect scale model and of placing deputies who were absent on certain votes but who voted on other similar ones.[3]

If a deputy then has a pattern of votes corresponding to a perfect scale type, he is assigned a scale score corresponding to the number of positive votes on the cutting points. If his pattern is not a perfect scale type, it is assigned to the nearest perfect type. In a few cases, if the divergence from any perfect type is great, no scale score is assigned.[4] The result of this procedure is that nearly every deputy in the parties being studied is placed in one of the segments or categories on each of the corresponding scales.

Ministrables and Cabinets

In placing deputies on scales, we have taken care not to count the votes of cabinet members—that is, to treat the votes as though those members voted neither positively nor negatively. The scale scores assigned to deputies who were members of certain cabinets thus depend entirely on the votes they cast at other times, when they were not in the cabinet. A few deputies who were in the innermost circles of the Assembly are therefore sometimes not given a score; others who served in the cabinet on several important votes are classified nearer the center of the scale than their actual votes would have placed them.

We have eliminated these votes in order to draw certain conclusions about the cabinets without biasing our results. The analysis of cabinet specificity of scales (Chapter 6) has already made use of this treatment. But it is also valuable for another purpose: the analysis of the votes of *ministrables* during periods when they were not in the cabinet.

A major reason often given for the overthrow of cabinets was the ambition of non-ministers to become ministers.[5] It is not surprising that the honor of being addressed as "Monsieur le Ministre" (for the rest of one's life) had its appeal; an amusing account of the effect of this possibility on a rank-and-file deputy is given in Pineau's novel, *Mon Cher Député*. Rémy Bellonday, his fictional deputy, eagerly accepts a cabinet post without bothering to ask what the cabinet's program will be.[6]

Among the critics of ministerial ambition some claimed that *ministrables* schemed to bring down cabinets, while others contended that *ministrables'* concern to enter cabinets led them to form coalitions hardly expected to last more than brief periods.[7] From still another perspective, Mendès-France was criticizing the system when in 1953 he asked his prospective ministers to promise not to join the *next* cabinet; he evidently feared coalitions that could be easily dissolved from within.[8]

These critics differ as to whether they see the vices of the system and the ambition of ministers operating through the deliberate destruction of cabinet coalitions from within or without. But they all call for an objective examination of what the *ministrables* actually did. Potential ministers outside the cabinet cast votes and were placed on our scales; the question is whether they differed from their rank-and-file party colleagues, and in what way.

We wish, then, to show the relations that existed between *ministrable* status and pro-cabinet positions on our scales. Let us first define a *ministrable* as a deputy who actually held a cabinet office during the Legislature under study, but who was not in the cabinet at the time of the particular vote considered. This is an approximate, operational definition, but it is enough to tell us the tendencies of potential ministers' votes.

We next consider each of the scales we have found and examine the cabinet's position on it. For the Moderates this position is typically the score on the extreme left (o), and for the Socialists on the right. For the center parties it sometimes happens that the position most consistently agreeing with the cabinet is central on the scale; in this case we shall "fold over" the scale categories so as to place the greatest agreement with the cabinet at one extreme, and the greatest disagreement at the other.[9] It also sometimes happened that the cabinet was divided or that its votes failed to fall perfectly into a scale pattern; this normally resulted when issues rather than cabinets were dominant and when successive cabinets took opposite stands on them.

For those scales where there was a definite score assignable to the cabinet, we can then study the association of *ministrable* status with support for the cabinet, that is, nearness to the cabinet's score. This relation can be expressed by the coefficient γ, just as in Chapters 4–6 it described the relation between two scales. It is only necessary to express the status of *ministrable* —and its absence—as a dichotomy, i.e., a score of 1 for *ministrables* and o for other deputies. These associations are presented in Table 7.2.

This table indicates clearly that the *ministrables* in every party shown tended to support the cabinet; the associations are largely positive. Moreover, there is one exception which, when taken into account, makes them even more positive. We have observed repeatedly that Mendès' cabinet was oriented "against the system." Many exceptions in the table reflect this fact. One scale for the Radicals in the Second Legislature (II-2) and two for the MRP (II-2 and 5) do not even reveal a consistent pro-cabinet position until we reverse the votes under Mendès, and count opposition to his cabinet as "pro-cabinet," that is, favorable to the dominant group in the Assembly. When we make this reversal, the associations for all three of these scales become positive. The only two scales on which the Moderate *ministrables* tended to oppose the cabinet (II-1 and 3) also show positive associations when their votes under Mendès are reversed. The Moderate and MRP *ministrables*, therefore, tended to oppose Mendès but support the other cabinets. An exception is the "Early Mendès" scale for the Moderates (II-5) on which, at this phase of his ministry, their *ministrables* tended slightly to favor him.

The Radicals' reaction to Mendès was more complex. On their Scale II-3, dealing with the Paris Agreements, their *ministrables* supported him strongly ($\gamma = +.42$); reversing these votes, which is quite inappropriate on this issue, destroys the positive association. Scales II-5 and II-7 included votes under the second Faure cabinet, and both had initially negative associations; this may well have been due to the fact that Mendès was then the legitimate leader of the party and Faure was thus governing against his own party's leadership.

The URAS apparently responded to Mendès not as an "antisystem" premier but as one premier among others, proposing action on the same issues. Thus in their Scales 2 and 3, dealing with colonial matters and with

Table 7.2 Association (γ) Between Ministrable *Status* and *Pro-Cabinet Scale Positions**

Legislature and Scale	Moderates	URAS	Rad.-UDSR	MRP	SFIO
I-1	+.73		+.35	**	+.54
I-2	+.60		+.64	+1.00	
I-3	+.56		+.47	+ .67	
I-4	+.74		+.38		
II-1	−.06 (+.06)	−.08	**	− .06	+.43
II-2	+.31	+.28 (**)	** (+.14)†	** (+.27)	
II-3	−.19 (+.19)	+.52 (**)	+.42 (−.42)	+ .12 (+.10)†	
II-4	+.24 (+.55)†	+.31	+.21†	− .02	
II-5	+.16 (−.16)	+.15	−.18	** (+.12)	
II-6	**	+.40	−.04† (+.05)	+ .18	
II-7	**		−.51† (+.26)		
III-1	+.66		+.28	+ .10	−.12
III-2	+.31		+.15		
III-3	+.33		+.25		
III-4	+.22		+.44		
III-5	+.14				
III-6	+.39				
Total					
+	13	5	10	5	2
−	2	1	3	2	1

*Figures in parentheses are based on classifying votes against Mendès-France as "pro-cabinet."
**No clear cabinet position is definable; either the cabinet was deeply divided or the positions of cabinets did not conform perfectly to a scale pattern.
†Scale scores rearranged to place pro-cabinet score at one extreme.

German rearmament, reversal of polarities under Mendès simply destroyed the scale patterns.

An exception remains for the Socialists. When they divided over de Gaulle in the Third Legislature, their *ministrables* were slightly more in opposition than support. The opposition may have been because of de Gaulle's hostility to the "system" (though his cabinet represented it well at first) or because these votes were free from the constraint of an official party position.

The general support by *ministrables* for the cabinet is even more striking if we consider an influence that might have been expected to work in the opposite direction. Not merely the machinations of ambition to bring the cabinet down but mere selectivity by the premier might have produced an opposite result. For suppose each premier had picked for his cabinet those members of other parties who were most congenial to his own position; those left out would have been most likely to oppose him. This remaining group would then have been negatively selected to include a disproportionate number of opponents of the cabinet. Clearly this effect did not occur; or if it did, it was counterbalanced by a general sympathy between all *ministrables* and the incumbent cabinet, setting all of them apart from the more indifferent or hostile rank and file.

The general tendency of the *ministrables* to support the cabinet reveals an important aspect of the French political system: the consensual subsystem of the Assembly. We consider the consequences of this fact in detail later in this chapter. First, however, we shall study the positions of individual deputies on the scales.

Factions and Leaders on the Right

The clusters of roll calls found for the parties of the right may now be used to order their deputies, according to the procedures just described. We select for discussion Scales I-1 and I-2; the former reflected the general division of the party into right and center factions over the controversy between Gaullism and the cabinet, and the latter the issue of the electoral law.[10]

The positions of the deputies on these two scales are shown in Table 7.3. The first, or general, scale (I-1) corresponds to the deputy's horizontal position in the table: column "0" includes the deputies most favorable to the center cabinet coalitions, while column 4 includes those most opposed. The second scale, dealing with the electoral law, corresponds to the deputy's vertical position: the top row (0) includes those most favorable to the electoral alliances among the center parties, and row 4 includes those most opposed to them. Row and column X give names of deputies who were not assigned scores on the scales because of death, absence, or change to membership in another party.[11] Deputies who served in the cabinet are now assigned pro-cabinet scale scores; thus Jacquinot, Pinay, and Roclore have been placed in the upper left cell of the table. The numbers opposite the dividing lines indicate the roll calls used for cutting points.

The major division of the rightist parties in the First Legislature was between the RI and the PRL, as Table 7.3 shows; the names of the latter are underlined. In rows 3 and 4, corresponding to greatest opposition to the electoral law, the proportion of PRL deputies was highest, and a number of them ran as Gaullists in 1951; those in the right-hand column (scale score 4) were most uniformly opposed to the cabinets of that period. The two scales can almost be condensed into one, as their high association ($\gamma = +.67$) indicates.

The deputies in the diagram may be distinguished in other ways as well. Many well-known deputies were favorable to the cabinet coalitions of that time: Pierre Garet, a former MRP deputy who later became president of the

RI Assembly group in the Second Legislature; Canon Kir, the mayor of Dijon; Paul Reynaud, frequently mentioned as a possibility for the premiership and for cabinet posts; Jacquinot and Pinay, themselves members of the Pleven cabinet; and René Coty, later President of the Republic. In the lower right-hand corner of the diagram are deputies (mostly PRL) who opposed the cabinets of that period. Those who later won seats as Gaullists included Barrachin, Bergasse, Bouvier O'Cottereau, Frédéric-Dupont, July, de Sesmaisons, and Rousseau. This group tended also to be strongly represented among the dissidents who supported Pinay's investiture in 1952 and then organized the ARS. Their presence among the Gaullists may have contributed to that party's reputation of "extreme rightism," and to alienating some of the support de Gaulle sought from former Radicals or Socialists.[12]

The RI and PRL deputies were distinguished from one another not only by their respective supporting and opposing the cabinet; they also differed in their social origins.[13] The PRL generally had higher social status than the RI deputies; this difference may have played its part in the fragmentation of the Right.

We may use Table 7.3 for further examination of the *ministrables'* votes. On both scales shown, a low score or "leftist" position corresponds to the greatest support for the cabinet. Thus the deputies listed in the upper left corner (Chastellain, Garet, et al.) supported the cabinet on every cutting point in both scales, while the group in the lower right corner (Barrachin, Bergasse, et al.) consistently opposed it.

We have identified as *ministrables* those deputies who served in cabinets in the First Legislature as ministers, secretaries, or undersecretaries of state. They are identified in Table 7.3 by initials in parentheses of the premiers under whom they served. We may compare *ministrable* status with position on Scale I-1 by locating the *ministrables* in the columns of the table. Of ten such deputies, two served in the Pleven cabinet and the final Queuille cabinet (Jacquinot and Pinay); their supporting votes on nos. 3407 and 3486 must be disregarded for our present purpose, since they were not merely *ministrables* but actual ministers during these votes. Of the other eight, four are in column 0 and four in column 1; they were clearly more favorable to cabinets in general than were their party colleagues. The same relation holds, but to a slightly lesser degree, for the *ministrables'* placement on Scale I-2. We thus fail to confirm the notion that leading deputies sought to bring down cabinets in order to obtain places in the next; though ministers in the cabinet may have shown a certain willingness to fall, potential ministers showed less overt effort to bring down the cabinet than did the rank and file. This finding will be supported in further detail by analyses for other parties and other Legislatures.

It may be argued, however, that the *ministrables'* votes fail to display all the subtle ways in which deputies and ministers can weaken a cabinet. For example, a characteristic tactic of the leading *ministrables* in the divided parties (Radicals and Moderates) is said to have been to encourage their "friends" to go into opposition without openly doing so themselves. Isorni refers to this process: "There were, in effect, some thirty of us 'national' deputies who, in the course of the last legislature of the IVᵉ, contributed to the

Table 7.3 *The Right in the First Legislature:* *Deputies' Scale Positions*

Scale I-2 (Electoral Law)	Scale I-1 (General Left-Right) 0	3407 3486	1	1172-1654b	2	1251-3419	3	2617-2153	4	X
0	Chastel'n(B) Garet Gavini Jacquinot (RBQ₂PlQ₃) Kir Lalle Pantaloni Pinay(Q₁PlQ₃) Roclore(R) Rollin Temple Thiriet		†Barbier †Coty(S_1S_2M) Jean-M(S_1Q_1) Reynaud(MQ_2)				Bougrain			Courant Marcellin Ramarony
101										
1	Becquet† †Betolaud(Q_1) Moustier†		Chamant						Bouvier Monin Moynet* Quilici Roulon	Delachenal Rigal
1942–3481										
2	Bruyneel Joubert		Clemenceau Felix Laniel(M)						Legendre Mutter Nisse	
3487–3856										
3	Montel P(Q_2)		Denais J		André P †Crouzier† Desjardins				Aumeran Christiaens† Dubois† Le Cacheux† Mallez Montillot†	
3205,3883										
4					Baudry d'A† Fredet July †Sesmaisons				Barrachin Bergasse Bouvier O'C Brusset Frédéric-D Geoffre Hénault Lefèvre-P Macouin Peytel Rousseau Schauffler Triboulet*	
X					Marin					Grousseaud Petit G Récy Sourbet Theetten Vieljeux

Deputies are arranged horizontally and vertically according to scale score; "X" designates those who were not scored on a given scale. Cabinet members have been reassigned scale scores based on their votes while in the cabinet. Between each pair of scale categories is an indication of the roll call numbers that separated that pair. When more than two roll calls were used to constitute a cutting point, only the numbers of the extreme roll calls in that group (in terms of p₊) are given, separated by a dash. Those whose names are underlined belonged to the PRL during at least part of the Legislature.

Letters in parentheses after a deputy's name are initials of premiers in whose cabinets he served.

*Nonscale type. †Ambiguous scale assignment. These symbols, before a deputy's name, refer to the horizontal scale; after, to the vertical. These notes and symbols hold for the similar tables following.

overthrow of the Mollet, Bourgès-Maunoury, and Gaillard cabinets by leaving the majority. Each time, we had only a single preoccupation, the safety of the franc and the safeguarding of Algeria. Almost always, we were pushed into it by some of our 'leaders' who regularly abandoned us at the moment of voting."[14] Another example is the action of Bourgès-Maunoury and Gaillard as "faithful seconds"[15] of René Mayer. Under the Bidault ministry in 1950 (no. 2218) they swung into opposition—conspicuously in relation to the Radicals' scales of that period—while Mayer was Minister of Justice. Later they were considered to have opposed Laniel at Mayer's behest while Mayer publicly supported the cabinet.[16]

One way to test the subtler hypothesis that *ministrables* support the cabinet while asking their friends or protégés to oppose it is to examine the votes of their friends. An approximate way of identifying "friends" is to select those deputies who ran on the same district list with a given *ministrable*. We have examined the votes of these running mates or *colistiers*, but they give no more support to the hypothesis of *ministrables'* opposition than do the *ministrables'* votes themselves.

Both scales shown for the right in the First Legislature reveal general support of the cabinet by *ministrables* compared to other deputies. But it is also useful to distinguish between these scales in the extent of this "*ministrable* effect," because the distinction illustrates differences between types of scales that appear repeatedly for other parties and Legislatures. The associations of these scales with *ministrable* status (Table 7.2) were $+.73$ and $+.60$ respectively. The difference suggests that Scale I-1, which contained seven roll calls dealing with the fate of cabinets, was closer to the Assembly's "game" in both content and factional voting than Scale I-2. The latter scale, we shall see in Chapter 10, was more closely related to the Moderates' divisions in later Legislatures, and presumably closer to constituency effects.

In the Second Legislature, although new issues arose, the Moderates' alignments still resembled those of the First. Their "Europe" scale (II-2) ranked them in a way closely associated ($\gamma = +.71$) with the electoral-law scale in the First Legislature.

Another major scale, II-1, divided the Moderates under the Mendès-France ministry chiefly on colonial issues. On this scale the *ministrables* tended to oppose the cabinet (Table 7.2). We select for examination, however, a scale based on roll calls earlier in the Mendès-France cabinet, II-5, because it is more clearly distinct from the "Europe" scale. Early in Mendès' ministry, from his investiture to his successful return from the Geneva conference, the *ministrables* actually tended slightly to support him. Later they began to attack him on foreign and colonial policy; nationalist opponents of European union were prominent among those Moderates shifting into

Table 7.4 Moderates, Second Legislature: Deputies' Scale Positions

Scale II-2 ("Europe")	Scale II-5 (Early Mendès)							
	0	2530	1	2570 / 2571	2	2529	3	X
0	Apithy Bardoux Beaumont[Me] Becquet Bettencourt [Me] Blachette Chamant(F_2) Chevallier J [Me] Courant (PlF_1Ma) Delachenal Jacquet M'l La Chambre [Me] Mazel Moustier Pantaloni Paternot Peltre Plantevin Temple [PlF_1PMe]		Anthonioz Boscary-M Christiaens(L) Colin Y *Detoeuf Garet(P) Gavini (PlF_1PMaL) Jacquinot (PlF_1MaL) Kir Lalle Laurens R Mamba Sano Montillot Ramarony (MaL) Ribeyre P (PlF_1PMaL) Reynaud(L) Sourbet(F_1F_2)		Boganda Chastl'n(L) Fourcade Lacombe Laniel (PlF_1L) Laurens C (PlF_1PMa) Le Cozannet *Lefèvre R *Montgolfier Mutter(L) *Tracol		Barbier Bruyneel (Pl) Delbez Jarrosson Joubert Montel P (PlF_1PMa) Noé Rolland Rousselot Salliard du R	Dommergue Kessous Litalien Pinay(PlF_1PF_2) Rollin
712–709								
1	Bessac Guichard Jean-M(PMa) Manceau Monin[Me] Moynet*[Me] Oopa Raffarin[Me]		Estèbe Olmi(L)		Isorni Saivre		Grimaud Petit G (PMa) Quilici	Pébellier 1
474–671								
2	André P Antier(PlF_2) Crouzier(F_2) Laborbe Leroy-L Liautey Loustanau-L Paquet Vassor Villeneuve		*Pupat		Deshors Pluchet		Aumeran Baudry d'A Denais Dixmier Fredet Guérard Guitton Toublanc	
X	Ben Tounès Pébellier 3 Renaud				Levacher Marcellin Naroun Vigier			Crouan Deboudt Frugier Joly Maurice- Petsche Pébellier 2 Pinvidic Valle

Underlined: Antier Peasants as of December 11, 1951.
Dashed underline: C. Laurens Peasants.

opposition. For this reason the later scale II-1 reflected a combination of the "Europe" scale and the earlier II-5.

Table 7.4 shows the Moderates' divisions on Scales II-2 and II-5. Those in the top row (0) were most favorable to European union; they constituted over half the party, included a disproportionate number of *ministrables,* and were largely Independents rather than Peasants. Those in the bottom row were most opposed to European union, but divided into two extreme groups in their attitudes toward Mendès-France; at the lower left were Antier Peasants (indicated by underlining) who supported him at first, while those who opposed consistently were less likely to be Peasants and more simply classifiable as on the "right."

The *ministrables* generally are distributed fairly uniformly across the four columns of the table; and this uniformity is more apparent if we omit from consideration the members of the Mendès-France cabinet, who were placed in column 0. This difference in position can be seen in the table, since those who served under Mendès are distinguished by brackets following their names enclosing the indications of their cabinet service.

For one *ministrable,* Antoine Pinay, there is additional evidence of his support for the cabinets of which he was a member. Pinay's "friends" constituted a well-known group rather distinct from the Laniel faction among the Independents. At one time they joined Pinay in abstaining on Laniel's financial bill.[17] They were Anthonioz, Chamant, Guichard, Jarrosson, Michel Jacquet, Jean-Moreau, and Pierre André; four of the seven are in the top row. They too were somewhat more favorable to the cabinet than were the other members of the party. The major exception was André, who strongly opposed European union and the cabinets favoring it.[18]

The deputies known to be representatives of particular economic interest groups tended to take somewhat more extreme anti-cabinet positions. André spoke for the steel industry. Liautey, representing the home distillers, also opposed European union. Joseph Denais, who had been a business spokesman under the Third Republic, and Marcellin, associated with small business, were strongly opposed to Mendès-France. On the other hand, Litalien, representing the trucking industry, took more pro-cabinet positions on Scale II-2.[19]

The Gaullists in the Second Legislature revealed by their scale positions that their party was structurally different from the others. Table 7.5 shows a cross tabulation of their deputies' positions on Scales II-1 (Economic) and II-3 (Germany). Those in the upper left corner of the diagram tended to be closest to General de Gaulle and to the early leadership of the RPF; they were on the "social" left wing of the party on domestic issues, and opposed German rearmament.[20] They tended also to oppose Faure's colonial policy (Scale II-6). Jacques Vendroux, General de Gaulle's brother-in-law, was on the extreme left of the party; near him were Pierre de Gaulle (the General's brother), as well as Jacques Soustelle and his *colistier,* Charret. Soustelle was president of the RPF parliamentary group in 1951, and was still considered a left-wing Gaullist when Mendès-France made him Governor-General of Algeria in 1955. Carlini, the mayor of Marseille, presided at the 1951 *conseil national* of the RPF. On the other hand, André Diethelm, who was president of the URAS Assembly group from 1952 until his death in 1954, occupied a central position on Scale II-1, more typical of elective leaders in

Table 7.5 URAS, Second Legislature: Deputies' Scale Positions

Scale II-3 (Germany)	|	Scale II-1 (Economic) 0	1807–1943 1	1867–1844 2	888–887 3	894–922 4	X
0		Carlini Noël L Vendroux	Charret-T Soustelle	Lebon			
2057							
1		Bricout Chatenay Commentry Damette Gaulle Nisse	Barrès Flandin Gaubert(P) Lipkowski Magendie Schmittlein (Me)	Briot Desgranges Furaud Gilliot Huel †Jacquet Marc (L)† †Koenig (Me F₂) Maurice-B Quinson	Bignon Brusset Gracia Seynat	Gaillemin Monsabert Prache	Barry-D†
2745–2744							
2			Dronne Durbet Gaumont Malbrant Sou	Bénouville †Corniglion-M(LF₂)† Deliaune †Ferri(L) Garnier Golvan* Guthmuller Haumesser †Lemaire (LMeP) Liquard †Palewski G (F₂) Palewski JP Serafini	†Fouques-D (Me)	Bouvier O'C Kauffmann Legendre Peytel Ritzenth'r Sidi el M Wolff	Tirolien
3264							
3		Clostermann	Bayrou(F₂) Catroux (MeP) Fouchet (Me)	Chaban-D (Me) Dassault Molinatti Triboulet(F₂)	Krieger	Hettier de B Prélot	
X		Vallon	Moatti	Diethelm Frugier Pinvidic	Ulver (LMe)	Bourgeois Georges Halleguen Hénault	

Initial "P" in parentheses stands for the unsuccessful Pineau cabinet of 1955.

divided parties.[21] The extreme positions of the other leaders suggest that they were chosen from above, rather than elected by the deputies, and that the parliamentary party may have been more fragile as a result. The only other major leader who occupied a right-center position on the scales was Jacques Chaban-Delmas, who significantly was among those favoring a more flexible position by the party before the Pinay investiture. He was one of the few to hold major office through the period of Gaullist weakness in the Third Legislature.

The lower right corner of the diagram would be occupied by most of the ARS deputies had they been included. Marcel Prélot, in this area of the diagram, had played the role of conciliator with the incipient ARS faction. Thus the internal divisions among the Gaullists reflected the ideological divisions that had prevailed in the RPF, and the distance of the leadership from the faction that had left to form the ARS.

An interesting feature of the URAS' positions on Scale II-1 is the lack of association between *ministrable* status and scale position. Their deputies who served under Mendès-France, and those who served under other premiers, do not appear in separate regions of the table. More of this group served under Mendès-France than under other premiers (those who wished portfolios under rightist premiers had left when the ARS split off); but neither the extreme left nor the extreme right of the URAS supplied a disproportionate number of ministers. Most URAS *ministrables* are in column 2, opposing Pinay but later supporting Laniel (in whose cabinet they were represented). They actually supported Pinay on Scale II-4, where the issue was economy, but opposed him on items in Scale II-1 that related to condoning violations of the tax law (Table 7.2).

By the end of the Second Legislature, several groups of deputies on the right had revealed consistent positions in spite of changing party names. One such group, chiefly on the right wing of the PRL, ran and were elected as Gaullists in 1951. Their "rightist" votes before 1951 expressed the same opposition to the cabinets that de Gaulle embodied.

In the Second Legislature these deputies were on the conservative but now pro-cabinet wing of the RPF. About thirty RPF deputies, including many of this same group, split off to support Pinay in 1952, rendering possible a rightist majority in the Assembly.[22] The more "loyal" Gaullists, as we have seen, were on the left wing of the party; this fact did not appear clearly in legislative voting, however, until after General de Gaulle had abandoned the movement. Thus, "right" in the sense of conservatism identifies an entirely different faction from "right" in the sense of opposition to the cabinet and the constitution.

The distinctions that must be made among the various currents of "rightist" politics can be clarified by reference to Rémond's classification. He traced three "rights" from 1815 to the early years of the Fourth Republic: the legitimist and monarchist tradition; the bourgeois, Orleanist, parliamentary tradition; and the Bonapartist appeal. The parallel between Bonapartism and Gaullism suggests itself, and the group of moderate rightists who resisted Gaullism and remained with the "system" seem to have represented a continuation of the Orleanist tradition. But Rémond sees the

Table 7.6 Moderates (IPAS), Third Legislature:
Deputies' Scale Positions

	Scale III-1 *(Algeria)*					
Scale III-3 (*Mollet-Domestic and Europe*)	0	171 239 / 1	690 / 2	807-710 / 3	706 777 / 4	X
0	Bettencourt Courant(P) Reynaud	Frédéric-D Gavini †Kir †La Chambre †Laniel †Plantevin Ribeyre(GPf) Vigier	Thébault			
363 **1**	Jacquinot† (PdG) Mutter(Pf)† Sourbet	†Barrachin (P) Boisdé †Boscary-M (GPf) Dixmier Garet(PGPf) Giscard(P) Huel Jacquet Michel Marcellin† (G) Mondon M† Pébellier Pianta †Pinay(PdG) Ramel† †Ritter †Temple Thiriet†	*Barennes *Bergasse(P) Coirre Couinaud† Crouan Gaillemin Goussu† Mignot Moustier† Pelleray Perroy Pinvidic	Bruyneel Coulon †Jean-M(P) †Priou Tremolet	Chamant† Jarrosson† Legendre† Montel P	Turc†
164 **2**	Delachenal*	Anthonioz Christiaens (G) Lalle Roclore Salliard du R Vayron	Febvay Féron Joubert	Baudry d'A †Georges Moynet Raingeard† Rousseau	Fourcade Isorni †Puy	
187, 419, 420 **3**		Brard Guitton Hénault Laurens C Petit G(P)	Alliot	†Chevigny †Crouzier Lefranc Sesmaisons	†André P	
X		†Chastel †Tardieu		†Fauchon	Fulchiron	Apithy

more antiparliamentary members of the PRL–RPF–ARS type as also embodying Orleanism; their changes of party affiliation may have resulted more from a desire to ride the electoral tide than from ideological differences with the other Independents.[23]

In the Third Legislature, three of the Moderates' scales dealt with the Algerian issue—Scales III-1, 2, and 4. The three others—III-3, 5, and 6—dealt with domestic issues, with the addition of some roll calls on the Common Market and on sub-Saharan Africa. To show the position of individual Moderates, we select the leading scale of each type, i.e., Scales III-1 and III-3. The deputies' scores on these scales are cross-tabulated in Table 7.6. Scale III-1 (horizontal) is most clearly related to the fate of cabinets (Chapter 6). On this scale, the *ministrables* tended to support the cabinet; their proportions are high in columns 0 and 1, but low in the columns to the right.

The major division on the horizontal scale, related to cabinets, is roll call no. 690, on which Bourgès-Maunoury fell. The forty-one Moderates to the right of this cutting point correspond at least approximately to "the forty" whom Duverger accused of overthrowing cabinet after cabinet. Those farthest to the right, when they spoke in the Assembly, tended to stress principles rather than the political situation of the cabinet; holding Algeria, for them, was a matter of the utmost importance, admitting of no compromise.

The vertical scale, no. III-3, shows a less clear concentration of *ministrables'* positions. Evidently domestic and European issues were not so closely related to the cabinets' fate as the Algerian question.[24] Moreover, Scale III-3 shows a higher degree of continuity with the Second Legislature than any other scale of the Third; it orders the Moderates who served in both similarly to Scale II-2 (Europe), with an association of .81. These two scales will be used in Chapter 10 in our analysis of constituency relations.

Factions and Leaders Among the Radicals

During the First Legislature, the Radicals[25] held generally consistent positions in relation to the cabinet—either supporting it or opposing it on the right. A fairly limited group of *ministrables* held office in one cabinet after another. Cabinet coalitions were typically to the left of the Radicals and the leaders of the party normally voted more leftist than the rank and file. The Gaullists who had been elected in 1946 and who joined the UDSR temporarily tended to oppose the cabinets and vote with the right wing of that party.

We select for examination the Radicals' leading scale in the First Legislature, I-1 (Schuman-Bidault) and the scale showing greatest continuity of deputies' positions with other Legislatures, I-2 (Marie-Queuille). The latter scale was also closely related to the fate of cabinets; six of its fifteen items involved investitures or cabinet interpellations, and its association with *ministrable* status was high (+.64). This association was heightened by the fact that investiture votes, when no cabinet existed, permitted all the *ministrables* to be scored; while on Scale I-1, some *ministrables* (Bourgès-Maunoury and Gaillard) opposed the MRP cabinets involved. On Scale I-1, Bidault's cabinet members were moved to the pro-cabinet score of 0 on the

Table 7.7 Radicals and UDSR, First Legislature: Deputies' Scale Positions

Scale I-2 (Marie-Queuille)	Scale I-1 (Schuman-Bidault)					
	0	2193-2113 / 1	839-2195 / 2	458-531 / 3	626-2856 / 4	X
0	Béné Billères Chassaing Chevallier P Delbos (RMQ_1B) Delcos(Q_2) Dézarnaulds Dupuy M'u Faure E$(Q_1$ $BQ_2PlQ_3)$ Forcinal Galy-G Garavel Jules-J(Q_1) Marie $(RS_1MS_2Q_1)$ Maroselli $(RS_1MBQ_2$ $PlQ_3)$ Mekki Mitterrand $(RS_1S_2Q_1$ $PlQ_3)$ Morice$(SMQ_1$ $BQ_2PlQ_3)$ Moro-G Pourtier Queuille $(MS_2Q_1BQ_2$ $PlQ_3)$ Rencurel Révillon (S_2Q_1) Smail	Baylet Caillavet Gaborit Mendès-F	Bourgès-M $(S_1MS_2Q_2PlQ_3)$ †Gaillard(S_1)		Hugues JA	Cudenet Mayer R $(S_1MS_2BQ_2$ $PlQ_3)$ Viollette
1143-1144 / 1	Devinat(Q_1Q_2) Herriot† Jeanmot†	Degoutte *Gervolino	†Bonnefous Bourdan(R) Petit E $(Q_1BQ_2Q_3)$ Pleven (BQ_2Q_3Pl)	David JP	Hugues E Médecin Olmi	
951-651 / 2		Bastid		Ahnne Ramonet	Daladier	
1145-1300 / 3	Horma Ould	*Babet	Badie	†Bayrou †Capitant †Castellani †Clostermann †Kauffmann †Kuehn †Malbrant †Raulin-L *Said M C	Anxionnaz Bégouin L Chaban-D Chevallier J Giacobbi (Q_2Pl) Godin Krieger Masson Mondon Vendroux Wolff	
X	Ben Aly C		†Fabre		Derdour Milcent	Varenne Zigliara

basis of their cabinet position.[26] The deputies' positions are shown in Table 7.7.

The major source of opposition to the cabinet was Gaullism. The only *ministrable* in row 3 or column 4 was Giacobbi; a Gaullist for most of the First Legislature, he joined the remainder of the Gaullist Radicals[27] in consistent opposition until he returned to the party in 1950. Bourgès-Maunoury, Gaillard, Petit, Pleven, and Bourdan were the only non-Gaullist *ministrables* to oppose the cabinet on Scale 1. But six other *ministrables* who did not hold office under Bidault still supported him: Delcos, Devinat, Jules-Julien, Marie, Mitterrand, and Révillon. Together with them in column 1 was Édouard Herriot, the grand old man of Radicalism and Jules-Julien's *colistier*.[28]

The positions of other deputies may be noted as a basis for subsequent discussion. In the upper left corner of Table 7.7, the party leaders were joined by some of the Radicals from the Southwest (Billères, Galy-Gasparrou), but others from this region supported the cabinet less fully (Baylet, Caillavet). Édouard Daladier was even more opposed to the cabinets of the First Legislature, and near him in the lower right part of the table was Jean-Paul David, a conservative "neo-Radical."[29]

Between the First Legislature and the Second the position of the Radicals in relation to the cabinet changed, and they were no longer clearly to the right of it. The cabinets of the First Legislature were characteristically coalitions of parties to the left of the Radicals; for a Radical to support the cabinet was therefore to take a leftist position. Among the Radicals' scales in the Second Legislature, Scale II-1 on school aid showed greatest continuity with the First Legislature. This scale centered about an issue, so much so that there was no clear cabinet position on it. The other scales for the Radicals in the Second Legislature showed very low associations (.37 or less) with any in the First. Some deputies reacted to the changed situation by voting in terms of issues while others voted in terms of support or opposition to the cabinet. Perhaps the most striking change of position was Daladier's, who continued to oppose the cabinet and moved from extreme right to extreme left. Some Gaullists, of course, underwent a similar change.

The positions taken by the Radical and UDSR deputies in the Second Legislature are shown in Table 7.8. For this table we choose Scale II-1 (school aid) and compare it with Scale II-7 (Mendès-Faure)—the latter reflecting both the conflict between two Radical leaders and the sharply contrasting attitudes toward the "system" that existed in different factions of the party in the latter part of the Second Legislature.

On the school aid scale, a majority of the party are found in the top row —the traditional "anticlerical" position of the Radicals. In the lower two rows (1 and 2) are found a number of overseas deputies, many of them Muslim, who supported school aid; neo-Radicals such as J.-P. David and de Léotard whose votes resembled the Moderates' more than the old-time Radicals'; and a number of UDSR deputies. In a sense, the lower two rows of the table largely include elements on the fringes of old-time Radicalism.[30]

The alignment of the party on Scale II-7 (Mendès-Faure) reveals the internal antagonisms that existed at the end of the Second Legislature. Table 7.8 shows not only the distinction between a "cabinet" and a "con-

Table 7.8 Radicals and UDSR, Second Legislature: Deputies' Scale Positions

Scale II-7 (Mendès-Faure)

Scale II-1 (School Aid)

Scale II-1 (School Aid)	0	1 (2823)	2 (3301 / 3376)	3 (2821)	X

0	Baylet
	Billères[Me]
	Galy-G[Me]
	Jules-J
	Laplace
	Mailhe
	Mitterrand
	  [F_1LMe]
	Mendès-F[Me]
	Valabrègue
		André
		Aubry P
		Béné
		Caillavet[MMe]
		Cavelier
		Chassaing
		†Coudert
		†Daladier
		Degoutte
		†Dézarnaulds
		Ducos
		Félice
		Forcinal
		Masson J
		  [F_1PiMMe]
		Massot
		Moro-G
		Perrin
		†Queuille
		  (PlF_1PiML)
		Saint-Cyr
		Souquès
		Trémouilhe
		Turines
			Cassagne
			Chabenat
			†Delbos(Pu)
			†Fabre
			Félix-Tch
			Garavel
			Houphouët-B
			Laforest(F_2)
			Mamadou K
			Morève
			Sid Cara
				Devinat(L)
				Faure M
				Gaborit
				Gaillard
				  (PlF_1PiM)
				Martinaud-D
				  (F_1PiML)
				Montjou
				Morice
				  (PlF_1Pi
				  MPuF_2)
				Ramonet
				Révillon(Pi)
				Smail
				Viollette
					Gardey
					Heuillard
					Nigay
					Rastel

1379–1174					
1	Delcos(Pl)	Caliot Lanet[MePu] Secrétain(Pu)	Bégouin L(F_1) Bengana Caillet* †Condat-M David JP Faggianelli Genton Hakiki †Verneuil	Badie(F_2) Marie (PlF_1PiML) Mayer R(PlM) Pierrebourg Saiah Savale	Goubert
3115–1401					

2	Babet
	Bénard F
	Bernard
	Duveau[Me]
		Herriot
		Labrousse
		Velonjara
			Barrier
			Chupin
			Hugues JA
			Lafay(F_1LF_2)
			Ould Cadi
			Ourabah
			Raveleson
			†Said MC
				Bonnefous
				  (F_1MPuF_2)
				Bourdelles
				Hugues E
				  [PlMLMePu]
				Legaret(Pu)
				Léotard
				Médecin(F_2)
				Petit E
				  [PlF_1PiMe]
				Pleven(PlPiML)
					Cadi Abd
					Zodi

X			Barry-D
			Bourgès-M
			  [PlF_1MMe
			  PuF_2]
			Faure E
			  [PlF_1LMeF_2]
			Deboudt
					Chevallier P
					  (Pl)
					Ducreux
					Mekki

stituency" scale, but also the realignment of the Radicals during the Second Legislature. The former left wing, including many of the *ministrables* of the First Legislature, was deeply divided in the controversy over Mendesism. In the left-hand column were those who failed to support Faure at his investiture; five of the six *ministrables* in this group had been in Mendès' cabinet (indicated by brackets). Similarly, in column 1 (supporting Mendès rather than Faure on the conditions for the elections) a majority of the *ministrables* were also former members of that cabinet. Joining them, however, was Henri Queuille; he supported his party leadership (i.e., Mendès) at this time, though he was later to break away with the Morice group.

The right-hand columns (2 and 3) include the deputies who sided with Faure. Most of the *ministrables* in this group had not served under Mendès. Faure himself and Bourgès-Maunoury, who had served under both, were placed in column 2; Émile Hugues and Petit, who resigned from Mendès' cabinet, were in column 3. Most of those who served in two or more cabinets, excluding Mendès', are in column 3, i.e., they failed to support Mendès at his fall (no. 2821). Thus the separation between Mendesist and non-Mendesist *ministrables* was as sharp among the Radicals as among the Moderates. Again it was only the Mendès-France cabinet that was clearly opposed by the *ministrables*. They supported the Faure cabinet fully, since by 1955 Faure had become an accepted member of the "system." And unlike Queuille's 1951 cabinet, Faure's was not expected to terminate the Legislature; the game of calculating combinations for the next cabinet was being played seriously up to the moment when Faure was overthrown by an absolute majority.

The reorientation shown by Scale II-7 corresponds to a division of the formerly united leadership of the party into two hostile camps. While in the First Legislature there had been a relatively united group of *ministrables* on the left wing of the party, the controversies of the Second Legislature divided them deeply. The two extremes on this scale correspond to those who failed to support Faure at his investiture (no. 2823) and those who failed to support Mendès at his fall. In the central scale positions were deputies devoted to the party as such (Herriot, Daladier), but a smaller proportion of *ministrables* than at the extremes.

The Third Legislature was to see the hardening of the lines between Mendesism and the rest of the party. The dominant scale, III-1, reflects this division. It was clearly a continuation of the conflict that existed under Faure's cabinet in 1955; but it is interesting to look earlier in the Second Legislature for the beginnings of this division. The roll calls in Scale II-2 (EDC) throw some light on the question. They represent not merely the issue of the European Army, but also a progressive disaffection of various elements of the party from the typical cabinets and the positions supported by the "system." Mendès-France was not the first to go into opposition, and it was actually on Laniel's Indo-China policy that he finally did. The Radicals who joined him at this time—not earlier or later—tended to be the ones who stood with him in the Third Legislature.[31]

The Third Legislature also saw a further reorientation among the Radicals. After Mendès-France left the Mollet cabinet, he was joined in opposition by some of his earlier followers as well as a group of new supporters elected in 1956. Remaining loyal to the cabinets were most of the Radicals who had served with Mendès under Mollet. These groups are shown in Table 7.9, where the most pro-Mendesist group appears in column 0 and the most pro-cabinet in column 4. The UDSR, including many of its overseas members, were also divided on this issue. The Morice Radicals are

Table 7.9 Radicals and UDSR, Third Legislature:
Scale III–1 and the Church–School Issue

	Scale III–1 (Mendesism)								
	0	846-265	1	693-963	2	762-772	3	714-646	4	Morice Radicals
Opposed to school aid	André A Anxionnaz(M₁) Béné Chatelain Ducos Dumas R Hovnanian Lecoeur C Masson J(M₁) Mendès-F(M₁) Mitterrand (M₁M₂) Moro-G	Barry-D Diallo	Caillavet Cassagne	Baylet Coulibaly Diori Lisette Mailhe Sagnol Sékou Touré	Billères (M₁BM₂G) Bonnaire Cupfer Daladier(M₂) Desouches Félice(M₁B) Galy-G(B) Keita(BM₂G) Laforest (M₁B) Leclercq Maroselli (M₁BM₂Pf) Pleven(M₂Pf) Soulié(B)	Gaborit Morice(BPi) Queuille(M₂) Révillon
19, 34, 64									
Favored continued school aid	Hernu Hersant Martin G Naudet Panier Said M C	†Babet Bégouin L Condat-M Guissou			Bailliencourt Bénard F(B) Bonnefous (BPiG) Bourgès-M (M₁BG) Brocas Chauvet Faure M (M₁BM₂GPf) Gaillard (BM₂G) Giacobbi(BG) Hugues JA Rolland	Arrighi Badie(PiPf) Devinat(PiM₂) Faggianelli(B) Hugues E(BG) Marie Morève Pierrebourg Ramonet(BdG)
X	Dubois Duveau(M₁) Souquès	Mahamoud		Bocoum B	Degoutte Houphouët-B (M₁BPiM₂ GPfdG) Trémouilhe	

Not placed on Scale III-1: Cerneau, Clostermann, Herriot, Lipkowski (Rad.), Konate (UDSR).

placed at the right of the table; although they are not included in the scale analysis for Radicals and UDSR (Scale III-1), they took a generally more conservative position than the Mendesists, sometimes supporting the cabinet and sometimes opposing it for the opposite reason, i.e., its lack of vigor (from their standpoint) in prosecuting the Algerian war.

The vertical dimension in Table 7.9 corresponds to the church-school question. Early in Mollet's ministry, the "anticlerical" forces proposed to abrogate the Barangé law, which gave some aid to private as well as public schools. Since their strength in the Assembly had increased, they expected to reverse the decision of the previous Legislature. The Assembly's agenda committee did not give this bill priority, and a motion was made from the floor to revise the agenda and consider the school question. This proposal was repeated three times, and each time defeated by a narrow margin. The three divisions (nos. 19, 34, 64) constitute the contrived item that separates the first and second rows in Table 7.9, the top row constituting the "anticlerical" wing of the party.

This scale was not included among those we considered previously for the Radicals and UDSR, because our criteria for selecting roll calls excluded some of its items from consideration; the UDSR were not sufficiently divided to permit its inclusion. It appeared, however, as part of a four-item cluster when the Radicals were analyzed alone, and two of its items also appeared as a "doublet" cluster for the Radicals and UDSR together. We use the three items of common content to construct the table.

The division over Mendesism was largely independent of the church-school issue; and the dominance of the former as the Third Legislature progressed suggested that it was forcing the historic school question, as well as others, into the background. But the school question remained the one constant division among the Radicals throughout all three Legislatures, and still had significance in the constituencies at the 1956 elections. Just as in the Second Legislature, Baylet and Daladier were "anticlerical," with André, Béné, and Ducos. But now the first two opposed Mendès-France and the last three supported him. Also "anticlerical," but now in a separate party, were Queuille, Révillon, and the leader of that party, Morice. Continuing to favor the Barangé law were J.-A. Hugues, Badie, Marie and others, but they too were divided by the party split.

Perhaps the most significant indication of the new divisions in the party are the several new Mendesist deputies in the second row, left-hand column: Hernu, Martin (Mendès' *colistier*), Naudet, and Panier. Even though these new men were "left" on the dominant issue of Mendesism and Algeria, they favored the continuation of the Barangé law.

The largest concentration of *ministrables* is in column 4, as our previous discussion of this scale suggested. But the difference in position between those who were ministers only under Mollet and those only under other premiers deserves special attention. In column 0, all of the *ministrables* served only under Mollet: they were the Mendesist ministers, who opposed the succeeding cabinets. On the other hand, seven of the Morice Radicals were ministers, but none in Mollet's first cabinet. It would seem that

Mendès-France, despite his lack of power in that cabinet, had at least exercised a veto over some of his party colleagues who had served frequently
in cabinets before.[32] Their secession from the party, like the secession of
the ARS from Gaullism, may well have been hastened by their exclusion
from the cabinet.

Factions and Leaders in the MRP

In the First Legislature the MRP was divided by three scales. On Scale
I-1 (Reynaud law, electoral law), small left and right wings were split off
from the main central segment. On each of the others, only one wing was
split off: the left on Scale I-2 (end of session) and the right on I-3 (cantonal
elections). The main central segment of the party supported the cabinets
and contained most of the *ministrables;* in all three Legislatures the MRP
had left and right dissident wings, while its pro-cabinet faction tended to be
in the center.

On Scale I-1, the leftist dissenters opposed the "Reynaud law" that gave
special powers to the Marie cabinet, and seemed motivated more by the defense of the Republic than by personal interests.[33] The right-wing dissidents on this scale split off on an amendment to the 1951 electoral law.
On the roll call (no. 3846) the cabinet was divided; its MRP members opposed the amendment and voted with their party's central segment. Scale I-2
marked off a leftist group who opposed adjourning the debates prior to the
1951 election, making common cause with the Communists to press the
claims of deprived groups; the Queuille cabinet wished to set aside these
claims in order to hold the elections on time. Also included in this group of
dissenters were some deputies pressing the claims of rural areas. The dissenters on Scale I-3 were marked off from the main body of the party by
three votes on the 1948 cantonal elections. A bill sponsored by the MRP
deputy Fonlupt-Espéraber was suspected by its opponents of aiming at postponement of these elections for fear of RPF encroachments on the MRP
vote. The right wing of the MRP—even after the Gaullists had left—opposed this bill.

These scales are cross-tabulated in Table 7.10. The three segments of
Scale I-1 are arrayed vertically; this scale best reflects the lasting divisions
in the party and is probably most closely related to constituency influences
(see Chapter 10). The segments of the party split off by Scales I-2 and I-3
are shown in the left and right columns of the table respectively; the names
of a few deputies who dissented on both these scales are shown twice.

Among the names in the top row are several deputies generally considered on the left wing of the party: Aragon, Boulet, Abbé Pierre, and
Abbé Gau;[34] the first three later left the party. Conversely, several of those
in the bottom row also appear on the right wing in subsequent Legislatures.
Among those in the right-hand column, center row—who opposed postponing the cantonal elections but did not deviate on the other scales—were
several who later left the MRP and ran as Moderates: Bessac (elected on a
"Taxpayers'" list in 1951), Caron, and Garet (later a leader of the Moder-
rates).

Table 7.10 MRP in First Legislature:
Deputies' Scale Positions

Scale I-1	Dissident on Scale I-2 (end of session)	Dissident on neither I-2 nor I-3	Dissident on Scale I-3 (cantonal elections)
Left (opposed Reynaud law)	Charpin Dominjon* Guérin M (Dissident on 2 after leaving party) Aragon Boulet* Pierre-Groues Thiriet	Bichet Cayol Couston Gau Mauroux Poinso-Chapuis(S_1) Prigent R(RQ_2) Valay(B) Verneyras	Boulet* Buron(BQ_2PlQ_3) Dhers Dominjon* Dumas Truffaut

Center	Asseray
	Bessac*
	Bonnet C
	Bouxom
	Denis A*
	Finet
	Guillou P
	Hubert
	Hulin
	Le Sciellour
	Martineau
	Mouchet
	Poimboeuf
		Abelin(S_1S_2)
		Augarde(S_1)
		Colin A(Q_1)
		Raymond-Laurent(BQ_2)
		Tinguy(BQ_2)
		+ 64 non-
		ministrables;
		
		(+mins. under Queuille$_3$:)
		Bacon(BQ_2PlQ_3)
		Bidault$(RS_1BQ_2Q_3)$
		Catoire$(S_2Q_1PlQ_3)$
		Letourneau
		  (RBQ_2PlQ_3)
		Louvel(Q_2PlQ_3)
		Monteil(PlQ_3)
		
		(+mins. under Marie:)
		Coste-F P$(RS_1MS_2Q_1Q_2)$
		Lecourt(MS_2Q_1)
		Teitgen PH(RS_1MB)
		
		(+mins. under both:)
		Pflimlin$(S_1MS_2Q_1BQ_2PlQ_3)$
		Schneiter$(S_1MS_2Q_1BQ_2$
		  $PlQ_3)$
		Schuman$(RS_1MS_2Q_1BQ_2$
		  $PlQ_3)$
			Bessac*
			Caron
			Coste-Floret A
			Coudray
			Delahoutre
			Denis A*
			Elain
			Farinez
			Gallet
			Garet
			Lambert EL
			Mehaignerie
			Michaud
			Moussu
			Prévert
			Schaff
			Schmidt
			Solinhac
			Taillade
			Thoral

Right (opposed 1951 electoral law)	Juglas* Laurelli	Bas Chevigné Dupraz$(S_1MS_2Q_1)$ Duveau Ihuel(B) Terpend	Burlot Charpentier Errecart Hutin-Desgrées Juglas* Tinaud Yvon

* Dissident on both Scales I-2 and I-3.

In Table 7.2 we omitted Scale I-1 from our computation of the *ministrable* effect, since the cabinet was divided on roll call no. 3846. We may examine the other cutting point separately, however, with the aid of Table 7.10. Out of twenty deputies in the top row who opposed the Reynaud law four, or one-fifth, were *ministrables* (Poinso-Chapuis, Prigent, Valay, and Buron). Of the remaining 114 deputies, eleven were *ministrables* who did not serve in the Marie cabinet; the proportion in this case was only one-tenth. The proportion of *ministrables* in the dissenting wing of the party on the Reynaud law was thus higher than in the rest of the party. This relation is an exception to our hypothesis that *ministrables* supported the cabinet disproportionately. But the dissenting *ministrables* were not those who had held the most cabinet posts.

On Scale I-2 there were no *ministrables* among the dissidents, and on Scale I-3 only one, Buron.[35] The difference in *ministrable* effect between these scales and Scale I-1 reflects the substance of the roll calls involved; for while the defeat of the Reynaud law did not threaten the Assembly's functioning itself, Gaullism did (in relation to Scale I-3), and a disorderly termination of the Legislature might have done so in a similar way (Scale I-2).

The absence of *ministrables'* opposition on Scale I-2 is not a test of our hypothesis, since Queuille's 1951 cabinet was expected to be the last of the Legislature; ambitious deputies could have gained little except their colleagues' hostility by an unsuccessful attempt to bring it down. It does suggest, however, that without ambition the *ministrables'* support might have been greater.

In the Second Legislature, the MRP was more deeply divided. Its lasting divisions are revealed by Scale II-4, which consisted largely of roll calls under Pinay. We present for comparison Scale II-2, centering about Mendès-France and the colonial question; on this scale there was some association between *ministrable* status and *opposition* to his cabinet ($\gamma = +.27$ in Table 7.2). A cross-tabulation of MRP deputies' positions on these scales is shown in Table 7.11.

The horizontal scale in Table 7.11 (Scale II-4) deals with economic questions under Pinay and Pleven; the farthest left segment (column 0) opposed Pinay and opposed Pleven at his fall. This group contains no *ministrables*. The group in column 3, on the other hand, supported Pinay; added to this group, in the lower righthand cell, are six deputies who served in the Pinay cabinet. Since these six are not included in the analysis of *ministrables'* positions on the horizontal scale, the relation for the remaining *ministrables* is negligible ($\gamma = -.02$). On the vertical scale, those at the top favored Mendès-France while those in the bottom row opposed him. The lowest cutting point on this scale (no. 1801) was the vote on Mendès' first unsuccessful investiture; the leading *ministrables* opposed him.[36] For this reason alone, the association of *ministrable* status with anti-Mendès (high) scores on the vertical scale is more pronounced ($\gamma = +.27$).

A further distinction is possible, on the vertical scale, among MRP *ministrables* who served in different cabinets. Near the top are the three who served in Mendès-France's cabinet—Buron, Monteil, and Juglas. Those who served in other cabinets, but not Pinay's, are more central on the vertical

Table 7.11 MRP in the Second Legislature:
Deputies' Scale Positions

	Scale II-4 (Early Cabinets)				
Scale II-2 (Mendès-Colonial)	0 671 1225	1 1053	2	3 893 947	X
0	†Bouret Denis A Lefebvre †Le Sciellour Reille-Soult†	Aubin †Billiemaz Buron [PlF₁MMe] Elain †Hulin Monteil[Me]	Couston	†Abelin(PF₂)	Sanogo Sékou
1971, 2529, 2571, 2597, 2618 **1**	†Bouxom† Fouyet †Gau	Bacon(PlF₁MF₂) Barangé Dumas(Pu) Gabelle †Solinhac	Fonlupt-E Gosset †Grimaud H †Ihuel	†Ait Ali Hutin-D Juglas[Me] Ranaivo †Wasmer	Mercier M Sauvage
2570 **2**	Schmitt A	Catoire Catrice Colin A(PlF₁M) Coste-F P (F₁ML) Delmotte Devemy Dienesch †Duquesne Lecanuet(F₂) Moisan(Pu) †Penoy† Poinso-Chapuis †Schaff Thibault(L)	Barrot Coudray Dorey* Lacaze Lecourt(Pu) Sauvajon Siefridt Simonnet Villard	Defos du Rau Halbout*	Peyroles†
1801 **3**	Meck	Cayeux Menthon Mouchet Teitgen PH(LF₂)	Ben Aly C Bichet Bidault(Pl F₁ML) Cartier G Coste-F A(Pu) †Lucas Martel L Mercier AF Michaud †Raymond-L Schneiter Taillade Tinguy Viatte	Bapst Burlot †Charpentier(Pu) †Dupraz(M) †Klock Mehaignerie (+ cabinet): Chevigné (PlF₁PiML) Letourneau (PlF₁PiM) Louvel(PlF₁ PiMLPu) Pflimlin (PlF₁PiF₂) Schuman (PlF₁PiPuF₂) Schumann (PlF₁PiML)	
X			Douala		Duveau Errecart

$$Scale\ II\text{-}4\ (0:\ 671,\ 1225;\quad 1:\ 1053;\quad 3:\ 893,\ 947)$$

scale; while all those who served in the Pinay cabinet also opposed Mendès, both at his first investiture attempt and later. This division suggests that in the Second Legislature the MRP *ministrables* had distinct positions on the issues, and entered cabinets by virtue of their positions on issues rather than because of any general propensity for cabinet support.

Even though the MRP lost or expelled both its extremes (as well as those who became Gaullists) in the transition from the First to the Second Legislature, some consistency in dissidence remained. Table 7.10 showing the division of the MRP in the First Legislature may be compared with Table 7.11. In Table 7.11 Scale II-4 divides the party into "left" and "right" at the cutting point (no. 1053) which nearly bisects the party. On the right wing (bottom row in Table 7.10) we then find a substantial overlap with Scale II-4: in column 3, Hutin-Desgrées, Juglas, Burlot, Charpentier, Dupraz, and Chevigné;[37] in column 2, Ihuel. On the left in both Legislatures are Gau (column 0), as well as Dumas, Buron, and Poinso-Chapuis (column 1). Only one deputy shifted from one wing to the other; Couston went from left to right.

In the Third Legislature, our procedure revealed only one politically significant division of the MRP, centering in the Mollet ministry. *Ministrables* showed a slight tendency to support Mollet ($\gamma = +.10$). The farthest left position, scale score 0, contained two *ministrables*—Bacon and Schuman. Over half the MRP deputies fell into scale category 1, approving Mollet's social legislation but reluctant to vote the taxes to pay for it.

If the segments to the left and right of this central segment are compared with the left and right wings in the Second Legislature (as divided by no. 1053 in Table 7.11), their continuity again appears: on the left in that table and in the Third Legislature as well were Lefebvre, Bouxom, Meck, Bacon, and Duquesne; in column 3 of that table, and continuing on the right, were Abelin, Wasmer, Dupraz, Klock, Mehaignerie, Chevigné, Louvel, and Pflimlin; and in column 2, Schneiter and Tinguy. Shifting from right to left were Schuman and Schumann, who supported Pinay, then Mollet; moving in the opposite direction was Schmitt.

Factions and Leaders Among the Socialists

The Socialists tended to divide more on roll-call votes on major issues than on the party's relations to the cabinet. Party councils frequently debated whether the party should support the cabinet, or participate in it, but the general strategy of the leaders was to insure unity in Assembly votes on cabinet participation. They could choose their positions to maximize the unity of the party; and since it was usually only the leaders who favored participation they could obtain unity by not participating in the cabinet or by refusing to support it.

What divided the party were major issues it would not easily escape by nonparticipation: support of Thorez in 1946, the electoral law of 1951, German rearmament in 1954. Only on the Algerian question in 1957 and de Gaulle's investiture in 1958 did Mollet take positions that divided the party between participation and opposition.

able 7.12 Socialist Factions Throughout the Fourth Republic

	Anti–de Gaulle	990	Pro–de Gaulle
		993	
		996	
ale II–1		1000	

Anti–Paris Agreements, Anti–EDC	("Popular Front")		("Nationalists")
	Auban(Bo)		Bouhey
	E Baurens		Lejeune(BS$_1$Q$_1$Bi PlQ$_3$//
	B Binot		M$_1$BoM$_2$GdG)
	EB Desson		Naegelen(BRS$_1$)
	EB Doutrellot		
	Gourdon		
	EB Mabrut		
	B Titeux		

Pro–Paris Agreements, Anti–EDC	EB Cartier Marcel		Arnal(Bo)
	Charlot		Lacoste(BRS$_1$MS$_2$Q$_1$Bi/Pu/
	E Guitton JB		M$_1$BoM$_2$G)
	B Henneguelle		B Lapie(BPlQ$_3$)
	T Leenhardt		Meunier J(BBi//Bo)
	E Levindrey		B Moch(BRS$_1$MS$_2$Q$_1$BiPlQ$_3$//
	Lussy		Pf)
	B Mayer D(BRS$_1$MS$_2$Q$_1$)**		Regaudie
	B Mazier		Segelle(BBi)

: Pro–Paris Agreements, Pro–EDC	("Republicans")		("Loyal Mollet Faction")
	B Coutant		T David M
	Darou		Degrond
	T Defferre(BPlQ$_3$/Pu/M$_1$)		Deixonne
	T Depreux(BRS$_1$)		Evrard
	B Durroux		Faraud
	Gazier(PBlQ$_3$/Pu/		Gernez
	M$_1$BoM$_2$Pf)		Gozard
	E Gouin(BR)		T Lamarque-Cando
	Guille(M$_1$M$_2$)		Minjoz(B/M$_1$BoM$_2$)
	Jaquet G(Pu/M$_1$BoM$_2$G)†		Mollet(BPlQ$_3$//M$_1$M$_2$PfdG)
	T Le Bail		Thomas E(BRS$_1$MS$_2$Q$_1$
	T Lempereur		Bi Pl Q$_3$/Pu/M$_1$BoM$_2$G)
	Loustau(Pu/M$_1$BoM$_2$)		Véry
	TE Mazuez		
	Métayer (BPlQ$_3$/Pu/		
	M$_1$BoM$_2$G)		
	Pineau(S$_1$MS$_2$Q$_1$Bi/Pu/		
	M$_1$BoM$_2$G)		
	Prigent T(BR//M$_1$)		
	TE Rincent		

*Table lists only those who voted as Socialists on enough of the issues cited to be placed in the categories
hown, and who sat in all three Legislatures.
**Opposed to Mollet, Daniel Mayer had left the party and the Assembly by the time of de Gaulle's investiture.
†G. Jaquet was pro-EDC and anti-Paris Agreements.

T: dissident on Thorez investiture Dec. 19, 1946.
E: dissident on one or more electoral-law votes, 1951 (Scale I-1).
B: dissident on Bourgès-Mannoury's request for special powers in Algeria, July 1957.
(/): transition between Legislatures.

A fuller interpretation of the divisions within the Socialist party emerges from a comparison of the positions taken during all three Legislatures by deputies who sat throughout.[38] Table 7.12 shows, in the first place, that the divisions on German rearmament (horizontal rows in the table) cut across the other major factional cleavages in the party. Among the strong opponents of German rearmament were two groups who voted differently on the other key roll calls dividing the party: the left or "popular front" wing of the party (upper left in Table 7.12) who also tended to oppose the electoral law of 1951 and Bourgès-Maunoury's special powers; and a smaller right or "nationalist" wing (Bouhey, Lejeune and Naegelen) who favored de Gaulle and generally did not dissent on the other party splits. The intermediate group in the right column of Table 7.12 also shared this characteristic.[39]

Among those who supported German rearmament (the bottom row of the table) there was also an important division on other issues. Those who opposed Thorez in 1946 appear chiefly in the lower left cell, that is, they also opposed de Gaulle. At first glance these positions seem contradictory—opposition to Thorez placing them on the "right" wing of the party, and to de Gaulle on the "left." But these may have been Socialists who supported the Republic against threats from either quarter; we thus name this group "Republicans." Another common source for these positions might have been opposition to Mollet.

In contrast, those who opposed the electoral law of 1951 are most frequent on the upper left and unlikely to have opposed Thorez. Opposition to the electoral law among the Socialists evidently reflected sympathy for the fellow Marxist party disadvantaged by the law, the Communists.

The apparent paucity of the "loyal Mollet faction" (lower right cell) results from our omitting the members who failed to serve in all three Legislatures. These junior members actually supported Mollet more fully than their senior colleagues, who had more independent bases of power. Mollet's reliance on junior members, and the multiplicity of divisions in the party, suggest that before the de Gaulle investiture he prevented the various oppositions from coalescing. The greatest previous threat to his leadership had been on EDC, where the "popular front" and "nationalist" opposition joined, as they did in the Assembly at large as well.[40]

The vital importance of this four-way division among the Socialists is revealed by the closeness of the de Gaulle investiture vote. Had the parliamentary group not supported de Gaulle,[41] and had the party's vote been unanimously against him, his majority might not have been sufficient to bring him the support and legitimacy he needed during the summer and fall of 1958. The coalescence of multiple sources of internal opposition in the Socialist party nearly had profound consequences for the future of France.

The Socialists' divisions in the Third Legislature constrained Mollet in his parliamentary strategy. On both Bourgès-Maunoury's request for special police powers and on the de Gaulle investiture Mollet met with opposition from a consistent minority. Some of this opposition went over into the PSA (later PSU), but its later electoral importance was small; Mollet kept the reins of the party in his hands during the early years of the Fifth Republic.

To interpret these divisions within the SFIO in relation to *ministrables* and the cabinet, we must first ask which votes favored the cabinet and the "system." Of all the issues dividing the party, the 1951 electoral law most clearly reflected this issue. The dissidents are indicated by the letter "E" in Table 7.12. None of this group served in a cabinet after their electoral-law dissent.

The other major divisions of the party were more matters of principle— German rearmament, civil liberties, personal power versus the Republic— than of coalition. Moreover, none of these issues alone clearly divided the Socialists in a way that set *ministrables* against the rank and file. The conjunction of these issues, however, did indeed divide the party into segments with high and low proportions of *ministrables,* as Table 7.12 shows. The "loyal Mollet faction" contained few such leaders. The segments that dissented on a single major issue alone (those segments above the loyal Mollet faction and to its left in Table 7.12) contained the greatest proportions of *ministrables;* with them were Lussy, Depreux, and Leenhardt, who were at various times group presidents. Those segments farthest from Mollet in the left-hand column again contained few *ministrables.*

This distribution of leaders may be interpreted in terms of intraparty relations more easily than by any cross-party consensus. We may presume that Mollet, concerned with his party's unity, used the patronage of cabinet posts to retain the loyalty of factions that were near his own position yet susceptible of dissent. The strongest dissenters, especially those in or near the "popular front" faction, scarcely ever sat in the cabinet; Daniel Mayer held no ministries after the First Legislature, while Lejeune was perhaps less disloyal in dissenting only on German rearmament.

Mollet's influence on Socialist representation in the cabinet enhanced his control of the party, but he had sources of strength within the party as well. Controlling his own large federation of the Pas-de-Calais, he needed only a few such others to dominate party congresses.[42] And while the Socialists were ideological compared with United States parties, the resources that helped to keep Mollet in office longer than any other premier were reminiscent of those of an American political boss.

The "System" and Cabinet Stability

We have examined the prevalent hypothesis that cabinets were overthrown by the ambitions of would-be ministers; yet statistical evidence for this has been hard to find. We might expect deputies voting against one cabinet and taking places in the next to exemplify this motive; but the major instances of such turnover in the Fourth Republic centered about the Mendès-France cabinet. The transitions from Laniel to Mendès and from Mendès to Faure showed high turnover of cabinet members. These transitions, however, marked clear policy alternatives; something more was at stake than mere positions. The new deputies who entered the Mendès-France cabinet expected policy changes in Indochina and the domestic economy; and even the old-timers who came back under Faure in 1955 wished to forestall these economic changes and hold the line in Algeria as much as recover their personal dominance of the cabinet.

If we study other cabinet transitions for evidence of personal ambition, we find isolated instances. In the First Legislature Mollet provoked Ramadier's fall; his ambition was to control the Socialist party more than to be a minister. Pleven engineered several combinations intended to invest cabinets more to his liking; he did so in Schuman's ministry and on Schuman's unsuccessful second attempt (1948), in Queuille's 1948 ministry, and at the crisis following Queuille's fall.[43] In the Second Legislature the Radicals who brought down Faure's 1952 cabinet were distrustful of young upstarts. Some of René Mayer's troubles with the Moderates in 1953 concerned personal ambitions, but it was eventually the Gaullists who brought him down. And late in the Third Legislature Fauvet wrote that the center wing of the Moderates, anxious for portfolios, were more disposed than the right wing to bring cabinets down.

In contrast to these individual incidents, our scale analysis has shown that potential ministers—those who had held or were later to hold cabinet posts in the same Legislature—disproportionately *supported* the sitting cabinet. At worst their distribution among scale scores was nearly the same as the rank and file, and in none of the parties did the *ministrables* show disproportionate opposition in their votes to a cabinet of the "system." Only with Mendès-France, and to a lesser extent Faure in 1952, was there evidence of their opposition. Thus our findings not only fail to support but directly contradict this prevalent diagnosis.

What seemed to have operated was a consensus among the leading *ministrables,* who had served together in many cabinets and gained from this experience a sense of the problems of government. This consensus was not unlike what has been observed in the United States Congress; the groups embodying it have been called the Senate "inner club" and the "priesthood of the House."[44] In a legislative body that governs with shifting and overlapping majorities, the leaders who participate in most of these majorities are likely to develop a sense of cooperation that mitigates their differences. Cooperation may not be so pronounced among the rank and file, or the ideologically extreme, or the fundamental critics of the system itself, who in turn do not enjoy so many of its courtesies. But it seems a general legislative phenomenon in both the United States and France. And whatever the lore of individualism and egoism in the Assembly, the actual votes of the leaders suggest that they did not share this individualism or dissensus as much as the rank and file of their parties.

This consensus may have differed somewhat from its counterpart in the United States because of the differences in legislative career patterns. In the Assembly a committee chairmanship was not normally the terminal point of a career but a step that might lead to the cabinet. Thus we would expect committee chairmen (especially if they had been ministers before) to share in the consensus of the leading group. They might also be more "generalist" than their American counterparts—a quality that the Assembly esteemed.

Our examination of the votes of potential ministers suggests that some "rules of the game" may have contributed to what brief tenure the cabinets had, rather than hastening their fall. Ministers apparently did evolve some understanding of problems of state; those most eligible for cabinet membership had been trained by previous experience and screened by crucial votes that rendered the sharp opponents of previous cabinets less eligible in the future. Moreover, members of an outgoing cabinet were expected automatically to support the next, often giving a few more votes to the supporting side. And Queuille, the most skilled conciliator among the Radicals, had a particular knack for being on the supporting side when a cabinet fell. Even the anti-cabinet Daladier moved into support of the Bourgès-Maunoury cabinet shortly before its fall; he was rewarded soon after with a position in the unsuccessful Mollet cabinet. The principle operative in this case was that of "sending back the elevator."[45]

How can this finding of predominant consensus among the *ministrables* be reconciled with real and frequent allusions by deputies and parliamentary reporters to the selfish calculations that undermined cabinets? Perhaps the difference is due to standards of comparison. Compared to the solidarity we might expect of an ideal cabinet, the members of real cabinets and their supporting factions were less than completely loyal to one another. Candid admission of the part played by self-interest, as well as verbalized hostility, were frequent; but also part of the culture of the Assembly was a set of rules inhibiting the expresssion of this self-interest and hostility by ministers or ex-ministers. If the *ministrables'* actions are compared with those of the rank and file, rather than with an ideal concept of cabinet solidarity, they may not seem so narrowly selfish.

An alternative explanation, which we shall consider below, is that the ministers *in* the cabinet, rather than their prospective successors outside, caused the coalitions to disintegrate. Their expectations of the meaning of the cabinet's compact may have played a part. On the one hand, ambition may have encouraged some deputies to join cabinets without deeply committing themselves to a compact or a policy; on the other, they may have regarded cabinets more as faithful reflections of the parts of their supporting majorities than as groups of men united to govern. And the hope of sitting ministers that they might enter later and different cabinets could have led them to resign more easily, in deference to the wishes of the Assembly. This dependence for future places on the parliamentary opposition, rather than on the voters as in Britain, is also seen as a source of cabinet instability. In this view either dissolution, or the prevention of ex-ministers from joining new cabinets, might have been a partial remedy.

Conflicts of Ideology and of Interest

If the *ministrables* were a stronger force for consensus than the rank and file, why then were cabinets so short-lived and impotent? We cannot ignore the fact of "parliamentary arithmetic": large blocs of intransigent deputies, mostly Communists, required a special majority among the rest for the formation of any cabinet. To attain a two-thirds majority is hard enough in passing legislation over the American presidential veto, or overcoming a filibuster in the United States Senate; but when the Communists and other antiparliamentary parties held two hundred votes, the majority required to invest a cabinet was even greater than two-thirds of the remainder. The unavailability of these votes undoubtedly magnified the effects of disagreement among the other parties.

We wish nevertheless to identify the characteristics of the pro-cabinet parties that contributed particularly to the divisions within and among them, and thus to the departure of certain elements from the cabinet's supporting majorities.

Among the many factors that contributed to these divisions, ideology seems to have predominated.[46] In the First and Third Legislatures, the most pervasive cause of cabinets' fall was the opposition between Socialists and Moderates. Although the bargaining power of the Moderates was greater in the Third Legislature, the arguments and complaints opposing the two parties were similar in both periods. For the Socialists it was a question of whether their ministers or their votes would support *libéral* (laisser faire) policies for the domestic economy. The militants hesitated to see their leaders collaborating with a party Mollet had called "the most stupid right in the world." Large private enterprises and the men who stood for them in the Assembly were regarded by the left as inherently suspect and contaminating.

Conversely, the Moderates were deterred by their suspicions of the Socialists from entering into any lasting agreements with such a "Marxist" party. The effects of Socialist *dirigisme* (state control) were seen as waste, bureaucracy, and high taxes. The Moderates continually sought reorganization of government enterprises, such as the social security administration and the nationalized railways, that would reduce expenses. New social legislation, which was Mollet's only excuse for presiding over a Socialist government in 1956–57, was the precise reason why the Moderates overthrew him as the time came to pay for it.

It may be debated whether these tenets are truly "ideology," "doctrine," or the like.[47] Perhaps they were little more than slogans to arouse the faithful in election campaigns and party meetings, or at best broad lines of policy. Yet they made a difference to the stability of cabinets; they were not primarily born of immediate parliamentary necessity; and they are thus to be distinguished from the other factors that brought cabinets down.

Other ideological considerations dominated the downfall of cabinets in the Second Legislature. The essential part played by the Gaullist URAS in cabinet coalitions brought with it the disadvantage of inconsistent alliances on different issues. The Gaullists were nationalist in external affairs but unwilling to ally themselves exclusively with the Right domestically. They had a well-defined configuration of positions on issues, which we may call an "ideology." The other parties were also separated by the perennial church-school question; though normally latent, it was enough to hasten the Socialists' move into opposition in 1952.

The Moderates' position on Algeria was also "ideological." They brought down Bourgès-Maunoury over his *loi-cadre* for Algeria. They went into opposition early when Mendès-France proposed "liberal" policies in North Africa; and even Edgar Faure suffered disaffection among the Moderates because of his Moroccan policy. The emphasis on firmness, the fear that the protectorates and Algeria would be gradually abandoned, played an important part in the Moderates' reactions.[48]

The vehicle of an ideology is not necessarily a party. Our analysis of intraparty division shows factions and segments within all the pro-cabinet parties, each faction with its own positions on certain issues. The Radicals were divided on the school question; the MRP on the conflict between its goals in domestic social legislation (obtainable in leftist coalitions) and in international policy (obtainable under Moderates); and so were all the parties except the Communists, on the Paris Agreements for German rearmament. A faction, even an individual, may hold a particular set of positions on major political issues, and do so consistently.

Reinforcing the differences of principle among parties and factions were differences of interest, often difficult to separate from the related principles. The factors that attenuated cabinet majorities were cumulative rather than mutually exclusive. Between its investiture and its fall, the same cabinet could find itself deserted by different sets of deputies for different reasons, all having contributed to its downfall. Thus we expect some cabinets to have been brought down by both "ideological" factors and "interests."

But can a clear distinction be made between "ideology" and "interest"? The Algerian settlers, for example, had a clear material interest in staying in Algeria and retaining political control; but it was supported by general arguments on the territorial integrity of France, the duty of a government to protect its citizens, and the alleged moral deficiencies of the Muslim rebels. Conversely, the defense of a principle such as *laïcité,* though it may not have been to the immediate economic advantage of Socialist politicians, may well have helped them retain their seats in the Assembly and directly aided their constituents, the public school teachers. Socialist defense of the nationalized industries was not only a matter of principle but also concerned the economic welfare and political power of party members. And the interest of a party leader such as Mollet could depend on his "falling to the left."

We shall ask simply whether nonparty groups organized to influence the Assembly played a part in cabinet instability; these are normally known as "interest groups." In some instances the activities of such groups involved the arguments and positions we have referred to as "ideology." The action of interest groups was normally not such as to aim at the overthrow of the cabinet. If a particular piece of legislation could be passed or stopped, interested groups could let the cabinet go its way on other matters. Only if the incumbent cabinet was resistant to influence would the group try to supplant it by another; an example might be René Mayer's role as a spokesman for the Algerian settlers in Mendès' fall. And not all groups that wished to change the personnel of the cabinet had the power to do so; although the home distillers opposed Mendès-France after his decrees on alcohol, they were not usually charged with major responsibility for his downfall.

A number of instances in which pressure groups played an important part in cabinets' fall are cited by Meynaud.[49] Marie fell in 1948 because the Socialists objected to Reynaud's raising the price of foodstuffs; this objection, in turn, came from those who would suffer most directly. Pleven's fall in January 1952 followed his effort to reform the railways and Social Security; pressure from the railway workers led the Socialists to withdraw their support. Pinay was brought down by the MRP when he asked to transfer certain contributions from family allowances to social security in general; again certain interested groups played their part. At Mayer's fall in 1953 both the RPF and pressure groups were considered responsible; his requests for economies had offended the beet growers, among others, while his position on EDC failed to satisfy the Gaullists. These examples are illustrative; but Meynaud also notes the difficulty of separating interest from ideology, and he judges ideology more important in cabinet crises.

If ideology and interests played a part in the disagreements among the parties supporting the cabinet, and if these differences were more pronounced among the rank-and-file deputies than among the *ministrables,* we must trace the sources outside the Assembly. Our ultimate conclusion that they were strongest among the party activists in the districts—as well as among the rank-and-file deputies—depends on our study of the social bases of voting behavior and of party differences in constituency relations (Chs. 8, 9, 10).

Consensus and Cabinet Weakness

We have sought some origins of cabinet instability in the dissensus among the parties' rank-and-file deputies and by inference in forces outside parliament. But paradoxically, they may also lie in the nature of the consensus that bound the *ministrables* of the "system" and led them to support the major cabinets in which their associates participated. For it may be that only certain sorts of cabinets could be invested in the first place, as a condition for gaining the *ministrables'* support, and that the cabinets' leaders themselves were overly willing to relinquish power. A selective effect may have prevented "outsiders" from dominating the cabinet most of the time; and the "insiders" selected, conforming to the "rules" by deferring to the Assembly's sovereignty, may have thus obtained the support of the other leaders in exchange.

This interpretation relates to another widespread explanation of the cabinets' immobility. It is often contended that the most active, decisive cabinets incurred opposition most rapidly and fell soonest.[50] To examine this question we must compare cabinets with one another, relating their policies to their duration.

Merely to put this question precisely reveals some of its ambiguities. What sort of action is meant? Was it the resolution of problems by the Assembly, the actual passage of legislation, or the public image of the premier that mattered? Edgar Faure, for example, was often considered an equivocator or conciliator; yet he carried through both the Tunisian agreements and the Paris agreements for German rearmament, started by the "decisive" Mendès-France. A premier's reputation for decisiveness may reflect a capacity for making enemies as well as for solving problems. Mendès is the obvious example, but there were others as well. Léon Blum failed of investiture in November 1947 by antagonizing the Gaullists, after having been successful in his earlier brief premiership;[51] and Paul Reynaud was also often compared with Mendès in his decisiveness, when both failed of investiture in 1953. Mendès, having drawn upon himself the hate of the MRP, the Radical leaders, and the nationalist right, as well as the muted distrust of some of the Socialists, was of course an extreme example.

A second problem in identifying "active" premiers is that there were at least two main types of action: on the parliamentary-political situation, and on the outside world (economic action, diplomacy, etc.). While Queuille acted in the first area, Mendès acted in the second.[52]

Let us start by arranging cabinets in order of duration and then contrast the actions of those that lasted for longer and shorter periods. We shall use for this purpose the calendar interval from the premier's investiture to the cabinet's fall.[53] The ordering of cabinets in the three Legislatures, according to this standard, is shown in Table 7.13.

Comparing shorter and longer-lasting cabinets suggests factors other than their activity that affected their periods in office. Mollet's cabinet, which endured longest, is often accused of *immobilisme,* as is Queuille's first cabinet, which lasted second longest. But *"immobilisme"* can refer simply to failure to act in a way or direction that the critic prefers. Queuille did indeed postpone economic problems, but he successfully fought off the Gaullist challenge of that time and postponed the cantonal elections. Mollet failed to negotiate a settlement with the Algerian Muslims, but he conducted forceful military action both in Algeria and at Suez.

The cabinets surviving longest seem to have been aided by two factors: unity against an external enemy and action that directly influenced the domestic political situation. For Mollet the external enemy was the Arab world; French non-Communist opinion was surprisingly united in seeing Cairo and the FLN as a single enemy.[54] For Laniel, the Indochinese war was a source of support until Dien Bien Phu showed the holding policy to be untenable. Under Queuille in 1948–49, it was opposition to the Gaullist threat—internal to France but external to "the Republic"—that united the parties of his majority. Moreover, each of these three premiers gained because his actions influenced the parliamentary situation. Queuille, well known as a master of conciliation and postponement, undoubtedly avoided antagonizing the deputies. Laniel and Mollet, though not following precisely the same policy, were each "reinvested" after a personal failure— Laniel after losing the presidential election to Coty in 1953, Mollet after the Suez invasion.

But even these explanations of the duration of the three longest ministries suffer from a certain *ad hoc* quality. Other cabinets besides Queuille's faced the Gaullist threat during the First Legislature; it was rather his skill at parliamentary politics that allowed him to stay in office longer. And in the Third Legislature Gaillard also gained some support from the country's unity in the face of foreign threats; yet when the "good offices" mission failed to attain what he had promised, he fell. Mendès himself did not fall much earlier in his ministry than did Faure afterward in his, in spite of their difference in style. Pinay, who exerted his influence on pressure groups and opinion, lasted only a little longer. Thus there are many exceptions to the hypothesis that the least active cabinets endured longest.

Among the cabinets that lasted from seven to ten months, not only is there little clear difference in duration, but also no related distinction between active and passive premiers, or between those who acted on the Assembly and those who acted on the external world. Those that lasted from one to six months (Marie, Pleven, Mayer, Faure in 1952, Gaillard, and Bourgès-Maunoury) seem to have had less clear "contracts" with the Assembly

Table 7.13 Duration of Cabinets in Months*

Months	Legislature		
	First	Second	Third
16			Mollet
15			
14			
13	Queuille₁		
12			
11		Laniel	
10	Ramadier		
9		Pinay	
		Faure₂	
8	Schuman₁, Bidault		
	Pleven	Mendès-France	
7			
6			Gaillard
5		Pleven	
		Mayer	
4			Bourgès-Maunoury
3	[Queuille₃]		
2	[Blum]	Faure₁	
1	Marie		
			[Pflimlin]
0	Schuman₂, Queuille₂		
Premier	Thorez 1946	Mayer 1951	Pinay 1957
not	Bidault 1946	Petsche 1951	Mollet 1957
invested	Blum 1947	Reynaud 1953	
	Moch 1949	Mendès-France 1953	
	R. Mayer 1949	Bidault 1953	
	Mollet 1951	Marie 1955	
		Pineau 1955	

*Measured from premier's investiture to his overthrow or the political end of his ministry.
[ ] Brackets indicate those cabinets that resigned for reasons other than an unfavorable vote in the Assembly.

at investiture. Faure's 1952 cabinet, as we have seen, also suffered from the leaders' distrust.

The clearest distinction between active and passive premiers emerges from examining unsuccessful efforts at investiture. Some of these must be set aside at the start as "mortgages" that had to be lifted in order to reveal the range of parliamentary possibilities at the start of the First and Second Legislatures: Thorez and Bidault in 1946, Mayer and Petsche in 1951. Others reflect the impossibility of a particular party's gaining a majority at a particular time, and are again "mortgages" or soundings of the parliamentary situation: thus the unsuccessful attempts of Moch and Mollet in the First Legislature and Pineau in the Second simply showed that a Socialist could not be invested. Pinay's unsuccessful try in the Third Legislature was also of this sort.[55] In the prolonged crisis of 1953 the failures of Bidault and Marie are not to be charged to their decisiveness. And Mollet's failure to be re-invested in 1957 reflected the Moderates' unwillingness to support a policy and a premier they had defeated in the recent past. The brief investitures of Schuman and Queuille in the First Legislature may also have ended in failure because of the recency of their previous fall.

The remainder of the short-lived or unsuccessful ministries, however, do seem to reflect the Assembly's dislike of clear-cut programs and decisive action. Blum and Mayer in the First Legislature were more decisive than the average premier-designate; when Mayer was finally invested in January 1953, after two failures, he was considered finally to have shown some parliamentary skill as well as his former "authority." And when he fell, he was considered to have ignored the "parliamentary health" of the cabinet, and disregarded Queuille's advice in this respect.[56] Queuille's second attempt to form a cabinet essayed a sharp break with the past, in omitting the Socialists from the supporting majority. In the Second Legislature Reynaud and Mendès-France lost in 1953 partly because they wanted more power to institute broad reforms. These were probably the major instances in which the Assembly showed its dislike of decisive action.

This analysis suggests that once a cabinet was invested, its duration was affected by conditions other than the Assembly's hostility to its activity; the initial step of investiture, on the other hand, reflected the Assembly's dislike of strong and innovating leaders.[57] Prospective premiers were well known to the Assembly, and their degree of decisiveness could be foreseen before their investiture. After a premier was invested, many factors other than his own plans and policies came to affect his success or failure. The international economic situation affected Queuille (1949) and Pinay; the rise of Gaullism affected Ramadier; the military situation affected Laniel, Faure (1955) and Mollet; and international negotiations influenced the date at which Mendès-France could bring up the Paris Agreements. Thus it is not surprising that the most accurate reflection of the Assembly's preferences should come at a stage where these external events mattered little—the initial investiture of premier and cabinet.

Even if a simple relation between duration and immobility is difficult to prove, there did exist relationships between a premier's tactics and his prospects for success in the short run. A premier might act on parliament itself, on the electoral situation, or on "external" problems such as inflation or German rearmament. The skill Queuille showed in fending off

Gaullism, first by postponing the cantonal elections of 1948, later by passing the 1951 electoral law, exemplifies "internal" action; Mendés' disdain for the parliamentary game, at least at the beginning of his ministry, exemplifies the "external." But Mendès' own apparent attempt to extend his majority in the traditional parliamentary manner—courting Gaullist support by appointing Soustelle while trying to appeal to the southwestern Radicals by sponsoring the *scrutin d'arrondissement*—actually hastened his enemies' attack rather than prolonging his ministry.

A tactic open to a premier who wished to prolong his ministry was to change the issues so as to mobilize a new or a different majority. The most obvious way to do this, either voluntarily or under duress, was to reorganize the cabinet; but after the departure of the Communists in 1947 this tactic was rarely successful. There were also many other occasions when the cabinet's base of support changed. Extreme and ill-advised attacks on the cabinet sometimes yielded augmented majorities in its favor, which, however, were often reduced when the cabinet resumed the initiative in favor of its own program. Events themselves altered the degree of support by particular groups for a cabinet: the Moderates, for example, moved into support of Mendès after his success at Geneva, and only later fell away from him.

The degree to which a premier could change the issues and party divisions under his ministry depended partly on the range of issues he could, or wished to, confront. It depended also on the stance of the various parties toward his cabinet, that is, on whether it was endowed by each particular party with a "dominant issue." When Faure introduced the electoral-law issue late in 1955, he prolonged his ministry somewhat. Mollet, wishing to raise taxes, tried to choose a moment in 1957 when the international situation would make his overthrow difficult; but he failed nevertheless. Other premiers prolonged their stay in office by avoiding issues, as Pleven did on the electoral law in 1951 and later on the Barangé law. Mendès' neutrality on EDC was an effort to avoid the fragmentation of his cabinet, but it was only partially successful.

Another possible basis for a change in issues (or at least in support for the cabinet) was a change in the parliamentary situation. The passage of a bill, or more generally the "lifting of a mortgage," might change the range of alternatives or remove the necessity for cooperation between two groups. This latter hypothesis has been put forward by Venezia.[58] He points out that in order to pass a given bill, heterogeneous cabinets were formed; but as soon as the law was passed which constituted the only common denominator of the two given groups, they denounced their pact. Examples of the fall of cabinets after the passage of a key bill are the Marie cabinet's fate after the Fonlupt-Espéraber bill in 1948, and Mendès' fall after the approval of the Paris Agreements.

As Leites has pointed out,[59] time was of great importance in the persistence or fall of cabinets. Time was related to the expectation of certain external events—elections or events in the international sphere. It was also measured by threats or promises made by the parties or party congresses that "came due" at certain times. There were also periods of "truce" resulting from parliamentary vacations; a cabinet would rarely be overthrown before a vacation, for example. Cabinets would also postpone controversial policy declarations until after a vacation period.

The tactics of individual premiers did thus affect the duration of their ministries; but a statistical demonstration of the Assembly's preference for weak and compromising premiers must apparently be limited to the initial step of investiture rather than the complex processes that followed.

That stronger premiers popular outside the Assembly could be occasionally invested and stay in office for a time was shown by the ministries of Pinay and Mendès-France. Invested partly because of an accident or an emergency, they developed support outside the Assembly and used it to stay in office longer. The leading deputies, though feeling the "rules" had been violated by these premiers' lack of subservience to the Assembly, could not easily defy their constituents' opinion. But after an opportune time had come for the Assembly to overthrow these men, each left the chamber with a lack of deference to the Assembly that well symbolized his outside sources of support.

An additional reason for the lack of association between the duration in office of a cabinet once invested and its activity was that cabinets were not brought down simply by the pressure of the Assembly. Some yielded to this pressure more than others, and often those who yielded more easily were the less innovating cabinets of the "system." Thus, as we have pointed out, the consensus of the leaders itself may not have contributed to either bold action or stability.

We conclude that bold, innovative activity—or a reputation for it—was harmful to premiers only at their initial investiture, or in the short run during their ministries. In the longer run, the effects of such activity could favor the premier's continuance in office (Chapter 11); his policies might prove successful and gain support outside the Assembly. Thus innovative action may have not so much impaired the longevity of the ministry as elicited a negative contribution to it from the Assembly.

This analysis suggests that two political subsystems existed under the Fourth Republic, and acted somewhat at cross purposes. On the one hand, there was the consensus of the parliamentary "system," whose members supported each other in the cabinet. On the other was the dissensus of ideologies and interests, rooted more in the constituencies than in the Assembly, together with a greater inclination toward protest and criticism of the government. The dissociation between these two systems may have been as important a source of the Fourth Republic's problems as the existence of either by itself (see Chapters 9 and 11). The consensus of the *ministrables* may have been too limited in substance. That is, the range of policies which this agreement permitted may not have been commensurate with either the demands of the citizenry or the needs of the times. Innovators, in or out of the Assembly, came to be viewed as somewhat disloyal to the Republic because they opposed the parliamentary "system"; and the reforms they proposed may have become more radical precisely because they were unable to penetrate that "system" and be coopted by it without excessive sacrifices.

The Legislative Parties and the Fate of Cabinets

Did the structure of the political parties—their indiscipline or their heterogeneity—contribute to the short life and weakness of the cabinets? This question, often asked, is not simple to answer. One difficulty is that the parties' differences in structure were reflected both in their legislative divisions and in their activities outside the Assembly (see Chapter 3). We cannot simply imagine a change in the legislative parties, therefore, without imagining a related change in their extra-legislative organizations. Nevertheless, we shall here consider the effects of the parliamentary parts of the parties alone, and postpone until later a consideration of their outside organization (Chapters 10, 12). Let us begin by examining contentions of other analysts of the Fourth Republic, with regard to the effects of the structure of the legislative (parliamentary) parties.

It has been suggested that the structure of the parties themselves, apart from their particular actions, contributed to cabinet instability. Aron, for example, argues that in the absence of a strong president party indiscipline necessarily undermined the cabinet; Britain and the stable multi-party democracies, in contrast to France, had disciplined parties that could conclude binding agreements. "When the government depends on temporary and revocable agreements between numerous parties, no one of which is subject to discipline when it comes to the vote, a certain ministerial instability is unavoidable."[60]

But, as Aron also points out, the French parties were not all equally indisciplined; the Socialists and MRP acted with considerable unanimity, and it was not in their ranks that the games for portfolios were played so much as among the Radicals, Moderates, and similar parties. Moreover, indiscipline could aid as well as harm the cabinet; Petsche and his fellow Moderate ministers in the First Legislature stayed in the cabinet at the expense of party membership. The southwestern Radicals also violated party discipline when they broke Mendès' hold on the Radical party in 1957, supporting the Mollet cabinet at its fall. Conversely, when a disciplined party went into opposition, its discipline was an additional hazard to the cabinet. The cabinets of the Third Legislature might have been brought down sooner if the Moderates had had more discipline.[61]

It is true that a highly fragmented legislative body will have a wide variety of possible majority coalitions. Fragmentation thus leads to the possibility of many small agreements, as contrasted with a few major agreements between cabinet and Assembly; either sort can conceivably be revoked. But a crucial factor is the relation of the executive to the fragments. As long as the executive has a supply of negotiable resources (such as those deriving from patronage or the support of public opinion), it may be able to marshal these shifting forces into a succession of supporting majorities. Small blocs may or may not have high bargaining power; to some extent the influential position of the UDSR in the First Legislature was due to the narrow margin of cabinet support created by the prior desertion of large blocs of votes. Had all the parties been fragmented, the power of the premier might thus have been enhanced. Mendès-France hoped to gain strength by negotiating with individuals rather than parties. Perhaps it would be more appropriate to say that the threats to the cabinets lay in the discipline of its opponents and the indiscipline of its supporters, but that each of these had a counterpart or converse tendency that could aid the cabinet.

A central problem then is why a cabinet, defeated by a mere plurality on an isolated issue, could not continue to govern. It was generally assumed that this could not be done, and the standards for a cabinet's agreement with its supporting majority were exacting. Siegfried well expressed this tacit assumption of the deputies:

> The instability of cabinets, independently of other reasons, undoubtedly derives from an excessive subtlety in the conception of ministerial responsibility: it is desired that at every instant and in all circumstances the government in power be located exactly in the political axis of the majority. If that axis is displaced, even slightly, a readjustment in the distribution of portfolios is required, so that the center of gravity of the cabinet may correspond exactly to the center of gravity of the Assembly.[62]

This assumption parallels the notion, prevalent at least during the Fourth Republic, that the votes of the citizenry should be mirrored exactly in the parties' distribution in the Assembly.

We have seen that the parties making the main contributions to the downfall of cabinets in the three Legislatures—Socialists, Gaullists, and Moderates—did so for largely ideological reasons. But in structure they differed widely, and the sources of their positions on issues were quite different from one another: the Socialists in their militants, the Gaullists in adherence to a general who had been their leader, and the Moderates in interests and views transmitted through an elite that was not completely embedded in professional politics.

The Socialist party reflected in clearest form a relation between Assembly and constituencies that held in varying degrees for most of the parties: the Assembly was a source of conciliation and compromise, the constituencies a source of conflict. For all the parties the approach of an election meant increased hostility in the Assembly; it was for this reason that Queuille proposed in 1951 to hold the election in June rather than November. Party congresses and committee meetings were often threats to the cabinet.[63] Moreover, each weekend, which sent the deputies home to their districts, meant an infusion of party and group hostility into the Assembly: increasing demands, higher prices for political bargains, reassertion of divisive partisan slogans.[64] To the extent that this relation held, the source of cabinet instability was to be seen primarily outside the Assembly. In succeeding chapters we shall argue that it was due more to party activists than to divisions in the public at large.

The Socialist party reflected this tendency thoroughly because it was controlled to a high degree by its local militants. More than ordinary voters, militants reflected partisan and doctrinal positions; and party leaders were often prevented by the influence of the militants at congresses from supporting viable long-run government policies in the cabinet. If the Socialists could have governed alone, internal party democracy might have been a virtue; but as members of a coalition, they actually contributed more to government stability when their oligarchic tendencies dominated.[65]

The Socialist party's divisions, which normally did not extend to roll-call votes, showed how party discipline could contribute either to a cabinet's fall or to its continuation. A persistent theme in the Socialists' internal controversies was Mollet's effort to gain and keep control of the party. In the early part of the First Legislature, this effort meant that the faction loyal to their secretary-general was opposed to participating in cabinets, even when the premier himself was a Socialist. Only by the party's unanimous respect in the Assembly of a narrow majority in its congress did Ramadier stay in office after the Communists left. Later in the First Legislature, as well as in the Second, unanimity normally meant opposition, as the party had only brief periods of participation. In the Third Legislature the relation was again reversed; Mollet then favored participation in cabinets which he felt he could dominate, or which continued his own policies. He was perhaps more able to do this after the party's *cure d'opposition* in the Second Legislature. Socialist discipline in the Third Legislature meant greater support for cabinets. In this change of position, Mollet moved from a "doctrinaire" position to support of the cabinet.

The case of the Gaullists in 1952-55 is entirely different from that of the Socialists. Their ideology was reinforced by adherence to the General's principles, not constituency pressure. Indeed, as the Second Legislature continued they had less and less constituency support, nor were there comparable organizations of Gaullist "militants" to exert pressure on them. Their contribution to cabinet instability, therefore, was more an accidental consequence of General de Gaulle's formation of the RPF as a means to gain power. Failing of its aim, the RPF became one more obstacle to cabinet stability.

The internal organization of the RPF was such as to beget fragmentation: a policy and leadership imposed from above became increasingly frustrating to an Assembly group whom the leaders did not fully represent. The RPF did fragment, and its fragments were drawn into cabinet coalitions. Its first division, and the formation of the ARS, increased the strength of the Moderates and their support in cabinets. Its later fragmentations gave some support to Mayer, Laniel, Mendès-France, and Faure; but even while divided, the URAS set demanding standards for the cabinet's performance, especially in European and colonial affairs.

Internal organization also affected the parties' support for cabinets through the measures that leaders found necessary to preserve party unity. If an important and determined minority within a party insisted on supporting the cabinet—as in the RPF after Pinay's investiture—the leadership might be forced to encourage unanimous abstention.[66] At the end of 1952 the RPF was induced to present Soustelle and then to back Mayer, again to keep the pro-cabinet faction in the party. But compromises in the opposite sense were more normal: the MRP under Pinay and the Radicals under Mollet gained greater unity by moving into opposition. At other times party unity could be preserved only by an alliance with another party, as when the MRP required Socialist participation in the cabinets of the Third Legislature; its deputies supported Mollet all the more strongly because they feared isolation and division under the rightist cabinet that might follow.

The Moderates, whose conflicts with the Socialists brought down cabinets in the First and Third Legislatures, derived their position from a different sort of organization. There were, of course, party officers and meetings of the parliamentary group, and these had some effect; but on questions of economic laisser-faire and "French Algeria," the main source of their strong positions was contact with influential persons in their constituencies and in the milieux in which they associated. On business questions, these views presumably came directly from employers, and on Algeria, from the settlers.

We conclude, therefore, that although the organization of the legislative parties was relevant to the successes and failures of cabinets, it did not affect them in any simple way. Rather, its effect was contingent on the position of party leaders for or against the cabinet—and on the resources the premier could command to gain the support of factions and coteries in the various parties.

We shall argue that the incapacity of cabinets to govern resulted from both an excess of dissensus in the constituencies and an excess of a somewhat misplaced consensus in the Assembly. Postponing the constituency question for the present, we must ask what sort of party structure in the Assembly could have fostered a serious consideration of alternative policies, with alternative sets of cabinet members to carry them out.

In phrasing the question in this way, we have in effect implied a diagnosis. The shortcoming of the "system" was that the same group of persons had to participate in the cabinets that were to implement alternative policies. This meant, in turn, that the cabinets of the "system" were constantly "solidary with their predecessors." To criticize the preceding cabinets meant to separate oneself from the legitimacy of the "system." Expressed otherwise, criticism of the parliamentary elite was too nearly synonymous with criticism of the regime itself. The function of a responsible opposition—proposing an alternative policy and providing an alternative set of persons to carry it out—was missing.[67]

What sort of party system could have provided alternative sets of persons to govern? The mere unavailability of the Communist votes was in itself enough to render this impossible during most of the Fourth Republic. Moreover, without a change in the composition of the Assembly by means of an election, it was arithmetically impossible for any cabinet to be succeeded by another whose supporting majority did not include some of the supporters of the first. There were certain occasions, however, when the Fourth Republic came as close as possible to this condition: when the Socialists moved in or out of the coalition supporting the cabinet. The investitures of Pinay and of Mèndes-France were major occasions on which this occurred.

The principal condition for an approximation to alternative majorities and alternative cabinets, within the limitations of the Fourth Republic, was therefore the formation of coalitions that included the extremes of the available segment of the political spectrum. Coalitions of the center of that segment produced the malfunctions we have observed. A center coalition fragments the opposition into two wings and therefore cannot be replaced by the opposition. This tactic may benefit the governing coalition, but it inhibits the representation of new demands.

Thus party structure cannot be considered in itself the key to the problems of the Fourth Republic. With many parties forming coalitions of the center, or with factions from a small number of fragmented parties doing the same thing, an effective opposition would have been impossible. The absence of such an opposition led to the paradoxical fact that while cabinets were brought down for ideological reasons, their successors' policies often showed little change.

Even though effective opposition is conceivable with undisciplined parties, the only examples in the Fourth Republic that approximated it involved a disciplined party—the Socialists. This implies that at least one way to obtain major changes in the policies and personnel of a cabinet coalition is to have large disciplined parties whose joining or leaving the coalition will make a considerable difference.

NOTES

1. The procedure involved is a modification of cumulative or Guttman scaling; see MacRae, "A Method for Identifying Issues."

2. *Ibid.*, 923–926.

3. See Samuel A. Stouffer, *et al.*, "A Technique for Improving Cumulative Scales."

4. For details of scale placement see Appendix B.

5. This criticism was a reason for the removal of cabinet members from Parliament under the Fifth Republic. See Aron, *France: Steadfast and Changing*, p. 124; Siegfried, *De la IVᵉ à la Vᵉ République*, pp. 195–196; Buron, *Le plus beau des métiers*, pp. 133ff.; Duverger, *The French Political System*, p. 138.

6. Pineau, *Mon Cher Député*, p. 167.

7. Chapsal, *La Vie politique*, p. 522, gives this explanation for the institution of the *suppléant* system in the Fifth Republic.

8. See Williams, *Crisis*, p. 40.

9. On the Radicals' Scale II-6, for example, score 2 corresponded to the greatest support for the cabinets involved. We therefore rearrange the categories in this order: 0; 1 and 3 together; 2. This set of three categories is then treated as an ordering related to support for these cabinets.

10. The electoral-law scale will be used in Chapter 10 for the study of constituency relations.

11. Members of the Peasant party for all or part of the First Legislature are omitted; the Peasant party voted distinctly from the RI and PRL.

12. Fauvet, in *La IVᵉ République*, p. 196, refers to these Gaullists of the right as only "Moderates who borrowed the R.P.F. ticket."

13. This finding is reported by Bartholomew in *The Politics of the Notable*.

14. Jacques Isorni, *Ainsi passent les républiques*, p. 136.

15. Jacques Fauvet, *Le Monde*, 21 October 1949.

16. Leites, *On the Game of Politics*, p. 61. Our scales give no indication of this action, however.

17. No. 1851; see Chapter 5 and *Le Monde*, 9 July 1953.

18. See Ehrmann, *Organized Business in France*, p. 250.

19. *Ibid.*, pp. 447, 242–243.

20. For biographical sketches of a number of leading Gaullists, see Viansson-Ponté, *The King and His Court*.

21. This hypothesis has been put forward for the U.S. Congress in MacRae, *Dimensions of Congressional Voting* and in Truman, *The Congressional Party*. Some exceptions to it have been pointed out in Samuel C. Patterson, "Legislative Leadership and Political Ideology."

22. The distinctive constituency characteristics of the ARS are pointed out in Williams, *Crisis*, p. 153.

23. Rémond, *The Right Wing in France*. He points out that the legitimist *ultracisme* had no counterpart among the major parties in the Fourth Republic (p. 344) and that the members of the PRL and ARS belonged to the moderate right (pp. 353, 373–374).

24. This difference between the two scales was shown in Table 7.2 by the respective associations of the scales with *ministrable* status: $+ .66$ and $+ .33$.

25. Including the UDSR; the two groups were combined in most of our scale analyses.

26. Two of them who were not moved, Petit and Pleven, opposed the Schuman cabinet on two votes on Germany, and were thus assigned to scale score 2 without ambiguity.

27. See de Tarr, *The French Radical Party*, Chapter 6. Almost all those in row 3, columns 3 and 4, were Gaullists for at least part of the First Legislature. These men later took a wide variety of positions in the URAS.

28. Herriot also favored the party's participation in cabinets, advocating this position at the Toulouse congress in 1949; see Soulié, *La Vie politique d'Édouard Herriot*, p. 563.

29. See de Tarr, *The French Radical Party*, p. 82.

30. Also in scale categories 1 and 2—the less "*laïc*" group—were Radicals who four years earlier had been listed as members of the *Association Parlementaire pour la Liberté de l'Enseignement*: Barrier, Bégouin, Bonnefous, Caliot, David, Faggianelli, J.-A. Hugues, Lafay, Bourdelles, de Léotard, and Pleven. Ducreux, also a member, did not live long enough to be placed on the scale. See *Le Monde*, 18 July 1951.

31. As Bardonnet writes: ". . . *L'opposition de M. Mendès-France au gouvernement de M. Laniel en 1953 rassemblait autour de lui un certain nombre de radicaux . . . ,*" *Évolution de la structure du parti radical*, p. 19n.

32. Most of the deputies who later joined Morice in seceding from the party had run in 1956 on platforms departing from that of the Republican Front, had failed to form electoral alliances with the Socialists, or had not been endorsed by *L'Express*. See Goguel in Duverger, Goguel, and Touchard, eds., *Les Elections du 2 janvier 1956*, pp. 468–469.

33. See Williams, *Crisis*, pp. 270–271. Roll calls nos. 986, 1012, and 1039 were concerned with this bill.

34. See Einaudi and Goguel, *Christian Democracy in Italy and France*, pp. 171–172.

35. This absence of dissent by the party leaders was reflected in the high associations of pro-cabinet votes on these scales with *ministrable* status in Table 7.2: $+ 1.00$ and $+ .67$, respectively.

36. See Williams, *Crisis*, p. 399n.

37. Chevigné was recognized as one of "*les plus modérés*"—Fauvet, *Le Monde*, 13 July 1951.

38. This interpretation, based on scales for individual Legislatures, is supported by an overall Q-matrix computed for the 58 Socialists who sat throughout all three Legislatures, combining all the votes on which they were significantly divided. Two major lines of cleavage were revealed: one dividing those who opposed Thorez in 1946 from those who opposed German rearmament in 1952–54 (including no. 709 on the European Army under Faure); and one combining the 1951 electoral-law dissidents with those who opposed de Gaulle in 1958. Also included in the latter was no. 831 in the First Legislature, on the Poinso-Chapuis decree relating to the church schools. The Q's for this group were generally higher than for the entire membership.

39. Among the deviant cases (favoring de Gaulle but opposing Bourgès-Maunoury) were Moch and Lapie, who had been with de Gaulle in London during the war. That the dissidence on EDC included more than the former left wing of the party is indicated in Gilles Martinet, "Y aura-t-il une scission socialiste?", *France-Observateur*, September 9, 1954, 10; and Roger Racier, "Quatre tendances au sein du parti socialiste," *France-Observateur*, February 3, 1955, 8–9.

40. The coalescence of two groups in opposition to Mollet on the de Gaulle investiture is pointed out in *France-Observateur*, 9, June 26, 1958, 3. These groups were the "traditional minority" in the party and another group who had formerly supported Mollet but did not wish to see the Republic done away with—the latter including Gazier, Jaquet, Métayer, Pineau, and Tanguy-Prigent, all "Republicans" in the table.

41. It required the aid of the Socialist Senators to reach a favorable decision.

42. Siegfried is quoted as saying: ". . . *Dans les votes du conseil national du parti socialiste, M. Guy Mollet était un peu comme ces présidents de sociétés par actions, disposant d'un nombre important de pouvoirs en blanc.*" Cited in Chapsal, *La Vie politique,* p. 257.

43. *Le Monde,* 13 March 1948, 9 September 1948, 31 July–1 August 1949, 25 October 1949. His position in Table 7.7 suggested this.

44. See William S. White, *Citadel;* MacNeil, *Forge of Democracy;* and the classical description of parliamentary consensus, de Jouvenel's *La République des camarades.* Williams describes the "club sense" of the Assembly in *Crisis,* pp. 430ff., and Elgey tells of its development in *La République des illusions,* pp. 302–303.

45. Melnik and Leites, *The House Without Windows,* p. 340. In France one rides up old-fashioned elevators but walks down. After one takes the elevator up, it is considered polite to send it down for the next user.

46. We contend this in spite of the fact that principled objection to one cabinet did not necessarily lead to an alteration in policy by the next. See Roy C. Macridis, "Cabinet Instability in the Fourth Republic (1946–1951)." The institution of the "crisis" made possible a re-patching of the old coalition; see Williams, *Crisis,* Chapter 29.

47. Leites, *On the Game of Politics,* Chapter 1.

48. The "French Algeria" position was more prevalent among the provincial militants than among the deputies; see Smith, "Algeria and the French *Modérés,*" p. 132.

49. Meynaud, *Les Groupes de pression en France,* pp. 163, 311–313.

50. See Leites, *On the Game of Politics,* pp. 145–147; Williams, *Crisis,* pp. 440ff.

51. For a favorable account of Blum's decisiveness see Matthews, *The Death of the Fourth Republic,* pp. 230–232.

52. Siegfried, *De la IVᵉ à la Vᵉ République,* p. 164.

53. It might be imagined that the period in which the Assembly actually held sessions would be a better measure, since ministerial crises were not normally provoked during vacations. But this measure, calculated from the number of issues of the *Journal Officiel,*

Débats Parlementaires, arranges the cabinets in almost exactly the same order as does simple calendar duration.

54. See Luethy and Rodnick, *French Motivations in the Suez Crisis.*

55. Although these failures are not to be charged primarily to the premier-designate's decisive personality, the very fact that they represented clear-cut moves away from the political center was enough to alienate some votes.

56. On Mayer's investiture and fall, see *Le Monde,* 8 January 1953, 23 May 1953.

57. See Williams, *Crisis,* pp. 440ff., and Chapter 11 below.

58. Venezia, "Les Fondements juridiques de l'instabilité ministérielle," 723.

59. Leites, *On the Game of Politics,* Ch. 4.

60. Aron, *France: Steadfast and Changing,* p. 21. For other assertions that party fragmentation led to cabinet instability see Nicholas Wahl, "Making and Unmaking a Government," in Beer and Ulam, eds., *Patterns of Government,* p. 282; and Duverger, *La VI⁰ République et le régime présidentiel,* p. 46.

61. *L'Année Politique,* 1954, p. 101. These examples are, of course, only particular instances of *ministrables'* consensus as we have described it.

62. Siegfried, *De la IV⁰ à la V⁰ République,* p. 164.

63. See *Le Monde,* 7–8 May 1950: *"Le ciel se couvre à l'approche des congrès ou des comités."*

64. Williams, *Crisis,* p. 232. The reverse was true under Pinay and Mendès-France.

65. Michels' distrust of oligarchy and *embourgeoisement* (expressed in his *Political Parties*) rested on the assumption that revolutionary socialism would govern by itself or not at all. See May, "Democracy, Organization, Michels."

66. *Le Monde,* 8 July 1952.

67. A similar critique of the French system of that time was made by Kirchheimer in "The Waning of Opposition in Parliamentary Regimes." Macridis also criticized the cabinets for failing to present alternatives to the electorate; see his "Cabinet Instability in the Fourth Republic (1946–1951)."

≫8≪

The Electorate: Stability in the Vote

THE CONTINUAL FRAGMENTATION OF THE National Assembly, and the effective exclusion of some of its fragments from cabinet coalitions, reflected a similar division on the part of the voting public. This division was expressed through a stable vote for a set of political parties that existed as of November 1946: the Communists, Socialists, MRP, Radicals, and Moderates. The transfers of votes between these parties were small. This immobility of the electorate was periodically broken, however, by large transfers of votes to new political movements: the RPF in 1947–53, the Mendesist wing of the Radicals in 1954–57, and the Poujadists in 1954–56. Each of these new movements, however, soon returned to the obscurity from which it had arisen.[1]

The simultaneous presence in the system of stable parties and these "surge" movements set limits on the possible distributions of the vote, and thus on possible party configurations in the Assembly. At the same time, widespread attitudes toward voting set limits on the electoral systems that might have been adopted.

In this chapter we shall examine the extent of the stability of the vote and its sources; the next chapter will consider the variation in the vote associated with "surge" movements. This analysis will draw on both electoral statistics and sample survey data. Neither survey data nor voting statistics provide a complete account of the process of voting decision, but they supplement one another. Surveys provide invaluable data on individuals' behavior and their attitudes, but the customary national sample provides too few cases for detailed local and regional comparisons. Aggregate statistics, on the other hand, are more valid and provide more local detail, but are limited by the variables that may be studied and by the indirectness of the inferences they permit about individuals.

Basic Attitudes Toward Voting

The proportion of adult citizens who voted under the Fourth Republic was very high compared with the United States.[2] It was not unusual for Europe; but perhaps more striking was the association of high voting participation with indications that citizens were unlikely to feel that it made much difference which party they voted for.[3] It was not always clear what policies would be aided by the election of a given party or deputy, as the cabinet coalitions he would support were hard to predict. Moreover, under the electoral alliance system, a vote for one deputy could elect another. Some voters may have felt that a particular deputy should be elected for the sake of personal favors and casework, even if his effect on cabinet coalitions was unpredictable.[4] But in general the combination of high participation and low predictability suggests that voting may have been more expressive than instrumental.[5] At least voting was not a clear means to influence public policy through actions of the Assembly as a whole.

Wylie refers to this attitude toward voting in his account of the 1956 election in Peyrane, in which one-quarter of the voters did not vote, one-quarter voted Poujadist, one-quarter voted Communist, and one-quarter voted for Moderate candidates:

> Peyrane is profoundly conservative. The vote does not mean that they want to change the order of things. It means quite the contrary, that they want to be left alone so they will not have to change. Not that the state of things is good as it is. It is neither good nor bad; it is tolerable. Or rather it would be tolerable if it were not for the malevolence of human beings organized into groups. For organization means power, and power means the oppression of the individual.
>
> Even at the local level where individuals know one another personally, we have seen that the only successful organizations are co-operatives whose benefits have been concretely demonstrated to outweigh their oppressive nature. Other groups lead a precarious life, and usually they disintegrate entirely. . . .
>
> They can ignore or disrupt local organizations, but whether they like it or not they are under the control of the French Government and the hidden forces which they believe run the Government. They react characteristically. The person who does not vote pretends to ignore the Government as he pretends to ignore a person with whom he is *brouillé*. He symbolically assassinates it. The person who votes adopts an even more popular form of defense. Just as he insults and gossips about his enemy, inflicting harm on him orally, so he uses the ballot as an insult to organized power. A few literal-minded voters . . . write insulting words on the ballot, even though they know the writing will cause the ballots to be thrown out.[6]

To express one's position might mean simply casting the ballot; or it might mean electing a deputy of one's own persuasion. This latter type of expression is emphasized by Chapsal: "A first goal of the choice of an electoral system . . . is to express as faithfully as possible all the opinions of the country and give them their chances proportionally."[7]

This French view of voting—as an opportunity to record one's preferences rather than to resolve differences—is further revealed by the way in which voting statistics were published in the early years of the Fourth Republic. Not only were the votes for each party given in early tabulations, but so too were the "unrepresented" votes.[8] The compiler evidently viewed it as a departure from true proportional representation if certain voters could not count themselves as represented in the Assembly by someone for whom they had voted. His ideal was to have an Assembly that mirrored the distribution of voters' preferences in the country. In the same perspective, the manipulation of the electoral system in 1951, permitting *apparentements* to win seats at the expense of Communists and Gaullists, was viewed by

232 Parliament, Parties, and Society in France 1946-1958

many as illegitimate. It did indeed seek the political advantage of the parties of the center coalition; but it distorted the distribution of party support far less than does the system used to elect the United States Congress. In our presidential elections, almost half the votes cast are "unrepresented" as are (in another sense) the minority votes for presidential electors in each state; but the President is considered the representative not only of all who voted for him, but of the public at large as well. A plurality electoral system, in contrast with proportional representation, may encourage more channels of representation that cross party lines.

The notion that votes for a candidate who was not elected were "unrepresented" is consistent with the vertical character of influence in France. It was not easy to regard one's erstwhile local political enemy as a channel of influence. To cross party lines on specific matters of local concern was difficult; and in this sense the failure to elect a candidate of one's own party may have meant an unrepresented vote.[9]

The use of the vote to express a particular political position, together with the multiple positions that might be expressed under a multi-party system, make possible a more detailed analysis of the vote than is possble for the United States. Detailed geographical studies of French regional and local politics, together with the very possibility of multiple regression analysis, reveal that voting in France was a qualitatively different phenomenon from voting in the United States.[10]

This state of affairs permits and encourages a closer scrutiny of the social bases of voting than does the system of the United States or Great Britain, where much research fails to go beyond a single dimension of social class or status. The *fonctionnaires'* vote for the Socialists, the small shopkeepers' support of Poujadism and related movements, the unique and insecure position of the MRP, and the urban "surges" for de Gaulle, all raise problems that cannot be solved in terms of a single dimension of "social class." Political system and social system, both more complex than in the United States, join to require a more detailed analysis.

Stability and Variation in the Vote

The distinction between stable and fluctuating segments of the vote may be shown by both aggregate statistics and survey data. Over the three legislative elections of the Fourth Republic and the two preceding elections to Constituent Assemblies, three parties held proportions of the vote that scarcely fluctuated more than two per cent—Communists, Radicals, and Moderates. Socialists and MRP each lost about half their 1945 voting support, but stabilized in 1951 and 1956. The Gaullists and Poujadists, however, rose suddenly to prominence and then declined precipitously (Table 8.1).[11] The aggregate stability of the vote for the stable parties might conceivably conceal considerable exchange of individual voters among them. That it does not can be shown more clearly by means of survey data. A series of surveys conducted by the Institut Français d'Opinion Publique (IFOP) during the Fourth Republic permits this individual analysis.[12]

Periodically, IFOP included in its surveys questions on the respondent's current party preference and his vote at the last parliamentary election.

Comparison of vote intention with retrospective reports of past vote provides valuable information on the types of individual changes in party preference that occurred. In a normal national sample by IFOP, about 2000 persons were interviewed, and some 50 to 60 per cent specified the party for which

Table 8.1 Stability and Variation in the Party Vote Under the Fourth Republic (Metropolitan France)

	Per Cent of Vote Cast at Election of				
	Oct. 21, 1945	*June 2, 1946*	*Nov. 10, 1946*	*June 17, 1951*	*Jan. 2, 1956*
Stable groupings:					
Communists	26.0	26.2	28.6	25.9	25.9
Radicals and UDSR*	11.1	12.8	12.4	11.2	13.5
Moderates	13.3	11.5	12.8	12.3	14.4
Stable after initial loss:					
Socialists	23.8	21.1	17.9	14.9	14.9
MRP	24.9	28.1	26.4	12.8	11.1
"Surge" move- ments					
Gaullism (RPF)	–	–	1.6	20.4	4.4
Poujadism (UFF)	–	–	–	–	11.5
*Total**	99.1	99.7	99.7	97.5	95.7
Turnout	79.8	81.8	78.1	77.3	79.6

*In October 1945 UDSR is counted with Socialists.
**Minor parties omitted.

Source: Party percentages are a combination of Fauvet, *La IVe République*, p. 373, and Williams, *Crisis*, p. 502. Turnout figures are from the volumes of election statistics published by *Le Monde* for 1945–46, and the official volumes of election statistics published by the Ministry of the Interior (Documentation Française).

they had voted. Although precise interpretations cannot normally be made when so many of the respondents are not classified, the information we do have shows the types of changes in preference that occurred, and their approximate magnitude, in various periods.

Cross-tabulation of vote intention by reported past vote provides "turn-over tables"[13] showing the types of transfers of political allegiance that occurred in a given period. A series of such tables will be shown below. We may consider them in sequence, dividing the Fourth Republic into five periods corresponding to the two Constituent Assemblies and the three Legislatures. These five periods start with the elections of October 21, 1945,

June 2, 1946, November 10, 1946, June 17, 1951, and January 2, 1956, respectively.[14]

Table 8.2 shows changes in party preference over the six-month period following the election of October 1945. Data are presented only for those respondents who gave a classifiable report of their previous votes. Among those who reported a Communist vote, for example, 88 per cent said they

Table 8.2 *Turnover in Party Preference, First
Constituent Assembly (1945–46)*

Preference April 1–15, 1946	Reported Vote October 1945 Election				
	Communist	*Socialist*	*Radical*	*MRP*	*Other Parties*
Communist	88%	7%	1%	1%	–
Socialist	4	72	16	4	5
Radical	1	3	66	4	3
MRP	–	3	7	61	12
PRL	–	1	2	16	37
Other parties	1	1	3	1	22
No Answer*	6	13	5	13	21
Total	100%	100%	100%	100%	100%

*This figure, not published in the source, is calculated by subtracting column totals from 100%. Comparison with other published tables suggests that this category was omitted.

Source: *Sondages*, May 1, 1947, No. 9, 111. This table was selected from four presented in *Sondages* for this period; turnover was relatively large in this table. A typical question wording for this and the following tables was: "If there were general elections now, for what party would you vote?"

would vote Communist again, while 4 per cent said they would vote Socialist and 1 per cent Radical. Party choice was relatively stable in this period; the major changes that occurred between "established" parties were a shift of 16 per cent of the former Radical voters to the Socialists and a shift of similar magnitude from the MRP to the newly formed PRL. The larger changes in the "other parties" column correspond to the coalescence of several small conservative parties into the PRL; these were mainly the *Alliance Démocratique* and the *Fédération Républicaine*, dating from the Third Republic.[15]

We have chosen to place the Radicals to the left of the MRP in these tables as a result of evidence contained in the tables themselves. The fact that the two large transfers of votes cited are from Radicals to Socialists, and from MRP to PRL, suggest that in the voters' minds the MRP had been more a party of the right. The placement of parties in terms of vote transfers is not necessarily the same as their placement in Assembly voting, even at the same time.[16]

Except for the coalescence of the parties of the right, the major parties held relatively stable clienteles during the First Constituent Assembly. Table 8.3 shows a similar stability during the Second Constituent Assembly in 1946; the largest change during that period was a shift of 16 per cent of the former MRP voters to the PRL. Apparently the formation of the PRL gave a more acceptable political home to some of the MRP's conservative sup-

Table 8.3 Turnover in Party Preference, Second
Constituent Assembly (1946)

Preference October 1946	Reported Vote June 2, 1946				
	Communist	*Socialist*	*Radical*	*MRP*	*PRL*
Communist	92%	2%	1%	–	–
Socialist	4	85	2	1	
Radical	–	6	71	4	3
MRP	–	3	6	71	5
PRL	–	–	3	16	67
NA (by diff.)	4	4	17	7	25
Total	100%	100%	100%	100%	100%

Source: *Sondages*, November 16, 1946, No. 20, 263.

porters; this trend was to be considerably amplified with the advent of the RPF and the increasing respectability of the later Moderate groupings.

Table 8.4 shows the changes that took place during the First Legislature (1946–51). Table 8.4A shows changes from November 1946 to April 1947, which were relatively small. Table 8.4B shows the changes brought about by the formation of the RPF; substantial shifts of voter preference toward Gaullism took place from all the major parties except the Communists. The preferences of former nonvoters are also shown here; they were disproportionately in favor of Gaullism as well, 23 per cent of this group choosing the RPF.[17] Because of the distribution of parties from which the RPF drew its support, we place it on the right center, between MRP and PRL.

By April 1951 the crest of the Gaullist wave had passed, and the parties from which the RPF had gained the most (MRP, PRL) had recovered much of their former support (Table 8.4C). Of the former non-voters, only 3 per cent now planned to vote RPF. At the same time the percentages in the "undecided" category increased. In the meantime the strength of the RPF had declined irregularly, with a recovery in September 1948 at a time of sharp conflict with the Communists.[18]

The decline of the RPF as a party was almost as rapid as its rise. By August 1953, only 52 per cent of its 1951 supporters said they would vote for it again, while 22 per cent did not give classifiable responses. This latter proportion gradually decreased until it was only 11 per cent in January, 1955 (Table 8.5).[19]

Table 8.4 *Turnover in Party Preference,*
First Legislature (1946–51)

	Reported Vote November 10, 1946						
	Com- munist	Social- ist	Radi- cal	MRP	PRL	Other parties	Did not vote
A. Preference April 1947							
Communist	88%	5%	2%	1%	–		
Socialist	5	84	12	3	2		
Radical	–	3	66	4	3		
MRP	1	1	6	73	5	(not given)	
PRL	–	–	3	5	80		
other, NA (by diff.)	6	7	11	14	10		
Total	100%	100%	100%	100%	100%		
B. Preference Dec. 1947:							
Communist	86%	3%	–	–	–	–	1
Socialist	4	74	2	1	–	5	9
Radical	–	2	62	1	1	–	3
MRP	–	1	1	34	1	3	3
RPF	–	8	26	54	70	54	23
PRL	–	–	–	1	19	–	1
other	–	1	4	1	1	30	–
NA (by diff.)	10	11	5	8	8	8	60
Total	100%	100%	100%	100%	100%	100%	100%
C. Vote inten- tion April 1951:							
Communist	81%	3%	1%	1%	–	3%	6%
Socialist	5	70	2	2	1	–	6
Radical	–	2	61	5	4	5	1
MRP	–	–	1	41	4	2	4
RPF	–	1	8	20	29	29	3
PRL	1	–	2	3	41	⎧48	2
other	2	1	2	4	5	⎨	8
Undecided	11	23	23	24	16	13	70
Total	100%	100%	100%	100%	100%	100%	100%

Sources: A. *Sondages*, May 1, 1947, No. 8, 95; B. February 1, 1948, No. 3, 37; C. 1951, No. 2, 46. Selected from nine such tables, or parts thereof, published in *Sondages* for this period. Table C
has also been augmented by means of data from Stoetzel, "Voting Behaviour in France."

Table 8.5 *Turnover in Party Preference, Second Legislature (1951–55)*

Preference January 1955	Reported Vote June 17, 1951							
	Communist	Socialist	Radical	MRP	RPF	Moderate	Other	Did not vote
Communist	88%	4%	–	–	–	–	6%	6%
Socialist	1	72	1	2	3	1	3	11
Radical	2	4	69	2	3	2	–	4
MRP	–	1	1	64	1	3	3	5
RPF	–	–	1	3	52	2	3	11
Moderate	*	3	5	13	27	82	3	2
Other	2	3	10	4	4	4	63	7
Won't vote, NA	5	12	14	13	11	6	18	54
Total	98%	99%	101%	101%	101%	100%	99%	100%
Per cent of sample	10	14	5	11	6	11	2	20 :

79%

Undetermined 20%

Total 99%

(N = 2044)

*Less than 1/2 per cent.

Source: Secondary analysis of data from IFOP survey no. 103. Selected from four such tables available to the author.

The distribution of new "Moderate" votes in 1955 shows an unexpectedly broad range of recruitment; they drew 3 per cent of the former Socialist voters, a proportion exceeded by the RPF in late 1947 but never by other parties of the "right." The RPF's losses are in fact less widely dispersed across the political spectrum than the "Moderates'" gains. One possible explanation of this anomaly seems to be that protests such as incipient Poujadism, not yet classified by IFOP as a distinct political movement, were rendering the recruitment of "Moderates" much more heterogeneous.[20]

In January 1955 the proportion of respondents whose preference was "other" or undetermined was higher among former Radical voters than among the supporters of any other major party (24 per cent). It is possible that the "other party" category reflected support for Mendesism at this time; Mendès-France had been a very popular premier, but he had made no move to take control of the Radical party and his overthrow was imminent at the time of the survey. When asked their current party preferences, some of the respondents replied, "for the new left" or "for Mendès-France"; these responses were coded as "other," and 10 per cent of the former Radicals fell in this category.

The fact that Mendès received little "party" support but much personal support indicates a certain lack of responsiveness of the system to the acts of the prime minister: there was no clear way in which voters could support a leader who pursued new policies, unless he embodied these policies in the program of a political party.[21] Mendès tried to do this later but failed.

The Radicals are still placed to the left of the MRP in Table 8.5. During the Second Legislature Radicals and MRP both lost significant fractions of their voters to the Moderates, but the MRP lost more. The Socialists, on the other hand, lost more to the Radicals. In these terms, therefore, the Radicals may be considered to the left of the MRP, apparently because the church-school question dominated economic issues in the voters' minds. But in the position of its deputies on economic issues, as well as in terms of party organization, MRP belonged farther to the left than the Radicals (see Chapters 3–6).

Table 8.6 shows the changes in vote intention that occurred during the Third Legislature, from January 1956 through March 1957. By November 1956 three major parties had been shaken by the events of the previous year: Communists, Radicals, and Poujadists. The brutal suppression of the Hungarian revolt caused many former Communist voters to report uncertainty in their preferences; but the March 1957 survey showed that this disaffection was only temporary, and that former Communist voters could not bring themselves to support the "bourgeois" parties.[22]

The disintegration of the Radicals associated with the conflict over Mendesism was shown at the Lyon Congress of November 1956 by the secession of the Morice faction of the party. Correspondingly, 28 per cent of the former Radicals reported uncertain party preference at that time. By March 1957 some of these returned, but 10 per cent of the former Radicals still indicated an intention to support the Socialists.

Poujadism showed a rapid decline from January 1956 through March 1957, though by January 1958 it had regained strength and held 51 per cent of its 1956 voters.[23] The direction of its potential losses was irregular: the largest single group moving from a Poujadist vote to another party went to the MRP in November 1956, then to the Moderates in March 1957. The reluctance of Poujadists to return to the other parties is suggested by the

Table 8.6 Turnover in Party Preference: Third Legislature (1956–58)

	Comm.	Soc.	Rad.	MRP	Mod.	Pouj.	Others	Did not vote
				Reported Vote January 1956				
A. Preference Nov. 1956								
Communist	68%	–	–	–	–	–	–	2%
Socialist	1	80	9	3	2	3	8	11
Radical	1	1	49	–	2	3	3	4
MRP	–	1	1	66	–	10	3	3
Moderate	–	–	8	4	76	7	6	3
Poujadist	–	1	–	–	2	40	–	–
Others	6	2	4	2	3	7	48	6
NA, Don't Know, Won't Vote	23	15	28	25	16	30	32	72
Total	99%	100%	99%	100%	101%	100%	100%	101%
Per cent of sample:	6	14	6	8	9	2	6	11: 62%

Undetermined : 38%
Total : 100%
(N = 1227)

	Comm.	Soc.	Rad.	MRP	Mod.	Pouj.	Others	Did not vote
B. Preference March 1957								
Communist	81%	–	–	–	–	–	–	1%
Socialist	2	82	10	4	2	8	11	5
Radical	1	–	60	–	–	5	4	2
MRP	–	–	1	80	1	2	7	1
Moderate	–	1	5	4	76	20	4	5
Poujadist	–	–	–	1	1	22	–	–
Others	3	2	1	–	–	5	63	2
DK, NA	13	14	22	12	20	38	11	84
Total	100%	99%	99%	101%	100%	100%	100%	100%

Source: *Sondages*, 1957, No. 3, 11.

fact that its former voters included a higher proportion of nonresponses and "don't knows" than did those of any other party.

The turnover tables we have examined reveal the stability of the major organized parties, as well as their positions relative to one another from the point of view of voter exchange. They show the political dispersion of the sources of the vote for the "surges," but what is more important in the study of stability, they reveal the block to certain transfers resulting from reluctance to move into a traditionally "enemy" party. This was true of the Communists after the Hungarian revolution; their disaffection was reflected by a transfer of preferences into the "undecided" category, from which they eventually returned to their source. When the RPF began its decline after the 1951 elections, its former voters also showed a disproportionate transfer to the "undecided" category.[24] The transfer of potential Mendesists into a nonparty category, on the other hand, reflected the unavailability of any party that corresponded clearly to their candidate preference.

Comparison of French turnover tables with similar tables for the United States suggests that the proportions of voters who shifted from one "stable" party to another in France were generally less than in the United States. In transitions between presidential elections in the United States from 1936 to 1960, from 13 to 21 per cent of those voting both times shifted from one major party to the other. In four of these six transitions, the losing party lost from 24 to 28 per cent of its former supporters; and even in the relatively stable transitions of 1940–44 and 1952–56, the losing party lost 16 per cent or more.[25]

Corresponding figures for French turnover tables may be obtained by considering only the transfers of preference from one "stable" party to another, and using as a base of percentages the total number of voters for a given "stable" party who either retained that preference or shifted to another "stable" party.[26] By this calculation the proportions shifting are not artificially lowered by the shifts that took place to a "surge" party such as the RPF. Proportions of shifters, calculated in this way, are shown in Table 8.7.

The most striking feature of Table 8.7 is that even with this adjusted calculation, there were three French parties for which the proportion of loss to all other stable parties was uniformly lower than the lowest proportion for losing parties in the United States (16 per cent)—Communists, Socialists, and Moderates. On only two occasions does the Moderates' loss exceed 16 per cent.

The Radicals exceeded this minimum proportion of loss several times, but they attained the degree of loss characteristic of the losing party in a major "swing" election in the United States (25 per cent or more) only three times: in April 1946 and April 1947, when they were losing to the Socialists, and in November 1956, when the party was disintegrating over the issue of Mendesism. The MRP, whose losses were heaviest, attained this degree of loss in two periods—1946, when it lost to the new PRL, and 1948–1951, when it lost to other parties as well as to the RPF. Of all the "stable" parties of the Fourth Republic, only the MRP showed a type and degree of loss of voters comparable with the major parties in the United States. The MRP, though more cohesive than the Radicals in the Assembly, was less so in holding the vote of the electorate—perhaps because the MRP itself was a new party after the Liberation, less deeply rooted than the others.

In demonstrating that most of the "stable" French parties held their vote firmly relative to one another, we have also understated the case in a sense.[27] When multiple parties exist, there is more opportunity for vote transfer than in a two-party system. Had we artificially divided the French parties into two groups, we should necessarily have reduced the proportions

Table 8.7 *Transfers of Votes Among the*
Stable Parties *

Previous election	Date of Survey	Reported Previous Vote				
		Communist	Socialist	Radical	MRP	Moderates*
Oct. 1945						
	Feb. 1946	3%	15%	9%	5%	**
	Apr. 1, 1946	5	16	28	29	**
	Apr. 16, 1946	4	15	22	31	**
	May 1946	5	12	16	27	**
June 1946						
	Oct. 1946	4	11	13	23	9%
Nov. 1946						
	Apr. 1947	6	10	26	15	11
	June 1947	4	11	12	15	7
	Dec. 1947	4	8	5	8	10
	July 1948	6	13	15	15	9
	Sept. 1948	3	12	14	24	12
	Mar. 1949	9	15	10	25	20
	Oct. 1949	9	15	15	24	14
	Apr. 1951	7	7	9	21	18
June 1951						
	Aug. 1953	1	10	12	19	4
	Aug. 1954	3	7	18	18	9
	Jan. 1955	3	14	10	21	7
Jan. 1956						
	Nov. 1956	3	2	27	8	5
	Mar. 1957	4	1	21	9	4

*Entries are shifters among those who reported preference for a stable party both times. The "stable" parties, for this analysis, are those listed in the column headings. The PRL, even though a new party in 1946, is included among the Moderates; substantial parts of the MRP losses in 1946 were to the PRL.

**In the turnover tables following the October 1945 election, the reports of previous Moderate votes are published only as part of the category "other parties"; for this reason no figures are given in the Moderate column for 1946.

of "shifting" votes; for some of the votes we have classified as shifts would then have moved only within one or the other of the two larger groups. Thus while the MRP showed proportions of loss comparable with those of the United States parties, it did so only with respect to parties that were relatively "near" it in principle and policy. Other things being the same, we should expect parties to have nearer ideological neighbors in a multi-party system than in a two-party system, and more transfers of votes to and from them.

We must conclude that French voters and party activists drew sharper distinctions between their stable parties than are customarily drawn between parties in the United States. The range of political positions was greater in France; but even neighboring party positions seem to have been distinguished more sharply. A voter's identification with one party carried with it views of the other parties as well; he knew what he was not as well as what he was. Political campaigns made much of these counter-identifications, and the new parties could circumvent them more easily than the old.[28] When new parties were unavailable, transfer to the "undecided" category was often easier than support for one's former political enemies. Thus there were real obstacles to the transfer of votes between the stable parties.

The stabilization of "normal" opinion, and sensitivity to sudden changes in opinion, have also been attributed by Duverger to proportional representation; but although there may be some truth in this interpretation, we are here stressing the very existence of sudden changes of opinion in France, with specific causes related to attitudes toward government and toward the opposing parties. Duverger also attributes the differentiation of party programs to a multi-party system, in which campaigning aims at stressing "the differences of detail which distinguish [a party] from its nearest rivals."[29] Detailed comparison with other multi-party systems is necessary to show whether this is a characteristic of these systems or particularly of France. Yet the susceptibility of the *scrutin d'arrondissement* to the Gaullist wave in November 1958—in which the strength of Gaullism was similar on the first ballot to what it had been in 1951—suggests that the dispositions of the voters, more than the electoral system, mattered in the system's reflection of a surge of opinion for a new party.[30]

An important consequence of this division (we shall argue) was the difficulty for an established party to gain enough strength, through an appeal to the electorate, to attain power and carry out its program.[31] Our findings from turnover tables emphasize the difficulty for the established parties to recruit voters from other established parties; but it was also difficult for them to draw voters from the young or the uninvolved because of a general distrust of the parliamentary system and its machinations.

This division among the stable parties was related to social divisions, but not identical with them. In France voting was more closely related to the voter's occupation than in the United States, especially in the smaller towns. French parties were more likely than American parties to have their own newspapers, narrowly attuned to party positions; and though the party press declined during the Fourth Republic, it was always more partisan than the American. The persistence of party positions was far greater than the association between party and occupation, and it would be absurd to say that social divisions were the only basis of party differences. Probably most clearly related to party choice was the degree of religious practice or religiosity,[32] with occupation next. But when we speak of social divisions that were politically significant, we must remember that past political differences may themselves have contributed to groupings and social relations that divided the public politically later.

Referenda and Stability of Party Division

The only votes between 1945 and 1958 on which all Frenchmen confronted identical alternatives were the referenda on constitutional questions, held at the beginning and end of the Fourth Republic. It might be imagined that because the questions thus posed were not formally linked to party, some freedom from party dictates could develop. In actuality, votes on the referenda were closely linked to party, especially for the Communists and Socialists.

Probably closest to the party vote was the referendum of May 5, 1946, at which an initial draft constitution, supported by Communists and Socialists, was defeated. The per cent "yes" on this referendum in the *départements* correlated +.99 with the proportion of vote for Communists and Socialists in the November 1946 election. The close relationship between party affiliation and vote intention at this referendum was also shown by survey data: among Communist voters, 95 per cent said they intended to vote yes and only 1 per cent no; for the Socialists these percentages were 74 and 18. This relationship was sharply reversed for the other parties: among MRP voters the percentages were 3 and 93; PRL, 2 and 93; and among Radicals, 3 and 78.[33]

More loosely related to a party vote was the first question on the referendum of October 21, 1945; should the assembly then elected draw up a new constitution? The Radicals were at that time more in favor of maintaining the constitution of the Third Republic than were any of the other parties; their vote at the 1945 election correlated +.30 with the proportion of "noes," and the regression slope indicated that at best only half the votes for Radical candidates were also cast in opposition to a new constitution.

The second question on that referendum dealt with the limitation of the powers of the Constituent Assembly, and on this the Communists joined the Radicals in opposition. The correlation between the per cent "no" and the combined vote for Communists and Radicals was +.77 on this question, reflecting the preponderant vote and higher discipline of the Communists.

The referendum of October 1946, in which the constitution of the Fourth Republic was approved, involved a greatly increased proportion of nonvoting. Although it has been suggested that this represented uncertainty on the part of Gaullist MRP voters,[34] the nonvoting rate by *départements* was very closely related to that in June 1946 (r = +.88), but multiplied by a factor of 1.63. Even the departures from this relation showed no clear relationship to the Gaullist or the MRP vote.

After de Gaulle's arrival in power in 1958, referenda still maintained an association with the party vote, but only the Communists seemed able to marshal a substantial part of their voting strength in opposition. In September 1958 the Communists were the only major party to advocate a "no" vote; for the *départements* of metropolitan France their 1956 vote correlated

+.80 with the proportion of "no" votes.[35] In the referendum of 1961, even though some rightists joined the Communists in opposition after Algerian independence was proposed, the greatest part of the "no" vote still came from the Communists.[36]

The response of Communist voters to the Gaullist referendum of 1958 resembled their response to the Hungarian crisis, in that they shifted to nonvoting rather than to other parties. This is suggested by the close relation between Communist strength and increases in nonvoting in Marseille.[37]

Social Correlates of the Vote: Regression at the National Level

We can gain a general perspective on the social bases of party voting by analyzing votes in the Fourth Republic as contrasted among metropolitan *départements*.[38] This analysis is possible because certain social and political divisions existed throughout the country; but it is also facilitated by France's administrative centralization. *Départements* are bases of division of electoral districts and of census tabulations; at the same time they coincide closely with the dioceses of the Catholic Church, and thus can be related to studies of religious practice.

Even though there are well-known and long-standing regional characteristics in French politics,[39] these do not mask local differences to the extent that they do in one-party areas of the United States. This situation makes possible regression analysis of the vote at the national level, in relation to characteristics of the population in the constituencies. We shall again consider the five legislative elections of October 1945, June 1946, November 1946, June 1951, and January 1956. To a large extent the legislative constituencies corresponded to the 90 *départements,* though some of the larger *départements* were subdivided to produce the 103 constituencies for the National Assembly in metropolitan France. From these districts were elected the 544 metropolitan deputies.

The particular variables used in this analysis were arrived at through deviant-case analysis. The total percentage vote for Communists, Socialists, and Radicals in the November 1946 election was chosen as most closely related to differences in the voters' religiosity; this was compared graphically with measures of religious intensity to reveal further significant social and economic variables. Deviant *départements* in this plot suggested the use of a rural–urban variable, and successive plots of residuals against new variables led in turn to the four predictor variables used. Conceivably a similar analysis carried out with another dependent variable (e.g., the Communist vote) might suggest somewhat different predictor variables.

The predictor variables used were defined as follows:

1. *Religious attitudes.* A persistent source of conflict was the question of state aid to church schools. The stable parties tended to take sides most clearly on this question, while the "surge" movements (Poujadism, and to a lesser extent Gaullism and Mendesism) were able to attract some of their clientele from both sides by taking ambiguous positions. Voters tended to take sides on this issue in relation to their religiosity.

The most desirable index of voters' religiosity, aside from a highly detailed opinion survey, would seem to be the actual church attendance of
the population. Detailed data on church attendance have been gathered by
sociologists in France, with the aid of the clergy, and promise to throw considerable light on this problem.[40] At the present time, however, these data
have not been published in quantitative form for more than a few *départements,* the major form in which they are available being cartographic.

As a fairly accurate substitute for the religious practice of the citizenry,
we shall therefore use the rate of ordination of priests by dioceses. This rate
is expressed as a quotient: the number of priests ordained in a five-year
period from a given area, divided by the number of young men aged 25–29
in that area. Statistics of this kind have been published by Canon Boulard
and appear to concide largely with other measures of the geographical
distribution of religious attitudes and practices.[41] The geographical distribution of ordination rates appears to be highly stable over time, except for
uniform increases and decreases, and there seems little risk in using ordination rates as an independent variable to account for votes from 1945 to
1956.

2. *Urbanization.* Among the various indices of rural–urban differences available,[42] there is some advantage in using one that corresponds to a fraction
of the population. This sort of index can most readily be compared with
party votes as fractions of the total vote; moreover, it provides the possibility
of comparison between regression analysis and survey results, if the same
population characteristics are identified in sample surveys.

Rural France, as we shall see below, presents a variety of socioeconomic
aspects that relate to the vote. A predominant one is the independent pro-
prietor with relatively small holdings who lives in a poorer area of the
country.[43] These proprietors and their families have tended to be suspicious
of the central government, city dwellers, and large economic enterprises;
setting aside the religious factor, they tended to live in regions of leftist
vote. In richer areas, at least those where middle-sized farms predominate,
there was more of a rightist tendency; this can be measured by the proportion of farm workers who are employed on middle-sized farms. Finally, there
are certain *départements* in the Paris Basin and on the Mediterranean coast
where farming is done on a relatively large scale, and the possibility of organizing the farm labor force again led to a leftist tendency.

Because of these multiple political tendencies in the rural population,
three distinct fractions of the employed male population will be used as
predictor variables: *a.* farm proprietors and family workers; *b.* hired
workers on farms hiring from one to nine such workers; *c.* hired workers on
farms hiring ten or more such workers.[44] The first of these three indices
will be taken as a measure of the "rural" proportion of the population.
Clearly, however, it differs from other measures that might be used. Thus
when we see below that rural areas were associated with a leftist vote, we
must recall that this particular definition has been used. The advantage of
this definition is that it appears to separate groups in the population that
are distinct in their political preferences.

3. *Agricultural wealth.* Index *b* suggested above (proportion of hired

farm workers on middle-sized farms) will be used for this purpose. Among the various possible alternatives[45] it seems best fitted to analysis based on complementary groups in the population.

4. *Agricultural proletarization.* Index c suggested above (proportion of hired farm workers on large farms) will be used for this purpose.

In addition to these four variables, it might be expected that social class would be significantly related to the vote. It is, but the geographical units necessary for comparison of the above variables on a national scale (*départements* or dioceses) preclude the distinction among *quartiers* of cities, which is necessary to show the significance of social class in terms of areas of residence. We shall consider this distinction below.

The dependent variables to be examined correspond to various categories of voters' choices. For each of the five elections to be considered, three comparable categories of the vote will be treated: *a.* the Communist vote; *b.* the vote for Communist and Socialist parties combined; and *c.* a broader category on the left, embracing not only Communists and Socialists but also the Radicals and related parties (up to 1951, this will be referred to as the "anticlerical" left; in 1956 it corresponds to the Communist vote plus that for the Republican Front). They will be expressed as proportions of valid votes cast (*suffrages exprimés*). Analysis of the vote for individual parties that were not politically "extreme" (SFIO or MRP) is not attempted here because of problems concerned with their competing for votes on "both sides."

Data from standard sources[46] were used to calculate the dependent variables. For categories *a* and *b*, the procedure was relatively straightforward. Occasional adjustments were made for the absence of a distinct Socialist or Communist list; the vote was allocated in proportion to that at an earlier or later election in the same district.

In category *c* more care was required. Most lists of the Radical party, UDSR, and RGR were placed on the "left" in elections preceding 1956; but a few were placed on the "right" because of the previous votes of the leading candidate or because of an electoral alliance with rightist groupings.[47] In the election of November 10, 1946, the Gaullist Union—a precursor of the RPF—presented lists in a number of districts. In sixteen of these districts these candidacies were judged to have so obscured the left–right distinction that figures for the "anticlerical" left in the preceding election (June 2, 1946) for the Constituent Assembly were substituted. The purpose of this substitution is to present the political cleavages of that time as though Gaullism had not existed as a political movement. In three other *départements*, coalition lists extending across the "clerical–anticlerical" boundary were also treated in this manner. In the 1956 election, Radical lists not associated with the Republican Front, together with all RGR lists, were placed on the "right," while all lists supporting the Republican Front were placed on the "left."[48]

In addition to these three comparable categories of the vote, two special categories will also be considered: the Gaullist gain (1946–51) and the Poujadist vote (1956).[49]

Regression coefficients were calculated for the predictor and dependent variables described above. Each calculation (except for the Poujadist vote) was based on a total of eighty-two *départements* or dioceses. It should be noted that this procedure emphasizes the less populous rural areas at the expense of those containing larger cities.

The results of the regression analysis, using the four predictor variables

Table 8.8 Standardized Regression Coefficients (b*) for Prediction of Political Variables

Date of Election: Predictor variables	Communists	Communists and Socialists	"Anticler- ical" left	
Oct. 21, 1945				
Religiosity	−.35	−.61	−.72	
Ruralism	+.19	+.30	+.49	
Agric. wealth	−.44	−.35	−.23	
Agric. proletarization	+.33	+.30	+.27	
Multiple R	.54	.64	.69	
June 2, 1946				
Religiosity	−.39	−.59	−.71	
Ruralism	+.23	+.33	+.47	
Agric. wealth	−.41	−.33	−.20	
Agric. proletarization	+.34	+.27	+.31	
Multiple R	.54	.63	.69	
Nov. 10, 1946				
Religiosity	−.35	−.56	−.75	
Ruralism	+.19	+.33	+.52	
Agric. wealth	−.32	−.23	−.20	
Agric. proletarization	+.30	+.26	+.26	
Multiple R	.53	.56	.71	
				Gaullist gain
June 17, 1951				
Religiosity	−.47	−.49	−.72	+.40
Ruralism	+.24	+.30	+.59	−.60
Agric. wealth	−.39	−.26	−.24	+.14
Agric. proletarization	+.32	+.25	+.31	−.17
Multiple R	.58	.56	.71	.51
				Poujadist vote
Jan. 2, 1956				
Religiosity	−.45	−.45	−.66	−.18
Ruralism	−.03	+.12	+.29	+.39
Agric. wealth	−.29	−.26	−.20	+.23
Agric. proletarization	+.24	+.24	+.21	−.07
Multiple R	.58	.52	.64	.44

*All political variables are expressed as proportions of valid votes cast (*suffrages exprimés*).

listed above, are shown in Table 8.8. Values of b* for the elections of 1945, June 1946, November 1946, 1951, and 1956 are shown separately; in each case the coefficients for various party groups can be compared for each indicator.[50]

We may begin the interpretation of Table 8.8 by considering the election of October 1945 for the First Constituent Assembly. The highest multiple correlation (*R*) for that election (.69) corresponds to the "anticlerical" left, in which the votes for Radicals, Socialists, and Communists are combined. This indicates that about half of the variance of the "clerical–anticlerical" division of the vote can be accounted for by the predictor variables used. In all probability, this degree of success in prediction is considerably greater than would obtain in the United States; the high association of the vote with religious practice would be matched in its uniformity only by the correlates of economic variables in state or regional analyses, or by the relation between occupation and urban political choice for the United States as a whole.[51] The remaining variance of French voting can profitably be studied by detailed regional investigations, with the use of regression analysis to highlight deviant cases.

The religious variable clearly contributes the most to this relationship (in the sense of having the highest b*, −.72). Although its relative importance varies somewhat from one election to another, and it is less important when we consider divisions farther to the left in the political spectrum, it is impressive to note that even among the correlates of the Communist vote it is uniformly highest or next highest.

While the religious variable contributes negatively to the "leftist" vote, ruralism contributes positively. In an overall sense, the rural regions of France tended to be somewhat more conservative than the urban;[52] but once the religious factor is set aside, what seems to emerge is the traditional leftist tendency of the small farmer. The value of b* (+.49) for ruralism is the second highest in predicting the "anticlerical" vote. We shall see below, however, that this relation is reversed within certain *départements,* and may be in part a regional effect.

The third predictor variable, intended to measure agricultural wealth, shows the expected positive association with "rightist" voting (b* = −.23 with the "anticlerical" left). And the fourth, though based on the tail of the same frequency distribution (hired farm workers by the number of such workers on a farm) shows the opposite effect of agricultural proletarization on the vote (b* = +.27). Thus the presence of a few hired workers on a farm indicates wealth and conservatism, with the workers' vote not necessarily canceling out the employers'; but when there are many workers on each farm, their presence indicates the likelihood of a leftist vote and a class cleavage in the countryside.

The pattern of signs of the b*'s (− + − +) remains the same for all the left–right divisions considered here—i.e., the divisions of the vote that consider Communists, Communists plus Socialists, or the entire "anticlerical" group of parties as the "left"—in every section of Table 8.8 but one. Within this pattern, we may proceed to compare the magnitudes of the b*'s as they vary from one point of division to another and over time.

As we move from an "anticlerical" left to more sharply delimited definitions of the left, we find that certain b*'s decrease and others increase. In particular, the relative importance of the religious variable declines (from −.72 to −.61 to −.35); that of ruralism also declines (+.49 to +.30 to +.19); while the importance of agricultural wealth and agricultural proletarization increase, particularly as regards the Communist vote. Thus as we move from the "anticlerical" definition of the left to the Communist vote, we find that economic variables (those related to agriculture) come to play a relatively more important part. Because of the general predominance of the religious variable, however, the multiple correlation R falls from .69 to .64 to .54 as we move toward the Communists.

The regression coefficients for the elections of June and November 1946 are very similar to those for October 1945. Apparently no major realignments of the electorate took place during this period.

In the 1951 election we find an increase in the association of the "anticlerical" left with rural areas (+.52 to +.59).[53] This change may be attributed to the presence of the Gaullist RPF on the scene; the RPF, although counted as on the right, drew some previously leftist votes as well,[54] and appealed particularly to the urban middle classes. Thus the remaining leftist vote in 1951 would have been more rural. The character of the Gaullist vote is indicated by the b*'s listed for the "Gaullist gain" (votes given to RPF lists in 1951 over and above those that could be attributed to support received by the same candidates on non-Gaullist lists in previous elections). This gain is seen to be less clearly "clerical," and slightly more urban, than the rightist vote in general had been before; the b*'s for the entire clerical right may be obtained, for comparison, simply by reversing the signs of those shown for the anticlerical left.

The Communist vote alone, over this period, showed a tendency to concentrate in the less religious *départements,* as its b* with religiosity changed from −.35 to −.47. This seems to reflect a loss of support that the party held in the early postwar years, in areas whose traditions were inconsistent with its ideology.[55] Aside from this, its relation to ruralism and to other agricultural variables changed little. The addition of the Socialist vote to the Communist, while it increases the negative association with religiosity in November 1946 (from −.35 to −.56), fails to make a comparable contribution in 1951 (−.47 to −.49) or in 1956.

In 1956 Poujadism and Mendesism appeared. Both these movements acted to reduce the relative importance of the religious variables: the former in an effort to amass protest votes over a wide range of the political spectrum, the latter because the Mendesist forces included some leftist-Catholic candidates and some Gaullists, while rejecting to the right the Faurist RGR and some Radical lists.[56] Thus the b* of the religious variable drops to −.66 in 1956, when we consider the Mendesists together with the Communists and Socialists.

The significance of the urban–rural variable also changes considerably by 1956. Whereas in 1951 the urban "floating vote" was taken by Gaullism to a considerable extent, in 1956 it was captured far more by the left in the form of Mendesism. Thus the earlier tendency of the anticlerical left to be relatively rural was heightened in 1951, but greatly reduced in 1956. (+.59 to +.29).[57] In 1956 the Communist *départements* also ceased to be predominantly rural.

All these categories of the leftist vote actually became more urban in 1956. For Socialists as well as Radicals this change might be attributed to Mendesism and their alliance in the Republican Front, but for the Communists another reason must be sought. We shall suggest, in spite of the absence of survey evidence to this effect, that the Poujadist surge may have taken some of the rural Communist vote.

The success of Poujade in straddling the clerical–anticlerical issue is illustrated by the low b* for the religious variable in predicting the Poujadist vote (−.18). The rural base of the Poujadist vote is evidenced by the b* of +.39. The third b* for the Poujadist vote runs counter to some expectations; it suggests that this vote was stronger in areas of agricultural wealth, while in fact crises in the market for some crops (e.g., the wine-growers' crisis) contributed to the Poujadist vote. Perhaps a better explanation is that these crises affected not merely farming areas, but particularly those with middle-sized farms including some hired hands. Possibly also it was those areas where commerce was more fully developed in the middle-sized villages that suffered more from modernization of trade and from taxes.[58]

By our regression analysis we can see not only the persistent associations between the vote for the stable parties and certain religious and socio-economic factors; we can also relate the changes in these associations to the "surge" movements. Thus the analysis of aggregate voting data, like the turnover tables considered above, permits a distinction between the consistent and selective recruitment of the stable parties and the more diverse recruitment, in terms of social categories as well as political parties, of the "surge" movements.

Contrary to what might be expected from the later importance of the Algerian issue, there is no clear evidence of increasing tension or cleavage in the metropolitan electorate over this period. Although the Communist vote lay increasingly along the lines of cleavage indicated by these variables (R rose from .54 to .58), the other multiple correlations fell slightly from 1945 to 1956. That the degree of cleavage in the electorate was not increasing, but may have declined over this period, is also suggested by survey data.[59] The high degree of internal cleavage remaining after the Liberation seems to have subsided, and the tensions of the Algerian conflict do not appear to have affected the 1956 vote strongly.

Regression Analysis Within Individual *Départements*

Analysis based on *départements* as units reveals something of the broader cleavages among population groups, but cannot tell us about some of the differences between smaller areas. For example, the analysis we have just considered will tell about the significance of urbanization, but not of class cleavages within urban *départements;* by failing to subdivide cities we have been dealing with all urban strata together, in economic functional units. For this reason, study of smaller sub-areas within cities is necessary if we are to reveal the significance of urban class differences through analysis of voting statistics.

At the same time, it is equally desirable to repeat and check those results through the detailed analysis of votes within individual *départments* at the cantonal level. Fortunately, data which permit tests of this sort are available for several *départements*. The limiting variable for this purpose is religiosity; only those *départements* for which statistical measures of religiosity are available at the level of the canton (or *doyenné*) permit this detailed analysis.

The *départements* for which analyses of this sort will be undertaken include Côte-d'Or, Côtes-du-Nord, Gard (with control for Protestantism), Ille-et-Vilaine, Isère, Nièvre, and Orne. In most cases, the data derive from detailed local voting studies in the tradition begun by André Siegfried. As the available data represent various regions of the country, and as somewhat different measures of the variables are available for different *départements*, they provide an indication of some of the limits of generalization of our regression analysis.

The association of religiosity with rightist voting, as observed for France in the preceding analysis, also appears within each of these *départements*, as the negative coefficients in the first column of Table 8.9 show. The tendency toward conservative voting in wealthy areas, which we observed for France as a whole, also exists within *départements*, as the first three entries in the second column show. This is true for Côtes-du-Nord, Isère, and Orne, with control on the other variables indicated. Thus in both these respects our analysis within *départements* gives similar results to those for France as a whole.

The relation between ruralism and leftist voting, however, is no longer clearly positive when examined within *départements*. The coefficients for Isère and Orne in part A of Table 8.9 begin to call this finding in question; and the further data presented in part B of the table sustain this impression. Unlike the relationships for France as a whole, the relations within *départements* show no strong associations between ruralism and leftist voting. Only in Ille-et-Vilaine is there a positive association, as for France as a whole; elsewhere the countryside is more conservative. It may be, then, that the general relation between ruralism and leftist voting is a regional and historical one rather than a direct economic relation; the traditionally leftist areas in the south happen also to be rural and to have a large proportion of owner-proprietors on small farms.[60]

The aggregate statistics we have used so far are useful for the study of rural in contrast with urban politics; but they throw little light on the different political leanings of various *quartiers* within cities. The study of areas within cities, though less frequent in the Siegfried tradition, has been carried out increasingly in recent years, by both cartographic methods and statistical approaches.[61] From these studies it appears that the relationship between working-class population and the Communist vote is extremely close, in an aggregate sense, even though the categories are not identical.

The relationship between working-class population and the Communist vote, though quite uniform within cities, is not so uniform from one city to another. Figure 8.1 superposes two sets of published data (for Paris and Marseille) with two additional sets of points, for Bordeaux and Rennes.[62] The points for the latter two cities lie consistently below those for Paris and Marseille, reflecting a less strong tendency toward Communist voting in Bordeaux and Rennes in *quartiers* of a given class composition. Possibly this difference can be attributed to the size of the cities: Paris and Marseille are the largest of the four (2.7 million and 0.6 million respectively), while Bordeaux and Rennes are smaller (0.25 and 0.1 million). This difference may

Table 8.9 Multiple Regression Coefficients Within Départements: Prediction of "Anticlerical" Leftist Vote, Nov. 10, 1946*

Département	Religiosity and Wealth Standardized regression coefficient (b*) for			
	Religiosity	Wealth	Ruralism	R
Côtes-du-Nord	−.41	−.42		.57
Isère	−.65	−.14	−.32	.88
Orne	−.89	−.17	−.34	.89
	Rural-urban differences (wealth omitted)			
	Protestantism			
Côte-d'Or	−.09		−.56	.56
Gard	−.36	+.72	−.07	.68
Ille-et-Vilaine	−.82		+.16	.73
Isère	−.62		−.35	.87
Nièvre	−.30		−.17	.39
Orne	−.74		−.40	.82
FRANCE	−.73		+.31	.66

*The dependent variable is the sum of percentages of the votes for Communists (including PCI), Socialists, and Radicals in those *départements* where these lists were present. The A.U.R. list in Nièvre was not included in the "left." The measure of religiosity was the proportion of Easter attendance among the adult population, except for the Côte-d'Or where seminary students per capita was used. The measure of ruralism was either the proportion of the population living from agriculture or the proportion of the employed population in agriculture.

Source:
Côte-d'Or: Long, *Les Élections Législatives en Côte d'Or depuis 1870*, pp. 219, 281.
Côtes-du-Nord: *Voir-Agir* (St. Brieuc, Les Presses Bretonnes, 1955); wealth as vehicle ownership per capita from *Bulletin Régionale de Statistique* (Rennes), 1956, No. 3, 12, and 1954, No. 4, 11.
Gard: Schram, *Protestantism and Politics in France*, pp. 183–184; ruralism from 1954 Census, $\frac{1}{20}$ sample.
Ille-et-Vilaine: F. Boulard, "La Pratique religieuse dans la Diocèse de Rennes," *Economie et Humanisme* (October 1951), 116; 1943 Census.
Isère: C. Leleu, "La Géographie des partis dans l'Isère," in Duverger, *et al.*, eds., *Les Élections du 2 janvier 1956*, pp. 371, 373 (wealth as agricultural tax rebate per farm), 375.
Nièvre: J. Pataut, *Sociologie électorale de la Nièvre au XXᵉ Siècle* (Paris: Cujas, 1956), Tome II, p. 5.
Orne: *Pratique religieuse et orientations pastorales* (Alençon; Direction des Oeuvres, 1956), wealth as farm owners among males 20 and over, and ruralism as agricultural workers among males 20 and older.
France: the measure of ruralism used here (for comparability) is the proportion of employed males in all agricultural occupations, i.e., the sum of the last three predictors employed in the national analysis reported above.

in turn reflect a difference in the size of industrial plants in the cities, with relative ease of Communist organization in the larger plants.[63] In any case, the difference does not appear explicable as a regional one.

The same sort of data that have been used for the study of the Communist vote are equally applicable to the study of the vote for other parties, but they have been used statistically for this purpose less often. They tend to show that the conservative parties draw votes from the well-to-do *quartiers*

Figure 8.1 Working–Class Population and Communist Vote in Four Cities, 1956

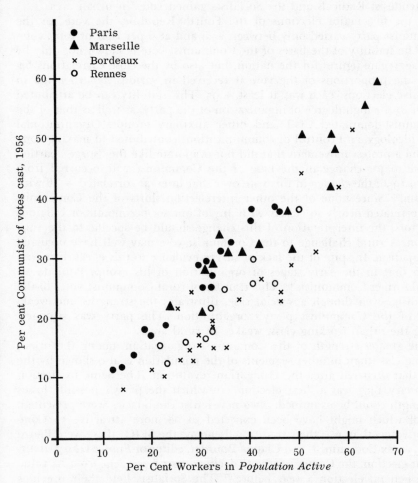

of cities, while the Socialists and Radicals have a less clear class base. Greater detail on particular occupational segments within a given class can best be obtained through local surveys.

The Geographical Strongholds of the Stable Parties

Each of the parties that attained a certain degree of stability in its vote depended on particular areas of France for its support, and most of them became more concentrated in those areas as the Fourth Republic continued. Thus the Communist party fell back somewhat from its rural areas of strength,[64] and held firmer in urban working-class *quartiers;* the Socialist and MRP vote, on the other hand, fell back on rural areas of long-standing political tradition. The Radicals came to depend on organizations led by local notables, and the Moderates combined rural strongholds with an appeal to the urban bourgeoisie. The major exception to this progressive stabilization seemed to be the Republican Front in the 1956 election; both the Mendesist Radicals and the Socialists gained votes in urban areas.

In the five major elections of the Fourth Republic, the vote for the Communist party varied only between 25.9 and 28.6 per cent of total votes cast. The stability of the bases of the Communist vote is shown not only by these aggregate figures for the nation, but also by the close correlations between the proportions of the vote it received in various *départements* in successive elections: each was at least +.95. This stability can be attributed in part to the high degree of organization of the party, as well as that of the Communist-dominated CGT and other auxiliary groups. Organizational work, ideology, and control of communications contributed to making communism a protest movement that did not evaporate like the "surge" parties.

The major change in the base of the Communist vote occurred from 1951 to 1956; the *change* in this vote over that interval correlated −.46 with ruralism.[65] Since none of the other interelection shifts of the Communist vote correlated nearly so closely with any of our socioeconomic or religious predictors, the interpretation of this change should be specific to the 1956 election. A rural challenge to the Communist vote may well have occurred in Poujadism. In spite of the lack of survey evidence to this effect, it is well known that in the early stages of organization of his group, Poujade attracted former Communists.[66] This transfer of rural Communist votes to the Poujadists, even though a special case, illustrates the strengths and weaknesses of the Communist party's organization. The party was strongest among the urban working class, weaker in rural areas.

The greater strength of the Communist organization among the urban working class than in other segments of the population is also shown by the shifts that occurred after the Hungarian revolution. The Seine by-election of January 1957 was a "test election" in which the party's possible losses of strength could be examined. Two new leftist candidacies were presented, each of which might have been expected to be more attractive to Communist voters than was their traditional enemy, the SFIO: these were Pierre Hervé, an ex-Communist, and Claude Bourdet, editor of *France-Observateur.* At that election, the Communist vote declined by 5.8 per cent from its value in the general election a year before.[67] The Socialists held their previous vote. What Communist vote was lost to the new candidacies seems to have gone over chiefly in the middle-class and intellectual *quartiers* rather than the working-class areas.

These directions of loss are consistent with the sources of stability of the PCF vote. The urban working class, with its low standard of living, concentrated in Communist neighborhoods and organized in the CGT, was most closely bound to the party. Rural Communism, a later source of support for the party, seems to have rested more on a traditional protest against government and the holders of power than specifically on Marxist notions of class conflict.

The perspective of the urban working-class Communist voter was highly organized around his own party and around attitudes toward other parties. This organized perspective rendered difficult any transfer of Communist votes to other "stable" parties, such as the Socialists or even the Mendesist Radicals. Rather, the few defections from the party went either to nonvoting or toward new parties or groupings that could present themselves as un-sullied by participation in the parliamentary "game." Moreover, these defections were least likely to occur among the urban working-class Communists.

The Socialist vote declined considerably from 1945 through 1951 before reaching a plateau of stability. Its greatest declines occurred from June to November 1946 and from 1946 to 1951. In the first of these periods, its losses were most closely related to demographic variables; both the Socialist vote, and the sum of Socialist and Communist votes, showed disproportionate losses in areas that were urban, anticlerical, and poor agriculturally.[68] But from 1946 to 1951, the Socialist vote appeared to withdraw to lines that were more related to historical traditions.

In each of these intervals, the Socialists lost some votes to the Communists.[69] Because of this competition on their left, the Socialists' competition with parties on their right can be isolated more clearly by adding the votes for the two leftist parties and examining the changes of this sum, which will then reflect the net loss of this segment to the other parties. In the transition from 1946 to 1951, which we shall consider, this net loss consisted largely of Socialist losses to parties farther to the right.

It was in areas that were traditionally leftist that the Socialists held their ground most successfully, from 1946 to 1951, relative to their competition on the right. A classification of the political traditions of French *départements*, summarizing elections from 1871 to 1946, has been made by Goguel.[70] This classification may be used to analyze the changes in the Communist and Socialist vote combined; from 1946 to 1951, they lost 5.7 per cent of the vote, divided roughly equally between the two parties.

The losses of the "left" (PCF plus SFIO) in this interval can be fruitfully examined by calculating them as a proportion of the November 1946 vote for both parties combined.[71] The proportional losses of the "left" may then be compared with the extent of traditional implantation of the "left" in various *départements*, as shown in Table 8.10. This table shows that the "left" lost the greatest proportion of its strength in *départements* that had been traditionally rightist, and lost the least, proportionally, in traditionally leftist areas. The fact that traditions dating back to 1871 make a difference here seems to imply that where the traditions are most pronounced, it has been possible for two or three generations to unite in maintaining a given political position in a community.[72]

The concentration of the MRP in regions such as Alsace and Brittany is well known. The geographical distribution of the Moderates' strength by 1956 somewhat resembled its distribution under the Third Republic, but also showed an unevenness related to particular candidacies. The Radicals and Socialists, as we have noted above, gained disproportionately in urban areas in 1956, rather than falling back to rural strongholds; these developments may have been associated with the "surges" of that year—the Re-

publican Front, of which they were members, and Poujadism, which may
have hurt them as well as the Communists in rural areas.[73]

Table 8.10 Historical Orientation of French Départements *and
Communist-Socialist Losses, 1946—1951*

Fractional loss of PCF plus SFIO:	To Left since:		To Right since:			
	1871–81	1902–46	1946	1919–36	1885–98	1871–81
less than .10	12*	5	1	2	1	1
.10 to .19	8	6	12	2	6	2
.20 to .29	–	2	7	5	3	1
.30 or more	–	–	–	1	2	2
Omitted (PCF or SFIO list missing)	1	2	1	2	1	2
Total	21	15	21	12	13	8

*Includes the *département* of Pyrénées-Orientales, where a dissident Socialist list is grouped with the SFIO, as done by Goguel in *Géographie des élections françaises*, p. 115.

Occupational Divisions and the Small-Town Vote

Our analysis of aggregate voting statistics has suggested that political and
social divisions extend more to the local level in France than in the United
States. Survey data may be used to confirm this hypothesis. In the United
States, survey studies have also shown a lesser association of education and
of nonfarm occupational status with the vote in rural than in urban areas.[74]
Yet it may be that the differences we have noted between the two countries
are due to the different variables that were used: occupational status for the
United States, religiosity the chief variable for France.[75] For this reason it
is well to examine occupational differences in France as they relate to the
vote, in urban and rural areas.

Survey data show a fairly clear-cut relation between occupations and the
vote under the Fourth Republic, as in Table 8.11. The working-class vote
tended to be more to the left, the middle class more to the right, and the
civil servants in between. We shall concentrate on the Communist and Socialist vote for purposes of comparison. The farmers' vote, which was
heavily Radical in the survey shown, will not be considered because of the
difficulty of assigning occupational status clearly to farmers.

French survey data indicate that the small town is not nearly so homogeneous politically in France as in the United States. Cleavages between
nonfarm occupational groups continue to have strong associations with party
choice in France even in towns less than 2,000 in size, as Table 8.12 shows.

In 1947 the proportion of Communist votes among workers was 57 per cent in the largest cities, and still remained 44 per cent in the small towns; the

Table 8.11 *Occupation of Head of Family by Respondent's Vote, 1955*

Occupation of head of family	Party preference 1955			Total	N
	Communists	Socialists	MRP, Radicals, Moderates, or Gaullists		
Worker	31%	29%	40%	(100%)	384
Civil servant	16	34	50	(100%)	122
Middle class*	12	20	68	(100%)	512
Farmer	9	15	76	(100%)	244

*This category includes white-collar workers, merchants, artisans, businessmen, professionals, retired persons, and a few housewives.

Source: Based on an IFOP survey conducted in January-February 1955.

corresponding proportions of the middle-class vote for the parties of the right and center were 68 per cent and 64 per cent. Thus the difference between working class and middle class remained substantial even in the small towns. In 1955 a higher proportion of the working-class vote was reported for the right and center parties, but this occurred in cities and towns of all sizes, and the degree of occupational division between Communists and the right-center parties remained nearly as high in the small towns as in the cities.

A quantitative comparison between these effects in France and the United States is possible, if we use the index employed by Ennis.[76] A measure of class voting is the difference between the proportions of Democrats in blue collar and white collar groups. For the three states on which he reports, this index is 40 to 43 per cent in metropolitan areas and only 1 to 16 per cent in rural areas. For the French data, let us substitute "Communist plus Socialist" for "Democratic," "worker" for "blue collar," and "middle class" for "white collar," in the data of Table 8.12. The corresponding indices in the four sizes of towns, from largest to smallest, in 1947 are 45, 29, 27, and 36 per cent respectively; and for 1955, 32, 24, 31, and 23. The decline in France is uniformly less; and class cleavage persists in the small towns even in 1955, a year of apparently lower status polarization.[77]

These data suggest that the structure of the small town as a political and decision-making unit was different in France from what it was in the United States. In one-party areas or towns in the United States, there is a tendency for a relatively homogeneous local elite to co-opt new members into a single dominant party affiliation. In France, on the other hand, the verticality of organizational structure corresponds to a relative lack of consensus at the local level, and to a vote which is expressive rather than instrumental in

Table 8.12 Occupational Cleavage by Size of City or Town, 1947 and 1955

| Size Place Occup.* | | Per Cent of Respondents in Each Occupational Group Who Preferred the Party Indicated, in | | | | | | |
| | | October 1947 | | | | January 1955 | | |
	PCF	SFIO	MRP, RGR, PRL, RPF	(N)	PCF	SFIO	MRP, RGR, Mod., URAS	(N)
Over 100,000:								
worker	57	20	23	(101)	38	25	37	(79)
civil servant	25	36	39	(28)	20	25	55	(20)
middle class	16	16	68	(165)	11	20	69	(145)
farmer	–	(100)	–	(1)	(25)	–	(75)	(4)
housewife	12	24	64	(102)				
20,000 to 100,000:								
worker	39	23	38	(66)	31	24	45	(80)
civil servant	19	37	44	(27)	14	29	57	(44)
middle class	13	20	67	(93)	15	16	68	(123)
farmer	11	–	89	(9)	–	–	(100)	(1)
housewife	13	29	58	(90)				
2,000 to 20,000:								
worker	44	17	39	(109)	32	34	34	(120)
civil servant	30	27	43	(33)	9	49	42	(33)
middle class	14	20	66	(103)	12	23	65	(151)
farmer	2	21	77	(58)	16	22	62	(37)
housewife	21	12	67	(96)				
Under 2,000:								
worker	44	28	28	(82)	25	28	47	(105)
civil servant	9	73	18	(22)	28	28	44	(25)
middle class	6	30	64	(95)	10	20	70	(93)
farmer	5	17	78	(169)	7	14	79	(202)
housewife	7	24	69	(81)				

*Occupations for the 1947 survey are the respondents'; for the 1955 survey, of the head of the respondent's family. "Worker" includes industrial and agricultural workers; "middle class" includes white-collar employees, merchants, artisans, owners and managers of industry, professionals, retired persons, those living on income, and (for 1955) a few housewives; "farmer" includes farm proprietors. The above tabulations are based on secondary analysis of data kindly furnished by the Institut Français d'Opinion Publique.

nature.[78] Lack of consensual processes in community or district permits a relation of "traditional enmity" between adjacent political parties, so that the transfer of votes even between adjacent parties is infrequent except when new "surge" movements arise. In this situation, one would expect to find multiple local elites, each perpetuating itself, rather than a single local elite.[79]

The relatively fewer functions of local government in France are consistent with a fragmentation of local elites. Local government in France is referred to as local "administration," and is under close control by the Ministry of the Interior. Because it has fewer functions, French local government produces local consensus on national issues far less than does American local government.[80] Politically important ties are more likely to go beyond the town in France rather than to unite it.

The intimate relation between local government and political cleavage is undoubtedly a reciprocal rather than a unilateral one. One cannot simply suggest a decentralized or federal government for France, with increased functions for municipal and *départemental* councils, without examining the real possibilities for consensus at the local level. The "trusteeship" in which the prefects hold these organs of government does occasionally have to be exercised when they fail to overcome their internal divisions.

This reciprocal relationship also involves the electoral system. Possibly proportional representation has contributed to political divisions in the small towns; even the two-ballot *scrutin d'arrondissement,* revived under the Fifth Republic, permits a certain degree of political fragmentation compared to the Anglo-American single-member, single-ballot system. But the very fact that France has scarcely ever tried the latter system may reflect the same local political division as does her administrative centralization.[81]

Stable Voting and Unstable Government

We have suggested that voting under the Fourth Republic, as far as it involved the parties persisting from 1945 to 1956, was remarkably stable in contrast with the United States. Underlying this stability are the meaning of the vote to the citizen (expressive rather than instrumental), the concentration of personal political contact within homogeneous circles, and the isolation of these circles from one another at the "grass roots." Both religious and class differences seemed to penetrate to the smallest communities and to serve as persistent bases of political division. The changes that occurred during the Fourth Republic in the bases of support for the "established" parties seemed to involve a settling down to a closer association between a party's strength and a characteristic base of support.

These characteristics of the vote combine to explain why it was so difficult for any of the established parties—or even any coalition—to win enough new votes at an election to dominate the Assembly and impose a policy. Campaigning, to fit into the pattern of voting, had to be directed toward the intraparty activities of mobilizing those who already favored one's party rather than toward convincing new voters to support the party. Appeals by the established parties to new types of voters from other parties and other social groups, such as bring victory to a winning party in the United States, would have met with resistance not only from those appealed to, but also from the militants of the party making the appeal.[82] The best example of these difficulties was the Radical party's resistance to Mendès-France's effort to enlarge and renovate its clientele.

A gain by an established party would have had particular advantages for putting a program into effect. First, the established party had a nucleus of experienced political leaders in the Assembly. Second, the new movements, even when they captured a significant share of the vote, were handicapped by unusually intense conflicts with the old parties, as well as by problems of their own internal organization. Although there were major transfers of the vote to new movements during the Fourth Republic, the new members who entered the Assembly as a result neither succeeded in enacting their programs nor ameliorated the conflicts of the "system."[83] Not until the Fifth Republic and the renewal of Gaullism was there before the voters a major party which realistically aimed at extensive conversion of voters from other parties, and at the same time had a substantial group of experienced political leaders; and even those leaders were dominated by de Gaulle.

This stability of voting, which limited the capacity of the system to absorb protest, has been traced back to the constituencies. The voters' preferences for the stable parties were more constant than in the United States. But at the same time, as Converse and Dupeux have shown, the electorate was *less* politicized in France than in the United States. Social divisions existed and were superimposed on one another; but they were not accompanied by the general intensity of ideological conviction that has sometimes been attributed to France. Both the extent of political participation by the general public, and the level of certain types of information, were lower there than in the United States. Moreover, the comparability of French and American data on these points is so close, within similar population groups, that the results seem not to be simply temporary effects of *dépolitisation* but expressions of general and persistent relationships common to both countries.

For this reason, we contend that France's social divisions were only *permissive* conditions for political division. They provided distinct channels through which divisive political communications could be sent; but the conditions under which these messages actually were sent must be sought elsewhere. Chief among them was the existence of a small, highly politicized group of political activists, more conscious of issues than its American counterpart. This group included some 5 per cent of the electorate. It can be identified approximately with the 5 per cent who claimed party membership.[84] Within this minority, a still smaller group could be considered "militants." It is to this group, in the deputies' districts, that we attribute the divisiveness and ideological character of French politics. The leading deputies, in contrast, had a consensus of their own, and the average French voter was no more involved politically than his American counterpart.

NOTES

1. These movements have been referred to by Converse and Dupeux as "flash" parties: "Politicization of the Electorate in France and the United States," 1. See also Aron, "France: Stability and Instability," 20. The creation of a new party configuration after the Liberation was also a marked change, but a more lasting one. The Socialists and MRP attained

their greatest strength in the early postwar elections, but fell from that strength to a stable lower percentage of the vote.

2. In presidential elections in the United States, 1948–1964, turnout in the non-Southern states ranged from 62 to 72 per cent of the eligible electorate; see Burnham, "The Changing Shape of the American Political Universe," 11. Under the Fourth Republic it ranged from 77 to 81 per cent of the electorate in the five general elections between 1945 and 1956 (see Table 8.1 below). Even allowing for difficulty of registration in the United States, the difference appears substantial.

3. In a comparison of seven nations on the question, "Do you think it will make a great difference whether one party or another is in power?", the lowest three were the United States (40 per cent "yes"), Canada (47 per cent), and France (49 per cent). The other nations compared were Great Britain, Norway, Sweden, and Denmark (70, 69, 61, 52 per cent respectively). See Sondages, January 1949, No. 16, 20.

4. See Williams, Crisis, pp. 313–314. The effects of cabinet unpredictability are also considered important by Grosser in "The Evolution of European Parliaments," Daedalus, 170. And La Palombara has suggested that "the deputy (and, perhaps, the average Frenchman) does not look to the legislature as an arena in which basic issues are to be confronted and resolved; he may judge that such resolution of conflict normally occurs, to take another example, in the administrative branch of government." "Political Party Systems and Crisis Government: French and Italian Contrasts," 138.

5. This distinction has been made in general by Talcott Parsons; see The Social System, pp. 385–386. Another alternative to instrumental voting in this sense is suggested by the concept "sense of citizen duty" which is distinguished from "sense of efficacy" in Angus Campbell, Gurin, and Miller, The Voter Decides, pp. 187–199; but this latter distinction does not seem so relevant to French voting. A related question concerning high turnout and low competition in municipal elections is raised in Kesselman, "French Local Politics."

6. Wylie, Village in the Vaucluse, pp. 330–331.

7. Chapsal, La Vie politique, p. 429.

8. See Élections et référendums des 13 oct., 10 et 24 nov., et 8 dec. 1946, pp. 262–265. French political scientists, in their analyses of representation, also often assume that a legislature accurately reflecting all types of opinion, or all parties, should be taken as a standard of comparison. See Duverger, Political Parties, pp. 372ff., and Cotteret, Emeri, and Lalumière, Lois électorales et inégalités de représentation en France 1936–1960. Related notions have received attention in the United States in controversies about redistricting, but they do not seem as deeply rooted as in France.

9. Analogous phenomena exist in the United States, and deserve more detailed study. In a closely contested congressional district, certain groups may have a more effective channel to Washington when a representative of a sympathetic party occupies the seat in question.

10. A somewhat comparable study, using aggregate statistics for the United States, is MacRae, "Occupations and the Congressional Vote, 1940–1950." It showed that national regression studies were relatively useless except in urban areas. This difference will also be illustrated below with survey data.

11. The contrast between stability and "surges" in France set her electoral behavior apart from that of the United States as well as that of other multi-party democracies. There are "surges" in the United States, but they normally favor the major parties rather than new parties; see Angus Campbell, "Surge and Decline: A Study of Electoral Change," showing that stable and surging electorate are distinguishable groups, but not on a basis of party preference. In Scandinavia, on the other hand, the "surging" component is less prominent; see Angus Campbell and Henry Valen, "Party Identification in Norway and the United States," 521–523.

12. Most of the data cited here are from *Sondages,* but some are based on secondary analysis of selected surveys, through the courtesy of the Institut Français d'Opinion Publique and the Roper Public Opinion Research Center.

13. Considerable work has been done on such tables in connection with panel studies of voting. See McPhee and Glaser, eds., *Public Opinion in Congressional Elections,* Chap. 4, and the references cited there. Data for six such tables, from 1946 to 1955, are given in Stoetzel, "Voting Behaviour in France," 112–114.

14. The two elections to the Constituent Assemblies are included here because they are relevant to the stability of the vote. The Constituent Assemblies were not analyzed in the preceding chapters, however, because they did not involve cabinet instability.

15. These parties and their leadership are discussed in Taylor, *The Fourth Republic of France,* pp. 87–89.

16. The same classification was made by the respondents in a 1955 survey, though this may have been due in part to the Mendesist image. See Institut Français d'Opinion Publique (IFOP), "À la Recherche de la 'gauche'", 1617. After the First Legislature, the Radicals exchanged votes with both Socialists and Moderates, but less with the MRP; thus Radicals and MRP did not completely resemble neighbors on a continuum. A more elaborate analysis of this problem is made in Philip E. Converse, "The Problem of Party Distances in Models of Voting Change," in M. Kent Jennings and L. Harmon Zeigler, eds., *Electoral Behavior.*

17. At this time the RPF received 31 per cent of all current party choices; but if we set aside the 60 per cent of the former non-voters who made no party choice in Table 8.4B, the Gaullist proportion is high among the remainder.

18. A turnover table for September 1948 shows the RPF winning nearly as many preferences as in 1947, and the Communists at the same time holding 95 per cent of their former vote.

19. The turnover table for August 1953 is given in *Sondages,* 1954, No. 1, 42; another for August–September 1954 was derived from secondary analysis of data supplied by IFOP.

20. The code category was "Paysans, Indépendants, Modérés."

21. Through November and December 1955 Mendès-France was by far the most popular choice for premier; 27 per cent of IFOP's sample named him, in contrast to only 2 per cent for Guy Mollet, who actually became premier after the election. *Sondages,* 1955, No. 4, 19.

22. The series of by-elections in early 1957 showed the same Communist recovery. While the Communist vote receded from its 1957 proportion in the Seine by-election of January 1957, by the summer it was attaining its previous local values in various parts of the country.

23. *Sondages,* 1960, No. 4, 21.

24. Twenty-two per cent, a higher proportion than for any other party. *Sondages,* 1954, No. 1, 42; this survey was conducted in August, 1953.

25. See Key, *The Responsible Electorate,* pp. 19, 24–25. For comparability with the French data, percentages are based on pre-election surveys. Figures for a two-year transition are given in McPhee and Glaser, *Public Opinion in Congressional Elections,* p. 67: "20 to 25 per cent . . . chose different parties for national office in 1948 and 1950." From 1958 to 1960, 23 per cent of those voting both times changed party; see Angus Campbell, "Surge and Decline," p. 411.

26. The "stable" parties are the Communists, Socialists, Radicals, MRP, and Moderates (including PRL). An example of this calculation may be given for the MRP's losses between November 1946 and April 1951 (Table 8.4C above). Of those reporting having voted for the MRP, only 52 per cent now indicated preference for a "stable" party. Of

these, 11 per cent shifted; on a base of 52 per cent, this gives 21 per cent of the stable-party voters who were shifters.

27. In another sense it may be overstated: omission of the large numbers of respondents who did not give definite party preferences removes persons of a type who are likely to shift, and the proportion of this type is greater in the French data than in the American surveys.

28. The notion of counter-identification is relevant to American voting as well. It is suggested as an explanation of third-party movements in rural areas in MacRae, "Occupations and the Congressional Vote, 1940–1950," 339. New parties may circumvent these counter-identifications; the RPF may have done this to the MRP, and third parties have done so in the United States as well, as suggested in MacRae and Meldrum, "Critical Elections in Illinois: 1888–1958," 675–677. See also Sellers, "The Equilibrium Cycle in Two-Party Politics," 27.

29. Duverger, *Political Parties*, pp. 314, 389.

30. See Maurice Duverger, "Paradoxes d'une réforme électorale," in Association Française de Science Politique, *L'Établissement de la Cinquième République*, pp. 221–240.

31. A related point was made by Macridis in "Cabinet Instability in the Fourth Republic (1946–1951)."

32. See *Sondages*, 1952, No. 4, and regression analyses below in this chapter.

33. *Sondages*, June 1, 1946, No. 11, 133.

34. These referenda are discussed in Williams, *Crisis*, pp. 20, 23.

35. For Paris the correlation was .99; see Desabie, "Le Référendum—Essai d'étude statistique," 168.

36. See Vangrevelinghe, "Étude statistique comparée des résultats des référendums de 1958 et 1961;" also Goguel, ed., *Le Référendum du 8 janvier 1961*, pp. 188–189.

37. See Olivesi and Roncayolo, *Géographie électorale des Bouches-du-Rhône sous la IVᵉ République*, p. 222.

38. The treatment that follows is adapted from MacRae, "Religious and Socioeconomic Factors in the French Vote, 1946–1956." A related analysis using improved data for rural *cantons* is given in Mattei Dogan, "Les Contextes politiques en France."

39. Characteristic political temperaments are associated with North and South, with Brittany, the Massif Central, and Alsace, for example. See Goguel, *Géographie des élections françaises de 1870 à 1951*.

40. The leader in this research has been Gabriel Le Bras; his two-volume *Études de sociologie religieuse* collects his writings over a long period.

41. Boulard, *Essor ou declin du clergé français*, opp. p. 30. The statistics used are based on the period 1940–1947, adjusted to an equivalent five-year period. They correlate closely with the number of priests per capita (pp. 467–469) and their geographical distribution closely resembles that of church attendance, but they agree less closely with statistics on the proportion of children enrolled in private schools.

42. Per cent of the population engaged in, or living from, agriculture; per cent in industry and transportation; proportion in various urban occupations, such as *ouvriers d'industrie;* per capita industrial production; etc. For sources of such data, see *L'Espace économique français*, prepared by the Institut National de la Statistique et des Études Économiques (INSEE); also *Recensement général de la population de mai 1954* (INSEE). The source actually used was the 1946 agricultural census, which provides unusually detailed data on numbers of hired workers per farm.

43. See Wylie, *Village in the Vaucluse*.

44. These figures were calculated from the *Recensement général de la population* (effectuée 10 mars 1946), pp. XLIX ff. Proprietors and family workers were combined because an introductory note to the volume implies that the two categories could not always be distinguished accurately. Only employed males were considered, because their occupational distribution was expected to be more closely related to the vote than that of females.

45. For example, the total proportion of hired farm workers among employed males (which would not permit construction of a separate index of "agricultural proletarization"); or the amount of fertilizer applied per hectare. I am indebted to M. Malassis of the École Nationale d'Agriculture at Rennes for pointing out the relation between the salaried labor force and other indicators of agricultural wealth; see Malassis, *Économie des exploitations agricoles,* pp. 62–69.

46. Husson, *Élections et référendums des 21 octobre 1945, 5 mai et 2 juin 1946; Élections et référendums des 13 oct., 10 et 24 nov. et 8 dec. 1946; Les Élections législatives du 17 juin 1951; Les Élections législatives du 2 janvier 1956.*

47. No adjustments for "pro-clerical" roll-call votes were made in the 1945 Radical classifications, but six Radical lists were classified as "right" in the June 1946 election, in terms of candidates' votes on March 15, 1946, on the school question. In the November 1946 election, those who had voted on the "clerical" side on May 14, 1946 (on *liberté d'enseignement* and the Rights of Man in the proposed constitution) were considered to be on the "right"; see *Journal Officiel, Debats de l'Assemblée Nationale Constituante,* (Vol. 1) 1946, 841–842. In 1951 those Radicals (and related groups) who formed joint lists with previously existing conservative groupings (*Indepéndants* but not *Contribuables*) were classed as "right."

48. A classification of Goguel's was used here; see Duverger, Goguel, and Touchard, eds., *Les Élections du 2 janvier 1956,* pp. 468–469. I am also indebted to M. Goguel for a private communication of his classification of these lists. A treatment of the Republican Front also appears in Schlesinger, "The French Radical Socialist Party and the Republican Front of 1956."

49. The Gaullist gain represents that part of the vote for RPF candidates in 1951 which exceeded the vote for the same candidates if they ran on non-Gaullist lists in the same districts in 1946. The Poujadist vote combines the votes for the one or more Poujadist lists in the ninety-five districts where such lists were presented.

50. The b*'s are regression coefficients obtained when all variables are converted to standard scores (sometimes designated as β's); see Walker and Lev, *Statistical Inference,* pp. 331–336.

51. Suggestive data for the United States, comparing correlations in rural and urban areas at the national level, are given in MacRae, "Occupations and the Congressional Vote," p. 333.

52. See Klatzmann, "Comment votent les paysans français," 22.

53. The corresponding coefficient for the Radical vote *alone* rose from + .40 to + .57. No corresponding change took place for the Communist and Socialist total. This suggests that while the RPF drew votes differentially from the Radicals in urban areas, it did not do so from the Socialists. Table 8.4C supports this inference. I am indebted to Arthur L. Stinchcombe for this analysis of the Radical vote.

54. An Institut National d'Opinion Publique (IFOP) survey shortly before the 1951 election indicated that 8 per cent of the former RGR (Radical) voters intended to switch to the RPF. See Table 8.4C.

55. A detailed geographical analysis of this change is given by Goguel in "Géographie des elections du 17 juin 1951," 350–351.

56. On Poujade's neutral position on the religious issue see Hoffmann, *Le Mouvement Poujade.* The Mendesist deputies, though numerically a small minority, were somewhat

more "proclerical" than the traditional Radicals; this reversal of scale polarity was discussed in Chapters 6 and 7.

57. This is owed in part to classification of several anti-Mendesist Radical lists as "rightist."

58. This possibility has been alluded to by Goguel in Duverger, Goguel, and Touchard, eds., *Les Élections du 2 janvier 1956*, p. 478. Rural but poor *départements* such as Ariège and the Landes gave low votes to Poujadist lists, while richer ones as Vienne and Mayenne gave considerably more.

59. Factor analysis of similar questions appearing in successive IFOP surveys suggests that the communalities were highest in 1947 and lower in 1954, rising again slightly in 1955. This conclusion is based on results presented in MacRae, "Une Analyse factorielle des préférences politiques," together with further unpublished research.

60. The six *départements* for which this analysis has been carried out do not contain any clear-cut examples of the leftism of southern France; only Gard might fall in this category, and the effect of ruralism there is obscured by Protestantism and by a relatively crude measure of religiosity among Catholics. Ehrmann has also pointed out that "prosperous and marginal systems of farming are concentrated in different areas," in "The French Peasant and Communism," 24. The map in Figure 9.2 shows the location of the *départements* in question.

61. One of the first statistical studies was Joseph Klatzmann, "Comportement électoral et classe sociale," in Duverger, Goguel, and Touchard, eds., *Les Élections du 2 janvier 1956*, pp. 254–285; his approach was followed in Olivesi and Roncayolo, *Géographie électoral des Bouches-du-Rhône*, pp. 243–264. Other studies of urban politics have also appeared in Cahiers Nos. 82 and 119 of the Fondation Nationale des Sciences Politiques.

62. For these data I am indebted to Professor Henri Krier of the University of Rennes, and to officials of the Hôtel de Ville and the Regional Statistical Office of Bordeaux.

63. I am indebted to Georges Dupeux for this hypothesis.

64. Much of this support had been gained in the Resistance and the immediate postwar period. For figures on the relative gains of party membership in industrial and agricultural areas, 1937–45, see Duverger, *Political Parties*, p. 34.

65. This confirms the interpretation of Table 8.8; but the effect is more pronounced when changes in the vote are examined. See MacRae and Meldrum, "Critical Elections in Illinois," 671–672.

66. See Hoffmann, *Le Mouvement Poujade*. One reason for the inadequacy of the surveys on this point is that no clear questions on intended vote are reported by IFOP in their analyses of late 1955 surveys. Another is the great underestimation of the retrospective Poujade vote in surveys of 1956 and later; former Communist voters may have been among those failing to answer. More detailed studies of local election statistics might also help. Goguel's analysis of the 1956 election also concludes that some Communist votes went to Poujade; see Duverger, Goguel, and Touchard, eds., *Les Élections du 2 janvier 1956*, p. 496.

67. We allow for reduced turnout by using percentages of votes cast. See Bodin and Touchard, "L'Élection partielle de la première circonscription de la Seine." These authors interpret the vote for Hervé as coming from ex-Communists because it was distributed spatially like the Communist vote.

68. A relative decline in their working-class support is also reported on the basis of IFOP data in Russell E. Planck, "Public Opinion in France After the Liberation, 1944–1949," in Komarovsky, ed., *Common Frontiers of the Social Sciences*, p. 196.

69. This transfer was shown in Tables 8.3 and 8.4C above. It is also indicated by the negative correlations between changes in Socialist and Communist percentages for these intervals, − .18 in both cases.

266 *Parliament, Parties, and Society in France 1946–1958*

70. Goguel, *Géographie des élections françaises de 1870 à 1951*, pp. 102–105.

71. When an organized party holds only a small fraction of the electorate and loses votes over a given interval, its losses in particular areas are often proportional to its previous strength there. Thus the ratio we use would show an approximately equal proportional loss in all areas were it not for differential effects related to the parties' implantation.

72. This and other indications of local political continuity in France require explanation in terms of social mechanisms of transmission. Converse and Dupeux present data suggesting that transmission of party orientations within the family is weak; see their "Politicization of the Electorate in France and the United States," pp. 11–14. Possibly channels of communication outside the family are important, or the transmission of non-political attitudes, e.g., toward the church, may play a part.

73. A detailed interpretation of the 1956 results is given by Goguel in Duverger, Goguel, and Touchard, eds., *Les Élections du 2 janvier 1956*, pp. 477–502. The non-statistical part of the present interpretation relies heavily on his judgments.

74. See Angus Campbell and Homer C. Cooper, *Group Differences in Attitudes and Votes*, pp. 27, 115–116; Philip Ennis, "The Contextual Dimension in Voting," in McPhee and Glaser, eds., *Public Opinion in Congressional Elections*, pp. 185–187; Angus Campbell, *et. al.*, *The American Voter*, pp. 356, 359.

75. Ennis ("The Contextual Dimension in Voting," p. 188) shows Protestant-Catholic differences in party choice in the United States that are greater in rural areas than urban. But these differences in religion may be between one town and another, while the occupational differences we shall discuss below are less likely to be so.

76. Ennis, *ibid.*, p. 187. This index is also used in Alford, *Party and Society*, defined at pp. 79ff. A relation between the extent of "class voting" and the urbanization of an entire nation is suggested there.

77. For the variation in status polarization from one election to another in the United States, see Campbell *et al.*, *The American Voter*, Chap. 13.

78. It should be emphasized that we have no direct data on the political homogeneity or decision processes of particular French towns; data of this kind are desirable in order to test our hypotheses more rigorously. Data for the United States, indicating one useful line of investigation, are given in Robert D. Putnam, "Political Attitudes and the Local Community."

79. These hypotheses refer especially to small-town dwellers rather than to farmers as such. Farmers' votes in the United States, at least in recent presidential elections, have shown neither the homogeneity nor the stability that a model of stable community elites would entail; see Campbell *et al.*, *The American Voter*, Chap. 15.

80. The legal status of local government is discussed in Chapman, *Introduction to French Local Government*, Chap. IV, and in Maspétiol and Laroque, *La Tutelle administrative*. The argument relating weak local government to dissensus goes back to Tocqueville; see *The Old Regime and the French Revolution*, Part II. But we refer here to national issues only, for on the issues that remained to the local community some consensus was attained; see Kesselman, *French Local Government*.

81. Though the fragmenting effect of proportional representation has often been discussed, it has rarely been measured by statistical comparison of individual districts in a country before and after a change of electoral system.

82. This consequence of proportional representation has been pointed out by Hogan in *Election and Representation*, pp. 63–65, and in the work of Ferdinand A. Hermens, whose diagnosis of the Fourth Republic appears in *The Representative Republic*, Ch. XIV. The absence of cross-party recruitment was part of Hoffmann's critique of French politics in "Politique d'abord!", 817.

83. Stanley Hoffmann has suggested that "the size and persistence of a floating mass of voters who shift their allegiances all over the political chessboard from election to election symbolizes [a] serious weakness of French democracy," in "The French Constitution of 1958," 350. But we contend it is not floating voters as such or their fickleness that caused difficulties, so much as the inconsistency of vote transfers with the strengthening of political parties that already possessed experienced leadership cadres.

It should be noted that local one-partyism in the United States, though it reflects tendencies toward consensus, has some of the same disadvantages as we have suggested for the French "surges": atrophy of local minority organizations deprives them of the leadership they may need when their party wins, as Key pointed out in *American State Politics*, Ch. 6.

84. The lower politicization of the French electorate and the characteristics of French political activists are shown in Converse and Dupeux, "Politicization of the Electorate in France and the United States." The corresponding figure on party membership was given in Table 2.1 above.

»9«

The Electorate: Variation in the Vote

W E HAVE SEEN THAT THE vote for the stable parties under the Fourth
Republic showed a greater constancy of division than in the United
States, consistent with a centralized and vertically organized society. France
shared this constancy with other multiparty systems; but side by side with it
were a series of political movements that brought about marked shifts in
the party vote. All these movements represented reactions to the immobility
of the system: Gaullism, Poujadism, and Mendesism, though in many ways
very different from one another, all embodied sharp criticism of the typical
cabinets of the Fourth Republic and proposed either a new style of government or fundamental change. The very novelty of these movements, and
their attacks on the system, in turn attracted the hostility of most of the men
and parties who had composed the major governing coalitions.

These changes in the vote must be examined and contrasted with those
of the "independent" vote in a two-party system. We shall see that although
the "surge" votes had some similarities to large-scale transfers of votes from
one American party to the other, they seemed more specific in their geographical or social bases and less concentrated among younger voters.[1] Thus
even these transfers, which did not easily conduce to the formation of new
governing majorities, had elements of specificity in their social bases that
distinguished them from the nationwide surges of support that often occur
in American presidential elections.

Gaullism and Poujadism

We have seen in the turnover tables for 1947–57 that both the Gaullist
RPF and the Poujadist UFF drew support from a wide variety of "traditional" parties. Yet these two movements had entirely different styles and
represented very different bases of support.

The Gaullist movement gained largely at the expense of the MRP and
the Moderates between 1946 and 1951 (Table 8.4). In 1945 and 1946 the
MRP still had the support of many conservative voters, who left it later for
Gaullism and subsequently for parties of the Right. And as we have seen by
tracing the voting records of a group of conservative deputies from PRL to
RPF to ARS, a segment of the conservative electorate were drawn into support of Gaullism as their deputies became temporary Gaullists. The Radicals
and Socialists also sustained initial losses to Gaullism, but by the 1951

elections they had regrouped their forces and their losses were small. And since General de Gaulle had taken a strongly anti-Communist stand, there were probably few Communist defections to the RPF.

In its social base, General de Gaulle's appeal in 1947–51 seems to have resembled Eisenhower's in the United States, and to have drawn an "independent vote" more like that of the United States than the votes that shifted to the Poujadists or between the stable parties. A survey study has shown the parallels between Eisenhower's appeal and de Gaulle's in 1958, and we may presume that in its breadth of recruitment among social groups, de Gaulle's in 1951 was not greatly different.[2] We have seen that the style of campaign activity by RPF voters—interpersonal persuasion of people who had voted for other parties—was most like American election activity (Table 3.3). And de Gaulle's appeal to a broad spectrum of urban middle-class voters was not unlike the characteristic appeal to "independent" voters in a two-party system with class-based parties.

The Poujadist movement, which at first glance might seem simply to have taken the place of Gaullism in 1956, was actually of a very different character. It appealed to an essentially negative attitude toward government. De Gaulle had appealed to the grandeur of France and asked for personal leadership; but Poujade based his campaign largely on attacks against the corrupt parliamentary system, and prided himself on being a small merchant and an ordinary Frenchman rather than a potential leader of the nation. A flavor of antisemitism and of vulgarity also distinguished Poujade's campaign from de Gaulle's.[3]

Moreover, the nucleus of the Poujadist movement—and its initial representation in the National Assembly—consisted largely of small merchants. Starting as a pressure group and metamorphosing into a political party, in the 1956 vote it was strong in *quartiers,* towns, and villages where small retail shops had been threatened with loss of business.[4] In its appeal to these merchants, as well as to winegrowers and others hit by economic hardships, Poujadism tended to reflect more the specific economic grievances of particular groups than the mobilization of a socially homogeneous "mass." The distribution of the Poujadist vote in urban areas resembled that of the RPF, since both appealed to segments of the middle class; but in the cities, Poujadism was more specifically a movement of small merchants, and it actually obtained its highest percentages of the vote in more rural areas.[5]

Regionally, Poujadism was also distinct from Gaullism. It appealed to the peasants of the South,[6] while the RPF had appealed more in the industrialized areas of the North. These differences may be seen most clearly by comparing the RPF losses (1951–56) with the Poujadist gains in the various districts.[7] Figure 9.1 shows the relation between these two changes in the form of a scatter diagram. The association between the two types of change is clearly *negative,* reflecting the completely different appeals of de Gaulle and Poujade. It is also possible to identify from this diagram those districts where the Gaullist loss exceeded the Poujadist vote by a given margin, and vice versa. These districts of relatively preponderant Gaullist or Poujadist strength are shown in Figure 9.2. The two types of districts are found in largely distinct regions of the country.

Poujade's relative failure in the north may have resulted partly from his appeal to "static" France, his distrust of large organizations and cities.

Figure 9.1 Contrast Between Gaullist and Poujadist Vote, 1951-56

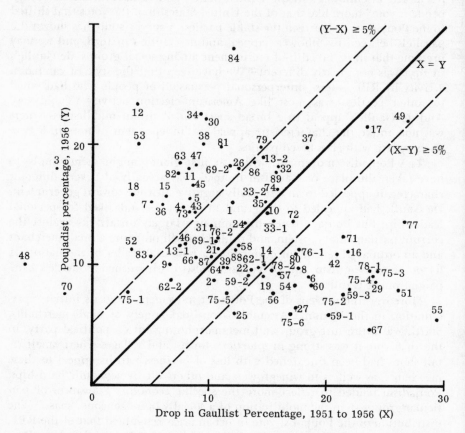

*The numbers identifying *départements* are in the conventional alphabetical order and are shown on the map in Fig. 9.2. Districts in divided *départements* are indicated by hyphenated numbers, e.g., 13-1 for the first district of Bouches-du-Rhône. *Départements* with no distinct RPF list in 1951, or Poujadist list in 1956, are omitted. Joint lists headed by ARS deputies in 1956 are considered "Gaullist."

But another source of the difference between the regional appeals of de Gaulle and Poujade may have been the persisting attitudes toward Vichy and the Resistance. Between 1940 and 1942, the Germans occupied the northern part of France but not the south. Figure 9.2 compares the relative attraction of the RPF and Poujadism with the division between the occupied and nonoccupied zones. All the districts with a Gaullist excess of 10 per cent or more lay all or partly in the occupied zone, while all but one with a similar Poujadist excess lay all or partly in the nonoccupied zone. It may be that the commitment to Vichy of many of the residents of the nonoccupied zone led to a lasting hostility to General de Gaulle, and perhaps to the Fourth Republic as well, which did not extend to Poujadism.[8]

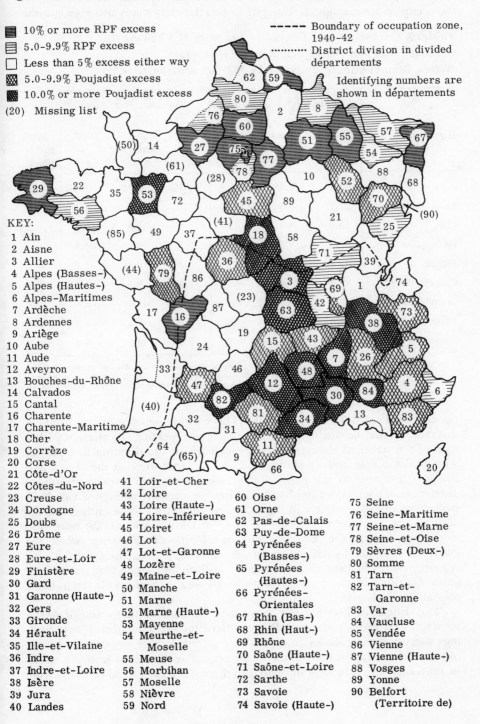

Figure 9.2 Districts of Relative Gaullist and Poujadist Strength, 1951–56

■ 10% or more RPF excess
▤ 5.0–9.9% RPF excess
☐ Less than 5% excess either way
▨ 5.0–9.9% Poujadist excess
■ 10.0% or more Poujadist excess
(20) Missing list

- - - - Boundary of occupation zone, 1940–42
·········· District division in divided départements

Identifying numbers are shown in départements

KEY:
1 Ain
2 Aisne
3 Allier
4 Alpes (Basses-)
5 Alpes (Hautes-)
6 Alpes-Maritimes
7 Ardèche
8 Ardennes
9 Ariège
10 Aube
11 Aude
12 Aveyron
13 Bouches-du-Rhône
14 Calvados
15 Cantal
16 Charente
17 Charente-Maritime
18 Cher
19 Corrèze
20 Corse
21 Côte-d'Or
22 Côtes-du-Nord
23 Creuse
24 Dordogne
25 Doubs
26 Drôme
27 Eure
28 Eure-et-Loir
29 Finistère
30 Gard
31 Garonne (Haute-)
32 Gers
33 Gironde
34 Hérault
35 Ille-et-Vilaine
36 Indre
37 Indre-et-Loire
38 Isère
39 Jura
40 Landes

41 Loir-et-Cher
42 Loire
43 Loire (Haute-)
44 Loire-Inférieure
45 Loiret
46 Lot
47 Lot-et-Garonne
48 Lozère
49 Maine-et-Loire
50 Manche
51 Marne
52 Marne (Haute-)
53 Mayenne
54 Meurthe-et-Moselle
55 Meuse
56 Morbihan
57 Moselle
58 Nièvre
59 Nord

60 Oise
61 Orne
62 Pas-de-Calais
63 Puy-de-Dome
64 Pyrénées (Basses-)
65 Pyrénées (Hautes-)
66 Pyrénées-Orientales
67 Rhin (Bas-)
68 Rhin (Haut-)
69 Rhône
70 Saône (Haute-)
71 Saône-et-Loire
72 Sarthe
73 Savoie
74 Savoie (Haute-)

75 Seine
76 Seine-Maritime
77 Seine-et-Marne
78 Seine-et-Oise
79 Sèvres (Deux-)
80 Somme
81 Tarn
82 Tarn-et-Garonne
83 Var
84 Vaucluse
85 Vendée
86 Vienne
87 Vienne (Haute-)
88 Vosges
89 Yonne
90 Belfort (Territoire de)

The division between a predominance of Gaullism in the north and of Poujadism in the south, although it coincides closely with the boundary of the occupied zone, might be thought to be related to many other geographi-

Table 9.1　Gaullist and Poujadist Votes in the Formerly Occupied and Non-Occupied Zones (1940–42) Within Départements *Crossed by the Occupation Line**

Département	Gaullist Loss, 1951–56			Poujadist Vote, 1956			
	Occu-pied Cantons	Non-Occupied Cantons	Diff.	Occu-pied Cantons	Non-Occupied Cantons	Diff.	Net Differ-ence
Jura	14.2%	6.1%	+8.1%	6.7%	9.0%	−2.3%	+10.4%
Saône-et-Loire	21.7	9.5	+12.2	11.8	12.8	−1.0	+13.2
Cher	20.0	9.4	+10.6	15.1	14.8	+ 0.3	+10.3
Indre-et-Loire	14.3	7.9	+6.4	17.8	19.7	−1.9	+8.3
Vienne	10.0	5.9	+4.1	18.2	16.6	+ 1.6	+2.5
Charente	18.3	10.4	+8.3	10.5	8.1	+ 2.4	+5.9
Gironde (2d)	10.9	4.7	+6.2	11.8	12.4	−0.6	+6.8
Landes	13.5	11.2	+2.3	6.9	7.1	−0.2	+2.5
Basses-Pyrénées	19.4	6.8	+12.6	18.8	19.0	−0.2	+12.8

*Calculations based on cantons lying entirely in one zone or the other. Allier, Indre and Dordogne had no cantons lying entirely in the non-occupied zone. The Poujadist vote is the sum for all Poujadist lists in the département in question; in the Basses-Pyrénées the Tixier-Vignancour vote is also included. In the Landes, the Besson vote is considered "Gaullist."

cal and political differences as well.[9] The various possible explanations of this relation may be distinguished somewhat by repeating the analysis within each of a number of *départements* through which the dividing line passed. The results of this analysis, shown in Table 9.1, indicate that the occupation line is still related to this political difference even when gross geographical differences are set aside. By distinguishing the cantons of each divided *département* that lay entirely in the occupied zone from those entirely in the nonoccupied zone,[10] we see that the losses of Gaullism (1951–56) were consistently greater in the occupied zone in all nine *départements,* while the Poujadist vote was slightly greater in the nonoccupied zone in six of the nine *départements.* The differential between Gaullism and Poujadism was greater (more Gaullist) in the occupied zone in all nine *départements* (right-hand column of Table 9.1).

The difference between the two zones, in each of these nine *départements* was far greater for the RPF vote than for the Poujadist. These findings suggest that attitudes toward Vichy in the former nonoccupied zone constituted an important barrier to the spread of Gaullism into the south in 1951, but were relatively unrelated to the northward spread of Poujadism.

It appears, then, that the RPF, in spite of its mass mobilization of voters, was prevented from winning more votes by the division over Vichy and the Resistance, which was still politically significant in 1951. This general appeal also stopped short of the formidable barriers separating it from the Communist party. Thus even the vote-transfer which most resembled the American "independent vote" was restricted from drawing support from certain segments of the population.

The similarity of the Poujadist proportions of the vote on both sides of the occupation line suggests that Poujade was successful in avoiding the Vichy–Resistance issue, just as he avoided the religious issue. The youth of Poujadism as a political party at the 1956 elections may have permitted it an ambiguity of platform that the RPF could not, or did not wish to, maintain between 1947 and 1951. Poujade's neutrality, in turn, may have earned him a greater degree of support from pro-Vichy elements than was available to the parties clearly identified with the Resistance and the Fourth Republic.

The possibility of neutrality by Poujadists with respect to Vichy and the Resistance is also suggested by the fact that nearly half of their deputies had failed to be active in the Resistance. Of those who were over 21 in 1943, 43 per cent had not been active in the Resistance; only the Moderates exceeded this proportion (45 per cent), while for Gaullist deputies the proportion was only 8 per cent.[11]

The Mendesist Vote

The third major voting surge of the Fourth Republic went to Mendesism in 1956. Gathering strength during the same period as Poujadism, it confronted the voters at the same time. Ideologically, Mendès' support was at almost the opposite pole from Poujade's: urban, internationalist, favoring economic progress, led by a Jewish deputy. Goguel, in interpreting the 1956 election, has asserted that the Radical gains of that year were essentially those of the Republican Front, were concentrated in northeastern industrial France, and came from much the same sources as the previous gains of the MRP in 1945–46 and the RPF in 1951.[12] Our regression coefficients have also shown that the Radical vote associated with the Republican Front became much more urban in its base in 1956 than before.

The actual behavior of the Radical vote in 1956 is somewhat more complicated, however. Both Republican Front Radicals and right-center Radicals gained in the North; both lost south of the Loire, presumably because of Poujadist competition. Goguel's own maps can be used to show this, if the Radicals' principal orientation in each district is cross-tabulated against their relative gain or loss; the resulting association is negligible.[13]

This lack of association is due not only to Poujadist inroads; it also reflects in part the loose definition of the Republican Front at the time. If we use hindsight to define Mendesism in terms of the *subsequent* division of the Radicals in the Third Legislature, a clearer relation between Mendesism and the party's voting gains (1951–56) emerges. Among those who were to be the strongest supporters of Mendesism in the Assembly (scores 0, 1, and 2 on Scale III-1) over two-thirds had overall Radical gains in their districts greater than the national gain. Among the other Valois Radicals, only 29 per cent came from such districts; and of the dissident Radicals, only 42 per cent. But at the 1956 election a number of Radicals who later opposed Mendès, and presumably were already lukewarm to him, had to be classified as belonging to the Republican Front, as they had not gone into open opposition. It was the thoroughgoing Mendesists, not simply the official endorsees, who attracted the extra votes.[14]

We can thus identify more clearly the voters and candidates involved in the Mendesist surge. We are dealing with only nineteen deputies from twelve *départements,* however; the thirteen who gained more than the national average came largely from the Paris area, Normandy, or areas to the west. These *départements* had earlier participated in the Gaullist surge, and for this limited group, Goguel's interpretation holds. Mendesism was undoubtedly taking segments of the former Gaullist vote—not merely on Gaullist tickets, but for Radical candidates.

But was the Mendesist surge really defined independently of Poujadism? North and south, urban and rural areas, distinguished Mendesism from Poujadism just as these characteristics distinguished the areas of Gaullist loss from those of Poujadist gain. One interpretation is that Mendesism and Poujadism limited one another in 1956: whatever "floating voters" were available for new movements in that election may have had to choose between the two. The rural voters of the south may have been more accustomed to the traditional "southwestern" Radicalism, and thus attuned more to Poujade than to Mendès-France. Certain urban voters of the north, more cosmopolitan and sophisticated, might have voted once for "left" Gaullism and later swung to Mendès—or outflanked him in the Jacobin Club of Paris.[15]

The relation between Mendesism and peasant protest was not, however, a constant one. At the beginning of Mendès' premiership he was supported enthusiastically by Paul Antier, who represented this protest and later allied himself with Poujade. But this alliance was weakened near the end of Mendès' term; Antier opposed Mendès at his fall. Mendès' steps toward the modernization of agriculture did not necessarily appeal to a peasant organization that wished to defend the status quo.[16] By the Third Legislature, Antier had swung to the extreme right in his opposition to the Mollet cabinet and its successors. And although it is true that Mendès also opposed Mollet, the peasants' opposition was more nationalist, as its junction with Poujade indicated, and diametrically opposed to that of Mendès.

How, then, could these groups have ever been allies? Their principal basis of agreement seemed to lie in their opposition to the "system"; on what should replace it they were less clearly agreed. Antier had earlier been a supporter of de Gaulle, and on that account had left Pleven's cabinet in 1952. But this too was an alliance in opposition rather than support for a policy. Thus Antier could be an electoral ally of Gaullism or Mendesism, but not so easily a political ally after Mendès came to power.

This reasoning, like our analysis of Gaullism and Poujadism, suggests that there was no single or constant source of "surge" votes in the Fourth Republic. There were indeed multiple sources of protest that could unite in the incipient phases of a new movement, but they did not easily remain united. Specific transfers occurred from the "stable" parties to new parties, related to local or regional culture and to specific interests.[17] Superimposed on these transfers were more amorphous ones—from nonvoters, minor party voters, new voters—but these latter were not always dominant. The capacity of new parties—or of partially renewed parties, such as Mendesist Radicalism—to free voters from the barriers that existed among the stable parties did not correspond to a general or uniform breakdown of these barriers. It affected some more than others, because of the very necessity for new parties to take stands, define their political styles, and thus establish particular affinities with some of the stable parties more than with others.

Social Bases of the Changing Vote

Of the three major surges during the Fourth Republic, the one about which survey data tell us the most is Gaullism. A 1947 survey, conducted at the height of the Gaullist wave, shows the RPF drawing support from a wide variety of occupational groups (Table 9.2). Of the IFOP sample, 25 per cent

Table 9.2 Party Preference by Occupational Groups, October 1947

Respondent's Occupation	PCF	SFIO	RGR	MRP	Mod., PRL	RPF	Others	Won't vote	NA	Total	N
Urban middle class											
Employers, managers	10	10	10	12	2	37	4	2	15	102%	52
Professionals	12	7	7	7	10	32	2	7	15	100%	41
White-collar	10	16	4	9	3	34	2	8	14	100%	172
Shopkeepers	9	8	8	9	2	38	2	6	18	100%	132
Artisans	14	31	3	3	–	26	3	3	17	100%	35
Civil servants	17	32	4	4	1	19	1	4	16	98%	141
"Ambiguous" occupations											
Students	7	23	13	–	3	33	3	10	7	99%	30
Retired	9	25	12	9	3	23	2	3	14	100%	129
Farm owners	3	13	15	11	3	29	1	6	20	101%	324
Housewives	10	16	7	8	3	27	2	9	19	101%	525
Workers											
Industrial	36	15	3	6	1	14	–	7	17	99%	397
Farm	33	20	6	5	–	6	1	10	19	100%	80

Source: Based on cards kindly furnished by IFOP.

said they would vote Gaullist if an election were held. Remarkably similar proportions gave this same answer in all but three occupational groups. The exceptions were workers (industrial and agricultural) and civil servants. Each of these occupational groups which failed to yield its quota to Gaullism was associated closely with one of the highly organized parties—workers with the Communists, civil servants with the Socialists. With these exceptions (in addition to the regionalism noted earlier), the Gaullist movement of that time resembled the socially homogeneous transfer of votes characteristic of "surge" elections in the United States.[18] Though RPF preferences in 1947 were selective regionally, they were neither sharply associated with social class nor drawn disproportionately from particular occupations. Even in early 1952 the RPF still drew support fairly uniformly from various occupational groups.[19]

Table 9.3 The January 1956 Vote by Occupational Groups, as Reported November 1956*

Occupation of Head of Family	PCF	SFIO	Rad.	MRP	Mod.	URAS	Pouj. UFF	Other	Abstained, DK, NA	Total	N
Professionals, executives	–	16	13	8	13	3	2	10	36	101%	62
White collar	3	18	6	8	6	3	1	5	50	100%	207
Shopkeepers	2	11	8	6	7	2	11	3	50	100%	101
Artisans	3	15	3	9	12	–	3	9	47	101%	34
Industrial workers	13	15	3	6	5	1	2	5	49	99%	384
Farmers	4	9	9	11	20	3	3	2	39	100%	186
Farm labor	8	16	6	4	10	–	–	–	57	101%	49
Other	3	12	6	12	11	–	1	3	52	100%	204

*Retrospective vote chosen to increase number of cases for Poujadists.

Source: These data were obtained through analysis of cards from the Roper Public Opinion Research Center.

The Gaullist vote of 1947 was not drawn disproportionately from younger or older voters; among IFOP's four age groups, the proportion preferring the RPF varied less than 2 per cent. This distribution contrasts with a general tendency in the United States, observed by McPhee and Ferguson, for younger voters to contribute disproportionately to electoral swings, including that of 1948–52.[20]

The occupational base of the Poujadist vote in the January 1956 election, as reported by respondents in November 1956, is shown in Table 9.3. Its clear-cut association with the occupation of "shopkeeper" suggests that Poujadism was more a reflection of specific discontents and interests than was the earlier support for the RPF.[21]

Tables 9.2 and 9.3 also indicate some of the continuities in the occupational correlates of party choice, as well as the problems of comparison of those correlates over time. The occupational groups contributing most to the reported Communist vote, in both cases, are the industrial and farm workers; but the Communist vote seems to have been greatly under-reported in November 1956, so that the magnitudes of the percentages are not reliable. Similarly, the Poujadist vote is considerably under-reported in 1956.

The main *associations* between particular occupations and the vote appear to persist, regardless of fluctuations in proportion reporting or in the popularity of the parties; but the relative strength of Communists versus Socialists among manual workers, for example, cannot be inferred reliably from these tables. The proportions not reporting party choice are shown, to indicate the possible magnitude of this bias. Apparently the surveys obtain definite party choices from a relatively active segment among each party's supporters, the depth of this segment varying with the party's legitimacy and success at the time of the survey.

Table 9.4 Age Differences in Shifts in Vote Intention at the Beginning and End of the Mendès-France Ministry

	August 1954			January 1955		
	Reported Former Voters Choosing		Reported Former Non-Voters Making Party Choice	Reported Former Voters Choosing		Reported Former Non-Voters Making Party Choice
Age	Same Party	Different Party		Same Party	Different Party	
18–34	77%	11% (345)	41%* (251)	70%	16% (327)	54%* (216)
35–49	79	11 (396)	26 (190)	74	12 (399)	32 (99)
50–64	74	13 (293)	25 (123)	73	13 (253)	29 (49)
65+	77	10 (193)	26 (89)	74	13 (191)	14 (52)

*In the approximately three years between the 1951 election and these surveys, those aged 21, 22, and 23 would have reached voting age and thus artificially inflated the proportions of non-voters making party choices. If all in these age groups had made party choices in 1954 and 1955, the proportions in the indicated cells would have been inflated by about 10 per cent each.

Although the Mendesist "surge" of January 1956 is difficult to distinguish from the orthodox Radical vote in surveys of that time, an earlier swing related to Mendès-France may be examined. During his ministry in 1954–55, two IFOP surveys were conducted, comparing respondents' past vote and their current preference.[22] Not only were some voters attracted to Mendès personally, but some moved into opposition. We shall consider all the changes of party preference that occurred during this period, in order to see whether changers tended to have the same social characteristics, in relation to nonchangers, as in the United States.

In particular we shall test the hypothesis that young voters participate more fully in changes than do older voters. We shall examine not only transfers among the parties, but separately transfers from nonvoting to party choice. The period under study is not one of a genuine "surge" movement, since no new parties or organized movements were clearly bidding for votes; Mendès' attraction was then personal rather than channeled into reorganization of the Radical party, and Poujadism was still a growing pressure group.

The results of this analysis are shown in Table 9.4. Looking first at the percentages of former voters choosing a different party, we see little difference among the age groups at either the beginning or the end of Mendès' ministry. But in the choices of former nonvoters there was a difference. Whereas the difference between the youngest and oldest groups was only 15 per cent in August 1954, it rose to 40 per cent by January 1955. These changes were not primarily to Mendès-France or the Radicals; the Moderates also attracted a number of new voters at the same time. Perhaps as a result of Mendès' term in office, an increasing number of voters began to feel that they had political demands or protests that could be expressed through the party system—the new Socialist supporters by an alliance with Mendès, Moderates by opposition to him, incipient Poujadists by moving into the "Moderate" category. This disproportionate change by youth would then appear not to be a general characteristic of voting in France, but a phenomenon that arose only under special circumstances. It may have corresponded more to the mobilization of nonvoters than to the transfer of votes among well-defined parties. The absence of a differential recruitment of youth to Gaullism in 1947 also calls in question the general variability of the vote of young adults, relative to their elders.[23]

These data suggest several differences between vote transfers in France and the United States. The changes of 1955, like those of the 1956 election, were not dominated by shifts of support to a single winning party, but consisted of several distinct shifts of voters in different directions.[24] Differential shifts by young voters were concentrated among those who had not voted in the previous election, rather than among shifters between parties. And except for the transfers of previous nonvoters in 1955, young voters were generally *not* more easily mobilized than old.

One possible explanation of this difference may lie in the earlier development of social barriers and political homogeneity of friendship choice in France than in the United States. The American phenomenon of "political immunization," to which McPhee and Ferguson refer, may result in part from the young adult's finding his place in the world. After his separation from the family he is likely to be socially and geographically mobile and to develop a stable, consistent organization of attitudes and friendships only in his thirties. The young adult in France may learn who he is and choose his path of life earlier, so that he arrives at voting age with a political preference that is not more changeable than his elders'.

This explanation does not deny the extensive shifts of political preference that occurred, or the "surges" with which they were chiefly associated; but it locates their incidence in different segments of the population from comparable political changes in other countries. Mannheim, for example, connects the development of "mass democracy" with an increasing importance of the younger generation.[25] But it is possible that in France the susceptibility to mass movements and movements of protest was not any greater proportionately among the young. Especially among those who had chosen a political party, this choice seemed just as stable in early adulthood as later.

The "Bandwagon Effect" and the Parties of the Center

The possibility of changing political preferences and arriving at consensus on policies may be examined, paradoxically, through attention to some of the apparent errors of survey research. It is well known that reports of respondents' votes at previous elections are subject to errors of recall. But these retrospective errors have systematic properties that may throw light on the political systems in which they occur. We expect respondents' reports of their votes immediately after an election to agree fairly well with the actual election statistics. But as time passes, American surveys tend to show a bias, known as the "bandwagon effect," toward the party that won the election. This may be noticed first in the preferences indicated after the election by those who did not report voting,[26] and it presumably influences the later results through over-reporting of the vote by nonvoters, as well as erroneous reports by those who did vote.

In the IFOP surveys the proportion of the sample reporting a definite party choice is normally less than the proportion of the electorate who voted; thus whatever "bandwagon effects" we observe are due to net under-reporting rather than over-reporting of the vote. Nevertheless, similar influences may be operating in the differential tendency to report voting for one party, at a later date, more than another.

In order to interpret these distortions in the reported vote we must first set a standard as to how large a change is to be considered significant. For this purpose we shall use the results of a survey conducted by IFOP only a few weeks after the January 1956 election—an interval so short as not to have permitted long-term distortions of memory or reporting. In this survey, the Communist vote and the vote for "other" parties were each underestimated by 4.5 per cent, and the Socialist overestimated by 4 per cent; all other discrepancies were smaller. We infer that errors of sampling and under-reporting alone were not likely to have exceeded 5 per cent in any category.[27]

With this baseline established, we turn to a series of retrospective distributions available for various periods during the Fourth Republic, starting with the period following the First Constituent Assembly election in October 1945 (Table 9.5). In interpreting this table we shall disregard those discrepancies of recalled vote from actual vote that fall below 5 per cent, and shall consider only those interelection intervals in which the "bandwagon effect" for a given party is uniform, i.e., in which the recalled vote always exceeds or always falls below the actual proportion of the vote.

According to this criterion, the only bandwagon effect in 1945-46 occurred for the "other" category, which increased; possibly this referred to the growing Moderate vote. At the same time (on one occasion) the MRP vote was under-reported. During the First Legislature the "other" category also increased somewhat; in this case one suspects the projection backward of Gaullist sympathies. But on the whole, there was little consistent evidence of a bandwagon effect before June 1951.[28]

Table 9.5 Percentage Distributions of the Vote at Previous Elections as Recalled by Respondents at Various Times

Election Survey	*PCF, MURF*	*Social-ist, UDSR*	*Rad.*	*MRP*				*Other*	*Total*	*(Turn-out)*	*% Report-ing Vote*	*N*
Oct. 1945	26	27	8	25				14	100%	(80%)		
*April 4–13, 1946	29	24	6	19				23	101%			
*April 16–23, 1946	26	22	7	21				24	100%			
*May 20–26, 1946	26	23	8	25				18	100%			
	PCF	*SFIO*	*RGR*	*MRP*	*Mod.*	*Gaull.*		*Other*				
Nov. 1946	29	18	12	26	13	2		0	100%	(78%)		
Jan. 1947	28	18	10	26	12			6	100%			
*June 1947	30	18	10	26	16				100%			
*Dec. 1947	28	18	11	31	5			8	101%			
*Sept. 1948	30	17	10	25	12			6	100%			
*March 1949	28	18	9	25	14			5	99%			
*Oct. 1949	28	17	13	26	15			2	101%			
*April 1951	29	17	9	24		21			100%			
June 1951	26	15	11	13	12	20		3	100%	(77%)		
Feb. 1952	19	21	12	16	12	20		**	100%		53%	1413
Aug. 1953	21	18	10	18	18	15			100%		57%	3458
Aug. 1954	18	26	9	16	20	10		1	100%		60%	2073
Jan.–Feb. 1955	17	25	9	19	18	10		3	101%		59%	2044
							Pouj.					
Jan. 1956	26	15	14	11	14	4	12	4	100%	(80%)		
Nov. 1956	12	26	12	16	18	3	5	8	100%		52%	1227
Nov. 1958	9	28	15	16	24	6	3	-	101%		50%	796

*Reconstructed by solution of simultaneous equations, based on turnover table and distribution of current preferences given in *Sondages*. The IBM 7094 was used for this purpose. Sample size and distribution of non-responses not given.

**Less than ½ per cent.

Source: Tables of recalled vote are given in *Sondages*, 1954, No. 1, 41, and in Association Francaise de Science Politique, *L'Établissement de la Cinquième République*, p. 146. Distributions for 1954, 1955, and 1956 surveys were obtained from IFOP cards.

From June 1951 to 1958 the picture changes. During the Second Legislature the recalled vote for Communists and Gaullists dropped with the passage of time; the Gaullists' actual support also dropped during this period, but the Communists' did not. During the Third Legislature and de Gaulle's period as premier (before he became president), the Communist and Poujadist recalled vote dropped precipitously. The Socialist, MRP, and Moderate vote, as recalled by respondents, was consistently higher than the actual vote during both Second and Third Legislatures.

One major difference between the two periods, before and after June 1951, was the institution of the *apparentements*. Before 1951 there were fewer "unrepresented" votes; proportional representation operated so that most voters could feel they were represented by deputies of their own persuasion. After 1951 the parties of systematic opposition were in fact under-represented: in 1951, both Communists and Gaullists, and in 1956, Communists and Poujadists to a lesser extent.[20] The invalidation of eleven Poujadist deputies may have added to this disparity. The Poujadists, like the RPF earlier, declined in popular support after their electoral success, but the Communists' actual vote did not decline nearly as much as their recalled (and reported) vote.

A second factor influencing retrospective distortion may have been the actual changes in support for the parties. Prior to 1951 the distortions in the "other" category may have been due to the rise in strength of the Moderates and then the Gaullists. In the Second Legislature the Gaullists' loss in popular support may have contributed to their greater retrospective decline than the Communists', and in the Third the same may have been true of the Poujadists. This leaves unexplained the Communists' sharp retrospective decline after 1956; perhaps this was due to a lesser feeling of legitimacy in reporting Communist votes, connected with the Hungarian affair, the Algerian issue, or the advent of the Fifth Republic.

The main trend of the "bandwagon effect" was toward greater support for the parties benefiting from electoral over-representation, which were also the ones that constituted most of the cabinets. But because this same trend ran parallel to fluctuations in popular support for rising or falling parties, we infer that the center coalition was receiving some increment of support or legitimacy. The exception to this trend was the Radical party, which continually played a part in cabinets but gained little if anything in the retrospective vote. Possibly its concentration on intraparliamentary matters, as we have seen it in the Radicals' scales, detracted from its ability to present a clear image to its supporters.

We infer that there were indeed swings of public support toward the center majority that governed France, but that these occurred only after 1951. The combination of an *un*representative electoral system, more like that of the single-member district, and a continuing series of coalitions among the parties that benefited from this system seems to have generated a bias toward the center that increased with the passage of time.[30] This bias, however, resembled the American "bandwagon effect" in not necessarily being convertible into votes at the following election.

Conclusion

Taken together, our analyses of sources of stability and change suggest the serious obstacles that hindered the election of an Assembly with a clearly different majority. The solid bases of support of the organized parties, and their isolation from one another even at the local level, constituted a stable structure that could be broken only by new and relatively radical "surge" movements.

The greatest variability in voting under the Fourth Republic was associated either with the decline of parties newly strengthened after the Liberation (SFIO and MRP) or with the surges and declines of RPF and Poujadism. (Mendesism, which was an assault more on party organization than on the preferences of the electorate, will be discussed further in Chapter 11.) An element shared by all these changes is that of hopes and disappointments. First the hopes of the Resistance, and later two movements for sweeping change and renovation, were shattered on the rocks of the electoral and parliamentary system. Proportional representation necessitated coalition government, rather than government by a clear-cut majority; and this in turn expressed the division among the parties, facilitated by the citizens' individualism and resistance to social pressure.

Stability of a party's vote, on the other hand, was associated with the existence of a clientele that could define itself as distinct from alternative political groups. For Communists and Socialists this distinctness was attained in terms of specifically political organization. For the MRP after its stabilization, its voters' religiosity, regionalism, and a particular philosophy of political action played their parts in maintaining distinctness. For the Radicals and Moderates association with certain local political leaders and hostility to their enemies constituted an alternative way of stabilizing the clientele.

Appeal to general "consensus" values[31] (*Rassemblement,* Estates General) rather than specific group values—or even "consensus" disvalues (*sortez les sortants*)—did not of itself create a specific and stable clientele. If a new movement tried to take votes from a variety of other parties, it carried with it the risk that an equally great variety of threats would confront the movement in its declining phase.[32] The appeal in terms of a leader's personal characteristics—especially when their controversial aspects were deliberately blurred in the campaign—was of this kind. Mendès and the Republican Front were somewhat less vague; but he too recruited support from groups whose views proved later to be in mutual conflict.

Even though proportional representation permitted the easy reflection in the vote of sudden changes of opinion expressed through new parties,[33] it did not alone account for the peculiarities of these "surge" movements. In contrast to an "independent" vote that might strengthen an established party on matters of general policy, the shifts in the vote went either to new movements breaking completely with the "system," or to expressions of very specific interests; Poujadism, in its career from pressure group to party, combined both but significantly failed to become absorbed in an established party. Thus the Fourth Republic did indeed know fluctuation of the vote; but the fluctuation was not such to permit a systematic alteration of government policy within a stable set of "rules of the game."

The contrast between stability and variation in the vote was also a contrast between government and opposition. There were, of course, two oppositions within the Assembly: the Communists, who held their one-fourth of the popular vote, and the pro-cabinet parties that were excluded from the cabinet coalition at any given time. But neither of these oppositions satisfied the desire of many voters for active protest against the government and its policies. This protest was expressed through "surge" movements.

Protest of this kind does not easily fit the conventional model of an alternating, symmetrical two-party system. In the United States it often finds expression through minor parties. Alternatively, when one major party has dominated the scene for a long time, the second major party may become more receptive to protest issues in order to regain power. The reality of a two-party system at a particular time may be not symmetry, but one-party dominance.

This dominance of one party can be seen most clearly in the politics of some large American cities. An entrenched organization normally controls the major elective offices. The geographical limits of the city contribute to the strength of this organization by excluding potential opposition votes. But periodically a reform movement develops, claiming to transcend political parties and organize city government on different lines. This movement gains control of the city government, holds it for a time, and then yields to organization politics again. The relation between organization and reform, like that between the stable and changing votes in the Fourth Republic, can usefully be understood in terms of two distinct political subsystems.[34]

Thus the phenomena of surge and decline, stability and change, government and opposition, which we see in the Fourth Republic, may well exemplify more general processes in the dynamics of representative government.

NOTES

———◆———

1. A closer parallel may in fact exist between the French "surges" and American third-party movements. The point, however, is that while transfers of votes between stable parties are dominant in the United States, transfers to new parties were dominant in France under the Fourth Republic.

2. Philip E. Converse and Georges Dupeux, "De Gaulle and Eisenhower: The Public Image of the Victorious General," in Angus Campbell, *et. al.*, *Elections and the Political Order*, pp. 292–345. On the relation of the geographical distribution of the 1951 RPF vote to that of the 1958 UNR vote, see Association Française de Science Politique, *L'Établissement de la Cinquième République*, pp. 361–371.

3. See Hoffmann, *Le Mouvement Poujade*. The early Gaullist campaign had its negative aspects, but did not depend so exclusively on them; for a summary of temporal changes in Gaullism, see Rémond, *The Right Wing in France,* pp. 367–368.

4. See Duverger, Goguel, and Touchard, eds., *Les Élections du 2 janvier 1956,* pp. 315–316, 343–350, 400–405, 420; also Hoffmann, *Le Mouvement Poujade,* pp. 12–13.

5. This contrast within the *département* of Côte d'Or, for example, is brought out by Long in *Les Élections législatives en Côte d'Or,* p. 166.

6. The sources of the Poujade vote are analyzed in Hoffmann, *Le Mouvement Poujade,* pp. 189–208. The winegrowers' crisis is emphasized in Schram, "Le Poujadisme dans le Gard." In the neighboring department of Bouches-du-Rhône, the Poujadist vote was swelled by vegetable growers; see Olivesi and Roncayolo, *Géographie électorale des Bouches-du-Rhône, pp.* 37ff., 75ff. For an indication of some of the other interests aggregated by Poujadism, see Hoffmann, *Le Mouvement Poujade,* pp. 13–14.

7. RPF losses, in *départements* where there were joint lists in 1951, are calculated by assuming the vote for such lists was not a "Gaullist" vote; the figure shown is the difference in percentages of vote cast at the two elections.

8. See Bourdet, "La Politique intérieure de la Résistance," 1845–1846. He points out that in the southern zone, *"les cadres de la société française étaient dans leur écrasante majorité,"* while in the northern zone these leaders had often taken an active part in the Resistance. The electoral results were also interpreted in these terms by Riès in "Tempéraments politiques et résultats électoraux," 131.

9. Further investigation might show that Gaullism was particularly strong in the area under complete control of the German army; see Aron, *De l'Armistice a l'insurrection nationale,* p. 25. On other differences between the two zones see *ibid,* pp. 27ff.; Fabre-Luce, *Journal de la France 1939–1944,* pp. 271ff.; Gordon Wright, "Reflections on the French Resistance (1940–44)," 339f.

10. This classification was performed with the aid of a detailed map from the German military archives, obtained from the National Archives and Records Service, Washington, D.C. The map used was an attachment to the Franco-German armistice agreement and is included in Nuremberg Document 1810–PS.

11. Mattei Dogan, "Political Ascent in a Class Society: French Deputies 1870–1958," in Marvick, ed., *Political Decision-Makers,* p. 86.

12. Duverger, Goguel, and Touchard, eds., *Les Élections du 2 janvier 1956,* pp. 488–489. For his classification of lists see pp. 468–469.

13. The maps used are nos. 15–16–17, *ibid.,* pp. 490–491. The resulting association between Republican Front predominance and relative vote gain is only $\gamma = +.09$.

14. An additional complication derives from possible transfers of votes among Radical lists, as Goguel's Map 17 examines only external transfers.

15. Gaullists with at least some connection with the Jacobin Club were Léon Nocher, Michel Debré, and Henri Ulver; see Coston, ed., "Partis, journaux, et hommes politiques d'hier et d'aujourd'hui," 425.

16. In the Third Legislature, Antier joined the extreme right wing; his alliance with Poujade and Dorgères is described in Fauvet and Mendras, eds., *Les Paysans et la politique,* pp. 139, 179–181. On Mendès-France's agricultural policy and the response to it see p. 116.

17. That not all extremist protest is "mass" protest, but some derives from specific interests, has been argued by Gusfield in "Mass Society and Extremist Politics."

18. These figures may be compared with the occupational distribution of voters who shifted toward Eisenhower from 1948 to 1952, given in Janowitz and Marvick, *Competitive Pressure and Democratic Consent,* p. 29. This group constituted 22.3 per cent of the re-

spondents, and its proportion among various occupational groups ranged from 21.7 to 25.5 per cent, except that only 14.6 per cent of the lower-lower class were pro-Eisenhower changers.

19. See Williams, *Crisis,* p. 509.

20. See William N. McPhee and Jack Ferguson, "Political Immunization," in McPhee and Glaser, eds., *Public Opinion in Congressional Elections,* p. 162. The published results of the Michigan studies do not show the changes for age cohorts (1948–1952) so clearly, but suggest a greater participation of young voters in the swing toward Eisenhower; see Angus Campbell, Gurin, and Miller, *The Voter Decides,* p. 70. It has also been shown that party identification is stronger among older voters; see Angus Campbell, Converse, Miller, and Stokes, *The American Voter,* pp. 161ff.

21. A comparable table is given in Lipset, *Political Man,* p. 225; this also shows the relatively high proportion of merchants who preferred Poujade. The same relation also existed in IFOP's survey in the Seine, January 1956, where the Poujadist vote was not under-reported; see Duverger, Goguel and Touchard, eds., *Les Élections du 2 janvier 1956,* p. 238.

22. Table 8.5 showed a turnover table from the second of these surveys.

23. A similar lack of differential shift of young voters to a new party was shown with respect to the rise of the UNR in 1958. Changes from 1956 to 1958 were actually slightly greater among older voters; see *Sondages,* 1960, No. 4, 26.

24. Changes of this kind do sometimes occur in the United States, however; see Converse, Campbell, Miller, and Stokes, "Stability and Change in 1960: A Reinstating Election."

25. Mannheim, *Man and Society in an Age of Reconstruction,* pp. 97–98.

26. See Angus Campbell *et al., The American Voter,* pp. 110–115.

27. See Jean Stoetzel and Pierre Hassner, "Résultats d'un sondage," in Duverger, Goguel, and Touchard, eds., *Les Élections du 2 janvier 1956,* pp. 199, 245, 249. Percentages are based only on those respondents who reported voting for a definite party—72 per cent of the sample.

28. Reconstruction of the vote from turnover tables involves neglecting the non-voters. If this group were negligible, or if they were distributed among the "now" vote categories in the same way as the rest of the sample, this approximation would cause no error. The error did not exceed 2.5 per cent in any category of the solution in one instance in which it was tried with a known answer.

29. The great declines in recalled vote for Communists and Poujadists in the Third Legislature thus cannot be fully explained in these terms.

30. That this bias owed more to the electoral system than to cabinet participation is suggested by the over-recall of the Socialist vote in 1953 and of the MRP vote in 1956.

31. This term is used in Lipset, Trow, and Coleman, *Union Democracy,* p. 294.

32. The appeals of the RPF, cutting across party lines, are described in Malterre and Benoist, *Les Partis politiques français,* pp. 130f.

33. Duverger, *Political Parties,* p. 313.

34. See Lowi, *At the Pleasure of the Mayor,* Ch. 8.

»10«

Assembly Votes and the Constituencies

MANY OF THE CONSTRAINTS placed on cabinet coalitions by "parliamentary arithmetic" can be traced to the compartmentalization of the electorate, especially with respect to shifts among the stable parties. But it is also possible that the divisions *within* the parties were traceable to conflicting pressures from the constituencies. When a segment of a party went into opposition, did this division reflect constituency pressures, organizational quarrels in the party, or considerations internal to the Assembly?

It has often been suggested that a major source of cabinet instability lay in constituency relations. As Williams has written, "The commonest cause of ministerial crises is the conviction, on the part of a party or a group of deputies, that some sacrifice demanded from them jeopardizes their whole electoral future."[1] A deputy's electoral future depended on the conditions in the one particular district in which he expected to run. These conditions differed considerably, within any of the parties that supported the cabinet, from one district to another. A party might make its reputation as a whole through its action in Paris, or it might gain or lose as a whole from major trends in opinion; but if the districts were important in cabinet instability, they should have exerted their influence differentially.

We shall see, however, that the relation between constituency influence and pressure on the cabinet was different in different parties. The basic divisions in the society, clearly reflected in the voters' choice of parties, were less clearly related to deputies' positions within their parties. More important correlates of these intraparty positions were specifically political conditions in the districts, such as the militants' positions or the alliances between parties—the former for the Socialists and MRP, the latter for the Radicals and Moderates.

General and Specific Constituency Influences

One may speak of leftist and rightist districts within a given party, or of districts where one interest or another exercised a strong influence on the Assembly. But to justify speaking in these terms, we must first ask whether these districts remained the same for all three Legislatures, and whether they were the same for different parties. We begin our analysis of constituency relations by asking how general or specific these district characteristics were. We presume that if there were organized constituency influences, affecting different deputies in different degrees, these influences produced consistent effects over time in the deputies' votes.[2]

286

To study the consistency of deputies' positions within a given party across the three Legislatures, we must examine many scales. Our previous analysis has shown that some scales were more consistently related over time than others.[3] These results are summarized in Table 10.1, which shows the scales with greatest continuity over time in their ranking of the deputies, within each of the parties. The associations (γ) between the scales chosen for different Legislatures are indicated in intermediate columns. For the Socialists, these associations are lower than for the other parties; but their continuity of position can be seen if we recognize that their deep divisions on EDC and on the de Gaulle investiture of 1958 each involved a coalition between the party's "left wing" and another dissenting faction. For all three of the other parties shown, sets of scales were found whose cross-Legislature associations were all .51 or higher.

Table 10.1 Scales Showing Greatest Continuity Across Legislatures

	First	γ_{12}	Second	γ_{23}	Third	γ_{13}
*Socialists**	I-1 (Electoral Law)	+.22	II-1 (German Rearmament)	+.41	a. III-1 (de Gaulle)	+1.00
				+.72	b. Votes at June 1957 congress	+ .53
				+.67	c. Scrutin no. 655 (July 1957)	+ .55
MRP	I-1 (Reynaud Law, Electoral)	+.68	II-4 (Pinay)	+.78	III-1 (Mollet)	+ .51
Rad.-UDSR	I-2 (Marie-Queuille)	+.66	II-1 (School Aid)	+.95	III-4 (School aid) (Radicals only)	+ .72
Moderates	I-2 (Electoral Law)	+.71	II-2 (Europe)	+.81	III-3 (Mollet—Domestic & Europe)	+ .51

*Three different indicators are used for the Socialists in the Third Legislature, as discussed in the text. Their associations with one another are: $\gamma_{ab} = +.72$; $\gamma_{ac} = +.61$; $\gamma_{bc} = +.88$.

It has been observed in both France and the United States that public opinion and party differences were more firmly anchored in domestic than in foreign policy.[4] The scales selected for greatest continuity tend to be concerned with domestic matters, with one major exception; the questions of Germany and of European union. For the Socialists and Moderates, the proposed European army elicited lasting divisions, and for the Moderates, European economic unification did so as well. Undoubtedly these were matters that affected Frenchmen deeply; the memory of the German occupation and the economic consequences of trade policy were directly significant to important groups of voters. Among the Radicals, however, the issue with greatest continuity of division was the church-school question;[5] and within the MRP, attitudes toward the Moderates (Reynaud, Pinay) as against the Socialists (Mollet) were a continuing source of differences. Both these latter parties were also divided on European and colonial policy, but not in ways that were so consistent over time.

We have also suggested that those scales reflecting consistent district pressures were not likely to be those most closely related to the fate of the cabinet. For the Socialists and MRP this inverse relation held. The Socialists' divisions were on issues, and when they divided over de Gaulle it was not simply another cabinet of the "system" that was in question. The most persistent divisions in the MRP, also, did not directly involve the investiture or fall of the cabinet.

For the Radicals and Moderates, on the other hand, the scales showing greatest continuity did in some cases involve the fate of the cabinet. The lasting division among the Radicals, as we have indicated, concerned the church-school question, especially in the Second and Third Legislatures. But their corresponding scale in the First Legislature was most closely related to the cabinet's fate, of all their scales during that period; it contained six votes on investitures or the cabinet. How could this have reflected constituency pressures? One possible source of this relation is a congruence between the position of the traditional Radicals, in the First Legislature, and the orientation of the cabinets in question. The cabinets included the Socialists; their premiers (in this scale) were Radicals on most of the votes in question; and the membership of the cabinets was strongly weighted with the leftist coalition that had emerged from the Resistance—Socialists and MRP. On the other hand, the opposition included a combination of Gaullists and Moderates. This configuration of forces was generally consistent with the lasting division in the party over the school question.

The scales selected for the Moderates are more closely related to the cabinet than those for the Radicals. Their electoral-law scale in the First Legislature involved one investiture vote, and their "Europe" scale in the Second had the highest proportion of confidence votes of any in that period. Although the issue of European union may well have affected the economic interests related to the Moderates differently in different districts (e.g., agriculture and industry), it also seemed fairly closely related to the cabinets' policy.

The relation between *ministrables'* votes and individual scales may also be used as an indirect test of whether the scales with continuity were those least related to the cabinet's fate. If we regard it as proven that the *ministrables* tended to support the cabinet at crucial junctures, then we should expect the associations between *ministrable* status and scale positions (in Table 7.2 above) to be least for the scales we have selected to measure constituency influences. This expectation can be tested, for each scale chosen in Table 10.1, by referring to Table 7.2 and comparing the *ministrable* effect for that scale with the effect for other scales for the same party and Legislature. This comparison cannot be made for a party that has only one scale in a given Legislature—the Socialists in all three Legislatures and the MRP in the Third. But for the MRP in the First and Second it is well confirmed: in the First the scale selected in Table 10.1 does not even have a defined cabinet position in Table 7.2,[6] and in the Second its *ministrable* effect is next to lowest among six scales. For the Radicals the divergence between *ministrable* effect and temporal continuity is less clear; the scale chosen for continuity in the First Legislature (Scale I-2 in Table 10.1) has the highest *ministrable* effect in Table 7.2 (+.64), but in the Second and Third there was no clear cabinet position on the school aid scales listed in Table 10.1. For the Moderates the scales chosen in Table 10.1 are next to lowest, highest, and intermediate in their *ministrable* effect in the three Legislatures respectively.

The overall result is a slight negative relation between *ministrable* effect and temporal continuity, clearest for the MRP and least clear for the Moderates. Superimposed on this relation is a general tendency toward a higher *ministrable* effect for Moderates and Radicals than for MRP.

The Socialists' scales, which we have contended were not related to the cabinet's fate, nevertheless show high associations with *ministrable* status in the First and Second Legislatures. To oppose the 1951 electoral law, as we have seen, was a sure way to remain out of the cabinet thereafter; and votes on EDC were also related to earlier and later cabinet positions. But what seems to have mattered here was whether a deputy was on Mollet's side; the *ministrable* effect in the Socialist party resulted from a persistent factional division *in the party* rather than from cooptation of Socialist *ministrables* into a consensual cross-party group in the Assembly.

Once we have chosen those scales that showed greatest consistency over the three Legislatures, we may examine the relations among the parties in a given constituency. The simplest such relation that one might imagine would result from a general constituency influence, affecting all deputies from a given district similarly. If this occurred, all the deputies representing rich, religious, rural areas might be on the right wings of their respective parties; or all deputies from urban working-class districts might be more favorable to social legislation than their party colleagues. Whatever the district influence might be, it would lead to similarity of scale positions of district colleagues from different parties.

We thus compare the scale positions of deputies in different parties who represented the same district. For the scales we have chosen, however, there was very little parallelism of this sort between district colleagues; the associations between their scale positions were uniformly low or negative.[7] Of the twenty-two possible cross-party associations of this sort in the three Legislatures, twelve were negative; and of those over .30 in magnitude, nine out of ten were negative. Not only is the hypothesis of "general district tendencies" not supported by the data; the parties[8] in a given district tended to take positions inversely related to one another, and this tendency increased somewhat from the First Legislature to the Third.

Because there were no general district tendencies for all parties, we must examine the constituency relations of each party separately. We shall consider in turn the temporal continuity of positions within each party; their relation to social and economic characteristics of the districts; and their relation to political characteristics of the districts, as indicated by the popular vote, the seats held, the electoral alliances formed, and the positions taken by deputies of other parties.

The lack of similarity of scale positions across parties does not, of course, deny that there were local interests to which all the deputies in a district bowed. Local products such as wine or industries such as fisheries did seem to attract support from all the deputies in their districts; but this support was not revealed in our·scales. The absence of such scales may have been due in part to the fact that these special interests called more for administrative than for legislative action, or to the relative unconcern of *L'Année Politique* with such matters.[9]

The Socialists

We first examine the constituency relations of the Socialist deputies because that party contributed so much to cabinet instability, especially up to 1952. It also had a higher degree of internal control than the other divided parties. We shall see that the positions taken by its deputies depended more on their militants' wishes, and less on coalitions and arrangements with other parties in the districts, than did the positions of the Radical and Moderate deputies.

The divergence of views between Socialist militants and deputies contributed to the uneasiness of the Socialists about cabinet participation throughout the Fourth Republic. Both the desire for a *cure d'opposition* in the First Legislature, and the haste with which Mollet seemed to encourage his own overthrow by the Moderates in October 1957, suggest the importance of a group within the party who were particularly frustrated by the compromises necessary to govern in coalition with the parties of the center and right.

The dissidence in the Socialist party was not unitary, however, as Table 7.12 showed. The two deepest divisions of the party on roll calls during the Fourth Republic occurred on EDC and the de Gaulle investiture; and on both of these, the opposition to Mollet was heterogeneous. Opposing EDC were both the leftist ("popular front") faction and a group we have called "nationalists"; opposing de Gaulle were both the leftists and another group we have called the "republicans." A substantial fraction of the "leftists" within the party can thus be identified by listing those who opposed both EDC and the de Gaulle investiture.[10] Such a list would also show association with dissent on the 1951 electoral-law votes and on the Algerian question prior to de Gaulle's investiture.[11]

The districts selected in this way, and the deputies who represented them, are shown in Table 10.2. Their tendency to leftist dissidence is reflected not only in the indices we have used to select them, but also in other positions they took within the party. Fifteen of these twenty-three departmental federations showed some dissent from a motion opposing unity of action with the Communists in July 1955. Of the sixteen federations supporting Philip's dissident motion at the Lille Congress of July 1956, eleven were on this list.[12] Several of these deputies were leaders in movements of dissent at other times.[13] And all but four of those listed as deputies in the Third Legislature indicated their dissidence by signing a manifesto supporting the publication *Tribune du Socialisme* against Mollet, or taking an active part in the dissident *Parti Socialiste Unifié*.[14]

The districts in question were not unusually concentrated in any particular region, nor were they predominantly urban or rural compared to others that ever had Socialist deputies.[15] Their presence was actually slightly associated with the religiosity of the districts. We infer that though there were consistently leftist federations and deputies within the SFIO, throughout

Table 10.2 The Left Wing of the Socialist Party:
*Deputies and Districts**

District	First Legislature	Second Legislature	Third Legislature
Aisne	Levindrey	Levindrey	Levindrey
Ardèche	(Froment)**	–	Palmero
Ardennes	Viénot Mme.	Desson	Desson
	Desson	Titeux	Titeux
Calvados	–	–	Margueritte
Charente	Maurellet	Maurellet	–
Côtes-du-Nord	Mazier	Mazier	Mazier
		(Thomas E)	
Drôme	Cartier Marcel	Cartier	Cartier
Garonne (Hte.)	Auriol	Auban	Auban
	Auban	Montel E	Montel
	Badiou	Rey	
Gers	Baurens	Baurens	Baurens
Isère	Hussel	Berthet	Berthet
Loire-Atl.	Guitton Jean	Guitton	Guitton
Lot-et-Garonne	–	Nenon	–
Maine-et-L.	Allonneau	–	–
Meurthe-et-M.	Lapie	Lapie	(Lapie)
Puy-de-Dôme	Mabrut	Mabrut	Mabrut
Rhin (Ht.)	Wagner	Wagner	–
Savoie	–	Sibué	–
Savoie (Hte.)	–	Briffod	Briffod
Seine 1	–	Verdier	Verdier
Seine 2	Mayer Daniel	Mayer	Mayer
Seine-et-Marne	–	Arbeltier	Arbeltier
Seine-Mar. 2	Binot	Binot	Binot
Somme	(Lejeune)	Lejeune	(Lejeune)
	Doutrellot	Doutrellot	Doutrellot
Vosges	Poirot	–	Poirot

*The left wing is defined in terms of dissent on the following occasions: (1) One or more dissident votes on electoral-law roll calls in Seale II-1, 1951; (2) Opposition to EDC on no. 2619, 1954; (3) Opposition to Bourgès-Maunoury's special powers, no. 655; (4) Federation favored Verdier motion on Algeria, June 1957; (5) Deputy opposed de Gaulle. The *départements* listed are those whose deputies or federations dissented on at least half of the occasions above on which they had an opportunity to be counted.

**Parentheses enclose the names of deputies who voted with the "right," i.e., opposed the Thorez investiture in 1946, favored EDC in 1954, or favored de Gaulle's investiture in 1958.

all three Legislatures, their presence was not associated with regional "leftism" or concentration of working-class voters.

The local leftist orientations of the Socialists also showed only a limited relation to the party's electoral alliances. In 1956 there was a tendency for leftist Socialist lists *not* to ally themselves with one Radical list against another; the Republican Front, which did form such alliances, was not a "popular front" coalition. But the leftist federations were equally likely to ally themselves with all the Radicals in their districts, or with none. The electoral alliances of the Socialists in 1951 were no more revealing of the lasting differences within the party. Those Socialists who had opposed the new electoral law did tend to refrain from electoral alliances, in comparison with their party colleagues; but the left-wing lists were actually slightly more likely to be allied with the Moderates than were other Socialists.

Another possible source of leftist dissent within the Socialist party might have been a political polarization in certain districts, in response to the presence of strong conservative forces; Zariski has observed this relation for the Italian Socialists. But in France, rightist strength was associated with Socialist dissidence only where the right was weak: districts with strong and medium rightist strength did not differ greatly in their proportions of leftist Socialists, while the thirteen districts with 60 per cent or more leftist vote included *no* dissident federations.[16]

The French Socialists did resemble the Italian, however, in their response to Communist strength in their districts; where the ratio of their vote to the Communists' was higher, they were less likely to be dissident. This relation held particularly in the areas where the French Socialists outpolled the Communists in 1951; of the nineteen districts of this kind, only one was leftist.[17] But the relation was not a simple linear one; at the other extreme, where the Communists had over three times the Socialists' vote, only two of eleven districts were leftist. The nine districts where the Socialists were outnumbered to this extent but not leftist included the urban areas Seine 4–6, Seine-et-Oise 1–2, and Rhône 1.[18] Among their representatives were Depreux and Philip, who were anti-Communist but opposed Mollet on other grounds. Possibly these were the areas in which trade-union or municipal-council experience with the Communists had counteracted the tendency of weaker federations to vote to the left.[19] Perhaps, too, the influence of stronger Socialist organizations in other parts of the *département* in the Seine and Rhône meant that the *département* rather than the district was the unit within which Socialist positions were taken.

Our finding that the Socialists tended toward the center when they outnumbered the local Communists, is interesting in contrast to what we shall find for other parties. The presence of a weaker neighboring party—a Radical federation unrepresented by a deputy—seems to have been an invitation for the Moderate deputies to move *toward* the neighboring party and absorb its vote. The Socialists' tendency was the opposite: to move toward a stronger party and away from a weaker. And for the Moderates in relation to the MRP, there was a less pronounced tendency to move toward the weaker ideological neighbor. The difference among these various cases may well have resulted from the degree of organization of the neighboring party. The Communists were so highly organized that in many districts a dominant Communist organization exercised an ideological attraction over the weaker Socialists. The MRP federations had enough militants so that the Moderates could not easily absorb them. The Radicals, however, were so weak in organization as to invite absorption presumably at the price of some ideological or other concessions to their local leaders.

Thus, while we can identify "leftist" federations and deputies in the Socialist party, there is little reason to attribute their positions either to district interests or to political bargaining outside the party. The leftist federations were not clearly associated with particular geographical areas. Their
positions antedated the formation of the 1951 electoral alliances and were
little associated with the Socialists' own alliances. Communist dominance in
the districts was somewhat associated with the presence of leftist Socialists.
But in comparison with the deputies of the other parties the Socialists
seemed to take their positions for reasons more internal to their party; their
positions were less closely related to those of district colleagues from other
parties with which they might have competed or bargained for votes. Having
a high degree of internal control and an active body of militants, the Socialist deputies took positions that were more nearly independent of the
influences of the other local parties or of their districts' electorates at large.

The MRP in the Constituencies

The MRP showed a clearer relation between deputies' scale positions
and districts. Its left wing tended to come from two types of districts: urban
ones, such as those of the Paris area, where the CFTC supplied a relatively
large part of the MRP vote and the deputies were consequently more concerned with social legislation; and districts in the South (e.g., the Aude or
the Dordogne), where religiosity was low and the MRP had to accent its
"social" rather than its religious aspect to win votes. The conservative wing
of the party, on the other hand, tended to come from the more religious
regions—Brittany, Alsace, the Massif Central. On the rare occasions when
the MRP wavered between support and opposition to a cabinet—notably at
the end of the Pinay ministry in 1953—the geographical differences did correspond somewhat to the party's division between support and opposition.

This division of the MRP between distinct types of districts existed as
early as the First Legislature. The left wing of the party, as shown in Table
7.10, represented districts that may be distinguished from others by their
voters' preferences for leftist parties—a characteristic shared by working-
class *quartiers* and the less religious South. The election of June 1946 for the
Second Constituent Assembly provides a fairly clear indication of votes for
left and right; at that time the MRP attracted a considerable share of
the conservative vote, and the Socialists were relatively strong.[20] We shall
use the proportion of the vote obtained by Socialists and Communists together, at that election, to measure the degree of general leftism of the
voters of a district. In these terms, the MRP deputies who voted on the left
wing of their party tended to come from districts whose electorate had also
voted on the left. This relation is shown, for all three Legislatures, in Table
10.3. For example, 17 districts whose MRP deputies scored 0 on Scale I-1
had had an average constituency vote of 51 per cent for the PCF and SFIO,
while 15 whose deputies scored 2 had an average leftist vote of only 41 per
cent.

The MRP differed from the SFIO in the relation of its internal divisions
to constituency characteristics, and from the Moderates and Radicals in the

consistency of its major scales (those with low numbers) over time.[21] Both these characteristics may be explained by the fact that the MRP was an organized party and also a new one. Building its organization after the Liberation, it recruited differently in different regions, and these organizations antedated the parliamentary party.[22]

Table 10.3 District Vote for Leftist Parties and MRP Deputies' Scale Scores

| | *MRP Deputies' Scale Position* | | | |
	0 *(left)*	*1*	*2*	*3* *(right)*
	Constituents' Support for PCF plus SFIO, June 1946			
First Legislature: Scale I-1	51% (17)*	45% (61)	41% (15)	
Second Legislature: Scale II-4	49% (5)	49% (21)	41% (21)	42% (12)
Third Legislature: Scale III-1	51% (5)	43% (27)	42% (6)	32% (3)

*In each table entry, the percentage is an average, over all the districts in which MRP deputies had the scale score indicated by the column head, of the vote for PCF plus SFIO. The number of such districts is given in parentheses. If the average scale score of two or more MRP deputies from a district (including ministers) fell half way between two categories, it was assigned to the more extreme category.

The scale positions of MRP deputies were related not only to the general political leanings of their districts, but also to the alliances their candidates concluded in the 1951 elections. Those MRP deputies who had been allied with the Socialists but not the Moderates in 1951 tended to be on the left in all three Legislatures; those who had been allied with the Moderates but not the Socialists were on the right.[23]

The Radicals' Constituency Relations

The Radicals' most consistent division, as we have noted, centered about the church-school issue.[24] To reveal this constancy, we used a relatively obscure cluster of roll calls on this subject that took place early in the Third Legislature; this cluster resembled the party's earlier divisions far more closely than did the dominant divisions on Mendesism and Algeria. The major alignments of the party changed so completely, in fact, that the "anti-clerical" Southwestern faction moved from cooperation with Mendés-France on the "left" of the party in 1946–1951, to hostility toward him and a place on what by 1957 was regarded as the party's "right."

Although the church-school issue was the one on which the Radical deputies' votes showed greatest continuity, conservative positions on these scales were not associated with the general religiosity of their constituencies. Rather, these positions were related inversely to it, like the Socialists', in all three Legislatures. Even more interesting is the fact that among the Radicals, leftism on the church-school issue was consistently associated with the more *rural* districts. This evidently reflected the history of the issue and its association with long-standing traditions that were mostly fully mainained in the countryside. No such clear association of leftist voting in the Assembly with rural districts was shown by any of the other parties.

The preponderance of left or right in the constituency vote was not, however, reflected in the Radical deputies' votes. For while the less religious rural areas tended to support "anticlerical" Radicals—and to vote for the left generally—this relation did not exist in the cities. There the working-class vote was high, and much of it went to Communists and Socialists, but the Radicals tended to resemble the Moderates.

Various writers have claimed that the Radicals' votes in the Assembly were related to their constituency alliances. Soulier suggested that under the Third Republic the weakest support for any cabinet was given by deputies whose own local coalitions included parties that were not members of the cabinet's coalition. Bardonnet links the Radicals' Assembly votes to constituency alliances. Goguel, stressing the affinity of the Central and Southwestern Radicals for Moderate votes, has made a similar suggestion. And Williams has related their votes on *laïcité* in 1951–52 to possible bids for conservative votes in their districts.[25]

This hypothesis receives some support from the relation between Scale II-1 and the Radicals' electoral alliances in 1951. If these alliances are ordered according to whether they were with SFIO only, both SFIO and Moderates, or Moderates only, this ordering is associated $(\gamma) + .33$ with the scale. This association is not as great as most of those we have interpreted for the other parties, however, and it does not persist as strongly in the Radicals' scale scores in the First and Third Legislatures.

A stronger and more consistent association was between the Radicals' scale scores and their alliances with the SFIO in 1956. Where the Socialists were allied with the only Radical list in the district, or with all of them, we infer that the Republican Front was not operating as a specifically Mendesist alliance. In districts of this sort, the Radicals' positions tended to be anticlerical in the Third Legislature, and to have been on the left since the First. Presumably the basis of the alliance was the traditional church-school question rather than Mendesism.

Williams suggests that Radicals' positions on the church-school issue were related not only to their electoral alliances, but also to their likelihood of attracting Moderate votes subsequently. Radicals "elected against strong Conservative competition" would thus be on the left, while in districts where the Moderates were weak the Radical deputies would be on the right.[26] A test of this hypothesis with Scale II-1 suggests that the relation is actually the reverse, if we use the absence of a Moderate deputy in the Second Legislature as an indicator of available Moderate votes.

A striking feature of the Radicals' scale positions was their inverse association with those of their MRP district colleagues. When the Radical in a district was on the right wing of his party, in the Second and Third Legislatures, if there was a local MRP deputy he tended to be on his party's left wing, and conversely.[27] This relation is of particular interest because the two parties in question are normally placed near one another on the political spectrum. It suggests that Radicals and MRP tended to form different kinds of electoral coalitions from one another in a given district, and to appeal to different clienteles.

While the positions of the two parties' deputies varied inversely, each party's deputies took positions related to alliances with Moderates or Socialists, as we have seen. It may be, therefore, that Radicals and MRP were alternate allies of the Moderates. One of these two parties would normally ally itself with the Moderates in a given district, and the other would take a position on the left. Or conversely, if one party took a leftist position in the district, an opening may then have existed on the right, permitting the other party to bid for votes or for an electoral coalition with the Moderates.[28] MRP and Radicals seem to have had relatively little to do with one another, differing not only on the religious and "social" issues but also in political style.[29]

The Moderates in the Constituencies

The scales that showed the greatest continuity over time for the Moderates were I-2 (Electoral Law), II-2 ("Europe"), and III-3 (Mollet-Domestic and Europe). The last two scales, both including roll calls on European integration, were very closely associated ($\gamma = .81$). The electoral-law scale in the First Legislature (I-2) showed higher associations with them than any other for that period. It was evidently not simply a reflection of the deputies' particular electoral situations, but involved a general issue, in a way that the question of single-member districts in 1955 (Scale II-6) did not. Associated with all these scales, but to a lesser degree,[30] was Scale III-1 (Algeria), which included the vote on which Bourgès-Maunoury fell. This scale was most closely related to the Moderates' action in bringing down cabinets in the Third Legislature.

The Moderates' scale positions showed less association with the urbanization or religiosity of their districts than those of any of the other parties we have considered. Neither of these variables had any associations (γ) greater than .25 with their scales in any of the three Legislatures.

Another negative finding, perhaps more surprising, concerns the relation between the Moderates' scale scores and the presence of competing lists that took more nationalist stands on Algeria.[31] The proportion of the vote for such lists in Moderate deputies' districts at the 1956 general election was actually associated with the Moderates' *support* for the cabinets rather than opposition. This relation, the reverse of that which some writers have suggested,[32] existed not only for Scale III-3, but also for the more cabinet-related Scale III-1. It is still conceivable that Poujadist and other right-wing pressure influenced the Moderates as the Third Legislature proceeded, but these data cast serious doubt on that relation and it has to be reconciled with them.[33]

In the First Legislature, the Moderate deputies' scale scores were inversely related to those of their MRP district colleagues ($\gamma = -.46$). This inverse relation did not recur during the Second or Third Legislature.[34] Probably the peculiar factor that produced this relation was the alternative, sharply posed for the Moderates in 1948–51, between alliance with the MRP and opposition with the Gaullists. The scales we have selected, for both parties, come from this period and are strongly weighted with this issue. Thus a leftist Moderate would be one who found it easier to ally himself with a local MRP colleague who was on the right wing of his own party. Conversely, in those districts where the MRP deputy had leftist inclinations, the Moderate would have found it harder to espouse a center coalition, locally or nationally.

Why did this negative relation cease to hold after the First Legislature? One reason may have been the lesser importance of Gaullism as an electoral issue to the deputies who were elected in 1951 and 1956. A number of the more pro-Gaullist Moderates moved to the RPF and could no longer be scaled with the Moderates in the Second Legislature. The MRP lost nearly half its seats in 1951, including many that had been won on conservative votes in 1946. The remaining MRP deputies may have included a much smaller proportion with propensities toward alliance with the Moderates. And the Moderates, we shall see below, seem to have been more interested in picking up Radical votes than MRP votes during the Second Legislature.

Our analysis of the Radicals has suggested that they and the MRP were alternative allies of the Moderates, particularly in the Second Legislature. This relation was reflected in part by the Moderates' scale positions, but only in relation to the Radicals. There was a clear association between Moderates' taking positions on the left wing of their party on Scale II-2, and the absence of Radical deputies in their districts. Of the districts represented by Moderates who were on the left of their party, scoring 0, only 32 per cent had Radical deputies; of the districts whose Moderates scored 1, 45 per cent elected Radical deputies; and of the districts whose Moderate deputies were on their party's right wing (scoring 2), 73 per cent had Radical deputies.[35] The percentages of MRP deputies in the same three types of districts were 55, 55, and 73 respectively—a much lower association. To explain this relation we shall test a series of hypotheses about the Moderates' constituency relations.

One reason the Moderates leaned to the left in districts with no sitting Radicals may have been to pick up the unrepresented Radical vote at the next election. This they may well have expected during the Second and Third Legislatures, because it was generally believed that the following election would also be fought under the system of *apparentements*. Under this system, a list too weak to elect a deputy would effectively give all its votes to its stronger allies. The Moderates could thus take advantage of a weaker Radical vote in their districts by an electoral alliance. An ambiguous title for the Moderates' list, acceptable to local Radicals, sometimes helped. This advantage was not so evident in the First Legislature, for another election under PR (as in 1946) would have required the local Radicals to take a secondary place (by withdrawing or taking second rank on a joint list) for the Moderates to benefit from their votes. Moderates' scale positions in the First Legislature seemed motivated more by their relationships with Gaullism or the cabinet at the national level,[36] or by local relations with the MRP, than by constituency combinations with the Radicals.

Although the Moderates in the Second Legislature seemed to have been interested in picking up or retaining small segments of Radical votes, this tendency did not extend to MRP votes to nearly so great an extent. The difference may have resulted from the greater importance of militants in the local MRP organizations: a Radical organization without a sitting deputy might have been more open to local bargaining than a similar MRP organization. Moreover, the Moderates regarded the Radicals as potential allies, while they viewed the MRP more distantly.[37] The Moderates could benefit locally from electoral alliances with strong MRP federations, as we have seen, but these alliances reflected more nearly a relation of equality, and it was less easy for them to absorb weak MRP lists. This inference is further supported by the fact that leftist Moderates were disproportionately likely to have formed electoral alliances with Radicals. This relation was less pronounced for Moderates and MRP.

This difference between Radicals and MRP as possible local allies of the Moderates was also reflected in the distributions of the parties' votes throughout the country. Moderates and Radicals tended to be implanted in different sections of the country, while there was a less negative association between Moderate and MRP strength in the constituencies.

Our analysis has suggested that the Moderate deputies, more than those of any other party, engaged in constituency alliances that were related to their intraparty positions. Both MRP and Radical deputies' positions within their parties were related to whether they had been allied with the local Moderates, though their own positions may have antedated the alliances. The Socialists, on the other hand, took consistent positions that seemed unrelated to their local alliances, with Moderates or other parties.

We have also seen that Moderates may have been a connecting link between the Radicals and MRP in those districts represented by deputies of the latter two parties; the negative association between Radical and MRP scale positions seems related to these parties' being alternative allies of the Moderates. They thus appeared to exchange votes with the Moderates more than with one another. Further evidence that this exchange actually occurred is provided by the vote transfers shown in turnover tables. In the First Legislature the relation did not hold; Radicals and MRP exchanged votes more with one another than with the PRL. In the Second Legislature it did hold; both Radicals and MRP gained *and* lost as much or more from the Moderates as they did from each other.[38] In the Third Legislature (Table 8.6) there was also a suggestion of such a relationship, but it was less clear.

What was cause and what was result in these inter-party relations? That Radicals and Moderates took intraparty positions related to their electoral alliances with each other suggests a reciprocal effect between these two parties. Similar in their structure—"cadre" parties in Duverger's terminology—they seem to have bid for a common clientele in various districts. The relation between Moderates and MRP in the Second Legislature, however, was less reciprocal. We have attributed this difference to the higher membership ratio of the MRP, which was more nearly a "mass" party.

In these terms, we suggest that the MRP took its positions in relation to the district, in creating its local organizations, and then formed coalitions as a result. The Moderates could take advantage of this if they wished, in the form of an *apparentement,* but they could not hope to absorb MRP votes as they could those of the Radicals.

The RPF in the Constituencies

We should expect the constituency relations of the Gaullists, as inferred from their scale positions after they began dividing on roll calls, to have been loose. In its early years, the Gaullist movement was ideological, and the most enthusiastic Gaullists took their stands as a matter of personal conviction rather than because they came from "Gaullist districts"—or conformed to them. Moreover, the electoral prospects of the Gaullists were difficult to predict after the General retired from politics in 1953 and partial elections revealed a decline in the Gaullist vote. In addition, the peculiar ideology of the Gaullists would have attracted and repelled traditional voters at the same time, by virtue of its "center" position on domestic issues combined with nationalism in foreign affairs.

Nevertheless, certain Gaullists may have been marked as on the right by their electoral alliances with the Moderates in 1951.[39] Perhaps those RPF deputies who continued to maintain alliances with local conservative forces throughout the Second Legislature were those same former Moderates, later ARS deputies, who became Moderates again in the Third Legislature.

This hypothesis is difficult to sustain for several reasons. The deputies who exemplified the temporary "marriage of convenience" with Gaullism most fully were Barrachin and Frédéric-Dupont of Paris and Bergasse of Marseille. But *apparentements* were not permitted in Paris and Bergasse did not form one in 1951. Moreover, the RPF *lists* were heterogeneous in individual districts: Frédéric-Dupont ran with Pierre de Gaulle, and Bergasse with Carlini—in each case a combination of a "temporary" Gaullist with a more loyal one whose votes placed him more to the left. The formation of the ARS was by no means a division between districts, but often divided Gaullists in the same district from one another. No less than eleven districts, most of them highly urban, elected two or more Gaullists in 1951, only to find them divided into URAS and ARS by 1955.

We conclude that the RPF in 1951 was still quite heterogeneous in its clientele; in this respect its deputies' later votes support the evidence of the turnover tables. Those deputies who wanted to build a base of electoral support for the next election tended to concentrate on a narrower segment of the initially diverse electorate than the RPF had bid for, usually on the right. More of the conservatives managed to retain their seats in the 1956 elections, while the loyal Gaullists were temporarily eclipsed.

Militants, Ideology, and District Influence

If cabinet instability reflected divisions in the constituencies, these divisions were more likely to make themselves felt through elections than through the positions taken within the parties by the deputies after their election. The parties that divided internally in accordance with social and religious differences among constituencies were not those that brought most cabinets down; and the scales most closely related to the fate of cabinets

were not always the ones that showed the greatest continuity and constituency influence. Continuous intraparty divisions existed on the most important scales, and were least related to constituency alliances, in the parties
with the highest membership ratios—the Socialists and MRP. The features
of the districts that seem to have held their deputies' positions stable, however, were not the general social and economic characteristics of their districts so much as the particular positions taken by their local militants.

The one party whose district delegations divided most consistently from
one another in relation to social and economic characteristics of the districts
was the MRP; and of all the parties, it was the one that supported the
cabinets most consistently. The Pinay cabinet was the only one whose downfall could be charged to constituency pressures on the MRP.

The other parties had consistent internal divisions as well. In the case
of the Socialists, these divisions occurred on the same issues that were said
to have divided deputies from militants; but no easy geographical explanation accounts well for the stands taken by individual deputies and federations. The personal and political histories of some of the senior Socialist
leaders may in fact go farther toward explaining these differences than do
the social characteristics of their districts. An example is the antagonism
between Daniel Mayer and Guy Mollet.

The Moderates brought down all three major cabinets in the Third
Legislature, and the divisions on which they did so are well represented by
Scale III-1. Insofar as the constituencies were beginning to be divided on the
Algerian issue, it is conceivable that the Moderates' split reflected divisions
in public opinion. Such a division would not, however, have necessarily
corresponded to the characteristic divisions between "static" and "dynamic"
France or to other lasting divisions that have been blamed for government
immobility; and the Moderates' opposition to the cabinet was not related to
the strength of extreme nationalist groups in their districts.

The Gaullists contributed to the downfall of several cabinets from 1953
through 1955; but this resulted more from the intransigence of the loyal
Gaullists than from the acts of the ARS, who (while seeking electoral support) tended to back the conservative cabinets of that period. One cannot,
therefore, charge the Gaullists' effect on cabinet instability to the splintering of the party by constituency pressures or the quest for electoral advantage.

The Radicals' scales divided into two distinct groups: those showing
continuity, reflecting the religious issue; and those showing less continuity,
reflecting cabinet coalitions. The changes in alignment of the party, from
one cabinet-related scale to another, furnish an indication that these scales
represented something other than a contest between constituency interests.

Insofar as divisions among ordinary French citizens influenced the downfall of cabinets, therefore, this influence worked primarily through "parliamentary arithmetic," i.e., the distribution of the parties' seats in the Assembly. Ordinary voters do not often vote for legislators in terms of particular
legislative issues,[40] and their ignorance of issues is probably greatest when
the party in question lacks the guidance of a strong and organized body of
militants. The issue-positions that were clearest and most continuous over
time were therefore those of the SFIO and MRP deputies, who were re-

sponsible to active local members; the Radicals were bidding for voters' more than militants' support, and may at the same time have been freer as individuals to play the parliamentary game. The Moderates, while maintaining some continuity in intraparty positions, also related these positions to the electoral situations in their districts.

The parties' internal divisions in the Assembly, even though they did not reflect pressures from the districts as entireties, may still have reflected important divisions among small subgroups within the districts: the political activists. While the ordinary French voter under the Fourth Republic was no more politicized or ideological than the American, French political activists were more conscious of issues.[41] And among the militants in the districts these divisions were undoubtedly more acute than among the active participants included in a survey sample. Thus the ideological aspect of Gaullism, the questions of principle that divided the Socialist party, and the unavailability of the MRP vote to absorption by the Moderates, reflected divisions in the politically active segment of the electorate—divisions that went beyond what Americans are accustomed to.[42] And even though we have observed that the consensus of the parliamentary leaders actually sustained the cabinet (Chapter 7), the divisions among the rank and file, under the influence of local militants, added their weight to "parliamentary arithmetic" in undermining the cabinets of the Fourth Republic.

The relative influence of members and voters in a party was thus associated with its ideological character and, in turn, the network of communication that restrained the party's voters from transfer to other parties. Among the stable parties, the most ideological were those with the highest ratios of members to voters—the Communists and Socialists. These were also the parties whose voters were most closely bound to them.[43] The one exception to this statement was the MRP, which lost more of its voters, even to other stable parties, than did the Moderates. While losing its voters, it held its militants, since the Moderates apparently did not try systematically to absorb the MRP organizations in the districts.

The stable parties with the lowest membership ratios were the Radicals and Moderates. These were the parties whose local organizations seem to have been most susceptible to a takeover by another party—the Radicals by the Moderates, and the Moderates by the Radicals in the Southwest or by the Gaullists. As long as the local support of a party was largely casual and based on the transactions of local *notables*, it could be bargained away or absorbed by a mass movement. In this respect the politics of the less organized parties was reminiscent of the American congressional district, which can be dominated by a sitting congressman even while its voters retain their presidential preferences. A minority organization can atrophy by failing to put up serious candidates rather than by a conversion of its former members to an identification with the local majority.[44] A party with a strong nucleus of local militants—atypical in the United States[45]—is less likely to bargain away its right to contest elections.

In this respect the RPF was only an apparent anomaly. At its peak it had a higher nominal membership ratio than any other party; and even after its division into URAS and ARS, the votes of its deputies revealed ideological concerns. One may suspect that it attracted members with strong political aims and interests, even though these interests ultimately proved to be diverse. The abundance of its membership—even after we discount the statistics—was not, however, a protection against loss of votes, because the vague issues of the *Rassemblement* and the stress on allegiance to the General, as means of recruitment of its members, did not further the organization of stable local federations. The Gaullists of 1947–55 were thus a very heterogeneous party containing strong and diverse ideological tendencies, unlike any of the stable parties. With a high membership ratio, the RPF was an ideological party; but its newness left it heterogeneous and susceptible to internal division, just as the MRP had been before it.

NOTES

1. Williams, *Politics*, p. 232.

2. This principle of selection emphasizes the influence of stable and organized groups at the expense of either general nationwide surges of opinion or specific and temporary protest movements such as those that contributed to the Poujadist vote.

3. See Chapter 7. The measurement of temporal consistency is complicated by the fact that the replacement of one deputy by another is likely to reduce it. This has been shown for the United States in Froman, *Congressmen and Their Constituencies*, Chap. 8; and Anderson, "Individuality in Voting in Congress: A Research Note." Actually, this reduction occurred for Radicals and Moderates but not for the MRP. It might be imagined that we could select scales with greatest constituency influence by choosing those on which the deputies from a given district tended to vote alike. But while district delegations did often vote alike, this principle of selection tends to pick votes on new issues, and to emphasize the votes of parties like the URAS that had weak constituency ties. We infer that bloc voting in district delegations resulted in part from consultation on issues where other guidelines were less clear; see Truman, *The Congressional Party*, pp. 256–260.

4. Converse and Dupeux, "Politicization of the Electorate in France and the United States," pp. 19, 21 (for domestic versus military policy in France); and Miller and Stokes, "Constituency Influence in Congress."

5. The reorientations of the Radicals and UDSR from one Legislature to another were so great that among the scales we have reported for them no set with adequate overall continuity could be found; every available combination of these scales had values of γ as low as .20. For this reason a scale for Radicals alone, dealing with the church-school question, was chosen.

6. This indeterminacy of the cabinet position results from the inclusion of a roll call on the electoral law. If this is omitted, the remaining division on the Reynaud law shows a *negative* association between *ministrable* status and cabinet support.

7. For the scales selected in each Legislature, associations between all possible pairs of the divided parties were examined. Associations were measured by the coefficient gamma, with each district being counted as a unit.

8. I.e., deputies, except for the Socialists, whose positions were classed as "left" or "right" even in some cases when they had no sitting deputy.

9. Only 3 per cent of our *Année Politique* sample of roll calls dealt with agriculture, as against 11 per cent in the random sample.

10. For this purpose we use vote no. 2619 on EDC, and the "de Gaulle" scale as shown in Table 6.6.

11. As indicators of dissent on Algeria we take votes on no. 655 under Bourgès-Maunoury, and the positions of the federations at the June 1957 Socialist congress. See *Le Monde*, 4 July 1957, and *France-Observateur*, 27 June 1957.

12. On the 1955 congress see *Le Monde*, 5 July 1955, and *France-Observateur*, 7 July 1955. The motion passed by 2890 to 52 with 588 abstentions, and only 28 metropolitan federations showed any dissent. On the 1956 congress, see *Le Monde*, 4 July 1957.

13. Sibué (*Le Monde*, 27 June 1953); Badiou (*Le Monde*, 14 July 1949); Margueritte (*Le Monde*, 3 May 1957); Lapie (*Le Monde*, 1 June 1957); and Mme. Viénot was one of a group who broke with the party in November 1956 (*France-Observateur*, 15 November 1956, p. 6). Only these deputies are mentioned because of their "incomplete" records of leftist dissent in the table.

14. *Tribune du Socialisme*, 15 March 1958, No. 3; cited in Coston, ed., "Partis, Journaux, et hommes politiques," 399–400; on PSU organization see also p. 414.

15. The proportion employed in agriculture in the *département*, for example, shows no uniform association with the existence of leftist federations. This situation differs from that found by Raphael Zariski for the leftist faction of the Italian Nenni Socialists; see his "The Italian Socialist Party," 389.

16. Rightist strength is measured by the proportion of the June 1946 vote cast for parties other than Communists or Socialists. This is in keeping with the definition used by Zariski, "The Italian Socialist Party," 385.

17. This is 5 per cent, as against 34 per cent for the rest of the party. The comparison is again with Zariski, *ibid*.

18. As well as Allier, Corsica, and Loire.

19. See Godfrey, *The Fate of the French Non-Communist Left*, p. 43. These exceptions were the more working-class districts of the Paris area, and Duverger notes (*Political Parties*, p. 112) that in working-class SFIO branches the militants were working-class, while in middle-class *quartiers* the militants were not workmen; thus they would have had less trade union experience.

20. The statistics for this election group the UDSR with the Socialists, reflecting a bipolar division of the electorate and a relative weakness of the center.

21. This latter feature was much more noticeable when continuity over time was analyzed by districts rather than by deputies.

22. The effects of this development on the parliamentary party were pointed out by Capelle in *The MRP and French Foreign Policy*, p. 149: "In . . . parties like the MRP, the militants tend to predominate over the parliamentarians for some time." Even when prospective deputies were sent out from Paris on local request, they usually voted so as to conform to their districts; see Munts, *Parties and Parliament in the Fourth French Republic*, p. 8on. See also Yates, "Power, Principle, and the Doctrine of the *Mouvement Républicain Populaire*," 436.

23. This effect was actually more pronounced in the First and Third Legislatures than in the Second. Goguel has noted that the electoral alliances between MRP and Moderates, excluding the anticlerical parties, tended to occur in the traditionally conservative regions; see his *France under the Fourth Republic*, p. 83.

24. This issue was most closely related to party in the voters' minds; see Converse and Dupeux, "Politicization of the Electorate in France and the United States," p. 19. But the Radicals were the only party with a major *internal* division on it.

25. Soulier, *L'Instabilité ministérielle sous la Troisième République*, pp. 398–399; Bardonnet, *Évolution de la structure du parti radical*, p. 59; Duverger, Goguel, and Touchard, eds., *Les Élections du 2 janvier 1956*, p. 489; Williams, *Politics*, p. 104n.

26. Williams, *Politics*, p. 104n.

27. The association (gamma) was − .77 in the Third Legislature, − .35 in the Second, and + .35 in the First. The reversal of sign in the First Legislature may have been due to a less direct connection of the scale with the school question, or to the different electoral system in effect prior to 1951.

28. The latter form of the hypothesis is the one suggested by Goguel; he considers the Radicals' relations with the Socialists to have influenced their decisions whether to seek support on the right; see Duverger, Goguel, and Touchard, eds., *Les Élections du 2 janvier 1956*, p. 489, and Goguel, *France under the Fourth Republic*, p. 82.

29. See Williams, *Crisis*, p. 113.

30. The gammas were .39, .59, and 41 respectively.

31. These are principally the Poujadist lists in the 1956 election, but we also include other lists classified in the official election statistics as "extreme right."

32. Williams, *Crisis*, p. 51, and Chapsal, *La Vie politique*, p. 245.

33. The inverse relation we have found holds only for the IPAS, since only these deputies were scaled.

34. These later associations were only + .16 and + .07, respectively. The numbers of districts involved were 33, 33, and 25 in the three Legislatures.

35. The numbers of districts were 34, 11, and 11 respectively. The association was weaker in the First and Third Legislatures.

36. See Marcel Merle, "Les Modérés," in Duverger, ed., *Partis politiques et classes sociales*, p. 243.

37. *France Indépendante*, 1951, *passim*. The comments of the Independents' newspaper on the Radicals seemed to take that party seriously, while the MRP was a target for both criticism and humor.

38. For exchanges of votes in the First Legislature, see Table 8.4. Our interpretation for the Second is based on Table 8.5 and on two other turnover tables not presented earlier (for August 1953 and August 1954). These three tables permit 12 comparisons of MRP and Radicals with each other and with the Moderates; in ten cases the per cent transfer is less to or from the other party (Radicals or MRP) than to or from the Moderates, and in the other two cases it is equal.

39. Goguel points out that RPF's few electoral alliances were with the right, in regions where the right was strong; *France under the Fourth Republic*, pp. 82–83.

40. Converse and Dupeux, "Politicization of the Electorate," and Miller and Stokes, "Constituency Influence in Congress."

41. Converse and Dupeux, "Politicization of the Electorate."

42. This assertion does not necessarily conflict with Leites' contention that ideologies were less pronounced than some French observers thought (Leites, *On the Game of Politics*); here the comparison is with the United States, rather than with the expectations of the French.

43. Table 8.7. A similar interpretation is made in McLellan, "Ministerial Instability and the Lack of Internal Cohesion in French Parties"; he attributes doctrinal concerns primarily to the militants as against the pro-cabinet factions in SFIO and MRP.

44. See Key, *American State Politics,* Chap. 6. But Key argued that the votes of the "outs" were not coopted by the "ins" prior to the direct primary, while the present analysis suggests that a major determinant of co-optation or absorption is the absence of militants.

45. Those atypical situations in the United States where members are numerous—the Democratic clubs and similar Republican organizations—place limits on bargaining by elected officials; see Wilson, *The Amateur Democrat.*

»11«

Organized Opinion and the Assembly

IN MANY RESPECTS THE ACTION of the Fourth Republic was constrained by the existence of a number of fairly distinct political compartments. Voters did not tend to transfer their preferences from one stable party to another. The more organized parties were given additional stability by their local militants. And these tendencies were reinforced by centralized politics and administration, vertical social relationships, and lack of consensus at the local level.

Yet together with these stable compartments were the periodic surges of opinion that supported movements for drastic change in the system. The surge movements were somehow separated from the stable parties: none of them simply went to strengthen a stable party, as surges or vote-transfers normally do in the United States. Moreover, these movements tended to advocate such fundamental change that they provoked defensive opposition from the stable pro-cabinet parties and their leaders.[1] The radicalism of the surge movements provoked a reflex of defense on the part of the leaders of the pro-cabinet parties, and this defensiveness helped to convince the dissatisfied that there was no hope for the solution of France's problems without drastic change.

This mutual reaction between the stable pro-cabinet parties and the surge movements reflected a lack of response of the parliamentary subsystem to certain kinds of fluctuations in public opinion. If this "system" had been better able to absorb or co-opt political dissent, the dissenters might have had greater confidence in the system.

Types of Opinion and Types of Response

The resistance of the Assembly's leaders to surges of opinion reflected not a general indifference to opinion, but rather a complex selective process. Certain types of opinion changes were indeed reflected in the Assembly: when the cantonal or municipal elections showed a gain for the conservatives, for example, the bargaining situation for prospective cabinet majorities was altered. Moreover, opinions of various interested groups on certain specific issues were well represented, and these groups often had spokesmen sitting in the Assembly. We must therefore distinguish among various sorts of "public opinion" and the Assembly's reactions to them.[2] We shall confine

306

the discussion to organized opinion, expressed through parties or pressure groups, or centering about political leaders.

The essential feature of the surge movements that brought opposition from party leaders was their direct criticism of the actions and policies of a dominant group of *ministrables* who participated in one cabinet after another. De Gaulle's proposals in 1946 for constitutional reform, for example, attacked a complex of principles and interests exemplified by Édouard Herriot. When Mendès-France criticized the Laniel cabinet, he attacked Bidault and his associates; when he chose cabinet members without consulting party leaders his action was taken as a criticism of Mollet as well as of the MRP leaders. These broadside criticisms enhanced the party leaders' opposition to the surge movements. The slow growth of conservative voting strength, however, did not have this effect.

The opinions represented by pressure groups did not threaten the deputies and their leaders in the same way as did the surge movements. Pressure groups, by definition, tried to affect government policy without themselves occupying elective office. They may have sought to reward their friends and punish their enemies at the next election, but they customarily gave the sitting legislators an opportunity first to become their friends. Parties, on the other hand, ran candidates for office. Once a demand, or a movement of opinion, became embodied in a "surge" party, it assumed a different character from the point of view of many sitting deputies. It could no longer be won over by concessions but was a clear competitor for seats in the Assembly. At the same time these movements challenged the justifying principles by which the leaders appraised their own and their associates' action in past cabinets. One possible tactic of compromise was to join the new movement temporarily, then abandon it when it lost momentum; some deputies pursued this tactic with respect to Gaullism and Mendesism. But those who supported these new movements, even temporarily, were not usually the Assembly's leaders. And the leaders' major response to the "surge" movements was resistance, through parliamentary action or infighting in the party councils.

Pressure groups were also received more easily in the Assembly than surge movements because they represented geographical, more than temporal, variations in opinion. The differences in opinion among various localities—in relation to economic interests, the church-school question, and other persistent domestic issues—had easy and direct channels of representation in the Assembly. For each such stable position, there were deputies who considered themselves its representatives and spokesmen, and had close ties with the corresponding pressure group. For some of these issues, the deputy's party position was also allied with that of the pressure group. But even if the issue cut across party lines, a deputy's career could be furthered by his close identification with an interest strong enough in his district to help re-elect him. If he sat on the committee concerned with that interest, his position was further strengthened.[3]

Thus stable geographical differences of opinion—or local interests— were so fully expressed through the Assembly and the parties that they were "built in" to the system. Their representatives may have had to bargain with one another in Parliament and the administration, but they had access to

these decision centers. Even sudden changes in demands by these local interests also found expression in the Assembly.[4] A change in agricultural
prices or a crop failure could bring rapid response from Peasants and others
in the chamber. Increases in the cost of living were reflected in pressure from
the trade unions and the parties with which they were affiliated. And prospective regulation affecting the interests of civil servants or of the recipients
of family allowances found direct channels for advocacy or opposition
through the Socialists or the MRP. If the interest group in question was
not closely affiliated with one or more parties, it might still be effectively
represented by a spokesman sitting in the Assembly, elected on a party list.
Thus representatives of the beet-growers' association, the home distillers, the
truckers, and the steel industry were among those who held seats. Certain
interests, such as that of the private schools, were also represented by associations of deputies.[5] Pressure-group action, or threats of it, often brought
concessions from the cabinet or led a party into opposition.[6]

A surge of opinion represented by a new party, however, or even by an
innovating faction in an old party, met the strongest of resistance. Several
explanations have been advanced for this resistance by the Assembly's
leaders. Probably most fundamental were the Assembly's desire for sovereignty, and the individual deputies' desire for security in office. Demands
that could be channeled through sitting deputies, and which would further
their careers, were welcomed. Demands that would lead to new elections
were regarded as threats. The defense of sitting deputies' seats, the defense
of the system, and the fear of abandonment of North Africa were joined in
the resistance to Mendesism.

A second explanation of why the demands of the "surges" were not
easily absorbed by the cabinet parties was that these demands were too
radical. Disillusion at the performance of the Third Republic in its last
years, as well as hostility to that of the Vichy regime, had led to widespread
hopes of total renovation. De Gaulle as well as Mendès-France wanted fundamental changes. While a limited number of demands in particular areas of
government policy can be absorbed by an existing party, demands for radical
change are harder to incorporate. The very optimism of expectations after
the Liberation may have heightened the disappointment with the Fourth
Republic's actual performance.

A third explanation lies in the personalities and actions of the leaders
themselves—de Gaulle and Mendès-France. Had de Gaulle been more skillful as a party organizer in 1946, or had he refrained from launching the
RPF until 1950, he might have succeeded more easily. Had Mendès made
fewer enemies, or had he moved to reorganize the Radical party while he
was premier, he too might have had greater success.

The failure of the system to absorb these movements was of crucial importance. In a parliamentary or presidential system, one expects that most
surges of public sentiment will encounter corresponding responses in government action. If surges occur without such action, we expect an increasing
disillusion with politics, i.e., a decrease in public support for the regime as
well as the government.[7]

The simplest way to prevent demands from exceeding government action
is to keep the demands low. A stable society, isolated from the impact of

international relations and limited in its rate of social change, may meet this requirement; France under the Fourth Republic did not. Even when certain issues were not brought to the public's attention (European union before 1951), a price was paid for this delay later.

A second way of rendering response commensurate to demand is the development of new policies by existing government personnel. It can take the form, in principle, of action by various agencies of government: local or national, legislation or case-work, private bills or administrative action. But once the demand has become associated with a diagnosis that the existing personnel are intrinsically incapable of responding to it, avenues of this sort are unavailable.

A third way in which a regime can respond to surges of demand is by change in government personnel. It is the inadequacy of this type of response with which we are primarily concerned in this chapter.

The Assembly resisted both dissolution—with the risk that elections would reflect new currents of opinion—and leaders who were popular with the voters. This resistance was manifested in the care with which absolute majorities were avoided at premiers' fall, and the extent to which advocacy of dissolution was counted against prospective premiers. In this sense the consensus that we have demonstrated among the leaders in the Assembly was not simply an agreement concerning the general interest, but perhaps also an agreement on their own personal interests as politicians.

To examine the Assembly's resistance to organized public opinion when this opinion threatened to bypass the deputies themselves, we shall first consider the deputies' reaction to premiers who were popular outside the Assembly. Then we shall consider the organizational obstacles which the deputies and the parties placed before two innovating leaders—de Gaulle and Mendès-France[8]—when they were seeking power but did not possess it.

Popular Premiers and the Assembly

Popular premiers were distrusted. They may have had long terms in office (if they succeeded in being invested), but only because the other deputies could not openly oppose them without themselves risking reprisal at the polls. But the Assembly brought them down when it could, and seemed particularly annoyed when these men (Pinay and Mendès-France) failed to express subservience to the Assembly at their fall. Pinay by resigning too soon and Mendès by trying to assert his position after being overthrown betrayed a feeling of independence from the Assembly's sovereignty, which their colleagues perceived and resented.

During the Fourth Republic, the French Institute of Public Opinion repeatedly asked its national sample, "Do you approve or disapprove of M. —— as Premier?" The responses were classified as approving, disapproving, or "no opinion." A list showing the highest and lowest proportions of approval obtained by the premiers about whom the question was asked is given in Table 11.1. First in the list (ranked in terms of highest approval obtained) was Charles de Gaulle, technically invested as a premier under the constitution of the Fourth Republic. Next were Mendès-France and Pinay, who were generally recognized as having appealed to the public over the heads of the deputies.[9] Next came a series of premiers who held office during the First Legislature—Ramadier, Schuman, Queuille, and Marie—these being the only others whose approval exceeded 40 per cent. Last on the list was René Mayer, appropriately the *"tombeur"* of the popular Mendès-France.

Table 11.1 Public "Approval" of Premiers
(IFOP national sample)*

Premier	Date		Approving	Premier	Date		Approving
de Gaulle	Aug.	1958	67%	Marie	Sept.	1948	41%
	Sept.	1958	60				
	Nov.	1958	73	Bourgès–M	July	1957	19
					Sept.	1957	38
Mendès–	Aug.	1954	62				
France	Jan.	1955	55	Mollet	April	1956	36
					July	1956	29
Pinay		1952**	56				
				Gaillard	Jan.	1958	32
Ramadier	March	1947	50				
	Oct.	1947	19	Bidault	Feb.	1950	29
Schuman	Dec.	1947	46	Pleven	Aug.	1950	23
	Jan.	1948	31		Oct.	1950	26
	April	1948	44				
				Laniel	Feb.	1954	22†
Queuille₁	Sept.	1948	28	Faure₂	March	1955	21
	March	1949	41				
	Oct.	1949	22	Mayer R	May	1953	15

*Premiers are arranged in order of highest per cent approval. Lowest per cent is also given.
**The question was not asked during Pinay's ministry. However, in May 1953, on the retrospective question, "Thinking of the governments we have had since the Liberation, are there any that you wished to fall?" 56 per cent said they had not wished Pinay to fall. This was the only cabinet for which over 50 per cent gave such an answer. See *Sondages*, 1954, No. 4, 45.
†A later issue of *Sondages* gives this figure as 30%.

These results suggest that certain men were clearly more popular than the rest—de Gaulle, Mendès-France, and Pinay. In addition, the figures may indicate a certain increment of support by the public for the regime in its earlier phases, since all the premiers holding office in 1947 and 1948, for whom results are available, ranked high on the list.[10] A gradual attenuation of support may then have occurred, but in this respect the support for the cabinets of the Third Legislature was as great as for the remaining cabinets of the First and Second. The premiers of the Third Legislature were "approved" by between 30 and 40 per cent, while the remaining premiers of the First and Second never received as much as 30 per cent approval.

Somewhat comparable data are available for the United States, since the American Institute of Public Opinion, under Gallup's direction, has asked a similar trend question since Roosevelt's presidency.[11] The proportion approving of Roosevelt ranged from 84 per cent to 50 per cent. When Eisenhower was first inaugurated, 78 per cent "approved" of him, and over his two terms, this figure never fell below 49 per cent. Truman was "approved" by 87 per cent when he succeeded Roosevelt, but in late 1946 his support fell to 32 per cent; and despite a rise to 69 per cent after his re-election, it again fell as low as 22 per cent in early 1952. The range of variation was therefore quite comparable in the United States and France; but in the United States the election of a new president revived public support,[12] while in France this support was revived only for the brief ministries of Pinay and Mendès, until de Gaulle's return to power. Over the same twelve-year period, the average popularity of the U. S. president was generally higher.

The leaders most popular with the public (whether deputies or not) were at the same time those against whom the Assembly's consensus defended itself most effectively. The senior *ministrables*, constituting a sort of "inner club," embodied the informal rules of the chamber and could punish those who broke them. The ideal member of this group, much like the "responsible legislator" in Congress,[13] was one who advanced slowly in his career, compromised rather than manifesting extreme opinions, and was skillful in rounding up support in the corridors of the Palais-Bourbon.

To appeal to the public over the heads of the deputies—and especially over the heads of these leaders—was to commit a double crime. A leader who did this threatened both to rob the Assembly of its sovereignty, after the manner of Gambetta in the 1870's[14] or General Boulanger in the 1890's; and at the same time he threatened the career interests and rules of the ruling group in the Assembly.

Probably the most important consequence of this attitude on the part of the Assembly's leaders was the circumvention of the constitutional provision that an absolute majority be required to bring a cabinet down. Once a cabinet fell in this way, another such fall within eighteen months would permit the dissolution of the Assembly. To be defeated by an absolute majority would then give the falling premier—or another soon after—a power over the deputies that they neither wished nor considered legitimate. Thus it was not merely the incapacity to govern effectively that led so many premiers to resign "prematurely"; it was also the likelihood that if they stood firm against the Assembly they would incur the enmity of their colleagues, on whose good will they depended for places in subsequent cabinets. Because of parliamentary arithmetic, the parties of the center coalition were "condemned to live together," and a division of the prospective parliamentary leaders into two mutually exclusive groups—cabinet and shadow cabinet—was not possible. Thus the interests of these leaders tended to become identified in their eyes with the maintenance of the Republic.[15]

There is ample evidence that the leading *ministrables* opposed both Mendès-France and de Gaulle;[16] but it will be well to consider Pinay in somewhat more detail here. Though popular outside the Assembly, Pinay did not challenge the system quite so openly as did other well-liked leaders.

Many observers recognized in Pinay the most popular premier of the Fourth Republic up to 1952. He was the first premier whom the moving-picture audiences had applauded since de Gaulle.[17] His success in curbing inflation lay partly in the fact that he succeeded in increasing public confidence. Moreover, his popularity was admittedly a factor in the longevity of his ministry, since any deputy or group openly to blame for opposing him risked retribution from public opinion. Unlike his predecessors, he customarily set votes of confidence on Tuesdays, *after* the deputies had returned from their constituencies.[18] As his fall neared, Faucher wrote: "From the left to the right, there are people who would like to bring down the Pinay cabinet, but who are afraid to do it too openly because M. Pinay has become a popular force."[19]

It is less easy, however, to demonstrate that Pinay's popularity outside the Assembly hurt him within the Palais-Bourbon. Various explanations are given for the fall of his cabinet: a coalescence of pro-Resistance forces in opposition to Pinay's association with Vichy; a sudden distrust on the part of the MRP when Pinay showed sympathy for Herriot's and Daladier's opposition to EDC;[20] and the ostensible issue of family allowances on which the MRP left his majority.

Nevertheless, there is some evidence that the *ministrables* opposed Pinay somewhat more than they did other premiers. The MRP, essentially the only party that split on its support of Pinay, failed to show the association of *ministrables* with support for his cabinet that it showed for other cabinets. Its two scales having negative associations with *ministrable* status (II-1 and II-4, Table 7.2) each included four roll calls under Pinay. These negative associations revealed a tendency for the leaders to support Pinay less than a premier of the "system," even though the scale pattern was not destroyed as it was for Mendès-France. At Pinay's fall, moreover, the leaders of the MRP were apparently most active in wishing to bring him down.[21]

The RPF *ministrables* showed a slight tendency to support Pinay—again not so pronounced as for other parties and other cabinets. Pinay's investiture, of course, was due to the defection of certain deputies (the future ARS) who were more willing than the loyal Gaullists to play the "game." But within the future URAS itself, those who served as ministers were also more inclined to support Pinay than were the rank and file of their party.

Pinay's later treatment at the hands of the Assembly did not reveal him to be clearly opposed to the "system"; he participated in several cabinets after his premiership. He did not, however, succeed in being reinvested; considered as a possibility at several succeeding crises, he either withdrew after finding he could not form a majority, or was voted down. When he withdrew from trying to form a cabinet after Mendès-France, the public was apparently disappointed that no popular premier could then be installed and that the Assembly was returning to the men of the "system."[22] in October 1957, however, he was considered to have been playing the "game" too much himself.[23]

The commentaries of the *Revue Politique et Parlementaire* suggest that in the latter part of his ministry Pinay was somewhat farther from the "system" than were other premiers. At one point de Gaulle accused Pinay of excessive solidarity with his predecessors; the commentator noted that Pinay would have liked not to be too close to them, but was exercising some care not to step on too many toes.[24] Later, after enumerating the ideological sources of opposition to Pinay, he notes that ". . . There are also those who cannot admit that Pinay might succeed where they failed. . . . Especially those who cannot accept being excluded, even temporarily, from power and its benefits."[25] Werth also attributes Pinay's fall partly to "his tendency to talk to 'the people' over the heads of Parliament," observing that this sort of appeal had long been unpopular with the deputies.[26] We may conclude, therefore, that while Pinay did not oppose the "system" as much as did de Gaulle or Mendès, he did to some extent and met a degree of opposition on this score that counteracted the benefits of his popularity.

The System Defends Itself: The RPF

In January 1946 General de Gaulle resigned from the premiership that he had held under the first Constituent Assembly, frustrated by the task of governing with the party coalition of that time. After the defeat of the first draft constitution in the referendum of May 1946, he spoke at Bayeux and proposed an alternative constitutional framework. But he failed to influence the constitution that was actually accepted; and by April 1947 he returned to political action, creating the *Rassemblement du Peuple Français*. Originally intended not to be a political party, the movement gradually took form and found itself limited to one part of the political spectrum. It was against this movement that some of the most effective defensive tactics of the "system" were directed.

The RPF opposed the constitution, the parliament, and the "system"; and in his campaigning, de Gaulle resorted to a demagogic appeal, with mass meetings and slogans, that was to be absent in 1958. Many observers identified the RPF as on the extreme right or "fascist."[27] But we now know that de Gaulle never wanted to be a dictator, and that the constitution might have benefited then from revision. Moreover, the Gaullists in the Assembly by no means represented simply the defense of privilege of the propertied classes; Gaullism in 1951 drew many active supporters from the Radicals, the MRP, and various groups in the UDSR, as well as from political amateurs. It was the right wing of the RPF, not the left, that broke Gaullist discipline to support Pinay; and when the remaining deputies were able to vote freely after the General's withdrawal from politics in 1953, they situated themselves in the center of the "social" spectrum, much as the UNR did later.

The essential grievance of many of the Assembly's leaders against de Gaulle in 1947–53 was precisely that he would be freer from their control than they wished. It was the "republican" defense-reflex against authority that united the anti-Gaullist forces and allowed the RPF to be defined as "extreme right." It would have been truer to call the RPF an antiparliamentary party of the "social center"; many French observers recognized this. Yet because de Gaulle wished more power than the parties would grant him —albeit within a constitutional framework—they engaged in a skillful defensive operation that showed the "system" at its best. In constructive, forward-looking policy, the "system" was less successful; but in "republican defense" it changed the electoral system, stabilized the cabinet, shortened ministerial crises, and postponed elections until the Gaullist tide receded.

The embodiment of this tactic of defense was Henri Queuille. Queuille's political biography represented almost perfectly the qualities necessary to become a leader in the "system." Moving steadily ahead throughout the Third and Fourth Republics, he spoke little, made few enemies, combined local interests with national office, and showed a talent for compromise.[28] He was 64 when he first became premier in 1948.

Three times premier as the First Legislature drew to a close, he played a leading part in the elastic defense against Gaullism. Shortly after his first investiture, he moved against de Gaulle by withdrawing an official "honor guard" from him after a violent RPF rally at Grenoble. Later he postponed the cantonal elections, to prevent another striking Gaullist victory such as the RPF had gained in the 1947 municipal elections. Finally, he shepherded the new electoral law through the Assembly, providing for the electoral coalitions that further reduced Gaullist representation in the Second Legislature. His final cabinet, though often divided on the church-school question as well as the electoral law, continued in office up to the elections of June 1951. Perhaps a final anti-Gaullist gesture on his part was to persuade business circles to support the small Pétainist UNIR party, expecting that they would take some votes from the RPF.[29]

Significantly, Queuille was one of the Radicals who joined with Morice to impede Mendès' attempt to remake the Radical party; in the Lyon division of the Radicals in 1956, he was one of the dissident leaders.

A second source of the opposition of the "system" to de Gaulle lay in the general's relations with Édouard Herriot. From the first meeting of these two men after the Liberation, a coolness developed between them which affected the Radicals' subsequent resistance to the RPF: "The France of yesterday and that of today did not understand one another." Herriot, representing the Third Republic, wanted it and his honors under it continued; de Gaulle gave him less deference than Herriot thought was his due. A sharp exchange about military decorations for officers loyal to Pétain set them further apart.[30]

Under the First Legislature, Herriot had several opportunities to use his influence in the Assembly to retard the Gaullist movement. Called by President Auriol to form a cabinet after Marie's fall, he declined but recommended his friend Queuille, who postponed the cantonal elections. And in the spring of 1951, when Queuille was about to leave the chamber after a narrow defeat on the electoral-law bill, Herriot as President of the Assembly quickly ruled that the bill should return to committee rather than be killed. This ruling saved the bill and thus maintained the numerical strength of the center coalition after the ensuing election.[31]

Herriot's stands within the Radical party also turned that party against the RPF. Arguing against Daladier at the Toulouse congress of 1949, he favored continued cabinet participation by the party, wishing to avoid popular movements of protest resulting from disillusionment with parliament.[32] Resigning his presidency of the party in February 1951, he forced the calling of a special party congress at which joint membership in RPF and the Radical party was forbidden.[33]

This opposition did not, however, carry over to Mendesism; rather, Herriot encouraged and assisted Mendès' efforts to remake the Radical party. Thus Mendès' channeling of his surge of popularity through an existing party, while it proved unsuccessful, did benefit from some support among older party leaders.

The leaders of the MRP also joined disproportionately in supporting the postponement of the cantonal elections in 1948. The Fonlupt-Espéraber bill, proposed by an MRP deputy, was a first step in this direction. Among the 33 MRP deputies who opposed it was only one (3 per cent) who held cabinet office in the First Legislature; fifteen of the party's *ministrables* who did not serve in the Marie cabinet (14 per cent) were among those who supported the bill.[34] Similarly, the *ministrables* of the RI and PRL showed a support for the cabinets of the First Legislature, and for the new electoral law, that was not equally shared by their rank and file. Thus the leaders' tendency to support the cabinet corresponded generally to a disproportionate anti-Gaullism during the First Legislature.

The RPF was defeated by the reflex of "republican defense," with the aid of the tactical skill that the leaders of the "system" commanded. But the defeat was also due in part to de Gaulle's timing. Early 1947—just *after* an election—was almost the worst possible time to initiate a new political movement. The law did not require a new election for nearly five years, and de Gaulle's appeals to the Assembly to dissolve itself were heeded only by a small pro-Gaullist minority of the deputies.

The long interval before the 1951 election allowed the Gaullist movement to lose momentum and to reveal its internal contradictions. A diffuse appeal to a wide public cannot easily be maintained for long without an increasing pressure for the movement to take stands on issues. And when de Gaulle did take positions, asking deputies to vote as he directed, he aided the parties to recover their straying members. Not until early 1951 did Herriot feel strong enough to come out against joint membership ("bigamy").

The leaders' opposition to de Gaulle in 1947–53 revealed the identification they made between the "system" and the Republic. De Gaulle learned his lesson. In 1958 the leaders supported him and entered his cabinet, regarding him now as more a defender of the Republic against a possible coup than its executioner. He then proceeded to make almost the same constitutional changes he had recommended in his Bayeux speech.

The System Defends Itself: Mendès-France

Whereas de Gaulle had tried to change French politics from outside the Assembly and outside the parties, Mendès-France operated within both. A deputy before the war, he had been with de Gaulle in London and Algiers; and though he was in de Gaulle's cabinet in 1945, he failed to persuade the General to institute an austerity program. Resigning from the cabinet, he remained in the Assembly, where until 1954 he was a lonely voice complaining that France's goals were out of proportion to her means and that drastic economic reforms were needed.[35] Failing of investiture in 1953, he succeeded in June 1954 after the defeat at Dien Bien Phu had brought home the need for a changed policy in Indochina.

The Assembly acquiesced in Mendès' investiture so that he could liquidate two continuing problems which previous premiers had been unable to resolve—Indochina and the EDC. His success at Geneva (later regarded as a failure by some of his initial supporters) permitted him to move on to the problems of North Africa, German armament, and the French economy. Before he could reach the domestic problems that had been his central concern, however, he was overthrown. Immediately afterward the Assembly shouted down his intended summary speech. In 1955 and 1956 he tried to control and reorganize the Radical party; but by 1957, having failed in this attempt, he was without strength in either the Assembly or the Radical party.

Mendès-France asserted his right to pick his own cabinet members without consulting the party leaders or the leading figures of the Assembly. Even at his unsuccessful investiture attempt of 1953, this choice marked him off from the premiers of the "system." When he finally formed his cabinet in 1954, he followed this principle. He bypassed the Socialists' leadership and thus failed to obtain their participation in his cabinet. He chose two MRP deputies from the rank and file, and they were immediately penalized by their party. But perhaps most significant was his omission of the leading *ministrables* of his own party from his cabinet. His was the first cabinet since July 1948 in which Queuille had not served; nor did any of the other Radicals who had served in four or more of the preceding cabinets of the Second Legislature find a place in Mendès' cabinet.[36]

The mutual disaffection between Mendès and the party leaders had already existed at his unsuccessful try for investiture in 1953. Even then the MRP leaders opposed him, except for those closest to rank-and-file opinion, and Mollet supported him only after being overruled by the Socialist deputies.[37] During his ministry the MRP opposed him nearly unanimously. The Socialists supported him but were kept from participating in his cabinet by a delaying action on Mollet's part. Among the Moderates and Radicals, the *ministrables* tended to oppose him (Table 7.2).

While he was premier, Mendès-France attained unusually high popularity with the public. He gave weekly radio chats (*"causeries du samedi"*), with a special appeal to youth. This appeal led to the recruitment of some young voters to his support; but at the time of his overthrow they did not know whether the Radical party was to be the vehicle for Mendesism.

The crucial defections from Mendès' majority occurred in the Radical party itself. His major enemies were Léon Martinaud-Déplat, administrative president of the party, and René Mayer.[38] Both were closely associated with North Africa,[39] and the outbreak of terrorism in Algeria provoked their opposition; they blamed the increasing unrest in North Africa on Mendès' lack of firmness. Mayer's delivery of the final blow to Mendès illustrated two of the factors in his defeat: hostility to weakness on the Algerian-colonial issue, and resentment of his popularity (Mayer had been the least popular premier).[40] The hostility of these two men to Mendès can also be traced to the relations between their own service in certain cabinets and Mendès' attacks on those cabinets. In June 1953, when Mendès sought investiture, the previous cabinet had been Mayer's, and Mendès made no pretense of following his predecessor's policies. Later in that year, Mendès' attacks on the Laniel cabinet brought him the enmity of Laniel's Minister of the Interior, Martinaud-Déplat.[41]

Mendès' overthrow led him to try to reorganize the Radical party and channel his newly won popular support to it, but his opponents' maneuvers cost him valuable months in this enterprise. First, his party colleague Faure became his successor, and did indeed carry some of Mendès' policies to completion. The choice of Faure made the organization of popular opposition more difficult.[42] But Faure initially took a neutral position in intraparty matters, and at a special party congress in May Mendès was able to win out over Martinaud-Déplat and start reorganizing the party. A "committee of action," in which deputies constituted only a small minority, proposed a series of structural reforms (including the abolition of Martinaud-Déplat's post) which were subsequently approved at a regular party congress in November.

Faure's decision to dissolve the Assembly, precipitating the January 1956 elections, allowed Mendès less time for his campaign than he had expected. The organization of the Republican Front was reduced to a hasty alliance between the Radicals and the Socialists. Mendès gave numerous endorsements, under this banner, to regular Radicals who later became his opponents. A few of Mendès' opponents were defeated, Martinaud-Déplat among them. But the result of the election failed to give Mendès the right to a sufficiently dominant place either in the cabinet (the Socialists outnumbered the Radicals in the new Assembly) or in his party.

The Republican Front won a victory in the 1956 elections, yet this victory was not as clear as it might have seemed. Mendès had seemingly increased the Radical vote markedly in urban areas; this and Poujadism were the major "surges" of that time. But President Coty offered the premiership to Mollet, leader of the largest party in the victorious coalition; the large-scale nullification of the majority provision of the *apparentements* by Poujadism led to a chamber elected almost by proportional representation; the MRP's veto deprived Mendès of the ministry of Foreign Affairs, and he rejected that of Finance. As a vice-premier, with relatively little control over policy, he saw Mollet falter in his liberal Algerian policy and Lacoste ally himself with the Algerian settlers.

While Mendès-France sat helplessly in Mollet's cabinet, he still retained nominal control of the Radical party. At the May 1955 congress, aided by Herriot, he had been elected first vice-president. He had then conducted a series of speaking trips and recruited new members to the party. When he broke with Faure in November 1955, he still had a substantial majority in the party congress. Throughout early 1956 recruitment of new members continued, though these applications were not always received enthusiastically by the local committees.[43] Even though Mendesists had been put in a number of key party posts, they were unable to exercise full control over the departmental federations.

Resigning from the Mollet cabinet in May 1956, Mendès continued to try to keep control of the party. He was met first with the secession of the Morice faction at the Lyon congress in November. He tried to obtain a binding agreement on a minimum of party discipline for the deputies who remained, and seemed to have obtained it at the conclave of Chartres

(March 1957). But at the fall of the Mollet cabinet, even these weakened rules of discipline could not be enforced. Mendès resigned from his party post, knowing he was beaten.[44] The Southwestern Radicals regained control of the party, and in September 1958 Gaillard assumed its leadership.

Perhaps Mendès could not have solved the Algerian problem even had he become premier. The successive revolts of the settlers and the army, starting in 1958, were challenging even for de Gaulle, whose support on the right was far firmer. Yet Mendès was thwarted not merely by the Algerian settlers, but also by the intrinsic character of the Radical party. To take a party that prided itself on its indiscipline—a party whose sources of power were essentially local and diverse—and to try to make it an instrument of policy, was to confront the most elastic and effective defenses of the "system." The same distrust of strong central power which defeated the RPF also deprived Mendès of the vehicle he needed for popularly based power, a reorganized Radical party.

A similarity between the defeats of Gaullism in 1953 and of Mendesism lay in the way certain notables joined each of the leaders, rode out his "surge," and then left him.[45] The PRL deputies who joined de Gaulle in the First Legislature, later left with the ARS and returned to the Moderates, used this tactic. Barrachin, for example, was said to have had great skill in surviving the demise of political parties with which he had been affiliated. And the Southwestern Radicals, who ultimately came to control their party, showed a similar willingness to wait until the Mendesist enthusiasm had subsided before asserting themselves. Queuille actually left the Radical party with the Morice faction in November 1956; but he had come as near as anyone to participating in the downfall of both surges. As the patient leader of the forces of the "system" in 1951 he had drawn the sting of the RPF. Then as Mendès challenged the notables' leadership of the Radical party in 1955 and 1956, Queuille swung into opposition with the Morice group.

In certain respects, de Gaulle and Mendès made very different appeals. De Gaulle favored constitutional reform while Mendès wished to change the governmental style without changing much more of the legal framework than the electoral law.[46] De Gaulle had extensive popular support, while Mendès had fewer voters and very few deputies who were completely loyal to him.[47] And de Gaulle was viewed as a man of the right, Mendès of the left. Yet beneath these superficial differences were deeper similarities. In the long run, constitutional reform may not have mattered so much as changes in the customs of parties and parliament—changes toward which both leaders strove. Even de Gaulle's surge of support was not completely his own, as the defections of deputies and voters after 1952 showed. And finally, neither de Gaulle nor Mendès could clearly be placed on the "right" or "left." The positions of the ex-RPF deputies on issues, as well as de Gaulle's own changes of position on Algeria, revealed this ambiguity; so too did Mendès' "heterogeneous" majority in the Assembly, and his apparent reversal of position from EDC to the Paris Agreements.[48]

Mendesism and the RPF also resembled one another, ironically, in producing effects on the Assembly that were opposite to those they intended. Each wished to break with the immobility of the "system" and institute bold new policies. Yet the legacy each left was another distinct group of votes in the Assembly, governed by strong convictions yet unlike any of the other blocs. The result in each case was to make cabinet coalitions still more difficult and to increase their immobility.

We therefore stress the similarities between these two movements, and between the types of resistance they met from the parliamentary leaders of the Fourth Republic. Both de Gaulle and Mendès-France were innovators; both aimed to strengthen the executive; both chose policies that made unexpected combinations of the left and right, framing them in view of France's real problems rather than party ideologies. And most important, both encountered the persistent and skillful opposition of the leading *ministrables,* and met defeat at their hands.

NOTES

1. The Communist party, of course, had stable support among the voters but was not pro-cabinet. When it moved to oppose the system, as during the strikes of 1947 and 1948, it did so by arousing its own segment of the public rather than a diffuse "public opinion" with a broader social base.

2. Some of the aspects of variation of public opinion in relation to issues and groups are discussed in Philip E. Converse, "The Nature of Belief Systems in Mass Publics," in David E. Apter, ed., *Ideology and Discontent,* pp. 245–246. It is also possible, of course, that a legislative body and its leaders can lead opinion; but the leaders who were most likely to do this were the ones least likely to receive the wholehearted support of the Assembly's "inner club."

3. See Williams, *Crisis,* pp. 246ff. and Chap. 26. This consonance between local interests and legislative specialization is also well known in the United States; but under proportional representation it may have been even greater, through selection of interests that were not so clearly separated geographically.

4. Contrast the responsiveness of the Assembly to Poujadism as a pressure group to its resistance after the group became a party. And in the summer of 1950, the Assembly spent several days on agricultural calamities but did not discuss Korea. *L'Année Politique,* 1950, p. 155; cited in Williams, *Crisis,* p. 375n.

5. On the specific representation of such groups see Ehrmann, *Organized Business in France,* pp. 249ff., and a series of articles by Bernard E. Brown: "Pressure Politics in France"; "Alcohol and Politics in France"; "Religious Schools and Politics in France."

6. See Chapter 7. A major exception to this responsiveness of the Assembly were the demands manifested through Communist-affiliated groups.

7. See Easton, *A Systems Analysis of Political Life,* Part 3.

8. We do not dwell on the system's resistance to Poujadism by invalidating elections because Poujade and his deputies never showed a capacity to govern or to propose serious policies.

9. See for example Fauvet, *La IVᵉ République,* p. 202, and Hoffmann, "Politique d'abord!"

10. Leon Blum's transitional ministry in 1946–47 also seemed popular, since a considerable transfer of voter preferences to the Socialists was noted on a question "Which party would you choose today?" asked at that time; *Sondages,* 1947, No. 5, 49.

11. "Do you approve or disapprove of the way _____ is handling his job as President?"

12. Eisenhower had 59 per cent approval in January 1961, and Kennedy was approved by 72 per cent in February. See also Katz and Piret, "Circuitous Participation in Politics."

13. See Huitt, "The Outsider in the Senate."

14. See Chevallier, *Histoire des institutions politiques,* p. 321.

15. One may conjecture that this identification of a central group with the values of the legislature as such is most likely to occur when there is a fluid set of parties or factions such that certain groups are essential for the formation of every governing coalition. In contrast, a system such as the British clearly excludes from a new governing group those who have held office in the preceding one. In France such a division tended to occur among the electorate but not the deputies.

16. De Gaulle as leader of the RPF was seen as a threat to the Republic, whereas de Gaulle in 1958 was both a means of saving the Republic against armed insurrection and a politically more skillful leader.

17. Ronald Matthews, *The Death of the Fourth Republic,* p. 297.

18. Goguel, *France under the Fourth Republic,* p. 185, and Williams, *Crisis,* p. 232n.

19. Faucher, *L'Agonie d'un régime,* p. 25; see also Williams, *Crisis,* p. 425.

20. For these two explanations see Faucher, *L'Agonie d'un régime,* p. 29, and Fauvet, *La IVᵉ République,* pp. 223–225.

21. *Le Monde,* 17 October 1957.

22. Faucher wrote (*L'Agonie d'un régime,* pp. 145–146): "*L'échec de Pinay survenant après la chute de Mendès prouve aux initiés qu'aucun style gouvernemental nouveau ne sera toléré par las forces occultes qui pèsent sur le Parlement. Jusqu'en 1956, seul pourra gouverner le syndicat des caïds du régime dont l'immobilisme est la vertu première. . . .*"

23. *Ibid.,* p. 214.

24. *Revue Politique et Parlementaire,* 208 (July–December 1952), 197.

25. *Ibid.,* p. 204.

26. Werth, *France 1940–1955,* p. 591.

27. A strong argument to this effect was made by H. Stuart Hughes before the 1951 elections in "Gaullism: Retrospect and Prospect," in Earle, ed., *Modern France.* But see also Werth, *France 1940–1955,* pp. 368ff. Lipset refers to de Gaulle as "a classic conservative" and links his support to that of the Moderates (*Political Man,* pp. 155–156).

28. See de Tarr, *The French Radical Party,* p. 159ff.

29. Isorni, *Ainsi passent les Républiques,* p. 9.

30. Soulié, *La Vie politique d'Édouard Herriot,* pp. 524, 533–534. The latter exchange took place in January 1946, four days before de Gaulle's resignation from the provisional presidency.

31. On the recommendation of Queuille, see *ibid.,* p. 557; on the electoral-law bill, *ibid.,* pp. 558–559.

32. *Ibid.,* p. 563.

33. *Ibid.,* p. 568.

34. See Chapter 4 and Table 7.10. "Opposition" is counted as on the contrived item (1097, 1099, 1112) used in that table.

35. For a summary of Mendès-France's career see Werth, *Lost Statesman*.

36. André Marie, like Queuille, had served in all five; Gaillard, Martinaud-Déplat, and Morice had served in four, as had Pleven (UDSR).

37. Williams, *Crisis*, p. 399n.

38. On the intra-party opposition during Mendès' ministry, as well as during his later attempts to reorganize the party, see Allen, "The Renovation that Failed"; also Bardonnet, *Evolution de la structure du parti radical*, pp. 19ff.

39. See Alain Gourdon, "Le Parti radical," in Duverger, ed., *Partis politiques et classes sociales*, pp. 238–239.

40. Table 11.1.

41. Bardonnet, *Évolution de la structure du parti radical*, p. 19n.

42. See Werth, *Lost Statesman*, p. 186.

43. See Bardonnet, *Évolution de la structure du parti radical*, pp. 48, 51n.

44. This episode is summarized in Bardonnet, *ibid.*, pp. 169–173; see also de Tarr, *The French Radical Party*, pp. 228–231.

45. See Williams, *Crisis*, p. 129.

46. See Allen, "The Renovation that Failed," p. 445.

47. Werth, *Lost Statesman*, p. 191.

48. During Mendès-France's premiership, between September 1954 and January 1955, the public's estimate of his position also changed. At the earlier of these dates, almost twice as many respondents in a national survey judged him to be a "man of the left" as a "man of the right" (31 vs. 16 per cent); while at the latter date, the proportions were nearly equal (24 and 25 per cent). See *Sondages*, 1955, No. 1, 37.

»12«

Basic Problems of the Fourth Republic

CABINET INSTABILITY WAS A MAJOR source of the weakness of the Fourth Republic. This instability, in turn, can be traced to a combination of three characteristics of the Assembly: "parliamentary arithmetic," including the two hundred normally unavailable votes; the multiple ideological divergences among the parties that did enter cabinet majorities; and the custom of resignation by premiers when the Constitution did not require them to do so.

These proximate causes of cabinet instability derived in turn from more remote causes. The distribution of party strength in the Assembly reflected a socially divided electorate, which could be mobilized by party action into voting for a system of multiple and diverse parties. This conversion of social into political divisions was made possible by the political differences among party activists in the districts. Both the multiplicity of parties and their ideological clashes could be traced partly to the centralization of state and society, which politicized problems and channeled them to the center. Centralization not only provided many occasions to overthrow cabinets but was consistent with a political style that was expressed through homogeneous protest groups rather than compromise at the local level. The fixed channels of vertical communication through parties and interest groups to Paris were periodically bypassed by "surge" movements, but these movements were resisted rather than absorbed by the stable pro-cabinet parties.

Our analysis of constituency relations and public opinion suggested that, aside from the surge movements, the general public played a rather passive role in the Assembly's conflicts. Party activists or militants, however, especially among the Socialists and MRP, seemed to pull the parties away from one another; they perpetuated these parties' internal divisions in the Assembly and heightened the dissension in Socialist congresses. The parties with fewer militants left their deputies freer to bargain in the constituencies and the Assembly. This bargaining normally favored the continuance of cabinets in office rather than their downfall. Cabinets so favored by parliamentary leaders were not always those that took the most decisive action; but had they expected, and been allowed, longer periods in office, they might have accomplished more.

In what respects do these aspects of the Fourth Republic constitute problems? If that regime were not so recent, we might view its deficiencies with the same detachment as we now regard the Articles of Confederation, which joined the United States loosely from 1781 to 1788.[1] Historical regimes may be diagnosed as examples of more abstract choices, which actual present choices resemble only in part. But even though the Fourth Republic no longer exists, its weaknesses have not been altogether remedied. The Fifth Republic, like the Fourth, may see substantial variations in political practice within the limits set by its Constitution. Deputies who received their political training under the Fourth Republic will be leaders in French politics for some time to come and may influence its practice, as the personnel of the Third influenced the practice of the Fourth. Centralization and social divisions have not disappeared, though they may be slowly changing. Thus France must still face many of the problems that she confronted during the Fourth Republic.

In considering the underlying causes of cabinet instability, we shall move from the more to the less manipulable.[2] The former are characteristically those to which French critics of the Fourth Republic have directed most attention: they included centralization, the Assembly's rules, and the parliamentary system itself.

Despite the importance of parliamentary institutions in the very definition of cabinet instability, we shall not consider the alternative of presidential government. A detailed comparison with the experience of the Fifth Republic would be needed, and that experience has depended heavily on its first President. The increase in the real powers of the President of the Republic—even more than in his formal powers—has been a striking change since the Fourth Republic. The direct popular election of the president may also have far-reaching effects. Should this office gain popular support and authority over Parliament independent of its occupant, major changes in the parties and in the public's attitudes might result. But until this occurs, we may continue to regard the problems of the Fourth Republic as of practical interest for France. We therefore consider the causes and remedies for the defects of the Fourth Republic, comparing it only with other variations of parliamentary government.

Within this framework, the principal formal changes proposed have concerned the rules and provisions governing the Assembly and centralization of government generally. Less closely regulated by the laws, but still important, are possible changes in party structure. Farthest from the proposals of French reformers, but nonetheless significant, are changes in ideology or in French national character. As we come to the end of this list, we are more nearly identifying "causes" than possible remedies, since they change so slowly and are so little open to voluntary alteration.

The Rules Governing the Assembly

The formal conditions under which the Assembly operated were altered both by the constitution of the Fifth Republic and by the new rules that the Assembly adopted in 1959.[3] Many of these changes aimed at reducing cabinet instability and increasing the effectiveness of government. They incorporated remedies for many of the alleged faults revealed by diagnoses of the Fourth Republic.

The major changes made by the new constitution concerning parliament were in the conditions for overthrow of the cabinet and dissolution of the

Assembly. An absolute majority against the cabinet on a vote of censure is now required to ovethrow the cabinet. The vote of censure originates from the Assembly, but may be put if the cabinet engages its existence on a piece of legislation. Moreover, the President of the Republic can now dissolve the Assembly.

Probably the most important effect of these changes is to facilitate the dissolution of the Assembly. The initiative for dissolution is removed from the fallen premier, and dissolution itself may become more closely linked to the downfall of a cabinet. A change of cabinets without a new election may be less likely, even in the face of parliamentary interests such as developed under the Fourth Republic. The threat of dissolution may thus contribute more to cabinet stability. But if dissolution itself is to produce a clearer majority, the election that follows must reveal a clearer "mandate" than did that, say, of 1956.

Several changes dealt with the general efficiency of the Assembly's operations, against both cluttering the agenda with irrelevancies and the abundance of legislative committees and their entrenched interests. The president of the Assembly was given greater control over debate; the number of committees was reduced; the types of possible amendments were limited; and electronic voting was introduced.[4] These changes are likely to help clear the agenda for important matters. Moreover, the cabinet's bills now have greater priority than before on the legislative calendar.

One change appears, in our analysis, to do more harm than good. This is the provision that deputies who become ministers must relinquish their seats in the Assembly. The Assembly will be deprived of able men, and the cabinet of supporters, in the event that ministers lose their posts before a new election becomes possible. To President de Gaulle, who has shown a preference for men trained outside the Assembly, this loss may not be a disadvantage; but ultimately, when the nation needs responsible political leaders, the restriction will show as defeat.

Even though informed commentators tell of ministers in office plotting to replace their current cabinet with another, our analysis does not support the thesis that *ministrables* outside the cabinet were a major source of cabinet instability. Rather, the rules of the parliamentary game required them to support the cabinet, even if only in their personal interest. The ex-ministers who sat in the Assembly, waiting for a return to the cabinet, supported the cabinet more in their votes than did the rank and file of their own parliamentary groups.

As regards the undermining of cabinets from within, the reform might appear more useful. Deputies will think more carefully before entering an ephemeral and tenuous combination. The cabinets formed will presumably have clearer "contracts." Yet the price of sacrificing valuable parliamentary personnel is severe. Perhaps a cheaper remedy would be to encourage the formation of successive cabinets that did not overlap in membership, i.e., a parliamentary system more nearly on the British model. It would involve, first, eliminating "unavailable" votes from the Assembly—no easy task; and second, rendering alternative cabinet coalitions responsible before the electorate. But if the latter step were taken, and the cabinet's fall automatically brought dissolution, then the reform would be no longer harmful but simply irrelevant.[5]

Centralization

Channeling political demands and issues to Paris and the Assembly has been a continual theme in our analysis as well as in others. Established under the monarchy prior to 1789, centralization has become a matter of republican faith; fear of the local powers has impaired the appeal of decentralization from the Girondins to the present. In 1792 the Girondins were attacked bitterly for wanting to institute a federalism resembling that of the United States. From the ultra-royalists of the early nineteenth century to the Action Française of the 1930's, hostility to centralization was a characteristic tenet of the conservative right. The Vichy régime continued the tradition by instituting regional administrative authority, and thus continued the association of decentralization with the right. Minor moves toward administrative decentralization ("deconcentration") or regional authority were made during the Fourth Republic, and the Fifth has pushed these farther. But there has been scarcely any transfer of political or budgetary authority to local elected representatives.[6]

Leftist advocacy of political decentralization has appeared recently; Brindillac recommended it, and Mendès-France suggested its value for economic development as well as civic participation. Other arguments on nonpolitical grounds might indeed strengthen its support;[7] and possibly wider support will render decentralization more feasible.

Decentralization has aroused the same sorts of concerns in the United States as well. Even though local *notables* in America do not include a nobility or an established church, local economic interests benefit from decentralized government. State government, local government, and decentralized federal administration are all subject to controls from local citizens of status, property, and power who might not be so influential were the same questions decided in Washington.[8]

Yet a striking deficiency of the Fourth Republic, which appears to be remediable, was that the central government was overloaded. Local problems played a part in the parliamentary game, even if they did not often give rise to major roll calls.[9] The deputies' capacity to influence the central administration or the prefects on behalf of local interests was coin of the parliamentary realm. The possibility (and often the necessity) of using Paris to influence the locality carried more problems to Paris, and thus provided more reasons for harassing cabinets and paralyzing their larger action.[10] In this particular sense a *politique du clocher* added its impediments to those resulting from ideology. Some local problems were politicized and added to ideological conflicts; others came to the center simply as bargaining points. Their effects cumulated. Thus any changes in the rules affecting the agenda were palliatives, rather than remedies for this more fundamental problem.

The broader choices confronting France as a whole might have been decided more easily could the local interests have confronted one another elsewhere. Greater powers to regions, *départements,* and merged communes might have kept some problems away from Paris, while providing for their solution and developing a spirit of compromise that might have affected politics and leadership generally. Decentralization might also permit local voluntary groups to interact more with one another, cultivating discussion and perhaps agreement.[11] The change from proportional representation to single-member districts is in fact a step in this direction, for it presses local interests into alliance by denying them separate channels to Paris.

This reduction of the load on the decision center might even have been worth some sacrifice of local justice. Local domination by nobles, notables, and the church—or by the "achieved notables" who have succeeded them[12] —might have been a small price to pay for greater decisiveness of the national government. Moreover, this local dominance, where it existed, might not have been restricted to the conservatives. The left, even the Communists, would undoubtedly have shared in the benefits of increased local autonomy. If there were any way of incorporating the Communist voters in meaningful political participation, perhaps it could have been done more easily in the localities than in the cabinet.

Decentralization appears thus to be a lesser evil. More effective national government, and not simply local support for government, can emerge from the devolution of functions to localities. These localities may not be the idyllic rural communities that some advocates of decentralization have pictured. They sometimes suppress their internal minorities or make policies at odds with those of the nation. Yet unless the efficiency of the central government in processing local demands can increase greatly, the long-run alternative may still be paralysis at the center and general loss of support by the central government.[13]

The Party System

Our analysis (like many others) has suggested that multiple parties with irreconcilable programs constituted a major source of cabinet instability. We might conclude that, if possible, France's party system should be changed. To permit cabinets to govern, stable majorities in the Assembly would be necessary. These might result either from a single disciplined party's gaining a majority, or from a coalition among two or more pragmatic, nonideological parties. Conceivably a coalition among several disciplined parties would lead to stable cabinets,[14] but this seems less likely in view of the ideological incompatibilities of the parties as they existed in the Fourth Republic. A system of multiple disciplined and organized parties, as in Scandinavia, requires a lower political temperature.

Only on rare occasions can there be a significant planned alteration in an established system of political parties. A major wave of public sentiment is needed to establish a new party; we have seen how parties established in this way were resisted. Changes in the electoral system may alter the party balance, but these too are characteristically opposed by the established parties unless they bolster the status quo. Divisions within existing parties may occur, but those that took place during the Fourth Republic did not enhance cabinet stability. Only at the founding of a representative regime, at the first establishment of parties in such a regime, or at certain major crises, can "planning" a party system be seriously considered.

One of France's greatest recent opportunities for party reform came at the Liberation. New institutions were to be formed, new leaders held power, older leaders were at least temporarily discredited. Yet in a few years the innovators were on the outside, and the leaders of the "system" that controlled the Assembly bore an unexpected resemblance to the élites of the Third Republic.

The foundation of the Fifth Republic seemed at first somewhat less auspicious for party reform. De Gaulle assumed the premiership surrounded by dignitaries of the Fourth Republic. The victory of the UNR in 1958 was regarded as a temporary aberration until it was repeated in 1962. In elections other than for the Assembly, the old parties still held much of their support.

Yet the general decline in party strength that took place in the later years of the Fourth Republic and continued in the Fifth may have made some parties more susceptible to change.[15] We have emphasized the part played by district party activists in maintaining distinctions among the established parties. The ordinary voters, however separated they may have been by divisions in the social structure, were not the chief source of divisions among the parties; they were willing to support municipal election lists formed by coalitions among the parties.[16] Nor did the *ministrables* seem to contribute as much to cabinet instability as did the rank-and-file deputies, closer to the local activists. Thus the weakening of the local party organizations in numbers and activity might be at least a necessary condition for party reform. It is not sufficient, of course, because new party organizations must supplant the old. Direct democracy does not appear an adequate solution for France's political problems.[17]

One alternative might be a system of parties engaging in political compromises, free to do so by their relative lack of active members or militants. To move in this direction would be to "Americanize" the French party system. And although a system of compromise and patronage has been viewed with some disdain by Duverger, it has found its supporters on this side of the Atlantic.[18] From this point of view parties of notables, bargaining without ideological commitments or the constraints of militants, would be a solution to France's dilemmas. Unpleasant as it would be to those who favor principles as the basis for party organization, it might have distinct advantages.

The argument in favor of parties of notables and patronage, however, is at best only part of the truth. Its insufficiency results from the fact that it is purely structural and says nothing about what policies and decisions are to result from the compromises, bargains, and deals that such parties foster. Militants join their parties and remain with them—and many voters support them—because they want to accomplish something, or at least express their demands, through politics. Some of these demands, to be sure, would die with the organizations. Others would persist; for example, the demands of certain segments of the population for rights and conditions of life which they consider their due. And if representative government is to make reasonable decisions affecting the many who are outside its constituency, principle and reflection must play their part.

But if French politics can still tolerate ideological parties, it cannot afford to have too many. Another viable alternative would be a system of two principled parties or firm coalitions. The Socialist ministers' vulnerability to their militants' pressure was most acute when their party was one among several members in a heterogeneous cabinet coalition. But if their party could form a cabinet alone, or if an enlarged party of the left could, the pressure for purity might be counteracted by the benefits of access to government and its influence. Even as leader of a coalition, Mollet held his party together in 1956–57 on domestic matters, and the incipient break came only on Algerian policy.

Two alternating parties of principle would require a break with the old habits of the "system"; no group of deputies could then be a permanent part of all cabinet coalitions. While such a group might remain under a system of compromise among undisciplined parties of patronage, its existence is inconsistent with a party system of the British type.

Another condition for the realignment of France's parties is to free the French Communist party or its voters from their isolation. This may not be a major condition for cabinet stability when only a few Communist deputies sit in the Assembly; the *scrutin d'arrondissement,* reintroduced in the Fifth Republic, has reduced their numbers. But the Communists retain a significant part of the popular vote and represent demands that are thus largely sealed off from satisfaction by government action. Moreover, any realignment approaching two-partyism would lead the leftist coalition to seek Communist votes.

A "new left" has long been the hope of French intellectuals, but the existing parties' possession of the leftist voters has prevented any new party from attaining strength. Perhaps the development of a new pole of attraction on the left would permit voters to transcend the bounds created by the Socialist and Communist organizations. If a long period of nonparty government, together with general amelioration in the standard of living of the working class, should weaken the voters' ties to the older leftist parties, perhaps a new coalition could be formed. This coalition might well have a strong membership organization, like the British Labour party. But such a development cannot be an easy or immediate one; the existing party organizations have great powers of resistance.

Another alternative is to loosen the ties that unite the UNR so that it is replaced by several blocs in the Assembly. Various cabinet coalitions might then be formed under the Fifth Republic as under the Fourth. And if France's problems become less onerous, with decolonization past and relations to Europe resolved, then only a moderate improvement on the authority of Fourth Republic cabinets may be necessary for effective government.

Ideology

The conduct of politics in terms of ideologies—elaborate diagnoses of, and remedies for, the political world—has often been attacked as lessening the chance of compromise and reducing support for government policies.

Even the somewhat dilute ideologies of the pro-cabinet parties of the Fourth Republic seem to have undermined cabinet stability. Moreover, the political elements most responsible for the divergences among the parties—the local activists—were also those to whom party principles meant the most. Thus one might imagine that a condition for cabinet stability would be the decline of party ideology as well as organization.

But we have suggested that the decline of organization is only a precondition for replacing the old party system by another. Likewise, the decline of ideology—or of principle—cannot itself solve the problems of policy formation. It might remove some problems from the "political" to the "technical" realm, to be treated merely in terms of means to agreed ends; but many vital problems would remain that could not be depoliticized in this way. Compromise cannot be an end in itself; it is at best a means to some desirable end. And without rational examination of the end, we can never be truly assured that we are in fact approaching it. To a Frenchman, trained in reasoning from first principles, this argument will be obvious. Its very lack of obviousness to some Americans reveals our need for preserving certain "ideological" characteristics that are found in French politics.

We have recommended decentralization, consensus, flexibility, as remedies for some of the persisting sources of the Fourth Republic's troubles. But in doing so, we seek a middle ground between French politics, or French styles of thought, and American. A principled view of the world is conducive not merely to disagreement, but also to coherent policy; to viewing politics in terms of its central issues rather than its peripheral bargains. It may enable statesmen to see beyond the necessities of the moment and pursue policies that will be viable in the long run.

Thus it is the ideologies of factions struggling for supremacy within a cabinet rather than the long-range policies of governments (actual or potential) that we criticize. The problem of the Fourth Republic, in this sense, was too many ideologies; but to discard principle altogether is not an adequate remedy. A two-party system with two coherent alternative policies does not necessarily hinder effective representative government. A highly organized view of the world, held by an individual or a party at any one time, does not necessarily imply deep cleavage or even rigidity. The point at which ideology becomes dangerous to continued political community is precisely the point at which it isolates the parties from one another. As long as persuasion and confrontation are possible, and the political balance may swing from one view of government to another, rational thought *and* continuing political life are both possible.

This criticism returns, then, to the notion of "ideology" itself. A most diversely used word, it has referred to everything from the beliefs of millenarian religious movements to the simple organization of a few consistent attitudes by a voter. But in the sense in which it has been criticized, it has come to mean both a detailed diagnosis of the world and an intensity of feeling that permits no alternatives. Ideology has thus come to mean "extremism," or intolerance of the rules of democratic politics. On occasion ideology has meant "totalism" for French protest movements.[19]

There is no need, however, to link ideology and "extremism" in this way. Ideology as a reasoned view of the world is not inconsistent with tolerance for alternative ideologies in the same political system. The weak ideologies that confronted one another in the Fourth Republic—chiefly those of the Socialists and Moderates—might not have prevented governments from functioning, if one or another had been permitted to govern alone. But the multiplicity of positions on a variety of issues, together with the special majorities required by the unavailability of some two hundred votes, made the strain too great.

National Character

Least susceptible to voluntary change, though not immutable, are those tendencies of a nation's citizens known as "national character." We shall not attempt to delineate French national character, or to distinguish it from American, in full detail.[20] There are, however, two French tendencies that impress American observers and are especially important for politics: the concern with general principles, and the resistance to interpersonal influence. From an American perspective, the French are both principled and impervious to persuasion. The notion that a matter of principle is involved, in fact, is almost equivalent to a Frenchman's saying that he cannot be moved.

Yet principles have two aspects in France. To say that one's position is *une question de principe* implies immobility. But to say that a statement, or a regulation, is true *en principe* implies that it is true only in general, and may be circumvented in particular cases. The latter meaning implies a certain detachment of principles from the actual objects or events that purport to exemplify them.[21] Political differences arose over words, and were reconciled by other words. To find a "formula"—even a meaningless parliamentary resolution with ambiguous phrases for all—was a normal task of the Assembly when a cabinet's policies were in question.[22]

This tendency can hardly have contributed to viable policies. It may indeed have been a source of the Assembly's reputation as a "house without windows." The earlier resolutions on EDC or the framework-laws on Algeria were verbal compromises patched together to maintain majorities in the Assembly.

If it is possible through choice of social institutions to bring political words closer to the matters to which they refer, it might take place in several ways. First, if the legislators are brought more directly into the oversight of the administration of the laws, they might be required to give concrete meaning to legal phrases. The alternative possibility of legislating only in general principles, leaving the details to be filled in by the cabinet or the administration, may have fostered the separation of words from things.[23] Second, the possibility of moving decisions to the localities or regions may increase the chances for decision-makers to see the effects of their action close at hand. Third, perhaps the combination of practical exercises with the general principles inculcated by the French educational system might link theory and practice, symbol and reality, more closely. Whatever advantages these proposals might have are of course not peculiar to France.

The resistance of Frenchmen to interpersonal persuasion is a second tendency often thought to have political consequences. The protection of the individual—an "individualism" of an entirely different sort from the individual enterprise cherished by the American creed—may contribute to France's political divisions. A compartmentalization of the social world has been connected with a logical compartmentalization of the worlds of nature and of ideas, as Gorer has suggested.

> The external world is limited and compartmentalized, both literally and figuratively. The "typical" landscape for Frenchmen is divided into contrasting segments, the greater part of which have been modified by human handiwork. The world of ideas is similarly compartmentalized, and "logic" consists of assigning things and motions to their proper compartments. Correct behavior, which will lead to *bonheur*, demands that the behavior appropriate to a compartment of life be exercised exclusively in this compartment; *malheur* follows inevitably if behavior suitable to one compartment is manifested in another. . . .[24]

The sociological counterpart of this hypothesis, discussed in Chapter 2, is that patterns of association tend to place the individual in groups that have this same non-overlapping character.

We suggested earlier that the lack of consensus in France is a general aspect of its society and results from the combination or cumulation of several norms that protect the integrity of the individual and his opinions. In the first place, fewer attempts at direct face-to-face persuasion are likely to be made, as they may be considered indiscreet.[25] Secondly, when there is face-to-face discussion of matters on which participants differ, the statements made are more likely to be expressive than to be directed at conversion of the other person or at agreement. Finally, even when attempts at conversion are made, they are less likely to be successful in France than elsewhere; the recipient feels that he can maintain his position legitimately.

Psychological experiments have been performed, using subjects in France and other European countries, that demonstrate the first and third norms in this sequence. The first is shown by some of the results of a cross-national experiment by Schachter et al.[26] The experiment was designed to test a complex hypothesis concerning how various conditions influence attitudes and persuasion directed toward a deviant member of a group. We shall ignore the effects of these conditions, and ask only whether systematic differences between France and other countries appeared throughout *all* the experimental conditions. For this purpose we may consider that four parallel and similar experiments were performed in each of four countries—Norway, Sweden, Holland, and France.[27]

In each of the four experiments in each country, a group of six or seven boys were brought together to form a "boys' aviation club." A competition among model airplanes was announced and each club had to decide what kind it would build. One of the boys, a confederate of the experimenter, consistently argued that the club should build a "rather dull glider" while the others were attracted to motor-driven planes. Observers recorded, in coded categories, who spoke to whom. After the discussion, subjects were asked to write down sociometric ratings of one another and to "vote" for the prospective president of the group.

On the sociometric preference scale, the French subjects showed the greatest rejection of the deviate, compared to their preferences for one another, in three of the four types of experiments. Similarly, on the vote for club president, they showed greater rejection of the deviate than the other three nationalities in three of the four experiments.[28] These findings do not support our hypotheses about social pressure in France; indeed they appear at first glance to contradict them, but they make the subsequent findings all the more impressive.

In spite of this rejection of the deviate, the French subjects tended *least* to try to influence him toward conformity. The communication measured was the proportion of task-relevant comments that could be classified as "intense" communications to the deviate. The French subjects were *lowest* in this kind of communication in three of the experiments, though highest on the fourth. In spite of a high private rejection of the deviate, they refrained from exerting social pressure on him.[29]

The second aspect of interpersonal communication we have noted, its expressive character, is difficult to demonstrate from available psychological research. The third, however, legitimacy of resistance to influence, has been shown to occur. Milgram performed comparable experiments with Norwegian and French students on their conformity to others' opinions.[30] In this case the pressure was exerted by the experimenter on the subject. A variation of Asch's classic experiment was used: the subject was asked to judge which of two tones heard through earphones lasted longer. Before his judging he heard the voices of five other "subjects" judging the same pair of tones, and in certain "critical" trials the five other voices judged the relative duration to be opposite from what it actually was. "Critical" trials constituted about half of all the trials in the experiment.

The tendency of French students to conform to the other "subjects" was somewhat less than the Norwegians', and when the judgment was expressed by secret ballot the difference between the two nationalities increased.[31] When a supposed "subject" made a critical remark to a real subject, such as "Voulez-vous vous faire remarquer?" ("Trying to be conspicuous?"), conformity increased in both Norway and France;[32] but while the Norwegian students accepted criticism without comment, more than half the French students made some retaliatory response.

In many respects the students of both nations responded similarly; but the differences between the two groups were consistently in the direction we might expect. This experiment does not prove resistance to social pressure causes French political fragmentation—or, indeed, that the reverse may hold, as Milgram also suggests. But it adds in a precise way to the selective impressions available from travelers. And even though each of these effects— the lesser exertion of social pressure and the greater resistance to it when exerted—is perhaps too small to bear the burden of explanation, they cumulate.

There is another way French society may inhibit personal persuasion: by reducing the number of occasions on which it can legitimately occur. Observation rather than experiment must assess this hypothesis. The centering of many aspects of life in the *foyer* and the family, and the isolation of personal matters from public discourse, may limit unexpected encounters.

But there are well-known situations in which Frenchmen discuss matters of contention—for example, the literary salon or the table of the local café. Siegfried referred to these two aspects of French sociability: "Where [the Frenchman's] family, his business, and his private affairs are concerned, he is reserved and almost impenetrable. In no other country can one feel so utterly alone as in France, where people barricade themselves in their homes as if they were fortresses. Yet these same people are usually charming and even prepossessing if you meet them on neutral ground."[33] To complete the story, we should have to know something of the frequency and content of encounters such as these.

Social Divisions and Political Activity

Many observers have suggested that French "individualism" is at the root of France's political difficulties. Yet even if this should be so, it requires reconciliation with our analysis. For we have attributed the major sources of principled political division in France to local political activists, not to the public at large. Following the findings of Converse and Dupeux, we cannot claim that the ordinary French voter (at least in 1958) was any more issue-conscious or moved by ideology than the average American voter. In fact, the opposite may have been true, for French and American voters were nearly equally involved in politics for a given number of years of education, but the average number of years of education was lower in France.[34] This lesser involvement of the French electorate implies that even if the public was more highly politicized in the early years of the Fourth Republic than in 1958, it was probably no more concerned with political issues than the American public.

We have therefore sought the source of France's political divisions in the attitudes of political activists, who were more politicized than American activists. Moreover, party *membership* was more prevalent in France. This difference, together with the apparently stabilizing effect of a high membership ratio on intraparty positions among the Socialists and MRP, suggested that the militants were of crucial importance for the divisions in the districts.

The divisive aspects of French political life that we have observed are not restricted to the activists, however. Occupational cleavage in survey data and regression analysis of aggregate voting statistics suggested that political divisions extended to the electorate as a whole and were more pronounced than in the United States. These divisions require explanation, in view of the lack of involvement of the average voter.

One possible explanation is that there were relatively fixed and non-overlapping *social* groupings that served periodically as channels for transmission of political information. The division in the village between the followers of the priest and the school teacher,[35] or in the city between bourgeoisie and workers, may not have involved clear political consciousness on everyone's part. But if separate leaders and separate media of communication had access to the different groups, the groups could have been moved to vote in accordance with their "social predispositions."

These mechanisms would permit political predispositions to be "inherited" without the child's actually knowing what his father's political leanings were.[36] A child would then grow up to resemble his parents politically if he remained in their social circles and received the political communications that passed through them. This process would account for the geographical stability of the vote over long periods, which Siegfried, Goguel, and their students have demonstrated.

To assume that these channels of communication account for certain salient characteristics of mass voting in France is also to qualify our observations about resistance to social pressure. We must assume that the resistance occurs especially when pressure comes from *outside* the accustomed circles— or from strangers, as is the case both for the experiments cited and for organized attempts at converting people from one political preference to another by personal influence. Political continuity would then result from the perpetuation of these channels, together with the continuity of the activist groups that send political communications through them.

The existence of social divisions in the community, ready to serve as largely passive channels for political communications, helps to explain another paradox of French local politics. While the small towns are divided on national politics, they often unite on local matters. The leaders of the various parties draw up a joint list, sufficient to get a majority of the votes, and present it to the local voters in an election without serious opposition. The list thus represents a sort of local consensus, but not the same in the American nonpartisan or one-party town.[37] The local joint list has to *combine* (but still preserve) the symbols that command support in the various separate subgroups. Whatever unity or consensus exists is a relation among the municipal party leaders, who work together in municipal affairs. They are not necessarily identical with the federations' militants, who keep the parties apart in the national campaigns.

To summarize, there were two sources of interparty consensus in France: relations among deputies in Paris, and relations among members of municipal (or departmental) councils in the localities. A contrasting source of dissensus were the separate groups of militants, each acting largely on its own members and supporters, directing their activity toward Paris rather than toward other parties in the localities. And there was a large but politically inactive source of votes, the general public, which could be reached normally only through separate and well-defined channels of communication.

This same fixity of group channels of communication, as well as the defensive character of groups, has been inferred by Pitts from the characteristics of the peer group as they develop in the early school years in France. A closely knit group with a defensive reflex he characterizes as a "delinquent community," pointing out that these groups are both stable and uninterested in long-term political change. Even the "surge" movements of French politics find meaning in this interpretation; he suggests that the "peer group must be bypassed rather than bargained with" by these charismatic movements.[38]

If the fixity of political preferences and the lack of absorption of new political movements by the old depended in this way on the existence of separate and defensive social groups, then two separate lines of reform are possible. One is simply reform from the top—reorganization of the party cadres and activists so as to send different communications through the pre-existing channels. This is akin to Debré's diagnosis in *Ces Princes qui nous gouvernent,* implying that it is the political leadership class rather than *nous,* the people, who need reform.[39] In a negative respect this reform has already occurred; throughout the Fourth Republic the political press steadily yielded its place to the nonpartisan press, and the numbers of activists in all parties declined. The Fifth Republic has continued this trend.

The alternative line of reform, however, would be to bring about a less exclusive set of social groupings, permitting political communications to reach competing groups more effectively in places other than Paris. As we have suggested, decentralization might be a means to this end.

If we attribute French political fragmentation to a general lack of interpersonal consensus, we must still consider two possible counterarguments. One is that it is not consensus—expressed in relations among equals—that matters so much as equality or inequality of status itself. It has been argued that what matters about America (seen by French eyes) is equality itself, and that the receptivity of Americans to communications by strangers flows from our basic belief in equality. In these terms, the important difference between France and the United States lies in the prevalence of status differences in France. These status differences may be associated with a certain "vertical" social distance, a more fundamental source of inhibitions on face-to-face communication across social barriers or between strangers.[40]

Coupled with this counterargument is another: that what we are describing are differences between America and Europe, between the New and the Old World, that are by no means specific to France. Were this the case, we could not even attempt to explain differences between French and American government in terms specific to France, for Europe contains many stable democracies that would then share the French lack of interpersonal consensus without sharing her political problems. French visitors have repeatedly observed that America was conformist; but we must also ask whether France is less conformist than her European neighbors.

The most direct rebuttal of these arguments would come from the study of English society. More hierarchical than America, it still seems to have greater tendencies toward consensus or compromise than France.[41] Moreover, other stable European democracies were used for comparison in the studies of Schachter et al., and of Milgram, showing less effective pressure toward consensus in France.

We suggest, although far more detailed comparisons are of course required to prove it, that it is neither authority relations as such nor the peculiar characteristics of the United States that account for the appearance of fragmentation and lack of consensus that French politics and society present to the American observer. Rather, French "individualism" has an independence that requires understanding in its own terms.

There is still time for France to remedy the defects of the Fourth Republic—to avoid falling back into the habits of that period. The Fifth Republic under de Gaulle has solved the Algerian problem and accustomed France to a stable and effective government. It has not, however, linked popular support with the process of government, nor has it provided the systematic testing grounds for political leadership that every representative democracy needs. Opportunities for major reforms occur at times of transition; both the advent of the Gaullist republic and its immediate sequel are such times. Once an organized and skillful political class develops again, it will impose many of its own rules on the political system.[42]

NOTES

1. Their faults were somewhat the opposite from those of the Fourth Republic, but they also led to the incapacity of a nation to govern itself. And even apart from the practical consequences of our study for France, there are similar consequences that the study of a past regime (the Fourth Republic or the Weimar Republic) may have for another present one (e.g., Italy).

2. An important aspect of the French system, as opposed to the American, was precisely the fact that so many fundamental matters were considered as susceptible to change.

3. On the changes brought about by the new constitution, see Hoffmann, "The French Constitution of 1958." On the Assembly's internal rules see Ruzié, "Le Nouveau Règlement de l'Assemblée Nationale."

4. See Ruzié, *ibid.*, pp. 880, 885, 893, 895. But in practice these rules were modified through the political conflict between the Gaullist leadership and the old parliamentary hands; see Charles Roig, "L'Évolution du parlement en 1959," in Guichard-Ayoub, pp. 43–166.

5. Its irrelevance up to 1964 is suggested in Goguel and Grosser, *La Politique en France*, p. 215.

6. The earlier history of this issue is traced in de Tocqueville, *The Old Regime and the French Revolution*, Part II; Stanley Hoffmann, "The Areal Division of Powers in the Writings of French Political Thinkers," in Maass, ed., *Area and Power;* and Chevallier, *Histoire des institutions politiques*, p. 78. Rightist views on the subject are traced in Rémond, *The Right Wing in France*, pp. 53, 242. Decentralization under Vichy is described in Chapman, *Introduction to French Local Government*, p. 25. On the creation of administrative tribunals see Langrod, "The French Council of State;" on the IGAME, Abbott and Sicard, "A Postwar Development in French Regional Government: The Super Préfet." Administrative decentralization under the Fifth Republic is discussed in *Administration traditionelle et planification régionale*, by the Institute d'Etudes Politiques of the University of Grenoble.

7. Brindillac, "Décoloniser la France"; Mendès-France, *A Modern French Republic*, Chap. 9. As regards other arguments for decentralization Joseph Ben-David has pointed out that centralization in France may have accounted for its slower development of science than Germany's; see his "Scientific Productivity and Academic Organization in Nineteenth Century Medicine."

8. See McConnell, *Private Power and American Democracy*. The complexities of decentralization and the myths surrounding it are also discussed in Fesler, "Approaches to the Understanding of Decentralization."

9. See Leites, *On the Game of Politics*, pp. 15f. Also illustrative is the fact that Mendès-France continued his duties as mayor of Louviers while at the Geneva conference on Indo-China.

10. An analogous "overloading of the center" by failure to resolve community conflicts at a level below the community itself is suggested by Coleman in *Community Conflict*.

11. See Mendès-France, *A Modern French Republic*, Chap. 10.

12. See Bartholomew, *The Politics of the Notable*.

13. President de Gaulle has obtained support for his actions through peculiar personal sources. Alternative avenues of support have been suggested, including the simplification of the political choices presented to the voter; see Converse and Dupeux, "Politicization of the Electorate in France and the United States," pp. 22–23. Though such sources of support might mitigate the overloading of the center, they seem unlikely to remedy it in the long run.

14. Suggested by Aron in *France: Steadfast and Changing*, p. 21.

15. Evidences of this susceptibility were the decline in party membership and in the circulation of the political press, as well as the inability of the established parties to persuade their voters to oppose de Gaulle. On this general development see Vedel, ed., *La Dépolitisation: mythe ou réalité;* but in one article in this volume, Rémond suggests that party strength stabilized after 1950 (pp. 89–90).

16. See Kesselman, *French Local Government*.

17. See Ehrmann, "Direct Democracy in France."

18. Duverger, *Political Parties*, pp. 1, 5, 22; and on the other side, Wilson, *The Amateur Democrat;* Daniel Bell, *The End of Ideology;* and other sociologists who have written in favor of "pluralism."

19. See Stanley Hoffmann, "Protest in Modern France," in Morton A. Kaplan, ed., *The Revolution in World Politics*, pp. 72–73.

20. In particular we do not deal with French attitudes toward authority. For a diagnosis of this aspect of French character see Crozier, "La France, terre de commandement," 779–798, and his *The Bureaucratic Phenomenon*, pp. 220–224. Our approach is closer to that of Crozier in "Le Citoyen," esp. pp. 205–211.

21. A general analysis of the separation of words from things has been made by Himmelstrand in *Social Pressures, Attitudes and Democratic Processes*.

22. This is also a function of American party platforms, but is seen less often in American legislative bodies.

23. Max Weber, analyzing the British parliamentary system of his time, saw the training it afforded in administrative oversight as particularly valuable; see *Staatssoziologie*, pp. 71–81. Many deputies felt themselves poorly informed on matters of legislation—perhaps associated with the fact that they were not expected to view legislation as concretely as legislators in other countries.

24. Cited in Métraux and Mead, *Themes in French Culture*, p. 39.

25. This is brought out in Leites, *L'Obsession du mal*, Chapter 19, "Regards interdits." Differences in types of political activity also reflect this norm, as we showed in Chapter 3.

26. Schachter, *et al.*, "Cross-Cultural Experiments on Threat and Rejection."

27. The authors judged that the experimental conditions were not met successfully in England, Belgium, and Germany; they therefore limited their interpretation to the four remaining countries; *ibid.*, p. 428. Most relevant here are the data on p. 421.

28. *Ibid.*, pp. 423, 424. Possibly this willingness to reject deviates in private communications is related to the frequency of anti-minority remarks (and *graffiti*) one encounters in France.

29. *Ibid.*, pp. 426, 427. This may reflect a repression of aggressive tendencies. See Métraux and Mead, *Themes in French Culture*, pp. 112–115; and Mead and Wolfenstein, eds., *Childhood in Contemporary Cultures,* pp. 104ff.

30. Milgram, "Nationality and Conformity."

31. The per cent of conforming responses was 62 vs. 50 and 56 vs. 48 for two initial experiments with twenty subjects of each nationality. In the response by secret ballot the percentages were 50 and 34 for Norwegians and French respectively.

32. The proportions rose to 75 and 59 per cent respectively.

33. Siegfried, *France: A Study in Nationality*, pp. 12–13. The last sentence quoted also suggests a qualification: French sociability and conversation may reflect the persuasive value of oratory or of well-styled speech. See Jesse R. Pitts, "The Family and Peer Groups," in Bell and Vogel, *A Modern Introduction to the Family*, p. 275.

34. Converse and Dupeux, "Politicization of the Electorate."

35. See for example Marcel Aymé's preface to Paul Serant, *Où va la droite?*

36. Widespread ignorance of father's politics was demonstrated by Converse and Dupeux, "Politicization of the Electorate."

37. For an account of local consensus see Kesselman, *French Local Government*. The nearest approach in the United States to this combination of national party symbols may have been the cross-filing system that once existed in California, which often permitted the candidate of one party to win the opposing party's primary. See Pitchell, "The Electoral System and Voting Behavior."

38. Pitts, "The Family and Peer Groups," in Bell and Vogel, *A Modern Introduction to the Family*.

39. Debré, *Ces Princes qui nous gouvernent*. A similar diagnosis is made by Stanley Hoffmann in "Paradoxes of the French Political Community," in Hoffmann, *et. al.*, *In Search of France*, p. 44–50. But this diagnosis attributes political division to leaders generally, rather than specifically to the militants.

40. Crozier, "France, terre de commandement" and *The Bureaucratic Phenomenon*.

41. On the hierarchical character of English society see Lipset, *The First New Nation*, Chap. 7; on cooperation in England relative to France, see de Madariaga, *Englishmen, Frenchmen, and Spaniards*, pp. 19ff.

42. This is a central contention in Lavau, "Réflexions sur le régime politique de la France."

Appendix A
Roll Calls and Data Processing

THE SAMPLE OF ROLL CALLS analyzed in this book consists of two parts: 739 were chosen because of their mention in *L'Année Politique*, and 150 were chosen by random sampling among the remainder. The criterion for selection from *L'Année Politique* was that the roll call be mentioned either in the text or in its appendix summaries (starting in 1950), and that the number of votes *pour* or *contre* be given.[1] These numbers correspond typically to the Assembly's preliminary or uncorrected totals, but are useful to identify the roll calls in the *Journal Officiel*. For the random samples, a table of random numbers was used to select fifty of the remaining roll calls in each Legislature. A list of the roll calls selected, with their page numbers in the *JO*, is given in Table A.2, at the end of this appendix.

The usefulness of this sample depends, in the last analysis, on the choices made by the editors of *L'Année Politique*. There is every reason to believe, however, that their choices of important roll calls agreed with the judgments of most other informed observers. All the roll calls selected by Williams[2] appear in our sample. Of a sample of 63 roll calls selected by Melnik and Leites[3] for study of the Second Legislature, 87 per cent are in our sample. Almost every roll call headlined in *Le Monde* throughout the Fourth Republic is also included; the only notable exception is a period in May–June 1947, which included a major budget vote headlined on June 25. Our random sample, by contrast, includes scarcely any votes in these three categories.

Sample selection involved a choice between costly data processing and the risk of losing important roll calls. As we have shown (Table 3.6), the preponderant majority of the 8550 roll calls conducted under the Fourth Republic were unimportant and unlikely to divide the parties. Had they all been examined, at least a thousand other useful roll calls would probably have been added; our random sample indicated that the Radicals alone would have been divided on this many. However, we felt the proportion of useful information in the more than 7800 other roll calls so small that examining them (scanning on the computer) was not worth the cost of tabulating them all.

Another indication of the adequacy of the *AP* sample was its relatively uniform distribution over the various ministries—a property not shared by any other available sample. This distribution is shown in Table A.1. Out of the 8550 roll calls that were conducted, 739 or 8.6 per cent were mentioned in the *AP,* according to our criteria. For the three Legislatures, the corresponding proportions were 7, 9, and 12 per cent, indicating a slightly increasing emphasis on roll calls by the *AP* as the Fourth Republic continued.

Table A.1 Roll-Call Sample, by Major Cabinets

Premier	Total Roll Calls	AP Sample Total	AP Sample Per Cent	Random Sample
I Legislature				
Ramadier	303	23	(8)	3
Schuman	626	36	(6)	7
Marie	193	16	(8)	5
Queuille$_1$	772	68	(9)	16
Bidault	696	41	(6)	6
Pleven	808	50	(6)	7
Queuille$_3$	747	66	(9)	6
Other	29	15	(52)	–
Total	4174	315	(7)	50
II Legislature				
Pleven	650	45	(7)	11
Faure$_1$	103	20	(19)	–
Pinay	678	73	(11)	5
Mayer	347	24	(7)	5
Laniel	722	40	(6)	12
Mendès-France	293	40	(14)	4
Faure$_2$	554	48	(9)	13
Other	29	12	(41)	–
Total	3376	302	(9)	50
III Legislature				
Mollet	568	71	(13)	29
Bourgès-Maunoury	117	11	(9)	10
Gaillard	278	28	(10)	8
Other	37	14	(38)	3
Total	1000	122	(12)	50
Grand total	8550	739	(8.6)	150

Among the major cabinets, the proportion of roll calls that entered the *AP* sample ranged from 6 to 19 per cent. Considerably higher proportions were chosen among the roll calls ("other" in Table A.1) that did not take place under a major (i.e., relatively lasting) cabinet; these involved a high proportion of votes on unsuccessful investitures and it is reasonable to think that more important votes occurred in these intervals (e.g., cabinet crises). One might try to interpret these percentages further, in relation to judgments of the intensity of political activity during particular cabinets (e.g., that of Mendès-France), but for our present purpose it suffices to show that the sample contains no egregious biases for or against particular cabinets, such as would obviously have distorted our interpretations.

For each roll call selected, the positions taken by all deputies were transferred to punch cards, ten cards being required for the approximately six hundred deputies' votes on a single roll call. These data were then transferred to magnetic tape, and the totals of *pour* and *contre* votes on the tape compared with the final official totals in the *Journal Officiel* by means of a computer routine.[4] When discrepancies were found (usually clerical errors, but occasionally errors in the *JO*), they were corrected on tape until the net discrepancy for the *pour* and for the *contre* total was two votes or less. Other indications of error, such as divisions in the cabinet or in the Communist party, were also traced and corrected. The data were then ready for processing.

It was possible for deputies to indicate changes of their votes after a roll call.[5] Such rectifications appear in the *JO*, sometimes immediately after the roll call in question, sometimes a session or more later. Because of the additional labor that would have been involved, only the rectifications appearing immediately after the roll call were incorporated in our data, and the others were ignored.

Table A.2 Roll-Call Sample

Scrutin	JO Page	Scrutin	JO Page	Scrutin	JO Page	Scrutin	JO Page
First Legislature		1948		1039	5838	1377R	364
		520	11	1044	5885	1382	444
1946		527	98	1047R	5889	1383	446
1	57	528	99	1048	5943	1384	447
2	67	529	101	1074R	5978	1391R	522
4	90	531	103	1080	6016	1399	616
6	127	535	109	1097	6159	1415	728
12	285	537	111	1098	6177	1444R	847
14	334	541	187	1099	6178	1448R	852
		555	316	1101	6181	1452	926
1947		558	338	1112	6237	1453	927
20	37	626	1038	1143	6432	1467	1249
21	84	640	1276	1144	6468	1468R	1287
22	85	649	1450	1145	6505	1502	1600
37	297	651	1485	1146	6536	1507	1618
45	417	671	1571	1172	6729	1508	1664
66	929	683	1690	1176	6768	1509	1665
67R*	961	725	2057	1191	6877	1510	1667
72	1037	737R	2294	1194	6881	1511R	1684
101	1473	751R	2460	1199	6915	1533	2068
102	1577	776	2695	1201	6930	1579R	2717
103	1578	783	2704	1210	7206	1584R	2744
122	2133	789	2712	1211	7207	1591R	2809
124	2212	799	2960	1212	7209	1594	2813
131R	2409	804	3091	1221	7383	1602	2927
158	2768	815	3199	1222	7385	1614R	3040
218R	3814	824R	3313	1223	7386	1616	3091
244	4207	830	3423	1224	7387	1618	3094
245	4249	831	3425	1251	7559	1630	3161
277	4561	838	3609	1253	7562	1634	3167
302	4745	839	3611	1276R	7743	1654	3381
304	4748	840	3612	1280	7972	1679	3646
305	4749	893	4404	1282	7974	1690	3797
313	4829	898	4432	1285	7978	1718	3982
314	4861	900	4450	1300	7998	1733R	4087
315	4876	949	4861	1308	8100	1754	4276
316	4989	950	4909	1324	8358	1755	4277
323	5120	951	4947	1340R	8379	1774	4343
324	5129	954	4994			1780	4432
326	5209	958	5084	1949		1785	4467
342R	5366	959R	5085	1351R	156	1790	4513
367	5501	971	5269	1363R	215	1811	4725
387R	5745	986R	5601	1369	331	1847	5103
391R	5750	992	5609	1370	332	1868	5361
432R	6190	1012	5705	1371	334	1869	5362
458	6224	1022R	5800	1372R	335	1870	5364

*"R" indicates a roll call in random subsample.

Table A.2 (continued)

Scrutin	JO Page	Scrutin	JO Page	Scrutin	JO Page	Scrutin	JO Page
1873	5413	2401	3030	3205	9961	3590	2557
1881	5477	2402	3031	3206	9962	3594	2563
1891	5530	2433	3263			3596	2566
1893	5567	2437	3320	1951		3598	2569
1899	5601	2438R	3321	3221	45	3614	2692
1912	5681	2439	3350	3236	156	3616	2721
1916	5824	2444	3399	3254	303	3618	2747
1917	5825	2459	3646	3255	305	3661R	2991
1919	5879	2510R	4245	3256	306	3732	3437
1920	5909	2579R	4833	3270	503	3837	4024
1921	5951	2607	5161	3290	628	3838	4025
1942	6394	2613	5275	3324	875	3839	4027
1949R	6481	2617	5341	3372	1275	3840	4028
1965R	6567	2618	5365	3399	1540	3842	4031
1986	6718	2619	5397	3400	1542	3846	4055
2031	7238	2620	5457	3402	1558	3847	4056
2046	7296	2631	5600	3403	1559	3849	4090
2065	7452	2643	5728	3404	1582	3856	4131
2093	7631	2651R	5817	3405	1584	3862R	4176
2094	7632	2676	6052	3406	1585	3870	4214
2097	7646	2819	7038	3407	1599	3871	4216
		2820	7039	3417	1661	3872	4217
		2821	7041	3419	1694	3873	4219
1950		2822	7042	3425	1735	3874	4220
2111	19	2824	7096	3426	1745	3883	4234
2112	21	2834	7243	3427	1792	3885	4237
2113	22	2836	7312	3428	1825	3901	4261
2148	187	2842R	7359	3429	1836	3923	4390
2150	319	2850	7371	3434	1843	3924	4404
2151	320	2856	7562	3453	1977	3958	4559
2153	323	2860R	7605	3454	1979	3967	4607
2180	731	2884	7758	3455	1980	4006	4794
2192	823	2903R	7852	3462	2016	4007	4795
2193	825	2928	8075	3470	2072	4008	4797
2194	826	2945	8243	3480	2169	4014R	4821
2195	828	2948	8247	3481	2170	4042	4943
2196	851	2960R	8342	3486	2178	4043	4945
2197	853	2985	8455	3489	2182	4046	4970
2198	854	2993R	8512	3505	2271	4047	4971
2203R	916	3003R	8527	3508	2274	4054R	5013
2218	1063	3023	8611	3518	2321	4062	5096
2227	1181	3054	8867	3544	2385	4071R	5213
2243	1360	3118	9294	3554	2503	4087R	5300
2310	1963	3138	9429	3564	2518	4115	5478
2314	2042	3160	9609	3569	2525	4131	5580
2318	2113	3176	9814	3571	2528	4164	5790
2321	2117	3202	9956	3573	2531	4168	5796
2400	3028	3204	9959	3579	2540	4172	5802

Table A.2 (*continued*)

Scrutin	JO Page	Scrutin	JO Page	Scrutin	JO Page	Scrutin	JO Page
4173	5803	361	8233	837	1766	1147	4791
4174	5805	362	8234	838	1793	1159	4938
		410	8475	841	1798	1174	5024
Second Legislature		463	9016	843	1801	1176	5027
		466	9050	852	1823	1214	5374
1	5940	469	9075	877	1969	1215	5391
4	5989	473	9141	879R	1972	1223R	5452
7	6023	474	9143	883	2015	1225	5455
9	6064	482	9182	884	2017	1244	5590
10	6091	501R	9319	885	2018	1269	5658
11	6092	574R	9776	886	2020	1285	5728
18	6200	603R	9965	887	2021	1286	5629
22	6280	612R	10019	888	2023	1303R	5816
28	6347	619	10046	889	2024	1306	5839
29R	6349	621	10070	893	2030	1318	5949
46	6524	626	10116	894	2032	1319	5979
51	6567	643	10185	895	2033	1321	5994
53R	6570	644	10186	899	2081	1322	6081
56	6582			904	2145	1360	6272
69R	6687	1952		922	2292	1370	6390
79	6773	661	102	927	2430	1379	6446
81	6797	671	195	931	2436	1401	6628
92	6823	672	285	947	2597	1445	7008
93	6825	673	318	948	2598	1447	7043
102	6852	676	350	952	2632		
115	6931	679	369	974R	2948	1953	
119	6957	680	371	986	3107	1453	54
121R	7013	688	416	987	3109	1457	138
122	7026	690	419	988	3110	1461	184
124	7029	696	537	989	3112	1469	251
134	7065	700	643	994	3119	1483	458
136	7068	701	645	995	3121	1495R	558
183	7183	709	781	996	3122	1499	564
198	7238	712	793	1005	3242	1501	567
210	7277	715	867	1012	3315	1512	583
213	7282	716	900	1014	3318	1523	634
217R	7311	718	903	1017	3343	1558	844
233R	7497	735	929	1019	3346	1568	906
248	7559	736	930	1048	3620	1576	1013
251	7572	740	936	1053	3656	1584	1059
259	7615	770	1152	1057	3723	1597	1162
266	7697	771	1154	1060R	3773	1612	1275
270	7737	775	1216	1070	3867	1624R	1343
308	7849	776	1254	1086	4151	1646R	1446
310	7867	821	1605	1119	4504	1649	1472
320	7951	830	1680	1121	4507	1654	1523
354	8135	832	1698	1134	4598	1693	1815
359R	8164	833	1760	1146	4789	1695	1818

Table A.2 (continued)

Scrutin	JO Page	Scrutin	JO Page	Scrutin	JO Page	Scrutin	JO Page
1698R	1864	2326	1150	2738	6545	3259	4977
1756	2309	2352	1478	2743	6644	3260	4979
1768	2351	2359	1526	2744	6861	3261	4980
1779R	2492	2368	1613	2745	6862	3262	4982
1784	2532	2382	1754	2748	6867	3263	4983
1798	2807	2384	1757	2749	6868	3264	4985
1799	2843	2387R	1795	2750	6901	3267	5120
1800	2891	2408	2013	2752	6959	3270	5125
1801	2982	2410	2057	2753R	6977	3271	5161
1802	3030	2414	2188	2762	7005	3279	5335
1804	3115	2431R	2287			3280	5337
1807	3170	2436R	2310	*1955*		3281	5344
1812	3207	2453	2412	2785	464	3286	5408
1844	3391	2504	2605	2809	522	3291	5438
1851	3402	2513	2706	2821	782	3292	5439
1867	3498	2521	2888	2822	863	3297	5455
1868	3521	2528	2988	2823	898	3298	5463
1886R	3654	2529	3037	2841	1097	3300R	5494
1906R	3700	2530	3085	2843	1206	3301	5496
1924	3818	2531	3115	2875R	1648	3325	5630
1942	3970	2536R	3220	2881	1703	3326	5632
1943	4209	2553R	3435	2882	1705	3327	5633
1944	4211	2567	3613	2883	1706	3328	5635
1962	4523	2570	3617	2892	1803	3330	5660
1967	4629	2571	3619	2900R	1891	3348	5789
1968	4630	2596	4067	2919R	2101	3355	5843
1970	4633	2597	4069	2922	2106	3361R	5898
1971	4635	2598	4092	2924	2149	3369	5970
1995R	4830	2608	4179	2925	2150	3376	6067
1999	4945	2611	4205	2926	2152		
2000	4947	2617	4370	2927	2153	*Third Legislature*	
2021	5094	2618	4371	2977	2289		
2026R	5183	2619	4473	2985R	2373	*1956*	
2033	5437	2620	4498	2992	2506	2	104
2044	5536	2622	4685	2994R	2509	5R	130
2056R	5619	2623	4740	2998R	2605	6	163
2057	5639	2634	4862	3010R	2792	9	228
2110R	6219	2646	4981	3018	2819	10	229
2116	6276	2649	5060	3038	2991	11	231
2117R	6291	2651R	5085	3040	3053	18	347
2182R	6810	2672	5433	3050R	3220	19	371
2247R	7255	2686	5568	3115R	3580	25R	413
		2691	5615	3151	3596	34	519
1954		2692	5616	3162	3780	35	562
2255	39	2693	5632	3177R	3946	36	564
2263	369	2697	5792	3188R	4029	37	565
2266	374	2716	6116	3232	4559	38	567
2305	788	2737	6543	3246	4580	45R	683

Table A.2 (continued)

Scrutin	JO Page	Scrutin	JO Page	Scrutin	JO Page	Scrutin	JO Page
47R	716	220	3583	539R	1580	745	5410
50	743	227	3735	543R	1727	748	5535
52	843	239	3862	544	1955	762R	5597
53	869	254	4330	568R	2527		
54	871	255	4365	569	2549		
55	872	265	4443	570	2551	1958	
56	874	272	4563	571	2622	772	111
60	1004	278R	4725	573	2678	777	229
64	1039	284R	4800	574	2734	778	231
70R	1151	302R	4929	577R	2845	793	343
82R	1221	303	4931	582	2925	798R	383
84	1324	317	5187	600R	3053	805R	415
85R	1326	320R	5258	608	3131	807	467
86	1389	323R	5371	609	3255	809R	470
96R	1486	344R	5579	613R	3421	813	527
103	1681	350R	5672	623	3495	823	695
104	1683	362	5818	629R	3556	838R	993
105	1684	363	5820	642R	3749	840	1036
106	1686	364	5821	646R	3755	841	1038
118	1807	365	5823	655	3827	846	1338
119	1808	366	5824	665R	3857	850	1390
120	1810	367	5826	668R	3915	873	1506
128R	1921	374	5923	673R	3922	880	1560
138	2049	383R	6035	674	3924	884	1678
144R	2143	387	6195	681	4334	898R	1749
147	2337	396	6283	682	4335	942	1895
151	2453	409	6401	686R	4341	961R	2042
152	2455			687	4411	963	2077
157	2743			690	4467	971	2203
162	2839	1957		692	4578	972	2295
163	2841	419	237	693	4627	974	2385
164	2842	420	239	694	4675	977	2417
168	3030	422R	265	701	4755	980R	2439
171	3057	424R	268	704	4895	983R	2515
184	3141	426R	271	705	4922	986	2521
187	3146	444R	499	706	4951	989	2553
193R	3165	467R	712	709	5095	990	2592
194R	3167	492R	904	710	5096	993	2609
210	3398	513	1219	713	5146	996	2633
211	3400	514R	1220	714	5154	1000	2639
212	3401	522	1351	715R	5194		

NOTES

———◆———

1. A list of roll calls concerned only with the electoral-law controversy, given in an appendix of the 1951 *Année Politique,* was not included.

2. Williams, *Crisis,* pp. 498–501.

3. Kindly furnished by Constantin Melnik.

4. Closely related versions of this and other routines used are described in MacRae, "IBM 1401 Q-Matrix and Editing Programs for Legislative Votes," 324.

5. Lidderdale, *The Parliament of France,* pp. 145–146.

Appendix B
Procedures for Cluster Analysis
and Cumulative Scaling

AFTER THE DATA WERE PLACED on tape and checked for accuracy, we next changed the votes of all cabinet members, as of a given roll call, to the equivalent of "not voting." This change removed any effect that cabinet solidarity might have on the appearance of clusters of votes specific to particular cabinets. If such clusters appeared, they would then be due to the votes of the other deputies in a given party or group of parties rather than to the ministers' votes.

At the same time, the proportion of dissidence within each party was calculated. A computer routine first prepared a cross-tabulation of votes by party groups, and then examined the distribution of votes for each party separately. The dissidence within each party was calculated as the proportion of politically meaningful votes that did not fall in the modal category on the given roll call. On a roll call conducted by the usual proxy voting procedure, politically meaningful votes included *pour, contre,* abstention, and *n'a pas pris part au vote (nppv)*. On a personal vote, the last category was omitted from this classification if all dissident votes were included in it.

A party or combination of parties was then chosen for examination of its vote structure in a given Legislature. The principal choice made here was of the four major pro-cabinet parties: Moderates, Radicals, MRP, Socialists; the Gaullists in the Second Legislature were also included. But for the first two of these, more than one parliamentary group was included in the analysis. This was considered useful because the related groups voted similarly in the Assembly and often divided on the same roll calls. A limit to the combination of parties was set by the frequency with which two similar parties (e.g., RI and Peasants in the First Legislature) were divided at the same time. If this frequency was small, the risk arose that the scales for the two parties jointly would reflect coalitions rather than issues. One major scale cluster could be expected to reflect the difference between the parties in question.[1] Other clusters would order the legislators in ways that differed from the first only by the shift of position of one party in relation to another. For this reason, parties that were rarely divided together were analyzed separately, and for those groups of parties that were analyzed together the only roll calls included were those on which both parties were divided.

The basic analysis for each party or combination of parties in each Legislature was conducted for all roll calls with at least 10 per cent dissidence. We made a list of deputies who were members of that party (or set of parties), and no other, during that Legislature, and chose the votes of these deputies on the selected roll calls for computation of the Q-matrix. When two or more parties were analyzed together, a roll call was selected only if each of these parties had at least 10 per cent dissidence, and if the three vote categories with the most votes were the same for all parties.[2] On personal votes, dissidence consisting entirely of the category *nppv* was not sufficient to permit the selection of a roll call for further study, except for the MRP and SFIO, for whom this category sometimes reflected politically significant dissent.

Our analysis of roll-call votes required that each be reduced first to a dichotomy. Occasionally, more than one distinct dichotomy could be used to represent the votes on a given roll call—as when a party had substantial fractions voting *pour, contre,* and abstaining. If the two possible dichotomies had values of p_+ differing by at least .20, both were used. If they did not, the polarity with p_+ nearer .50 was chosen. For each dichotomy, "positive" (rightist) and "negative" sets of vote categories (polarities) were defined. We judged which votes were "positive" largely by inspecting the tabulation of votes by parties; but if this proved to be erroneous, a correction could easily be made at a later stage of the analysis. A few more roll calls were eliminated at this stage, if no politically meaningful polarities could be found which still had at least 10 per cent dissidence; for example, a party with 90 per cent abstention, 5 per cent *pour,* and 5 per cent *contre* would fail this requirement, since *pour* and *contre* were required always to be of opposite polarities. A related requirement was that abstention and *nppv* were never classified into opposite polarities.

Every pair of dichotomies thus selected was compared with every other in a fourfold table, the measure of similarity used being Yule's Q.[3] The reasoning leading to this choice follows that of Goodman and Kruskal,[4] starting from a consideration of the relative frequencies of consistent and inconsistent orderings of pairs of cases on the two variables in question. Although this reasoning can include trichotomies, the operation was restricted to dichotomies because another item might be scalable with "part" of a trichotomy (one dichomization of it) but not with another "part." This property necessitates introducing trichotomies as pairs of dichotomies for complete study of their scale properties.

The index of association Q has the additional desirable property of giving results very similar to those previously obtained by an exponential model in the study of scalability.[5] When the "zero box" is empty, the coefficient is unity. The error allowed by this model in the "zero box" for a given value of Q then varies approximately inversely with the distance between the items. This distance is measured roughly by the proportion in the cell diagonally opposite the "zero box." The use of Q amounts to substituting a hyperbolic function for an exponential one. If we construct fourfold tables that just meet the requirements of the exponential model, with the

++ and −− cells in the table equal in size, then for k = 10, Q varies from .94 to .95, and for k = 5, Q varies from .61 to .69, as the distance between the two items varies from zero to .30. Thus the two models are quite similar, but the use of Q is far more convenient.

The Q-matrix (or its section above the diagonal, since it is symmetrical) was obtained from the computer and used to select clusters of roll calls. A threshold value of Q = .8 was chosen so as to reveal the divisions in the various parties; clusters existing at higher or lower thresholds are also interesting, but they are not considered here because they would complicate the analysis and presentation.

The largest cluster in the matrix, i.e., the largest group of roll calls such that each had a Q of at least .8 with each other, was first sought by inspection.[6] For this purpose, two polarities of a single roll call were counted as one roll call only. After this first cluster was found, the roll calls in it were eliminated from consideration and the procedure was repeated, until no further cluster containing as many as four roll calls could be found. The resulting sets of roll calls (clusters) are those presented in Chapters 4, 5, and 6. If two clusters containing equal numbers of roll calls were found, that cluster with the higher average value of Q was preferred.

This procedure was chosen as a simple and intelligible one that we believe parallels closely the results obtainable by factor analysis. Either the multiple-group method of factor analysis, or principal component analysis followed by oblique analytic rotation, is expected to yield results similar to those presented here.[7] The major difference is that where a general factor exists, its variance is forced largely into our first scale at the expense of subsequent ones.

Each cluster thus defined could be studied in terms of its content (as in Chapters 4, 5, 6) and in terms of the placement of legislators on the corresponding dimension (Chapter 7). For placement of legislators, a procedure was devised that was completely objective and produced scale placements corresponding approximately to the criteria customary in Guttman scaling.

The roll calls in a given cluster were all used in placing legislators. Each roll call was used, either as an item alone, or as part of a contrived item. This procedure eliminated the subjective judgments that might otherwise have been involved in using some roll calls but not others from a given cluster. The assignment of roll calls to items in the scale was made on the basis of their marginals (p_+). The values of p_+ for the roll calls in a given cluster were arranged in decreasing order, and then partitioned so as to produce subgroups of roll calls whose average values of p_+ were separated from one another by approximately .10, where possible. This partitioning was done by the following sequence of steps:

1. Having set an interval of .1, we scanned the marginals in order and marked off a division wherever the interval between adjacent items in the sequence was .1 or greater.

2. The first step divided items into potential intervals that could define contrived items; however, some might be too large. Subgroups whose range of marginals was greater than .15 were further divided, as follows:

3. Procedure for subdivision: We used the extreme values of p_+ in the subgroup, in order to define the range of marginals in the subgroup. We divided this range by 0.1; the quotient, rounded to the nearest integer, was the number of contrived items to be formed from this subgroup. Then the range of marginals was divided by this integer; the quotient was the length of each subinterval. (Normally each such subinterval contained at least one roll call.) We marked off the endpoints of the subintervals in this way, and combined the items between each adjacent pair of endpoints into a contrived item (including as a limiting case a single roll call).

Note: If more than one polarity for a given roll call could fit into the cluster in question, at this point (but not earlier in the process, i.e., not in counting cluster size) a second polarity could be added for the purpose of placing legislators.

4. The subgroups of items separated by the division thus made were the contrived items; any number of items from 1 to the total number of items in the scale could thus enter into a contrived item, and every item in the original cluster entered in some way into the scale.

After the items in the scale were selected in this way, each legislator was assigned an equivalent "vote" ($+$, $-$, or 0) on each item. For a contrived item, this "vote" was determined by the predominant sign of the votes on the corresponding roll calls. Where all responses were "0," or where there were an equal number of "$+$" and "$-$" votes, the resulting "vote" assigned on the contrived item was "0."

The next step was to assign scale scores to the legislators on the basis of their "votes" on the items in the scale.[8] The following procedure was used:

1. We arranged the contrived items in decreasing order of average positive marginals (e.g., as columns in a data matrix whose rows are legislators).

   a. If in the Q-matrix the original assumed polarity had to be reversed relative to the other items in its cluster, then $(1 - p_+)$ was substituted for p_+.

   b. Occasionally it had been found that a set of items scale in an order other than that of their marginals—owing to special distributions of "0" responses—but no such instances have been observed with marginals at least .1 apart.

2. If a legislator's pattern of contrived-item responses consisted of a series of $+$'s followed by a series of $-$'s, we assigned him a scale score equal to the total number of contrived $+$'s. Thus, the smallest score assigned (normally for those least conservative) was 0, and the largest score was equal to the number of items. According to the standards as stated here, the number of items could not exceed 9, and the number of these "perfect scale types," 10 (0 to 9).

3. If the pattern of contrived-item responses consisted only of $+$'s and $-$'s but did not fit condition (2), we examined whether it could be made to fit that condition by interchange of an adjacent $+$ and $-$; i.e., if it consisted of a set of $+$'s, (0 to $n-2$ in number) followed by "$- +$", followed by a set of $-$'s. If this was possible, we assigned the scale score corresponding to the number of $+$'s.

4. If the pattern consisted of +'s and −'s only, and could be made to fit condition (2) by the alteration of a single response (+ to − or − to +), we assigned the scale score that this altered pattern would have (number of +'s after alteration).

5. If more than one response had to be changed to attain a perfect scale type (condition 2), no scale score was assigned (designation "X").

6. If "indeterminate" (o) responses occurred, the response pattern could be classified as "simple indeterminate" (no case of a − followed by a +) or "error-indeterminate" (o *and* at least one − followed by a +).

a. Simple indeterminate patterns. Any "o" followed by a + became a +; any "o" preceded by a − becomes a −. This would either change the pattern to a perfect scale type or make it into:

b. (Sequence of +'s), (sequence of o's), (sequence of −'s). For this type of pattern, we listed all scale types to which it could be converted by alteration of the sequence of o's. If they spanned more than half the possible scale types, we assigned "X."[9] If half or less, we first reconsidered "o" responses resulting from ties on contrived items having two or four roll calls. For each such item, we defined as a "tie-breaker" that roll call with the highest average Q in the cluster. By giving additional weight to the tie-breakers, we assigned the "vote" + or − to legislators on those items where possible. We also did the same for the patterns +o and o− if the o could be resolved by a tie-breaker.

c. We considered all possible scale configurations to which the actual response pattern could be assigned and averaged the corresponding scale scores. We assigned as the score this average, or its rounded value if it contained a fraction other than $1/2$. If the average was a half-integer, we assigned toward the median, i.e., that scale category that contained the median legislator.

d. Error-indeterminate patterns.

1. We corrected a single error in such a way as to change the scale pattern to "simple indeterminate." If this could be done in only one way, we proceeded as in 6b-c.

2. If the error could be corrected in two ways (case 3), we then considered each of these possible scale patterns and treated each as in 6b-c. If the result was a set of possible scale types (considering both ways of removing the error) that spanned more than half the possible scale types, we assigned "X." Otherwise, we would assign the average as in 6b-c.

7. Notation for assigned scale scores: Those assigned by alteration of error or of error-indeterminate patterns were designated by "*"; those assigned by alteration of "indeterminates" alone, by a dagger (†). This notation applied to scores resolved by tie-breakers as well as to those assigned by changing an "o" to a + or −.

This procedure for assigning scale scores was followed not only for the deputies included in the Q-matrix, but also for all deputies who served in the party or parties in question at some time during the Legislature. For this latter group, only their votes cast while members of the party were considered; all others were treated as "o". It was possible to assign scores to a number of additional deputies in this way.

NOTES

———◆———

1. Such dominant scales have been found for the Republicans and Democrats together in the U.S. House of Representatives; see MacRae, "A Method for Identifying Issues."

2. If this condition could be attained with the alteration of a single vote, the roll call was also considered acceptable. The two Peasant groups in the Second Legislature were considered one party for this purpose.

3. Yule, *An Introduction to the Theory of Statistics,* p. 38.

4. Goodman and Kruskal, "Measures of Association for Cross Classifications," 748ff.

5. MacRae, "An Exponential Model for Assessing Fourfold Tables;" also applied in *Dimensions of Congressional Voting.*

6. For Q-matrices that were relatively small (such as those for the Socialists), this procedure was also possible on the computer; routines for performing this search were written by Frank K. Bamberger and Robert Axelrod. But since they used a great deal of computer time, they were replaced by visual inspection.

7. See MacRae, "Cluster Analysis of Congressional Votes with the BC TRY System."

8. The procedure to be described is essentially the same as that used in MacRae, *Dimensions of Congressional Voting,* pp. 321–322.

9. We did not assign "X" to the patterns +o and o— if the "o" could be resolved by means of a tie-breaker (see below). And for tabular presentation, some "X" responses and ambiguous responses were resolved in terms of a minister's votes while in the cabinet.

Bibliography

Abbott, Roger S., and Roger Sicard, "A Postwar Development in French Regional Government: The Super Préfet." *American Political Science Review*, 44 (June 1950), 426–431.

Alford, Robert R., *Party and Society*. Chicago, Rand McNally, 1963.

Allen, Luther A., "The Renovation that Failed: Mendès-France and the Radical Party." *Western Political Quarterly*, 13 (June 1960), 445–463.

Almond, Gabriel A., and Sidney Verba, *The Civic Culture*. Princeton, Princeton University Press, 1963.

Ambler, John S., *The French Army in Politics, 1945–1962*. Columbus, Ohio, Ohio State University Press, 1966.

Anderson, Lee F., "Individuality in Voting in Congress: A Research Note." *Midwest Journal of Political Science*, 8 (November 1964), 425–429.

Andrews, William G., "Swan Song of the Fourth Republic: The Committees of the Majority." *Parliamentary Affairs*, 15 (Autumn 1962), 485–499.

L'Année Politique. Various issues.

Annuaire de l'Assemblée Nationale, 10 November 1946. Paris, Office Française d'Éditions Documentaires, 1954.

Annuaire de l'Assemblée Nationale, II⁼ Législature. Paris, Société Générale de Presse, 1955.

Apter, David E., ed., *Ideology and Discontent*. New York, Free Press. 1964.

Aron, Raymond, *De l'Armistice à l'insurrection nationale*. Paris, Gallimard, 1945.

———, "France: Stability and Instability." *Yale French Studies*, 15 (1955), 17–23.

———, *France: Steadfast and Changing*. Cambridge, Harvard University Press, 1960.

Arrighi, Pascal, *La Corse, atout décisif*. Paris, Plon, 1958.

Association Française de Science Politique, *L'Établissement de la Cinquième République: Le Référendum de septembre et les élections de novembre 1958*. Cahier No. 109. Paris, A. Colin, 1960.

Bardonnet, Daniel, *Évolution de la structure du parti radical*. Paris, Montchrestien, 1960.

Bartholomew, Reginald, *The Politics of the Notable*. Unpublished Ph.D. dissertation, University of Chicago (in preparation).

Bauchet, Pierre, *Economic Planning: The French Experience*, trans. by Daphne Woodward. New York, Praeger, 1964.

Baum, Warren C., *The French Economy and the State*. Princeton, Princeton University Press, 1958.

Beauvoir, Simone de, *The Mandarins*, trans. by Leonard M. Friedman. Cleveland, World, 1956.

Beer, Samuel H., and Adam B. Ulam, eds., *Patterns of Government*. New York, Random House, 1958.

Bell, Daniel, *The End of Ideology*. New York, Free Press, 1960.

Bell, Norman W., and Ezra F. Vogel, eds., *A Modern Introduction to the Family*. New York, Free Press, 1960.

Beltramone, André, "Sur la Mesure des migrations intérieures au moyen des données fournies par les recensements." *Population*, 17 (October-December 1962), 703–724.

Ben-David, Joseph, "Scientific Productivity and Academic Organization in Nineteenth Century Medicine." *American Sociological Review*, 25 (December 1960), 828–843.

Bendix, Reinhard, and Seymour Martin Lipset, eds., *Class, Status, and Power*. New York, Free Press, 1953.

Bettelheim, Charles, and Suzanne Frère, *Une Ville française moyenne: Auxerre en 1950.* Cahiers de la Fondation Nationale des Sciences Politiques, No. 17. Paris, Colin, 1950.

Blanchet, André, *L'Itinéraire des partis africains depuis Bamako.* Paris, Plon, 1958.

Bodin, Louis, and Jean Touchard, "L'Élection partielle de le première circonscription de la Seine." *Revue Française de Science Politique,* 7 (April–June 1957), 299–304.

Bosworth, William, *Catholicism and Crisis in Modern France.* Princeton, Princeton University Press, 1962.

Bottomore, Thomas, "La Mobilité sociale dans la haute administration française." *Cahiers Internationaux de Sociologie,* 13 (1952), 167–178.

Boulard, F., *Essor ou declin du clergé français.* Paris, Editions du Cerf, 1950.

Bourdet, Claude, "La Politique intérieure de la Résistance." *Les Temps Modernes,* 112–113 (May 1955), 1837–1862.

Bourdieu, Pierre, *Sociologie de l'Algérie.* Paris, Presses Universitaires de France, 1958.

Bresard, M., "Mobilité sociale et dimension de la famille." *Population,* 5 (1950), 533–566.

Brindillac, Charles, "Décoloniser la France." *Esprit,* 25 (December 1957), 862–877.

———, "Les Hauts Fonctionnaires." *Esprit,* 21 June 1953), 862–877.

Bromberger, Merry and Serge, *Les 13 Complots du 13 mai.* Paris, A. Fayard, 1959.

Brown, Bernard E., "Alcohol and Politics in France." *American Political Science Review,* 51 (December 1957), 976–994.

———, "Pressure Politics in France." *Journal of Politics,* 18 (November 1956), 702–719.

———, "Religious Schools and Politics in France." *Midwest Journal of Political Science,* 2 (May 1958), 160–178.

Burnham, Walter Dean, "The Changing Shape of the American Political Universe." *American Political Science Review,* 59 (March 1965), 7–28.

Buron, Robert, *Le Plus beau des métiers.* Paris, Plon, 1963.

Campbell, Angus, "Surge and Decline: A Study of Electoral Change." *Public Opinion Quarterly,* 24 (Fall 1960), 397–418.

———, and Homer C. Cooper, *Group Differences in Attitudes and Votes.* Ann Arbor, Survey Research Center, 1956.

———, and Henry Valen, "Party Identification in Norway and the United States." *Public Opinion Quarterly,* 25 (Winter 1961), 505–525.

———, Gerald Gurin, and Warren E. Miller, *The Voter Decides.* Evanston, Row, Peterson, 1954.

———, Philip E. Converse, Warren E. Miller, and Donald E. Stokes, *The American Voter.* New York, Wiley, 1960.

———, *Elections and the Political Order.* New York, Wiley, 1966.

Campbell, Peter, "Discipline and Loyalty in the French Parliament During the Pinay Government." *Political Studies,* 1 (September 1953), 247–257.

———, *French Electoral Systems and Elections.* New York, Praeger, 1958.

———, "French Party Congress." *Parliamentary Affairs,* 10 (Autumn 1957), 413–423.

Capelle, Russell B., *The MRP and French Foreign Policy.* New York, Praeger, 1963.

Centers, Richard, "Marital Selection and Occupational Strata." *American Journal of Sociology,* 54 (May 1949), 530–535.

Chapman, Brian, *Introduction to French Local Government.* London, G. Allen and Unwin, 1953.

Chapsal, Jacques, *La Vie politique et les partis en France depuis 1940.* Paris, Les Cours du Droit, 1960–61.

Chenery, Hollis B., "Patterns of Industrial Growth." *American Economic Review,* 50 (September 1960), 624–654.

Chevallier, J.-J., *Histoire des institutions politiques de la France de 1789 à nos jours.* Paris, Dalloz, 1952.

Chombart de Lauwe, P.-H., *et. al., Paris et l'agglomération parisienne,* Vol. I. Paris, Presses Universitaires de France, 1952.

Churchill, Winston S., *Triumph and Tragedy.* Boston, Houghton Mifflin, 1953.

Coleman, James Samuel, *Community Conflict.* New York, Free Press, 1956.

Colliard, C.-A., "La Pratique de la question de confiance sous la IVᵉ République." *Revue du Droit Public et de la Science Politique,* 64 (1948), 220–237.

Converse, Philip E., and Georges Dupeux, "Politicization of the Electorate in France and the United States." *Public Opinion Quarterly,* 26 (Spring 1962), 1–23.

————, Angus Campbell, Warren E. Miller, and Donald E. Stokes, "Stability and Change in 1960: A Reinstating Election." *American Political Science Review*, 55 (June 1961), 269–280.

Coston, Henry, ed., "Partis, journaux, et hommes politiques d'hier et d'aujourd'hui." *Lectures Françaises*, Special Number (December 1960).

Cotteret, Jean-Marie, Claude Emeri, and Pierre Lalumière, *Lois électorales et inégalités de représentation en France 1936–1960*. Cahiers de la Fondation Nationale des Sciences Politiques, No. 107. Paris, A. Colin, 1960.

Crozier, Michel, *The Bureaucratic Phenomenon*. Chicago, University of Chicago Press, 1964.

————, "Le Citoyen." *Esprit*, 29 (February 1961), 193–211.

————, "La France, terre de commandement." *Esprit*, 25 (September 1957), 779–798.

————, "Pour une Analyse sociologique de la planification française." *Revue Française de Sociologie*, 7 (April–June 1965), 147–163.

Daedalus, "A New Europe," 93 (Special issue, Winter 1964).

Dahrendorf, Ralf, *Class and Class Conflict in Industrial Society*. Stanford, Stanford University Press, 1959.

Debré, Michel, *Ces Princes qui nous gouvernent*. Paris, Plon, 1957.

de Madariaga, Salvador, *Englishmen, Frenchmen, and Spaniards*. London, Oxford, 1928.

Derruau-Boniol, S., "Le Département de la Creuse: Structure sociale et évolution politique." *Revue Française de Science Politique*, 7 (January–March 1957), 38–66.

Desabie, Jacques, "Le Référendum—Essai d'étude statistique." *Journal de la Société de Statistique de Paris*, 7–8–9 (July–September 1959), 166–180.

Dogan, Mattei, "Les Contextes politiques en France," *Proceedings of the Symposium on Quantitative Ecological Analysis in the Social Sciences*, Evian, September 1966 (in press).

Dupeux, Georges, "France." *International Social Science Journal*, 12 (1960), 40–53.

Duverger, Maurice, *Demain la République*. Paris, Julliard, 1958.

————, *The French Political System*. Chicago, University of Chicago Press, 1958.

————, *Political Parties*, trans. by B. and R. North, 2d ed. London, Methuen, 1959.

————, *La VIᵉ République et le régime présidentiel*. Paris, A. Fayard, 1961.

————, ed., *Partis politiques et classes sociales en France*. Cahiers de la Fondation Nationale des Sciences Politiques, No. 74. Paris, A. Colin, 1955.

————, François Goguel, and Jean Touchard, eds., *Les Élections du 2 janvier 1956*. Cahiers de la Fondation Nationale des Sciences Politiques, No. 82. Paris, A. Colin, 1957.

Earle, Edward M., ed., *Modern France*. Princeton, Princeton University Press, 1951.

Easton, David, *A Systems Analysis of Political Life*. New York, Wiley, 1965.

Ehrmann, Henry W., "Direct Democracy in France." *American Political Science Review*, 57 (December 1963), 883–901.

————, "The French Peasant and Communism." *American Political Science Review*, 46 (March 1952), 19–43.

————, *Organized Business in France*. Princeton, Princeton University Press, 1957.

————, ed., *Interest Groups on Four Continents*. Pittsburgh, University of Pittsburgh Press, 1958.

Einaudi, Mario, and François Goguel, *Christian Democracy in Italy and France*. Notre Dame, Ind., University of Notre Dame Press, 1952.

Élections et référendums des 13 oct., 10 et 24 nov. et 8 dec. 1946. Paris, Le Monde, 1947.

Les Élections législatives du 17 juin 1951. Paris, Documentation Française, 1953.

Les Élections législatives du 2 janvier 1956. Paris, Documentation Française, 1958.

Elgey, Georgette, *La République des illusions 1945–1951*. Paris, A. Fayard, 1965.

Etzioni, Amitai, *A Comparative Analysis of Complex Organizations*. New York, Free Press, 1961.

Fabre-Luce, Alfred, *Journal de la France 1939–1944*. Paris, Amiot-Dumont, 1947.

Faucher, J.-L., *L'Agonie d'un régime*. Paris, Atlantic, 1959.

Fauvet, Jacques, *The Cockpit of France*, trans. by Nancy Pearson. London, Harvill, 1960.

————, *Histoire du parti communiste français*, Vol. II. Paris, A. Fayard, 1965.

————, *La IVᵉ République*. Paris, A. Fayard, 1959.

————, and Henri Mendras, eds., *Les Paysans et la politique dans la France contemporaine*. Cahiers de la Fondation Nationale des Sciences Politiques, No. 94. Paris, A. Colin, 1958.

Fesler, James W., "Approaches to the Understanding of Decentralization." *Journal of Politics*, 27 (August 1965), 536–566.

Finer, Herman, *Dulles Over Suez*. Chicago, Quadrangle, 1964.

Fourastié, Jean, ed., *Migrations professionelles: Données statistiques sur leur évolution en divers pays de 1900 à 1955*. Cahiers de l'Institut National d'Études Démographiques, No. 31. Paris, Presses Universitaires de France, 1957.

France Indépendante. Various issues.

France-Observateur. Various issues.

Froman, Lewis A., Jr., *Congressmen and their Constituencies*. Chicago, Rand NcNally, 1963.

Gallagher, Orvoell R., "Voluntary Associations in France." *Social Forces*, 36 (December 1957), 153–160.

Gerth, Hans H., and C. Wright Mills, eds., *From Max Weber: Essays in Sociology*. New York, Oxford, 1946.

Girard, Alain, and Jean Stoetzel, eds., *Français et immigrés*. Cahiers de l'Institut National d'Études Démographiques, Nos. 19 and 20. Paris, Presses Universitaires de France, 1953.

Godfrey, E. Drexel, *The Fate of the French Non-Communist Left*. New York, Doubleday, 1955.

Goguel, François, *France under the Fourth Republic*. Ithaca, Cornell University Press, 1952.

——, "Géographie des élections du 17 juin 1951." *Esprit*, 19 (September 1951), 343–364.

——, *Geographie des élections françaises de 1870 à 1951*. Cahiers de la Fondation Nationale des Sciences Politiques, No. 27. Paris, A. Colin, 1951.

——, ed., *Le Référendum du 8 janvier 1961*. Cahiers de la Fondation Nationale des Sciences Politiques, No. 119. Paris, A. Colin, 1962.

——, and Alfred Grosser, *La Politique en France*, 2d ed. Paris, A. Colin, 1964.

Goodman, Leo A., and William H. Kruskal, "Measures of Association for Cross Classifications." *Journal of the American Statistical Association*, 49 (December 1954), 723–764.

Goreux, L. M., "Les Migrations agricoles en France depuis un siècle et leurs relations avec certains facteurs économiques," *Études et Conjoncture*, 11 (April 1956), 327–345.

Gravier, Jean-François, *Décentralisation et progrès technique*. Paris, Le Portulan, 1953.

——, *Paris et le désert français*. Paris, Flammarion, 1947.

Grosser, Alfred, *La IVe République et sa politique extérieure*. Paris, A. Colin, 1961.

Guichard, Éliane, Charles Roig, and Jean Grangé, *Études sur le Parlement de la Ve République*. Paris, Presses Universitaires de France, 1965.

Gurvitch, Georges, "Social Structure of Pre-War France." *American Journal of Sociology*, 48 (March 1943), 535–554.

Gusfield, Joseph R., "Mass Society and Extremist Politics." *American Sociological Review*, 27 (February 1962), 19–30.

Hamon, Léo, "Introduction à l'étude des partis politiques de l'Afrique française." *Revue Juridique et Politique d'Outre-mer*, 13 (April–June 1959), 149–196.

Hartz, Louis, *The Liberal Tradition in America*. New York, Harcourt, Brace & World, 1955.

Hausknecht, Murray, *The Joiners*. Totowa, N.J., Bedminister, 1962.

Heberle, Rudolf, "A Note on Riesman's *The Lonely Crowd*." *American Journal of Sociology*, 42 (July 1956), 34–36.

Hermens, Ferdinand A., *The Representative Republic*. Notre Dame, Ind., University of Notre Dame Press, 1958.

Himmelstrand, Ulf, *Social Pressures, Attitudes and Democratic Processes*. Stockholm, Almqvist & Wiksell, 1960.

Hodgkin, Thomas, and Ruth Schachter, "French-Speaking West Africa in Transition." *International Conciliation*, 528 (May 1960), 375–436.

Hoffmann, Stanley, "The French Constitution of 1958: I. The Final Text and Its Prospects." *American Political Science Review*, 53 (June 1959), 332–357.

——, *Le Mouvement Poujade*. Cahiers de la Fondation Nationale des Sciences Politiques, No. 81. Paris, A. Colin, 1956.

——, "Politique d'abord!" *Esprit*, 25 (December 1957), 813–832.

——, et. al., *In Search of France*. Cambridge, Harvard University Press, 1963.

Hogan, James, *Election and Representation*. Cork, Cork University Press, 1945.

Hughes, H. Stuart, "De Gaulle in Power." *Commentary*, 26 (September 1958), 185–193.

Huitt, Ralph, "The Outsider in the Senate." *American Political Science Review*, 55 (September 1961), 566–575.

Hurtig, Serge, "La S.F.I.O. face à la Vᵉ République: majorité et minorité." *Revue Française de Science Politique*, 14 (June 1964), 526–556.

Husson, Raoul, *Élections et référendums des 21 octobre 1945, 5 mai et 2 juin 1946*. Paris, Le Monde, 1946.

Institut d'Études Politiques de l'Université de Grenoble, *Administration traditionelle et planification régionale*. Cahiers de la Fondation Nationale des Sciences Politiques, No. 135. Paris, A. Colin, 1964.

Institut Français d'Opinion Publique, "À la Recherche de la 'gauche.'" *Les Temps Modernes*, Nos. 112–113 (May 1955), 1576–1625.

Institut National de la Statistique et des Études Économiques, "L'Enquête par sondage sur l'emploi de juin 1953." *Bulletin Mensuel de Statistique*, 5 (Suppl., October–December 1954), 32–40.

——, *L'Espace économique français*. Paris, Presses Universitaires de France, 1955.

——, (Croze), "Les Migrations d'électeurs de 1949 à 1953." *Bulletin Mensuel de Statistique*, (Suppl., April–June 1955), 1–29.

——, *Recensement général de la population de mai 1954*. Paris, Presses Universitaires de France, 1956.

Isorni, Jacques, *Ainsi passent les Républiques*. Paris, Flammarion, 1959.

Janowitz, Morris, and Dwaine Marvick, *Competitive Pressure and Democratic Consent*. Ann Arbor, University of Michigan Press, 1956.

Jennings, M. Kent, and L. Harmon Zeigler, eds., *Electoral Behavior*. New York, Prentice-Hall, 1966.

Journal Officiel de la République Française, Débats Parlementaires, Assemblée Nationale. Various issues.

Jouvenel, Robert de, *La République des camarades*. Paris, Bernard Grasset, 1914.

Kaplan, Morton A., ed., *The Revolution in World Politics*. New York, Wiley, 1962.

Katz, Fred E., and Fern V. Piret, "Circuitous Participation in Politics." *American Journal of Sociology*, 69 (January 1964), 367–373.

Kesselman, Mark J., *French Local Government: The Politics of Consensus*. New York, Knopf, 1967.

——, "French Local Politics: A Statistical Examination of Grass Roots Consensus," *American Political Science Review*, 60 (December 1966), 963–973.

——, "Presidential Leadership in Congress on Foreign Policy." *Midwest Journal of Political Science*, 5 (August 1961), 284–289.

——, "Presidential Leadership in Congress on Foreign Policy: A Replication of a Hypothesis." *Midwest Journal of Political Science*, 9 (November 1965), 401–406.

Key, V. O., Jr., *American State Politics*. New York, Knopf, 1956.

——, *The Responsible Electorate*. Cambridge, Harvard University Press, 1966.

——, *Southern Politics*. New York, Knopf, 1949.

Kirchheimer, Otto, "The Waning of Opposition in Parliamentary Regimes." *Social Research*, 24 (Summer 1957), 127–156.

Klatzmann, Joseph, "Comment votent les paysans français." *Revue Française de Science Politique*, 8 (March 1958), 13–41.

Komarovsky, Mirra, ed., *Common Frontiers of the Social Sciences*. New York, Free Press, 1957.

Kornhauser, William, *The Politics of Mass Society*. New York, Free Press, 1959.

Lancelot, Marie-Thérèse, "Le Courrier d'un parlementaire." *Revue Française de Science Politique*, 12 (June 1962), 426–432.

Landes, David S., "Observations on France: Economy, Society, Polity." *World Politics*, 3 (April 1957), 329–350.

Lane, Robert E., *The Regulation of Businessmen*. New Haven, Yale University Press, 1954.

Langrod, Georges, "The French Council of State: Its Role in the Formulation and Implementation of Administrative Law." *American Political Science Review*, 49 (September 1955), 683–687.

——, *Some Current Problems of Administration in France Today*. San Juan, University of Puerto Rico School of Public Administration, 1961.

La Palombara, Joseph, "Political Party Systems and Crisis Government: French and Italian Contrasts." *Midwest Journal of Political Science*, 2 (May 1958), 117–142.

Lavau, Georges-E., *Partis politiques et réalités sociales*. Cahiers de la Fondation Nationale des Sciences Politiques, No. 38. Paris, A. Colin, 1952.

———, "Réflexions sur le régime politique de la France." *Revue Française de Science Politique*, 12 (December 1962), 813–844.

———, "La Réforme des institutions." *Esprit*, 26 (September 1958), 230–257.

Lavergne, Bernard, "La Chute de la IVᵉ République et la nouvelle Constitution." *L'Année Politique et Économique*, (July–October 1958), 189–246.

Le Bras, Gabriel, *Études de sociologie religieuse*. Paris, Presses Universitaires de France, 1956.

Leiserson, Avery, *Parties and Politics*. New York, Knopf, 1958.

Leites, Nathan, *L'Obsession du mal*. Unpublished manuscript.

———, *On the Game of Politics in France*. Stanford, Stanford University Press, 1959.

Le Monde. Various issues.

Lerner, Daniel, "The 'Hard-Headed' Frenchman." *Encounter*, 8 (March 1957), 27–32.

———, "Interviewing Frenchmen." *American Journal of Sociology*, 62 (September 1956), 187–194.

———, and Raymond Aron, eds., *France Defeats EDC*. New York, Praeger, 1958.

Lesire-Ogrel, H., "Systèmes électoraux et vie politique." *Formation*, (November 1958), 1–6.

Lewis, Edward G., "The Operation of the French Economic Council." *American Political Science Review*, 49 (March 1955), 161–172.

Lidderdale, D. W. S., *The Parliament of France*. London, Hansard Society, 1951.

Lipset, Seymour Martin, *The First New Nation*. New York, Basic Books, 1963.

———, *Political Man*. New York, Doubleday, 1960.

———, and Reinhard Bendix, *Social Mobility in Industrial Society*. Berkeley, University of California Press, 1959.

———, Martin A. Trow, and James S. Coleman, *Union Democracy*. New York, Free Press, 1956.

Little, Kenneth, "West African Urbanization as a Social Process." *Cahiers d'Études Africaines*, 3 (October 1960), 90–102.

Long, Raymond, *Les Élections législatives en Côte d'Or*. Cahiers de la Fondation Nationale des Sciences Politiques, No. 96. Paris, A. Colin, 1958.

Lowi, Theodore J., *At the Pleasure of the Mayor*. New York, Free Press, 1964.

Luethy, Herbert, *France Against Herself*. New York, Praeger, 1955.

———, and David Rodnick, *French Motivations in the Suez Crisis*. Princeton, Institute for International Social Research, 1956.

Maass, Arthur A., ed., *Area and Power*. New York, Free Press, 1959.

McConnell, Grant, *Private Power and American Democracy*. New York, Knopf, 1966.

McLellan, David S., "Ministerial Instability and the Lack of Internal Cohesion in French Parties." *World Affairs Quarterly*, 28 (April 1957), 3–24.

MacNeil, Neil, *Forge of Democracy*. New York, David McKay, 1963.

McPhee, William N., and William Glaser, eds., *Public Opinion in Congressional Elections*. New York, Free Press, 1962.

MacRae, Duncan, Jr., "Une Analyse factorielle des préférences politiques." *Revue Française de Science Politique*, 8 (March 1958), 95–109.

———, "Cluster Analysis of Congressional Votes with the BC TRY System." *Western Political Quarterly*, 19 (December 1966), 631–638.

———, *Dimensions of Congressional Voting*. University of California Publications in Sociology and Social Institutions, Vol. 1, No. 3. Berkeley, University of California Press, 1958.

———, "An Exponential Model for Assessing Fourfold Tables." *Sociometry*, 19 (June 1956), 84–94.

———, "IBM 1401 Q-Matrix and Editing Programs for Legislative Roll-Call Votes." *Behavioral Science*, 10 (July 1965), 324.

———, "Intraparty Divisions and Cabinet Coalitions in the Fourth French Republic." *Comparative Studies in Society and History*, 5 (January 1963), 164–211.

———, "A Method for Identifying Issues and Factions from Legislative Votes." *American Political Science Review*, 59 (December 1965), 909–926.

———, "Occupations and the Congressional Vote, 1940–1950." *American Sociological Review*, 20 (June 1955), 332–340.

———, "Religious and Socioeconomic Factors in the French Vote, 1946–1956." *American Journal of Sociology*, 64 (November 1958), 290–298.

————, and James A. Meldrum, "Critical Elections in Illinois: 1888–1958." *American Political Science Review*, 54 (September 1960), 669–683.

Macridis, Roy C., "Cabinet Instability in the French Republic (1946–1951)." *Journal of Politics*, 14 (November 1952), 643–658.

————, "The Immobility of the French Communist Party." *Journal of Politics*, 20 (November 1958), 613–634.

————, "A Note on the Revision of the Constitution of the Fourth Republic." *American Political Science Review*, 50 (December 1956), 1011–1022.

————, "The Predicament of French Socialism." *Antioch Review*, 20 (Summer 1960), 153–162.

Madinier, Philippe, "La Mobilité du travail aux États-Unis et en France." *Revue Économique* (Paris), 4 (July 1959), 549–574.

Malassis, Louis, *Économie des exploitations agricoles*. Paris, Colin, 1958.

Malterre, Jacques, and Paul Benoist, *Les Partis politiques français*. Paris, Bibliothèque de l'Homme d'Action, 1956(?).

Mannheim, Karl, *Man and Society in an Age of Reconstruction*. New York, Harcourt, Brace & World, 1941.

Marvick, Dwaine, ed., *Political Decision Makers*. New York, Free Press, 1961.

Maspétiol, Roland, and Pierre Laroque, *La Tutelle administrative*. Paris, Recueil Sirey, 1930.

Matthews, Ronald, *The Death of the Fourth Republic*. New York, Praeger, 1954.

May, John D., "Democracy, Organization, Michels." *American Political Science Review*, 59 (June 1965), 417–429.

Mead, Margaret, and Martha Wolfenstein, eds., *Childhood in Contemporary Cultures*. Chicago, University of Chicago Press, 1955.

Meisel, James H., *The Fall of the Republic*. Ann Arbor, University of Michigan Press, 1962.

Melnik, Constantin, and Nathan Leites, *The House Without Windows*. Evanston, Row, Peterson, 1958.

Mendès-France, Pierre, *Dire la vérité: Causeries du samedi, juin 1954-février 1955*. Paris, Julliard, 1955.

————, *A Modern French Republic*, trans. by Anne Carter. New York, Hill and Wang, 1963.

Mendras, Henri, *Sociologie de la campagne française*. Paris, Presses Universitaires de France, 1959.

Merton, Robert K., *Social Theory and Social Structure*, rev. ed. New York, Free Press, 1957.

Métraux, Rhoda, and Margaret Mead, *Themes in French Culture: A Preface to a Study of French Community*. Hoover Institute Studies, Series D, No. 1. Stanford, Stanford University Press, 1954.

Meynaud, Jean, *Les Groupes de pression en France*. Cahiers de la Fondation Nationale des Sciences Politiques, No. 95. Paris, A. Colin, 1958.

Michels, Robert, *Political Parties*, trans. by Eden and Cedar Paul. New York, Free Press, 1949.

Middleton, W. L., *The French Political System*. New York, Dutton, 1933.

Milgram, Stanley, "Nationality and Conformity." *Scientific American*, 205 (December 1961), 45–51.

Miller, Warren E., and Donald E. Stokes, "Constituency Influence in Congress." *American Political Science Review*, 57 (March 1963), 45–56.

Morazé, Charles, *The French and the Republic*, trans. by Jean-Jacques Demorest. Ithaca, Cornell University Press, 1958.

Morgenthau, Ruth Schachter, *Political Parties in French-Speaking West Africa*. New York, Oxford, 1964.

Morris-Jones, W. H., *The Government and Politics of India*. London, Hutchinson, 1964.

Munts, Raymond, *Parties and Parliament in the Fourth French Republic*. Unpublished M.A. thesis, University of Chicago, 1949.

Murphy, Robert, *Diplomat Among Warriors*. New York, Doubleday, 1964.

Neumann, Robert G., "The Struggle for Electoral Reform in France." *American Political Science Review*, 45 (September 1951), 741–755.

New York Times. Various issues.

Nordlinger, Eric A., "Democratic Stability and Instability: The French Case." *World Politics*, 18 (October 1965), 127–157.

Olivesi, Antoine, and Marcel Roncayolo, *Géographie électorale des Bouches-du-Rhône sous la IVᵉ République.* Cahiers de la Fondation Nationale des Sciences Politiques, No. 113. Paris, A. Colin, 1961.

Organisation for Economic Co-Operation and Development, *Joint International Seminar on Geographical and Occupational Mobility of Manpower,* Castelfusano, 1963, Supplement to the Final Report. Paris: Organisation for Economic Co-Operation and Development, 1964.

Parsons, Talcott, *The Social System.* New York, Free Press, 1951.

Patterson, Samuel C., "Legislative Leadership and Political Ideology." *Public Opinion Quarterly,* 27 (Fall 1963), 339–410.

Pickles, Dorothy, *Algeria and France.* New York, Praeger, 1963.

Pineau, Christian, *Mon Cher Député.* Paris, René Julliard, 1959.

Pitchell, Robert J., "The Electoral System and Voting Behavior: The Case of California's Cross-Filing." *Western Political Quarterly,* 12 (June 1959), 459–484.

Pitt-Rivers, Julian A., "Social Class in a French Village." *Anthropological Quarterly,* 33 (January 1960), 1–13.

Pitts, Jesse R., *The Bourgeois Family and French Economic Retardation.* Unpublished Ph.D. dissertation, Harvard University, 1957.

Promotions, 35 (October–December 1955), 109–116.

Putnam, Robert D., "Political Attitudes and the Local Community," *American Political Science Review,* 60 (September 1966), 640–654.

Recensement général de la population (effectuée le 10 mars 1946), Vol. VII, *Exploitations agricoles.* Paris, Presses Universitaires de France, 1950.

Rémond, René, "Les Anciens Combattants et la politique." *Revue Française de Science Politique,* 5 (June 1955), 267–290.

———, *The Right Wing in France: From 1815 to de Gaulle,* trans. by J. M. Laux. Philadelphia, University of Pennsylvania Press, 1966.

Revue Politique et Parlementaire, 208 (July–December 1952).

Riès, J., "Tempéraments politiques et résultats électoraux." *Revue Socialiste,* (February 1956), 119–131.

Rose, Arnold M., *Theory and Method in the Social Sciences.* Minneapolis, University of Minnesota Press, 1954.

———, ed., *The Institutions of Advanced Societies.* Minneapolis, University of Minnesota Press, 1958.

Rouanet, Pierre, *Mendès France au pouvoir (18 juin 1954–6 février 1955).* Paris, Robert Laffont, 1965.

Ruzié, David, "Le Nouveau Règlement de l'Assemblée Nationale." *Revue du Droit Public et de Science Politique,* 75 (September–October 1959), 863–914.

Schachter, Stanley, *et al.,* "Cross-Cultural Experiments on Threat and Rejection." *Human Relations,* 7 (November 1954), 403–440.

Scheinman, Laurence, *Atomic Energy Policy in France under the Fourth Republic.* Princeton, Princeton University Press, 1965.

Schlesinger, Joseph A., "The French Radical Socialist Party and the Republican Front of 1956." *Western Political Quarterly,* 11 (March 1958), 71–85.

Schram, Stuart R., "Le Poujadisme dans le Gard." *Christianisme Social,* 62 (March–April 1956), 195–207.

———, *Protestantism and Politics in France.* Alençon, Corbière and Jugain, 1954.

Sellers, Charles G., "The Equilibrium Cycle in Two-Party Politics." *Public Opinion Quarterly,* 29 (Spring 1965), 16–38.

Serant, Paul, *Où va la droite?* Paris, Plon, 1958.

Siegfried, André, *De la IVᵉ à la Vᵉ République.* Paris, Grasset, 1958.

———, *France: A Study in Nationality.* New Haven, Yale University Press, 1930.

Smith, T. Alexander, "Algeria and the French *Modérés:* The Politics of Immoderation?" *Western Political Quarterly,* 18 (March 1965), 118–134.

Snowiss, Leo M., *The Metropolitan Congressman.* San Francisco, Chandler, 1968.

Sondages. Various issues.

Soulié, Michel, *La Vie politique d'Édouard Herriot.* Paris, A. Colin, 1962.

Soulier, Auguste, *L'Instabilité ministérielle sous la Troisième République.* Paris, Recueil Sirey, 1939.

Statistical Abstract of the United States. Washington, U.S. Government Printing Office. Various issues.

Stoetzel, Jean, "Voting Behavior in France." *British Journal of Sociology,* 6 (June 1955), 104–122.

Stouffer, Samuel A., Edgar F. Borgatta, David G. Hays, and Andrew F. Henry, "A Technique for Improving Cumulative Scales." *Public Opinion Quarterly,* 16 (Summer 1952), 273–291.

Tannenbaum, Edward R., *The New France.* Chicago, University of Chicago Press, 1961.

Tarr, Francis de, *The French Radical Party from Herriot to Mendès-France.* New York, Oxford, 1961.

Taylor, O. R., *The Fourth Republic of France.* London, Royal Institute of International Affairs, 1951.

Thibaudet, Albert, *Les Idées politiques de la France.* Paris, Stock, 1932.

Thompson, Virginia, and Richard Adloff, *The Emerging States of French Equatorial Africa.* Stanford, Stanford University Press, 1960.

———, *French West Africa.* Stanford, Stanford University Press, 1958.

Tocqueville, Alexis de, *The Old Regime and the French Revolution.* Garden City, Doubleday, 1955.

Tournoux, J.-R., *Carnets secrets de la politique.* Paris, Plon, 1958.

———, *Secrets d'état.* Paris, Plon, 1960.

Tribune du Socialisme, No. 3, 15 March 1958.

Truman, David B., *The Congressional Party.* New York, Wiley, 1959.

United States Bureau of the Census, *Historical Statistics of the United States, Colonial Times to 1957: Continuation to 1962 and Revisions* (Washington, D.C.: U.S. Government Printing Office, 1965).

Vangrevelinghe, G., "Étude statistique comparée des résultats des référendums de 1958 et 1961." *Revue de Statistique Appliquée,* 9 (1961), 83–100.

Vedel, Georges, ed., *La Dépolitisation: Mythe ou réalité?* Cahiers de la Fondation Nationale des Sciences Politiques, No. 120. Paris, A. Colin, 1962.

Venezia, Jean-Claude, "Les Fondements juridiques de l'instabilité ministérielle." *Revue du Droit Public et de Science Politique,* 75 (July–August 1959), 718–755.

Viansson-Ponté, Pierre, *The King and His Court,* trans. by Elaine P. Halperin. Boston, Houghton Mifflin, 1964.

Vulpian, Alain de, "Physionomie agraire et orientation politique dans le département des Côtes-du-Nord." *Revue Française de Science Politique,* 1 (January–June 1951), 110–132.

Walker, Helen M., and Joseph Lev., *Statistical Inference.* New York, Holt, Rinehart & Winston, 1953.

Weber, Max, *The Theory of Social and Economic Organization,* trans. by A. M. Henderson and Talcott Parsons. New York, Oxford, 1947.

———, *Staatssoziologie,* ed. by Johannes Winckelmann. Berlin, Duncker & Humblot, 1956.

Werth, Alexander, *France 1940–1955.* New York, Holt, Rinehart & Winston, 1956.

———, *Lost Statesman: The Strange History of Pierre Mendès-France.* New York, Abelard-Schuman, 1958.

White, William S., *Citadel.* New York, Harper & Brothers, 1957.

White, Winston, *Beyond Conformity.* New York, Free Press, 1961.

Williams, Philip M., "Compromise and Crisis in French Politics." *Political Science Quarterly,* 72 (September 1957), 321–339.

———, *Crisis and Compromise.* Hamden, Conn., Archon Books, Shoestring Press, 1964.

———, "Political Compromise in France and America." *American Scholar,* 26 (Summer 1957), 273–288.

———, *Politics in Post-War France,* 2d ed. London, Longmans, 1958.

Wilson, James Q., *The Amateur Democrat.* Chicago, University of Chicago Press, 1962.

Wood, David M., "Issue Dimensions in a Multi-Party System: The French National Assembly and European Integration." *Midwest Journal of Political Science,* 8 (August 1964), 255–276.

Wright, Charles R., and Herbert H. Hyman, "Voluntary Association Memberships of American Adults: Evidence from National Sample Surveys." *American Sociological Review,* 23 (June 1958), 284–294.

Wright, Gordon, "Reflections on the French Resistance (1940–44)." *Political Science Quarterly,* 77 (September 1962), 336–349.

————, *The Reshaping of French Democracy*. New York, Reynal and Hitchcock, 1948.

————, *Rural Revolution in France*. Stanford, Stanford University Press, 1964.

Wylie, Laurence, *Village in the Vaucluse*. Cambridge, Harvard University Press, 1957.

Yates, W. Ross, "Power, Principle, and the Doctrine of the *Mouvement Républicain Populaire*." *American Political Science Review*, 52 (June 1958), 419–436.

Yule, G. Udny, *Introduction to the Theory of Statistics*. London, Griffin, 1911.

Zariski, Raphael, "The Italian Socialist Party: A Case Study in Factional Conflict." *American Political Science Review*, 56 (June 1962), 372–390.

INDEX

A

Abbott, Roger S., 336

Abelin, Pierre, 208

Académie Française, and uniformity of standards, 31

Action Républicaine et Sociale (ARS), support for Pinay, 120; continuity of deputies' position, 195; and constituencies, 299

Adloff, Richard, 62

Africa, sub-Saharan, political leaders, 24; parties, 44

Agricultural proletarization, and vote, 246

Agricultural wealth, and vote, 245

Alford, Robert R., 266

Algeria, 1; legal status, 24; social groupings in, 24; settlers, 25; Mendès-France and, 127, 128; emergency law (1955), 130; terrorism (1956), 159. *See also* National Liberation Front

Algerian statute (1947), 73

Allen, Luther A., 321

Almond, Gabriel A., 29, 39

Ambler, John S., 13

American cities, cycles of protest in, 283

American presidents, popularity, 310

Anderson, Lee F., 302

André, Pierre, 193, 203

Andrews, William G., 179

Année Politique, L', 339; sample of votes, 55

Antier, Paul, 274

Anti-Semitism, 23

Apparentements. See, Electoral alliances

Apter, David E., 319

Aragon, Charles d', 204

Arboussier, Gabriel d', 26

Aron, Raymond, 12, 40, 89, 108, 111, 156, 222, 226, 229, 260, 284, 337

Arrighi, Pascal, 12, 179; suspension of parliamentary immunity, 165

ARS. *See Action Républicaine et Sociale*

Assemblée Nationale. See Deputies; *Ministrables;* National Assembly; Parliamentary customs; Parliamentary groups; Roll-call votes

Associations, voluntary. *See* Voluntary groups

Auerbach, P. H., 112

Auriol, Vincent, President of the Republic, 71, 76, 77, 80, 116, 124, 314

Axelrod, Robert, 353

Aymé, Marcel, 338

B

Bacon, Paul, 208

Badie, Vincent, 203

Badiou, Raymond, 303

Bamberger, Frank K., 353

Bandwagon effect, 279

Barangé bill for school aid, 115, 203

Bardonnet, Daniel, 61, 62, 227, 304, 321

Barrachin, Edmond, 189

Barrès, Philippe, 121

Barriers. *See* Social structure; Boundaries

Barrillon, Raymond, 108, 156

Bartholomew, Reginald, 62, 226, 337

Bauchet, Pierre, 13, 39

Baum, Warren C., 38

Baylet, Jean, 199, 203

Beauvoir, Simone de, 37

Beer, Samuel H., 229

Bell, Daniel, 337

Bell, Norman W., 37, 338

Ben-David, Joseph, 336

Bendix, Reinhard, 36, 40

Béné, Maurice, 203

Benoist, Paul, 156, 285

Bergasse, Henri, 189, 299

Bessac, Abel, 204

Bettelheim, Charles, 39

Bidault, Georges, 71, 81, 307; cabinet and its support, 81; fall of cabinet, 82; replaces Schuman in Mayer cabinet, 121

Billères, René, 199

Blanchet, André, 62

Blum, Léon, 71, 74, 76

Bodin, Louis, 265

Bosworth, William, 38

Bottomore, Thomas, 37

Bouhey, Jean, 210

Bouilleurs de cru. See Home distillers

Boulanger, General Georges, 43, 311

Boulard, Canon Fernand, 263

Boulet, Paul, 204

Boundaries, between groups, 16, 33. *See also* Social structure

Bourdet, Claude, 254, 284

Bourdieu, Pierre, 38

Bourgès-Maunoury, Maurice, 108, 197, 213; in Mendès-France cabinet, 126; investiture, 161; cabinet and its support, 162; relation to René Mayer, 191

Bourguiba, Habib, 116, 163

Bourricaud, François, 38

Boutemy, André, 121

Bouvier O'Cottereau, Jean-Marie, 189

Bouxom, Fernand, 208

Bresard, M., 36

Brindillac, Charles, 37, 39, 40, 62, 336

Bromberger, Merry, 179

Bromberger, Serge, 179

Brown, Bernard E., 38, 319

Bureaucracies, relation to parties, 45

Burlot, André, 208

Burnham, Walter Dean, 261

Buron, Robert, 13, 206, 208, 226

C

Cabinet instability, sources, 6. *See also* Ideology; *Rassemblement du Peuple Français* (RPF); Radical Party

Cabinets, support and opposition votes, 58, 59; weakness 65; investiture process, 67; types of action, 68; rumors of fall, 69; duration, 217; consensus and relation to preceding cabinets, 225

Caillavet, Henri, 199

Campbell, Angus, 63, 261, 262, 266, 283, 285

Campbell, Peter, 61, 62, 63, 112

Capelle, Russell B., 62, 303

Carlini, Michel, 193, 299

Caron, Paul, 204

Catholicism, conservative, 43; social, 43

Catroux, General Georges, 159

Centers, Richard, 36

Centralization, 319; of society, 32; in political parties, 47

Chaban-Delmas, Jacques, 13, 71, 121, 195

Chambord, Count de, 43

Chapman, Brian, 38, 266, 336

Chapsal, Jacques, 109, 154, 155, 179, 226, 228, 261

Charpentier, René, 208

Chênebenoit, André, 109, 179

Chenery, Hollis B., 36

Chevallier, J.-J., 61, 62, 320, 336

Chevigné, Pierre de, 208

Chombart de Lauwe, P.-H., 36, 37

Church-school question, position of African leaders, 25; and Radicals' divisions, 203; continuity of Radicals' divisions on, 288. *See also* Barangé bill; Marie, André

Church schools, 22

Churchill, Winston S., 13; talks with Mendès-France, 127

Civil servants, 19; higher, 20

Coleman, James Samuel, 36, 38, 39, 285, 337

Colliard, C.-A., 109

Colonial issues, in Second Legislature, 135, 136

Colonies. *See* Overseas France

Common Market, passage of bill for (1957), 161

Communication, channels of, 15

Communist party, occupations of deputies, 52, 53; opposition to Ramadier, 71, 72; and working-class population, 251; changes in vote for, 254

Community, 17

Compartmentalization, and French national character, 330. *See also* Boundaries between groups

Confédération Générale du Travail (CGT), 27

Congress, U.S., leadership groups, 311

Consensus, norms regarding, 16. *See also* Group pressure

Constituencies, influence on Assembly, 10; influences on roll-call votes, general and specific, 286

Converse, Philip E., 63, 260, 262, 266, 267, 283, 285, 302, 303, 304, 319, 337, 338

Cooper, Homer C., 266

Coston, Henry, 284, 303

Cotteret, Jean-Marie, 261

Coty, René, President of the Republic, 125, 129, 130, 165, 189; elected President of the Republic, 125; chooses Mollet as Premier (1956), 317

Council of the Republic, and 1951 electoral law, 86

Cross-cutting social ties. *See* Social structure, superposition

Crozier, Michel, 13, 36, 38, 39, 337, 338

Cumul. See Deputies, as mayors

D

Dahrendorf, Ralf, 36

Daladier, Édouard, 81, 89, 124, 199, 201, 203, 314

David, Jean-Paul, 199

Debré, Michel, 7, 13, 335, 338

Decentralization, leftist advocacy, 325

Defferre, Gaston, in Mollet cabinet, 159

de Gaulle, Charles. *See* Gaulle, Charles de

de Gaulle, Pierre. *See* Gaulle, Pierre de

Deixonne, Maurice, 75

Delahoutre, Eugène, 81

de Madariaga, Salvador, 338

Demands, political, and government response, 306

Denais, Joseph, 193

Depreux, Édouard, 106, 211, 292

Deputies, nonpolitical occupations, 52, 53; as mayors, 54; scale positions, how related to votes, 182; scale positions and constituencies, 286. *See also* Scale positions; names of individual parties

Derruau-Boniol, S., 36

Desabie, Jacques, 263

Devinat, Paul, 199

Dien Bien Phu, fall, 125; and Mendès-France investiture, 315

Diethelm, André, 122, 193

Distillers, home. *See* Home distillers

Dogan, Mattei, 63, 263, 284

Dronne, Raymond, 164

Duchet, Roger, 124

Ducos, Hippolyte, 203

Dumas, Joseph, 208

Dupeux, Georges, 39, 63, 260, 265, 266, 267, 283, 302, 304, 333, 337, 338

Dupraz, Joannès, 208

Duquesne, Jules, 208

Duverger, Maurice, 13, 14, 37, 39, 50, 61, 62, 63, 155, 156, 179, 226, 227, 229, 261, 263, 264, 265, 266, 284, 285, 303, 304, 321,

337; classification of parties, 46; and effects of electoral systems, 242

E

Earle, Edward M., 36, 320

Easton, David, 319

Écoles libres. See Schools, church

École Nationale d'Administration (ENA), 21

Economic development under Fourth Republic, 4; compared to rest of Europe, 16

EDC. *See* European Defense Community

Educational system. *See* Schools, public

Ehrmann, Henry W., 38, 227, 265, 319, 337

Einaudi, Mario, 227

Eisenhower, Dwight D., appeal of, compared with Gaullism, 269

Elections, non-parliamentary, effects on Assembly, 68; municipal (1947) and RPF gains, 73; legislative, July 1951, 114

Electoral alliances, law providing for, 84; effects of, 42, 278, 317; effects in 1951 election, 113

Electoral law, and Pleven cabinet, 84; 1951, Radicals' positions on, 102

Electoral system, changes in, 9; and multipartyism, 42. *See also* Plurality electoral law; Proportional representation; Duverger, Maurice

Elgey, Georgette, 109, 228

Ély, General Paul, 159, 164

Emeri, Claude, 261

Ennis, Philip, 266

Etzioni, Amitai, 62

Euratom, 160; passage of bill for (1957), 161

European Army, debate on (1952), 115. *See also* European Defense Community

European Coal and Steel Community (CECA), 82, 116

European Defense Community (EDC), 113, 287; and RPF votes, 122; Socialist resolution on, 124; debated under Laniel, 124; negotiations on, 125, 126; Mendès-France and, 126; defeat, 127; ideological positions on, 133

European union, parliamentary issue, 115, 133; continuity of intraparty divisions on, 287

Express, L', 131; test votes on Mendesism, 128

F

Fabre-Luce, Alfred, 284

Family. *See* Kinship

Faucher, J.-L., 153, 320

Faure, Edgar, 196, 310; investiture (1952), 116; first cabinet and its support, 116, 117; fall (1952), 118; *ministrables'* opposition to (1952), 118; minister of finance under Mendès-France, 126; investiture (1955), 129; second cabinet (1955) and its support, 130; fall (1955), 132; exclusion from Radical party, 132

Faure, Marcel, 38

Fauvet, Jacques, 12, 38, 108, 109, 110, 111, 122, 153, 154, 155, 156, 179, 226, 227, 284, 319

Ferguson, Jack, 276, 278, 285

Fesler, James W., 336

Finer, Herman, 179

First Legislature (1946–1951), cabinets and issues, 66

FLN. *See* National Liberation Front

Fonctionnaires. See Civil servants

Fonlupt-Espéraber bill on cantonal elections, 77, 79, 315

Fourastié, Jean, 40

Fourth Republic, basic problems, 322

Frédéric-Dupont, Édouard, 189, 299

Frère, Suzanne, 39

Froman, Lewis A., Jr., 302

Front de Libération Nationale. See National Liberation Front

Furaud, Jacques, 103

G

Gaillard, Félix, investiture, 163; cabinet and its support, 164; relation to René Mayer, 191; becomes Radical leader (1958), 318

Gallagher, Orvoell R., 38

Galy-Gasparrou, Georges, 199

Gambetta, Léon, 311

Gamma (γ), coefficient of association between scales, 97

Garet, Pierre, 124, 188, 204

Gau, Abbé Albert, 204, 208

Gaulle, Charles de, Premier, 1; sources of support, 3; and RPF, 70; socialist opposition to, 105; meeting with Mendès-France, 128; investiture (1958), 165, 211; as renovator, 307

Gaulle, Pierre de, 193, 299

Gaullism, November 1958 legislative election, 242; and Mendesism, similarities, 318. *See also Rassemblement du Peuple Français; Union Républicaine d'Action Sociale; Action Républicaine et Sociale*

Gaullist deputies, voting patterns in Second Legislature, 133; positions on issues, 141, 142

Generals, affair of, 83, 84

Generations, transmission of political attitudes between, 334

Geneva Conference. *See* Indochina

German zone of occupation (1940–42), and vote, 270

Germany, Federal Republic, association with Ruhr, 79; rearmament, 89; continuity of intraparty division on, 287. *See also* London Agreements; Paris Agreements

Gerth, Hans H., 62

Giacobbi, Paul, 78, 199; in Queuille cabinet (1950), 82

Girard, Alain, 37

Girondin tradition, 43

Glaser, William, 262, 266, 285

Godfrey, E. Drexel, 303

Goguel, François, 38, 155, 227, 263, 264, 265, 266, 284, 285, 303, 304, 320, 336

Goodman, Leo A., 97, 112, 349, 353

Gourdon, Alain, 321

Government impotence. *See Immobilisme*

Grandval, Gilbert, 131

Gravier, Jean-François, 31, 39

Grosser, Alfred, 12, 155, 261, 336

Group pressure, on deviate, cross-national study, 332; response to, France *vs.* Norway, 332

Groups, voluntary. *See* Voluntary groups

Guichard-Ayoub, Éliane, 336

Gurin, Gerald, 63, 261, 285

Gurvitch, Georges, 36, 37

Gusfield, Joseph R., 40, 284

H

Hamon, Léo, 38, 62

Hartz, Louis, 61

Hassner, Pierre, 285

Hausknecht, Murray, 39

Heberle, Rudolf, 40

Hermens, Ferdinand A., 266

Hernu, Charles, 203

Herriot, Édouard, 13, 199, 201, 307, 314; President of Assembly, 87; preconditions for EDC, 127; opposition to German rearmament, 129; and defense against Gaullism, 314

Hervé, Pierre, 254

Himmelstrand, Ulf, 337

Hodgkin, Thomas, 38

Hoffmann, Stanley, 2, 12, 13, 37, 39, 40, 62, 264, 265, 266, 267, 284, 319, 336, 337, 338

Hogan, James, 266

Home distillers, 27

Hughes, H. Stuart, 13, 320

Hugues, Émile, 126, 201

Hugues, J.-André, 203

Huitt, Ralph K., 320

Hurtig, Serge, 179

Husson, Raoul, 264

Hutin-Desgrées, Paul, 208

Hyman, Herbert H., 39

I

Ideology, 328; and cabinet instability, 176; and political divisions, 213

Ihuel, Paul, 208

Immigrants, absorption of, 22

Immobilisme, 1, 4, 66; definition, 2

Incivisme, 3

Indochina, debated under Laniel, 122; Geneva Conference on, 126; partitioning, 126

Institut Français d'Opinion Publique (IFOP). *See* Surveys

Intellectuals, political tendencies of, 21

Interest groups, centralized action, 26; *vs.* parties, 306; spokesmen in the Assembly, 307

IOM (*Indépendants d'Outre-Mer*), 44

Isorni, Jacques, 226, 320

Italian Socialists, 292

J

Jacobin Club, 43, 274

Jacobin tradition, 43

Janowitz, Morris, 284

Jennings, M. Kent, 262

Joan of Arc, 43

Jouvenel, Robert de, 228

Juglas, Jean-Jacques, 208

Jules-Julien, Alfred, 199

July, Pierre, 189

K

Kaplan, Morton A., 37, 337

Katz, Fred E., 320

Kesselman, Mark J., 38, 111, 261, 266, 337, 338

Key, V. O., Jr., 61, 262, 267, 305

Kindelberger, Charles R., 13

Kinship, 17, 18; and stratification, 19, 20; and mass society, 32

Kir, Canon Félix, 189

Kirchheimer, Otto, 229

Klatzmann, Joseph, 264, 265

Klock, Joseph, 208

Koenig, General Pierre, in Mendès-France cabinet, 126

Komarovsky, Mirra, 265

Kornhauser, William, 28, 31, 32, 38, 39, 40

Krier, Henri, 265

Kruskal, William H., 97, 112, 349, 353

L

Lacoste, Robert, 317; Resident General of Algeria, 159, 160

Lalumière, Pierre, 261

Lancelot, Marie-Thérèse, 38

Landes, David S., 36, 37

Lane, Robert E., 14

Langrod, Georges, 37, 336

Laniel, Joseph, 307, 317; investiture, 122; cabinet and its support, 123; fall, 125

La Palombara, Joseph, 110, 261

Lapie, Pierre-Olivier, 303

Laroque, Pierre, 266

Laurens, Camille, 135

Lavau, Georges-E., 38, 61, 338

Lavergne, Bernard, 13

Le Bras, Gabriel, 263

Lecourt, Robert, 69

Leenhardt, Francis, 211

Lefebvre, Mme. Francine, 208

Legislative parties. *See* Parliamentary groups

Leiserson, Avery, 62

Leites, Nathan, 12, 13, 90, 108, 109, 111, 154, 179, 226, 228, 229, 304, 337

Lejeune, Max, 210; opposition to EDC, 127

Léotard, Pierre de, 199

Lerner, Daniel, 36, 40, 156

Lesire-Ogrel, H., 63

Lespès, Henri, 103

Lev, Joseph, 264

Lewis, Edward G., 64

Liautey, André, 193

Lidderdale, D. W. S., 63, 64, 109, 155, 179, 347

Lipset, Seymour Martin, 36, 37, 38, 40, 285, 320, 338

Liquard, Émile, 103

Litalien, Georges, 193

Little, Kenneth, 38

Livry-Level, Philippe, 103

Local decision centers, weakness, 26

Local government, activities of citizens in, 29

Local politics, 333

Localism, 325

Lois-cadres, civil service reform, 1951, 116

London Agreements, for German rearmament, 128

Long, Raymond, 284

Louis Philippe, support for, 43

Louvel, Jean-Marie, 208

Lowi, Theodore J., 285

Luethy, Herbert, 13, 14, 61, 229

Lussy, Charles, 211

M

Maass, Arthur, A., 39, 336

MacMahon, Marshal, 9

McConnell, Grant, 336

McLellan, David S., 304

McPhee, William N., 262, 266, 276, 278, 285

MacRae, Duncan, Jr., 111, 226, 227, 261, 263, 264, 265, 347, 353

Macridis, Roy C., 38, 61, 111, 155, 228, 229, 263

Madinier, Philippe, 40

Malassis, Louis, 264

Malterre, Jacques, 156, 285

Mamy, Georges, 155, 179

Mannheim, Karl, 278, 285

Mannoni, Eugène, 179

Marcellin, Raymond, 193

Margueritte, Charles, 303

Marie, André, 91, 92, 104, 197, 203, 314; investiture, 76; cabinet and its support, 76, 77; attacks on (1949), 79; school-aid bill (1951), 115; attempt at investiture (1953), 120

Marshall Plan, adoption, 75

Martin, Gilbert, 203

Martinaud-Déplat, Léon, 316, 317; abolition of party office, 131

Martinet, Gilles, 228

Marvick, Dwaine, 284

Maspétiol, Roland, 266

Mass society. *See* Voluntary groups

Matthews, Ronald, 110, 154, 228, 320

Maurice-Petsche. *See* Petsche, Maurice

May, John D., 229

Mayer, Daniel, 80, 106, 211; opposition to EDC, 127; opposed to Mollet, 300

Mayer, René, 80, 191, 316; Minister of Finance (1947–48), 72; and church-school question, 115; attempt at investiture (1951), 114; Minister of Finance under Pleven (1951), 115; investiture, 120; cabinet and its support, 120; fall, 122, 212; and fall of Mendès-France, 120, 133

Mead, Margaret, 36, 337, 338

Meck, Henri, 208

Mehaignerie, Alexis, 208

Meldrum, James A., 263, 265

Melnik, Constantin, 111, 154, 228, 347

Membership ratios, parties and constituencies, 300

Mendès-France, Pierre, 103, 307, 336, 337; support for, 43; attempt at investiture (1953), 122; opposes Laniel cabinet, 125; investiture, 125; formation of cabinet (1954), 125; cabinet and its support, 125; fall, 129; in Mollet cabinet (1956), 159; resigns from Mollet cabinet, 160; loses control of Radical party, 161; as renovator, 307; selection of cabinet, 316; opposition of party leaders to, 316; radio chats, 316; MRP coolness toward, 316

Mendesism, support for, 238; support by voters (1956), 249; sources of vote for, 273; inverse relation to Poujadism among electorate, 274. *See also* Radical party

Mendras, Henri, 36, 37, 38, 39, 156, 284

Merle, Marcel, 62, 112, 156, 304

Merton, Robert K., 36, 39

Métraux, Rhoda, 36, 337, 338

Meynaud, Jean, 38, 228

Michelet, Edmond, 103

Michels, Robert, 62

Middle classes, 20

Middleton, W. L., 61

Milgram, Stanley, 332, 338

Militants. See Parties, political

Miller, Warren E., 63, 261, 285, 302, 304

Mills, C. Wright, 62

Ministers, ineligibility for seats in Assembly under Fifth Republic, 324. *See also Ministrables*

Ministrables, 70; view of politics, 5; support for cabinet, 8, 185; opposition to new men, 147; analysis of votes of, 186; support for cabinet, related to scales, 186; support for cabinet, and temporal continuity of scales, 288; consensus among, 212; similarity to Congressional leadership groups, 311

Mitterrand, François, 199; opposes Laniel cabinet, 125; Minister of Interior under Mendès-France, 129

Moch, Jules, 80, 83; opposition to EDC, 127

Moderates, definition, 134; Second Legislature, roll calls in scales, 134; Second Legislature, subject matter of scales, 135; Third Legislature, scale clusters, 166; Third Legislature, roll calls in scales, 166; Third Legislature, subject matter of scales, 166, 168, 169; scale positions, Second Legislature, 193; scale positions, Third Legislature, 197; recruitment of electoral support (1955), 238; constituency relations and scale positions, 296. *See also Mouvement Républicain Populaire;* Radical party; Socialist party

Mollet, Guy, 65, 68, 70, 72, 106, 122, 211, 290; *mission d'information* (1950), 82; investiture attempt (1951), 85; investiture, 157; cabinet and its support, 158; fall, 161; attitudes of MRP deputies toward, 288; Socialist opposition to, 292, 300; delays Socialist participation in Mendès-France cabinet (1954), 316

Morazé, Charles, 37

Morgenthau, Ruth Schachter, 38, 62

Morice, André, 160, 203, 314

Morice Radicals, 49, 171, 203

Morocco, 127; deposition of Sultan, 124; Faure and, 131

Morris-Jones, W. H., 36

Moslems. *See* Muslims

Mouvement Républicain Populaire (MRP), 102, 204; First Legislature, roll calls in scales, 103; Second Legislature, roll calls in scales, 148; Second Legislature,

subject matter of scales, 148; Third legislature, roll calls in scales, 173; scale positions, First Legislature, 204; scale positions, Second Legislature, 206; shift of voters to PRL (1946), 234; constituency relations, 293; deputies' scale positions and leftist vote in districts, 293; relation to Moderates in constituencies, 296

MRP. *See Mouvement Républicain Populaire*

Munts, Raymond, 303

Murphy, Robert, 13, 179

Muslims, status in Algeria, 25

N

Naegelen, Marcel-Edmond, 83, 109, 210

National Assembly, rules, changes under Fifth Republic, 323; dissolution of, 324. *See also* Deputies; *Ministrables;* Parliamentary customs; Parliamentary groups; Roll-call votes

National character, 330

National Liberation Front (FLN), 45, 164; and Cairo, 217

Naudet, Pierre, 203

Neo-Radicals, 199

Neumann, Robert G., 110

Nordlinger, Eric A., 39

Notables, 301; and party structure, 46; in America, 325

O

Occupations, and stratification, 19; changes in distribution, 33; inheritance rates, 34; of head of family and vote, 256; and vote, by size of city or town, 257; and voters' party preference (October 1947), 275; and voters' party preference (January 1956), 276. *See also* Deputies

Old Age Fund, Mollet bill, 159

Olivesi, Antoine, 263, 265, 284

Opinion, and Assembly, 306; types of, 307; geographical *vs.* temporal variations, 307

Opposition, in Assembly, "unavailable" votes, 59; conditions for, 224

Oradour-sur-Glane massacre, trial, 121

Overseas France, representation of, 24

P

Palewski, Gaston, 121

Palewski, Jean-Paul, 103

372 *Index*

Panier, Claude, 203

Paris Agreements on German rearmament, 128; vote on, 129; ratification, 130

Parliamentary customs, 7. *See also Ministrables*

Parliamentary groups, cohesion, 55

Parsons, Talcott, 36, 261

Parti Républicain de la Liberté (PRL), 70, 75, 76, 92, 96, 234

Parti Socialiste Unifié (PSU), 290

Participation, political, 15, 50; types, by party, 50; in voting, 230, 231

Parties, political, "surge," 9, 10, 240, 307, 322; members' activity, 29; system of, 42; historical persistence, 42, 43; active members (*militants*), 45, 322; *militants* and constituencies, 299; activists and distinction between, 242; structure, 45; congresses, 48; membership ratio, 50; influence on voters, 49, 50; divisions in Assembly, 57; stable vote for, 230; identification with, 242; ideological, and constituency relations, 301; atrophy of minority organization, 301; compromises and ideology, 327. *See also* Membership ratios; *Notables;* Parliamentary groups; names of particular parties

Party preference, turnover in First Constituent Assembly, 235; turnover in Second Constituent Assembly, 235; turnover in First Legislature, 235; turnover in Second Legislature, 238; turnover in Third Legislature, 238. *See also* Occupations; Turnover tables; Voting of electorate

Party system, reform of, 326

Patterson, Samuel C., 227

Paysans. See Peasants, Peasant party

Peasant party, Antier faction, 116; in Second Legislature, 134; factional differences, 135

Peasants, social characteristics, 18, 20; distrust of government, 27; and Poujadism, 269

Peer groups, in schools, 23

Personal vote in Assembly, 55

Petit, Eugène (Claudius), 201

Petsche, Maurice, 79; attempt at investiture (1951), 115

Pflimlin, Pierre, 13, 129, 208; fails to form cabinet (1957), 161; investiture, 165

Philip, André, 106; dissidence in Socialist party, 290

Pickles, Dorothy, 109

Pierre, Abbé (Groués), 204

Pinay, Antoine, 122, 123, 129; tax amnesty, 119; investiture, 118; cabinet and its support, 118; resignation as premier, 120; friends of, 193; attitudes of MRP deputies toward, 288; opposition from *ministrables,* 311, 312; lack of support from MRP *ministrables,* 311, 312

Pineau, Christian, 116, 226; attempt at investiture (1955), 129

Piret, Fern V., 320

Pitchell, Robert J., 338

Pitt-Rivers, Julian A., 36, 37

Pitts, Jesse R., 36, 37, 334, 338

Planck, Russell, E., 265

Pleven Plan. *See* European Defense Community

Pleven, René, 78, 84, 189, 274; premier, 82; cabinet (1950) and its support, 83; investiture (1951), 115; cabinet (1951) and its support, 116

Plurality electoral law, 42, 84, 220, 242; localism of, 44; proposed by Mendès-France, 1955, 129; considered by Assembly, 1955, 129

Poinso-Chapuis, Mme. Germaine, 206, 208

Polarities of roll calls, 348

Political involvement. *See* Participation, political

Political movements. *See* Parties, "surge"

Political participation. *See* Participation, political

Political parties. See Parties, political

Politicization, France vs. United States, 333

Population density, 16

Poujadism, decline of, and voter support, 238, 239

Poujadist vote, 268; in middle-sized towns, 19; appearance of (1956), 249; sources, 269; relation to Gaullism, 268; and Gaullist vote (1951–56), 269; strength by districts; 269; in occupied and nonoccupied zones (1940–42), 270

Poujadists, positions of, contrasted with American groups, 14; ideology, 269

Prefects, functions of, 26

Prélot, Marcel, 195

Premiers, popularity, 217, 309; Assembly's reactions to popularity, 309; public approval of, 309

President of the Republic, 1953 election, 124, 125

Pressure groups. *See* Interest groups

Prigent, Robert, 206

PRL. *See Parti Républicain de la Liberté*

Proportional representation, 231; effects of, 259

Protest, political expression of, 283

Proxy vote in Assembly, 55

Public opinion. *See* Opinion

Puissesseau, René, 108, 109

Putnam, Robert D., 266

Q

Q-coefficient, 93

Q-matrix, 93, 349; for Moderates in First Legislature, 94, 95, 96

Question of confidence, "unofficial," under Ramadier, 73

Queuille, Henry, 79, 92, 107, 197, 201, 217, 316; first cabinet (1948) and its support, 79; second cabinet (1950), 82; investiture (1951), 85; third cabinet (1951) and its support, 85; and defense against Gaullism, 313

R

Racier, Roger, 228

Radical party, Cadillac committee, 45; reform by Mendès-France, 50; Lyon congress (1956), 49, 115, 160, 317; and cabinet instability, 173; antagonisms in, 197; southwestern faction, 199, 318; disintegration of, and voter support, 238; constituency relations, 294; scale positions, inverse association with MRP, 295; relation to Moderates in constituencies, 295, 296; structure, 317. *See also* Mendès-France; Morice Radicals; Radicals and UDSR; *Rassemblement des Gauches Républicaines*

Radicals and UDSR, scales in First Legislature, 96, 97, 100, 102; scales in Second Legislature, 143, 145, 147; scales in Third Legislature, 169, 171, 173; scale positions in First Legislature, 197; scale positions in Second Legislature, 199; scale positions in Third Legislature, 201, 202, 203

Ramadier, Paul, 77, 88; investiture, 71; cabinet, 71; support for cabinet, 72, 73

Rassemblement Démocratique Africain (RDA), 44

Rassemblement des Gauches Républicaines (RGR), 102

Rassemblement du Peuple Français (RPF), 113; cohesion, 57; founded, 70; dissidence on Pinay investiture, 118; decline of, 235; shifts of votes toward, 235;

votes for, 268, 273; campaign activity, 269; relation of votes to Poujadist vote, 270; strength of vote by districts, 269; votes in occupied and nonoccupied zones (1940–42), 270; constituency relations, 299; Assembly leaders' defense against, 313

Referenda, 243

Regionalism and politics, 22

Regression coefficients, standardized, for prediction of political variables, 244; multiple, within *départements*, 250

Religion, attitudes toward, 22. *See also* Catholicism; Church-school question; Voting of the electorate

Rémond, René, 37, 40, 50, 61, 227, 284, 336, 337

Representation, by political parties, 41. *See also* Voting of the electorate

"Republican" defense, 313, 314

Republican Front, 246, 249, 254, 255–56, 273, 274, 317

Resistance, 44, 273

Révillon, Tony, 199, 203

"Reynaud law" (1948), 88

Reynaud, Paul, 74, 77, 81, 89, 189; in Marie cabinet, 76; in Queuille cabinet (1950), 82; legislation under Marie cabinet, 104; attempt at investiture (1953), 122; attitudes of MRP deputies toward, 288

RI (*Républicains Indépendants*), 96. *See also* Moderates; Parties, political

Riès, J,. 284

Right center, and large industrial organizations, 145

Rightist parties, divisions in First Legislature, 96; scales in First Legislature, 97; in Second Legislature, 134; deputies' scale positions, 188. *See also* Moderates

Robespierre, Maximilien, 43

Rodnick, David, 13, 229

Roig, Charles, 336

Roll-call votes, cabinet specificity, 66, 89, 176; issue specificity, 66, 89, 176; clusters, interpretation, 66, 91; index of similarity (Q), 92; polarity, 96, 182; and constituencies, 286. *See also* Constituencies; Personal vote, Proxy vote

Roll-call votes in scales, lists. *See* names of individual parties

Roll calls, subject classifications, 137, 138; sample, 339; sample, by major cabinets, 340; list of, 342–346

Roncayolo, Marcel, 263, 265, 284

Rose, Arnold M., 29, 38, 39

Rouanet, Pierre, 153
"Round table" (conference of party leaders) of 1957, 162
Rousseau, Charles, 189
RPF. *See Rassemblement du Peuple Français*
Ruzié, David, 336

S

Saar, 127
Sakhiet-Sidi-Youssef, bombing, 164
Salary scale bill, provisions, 115; under Faure (1952), 116
Sawyer, John E., 36
Scale positions, continuity of deputies', 287
Scales, interpretation, 181; cutting points, 182; placement of deputies on, procedure, 182; showing continuity across Legislatures, 287
Scaling, procedures, 348
Schachter, Stanley, 331, 337
Scheinman, Laurence, 179
Schlesinger, Joseph A., 264
Schmitt, René, 208
Schneiter, Pierre, 208
School system. *See* Schools, public
Schools, church, 22. *See also* Church-school question
Schools, public, 23, 24
Schram, Stuart R., 37, 284
Schuman Plan. *See* European Coal and Steel Community
Schuman, Robert, 76, 121, 208; premier (1947–48), 74, 75; cabinet and its support, 74
Schumann, Maurice, 208
Scrutin d'arrondissement. See Plurality electoral law.
Sellers, Charles G., 263
Serant, Paul, 338
Sesmaisons, Olivier de, 189
SFIO. *See* Socialist party
Sibué, Louis, 303
Sicard, Roger, 336
Siegfried, André, 3, 12, 13, 64, 108, 180, 223, 226, 228, 229, 333, 338
Smith, T. Alexander, 180, 228
Snowiss, Leo M., 63
Social divisions. *See* Social structure
Social mobility, 32

Social structure, divisions in, 5; superposition of cleavages, 15, 16; norms regarding interaction, 16; divisions, and political activity, 333; and party vote, 242. *See also* Boundaries between groups; Kinship; *Notables;* Occupations, Social mobility.
Socialist party (SFIO), 43; incompatibility with Moderates in cabinet coalition, 82; and downfall of cabinets in First Legislature, 87; First Legislature, roll calls in scale, 105; scale in Second Legislature, 150; scale in Third Legislature, 174; factions and leaders in, 208; militants, 223; militants and deputies, 290; changes in vote for, 255; constituency relations, 290; left wing, deputies and districts, 290, 291; relation to Communists in districts, 292. *See also* Gaulle, Charles de; Mollet, Guy
Soulié, Michel, 320
Soulier, Auguste, 108, 304
Soustelle, Jacques, 116, 120, 193; Governor General of Algeria, 129, 131
Spaak, Paul-Henri, 126
"Static" France and Poujadism, 270
Stinchcombe, Arthur L., 264
Stoetzel, Jean, 7, 262, 285
Stokes, Donald E., 285, 302, 304
Stouffer, Samuel A., 226
Stratification, social. *See* Kinship; Occupations; Social Structure
Subsystems, political, 4
Suez invasion, 160
"Surge" parties or movements. *See* Parties, "surge"; Gaullism; Mendès-France; Poujadism; *Rassemblement du Peuple Français*
Surveys of voting preferences, 230

T

Tannenbaum, Edward R., 40
Tarr, Francis de, 156, 179, 180, 227, 320, 321
Taylor, O. R., 108, 262
Terrenoire, Louis, 103
Thibaudet, Labert, 27, 62
Thompson, Virginia, 62
Thorez, Maurice, 71, 72, 105, 208, 210
Tinguy du Pouet, Lionel de, 208
Tocqueville, Alexis de, 31, 266, 336
Tony-Révillon. *See* Révillon, Tony
Touchard, Jean, 155, 227, 264, 265, 266, 284, 285, 304

Tournoux, J.-R., 178

Trow, Martin A., 36, 38, 285

Truman, David B., 227, 302

Tunisia, and Faure investiture (1952), 116; debate on, 119; negotiations (1954), 127; agreements on (1955), 130

Turnover tables, 232; French and American, comparison, 240

U

UDSR. *See Union Démocratique et Socialiste de la Résistance*

UFF. *See* Poujadists

Ulam, Adam B., 229

Ulver, Henri, 121

Union Démocratique et Socialiste de la Résistance (UDSR), 76, 78, 79, 97. *See also* Radicals and UDSR

Union et Fraternité Française. See Poujadists

Union Républicaine d'Action Sociale (URAS), Second Legislature, roll calls in scales, 141, 142; scale positions of deputies, 195; and cabinet instability, 224

Urbanization, as predictor of vote, 245; and votes in 1951 election, 249; and 1956 votes, 249

V

Valay, Gabriel, 206

Valen, Henry, 261

Vangrevelinghe, G., 263

Vedel, Georges, 63, 337

Vendroux, Jacques, 193

Venezia, Jean-Claude, 220, 229

Verba, Sidney, 29, 39

Vertical communication, 322. *See also* Social Structure; Voting of electorate

Viansson-Ponté, Pierre, 227

Vichy, attitudes toward, and vote, 272, 273

Vichy amnesty bill, 119; passage, 83, 122; second reading, 124

Viénot, Mme. Andrée, 303

Vogel, Ezra F., 37, 338

Voluntary groups, in mass society, 28; membership, 28

Voting by deputies. *See* Roll-call votes

Voting of electorate, 10; attitude of voters toward, 230; stability and variation, 232; stability, effects on government, 259; shifts, France vs. United States, 240; transfers of votes among stable parties, 242; and vertical influence, 232; unrepresented votes, 231, 232; and religious attitudes, 244; floating vote, 249; regression analysis within individual *départements*, 250; historical traditions and change, 255; in cities vs. towns, 253; changes, and social bases, 275; changes, and age, 276; retrospective distributions, 279. *See also* Social structure; Surveys; Turnover tables; names of individual parties

Vulpian, Alain de, 36

W

Wahl, Nicholas, 229

Walker, Helen M., 264

Wasmer, Joseph, 208

Weber, Max, 62, 337

Werth, Alexander, 110, 155, 178, 179, 320, 321

White, William S., 228

White, Winston, 39

Williams, Philip M., 13, 37, 61, 62, 63, 64, 108, 109, 110, 112, 153, 155, 226, 227, 228, 229, 261, 263, 284, 302, 304, 319, 320, 321, 347

Wilson, James Q., 39, 305, 337

Wolfenstein, Martha, 36, 338

Wood, David M., 111

Working class, and Communist party, 26, 27; proportion of, in relation to Communist vote, 251; separation from centers of power, 26

World War II, effects on France, 2

Wright, Charles R., 39

Wright, Gordon, 40, 109, 284

Wylie, Laurence, 36, 37, 39, 261, 263; on attitude toward voting, 231

Y

Yates, W. Ross, 156, 303

Yule, G. Udny, 90, 111, 353

Z

Zariski, Raphael, 292, 303

Zeigler, L. Harmon, 262

Zeller, General André, 159